ANNALS OF COMMUNISM

Each volume in the series Annals of Communism will publish selected and previously inaccessible documents from former Soviet state and party archives in a narrative that develops a particular topic in the history of Soviet and international communism. Separate English and Russian editions will be prepared. Russian and American scholars work together to prepare the documents for each volume. Documents are chosen not for their support of any single interpretation but for their particular historical importance or their general value in deepening understanding and facilitating discussion. The volumes are designed to be useful to students, scholars, and interested general readers.

# Spain Betrayed

*The Soviet Union in the Spanish Civil War*

Edited by
Ronald Radosh, Mary R. Habeck, and
Grigory Sevostianov

Yale University Press

New Haven and London

This volume has been prepared with the cooperation of the Russian State Military Archive (RGVA) and the Russian Institute of General History of the Russian Academy of Sciences.

Published with assistance from the foundation established in memory of Henry Weldon Barnes of the Class of 1882, Yale College.

Designed by James J. Johnson and set in Sabon Roman and Melior types by The Composing Room of Michigan, Inc. Printed in the United States of America by Vail-Ballou Press, Binghamton, New York.

*Library of Congress Cataloging-in-Publication Data*

Spain betrayed : the Soviet Union in the Spanish Civil War / edited by Ronald Radosh, Mary R. Habeck, and Grigory Sevostianov.
    p.  cm. — (Annals of Communism)
    Translations of documents from former Soviet state and party archives.
    Includes index.
    ISBN 0-300-08981-3

    1. Spain—History—Civil War, 1936–1939—Participation, Russian. 2. Communism—Spain—History—20th century. I. Radosh, Ronald. II. Habeck, Mary R. III. Sevost'ianov, Grigorii Nikolaevich. IV. Series.
DP269.47.R8 S63 2001
946.081′347—dc21                                   00-054646

A catalogue record for this book is available from the British Library.

The paper in this book meets the guidelines for permanence and durability of the Committee on Production Guidelines for Book Longevity of the Council on Library Resources.

10  9  8  7  6  5  4  3  2  1

Yale University Press gratefully acknowledges the financial support given for this publication by the John M. Olin Foundation, the Lynde and Harry Bradley Foundation, the Historical Research Foundation, Roger Milliken, Lloyd H. Smith, Keith Young, the William H. Donner Foundation, Joseph W. Donner, Jeremiah Milbank, the David Woods Kemper Memorial Foundation, the Daphne Seybolt Culpeper Foundation, and the Milton V. Brown Foundation.

For my late uncle,
Irving Keith (born Kreichman),
*who died believing that he was fighting "the good fight,"*
*and*
for Bill Herrick,
*a great and humane man who has lived for the truth*

RR

For my family,
*who taught me to see both sides of every question*

MRH

# Contents

# Illustrations

# Acknowledgments

I would like to acknowledge the support and assistance of the Russian archivists that made this volume possible.

MARY R. HABECK

Many people helped work on this project. At Yale University Press, I would like to thank Vadim Staklo and Susan Abel, for their hard work, expertise, and patience. Above all, I wish to thank our superb editor, my friend Jonathan Brent. Without his understanding, commitment, and comprehension of the importance of this project, the book would not exist.

I am indebted to Amitai Etzioni, director of the Center for Communitarian Policy Studies at George Washington University, and to Stephen Joel Trachtenberg, the president of George Washington University, for giving me a home at their institution while I was working on this project. I am greatly appreciative of their personal support for my work.

Finally, I thank the John M. Olin Foundation for numerous grants. The foundation's support enabled me to carry out the work on this book.

RONALD RADOSH

Yale University Press and the editors are grateful to Stephen Schwartz for his careful fact-checking of our manuscript for errors and omissions, and for his expert suggestions and advice on many issues of fact and interpretation.

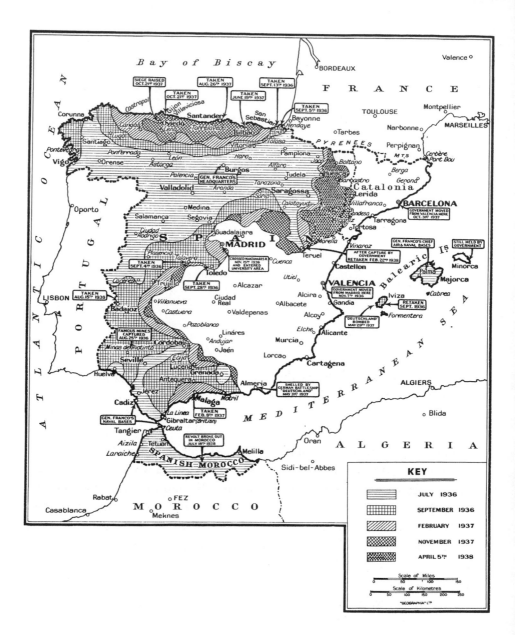

Franco's Advances in Spain up to April 1938.

"Atlantic to Mediterranean: Franco's Gradual Advances in Spain," reproduced by permission from the *Illustrated London News,* April 9, 1938, p. 607.

# Introduction

On 16 July 1936, a large part of the Spanish officer corps rose up in revolt against the legitimately elected Popular Front government of Spain. The coup by the rebellious generals led not to a successful takeover, but instead to a civil war, a battle in which the sympathies and solidarity of millions around the world were enlisted on one side or the other. Spain, a nation that had long been relegated to the sidelines of history, suddenly thrust itself on the world's attention. It became the focus of other nations' foreign policy—and also of a desire on the part of idealistic volunteers to come to the aid of the embattled Republic. From that time on, the Spanish Civil War became not just a part of history but a parable about the need to respond when the forces of tyranny attempt to crush progressive movements seeking democracy, social change, and freedom.

## The Significance of the Spanish Civil War Today

The fight to save the Spanish Republic in fact became the stuff of legend. Once thousands of brave young men, most of them organized by the communist parties in the West, rushed to Spain to join the battle on the behalf of the Republic, it was inevitable that Spain would become the symbol for what was later to be spoken of as "the good fight"—the kind of warfare that those on the right side wage to defeat the powerful enemies of democracy. The new modern enemy was fascism—the scourge unleashed on the world by Hitler in Germany and Mussolini in Italy. Spain was fated to be the first nation in which the three great ideologies and political systems—democracy, fascism, and communism—would fight it out.

According to compelling legend that was born with the decisive defeat of the Republic and that echoes down to the present day, Joseph Stalin and the Soviet Union led the effort to stop "fascism" in Spain. The Communist International (Comintern) issued orders to its cadres around the world to organize volunteers immediately from the national communist parties into military units that would fight alongside the Republican army. For these mainly young and idealistic volunteers, the Spanish conflict was a noble crusade against Hitler and Mussolini and their Spanish puppet Franco. Many years later the volunteers would describe themselves proudly as "premature antifascists," those who had the prescience to understand what the rest of the West came to realize only after American entry into World War II. Survivors from the International Brigades would describe the effort to save the Republic as one of the noblest and most selfless undertakings of the international communist movement, under the aegis of the Soviet Union. History may have proved Stalin to be one of the worst tyrants and murderers of the twentieth century, but in Spain, the story goes, he stood on the right side and mobilized his weak nation and its international allies to save a democratic Republic.

It is this claim about the meaning of the war that led the British journalist and historian Paul Johnson to comment, aptly, that "no episode in the 1930s has been more lied about than this one, and only in recent years have historians begun to dig it out from the mountain of mendacity beneath which it was buried for a generation."[1] Indeed, even as Johnson wrote those words in the 1980s, it was clear that for many intellectuals, Spain was a cause to be celebrated rather than explored anew. The late Alfred Kazin, one of the most distinguished American literary critics, described the Spanish Civil War as "the wound that will not heal"; he declared, therefore, that the "destroyers of the Spanish Republic would always be my enemies."[2] For men of that generation, Spain was "their" war—the one noble cause that they could not let go. The journalist Murray Kempton explained the roots of such loyal conviction. It came from a "small segment of my generation," Kempton wrote, "which felt a personal commitment to the revolution."[3] Like Vietnam for the young men and women of the New Left in the 1960s, Spain, for those who came to adulthood in the 1930s, was a historical event never to be reexamined, which was to serve as a source of never-ending inspiration.

The truth, of course, is not so simple. The Spanish Civil War took place because indecisive elections in February 1936 revealed a nation divided; the irresponsible militancy of sectors of the more extreme Left fed the aims of the insurgent generals. Once civil war broke out, both sides were responsible for unspeakable atrocities. The intervention of Germany and Italy prevented Franco's defeat, even as Soviet military aid gave the Republic the means to beat back the initial advance by Franco's forces.

The problem was that the Soviet Union exacted a harsh price from the Spanish Republic for the delivery of that military aid. The British historian Gerald Howson has furnished overwhelming evidence showing the extent to which Stalin shortchanged and double-crossed the Spanish Republic. As a result of Howson's extensive research, no longer can it be claimed that the Soviet Union was a bastion in the struggle against Franco. Rather, Stalin in effect swindled the Republic out of several hundred million dollars in arms deals. This was done through a secret cooking of the account books. The Soviets faked the prices of arms—guns, planes, and tanks—in order to obtain the gold reserves of Spain. They accomplished it in the following manner. The official exchange rate was 5.3 rubles to the dollar, but the Russians created special exchange rates, favorable to themselves, for the weapons that they sold to the Spanish. Thus, the "coefficient" exchange rate of 2.5 rubles to a dollar for a Russian Maxim machine gun made the guns almost twice as expensive as it should have been for the Spanish to purchase with their gold. On two aircraft alone, Stalin stole more than fifty million dollars from the Republic. In addition, many of the items supplied were ancient and unusable, often delivered without ammunition. As Howson writes, of all the "swindles, cheatings, robberies and betrayals the Republicans had to put up with, this barrow-boy behavior by Stalin and the high officials of the Soviet nomenklatura is surely the most squalid, the most treacherous and the most indefensible." One of course expected *opponents* of the Republic to try to do it in; but as Howson writes, by defrauding the Spanish Republican government of millions of dollars, "by secretly manipulating the exchange rates when setting the prices for the goods they were supplying," the Soviets "belied everything they professed to stand for."[4]

In addition, the price the Republicans paid for the Soviet aid was the very factor that led to the Republic's eventual demise. In exchange for military aid, Stalin demanded the transformation of the Republic into a prototype for the so-called People's Democracies of postwar Eastern and Central Europe. In addition to generals and supplies, Stalin sent the Soviet secret police (the NKVD) and the military intelligence unit (the GRU) to Spain. There the GRU established secret prisons, carried out assassinations and kidnappings, and func-

tioned under its own rules and laws, independent of the Republican government. Years ago, one of the first Soviet defectors from the NKVD, Walter Krivitsky, argued that "the Soviet Union seemed to have a grip on Loyalist Spain,
as if it were already a Soviet possession."[5] For years, Krivitsky's account was
deemed unreliable, suspect because of his status as a defector; but as the
decades have passed, a consensus has emerged among historians that Krivitsky's telling assessment was essentially correct.[6] E. H. Carr, the late British historian, whose sympathies were always with the Soviets, accordingly wrote in
his last, posthumously published book that the Spanish Republic had become
"what its enemies called it, the puppet of Moscow."[7]

The most recent works on Spain, therefore, make clear that the Spanish government's greatest supporters—including the Soviet Union, which controlled
the participation of European leftist volunteers in the war—had mixed, if not
completely sinister, motives for helping the Republicans. The point of view is
hardly new: scholars have long argued that for its own ends, the Soviet Union,
acting largely through the Comintern and the secret police, manipulated the
Spanish Republic. The difficulty, however, has lain in proving the common allegation about Soviet intentions during the war. Until now we have been dependent on a few documents made available by Comintern members, some
documentation from Spanish archives, and the memoirs of participants. Although many of these touched on the Soviet role, direct evidence covering the
USSR's intervention in Spain has been lacking. In 1991 and 1992, as previously closed Soviet archives began to be opened, it became possible to investigate the period anew. For the first time, an entire group of records dedicated to
the Spanish Civil War came to light in the Russian State Military Archives.
Searches in this and other depositories in Moscow unearthed a new batch of
relevant Comintern, Politburo, and intelligence agency documents.

The significance of the new material cannot be overstated. We now have, for
the first time, hard evidence that proves what many had suspected since the beginning of the Spanish Civil War: that Stalin sought from the very beginning to
control events in Spain and to manage or prevent the spread of actual social
revolution. Using officials from the military, intelligence, and the Comintern,
Moscow attempted to take over and run the Spanish economy, government,
and armed forces. Of course, Stalin did not find it easy simply to dictate events.
He faced opposition from such men as Premier Francisco Largo Caballero, as
well as other moderates in the Popular Front government. The Soviet advisers
sent to Madrid thus found it more difficult than they expected to impose their
will on the Spanish Republic; yet, using the possibility of aid as virtual black-

mail, these men would eventually succeed in implementing almost every important decision that Moscow dictated, while pushing out of power those Spaniards who tried to oppose them.

Some contemporary historians try to resist such conclusions. A British historian, Tim Rees, has argued that in reality the Comintern, and hence the Soviet Union, were "unable to achieve a high level of control over the PCE [Communist Party of Spain] and hence over developments through it." Rees agrees about the general political development in the Republic as outlined by most historians, but he argues strongly that the Soviets exercised no "central direction" and that the PCE acted independently, merely seeking Comintern endorsement for its actions. Rees's analysis mirrors that of the revisionist historians of American Communism, who in their works portray the American Communist party as composed of militants who responded to local conditions and cared little about the dictates from the Soviet Union and the Comintern. Rees's observation about "the absence of Comintern guidance," however, is shown to be false by the documentary material contained within these pages. Thanks to the regular flow of now decoded "MASK" documents[8] from the Comintern to the PCE in 1936 and to the intervention of Soviet officers and Comintern agents, Soviet influence and control over the Spanish Communist party was nearly total. Rees's claim, for example, that the brutality shown by PCE cadres in the "campaign to suppress the POUM owed far more to feeling on the ground than any dictates from Moscow" is, in light of the huge amount of evidence to the contrary, simply untenable.[9]

Until the release of this new archival material, historians writing about the Spanish Civil War have tended to fall into two groups, some following Rees's interpretation and others dissenting from his view. To point up the contrast, we can take as examples the work of two writers: the distinguished British historian Paul Preston, the author of numerous books and articles pertaining to the war, including his best-known work, published in 1986, *The Spanish Civil War: 1936–39*,[10] and the journalist-historian Burnett Bolloten, who as a young man sympathetic to the Communists covered the war for the American press, and who later devoted the rest of his life to a thorough academic study of the Communist role in Spain. Bolloten's classic, completed shortly before his death, appeared in 1991, under the title *The Spanish Civil War: Revolution and Counterrevolution*.[11] Examining these two works of history, readers can immediately see that each of the scholars, despite adhering to traditional academic norms of presentation, comes to the subject with a definite point of view. Preston, in his most recent revised edition of his major work on the war, makes his sympathies clear from the start, when he dedicates his book to "the men and women of the International Brigades who fought and died fighting fascism in Spain." The accolade makes it clear that Preston writes as one sympathetic to the general communist version of events. This is not to deny that there is much of great value in Preston's work. He is fully aware of the most recent scholarship on the war, and when analyzing Stalin's foreign policy and reasons for intervention in the conflict, Preston endorses the historical consensus that "Stalin helped the Spanish Republic not in order to hasten its victory but rather to prolong its existence sufficiently to keep Hitler bogged down in an expensive venture."[12]

When Preston turns to the internal politics of the Republic, though, his bias in favor of the moderates of the Front leads him to calumny people who favor a different interpretation. One of the central questions facing the Republic and the opponents of Franco was whether the war should be fought to preserve a middle-class republic or to inaugurate social revolution—this was the question that caused the most profound rift between the Communists and moderate Socialists on the one hand and the anarchists and the revolutionaries in the POUM (Workers Party of Marxist Unity) on the other. Preston, however, writes that Cold Warriors in the West used this debate "to disseminate the idea that it was the Stalinist suffocation of the revolution in Spain which led to Franco's victory," and he further charges, without evidence, that works presenting this point of view "were sponsored by the CIA-funded Congress for Cultural Freedom to propagate this idea," and that the result was "an unholy alliance of anarchists, Trotskyists and Cold Warriors." The rhetoric this historian engages in bears a striking resemblance to the canards and attacks launched by the Soviet Union and the PCE against their ideological enemies at the height of the Civil War. At the very least, the accusation serves to cut off analysis and debate, by dismissing interpretations contrary to Preston's own as discredited Cold War views. Of course, it skirts the issue of whether the other interpretation has any merit.[13]

Bolloten, by contrast, wrote the most complex account so far of how the Communists gained hegemony in the Republic. In contradistinction to other scholars, Bolloten argued that in fact an actual social revolution had taken place in Spain, one that, as historian Stanley Payne puts it in the introduction to Bolloten's grand work, was completely "pluralist" and authentic. Whereas outsiders saw the events as "a contest between democracy and fascism," Bolloten (and Payne) portrayed it as something of greater substance, a war that took place within an actual revolution that broke out within the Republican zone. The aim of the Communists, according to the thesis that Bolloten develops in exhaustive detail, was to expand their power gradually and gain influence over the army, police, and political apparatus. Because this was the focus of his work—earlier versions appeared first in 1961—Bolloten was regarded as attempting "in some fashion to impugn or besmirch the Republican cause." As Stanley Payne notes, although Bolloten refuted the Francoist charge that a Communist plot to overthrow the Republic existed in 1936, he was nonetheless accused of having written his work at the behest of the CIA—precisely the charge that Preston still repeats.[14]

If the foregoing discussion indicates anything, it is that the Spanish Civil War remains to this day a highly charged issue. It is history, but to those who are writing it, as well as those who have a romantic or political attachment to the events, the issues are still vital and worth fighting about. There is one overriding question that historians address in different ways, according to their individual political sympathies. Were the Communists and the Soviet Union correct in maintaining that the only issue was to fight the war, or were the POUM and the anarchists right when they argued that the only way to fight the war successfully was to carry out a genuine social revolution? Historians answer it in two ways. First, once again, let us see what Paul Preston says:

> The ultimate issue was to do with the primacy of war or revolution. The view argued by the Communist party, the right wing of the Socialist Party and the bourgeois Republican politicians was that the war must be won first in order to give the revolution any possibility of triumphing later. For the anarcho-syndicalist CNT, the more or less Trotskyist POUM and the left wing of the PSOE, proletarian revolution was itself the essential precondition for the defeat of fascism. After 1939, Spanish Republicans engaged in bitter polemics. The position put forward by the Communists and their allies was that the Spanish Civil War was fought between fascism and a popular, democratic anti-fascist Republic. In this view, popular revolutionary movements were an obstacle which not only hindered the central task . . . but also threatened to bring down on the head of the Republic an alliance of the conservative Western democracies with the Axis powers. The contrary position was [that] only a full-scale proletarian revolution could destroy the capitalism that spawned fascism.[15]

Preston's explanation of the difference between the Spanish Communists' approach toward the war and that taken by the revolutionaries is written in such a manner that the reader can reach but one conclusion: that the position taken by Moscow and the Communist Party of Spain is the only one that makes sense. Preston acknowledges that the Communists ignored the dilemma that the Republic's unique weapon was "popular enthusiasm," which tended to disappear as the Republic advanced solely the goals of the upper middle class; but he argues that the revolutionary forces ignored the international situation and the conventional military might of the Francoist forces. Preston recognizes that when the Republic eventually lost the war, it was easy for the defeated revolutionary forces—the POUM, the anarchists, and the Trotskyists—to argue that had the Republic not adopted the Communist position, Republican troops would have been able to win. He argues, however, that the evidence proves the Communists to have been correct, and he points to the "indisputable perception of the Communists that once the uprising had developed into a civil war, then the first priority had to be to win that war."[16]

Other scholars have challenged that argument. Robert Alexander takes up this analysis directly:

> There can be little doubt about the fact that this unremitting drive to establish in Republican Spain a replica of Stalin's Soviet Union greatly undermined the morale of those fighting and working for the Republican cause. Certainly, creating a situation in which large numbers of Republican officers and men feared more the Stalinists who were in their midst, than they did the Franco troops on the other side of the trenches, did not stimulate those soldiers' will to carry on the struggle against the Rebels. Since most of the members of the Republican forces were workers and peasants who had participated to one or another degree in the Revolution of the early phase of the war, the efforts of the Stalinists to destroy that Revolution also could not be anything but a negative contribution to the war effort. Similarly, those efforts certainly increasingly raised troubling questions in the minds of the workers and peasants in the rearguard about whether their sacrifices for the struggle were any longer worthwhile.[17]

The present collection of documents provides new and sometimes startling data that help shed light on these and other controversial areas of the Spanish Civil War. The archives generally confirm the view of events held by one of the groups of historians—-including such luminaries as Víctor Alba, Antony Beevor, Burnett Bolloten, Pierre Broué and Emile Témime, E. H. Carr, Gabriel Jackson, Stanley Payne, and Stephen Schwartz. For many years, and working independently, these scholars have traced the duplicitous maneuvers of the Soviet Union in the Spanish Republic during the Civil War. That our findings substantiate their research only deepens our respect for those who got so much right without access to the information now at our disposal.

The documents that we offer also shed light on many of the disputed episodes of the war. These include the timing of the Republican request for assistance from the Soviet Union; the civil war within the Civil War (the fighting in Barcelona in May of 1937); the rise and fall of the International Brigades; the internal workings of the Comintern and its influence on Spain; and much else. Readers will find many documents that detail the involvement of the top Soviet leaders, including Voroshilov and Stalin, as well as major figures in the Comintern, in the unfolding of events in the Spanish Republic. The documents included here address the entire spectrum of Soviet diplomatic, military, economic, and political policies in Spain. They show us what the Soviet leaders thought about their involvement, how they viewed their role in the war, and what they envisioned for the future of Spain.

The most important aspect of the archival evidence is thus not startling new revelations, but rather the more complete understanding of Soviet and Comintern participation in the war and the politics of the Spanish Republic that the documents provide. As some historians have long suspected, the documents prove that advisers from Moscow were indeed attempting to "Sovietize" Spain and turn it into what would have been one of the first "People's Republics," with a Stalinist-style economy, army, and political structure. Yet the documents also reveal a hitherto unknown incompetence on the part of many Soviet advisers, as they tried to influence and ultimately control the Republican government. In the same way, the speeches and reports from Comintern officials, while demonstrating their desire to obtain a complete hold over the Spanish Communist party, also reveal the problems that they had achieving total control. In the end, the documents suggest that the Soviets achieved so much in Spain not because of their overwhelming efficiency, but rather because they were more competent and united than their hapless opponents.

In some ways, then, this volume fits into a larger body of work that appeared at the end of the twentieth century: works that attempt to make sense of the part that Communism and the Soviet Union played in the twentieth century. Two recently published books in particular make the same connection between the meaning of Communism and the Spanish Civil War that is made in this volume. Both created a stir, particularly in France, where the Communist movement had gained a foothold because of the role that Communists played in the Resistance during World War II. One of these, *The Black Book of Communism: Crimes, Terror, Repression,* edited by Stéphane Courtois and a group of distinguished scholars of the Left, attempted a worldwide analysis of the effect of Communism in different countries and presented a compelling portrait of Communism as inherently an "evil" system. The other, by the late historian François Furet, *The Passing of an Illusion: The Idea of Communism in the Twentieth Century,* is a lengthy essay by France's leading historian of the French Revolution, himself a former Communist, assessing the mythology and impact of Communism on the entire West and its intellectual life.

The provocative reevaluations of the nature of Communism and the Spanish Civil War in these books are confirmed by the documents in this volume. Furet, in a brief but thorough and exceptional summary of the Republic's tempestuous chronology, offers a sober evaluation of Stalin's goal, which was, he writes, "to put republican Spain under the Soviet influence and to make it a 'friend of the USSR,' an expression that implied leaving the bourgeoisie in place so long as it was pro-Soviet." Such a goal, he explains, was both defensive and offensive, and could serve "either as a basis for negotiations in case of a setback or as a chance to move toward a Soviet-style revolution of the sort that would occur in Central and Eastern Europe after World War II." Furet notes that though pressure from the Communists may have unified the military organization, it also destroyed the foundations of authentic Spanish antifascism. With the crushing of the popular revolution, the destruction of the POUM, and the alienation of the left and right wings of the Socialist party, the "flame of the Spanish Republic [was] extinguished." Nonintervention was a charade, he emphasizes, and Western policy allowed the Soviets to blackmail the Republican government more easily. But Moscow's antifascist logic was false; its version of antifascism "went so far as to kill republican energy under the pretext of organizing it, just as it compromised the republican cause under the semblance of defending it." In the Soviets' unique fashion, the concept of solidarity and antifascism "perpetually concealed the pursuit of power and the confiscation of liberty."[18] Stéphane Courtois and Jean-Louis Panne offer much of the same analysis in their essay for *The Black Book of Communism.* The Communists' goal, they write, "was to occupy more and more positions in the Republican government so as to direct policy in accordance with the interests of the Soviet Union." Their essay, however, deliberately concentrates on the ugly details of the brutality of the NKVD in Spain, during its lengthy effort to wipe out all self-proclaimed "counterrevolutionary" elements, especially the anarchists and the leadership of the POUM. Agreeing with Furet, Courtois and Panne conclude that "Moscow's intervention was intended solely to promote Soviet interests while pretending it was essential for the struggle against fascism." Stalin's real goal, they write, "was to take control of the destiny of the Republic. To that end, the liquidation of left-wing opposition to the Communists—Socialists, anarchosyndicalists, POUMists and Trotskyites—was no less important than the military defeat of Franco."[19]

It is good to see Paul Johnson's hope that the lies and obfuscation surrounding the history of the Spanish Civil War are finally being subjected to the light of day. Our book, we hope, is part of the process and joins the Furet and Courtois volumes, as well as those of Víctor Alba, Stephen Schwartz, and Robert Alexander, in setting the record straight. By providing the next generation of scholars with the tools necessary to reexamine the role of the Soviet Union and Communism in Spain, the documents offered in our book will help curb the tendency to turn the conflict into a modern-day legend. It may have been true, as Furet wrote, that "the history of the Spanish Civil War was covered with a blanket of silence and lies that would remain in place throughout the twentieth century."[20] Thanks to the material we have found in the Moscow archives, as well as the pioneering work of the scholars we cite, in the new century such an outcome is no longer possible.

# Historical Background

The attempted coup that began the Spanish Civil War was the culmination of long-standing tensions and social strife that no government had been able to address satisfactorily. The divide between rich and poor in Spain was immense, and the powerful Catholic hierarchy did little to ameliorate conditions. The result was that destitute peasants and dissatisfied workers supported either radical anarchism or socialism, buttressed by a bitter anticlericalism, while liberalism in Spain tended to be more extreme than in most of Europe. Yet the wealthy landowners and certain areas of the country, especially the north, maintained a staunchly conservative outlook that precluded any serious reconsideration of the nation's social ills. Many Spaniards in fact had monarchist leanings and believed that their country's salvation lay in native Spanish traditions and a strong centralized government. Meanwhile, nationalist movements in the Basque provinces and Catalonia encouraged these people to think of themselves as distinct from the Castilians who ruled in Madrid, and as deserving of more autonomy or even outright independence from the central government. Even apart from other considerations, though, the fact that most of Spain's industrial capacity was centered in these regions of the country would make even liberal Spanish regimes resistant to granting any but limited autonomy to the provinces.

As a result, political instability prevailed throughout the nineteenth and early twentieth centuries. This period was characterized by numerous military coups, a short-lived republic, and monarchies with varying amounts of political power. Many workers and peasants responded by joining or creating their own unions and associations, most of which were either anarchist in nature, like the anarcho-syndicalist National Labor Confederation (CNT) and later the more radical Iberian Anarchist Federation (FAI), or socialist, like the General Workers' Union (UGT). To a lesser extent, the workers and peasants supported various radical, socialist, and communist parties. In 1923, on the heels of military defeats in Morocco, the constitutional monarchy that had lasted since 1874 was set aside by a military *pronunciamiento,* which dismissed the parliament (Cortes) but retained King Alfonso as the nominal head of government. The ensuing dictatorship of General Primo de Rivera lasted until 1930, when growing discontent allowed the king to ask for his resignation. Not long thereafter, continuing unrest pushed Alfonso into exile and ushered in the Second Republic.

From the first there were signs that the new republic, dominated by the Spanish form of radical liberalism, faced serious problems. Anticlerical provisions in the new constitution, along with strikes, agrarian revolts, and burning of churches by anarchists and attempts to rein in the power of the army, appalled Catholic and traditionalist Spaniards. In November 1933, a general election gave power to a center-right coalition, which set about undoing the "damage" done by the previous government. Social unrest increased dramatically and came to a head in an Asturian revolt of October 1934 that was brutally suppressed by the army, led by Generals Francisco Franco and Manuel Goded. This in turn outraged both the liberal Republican parties and the socialists, who for the first time agreed to work together in the Popular Front (P.F.), which they formed to combat the rightist coalition. In new elections held February 1936, the P.F. won overwhelming control of the Cortes, even though it obtained less than half of the popular vote.

It was not obvious at first that this would lead to civil war in Spain. Immediately after its electoral victory, the new P.F. pursued a moderate course. Socialists did not dominate the first cabinets; Manuel Azaña, leader of the Republican Left, became prime minister (and later president). Limits were placed on the influence of the Catholic Church and large industrialists and landowners, and social services were introduced to help the large working-class majority in the cities as well as the unemployed poor. This was, however, too much for conservatives and too little for the anarchists and socialists who supported the P.F. Radicals in the front began to talk about the need for a "dictatorship of the proletariat," an end to all private property, and the inevitability of a Spanish revolution to rival that which had taken place in the Soviet Union.

In certain sections of the country, peasants and workers had already acted to take matters into their own hands. Demanding immediate social justice, peasants seized the property of landowners, and anarchists again proceeded to burn down churches, that visible symbol of the power and wealth of the Catholic hierarchy. Large cities and rural areas alike suffered crippling strikes, and radical youth marched in huge demonstrations. Traditionalists and conservative Spaniards were frightened by these events, which suggested to them that even more than in 1931, the country was headed toward a Bolshevik future. Throughout the summer, Left and Right carried out politically motivated assassinations, and the country slid inexorably toward chaos.

As Spain descended into lawlessness, a large portion of the officer corps became convinced that only they could save Spain from ruin at the hands of those they collectively termed communists. Generals Emilio Mola and José Sanjurjo organized a well-coordinated rebellion to overthrow the Republican government quickly and painlessly. Unfortunately for their plans, the rebels failed to achieve their goal immediately, and thus the path was opened for a prolonged and bloody civil war, as well as something more than just an internal conflict. When both Nationalists and Republicans realized that they needed outside assistance, each side appealed to its "natural" ally in the world's political spectrum. Soon after the fighting began, General Francisco Franco, at first just one of many supporters of the revolt, sent emissaries to Hitler and Mussolini asking for their help in transporting troops. For their part, the Republicans turned to the democracies of the West, especially those whose governments—like the one in France—had moved to the left. With the Soviet Union standing alone as the world's first socialist nation, the Spanish Republic also requested aid from Stalin. The Fascist and Nazi leaders decided to intervene early, and they gradually escalated the nature of their assistance from transportation to direct military involvement. Mussolini contributed the largest number of men and a great deal of matériel. Hitler sent a sizable contingent of pilots—the notorious Condor Legion—as well as his best tanks and aircraft. Stalin was not far behind. By late autumn of 1936, Germany, Italy, and the Soviet Union were all deeply involved in the Spanish conflict, and they would remain so until the war's end.

The internationalization of the war would have far-reaching consequences. In addition to ensuring that the conflict would be lengthier and deadlier than it might otherwise have been, the spread of hostilities also divided the societies of Europe, and the United States, into two opposing groups. On the one side were those who feared either a "Sovietization" of Spain and the eventual absorption of the country into the Soviet sphere or a broadening of the war into a general European conflict. These "moderates" would not support the intervention of Hitler and Mussolini; they also eschewed any aid for the Republicans and favored what they called a policy of nonintervention. The British government, dominated by men who thought along these lines, worked hard to ensure that the great powers agreed on a nonintervention treaty and then implemented it as fully as possible. The United States, and eventually France, would also decide that partisan involvement was far too dangerous and that isolating Spain was the only practical way to contain the conflict. On the other side stood the majority of the European Left, which saw the war as an attempt by "international fascism" to impose its ideology and system through open battle. For these forces, the Spanish conflict was actually a side door to a military struggle against Hitler and Mussolini. As for the Soviet Union, which was soon to supply arms and "advisers" to the Republic, it pursued a dual goal. Any intervention was to take place within the framework of the overall Soviet policy of seeking alliances with France and Britain. Hence, Stalin would provide enough military aid to allow the Republic to defend itself, but not enough to frighten or outrage the West. Moreover, his aid included internal intervention in the policies of the Republic; intervention meant to gain control over the war and to prevent any elements of the Spanish far Left—including anarchists and revolutionary Communists—from fomenting social revolution. Such a step, Stalin believed, would strike fear into the minds of the leaders of the conservative West; it had to be avoided. The Communists in Spain, acting under Soviet guidance, would become a bulwark against revolution, collectivization, and social disorder, while seeking to manipulate and control events for their own ends.

# Note on the Documents

Mary Habeck translated into English most of the original documents from Russian, along with a handful from other languages. William McKone also supplied several English translations of Russian documents, and John Monroe translated the documents written only in French. Translation or transliteration was often problematic: certain letters or reports had originally been written in French, for instance, before being translated first into Russian and then from Russian into English. Every effort has been made to verify the names of people or places that were transliterated into Cyrillic from Spanish or French (for example) and then back again into the Roman alphabet for this publication. Nevertheless, mistakes are almost certain to have occurred: our apologies for any errors of transliteration that remain.

In most cases, documents are identified by archive name and by fond (collection), opis (inventory), delo (file), and list (page) number, abbreviated respectively f., op., d., and l. Ellipses appearing on a separate line in this book mark an omission by the editors, as do ellipses appearing inside square brackets in running text. All other ellipses were in the original documents.

# Abbreviations and Acronyms

| | |
|---|---|
| CC | Central Committee [of a party] |
| CNT | National Labor Confederation—the anarcho-syndicalist trade union |
| ECCI | Communist International or Comintern |
| FAI | Iberian Anarchist Federation |
| GRU | Main Intelligence Directorate—Soviet military intelligence agency |
| JSU | Unified Socialist Youth |
| MOPR | International Red Aid; Organization for Aid to Imprisoned Fighters for the Revolution |
| NKID | People's Commissariat of Foreign Affairs |
| NKVD | People's Commissariat of Internal Affairs— precursor of the KGB |
| P.B. | Politburo |
| PCE | Communist Party of Spain |
| POUM | Workers' Party of Marxist Unity |
| PSOE | Socialist Workers' Party of Spain |

PSUC        Unified Socialist Party of Catalonia

PUR         Political Directorate of the Revolutionary Military
            Council of the Worker-Peasant Red Army—the
            political arm of the Bolshevik Party within the Red
            Army that controlled the commissars

RKKA        Worker-Peasant Red Army—Soviet Red Army

UGT         General Workers' Union—union dominated
            by the Socialists and Communists

VKP(b)      All-Russian Communist Party (Bolshevik)—official
            name of the ruling party of the Soviet Union

Spain Betrayed

# CHAPTER ONE

# 1936

## Moscow and the Comintern Set the Stage

THE FIRST FEW MONTHS of the Spanish Civil War set the stage for all that would follow. From the beginning of the July uprising through December 1936, the battle lines between Nationalists and Republicans were drawn; international actors made their decisions to intervene or not; and the internal dynamics of the Republic, the interplay among the diverse parties, unions, and factions within the "Loyalist" camp, took shape. Perhaps the most vital foundation laid during this first critical period was the response of international Communism to the events in Spain. Nowhere is this more dramatically illustrated than in the MASK intercepts, the encrypted telegrams that Comintern and other Soviet authorities in Moscow sent to their subordinates throughout Europe. The very day that the war began, Moscow sent the Spanish Communist party directives for responding to the "alarming situation." **Document 1** exemplifies both the tone that the Soviets, and the Comintern, took in dealing with their Spanish comrades and the principal policies that the Communists would adopt in responding to the crisis. Although the telegram described these as "proposals" and advice, the imperative tone taken by Moscow made it clear that there was little room for argument or maneuver by the small and relatively powerless PCE (Communist Party of Spain). As for the content of the "proposals": the word from Moscow was that the party had at all costs to preserve the Popular Front, "as any split there would be utilised by the Fascists in their fight against the people." Unity was vital not only in order to present a unified front to the enemy—it also created the impression that the steps the Comintern desired emanated from the entire Spanish polity rather than just the Communists. Therefore, the PCE was to "endeavour to get all parties of the Popular Front to agree on the most important measures [that is, the measures that the party considered the most important] and to carry them out as measures of the Popular Front." The PCE would do this using all of the means at its disposal—demonstrations, resolutions, and delegations of workers and peasants—to pressure the government into agreeing to Communist strategies for winning the war.

Not surprisingly, these strategies coincided with Soviet policy. Thus, the directive to push the Republican government to deal as firmly as possible with anyone who aided the Nationalists (internal "enemies of the people," the aristocracy, and even parliamentary leaders) and to marginalize the anarchists fit in with Stalin's aspiration to purge political and class enemies. The political atmosphere in the Soviet Union at the time may have made this aim even more urgent for the Comintern. Just as the war in Spain began, Stalin was embarking on the show trials of his last important opponents, Kamenev, Zinoviev, and eventually Bukharin.[1] Efforts to purge the Spanish military and other institutions of "adventurers, terrorists, conspirators, and Fascist rebels" began at about the same time and continued until the defeat of the Republic. The only changes over the next three years were to the definition of "enemy of the people" and in the lengths to which the party would go to be rid of such enemies.

The attitude toward the anarchists is especially significant. Spanish anarchism had very deep roots in both the peasantry and the growing industrial working classes. Inspired by the Russian founder of modern anarchism, Mikhail Bakunin, Spanish anarchists abhorred organized parties of any sort; yet they also formed the Iberian Anarchist Federation (FAI)—that dominated the largest workers' union, the National Labor Confederation (CNT). Because of their opposition to the state, no matter what its form or composition, the anarchists contested Stalin's vision of the Communist regime.[2] This attitude, combined with their widespread appeal and influence among the poor, meant that the anarchists constituted the largest threat to the PCE and the Comintern in Spain. The Spanish Communists had stormy relations with the anarchists, and the Civil War only exacerbated tensions between the two groups. Throughout the conflict, Soviet and Comintern advisers would decry the "subversive" activities of the anarchists, and particularly their refusal to curtail revolutionary activities or to allow the formation of a regular, disciplined army. Document 1 confirms, however, that their hatred of the anarchists was not inspired solely by the syndicalists' activities. Describing them as little better than pawns of the fascists, it shows that the Communists had determined to destroy the anarchists from the very beginning of the war, before their opponents had articulated, let alone put into effect, their wartime policies.

Linked to this demand, and no less intertwined with Soviet policy, was the order to pursue the unification of the Communist-dominated General Workers' Union (UGT) and the CNT. With the adoption of the Popular Front platform in 1935, Communists worldwide were instructed to work with any leftists except the "Trotskyists" (a code word for all "enemies of the people"). The demand to establish a single union also stemmed from a new understanding of how to construct a socialist state: not through open revolution, but through the absorption of independent unions or parties into a single entity controlled by the Communists. After World War II, a similar strategy would result in the creation of the "People's Democracies" of Eastern Europe. Document 2, sent out just a few days later, also held out the possibility of forming a new government that would include Communists. This too was part of the Popular Front strategy, but one that was less desirable to Moscow and the Comintern in Spanish circumstances. In this telegram it is clear that the PCE was to join the government only if the current regime continued to vacillate in its attitudes toward the rebels and the war. One reason for the hesitation over direct participation was a desire to present Republican Spain to the rest of

Western Europe as a democratic bourgeois state rather than a revolutionary Communist regime. Only thus could Spain hope to win support from France or Britain in its struggle to defeat the Nationalists.[3] These three tactics—purges, the unification of Socialists and Communists, and direct participation in a bourgeois government—formed the basis for subsequent policies that the Comintern, the PCE, and the Soviet advisers followed throughout the war in Spain.

Despite the urgency expressed in these telegrams, there was every reason for Spanish Communists to believe that the government would quickly suppress the uprising. Rebel troops had seized only a few cities in the extreme north and south of the country, while Loyalist forces managed to hold the largest urban areas. Without reinforcements from Africa, where the majority of Nationalist soldiers were apparently trapped, the rebellion seemed doomed. The earliest reports by the PCE on the situation in Spain, exemplified by **Document 3** and **Document 4,** reflected their optimism. It also showed what they hoped would come of this attempt to extinguish the Popular Front: a further development of the bourgeois revolution, and "the realisation of the revolutionary democratic programme," which would include the seizure of private property and the application of revolutionary law. They saw too that this was a key opportunity to increase the power and influence of the party and might result in their direct participation in the government. Like the Comintern, they viewed the anarchists, who would have to be dealt with through "revolutionary law"—that is, executions—if they continued their "acts of provocation," as the one black spot. It should be noted that one of the authors of this message was not even Spanish. "Luis" was the code name for Vittorio Codovilla, an Argentinean Communist who had been sent to Spain earlier in the decade as the Comintern representative to the PCE. His signature on this document and others, and his later actions, would show that he was much more than just an observer, however. In time he would virtually run the PCE, treating the Spanish "comrades" as second-class citizens in their own party.

The next three pieces of evidence show that the Comintern (or ECCI) was not so sanguine about the future of the conflict. Comintern members saw, more clearly than their Spanish comrades,

that the uprising might not be easily crushed and that a prolonga-
tion of the conflict would radically affect PCE behavior during the
crisis. On 23 July, a meeting of the ECCI was held at which the
secretariat discussed how Communists should react to events in
Spain. There has been much speculation about the timing of this
Comintern response to the war. Hugh Thomas used Nationalist
sources with Communist confirmation to suggest a joint gathering
of the secretariats of the Comintern and Profintern on 21 July and
another on the 26th. But he knew no more than anyone else what
was discussed and decided in these meetings.[4] E. H. Carr thought
that the ECCI secretariat had not assembled until mid-September
to define its approach toward the Spanish events.[5] In fact, only after this meeting on 23 July would the secretariat issue its first sub-
stantive directives for the PCE. **Document 5,** Dimitrov's report at
the meeting, reveals the reasoning behind Comintern and Soviet
policies and the concrete measures they wanted taken. His most
important conclusion was that Spain was not *yet* ready for a true
revolution. The party should not act precipitately, as if the war
were already won, he stressed, and therefore "we should not assign
the task, *at the present stage,* of creating soviets and seeking to
establish a dictatorship of the proletariat in Spain" [emphasis
added]. The Communists had to strengthen the democratic republic "*at the present stage*" by destroying the fascists; once "our positions have been strengthened, then we can go further" [emphasis
added]. The Spanish comrades had to resist the temptation to
"rush ahead and get carried away" and instead should work on
tasks suited to "the present moment" and the current strength of
the Communists. Then, even more clearly, Dimitrov argued that if
the army had managed to seize the Madrid garrison, conditions
would have been ripe for a true seizure of power. The Communists
could have "overthrown the Azaña government early in the morning, issued a manifest from the new government, a real republican
democratic government." Because the Popular Front had managed
to hold on to power, though, the Communists had to work with
them, not against them. The very careful use of these terms, as
well as the injunction to "act under the semblance of defending the
republic," supports the contention of some scholars that the
Communists purposely disguised their true objective, social revo-

lution.[6] They would do this in the first place by pretending that their ultimate goal was merely a bourgeois democratic regime and in the second by concentrating on winning the war with the Nationalists *first*. Afterward, anything was possible.

The result of this meeting was **Document 6,** a telegram instructing the PCE on the proper course to take in the developing war. The secretariat once again stressed that the party should not get carried away with schemes that could be realized after victory. The document then repeated most of the instructions given in Document 1 and discussed at the Comintern gathering. The two major additions (given as Points 5 and 6) are striking and deserve special attention. At the end of his report, Dimitrov had hesitated over whether the Spanish Communists should support a regular army or a people's militia. Although it was obvious that the Spanish people needed an armed force of some sort, it is unclear from his discussion which type of force he thought would best serve the Republic. He ended his report by mentioning that he would ask "the comrade secretary" (that is, Stalin) if he had any comments on these points. The telegram, sent the next day, apparently reflected Dimitrov's remarks as amended by Stalin. Point 6 endorsed the use of a regular army, along with the militia, as the proper response to the rebellion and to enemies "from without and within." This endorsement paved the way for the creation of the People's Army, a force that the Communist party would come to dominate. Perhaps even more important is Point 5, which shows that the Comintern, and Stalin, still viewed the PCE's potential inclusion in the Republican government with extreme caution. As earlier, the party was told not to participate simply in order "to preserve the unity of the Popular Front." Much stricter conditions were also laid down for direct participation, which could occur only if it was "urgent and absolutely necessary" to win the war. As we shall see, this point would become significant when the new Largo Caballero government was formed in early September.

Still, the Comintern and Moscow realized that they could not allow the PCE to advocate openly the policies outlined by these documents. The next piece of evidence, **Document 7,** adds to our understanding of why the Communists in Spain, after their first enthusiastic involvement in the heady revolutionary days of July and August, suddenly declared their support for a bourgeois democracy and portrayed themselves throughout the war as moderates. A few scholars, such as Pierre Broué and Emile Témime, have believed the party line that the Communists were in truth the "champions of moderation and loyalty to the Republican regime."[7] Víctor Alba, too, concluded that the slogans were reality; the Communists wanted first to suppress and then to appropriate the revolution.[8] Most others have thought that the primary reason for this change of course, whether real or only apparent, was a desire to win over the Western democracies by calming their fears about the nature of the Spanish government.[9] This document confirms that, in addition to the desire to defeat the rebellion first and then worry about further developing the revolution, the Comintern advocated this tactic as the only way to obtain help from Britain, France, and the United States. They correctly assumed that none of the Western nations, including the usually sympathetic France, would give aid to a government that they even suspected of being Communist. It is interesting to note that both Document 1 and Dimitrov's report of 23 July directly contradicted Points 2 and 3 of this telegram: the PCE had, in fact, been ordered to support the confiscation of the land belonging to the Church and to the large landowners "directly or indirectly" involved in the rebellion. Later events were also to prove that only one part of Point 1, the struggle against "anarchy," was the literal truth.

## Document 1

MASK Intercept

MOST SECRET.
N°. 6485/Sp.
Date: 22nd July 1936
From: Moscow
To: Spain
N°: 266–275
Date: 17th July 1936

MEDIDA and B.P.
After considering the alarming situation in connexion with the Fascist conspiracy in SPAIN, we advise you:—

1. To preserve intact, at any cost, the ranks of the Popular Front, as any split there would be utilised by the Fascists in their fight against the people. Therefore you must endeavour to get all parties of the Popular Front to agree on the most important measures and to carry them out as measures of the Popular Front. Having done this you must use all forms of pressure on the Government—meetings, resolutions in the Assemblies, delegations of workers and peasants to the Government to negotiate etc; in order to bring about a decisive rebuff for Fascism, and to negotiate energetic steps on the part of the Government against the insurgents.

2. Demand the immediate arrest of those parliamentary leaders who (one group)[10] the Republican Government and have this carried out immediately without further hesitation. Rid the army, the police and the organisations of authority from top to bottom, from the enemies of the people. Deprive the aristocracy (?) who are behind the conspirators, of all rights of citizenship and confiscate all their goods. Expel them from the country and prohibit their press (?).

It is necessary to set up a special court for adventurers, terrorists, conspirators, and Fascist rebels and to apply the maximum penalty on these including (?) confiscation of their goods.

3. To do now what you have omitted to do before, due to lack of firmness on the part of your allies in the Popular Front, that is to say, taking full and immediate advantage of the present alarming situation, create, in conjunction with the other parties of the Popular Front, alliances of workers and peasants, elected as mass organisations, to fight against the conspirators in defence of the Republic and at the same time to develop the formation of the workers' and peasants' militia.

4. It is necessary to take preventative measures with the greatest urgency against the putchist attempts of the anarchists, behind which the hand of the Fascists is hidden.

With this end in view, and taking as a basis the declaration of the administration of C.N.T. on solidarity, the C.G.T. [U.] ought to propose to C.N.T. the immediate construction in the centre and locally of joint committees to fight against the Fascist insurgents and to prepare the unification of the syndicates.

If the anarchist administration should refuse this proposition, you must take up a stand, together with all the organisations linked up with the Popular Front, against the anarchists as strike breakers of the struggle against fascism in the working classes.

At the same time you must establish broad social legislation, with extensive rights reserved in the unified C.G.T., so that the workers which have interests (2 groups) syndical organisations: conclusion of collective contracts.

. . . (Next 10 groups too corrupt to decypher [*sic*])—which is important in the fight against the fascist conspirators: (several groups corrupt) for our campaign and under pressure of the masses (2 groups) the necessity of a law for

## Document 1 *continued*

handing over the land of the land-owners and the church to the peasants as a retort to the seditious attempts to establish Fascist dictatorship on the part of the reactionaries.

Such measures will be a decisive blow to fascism, will undermine its material foundation, will arouse among the peasants' sons in the army enthusiasm and desire to defend the republic, thus making the Republican regime inviolable against the fascists.

Please let us know your opinions on our proposals.

DIOS MAYOR

## Document 2

MASK Intercept

MOST SECRET.
N°. 6484/Sp.
Date: 22nd July 1936
From: Moscow
To: Spain
N°: 268–271
Date: 20th July 1936

DIAZ and LUIS.

We are intensely anxious that the Party should activate all (one group) forces to crush the counter-revolutionary rebellion in a decisive manner, and to defend the republic.

The joint action of all the forces of the Popular Front, the equipment of the masses, the fraternisation of the people with the army and its combined action against the counter-revolution, the support of every means of the Government's measures against the rebels—these are the conditions of victory.

Vacillation by the Government might break up the cause of the Republic.

For this reason, if the Government, in spite of the mass support of the Popular Front, is going to vacillate, it will be necessary to raise the question of forming a Government to defend the Republic and to save the Spanish people with the participation of all parties of the Popular Front, Communist and Socialist.

In order to get the active participation of the masses in the fight against the counter revolution, it is necessary, together with the other organisations of the Popular Front, to begin creating a committee of defence of the Republic of all anti-Fascist organisations and of the working population locally.

DIOS, Mayor

9

# Document 3

MASK Intercept

MOST SECRET.
N°. 6509/Sp.
Date: 23rd July 1936
From: Spain
To: Moscow
N°: 267–270
Date: 21st July 1936

DIOS and MAYOR.

MADRID is entirely in the hands of the militias and Government forces. In the rest of the country they are reducing the last (two groups) of the rebellion. The popular militias are arming throughout the country. Those, together with the forces loyal to the Government, constitute the army of defence of the democratic republic. The militias are considered as official organisations and the militia men receive salaries. Various columns of the militias left MADRID to attack the fascist armies of TOLEDO, SARAGOSSA, VALLADOLID and BURGOS.

In the majority of cases they are already applying the revolutionary law and confiscating enemy goods.

The forces of the Popular Front and the Government are closely united and the enthusiasm of the people is enormous.

We are convinced that we shall crush the enemy decisively, and that this will be the first step in the realisation of the revolutionary democratic programme.

The one black spot are [sic] the anarchists who are pillaging and burning. They have been warned (4 groups), but if they persist in acts of provocation, the revolutionary law will be applied.

LUIS and DIAZ

# Document 4

MASK Intercept

MOST SECRET.
N°. 6517/Sp.
Date: 23rd July 1936
From: Spain
To: Moscow
N°: 274, 275
Date: 21st July 1936

## Document 4 *continued*

MAYOR and DIOS.

The political situation can be summarised as follows:—

Until now the Government has been identified with our policy of the Popular Front and with the revolutionary steps which are being taken.

The hatred against fascism and the military party is (one group) that it carries away even the most timid to justify any kind of revolutionary measure, but it is quite clear that the measures which will be taken will raise us, within a very short time, to the Government of the Popular Front, in the conditions of a huge development of the bourgeois democratic revolution, in which event we think we ought to take part.

Give us your opinion.

LUIS, DIAZ

## Document 5

RGASPI, f. 495, op. 18, d. 1101, ll. 21–23

Secretariat ECCI. 23/7/36
Spanish Question

DIMITROV. I believe that the policy carried out so far is correct. We cannot permit our comrades to approach the development of these events as if we were anticipating the destruction of the rebels and we were rushing ahead. We should not, at the present stage, assign the task of creating soviets and try to establish a dictatorship of the proletariat in Spain. That would be a fatal mistake. Therefore we must say: act in the guise[11] of defending the Republic; do not abandon the positions of the democratic regime in Spain at this point, when the workers have weapons in their hands, that this has great significance for achieving victory over the rebels. We ought to advise them to go forward with these weapons, as we have done in other situations, seeking to maintain unity with the petty bourgeoisie and the peasants and the radical intelligentsia, establishing and strengthening the democratic Republic at the present stage through the complete destruction of the fascist counterrevolutionary elements, and then we can proceed from there, resolving concrete questions.

In other words, comrades, we believe that in the present international situation it is advantageous and necessary for us to carry out a policy that would preserve our opportunity to organize, educate, unify the masses and to strengthen our own positions in a number of countries—in Spain, France, Belgium and so on—where there are governments dependent on the Popular Front and where the Communist party has extensive opportunities. When our positions have been strengthened, then we can go further.

We have been interested for some time in having a democratic regime like this, so that through the general pressure of the masses and the Popular Front in a number of European countries (among which are the fascist countries—Germany, Italy, and so on), we [could] influence the mass of workers. The example of Spain shows how the masses operate, how the proletariat, the petty-bourgeois, radical intelligentsia, and peasants can form a common democratic platform against reaction and fascism. We have a number of examples in European circumstances where the masses, through the policy of the Popular Front, under pressure from fascism and reaction, are strengthening their position and are shaping conditions for the final victory of the proletariat. This is a somewhat different path than we had imagined earlier. But this path is closer to the German and Italian proletariat.

We should be able to influence the masses of these countries a great deal, and therefore the struggle in Spain has immense significance. It seems to me that we must push this point, and we hope that we will in fact be victorious over the enemies of the Popular Front, who desire the destruction and discrediting of the Popular Front.

It must be said that the Spanish comrades have a lot of temptations. For example, *Mundo Obrero* has appropriated *Acción Popular's* wonderful building. This is fine. But if our [people] begin to confiscate factories and enterprises and wreak further havoc, the petty bourgeoisie, the radical intelligentsia, and part of the peasantry may move away, and our forces are still not sufficient for a struggle against the counterrevolutionaries. Therefore, we must place before the proletariat and the broad working masses those tasks that suit the concrete conditions of the present moment, that suit the strength of the party, the strength of the proletariat. Do not rush ahead and get carried away.

This question is also connected with the army. The army is smashed to pieces. The [rebellion] began in the army units in Morocco. If the garrison in the center had been seized, we might, in the Bulgarian or Greek way, have carried out a revolution in twenty-four hours, overthrown the Azaña government early in the morning, issued a manifesto from the new government, a real Republican democratic government, and so on. The Popular Front actually has the predominant position in Madrid.

From this comes the question that is before our comrades: Is it expedient to replace the army, which is in reality disbanded and destroyed, with a people's militia? It is necessary to create a people's Republican army and to attract to it all of the officers and generals who have remained loyal to the Republic. But to put in a people's worker-peasant militia in place of the army actually means to follow a different line. That is a different policy. An army is necessary in the cities as the state's armed organization. There ought to be a Republican army, [and] that entails a purging of the elements of the old army that are shirking their duties, [and] a use of the army's command staff that is not treasonous. The Spanish people are in need of an armed state force. This question requires some serious thought. We must be more far-sighted than petty-bourgeois politics, which join with us today and can change tomorrow.

## Document 5 *continued*

That is one question. The other question concerns the confiscation of land. Some people say: Let's seize the land, appropriate the land of the landowners and the Church. I think that this is correct. The land of the largest landowners must be taken, regardless of whether they participated in the rebellion or not; this land must be distributed to the peasants and thus disrupt the landowners, [who] say that this does not concern them because they still have their land. The property and land of all the landowners who directly or indirectly participated in the rebellion must also be confiscated. Another position is now impossible.

I am asking the comrade secretary if there are any doubts about this question or any comments. This will be helpful for our Spanish comrades.

## Document 6

MASK Intercept[12]

MOST SECRET.
N°. 6524/Sp.
Date: 24th July 1936
From: Moscow
To: Spain
N°: 279–283
Date: 24th July 1936

DIAZ.
Your information is insufficient; it is not concrete but sentimental. Once again we ask you to send us serious and effective news. We urgently recommend you to:—

1. Concentrate on the most important business of the moment, that is to say, on the rapid suppression and definite liquidation of the Fascist insurrection, and do not let yourselves be carried away by schemes which can be realised after the victory.

2. Avoid any measures which might break up the unity of the Popular Front in its fight against the insurgents.

3. We warn you not to deviate, through exaggeration, with respect to our own forces and the forces of the Popular Front, and do not minimise the difficulties and new dangers.

4. Do not (one group) [run ahead of], do not abandon the positions of the democratic regime and do not [exceed the limits of a struggle for a truly democratic republic].

5. As much as possible do not let the Communists (?) take direct part in the Government. It is opportune not to participate in the Government as, in this

## Document 6 *continued*

way, it will be [easier] to preserve the unity of the Popular Front. Only participate in the Government if it is urgent and absolutely necessary in order to
crush the insurrection.

6. We consider it inopportune, at this moment, to bring up the question of
replacing the regular army by the popular militia, as it is necessary to concentrate all forces, the militia as well as the troops loyal to the Government, in
order to suppress the rebellion, all the more so as, in the present struggle, it
will be the new republican army, fighting side by side with the militia, which
will be the support of the Republican regime against enemies both from without and within. [Attract loyal Republican officers to the side of the people in
every way possible and get rebel units to go over to the side of the Popular
Front. It is essential for the Government to declare amnesty for those who immediately abandon the ranks of the rebels and go over to the people's side.]

## Document 7

MASK Intercept

MOST SECRET.
N°. 6595/Sp.
Date: 4th August 1936
From: Moscow
To: Spain
N°: 297–300
Date: 31st July 1936

For the purpose of facilitating real and effective help for the Spanish people, and in order to paralyze the campaign in the reactionary world press, we
advise you to intervene with the Government that it may make a declaration
as follows:—

(1) That the Spanish people, under their Republican government, are fighting for the defence of the democratic republic, for democracy, for republican
order against Fascism, anarchy and counter-revolution.

(2) All the confiscations that take place now are not directed against private
property in general but against those taking part in the rebellion.

(3) The Government must also declare that the Spanish people and its Government appreciate the religious feelings of the people, and that the only reason why certain monasteries were occupied during the struggle was that they
were strategical military positions of the rebels.

(4) The Government guarantees the interests of foreign citizens in Spain
and the inviolability of their property.

Moreover the Government will carry out all agreements made with other

14

countries, but states, in the name of the Spanish people that (groups missing: ? it denies) the validity of any international agreement made on the part of the rebel adventurers.

The workers' organisations affiliated to the Popular Front should make similar declarations.

Secretariat

## Early Political Maneuvers

Over the next several months the Spanish Communist party faithfully carried out the instructions sent to it from headquarters in Moscow. Almost all the Communist leaders, including the head of the JSU (the Unified Socialist Youth), Dolores Ibárruri ("La Pasionaria"), José Díaz (the head of the party), and Jesús Hernández (a prominent party member), repeatedly denied that the PCE wanted anything more than the defeat of the enemy and the restoration of a bourgeois democracy throughout Spanish territory.[13] But not everything in the political sphere went the way that the Communists, whether in Moscow or Spain, hoped. On 25 July four of the small leftist parties in Catalonia, including the Communist party of Catalonia, came together to form the Unified Socialist Party of Catalonia (PSUC). Within a few days the new party had joined the Third International, and throughout the war the PSUC acted in concert with the PCE as the arm of the Comintern in Catalonia. It has always been assumed that the Comintern (and the Soviets) approved of this move and perhaps even maneuvered to have it carried out as part of an overall plan to dominate politics in Spain. As Víctor Alba points out, the PSUC followed PCE directions from the outset, a situation that seemed only to confirm this interpretation.[14] It also fit well with the Communist policy of seeking to unite leftists, a policy illustrated in Document 1. **Document 8** shows that this view of events is not, in fact, correct. In agreeing to merge with the three other parties, the Catalan Communist party had actually acted on its own, "contrary to the instructions given." The PCE leaders thought that the move was a "serious mistake" but saw no choice other than to accept the action and to work on the "ideological enlightenment" of the new grouping. Fortunately, the Catalan Communists had apparently made mem-

15

bership in the Third International one of the conditions for their participation in the party, and the PSUC was soon under Stalinist discipline within the Comintern.

The justifications the Catalan Communists gave for their decision are also quite revealing. Like the PCE and the Comintern, the Catalans thought that unity was the best way to deal with the danger represented by the anarchists and also "to strike a serious blow at the Trotzkyites." The linkage of these two groups is significant for later events. "Trotskyism," here as elsewhere, meant any enemy of Stalin or the international communism that he dominated. In Spain the Soviets and the PCE specifically applied the term to the Workers Party of Marxist Unity (POUM), an anti-Stalinist Socialist party that had only a few thousand members, mostly in Catalonia. Trotsky had actually repudiated the POUM, and it was not connected at this point with his movement. The majority of its support resulted from the undoubted credibility of its leaders, Andrés Nin and Joaquín Maurín. Although the anarchists and the POUM did not like each other and never worked together, their anti-Stalinist attitudes meant that the Communists saw them as one and the same. Both were viewed as major threats to Communist power in Spain, and especially in Catalonia. Throughout the war, the Soviets, the PCE, and the Comintern would work to exclude them from power and limit their influence among the workers and peasants—and eventually would turn to outright murder.

Several weeks after the creation of the PSUC, the PCE found itself forced to make a decision that had even greater consequences. The Giral administration, unable to deal effectively with the rebellion, collapsed, and President Azaña asked Francisco Largo Caballero to form a government on 4 September. Largo Caballero was a well-known leftist Socialist who had earlier in the year been praised as the "Spanish Lenin" by the PCE and others. In a rather strange move for a man who would soon show his complete independence from Moscow's control, Largo Caballero refused to form an administration without the participation of the Communists. Although the PCE was willing to join a Popular Front government as early as 21 July, subsequent instructions from Moscow, as shown by Document 2, made the Communists at first refuse to accept Largo Caballero's invitation. Very shortly thereafter, though, the PCE changed course and decided to participate in a bourgeois government; it was the first European Communist party to ever do so.[15] **Document 9,** in connection with other evidence from the archives, shows that the Largo Caballero government was not the favored option and that the permission they received to join the Popular Front was given reluctantly, and then only on condition that Giral remain as the head of the government.[16] This explains why Díaz felt it necessary to write that "despite our efforts, we were not able to avoid a Caballero government." The comment is also important to consider in evaluating the events of the next several months. Even before they became disaffected, the Communists already had reservations about a Largo Caballero government, reservations that would explode into open confrontation in the spring of 1937.

---

## Document 8

MASK Intercept

---

MOST SECRET.
N°. 6579/Sp.
Date: 31st July 1936
From: Spain
To: Moscow
N°: 302–305
Date: 30th July 1936

MAYOR DIOS
Contrary to the instructions given, the comrades directing our party in CATALONIA have formed, together with the Socialist union, the Catalan proletariat party and the Socialist federation, a Socialist Party—(the last ten groups of this part missing).

The comrades say that they did this as a symbolical act in order to render the armed fight against fascism more effective, and to present a solid front against the untimely behaviour of the anarchists, and also to strike a serious blow at the Trotskyites [sic].

They say—(next 30 groups corrupt) secretary VALDES. The Communists have not got a majority on the committee, although there are comrades identified with our party.

We consider this action was a serious mistake, but in view of the critical sit-

## Document 8 *continued*

uation, the only thing to do is to accept it, [to] increase the work of ideological enlightenment in the heart of the new party, and to make thorough preparations for the congress.

A comrade will leave here to obtain better information.

DIAZ LUIS

## Document 9

RGVA, f. 33987, op. 3, d. 852, l. 46

To Com. Voroshilov

From Madrid we have received the following telegram (dated 4/9) from Com. Díaz, the secretary of the C.P. of Spain, and Com. Duclos, the secretary of the C.P. of France.

"Despite our efforts, we were not able to avoid a Caballero government. We succeeded in placing Giral as minister without portfolio and also an expansion in the Esquerra cabinet in Catalonia and among the Basque nationalists. Number of Republicans of all shades—4; three Socialists of every tendency, two Communists. *CNT* is making a declaration about supporting the government and is taking part in the commission's work. We found out . . . through very great difficulties, which might have important political and military consequences. To prevent that, we are acting to put an end to the government crisis today. Everyone emphatically insisted on the participation of the Communists in the new government, and it was impossible to avoid without creating a very dangerous situation. We are taking the necessary measures to organize the work of our ministers."

G. Dimitrov
8/9/36

## The Soviets Intervene

Throughout these political machinations the Republican forces and the Nationalists battled on. By September the rebels had managed to expand the area that they controlled from the two strips of land in the extreme north and south of the country to include almost half of Spain's territory. Rather surprisingly, given the Nationalists' feelings about foreign influence, they had relied on assistance from abroad for this success. The request for aid came very early in the conflict. Franco, in July just one of several conspirators, controlled the Moroccan troops, the best-armed and led units of the Spanish army. Most of these forces were, however, trapped in Africa during the first week of the uprising. Fearing that the Republicans would crush the rebellion in detail while its salvation sat idle in Morocco, Franco sent messengers to Hitler and Mussolini asking for aid. After some initial wavering, both decided to support his cause. Airlifts of nationalist troops, conducted mostly by Italian and German aircraft, brought in the reinforcements from Morocco and allowed the rebels to break out of their confinement in southern Spain. Over the next several months the scope of Italian and German intervention would expand to include tanks and other war matériel as well as several thousand regular troops and scores of pilots.

While Franco was appealing to the Nazis and Fascists, the leaders of the Republic realized that they too would need help from the outside world. Arguing that Popular Front governments had to stand together against the fascist threat, José Giral asked France for aid on 19 July. Léon Blum, for both ideological and strategic reasons, agreed and promised to send matériel to Republican Spain. French suppliers also had a long-standing relationship with the Spanish military and were, in fact, in the process of shipping aircraft to Spain. One week later, convinced by the British refusal to intervene, an internal furor created by the rightist press, and the possibility that the war might spread and cause another general European conflagration, the Blum cabinet reversed its decision. The French shortly afterward proposed and then strongly promoted a policy of noninterference in Spanish affairs.[17] The conservative British government was even less open to aiding the Republicans, and it never seriously considered intervening in the Civil War, while the Americans determined to uphold their neutrality laws from the very start.

At some point during the first few months of the war, the Soviet Union, in contrast to the Western democracies, decided to assist the Republic. In September, shipments of food from the "Soviet people" arrived openly at Spanish ports and T-26 tanks took part in battles near Madrid in late October. It is unclear exactly why the Soviets determined to help the Spanish, and the available documents are not helpful on this point.[18] A desire to aid ideological comrades, fears about encouraging aggression if the Nationalists were not stopped, and a willingness to support France's strategic position all may have played their part in the decision.[19] What the archival materials do help to clarify is the precise timing of both the Spanish request for aid and the Soviet decision to intervene. Some scholars have argued that it was only after the West abandoned Spain that the Republicans were forced into the Soviets' arms.[20] **Document 10,** a letter from Giral addressed to the Soviet ambassador in France, contradicts this view. The date on this correspondence is especially important. On the evening of 25 July the French cabinet met to decide whether to honor Blum's promise and send the aircraft to Spain. For the reasons already discussed, they changed their minds about intervening in the war; yet the first promise to send aircraft was actually honored, and thus it was only after several days had passed that it became apparent to the outside world that the French had altered their policy. This letter, then, was sent when the Republicans still thought that they could count on the French for at least the aircraft, if not more substantial aid. It was not Western inaction that forced the Spanish government into the Soviet sphere; the Republicans had already decided to request Soviet aid, not realizing how dependent they would become on the Russian bear.

As for the Soviet response to this request, the general consensus among scholars has been that Stalin determined to intervene only in late September or early October. Most historians have discounted the allegation by Walter Krivitsky, an NKVD agent who defected to the West during the war, that Stalin and the Politburo met in August and decided then to send weapons.[21] These scholars point out that Stalin elected to join the rest of Europe in signing a nonintervention agreement and actively participated in the Non-Intervention Committee, which met in London. Both these instruments were supposed to prevent a widening of the war by restraining the great powers from sending men or weapons of war to either of the belligerents in Spain. The Soviet Union, they argue, sent food and other humanitarian aid in September, and shipped only tanks, aircraft, and other military matériel after 8 October.[22] On that date the Soviet delegate to the committee, Ivan Maisky, warned that the Soviet Union would henceforth feel itself bound to the agreement to no greater degree than any of the other participants. This was an obvious reference to Italy and Germany, whose violations of the agreement were by this time too blatant to ignore. The apparent hesitation on the part of Stalin after 18 July, and his sudden change of policy, have required some explanation. Historians point to Stalin's desire to work with the West against fascism—the developing policy of "collective security"—and the purges then taking place, which may have distracted his attention from Spain.[23] In addition, military dispatches from the front lines suggested that the Republicans would collapse if they did not receive immediate and massive aid.[24] Then there were the reports from the first Soviet advisers on the scene, which emphasized the lack of modern technology in Spain and the dangers that this represented.[25] All these considerations, added to the blatant disregard that Hitler and Mussolini showed for the agreement, may have convinced Stalin to push beyond small arms and begin sending tanks, airplanes, and greater numbers of men in early October.

## Document 10

RGVA, f. 33987, op. 3, d. 991, ll. 56–59

Chairman of the Council of Ministers
Madrid, 25 July 1936
To the Ambassador of the USSR in France

Dear Sir:

The government of the Republic of Spain needs to supply its army with modern armaments in significant quantities to conduct the struggle against those who began and are continuing the civil war against the legal authority and constitutional government and who are being supplied with weapons and ammunition from abroad in abundant quantities. The government I head, knowing what sorts of means and availability of military matériel are at the disposal of the USSR, decided to appeal to you to notify your government about the desire and necessity, which our government is experiencing, for supplies of armaments and ammunition of all categories, and in very great quantities, from your country.

Taking the opportunity, etc.

Signature: José Giral

## The Advisers Begin Their Work

The Soviet Union responded to the Spanish request for aid with more than just weaponry. In August and September the first men arrived in Spain to help organize the war against the Nationalists. By late November, there were more than seven hundred Soviet military advisers (most of whom doubled as GRU workers), NKVD agents, diplomatic representatives, and economic experts in Spain. Before the outbreak of the war, Spain and the Soviet Union had not even maintained diplomatic relations. These were restored in late August with the arrival of Vladimir Antonov-Ovseenko and Marcel Rosenberg, the consul in Barcelona and the ambassador to Spain respectively. The military advisers were under the leadership of Yan Berzin (real name, Pavel Ivanovich Kiuzis Peteris), who was the head of the GRU until he left for Spain. He was aided by Grigory Shtern, the chief military adviser; Vladimir Gorev, military attaché; Nikolai Voronov, the official in charge of artillery; Boris Sveshnikov, adviser for the air forces; and Semyon Krivoshein, the commander of the tank units. The economy was to be put right by Artur Stashevsky. The Comintern, which already had representatives such as Codovilla in place before the war broke out, also sent dozens of its own people to help the Republicans. These included men like André Marty (who organized the International Brigades) and Palmiro Togliatti, the Italian Communist leader. Within a few months all of the International Brigades would have Comintern or regular Red Army officers as their commanders.

The major unanswered question is how exactly the Soviet Union (and the Comintern) conceived of the role of these men in Spain. From the new evidence it is clear that almost from the start, the Soviets saw themselves as much more than just "advisers," although they would continue to use the title throughout the war. They believed that they were in Spain to help win the war, whatever the cost. If it meant seizing control of the army, military operations, the Spanish economy, and eventually the Spanish political system, they were willing to do so. They complained about the incompetence of the Spanish, expected them to follow Soviet advice entirely, and would force out of power those who stood in the way. Comintern officials had a more ambiguous relationship with their Spanish

comrades and the Spanish government. On the one hand, they often decried the interference of the Soviets in Spanish affairs, complaining that it left very little room for the indigenous Communists
to develop their own party and run their own war. On the other
hand, they agreed that the Spanish were incompetent in both political and military matters and understood all too well the desire to
take control into one's own hands. This ambiguity would allow in-
dependent-minded Comintern representatives to act as the Soviets
did, gradually taking over the PCE and important sectors of the
war effort.

## ILYA EHRENBURG

The dispatches that these men sent back to the Comintern Secretariat and to Moscow constitute our best evidence of the way that
the Soviets and Comintern viewed the war in Spain and of the political maneuvering that went on behind the scenes. One of our first
glimpses of Soviet thinking about Spain comes from three letters by
Ilya Ehrenburg, a reporter and writer. Ehrenburg was much more
than simply an *Izvestia* correspondent, however. He in fact used his
nonthreatening position to talk frankly with the highest officials in
Spain and to determine their views of the political and military situation. In three pieces of correspondence, in particular, given here
as **Documents 11, 12, and 13,** he focused primarily on the political
situation. He then reported back to Rosenberg, who sent Ehrenburg's letters on to Stalin and other Politburo members. Ehrenburg's meetings with Luis Companys y Jover, the president of the
Catalan generalitat, revealed to Moscow the growing split between
Catalonia and the government in Madrid. The friction between the
two centers would create some of the biggest headaches for the Soviets, who naturally preferred to centralize authority, preferably in
Madrid. One of the strongest reasons for suspicion of the Barcelona
administration was the strength of the anarchists and "Trotskyists" (POUM) in Catalonia. From these letters it is clear that the Soviets saw their relationship with the anarchists as close to open
warfare. In the first letter, Ehrenburg described Juan García Oliver,
one of the best-known anarchist leaders, as "frenzied," "intransigent," "raving." He reported that FAI members purposely kept

ammunition away from the Communists and committed other "petty tyrannies." He commented in the second letter about the anarchists' lack of responsibility when it came to industry. The one positive note was Companys, who seemed more willing to support the Soviet Union and work against the anarchists. Ehrenburg thought that he should be sent "a steamship, even if it held only sugar," to soften his heart. The postscript to the letter in which this quotation appears showed that his advice to García Oliver had also produced concrete results.

Within a week the situation once again looked grim. In his third letter, Ehrenburg wrote that the war was not going well and that the anarchists, infiltrated by German intelligence agents, were at least partially responsible for the defeats and demoralization at the front. The "Trotskyists" had contributed to the problem by undermining the party in Catalonia, attracting away good leaders like Maurín, and carrying out "provocative activities." Meanwhile, the weak and disorganized party was incapable of improving matters. One reason was the interference of someone Ehrenburg called the "real" leader of the PCE. From the document it is obvious that it was one of the foreign Communists sent to advise the PCE, very probably either Boris Stepanov (as the Bulgarian Comintern representative in Spain was called) or Codovilla, who had signed the earliest dispatches from the PCE to Moscow.[26] Ehrenburg accused this man of taking the place of the Spaniards in the party, damaging the reputation of both the party and the Comintern, and hindering the formation of an independent Spanish leadership. Similar accusations would be made by other Soviet and Comintern officials, but Moscow would do nothing to rein in men who were, after all, simply following orders. Ehrenburg thought that the only bright spots were that Largo Caballero and Prieto listened to "everything that we say," and that it might not be necessary to merge the Socialist and Communist parties immediately. The Communists already had so much influence inside the UGT that he did not see any need to rush into uniting the two parties at that point in the war.

# Document 11

RGVA, f. 33987, op. 3, d. 852, l. 150

*Secret.*

To Com. *Stalin.*

Copies: to Comrades Molotov, Kaganovich, Voroshilov.

At the request of Com. Rosenberg, I am forwarding to you copies of three letters from Ehrenburg in Barcelona to Rosenberg in Madrid, which arrived in yesterday's diplomatic pouch.

/N. Krestinsky/

*9 Copies. vr/mm*
1–5—to addressees
6—to Com. Litvinov
7—to Com. Stomoniakov
8—to Com. Neiman
9—file

Copy N° 5.

[ll. 156–159]

17 September

Dear Marcel Israelevich [Rosenberg],

To add to today's telephone conversation, I report: Companys was in a very nervous state. I spoke with him for more than two hours, while all he did the whole time was complain about Madrid. His arguments: the new government has not changed anything; slights Catalonia as if it were a province, and this is an autonomous republic; sends instructions like to the other governors; refuses to turn over religious schools to the generalitat; demands soldiers and does not give out any of the weapons bought abroad, not one airplane, and so on. He said that he had received letters from the officers commanding units on the Talavera-Ávila front requesting that they be recalled to Catalonia. He very much wanted a Soviet consulate in Barcelona but thought that Madrid had shelved that question. He said that they had succeeded in conveying the gold to France, but the Spanish government in Paris suggested to the French banks (?) that they not take the gold. He cited dozens more examples. He said that the economic adviser that they sent to Madrid ought to state all of their claims. That issue still needs to be resolved. As yet, neither Caballero nor Prieto has managed to find time to receive him. And so on. He explained that if they did not receive cotton or hard currency for cotton within three weeks there would be a hundred thousand out of work. He very much wanted to trade with the Union.[27] He believed that any sign of attention being paid to Catalonia by the Union was important. As for the internal situation, he spoke rather optimistically: the influence of FAI was decreasing, the role of the government growing.

Gassol, the minister of education, also accused Madrid of contempt for Catalonia.

The head of Companys's cabinet (I forget his name) assured me that FAI was weakening.

According to him, the day before yesterday the Guardias de Asalto and the Guardia Civil openly spoke out against the CNT (I ought to note that the Communists, confirming this fact, attribute it to his growing influence over the UGT). It is worth mentioning that the black-and-red flag[28] was taken down from the courthouse yesterday. The anarchists threatened to start a row but gave it up.

I spoke with García Oliver. He was also in a frenzied state. Intransigent. At the same time that López, the leader of the Madrid syndicalists, was declaring to me that they had not permitted and would not permit attacks on the Union in the *CNT* newspaper, Oliver declared that they had said that they were "criticizing" the Union because it was not an ally, since it had signed the non-interference pact, and so on. Durruti, who has been at the front, has learned a lot, whereas Oliver, in Barcelona, is still nine-tenths anarchist ravings. For instance, he is against a unified command on the Aragon front; a unified command is necessary only when a general offensive begins. Sandino, who was present during this part of the conversation, spoke out for a unified command. They touched on the question of mobilization and the transformation of the militia into an army. Durruti made much of the mobilization plans (I do not know why—there are volunteers but no guns). Oliver said that he agreed with Durruti, since "Communists and Socialists are hiding themselves in the rear and pushing the FAI-ists out of the cities and villages." At this point he was almost raving. I would not have been surprised if he had shot me.

I spoke with Trueba, the PSUC (Communist) political commissar. He complained about the FAI-ists. They are not giving our men ammunition. We have only thirty-six bullets left per man. The anarchists have reserves of a million and a half. Col. Villalba's soldiers only have a hundred cartridges each. He cited many instances of the petty tyrannies of FAI. People from the CNT complained to me that Fronsosa, the leader of PSUC [*sic*], gave a speech at a demonstration in San Boi in which he said that the Catalans should not be given even one gun, since the guns would just fall into the hands of the anarchists. In general, during the ten days that I was in Catalonia, relations between Madrid and the generalitat on the one hand, and that between the Communists and the anarchists on the other, became very much more strained. Companys is wavering; either he gravitates toward the anarchists, who have

## Document 11 *continued*

agreed to recognize the national and even nationalistic demands of the Esquerra, or he depends on the PSUC in the struggle against FAI. His circle is divided between supporters of the former and of the latter solutions. If the situation on the Talavera front worsens, we can expect him to come out on one or
the other side. We must improve relations between the PSUC and the CNT
and then try to get closer to Companys.

In Valencia our party is working well, and the influence of the UGT is growing. But the CNT has free rein there. The governor takes their side completely.
This is what happened when I was there: sixty anarchists with two machine
guns turned up from the front, as their commander had been killed. In Valencia they burned the archives and then wanted to break into the prison to free
the criminals. The censor (this is under López, the leader of the CNT) prohibited our newspaper from reporting about any of this outrage, and in the CNT
paper there was a note that the "free masses destroyed the law archives as
[part of] the accursed past."

A meeting of Catalan writers is now taking place with Bergamín, who came
with me. I hope that on the intelligentsia front they succeed in uniting the
Spanish and the Catalans. Tomorrow a mass meeting with ten thousand people will be held with this goal, at which I will give a speech from the secretariat of the International Union of Workers for the Protection of Culture.

As this letter has several vital corrections for what I gave you for Moscow,
please send this as well to Moscow.

Day after tomorrow I am leaving for Paris. If you wish to communicate anything, please do it through our embassy.

Heartfelt greetings,
Ilya Ehrenburg

Postscript by Com. Rosenberg:
Thanks to dependence on the Spanish market, the vain attempt at an "independent" Catalonia has been held up by "dependence" on the general Spanish economy.
M.R.

## Document 12

RGVA, f. 33987, op. 3, d. 852, ll. 160–162

18 September

Dear M. I.,

Today I again had a long conversation with C. He was calmer. His point:
Robles was indulging the anarchists. It was hard to come to an agreement

with them. The plan of the "advisers" was not an ultimatum but a desire. He proposed to form a local government in this way: half Esquerra, half CNT and UGT. He said that he would reserve for himself finance and the police. After my words on the fact that the anarchists' lack of personal responsibility would interfere with manufacturing, he declared that he "agreed" to put a Marxist at the head of industry. He called Oliver a fanatic. He reproached the PSUC for not answering the terror of the anarchists with the same. On the conduct of the Catalan militia in Madrid, he said that that was the FAI-ists and that the national Guardia and the Esquerrists would fight anyone. He said that Madrid itself wanted the CNT militia, while not hiding the fact that the latter left to "establish order in Madrid." He advised sending them back from Madrid. He said that when Tardiella arrived (no doubt I've gotten the name mixed up—he's the one that went to Madrid) he would gather the CNT and the UGT and suggest forming a new government under his presidency.[29] He assured me that the *consejos* in that form would preserve the facade of a constitutional government. The whole time he cursed the FAI. He knew that I was going from him to the CNT and was very interested in how the FAI-ists would converse with me. He requested that I communicate the results [of the conversation] with him. He complained that the FAI-ists were against Russia, were carrying out anti-Soviet propaganda, or more accurately, carried out, but that he was our friend, and so on. A steamship, even if it held only sugar, would soften his heart.

With the CNT I spoke with Herrera. He was much more modest than Oliver. On stopping the anti-Soviet outbursts: he immediately agreed with me. On the advisers, he stands with his (!) Madrid government; party, Marxist. It is necessary to create a true workers' government, and so on. All the same, at the end of the visit, when I pointed out to him the diplomatic fallout from a break with constitutional succession, he gave in a little. But at this point all sorts of international anarchists descended on us and I left. The following is interesting: attacking the Madrid government, Herrera cited the same facts that Companys did yesterday—the delay with the two wagons, the story about the gold, the refusal to supply Catalonia with weapons, and so on. Moreover, he spoke with the tone of Catalan patriotism. Undoubtedly there is close contact between the generalitat and the CNT. The question is to what conclusion Companys will come.

Today in the *Solidaridad Obrera* an appeal by the CNT was printed with a call to protect small proprietors, peasants, shopkeepers, and so on. A favorable fact.

As for the trip by lawyers to the Union, that is either stupidity or desertion. We'll clarify it.

The great writer Bergamín (a Catholic antifascist) is personally handing you a letter. Snuggle up to him.

Miravitlles told me that the FAI-ists are already starting to talk about a

## Document 12 *continued*

"desperate defense of Barcelona," and so on. Herrera, among the other things he said, accused Madrid of doing away with the landing on Majorca, as the fascists will start to bomb Barcelona.

Sincerely yours,
Ilya Ehrenburg

There is a mass meeting today. Tomorrow morning I leave for Paris.

18 September
The mass meeting went off with a great deal of enthusiasm. The majority were CNT; however, when I spoke, I managed to get everyone to give a round of applause for the Union and the Spanish Republic. I appealed for unity. The council of the antifascist militia is now meeting. The members promised me that they would implement a conciliatory policy on the question of reorganizing the Catalan government.
The "tourists" are honest but stupid.

Yours,
I. Ehrenburg

18.

Addendum to the telephone conversation and letter:
Although Oliver was intransigent, I know that yesterday he nevertheless said in the *Sol. Obrera* to stop the attacks against the USSR. And indeed, two telegrams from Moscow were printed today in the *S.O.* with favorable headlines. So the conversation was not in vain.
I. E.

## Document 13

RGVA, f. 33987, op. 3, d. 852, ll. 151–155

N° 13 26/9/36
vkh N° 5186
30/9/36                                                                    Top Secret!
In such dynamic circumstances, when the comparatively small strength of the rebels is preparing to cut Madrid's rail communications and when everything depends on the morale of units which, under the influence of a new political enthusiasm, may yet, in the face of the direct danger threatening Madrid, reveal a capacity to resist which up to this time they have seemed in-

capable of—it is difficult to predict the further development of the struggle.

Only in the course of the civil war's development will the weight of the industrial north, now cut off by the front line and equipped with a certain amount of weaponry shipped recently from abroad, reveal its influence on the outcome of the struggle.

There are still a lot of unknowns, including such extremely vital factors as the internal situation in Portugal itself, which since the beginning of the rebellion has become a virtual base for the rebels; the situation in Morocco; and finally, such nontrivial factors as the size of further deliveries and resupplies of airplanes and tanks for the rebels on the part of Germany and Italy.

This last factor will play a paramount role for a reason that has already been noticed repeatedly—the lack of military experience among the Spanish workers and the resulting weak resistance in the face of modern military technology.

Inexperienced units panic not only in the face of an air bombardment, but also when faced with machine guns and other types of automatic weaponry.

The classic example showing that the militia is still not capable of decisive action is the story of the capture, or rather the noncapture, of Alcázar.

The demoralization of units is also explained in part by the deaths of the best self-sacrificing elements of the proletariat, which fell in street battles during the first days of the rebellion in Madrid, Barcelona, and other cities.

I will not dwell on the fact that the anarchist tradition, deeply sown in the consciousness of Spanish workers, even if they have not directly joined with the anarchists, plays its own negative role.

Undoubtedly one of the main tasks is to attract to the revolution's side, at this stage, the healthier elements from among the anarchists. It is characteristic that in the last conversation that I had with Galarza, the minister of the interior (a Socialist), he mentioned that his attempt at cooperation with the anarchist labor federation had produced positive results, and that lately several of the confederation leaders had begun to recognize that many alien elements were interspersed among their members. One of the anarchists' "idols," who provokes great doubts of a nonideological sort, is Juan López, who is now the boss of Valencia and who, by the way, directed some "compliments" at me in a speech delivered at a demonstration.

I will not again go over the diversionary work insinuated into the periphery of the anarchists by German intelligence, which I mentioned in my previous dispatch.

The question of possibly merging the Socialists and the Communists into one party (as in Catalonia) does not have, according to my preliminary impression, any immediate, current significance since the Socialist party, as such, at least in the central region, does not make itself much felt and since the Socialists and Communists act in concert within the framework of a union organization—the General Workers' Union—headed by Caballero (abbreviated UGT), the activity and influence of which far exceed the limits of a union.

Except for La Pasionaria, the leadership of the Communist party consists of people who do not yet have authority on the national level. The party's real general secretary was an individual about whom I wrote you. Because he occupied just such a position not only within the Central Committee but also outside it, he besmirched the reputations of two institutions with all the people in the Popular Front. However we evaluate his role, in any case, the fact that he himself took the place of the leadership hindered the formation, from the leadership cadres, of independent political leaders.

The Communist party, which has attracted some of the more politically conscious elements of the working class, is, all the same, insufficiently organized and politically strong to take on even to the slightest degree the political work for the armed forces of the revolution. In Catalonia, about which I can judge only through partial evidence, the party is significantly weaker and undoubtedly suffers from the provocative activities of Trotskyists, who have won over several active leaders, like, for example, Maurín. Undoubtedly the party is still incapable of independently rousing the masses to some kind of large-scale action, or of concentrating all the strength of the leadership on such an action. What is more the example of Alcázar has been in this connection a notoriously negative test for the party. However, I will not give a more definite evaluation of the cadres and strength of the party, since this is the only organization with which I have had insufficient contact.

What are our channels for action in this situation? We support close contact with the majority of the members of the government, chiefly with Caballero and Prieto. Both of them, through their personal and public authority, stand incomparably higher than the other members of the government and play a leading role for them. Both of them very attentively listen to everything that we say. Prieto at this particular time is trying at all costs to avoid conflict with Caballero and therefore is trying not to focus on the issues.

I think it unnecessary to dwell at this time on the problem of how an aggravation in class contradictions might take shape during a protracted civil war and the difficulties with the economy that might result (supplying the army, the workers, and so on), especially as I think it futile to explore a more distant prospect while the situation at the front still places all the issues of the revolution under a question mark.

In this kind of circumstance, such as I have touched on above and which I went into in my summary telegram, there is no need to prove that supplying [the Spanish] with technology may turn out to have a huge influence on the final outcome of the civil war. It is clear that however significant the temporary successes of the rebels may be, they have in no way guaranteed a definitive advantage. The steadfast military cadres of the revolution will be forged in the very process of the civil war.

## Document 13 *continued*

In this letter I have managed to touch superficially upon only some of the questions relating to an analysis of the entire situation—I will leave my summary telegram at the base.

25/9/1936[Rosenberg]

x) As I have already informed you, the syndicalist form of power proposed by the anarchists actually amounts to the creation of rev.[olutionary] com.[mittees] from the anarchist confederation of labor (CNT) and the union organization headed by Caballero (UGT) with a fictitious Republican adjunct to that. This formula in the provinces is nearly always put into effect in the bloc CNT with UGT, and in Castile as the bloc UGT with CNT.

---

ANDRÉ MARTY

André Marty's experiences in Spain supported Ehrenburg's analysis of the party. Marty's reputation was as a strict Stalinist, suspicious of virtually everyone and willing to shoot anyone that he suspected of deviations or treachery.[30] The two documents in this chapter lend credence to this contention, while adding a few nuances. He thought, for instance, that the Communists were quite capable of making mistakes on their own, quite apart from the insidious sabotage of the anarchists and "Trotskyists." He also believed that it was wrong to take control over the PCE away from the Spanish, but on this point he would find no more of an audience than Ehrenburg did. In **Document 14,** a report to the Comintern on the condition of the PCE, Marty detailed exhaustively the weaknesses of the Communists and the difficulties that they faced in trying to respond to the war. Although the party was growing at a "very rapid pace," it was actually doing very little and planning even less for the future. It apparently had no concrete policies on military matters or the unions, and the agrarian line, though correct, was not publicized. He viewed the PSUC, formed without the permission of the Comintern, with great suspicion and thought its policies "erratic" and its leaders suspect. He reserved his most severe criticism, however, for the leadership of the PCE. The Central Committee no longer existed, the work of the Politburo was "terribly primitive," and the only capable Spanish leader was ill. Instead "Codo" (short for Codovilla) had taken over running the party, which he apparently viewed as his own personal preserve. The Hungarian representative Erno Gerö imitated Codovilla as well, taking the place of the Spanish Politburo members. It is significant that, though Marty severely criticized both these men for their high-handed actions, he also was frustrated by the poor functioning of the Spanish government and the PCE. He understood all too well the advisers' desire to seize control and run the country themselves. The appraisals of the Communist party made by Marty and Ehrenburg confirm the accusations of historians such as Víctor Alba that the PCE, completely subordinated to Moscow before the war began, did not have an independent life during the conflict.[31] Instead, it was the international Communist movement that ran the party, using mouthpieces such as Dolores Ibárruri ("La Pasionaria") to give the illusion of Spanish control. Erno Gerö was in fact rewarded for his attitude toward the Spanish comrades. As Marty mentioned, he was ordered to Barcelona to oversee the PSUC in early October. There he directed that party from behind the scenes, as Bolloten writes, "with extraordinary energy, tact, and efficiency."[32]

The day before he gave this report, Marty had presented a longer summary of the general situation in Spain (**Document 15**). In contrast to the report on the PCE, which had a more limited distribution, here Marty said very little about the Communists' weaknesses and instead stressed their increasing political influence and successful policies. There were two areas for concern—the subversive anti-Communist activities of the anarchists and Largo Caballero—which he thought were linked. From this report and others from Soviet advisers, it is clear that by early October the honeymoon between the Communists and Largo Caballero was already over. Marty, like the rest of the foreign representatives and advisers in Spain, had decided that Largo Caballero was not going to implement Communist policies and was far too favorable toward the anarchists. The Spanish leader also did nothing about the "treachery" that was going on in the state bureaucracy and military apparatus. Only when he "changed for the better" and began to pay more attention to the Communists did Marty find anything good to say about the man who had once been called the Spanish Lenin. Meanwhile, the anarchists continued unchecked their "wrecking" (sabotage) in industry, agriculture, and the army. Marty had to admit several times that the anarchists enjoyed a great deal of prestige and that their proposals were extremely popular, but this was owing to good campaigning and propaganda, not to the true support of the people.

Like other Communists, Marty distinguished various strata among the anarchist leaders and their masses. There were a few "good" anarchists and many "bad" anarchists, and the Communists hoped to be able to encourage the first, while working to destroy the latter. The most ominous warning that Marty gave throughout his report was that the "bad" anarchists were gathering weapons and were better armed than the Communists. He also mentioned a report by Codovilla that the anarchists (working with Largo Caballero) had prepared a coup in August to overthrow the government. None of the scholars who have studied the Civil War mention any such preparations, and it seems unlikely, given a whole variety of factors.[33] In light of the events of the following May, however, it is significant that in October 1936 the Communists already anticipated a use of force by their main political enemies. Marty's most important statement on his views of the anarchists and the future of Spain came at the very end of the report. There he noted that "to fight with [the anarchists] in the face of fascism—this [would be] the end. This means that we should not stop at conceding something to them, and after victory we will get even with them, all the more so since at that point we will have a strong army." Throughout the war, the Communists never lost sight of what they needed in order to shape postwar Spain. Their insistence on control over the Spanish police, army, and secret services made chilling sense and is yet another reminder that similar tactics would be used in postwar Eastern Europe.

# Document 14

RGASPI, f. 495, op. 74, d. 199, ll. 61–64

14 October 1936
Secret
Remarks About the CP of Spain

André Marty

In the period from 18 July to 1 September, the members of the party were absorbed with the armed struggle. Thus, all of the work of the party was reduced to military action, but largely in an individual sense, rather than from the standpoint of political leadership of the struggle. At best, the party committees discussed urgent questions (the collection of weapons and explosives, supplies, questions of housing, and so on) but without setting forth perspectives [for the future] or still less following a general plan.

Beginning on 18 July, many leaders headed the struggle and remained at this work later, during the formation of the columns. For example, Cordón is the assistant commander of the Estremadura column; Uribe, the deputy for Valencia has the same position in the Teruda column; and Romero is in the column that is at Málaga; del Barrio is in the column at Saragossa. But it must be said that only a very few of the leaders have the requisite military abilities (I do not mean personal bravery). Thus, of the four just mentioned, Cordón is a brilliant commander, del Barrio is quite good, and the rest are worthless from a military point of view.

The political activity of the party has been reduced to the work of the leadership (editorship of the newspapers, several cells, démarches to the ministries). Party agitation, not counting what is carried out in the press, has come to naught. Internal party life has been reduced to the discussion of important, but essentially practical and secondary, questions.

Meanwhile, recruiting has moved and continues to move at a very rapid pace. The influx of new members into the party is huge. For the first time intellectuals and even officers are being drawn into the party (I am not talking about those like Asen[s]io, whose declaration about admittance was, apparently, dictated by personal ambition).

But on the other hand, the party has not worked on military matters. Comrade CODO declared, "Not being a military man myself, I cannot give you my opinion." But already the most active elements from the middle cadres began in July to set up militia units which subsequently were transformed into the Fifth Regiment. The general staff of the Fifth Regiment, consisting of workers or officers who are Communists or sympathizers—this is the best thing that we have in the entire fighting army. As the Politburo has not given anything but general directives, it is understandable that friction has ensued. For the first time, in the middle of September, the general staff heard a political report by MIJE. They were extremely satisfied.

The Central Committee no longer exists. Several members of the CC were killed; others were expelled or removed for various reasons. Around the Politburo (see the details in the report to the secretariat from the 10th) only a few members of the CC remain (URIBES [*sic*], ROMERO, and so on).

Even at the moment of the formation of the ministry, the P.B.'s understanding consisted solely of the need to defeat the enemy, the need to make war.

Thus, Comrade CASTRO, who as the commander of the Fifth Regiment enjoyed colossal authority, was removed and named director of the Institute of Agrarian Reform. We lost ten days on that, searching for a new deputy for Lister's regiment. The CPF, in agreement with the PCE, sent Comrade Gayman for work in the military commission, at the disposal of the PCE. In the course of twenty days, the party secretariat, and in particular Comrade CODO, had not given him any directives and had not used any of his work. When I arrived in Madrid, he was already ready to leave.

Beginning with the first days of September, the external agitation of the party (mass meetings) began progressively to develop. Simultaneously with that, mainly through the help of Gerö, we changed the line in *Mundo Obrero:* instead of [one on] a sacred optimism, we began a campaign on the need to organize the war. Three CC instructors were sent to the Levant to strengthen the party's organization and for the political leadership of the new military units, which are forming with the Fifth Regiment. At the end of September we set up the organization of the party organs in the military units on the following basis: a front committee, with the rights of a provincial committee, which will lead the Communist groups and the political sections[34] that are being set up in the new units; behind them is the provincial committee, responsible for the political sections and groups in the units that are in their territory.

This decision was very well received by the party and the comrades that are in the army. But all the same, this directive has still not been put into effect; such an organization has only begun. The internal activity of the party: this continues to be very weak and limited to the resolution of routine questions, but the political problems have not been discussed and are not being discussed now.

THE PARTY LEADERSHIP. The current leadership exists only in Madrid and Valencia. In addition, the leadership in Valencia is very weak politically, which is reflected in the newspaper (*Verdad*). In all of the provinces of the Levant, our influence is very strong both in the cities and in the villages. But with the exception of the provincial committees in Alicante and Murcia, all of the rest of the committees are very weak. The Cartagena Committee works very well from a practical point of view (thanks to the influence of the workers of the naval arsenal and the sailors, both of whom are under our influence. The commander of the cruiser *Núñez* is a Communist, a sea mechanic for twenty-eight years). Our party is still very young in this entire area, and it still needs to learn everything.

CATALONIA. Our party (the Unified Socialist Party of Catalonia—PSUC—in Comintern) is not united. It continues to remain [merely] the sum of the four component parties from which it was created. From the point of view of the Communist [party], despite the fact that the leadership is in our hands, it does not have an ideological backbone. There is significant friction from this. Despite this fact, [the party's] correct policy vis-à-vis the peasantry and petty bourgeoisie enhances its powerful influence daily. The PSUC is the third party in Catalonia (after Esquerra and the CNT). A majority of the members of the party are members of the UGT, which has significantly increased the number of its members. Unfortunately, the erratic policy of the party, especially on the question of cadres, gave the opportunity to raise SESÉ to the head of the UGT—a man who is suspect from every point of view (see the protocols of the Catalan Commission at the Seventh Congress of the Comintern International in September 1935). Arlandis (see the same document) continues to remain in the leadership. He is constantly in France under the pretext of buying weapons and refused to carry out a party resolution (P.B. PCE) that recalled him to Madrid. The leadership of the Socialist party in MADRID (the Workers' Party of Spain) continues to work in the PSUC, and it often happens that the local groups direct their letters to it instead of writing to the CC PCE. On the other hand, Caballero is striving to seize the leadership. Fifteen days ago in Madrid he handed three million pesetas to COMORERA, the general secretary of the PSUC, for whom we sent to discuss the question of Catalonia, and we heard this information about him.

The party's union policy. Nothing practical has been done. The CNT continues to follow an ever increasing number of UGT declarations, but generally for political reasons. Our groups assemble but do not work on the problems of everyday demands. In general, our activists remain in the UGT (the work is easier). It is my opinion that the struggle for the unification of the unions is becoming a pressing task. I proposed that the unions that are under our influence appeal for unification with two aims: 1) unity of the working class to defend the interests of the workers against the employers; 2) unity in production to defeat fascism. Mije in principle accepted this proposal on unification (without pointing out the aims) at a large mass meeting organized by the party in Madrid on 27 September. This proposal elicited very strong applause, but I would have preferred that this had been done as I proposed. It is my opinion that union work requires radical restructuring.

This will give us the opportunity to smash the sectarian attitude of our party toward the anarchists in the workers' committees.

Agrarian policy. In general the policy is correct (see the decision by the Ministry of Agriculture on the question of land), but it has not been popularized in the villages. They do not demonstrate the deep difference between our line and the methods of the anarchists. And in this area a colossal work still must be accomplished.

Life of the party. The organization of several regional conferences is foreseen. The Asturian conference should have taken place on 4 October. The Politburo could not send anyone (Pasionaria, who was selected, could not get an airplane). Thus I do not have any information about how it went. But it seems that MANSO, our deputy (leader since October 1934) was completely outdone by the Socialists. I have not heard anywhere that the question about the future leadership of Asturias is being discussed.

Work of the P.B. Terribly primitive. I managed to go to three meetings, for unfortunately these meetings are conducted in circumstances which allow nonresident comrades to remain at the meetings and hear everything that is discussed there. The same kind of sickness exists in the P.B., and in many party committees. They are discussing one question, a thousand others are joined to it, and finally no exact decisions are resolved on, nor are there any methods offered to put such decisions into effect, nor is it indicated who is responsible for carrying them out.

Despite the fact that a mass of secret documents are strewn about the tables, I never saw any written decisions from either the secretariat or the Politburo.

The only person capable of leading the P.B. and making decisions is DÍAZ—the general secretary. Unfortunately, the state of his health is such that he ought not to work.

Proposals:

It is necessary to define more precisely the policy of the party on the following questions:

a) Economic measures (industry and agriculture) and social policy in the current circumstances. (The party has still not spoken on such measures as commandeering, committees of workers' control that have been put into effect by the anarchists; the organizations have not received any kind of directives on these questions.) What must be undertaken in order to carry this out and to popularize it (the creation of a large agitprop department)?

b) Organizational measures of the party (1. usual organizations in the Republican zone and organizations in the military units, 2. illegal organizations in the zone occupied by the fascists, and 3. finances of the party).

c) The strengthening of the leadership in every organization and the appointment of a new Central Committee.

At the current time it is without doubt difficult to convene a party congress quickly, but then, it is possible to conduct a provincial conference relatively easily (even including Catalonia) and a party conference.

Remarks about the dispatch of representatives and instructors to Spain.

I was very surprised on my arrival in Madrid by the work of Codo. There is no other term for this than "ka" [*sic*]. He does everything himself. He works in the former office of Gil Robles (the party is housed in the former building of

CEDA). At 9 o'clock in the morning, he receives everyone and right there decides all the questions himself. Before his arrival in September, he wrote many of the editorials for *Mundo Obrero* himself.

This kind of conduct, it seems to me, completely contradicts the directive of the Seventh Congress and of Comrade Dimitrov. The result of this is that the members of the party have been turned into nothing but executors [of orders], they completely lose any feeling of responsibility, and [this] impedes the organizing of cadres. Thus, for example, Com. Checa, upon whom has been laid responsibility for organizing the police, spends three-quarters of his day signing passes, searching rooms, and dealing with petty problems.

Codo views the party as his own property. On his return from Moscow, he gave a very concise report; I feel now that it was nowhere near complete. In particular, he said absolutely nothing about the criticism put forward here.

In my opinion this kind of behavior is intolerable. Either he ought to be a member of the Spanish Communist party, in which case he can be appointed general secretary, and then only if he changes his work methods.

Or he remains a representative of the Comintern, and in that case, he ought not to take the place of the secretary of the party, he ought to act through the councils and not take the place of the party's leadership under any circumstances.

By the way, it was not surprising to me that when coming here, on the way here and on the way back, he sat each time in Paris for five days, despite the serious situation.

Comrade Gerö imitates him on a lesser scale, but in the same vein. After his departure from here, Comrade Gerö arrived in Madrid before I did. He took a post and imitated Codo's working methods, perhaps to a lesser degree. In particular, he did not write articles for the newspaper himself but inspired those who did write them. I pointed out to him in a very comradely way that it was not good to take the place of the P.B. members. So, for example, he alone heard the reports from the regional, district, and so on, secretaries and issued directives. Comrade Checa, the secretary of the organization, was never present at these conversations. To my remarks, Comrade Gerö declared to me that now was not the time to be occupied with experiments. I believe that his methods, although it is true that they are not as authoritarian, are just as bad as Codo's methods.

Of course, it is clear that when you are in Madrid and you see the sabotage of the government bureaucracy, the indisputable delays in carrying out directives by the organs of the party, you try to take control into your own hands. But all the same I believe that this method is not good. First, because one should not take the place of the leadership. Second, because we are lessening the authority of the Politburo by giving directives personally to the regional secretaries and other individuals. And finally, because by doing this, we are delaying the development of cadres.

As for me, I am content that I am making my own proposals. In the best case about 40 percent were accepted. I am convinced that the best method is to persuade patiently. This method, in my opinion, will have the greatest results. Even on the general staff of the Fifth Regiment I never gave any directives and never approved directives, even if I myself was in agreement with them. I always asked that these directives be approved by the P.B., or at the least by responsible members of the Politburo.

Comrade Gerö, carrying out the directive that was received from here, is now in Catalonia. I think that he will not take the place of the party leadership in Barcelona, thanks to the peculiarities of that party (groups of leaders, consisting of the former leadership of the four parties), but in Madrid matters are very much amiss.

3 copies
1 copy to Com. Manuilsky
2 copies to Com. Moskvin

22 Outgoing N° 985/o
11 Oct. 1936

## Document 15

RGVA, f. 33987, op. 3, d. 832, ll. 70–107

*Top Secret*

To Comrade Voroshilov K.E.

Accompanying this is a stenogram of a report just given by Com. Marty (when he arrived from Madrid) at a meeting of the secretariat of the Comintern on 10/10/1936.

17/10/36
[signed] /D. Manuilsky/

*Secret*

(6) la.
17/10/36

### On the Situation in Spain

Report by Com. André Marty at a meeting of the secretariat of the ECCI
on 10 October 1936

In this report I will touch on three topics: the political situation in the country, the military situation, and also the near-term prospect.

# Document 15 *continued*

### 1. *Political Situation*

I left Madrid on 2 October, at a moment fraught with tension for Spain's political and military situation.

The Caballero government, set up on 3 September, met with enormous enthusiasm both at the rear and at the front. Now that government is just as discredited as the Giral administration was then.

The government is losing its authority by showing weakness toward the anarchists, who are destroying industry with their experiments. To this must be added the distress that the military defeats have caused the people.

The breakthrough at Talavera led to the fall of Giral's government. Now the situation at the front is worse. In the last few days of September, Torrijos fell, leading to the surrender of Toledo. On 9 October the enemy seized two important points—Navalperal and Santa Cruz del Retamarro. The fall of Toledo created panic in Madrid. The people were convinced that the enemy would be in the capital within a few hours. And if the fascists had that minute thrown a column of armored cars and a cavalry squad at Madrid, the city might have been taken by them without a fight.

The government is also losing its authority because they were unable to make any changes in providing supplies for the country. Despite the fact that Madrid still has lines of communication open with the richer areas of Levant, there are not enough sugar, milk, coffee, potatoes, beans.

### A. *Weakness and Indecisiveness of the Government*

The internal discord within the Caballero administration has not ended. Caballero is a sort of bad union bureaucrat. Prieto is undoubtedly a capable man, but he is completely absorbed in thinking about how to play dirty tricks on his "friend" Caballero. The newspapers *Claridad* (Caballero's organ) and *El Socialista* (Prieto's organ) excel in attacking each other. The other ministers go along. Only the two Communist ministers use all their might to weld together the government with concrete proposals directed at strengthening the struggle against fascism. Unfortunately, many of these proposals, because of Caballero's opposition, are rejected and, even if they are adopted, are not put into effect. One serious and helpful man in the ministries is the Left Republican Just (the minister of social work). The minister of internal affairs (a Socialist from Caballero's group) is a very energetic man. Del Vayo, the minister of foreign affairs, also has clear and correct purposes. But the work methods of these people are extremely primitive. Prieto, the minister of the navy and aviation, does all the technical work himself at the ministry: he calls up the various institutions himself, dictates to the typist, hunts for people—and this is one of the best organizers.

Anyone can walk into the building of the War Ministry unimpeded and unchecked. At the reception for the ministry there is always a crush: officers, militia commanders, union workers helping everyone there, sometimes on highly secret matters. The ministry workers dictate to typists there. As a prime example: the minister's secretary is not in the military, but is a union worker. Women workers for the MOPR go into the minister's office without permission. Of course this kind of situation does not protect the interests of the work done by the minister of security. And we were very happy that the work for fortifying Madrid was given to the Ministry of Social Work under the leadership of Just [a Communist] and not to the War Ministry headed by Caballero.

Azaña, the president of the Republic, is fully aware of his situation, but his power is limited by law and he is the kind of man who can never let himself step outside the bounds of the law.

This is a rough characterization of the government's work, which has not been able to use the enthusiasm of the masses or to create a genuine antifascist unity. One of the reasons for this disorder, in my opinion, is that it has never given the masses an answer to the question, What are we fighting for? The government says that the goal for the struggle is victory over fascism. That kind of formula may unify all the revolutionary elements, but it is beside the point for the rest of the population. From my point of view, that kind of formulation is insufficient.

B. *On the Situation in the Machinery of State*

The machinery of state is either destroyed or paralyzed. In the best-case scenario it just does not have any authority. Every step is [marked by] treachery. It is absolutely obvious, for instance, that provincial governors and the higher officer corps are betraying us.

Thus the civilian and military governor of Málaga came to the conclusion that to protect the city from the enemy, it was necessary to pull back all forces as close as possible to the city. They thus left all the high ground unprotected and allowed the enemy to cut off communications to the city. From the very beginning of the fascist rebellion, the workers' organizations in Málaga asked the government to replace both governors, but neither Giral nor Caballero would agree to this demand. The result is that these wreckers,[35] who have no authority among the population, destroyed the city's defenses.

The governor of Valencia allowed a "steel column" of anarchists, who had remained in positions without authorization, to enter the city. The anarchists began to disarm the Republican militia and the Guardia Civil; they paraded around the city militia men who had been stripped of their clothing. Only the Communists managed to put a stop to this disgrace and disarm this unrestrained gang. This time the governor was removed from his post.

The lack of discipline in parts of the state, which has treachery lodged within, means that the antifascist elements in the government that are dedicated to us remain half paralyzed. We must pay very serious attention to the machinery of state.

# Document 15 *continued*

## C. *The Situation in Industry*

The anarchists set up worker control everywhere, transforming the workers into factory owners. The movement for worker control began in Catalonia, then spread to the Levant and gripped Madrid. Even foreign enterprises—for example, a branch of the French Renault factory—are in the hands of workers' committees. Almost all private enterprises, even those whose owners did not go over to the rebels, went into the hands of workers' committees. The social services in the large cities are in the same situation: trams, gas, electricity. All automobiles have been requisitioned by workers' organizations.

I will give the example of the decision by the anarchist CNT (National Labor Confederation) and FAI (Iberian Anarchist Federation), which are always linked with each other. The decision reads: "The workers of all branches of industry must quickly begin the sequestration of all enterprises through their collectivization. This should be done in the shortest possible time, after which workers' councils will be elected, which will direct industry with the help of the appropriate technical personnel.

In the absence of such personnel, demands will be handled by the FAI's Technical Control Committee.

There should be a representative of the Economic Council in the councils."

I have in my hands decisions showing how this socialization will take place. Here, for example, is a copy of an act on sequestering gas works and electric stations.

. . .

What is the danger here? The danger is that these decisions nearly always affect the interests of small and midsize industry, small and midsize trade, and even small shops. In Barcelona all bakeries, small bread shops, chocolate factories, and so on, were nationalized. This movement has swept through the provinces. In Madrid they even nationalized the beauty shops. The owner of a beauty shop will have equal pay with his or her workers. The anarchist organization in Madrid, and with it all anarchist newspapers, are promoting the slogan of equal pay. In Catalonia this slogan has already been put into effect.

. . .

We see then that the Committee of Workers' Control will not only regulate the conditions of work but also control the entire life of the enterprise. These committees exist not only in Catalonia but also in many large cities of the Levant and even in Madrid.

The anarchists are very active and are trying to carry out this same kind of work in the south. During the war, they declare, we need to intensify production and at the same time carry out a social revolution. The anarchists do not miss any chance to emphasize their constructive capabilities. They do not tire of writing about that in their papers. I dwell at length on this question because the anarchists have a decisive influence for the entire country and even for Madrid, where the government is located.

## Document 15 *continued*

### D. *The Agrarian Question*

A very popular anarchist slogan is on the reconstruction of agriculture: "We need to destroy the economic base of fascism." Under this slogan, all the anarchists are agitating for the collectivization and nationalization of land. In all their decisions, in all their press, they insist on the need for collectivization, so that "the peasants can catch up with what cuts them off from the industrial workers." They extol all the advantages of collectivization.

A congress of Catalan peasants which representatives of two hundred unions attended decided that:

"All sequestration of land will be under the control and direction of unions and the cultivation of their collective means favorably affects, in the first place, the unions and, in general, all workers."

In this decision, as in a whole series of other documents and pronouncements, they stipulate the need to implement collectivization voluntarily, the need to treat the small property owners with respect, not to hurt their interests, and so on.

In fact, it happens that even in Catalonia, where small landowners (rabassaires) are very widespread, the anarchists are attacking them. Their land is subject to requisition. Requisitioned land either is not paid for at all or is paid for with vouchers, which are worth precisely nothing. Villages are often hit with fines.

What are the results of this kind of policy? I personally visited Murcia, a rich area famous for its gardens. Noticing that the peasants when meeting did not greet each other with the Republican salutation, as in all the other villages, I ask the secretary of the provincial party committee what this meant. He answered me: "The situation here is very difficult. The peasants say that earlier they paid the landowner and now they pay the union, meaning that nothing has really changed."

### E. *Problems in Catalonia*

The comrades know that the new Catalan government is completely independent from Madrid. But, until lately, power in Catalonia rested, essentially, not in the hands of the Catalan government, but in the hands of the Central Committee of militia, led by the anarchists. This Central Committee advanced the slogan of the creation of committees of workers, peasants, soldiers, and militiamen. Not long ago the CC militia was disbanded, but all its members went into the government.

The current Catalan government consists of three Left Republican councillors, three representatives from the CNT, two from the Unified Socialist Party (formed as a result of the merging of the Communist and two Socialist parties in Catalonia), one from the peasant's union (Rabassaires), one from the Workers Party of Marxist Unity (Maurín's group, uniting with the Trotskyists; their representative in the government is Nin), one from the Independent Party, one representative from the petty-bourgeois party Acció Catalá. We have two portfolios in this government: the Ministry of Communal Economy and Labor and the Ministry of Social Work. The program of the new government does not differ at all from the anarchist program that was published in the *Solidaridad Obrera* from 29 October:

. . .

Thus, in short outline, the characteristics of the country's economic situation. The workers manage the enterprises but do not know how to run them. In actual fact, the anarchists are in control of everything.

The anarchists in Barcelona say: We are working on the war. They turn out armored cars, but they are so heavy that they can move only on flat terrain and very quickly break down. And so far the anarchists have wastefully consumed all the raw materials they found at the enterprises. But the reserves are coming to an end, and they are being forced to buy from abroad, mainly from France. Their legations go abroad with gold and valuables that they have seized. And often they just buy all kinds of trash. In Barcelona, meanwhile, the impression is created that they are very active and energetic. The workers are actually working hard and even many foreign specialists, who are not in any position to understand this complicated social mess, are won over by the enthusiasm of the masses. Thus, for example, one aviation engineer—Serre— the technical director of a French company, Air France, who was in Barcelona for three days to study the possibility of repairing and producing airplanes, declared to me, "Everything is going well in Barcelona. I spoke with the workers' committee, with the engineers; they will repair and even produce new machines." After I checked, it turned out that factory could not do anything in less than a month. All sorts of rogues and frauds have flocked to the workers' committees with the most fantastic proposals. The engineers do not dare to object, because they are afraid that they will be shot as saboteurs. The result is that Catalan industry is almost paralyzed by the anarchists. The little that they still manufacture remains in Catalonia itself; the anarchists give nothing to Madrid.

F. *On the Position and Activities of the Anarchists*

Which forces play the main role in the current situation? Only two forces are present: the anarchists and the Communists. The Socialists have withdrawn to the background, owing to internal discord and incapacity to seize the initiative.

The prestige of the anarchists has grown appreciably. In Barcelona itself this coincided with their active role in the suppression of the rebellion of 18– 19 July. It was then that the prominent anarchist leader Ascaso died. One of the leaders of the anarchists, Durruti, leads operations on the Aragon front; the other leader, García Oliver, commands the militia forces in Barcelona. Both of them are always at the fronts. The prestige of the anarchists has also grown in Madrid. In general, the anarchist union enjoys no less influence than Caballero's union. The influence of the anarchists has also grown among

45

the peasants. But they are especially strong among the sailors of the navy. There are also many officers connected with the anarchists, but part of the officers go along with us. The anarchist militia is better armed than ours, since the anarchists appropriated weapons everywhere that they could. They have not only rifles but machine guns, as well.

Com. Codovilla told the presidium how the anarchists, together with Caballero, at the end of August prepared a coup to overthrow the government. After Caballero came to power, they quieted down somewhat. At first they supported the new government, but when they became convinced that Caballero was not ensuring victory, they began a campaign even against Caballero's government. A plenum of all regional organizations of the CNT was held on 18 September. The plenum adopted a resolution demanding the creation of a national defense council, in which there would be representatives from all the proletarian organizations fighting against fascism: five delegates from the General Workers' Union, five from the National Labor Confederation, and four from the Republicans. The chairman of the defense council would be Largo Caballero. In that resolution there was not one mention of the Communists. But two days later a delegation from the anarchists came to the CC of the Communist party, declaring that they had nothing against the Communists, but since the Communists were in the UGT, they could receive representation on the council through that union; they said that they had reached an understanding with the Socialists to divide positions [on the council] between them.

In the same resolution the plenum of the CNT regional committees advanced demands for the reorganization of the ministries and their conversion into departments; for the creation of a unified people's militia on the basis of universal military service; for control over militias by the councils of workers and militiamen, created by the General Workers' Union and the National Labor Confederation; for the creation of a unified military command in the form of a military commissariat, appointed by a national council from among representatives of the three sectors that are fighting against fascism. Concerning the economy, the resolution envisaged the socialization of banks; the socialization of property of the Church, which controls large amounts of land, of large industrial enterprises, of wholesale trade, of transport, and of all enterprises whose owners were involved in the rebellion; workers' control over industry and private commerce; the use by workers' unions of all the socialized means of production and exchange; freedom of experimentation in the villages, the implementation of which would not hinder the normal economic life of the country; [centralized] planning for large-scale industry and agriculture. At the same time, they resolved to call a plenary meeting in ten days of CNT regional organizations, to decide the question of putting into action the adopted resolution.

On 25 September the CNT held four large mass meetings in Barcelona,

Madrid, Valencia, and Málaga. The meetings were very successful, since the anarchists came with concrete proposals. In Madrid, López, a very popular anarchist from Valencia, declared in his speech (and this was printed in all the newspapers), "There is one party that wants to monopolize the revolution. If that party continues its policy, we have decided to crush it. There is a foreign ambassador in Madrid who is interfering in Spanish affairs. We warn him that Spanish affairs concern only the Spanish." This was the first public speech by the anarchists [directed] against us and against the Soviet plenipotentiary. About this I need to say that, while attacking the "disloyal" Soviet plenipotentiary, López did not utter one word about the destructive work done by the German, Italian, and Portuguese ambassadors against Spain.

Not one of the organizations decided to give an immediate answer to the anarchists' resolution/ultimatum. All were waiting for a change at the front, counting on the fact that even the most insignificant victory would allow them to avoid giving an answer. The president of the Republic refused to receive a delegation from the CNT, and Caballero would not receive them, either. The only party that approved the anarchists' proposal without reservations was the small Federal Republican Party, which does not play any role at all. On 25 September the Socialists formally replied that the question posed by them concerned the government and that the government ought to answer it.

The General Workers' Union responded on 26 September. In the answer they said that the unions agreed to the formulation of the question on unity but that they did not agree to change the constitution and so on. Our answer was published in *Mundo Obrero* on 29 September. We said that we welcomed everything in the anarchists' proposal that furthered the achievement of unity, discipline, and real coordination of all forces. We agreed that it was necessary to quickly recruit all antifascist forces for the organization of struggle and victory. Believing that the decision of the CNT plenum will rally all of the organizations who are responsible before the masses and before history for the final victory over fascism, we propose calling a meeting of the representatives of all organizations and parties to come to the desired agreement.

At the same time, we introduced a number of practical suggestions, which anticipated the involvement of the anarchists in all important existing government organizations, to heighten, in this way, their feeling of responsibility toward the common cause.

On the following day the CNT newspaper published an article in which it was said that the Communists completely agreed with the anarchist proposals. This is evidence of the fact that our answer on unity, on the use of the proposal made by CNT, awoke a response among the anarchist masses.

The anarchists published a new appeal on 29 September, less provocative in tone. But at the same time, an article was published in their paper whose headline said that only counterrevolutionary parties could be against the CNT proposals. From that day on, the anarchists have tirelessly repeated,

"Why is everyone so slow to create a national defense council? This silence aids the enemy." *Solidaridad Obrera* has strengthened its assault on the government, attacking the Basque nationalists, the Catholics, and so on.

We have to take all of this into consideration. The anarchists have under their control, either directly or indirectly, all major industry and part of the agriculture of this country. They contrast the creation of a national defense council with the Council of Ministers. But the thought of creating such a council finds a wide response even among the masses that are not under the anarchists' influence. We must find the right tone for discussions and conversations with the anarchists. The antagonism between the anarchist and the Communist workers in Spain is very great. It is especially dangerous now, because both sides are armed.

At the same time, we must not see all anarchists as one solid mass. Among their leaders we must differentiate three groups. Some, like Durruti and Oliver, are fighting with weapons in hand against fascism. They understand that without unity they will be defeated. They are for the introduction of military discipline, for unified command, which contradicts anarchist "theories." These leaders reflect the mood of their masses who understand the seriousness of the current situation. The second group is represented by López, who spoke out against the Communist party and the USSR. All kinds of foreigners have joined that group, like our old acquaintance Pierre Besnard and Emmy [*sic*] Goldman, who is passing herself off as English, but who is really a Russian Jew. I must say that anarchists from every corner of the world are thronging to Barcelona now. This second group consists of old politicians, people who consort with Lerroux, who has now officially gone over to Franco's side.

Finally, the third group—manifestly provocateurs, fascists calling themselves anarchists. We discovered in Madrid a secret store of weapons, belonging to these "fascist-anarchists." Yet, as we are fighting the anarchists, publicly proving that among them are many fascist provocateurs, it is dangerous, for the anarchist demagogues try to stir up their masses against us.

We must distinguish two strata among the anarchist masses: the majority of them are honest Spanish workers who exert influence both on the "left" Socialists and even on the Communists. These people honestly believe that they are called to carry out a social revolution. With these people we must secure a united front, even if we have to make serious concessions. The second stratum are the lumpen proletariat: all the thieves, bandits, prostitutes are declaring that they belong to the anarchists, because only thus can they get the weapons necessary for their dark deeds. They make short work of our people. Not long ago in Valencia they killed one of our workers—a transport worker. The funeral of the murdered worker turned into a powerful demonstration, in which fifty thousand people participated. On that day the anarchist organization was forced to broadcast on the radio that the anarchists had nothing to do with the murderers. This shows that, under pressure from the masses, the leaders of the CNT are beginning to understand the necessity of getting rid of their dark, criminal element. This understanding makes easier the task of creating a united front between the anarchist and the Communist workers.

G. *The Role and Influence of the Communist Party*

I have already said that the second basic force in Spain was our party. The political influence of the Communist party has exceeded all expectations. A month ago the president of the Republic, Azaña said, "If you wish to have a correct evaluation of the situation, if you wish to see people who know what they want, read *Mundo Obrero.*" I will cite a small fact that characterizes the composure and self-possession of our party in circumstances where often chaos reigns all about, where people lose their heads over the smallest trifle.

On 20 September in Madrid a small demonstration took place, devoted to the Fifth Regiment of the people's militia in connection with the naming of a new company commander—Lister. At three in the afternoon an officer of the general staff burst into the center of the demonstration and cried out in despair, "The front on the Tajo has been broken through—everyone is running! Give me two battalions, or the enemy will be in Madrid by this evening." The political commissar of the company, Com. Carlos, who was at the demonstration, rebuffed the terrified officer and, calming the demonstrators, assured them that there was no reason to panic. The demonstration went on in the strictest order.

Only our party knows what must be done. The slogans of the party are quickly taken up and reprinted by all the newspapers. [ . . . ]

Our party was the first seriously to pose the question of rapprochement with the Catholics. We drew in a former minister during the monarchy, a prominent figure in the Catholic movement, Ossorio y Gallardo, for a speech on the radio to address Catholics. For the first time on our radio, a priest spoke, who began his speech with the statement: "A priest is speaking with you. I greet the people of Spain with a clenched fist raised high. Long live the Republic! Long live the Spanish people!" Then he began arguing with the pope, proving to the latter that he was poorly informed about the situation in Spain. This speech by a priest produced a strong impression and called forth a great response.

Our party took the right position vis-à-vis the Moroccans. All the papers were constantly cursing the Moroccans. We made the first attempt to win over the Moroccan people. With this goal in mind, we put on the radio an Arab public speaker. It is possible that the Moroccans did not understand him since he spoke in the literary language, which is different from the common Arabian language. But the first step was taken, and it had significant consequences. The anarchist organ began to write "about our brothers, the Moroccan soldiers." And we made it so that captured Moroccan soldiers could freely walk the streets of Madrid without risking their lives.

Our party supplies cadres for the police. The party guarantees the protection of the arrested during interrogation.

But the main strength of the army has been directed toward the creation of what has become the pride of the People's Army—the Fifth Regiment of the militia. The Fifth Regiment, enjoying well-deserved military glory, numbers twenty thousand warriors. All the commanders of the regiment are Communists—either Communist workers or officers of the old army who are committed to us.

The party is carrying out a great work, but there are still significant weaknesses. In the first period from the beginning of the rebellion until the beginning of September, the large role of the party often faded away. The party did not appear as an independent power. That is why the CNT was able to come forward as the savior of the situation, with its ideas about the national defense council. The party has been carrying out a colossal work, but the masses do not feel that our party is an all-uniting force that is capable of changing the situation. Now the party is organizing large mass meetings, organizing appearances by its ministers. The first few days in September, a large gathering of Communists was called in Madrid, which, in point of fact, was the first inner-party gathering since the beginning of the war.

The leadership of the party has little studied military affairs, declaring that we are not military men. There was some friction with the military leadership of the Fifth Reg., which complained about the lack of attention from the party. The party, not infrequently forgetting that cadres decide everything, did not devote much attention to training cadres. There are not enough experienced, expert Communists. After our comrades entered the government, we put Communists into the Ministry of Agriculture and into the Ministry of Education. But this "expenditure" was repaid, for we have the opportunity to use these ministries for our agitation and for other goals of our own.

Our party in Catalonia merged with two existing Socialist organizations. The unified party is not strong enough and often it backs down before the anarchists and supports its political slogans.

The leadership of the party is represented by the Politburo alone. Outside of the members of the Politburo and the four to five other members of the Central Committee, the rest of the members were either killed at the front or expelled from the party.

A few words about individual leading workers of the party.

The general secretary of the party is *Com. Díaz*—an excellent comrade, a very good Bolshevik. But he suffers from an extraordinarily serious illness of the liver and the doctors have forbidden him to work for more than one hour a day. Of course he does not obey the doctor's orders and works a great deal. He is head and shoulders above the rest of the members of the Politburo. He is a very concrete and practical man—quite a rare phenomenon among the

Spanish. At meetings of the Politburo he renders concrete everything proposed and on the spot gives directives on how to put into action the decisions that are adopted.

*Com. Mije* is very overworked. He is the political editor of *Mundo Obrero*. He spends not less than an hour and a half every morning at work on the paper. He maintains the connection between the party and the War Ministry, where he must be two times a day for meetings with Caballero or with the general staff. He is also responsible for the Madrid party committee, for the Madrid committee of the people's front. In general, he works not less than twenty hours a day.

*Com. Checa* is the organizational secretary for the country and for the army, responsible also for the work of the Communists in the police. He gives directives for conducting the interrogation of those under serious arrest.

Ministers *Hernández and Uribe* are both busy with work in the ministries, visit the fronts, travel in the provinces for propaganda.

*Com. Cordón* is the military assistant of the chief of the Estremadura column. He travels to Madrid only once every ten days, when he can get away from the front.

*Com. Pasionaria* carries out propaganda and work among women.

Com. Antonio also attends meetings of the Politburo. He is the former secretary of the Komsomol and now the secretary of the Madrid party committee. But he has not been in Madrid more than two months, as he commanded a column of youths at the front.

The party, of course, has middle cadres, formed during the struggle. Among them are energetic organizers. I must add also the military cadres, which are forming very quickly. But, all the same, the shortcomings of these people are quickly sensed.

The general staff of the Fifth Regiment makes an excellent impression. There is only one foreigner among their number (the political commissar), who is all the same considered Spanish, for he has lived for a long time in Spain. The Fifth Regiment's general staff has an operations department led by comrade workers. The work of the general staff is based on the type of work done by the general staff of a normal army. The officer of each battalion receives a geographical military map of his sector, prepared by the Fifth Regiment. Even the general staff of the War Ministry does not have an operations department and works very primitively.

The Fifth Regiment's general staff carefully trains officers for a month in advance. Lister, the commander of the Fifth Regiment, a bricklayer, is a great comrade, a real military leader. But it is clear that our people still do not have enough knowledge, experience, practice. It is difficult to learn everything in two months, but they have learned a lot. The military comrades also are very overworked. And here, of course, there are few people. We need about ten times as many people.

## Document 15 *continued*

### 2. *The Military Situation*

. . .

*Prospects.* Our party is working under very difficult circumstances. A great deal of tact and skill is required of it, especially when we need to get something from Largo Caballero. I will present just two facts: on the Tajo front on 17 September, a difficult situation was created. The commanders directly demanded reinforcement, but Madrid could not help them, since at that time they did not have any reserves. Mije went to the War Ministry to speak with Caballero. The conversation took place without witnesses, because Largo is very proud and touchy. Mije brought out the following proposals:

1) Appeal to the people.

2) Quickly set up a military committee that would be under the general leadership of the government and would plan and carry out all the necessary military measures. Each decision of this military committee would be unconditionally put into effect, like a military order.

In the military committee ought to be

> Largo Caballero—as chairman
>
> Indalecio Prieto—responsible for national defense and operative units
>
> Antonio Mije—responsible for organizing reserves and military industry
>
> Julio Just—responsible for transport
>
> Chairman of the CNT—responsible for supplies

3) Organize the defense of Madrid.

4) Mobilize the whole rear.

5) Quickly create in the Levant a reserve army, and so on.

Mije advised that Caballero himself, on his own initiative, ought to put these measures into effect and promised that the party would come out with its own proposals only if he, Caballero, wanted that. Mije also introduced several proposals about the air forces (decentralization of the aerodromes and the centralization of the command).

Caballero refused even to consider these questions.

On 20 Sept. we repeated our previous proposals, adding only the suggestion about creating a fortified line halfway between Madrid and the Tajo front and several new proposals on aviation. Mije in particular insisted on the necessity for carrying out a number of measures for anti-air defense. People are running to the front not knowing how to save themselves from enemy fire. We need to teach them to keep their heads and not shoot every tenth person, as is now done. Give people picks and shovels, let them learn to dig trenches. Caballero has spoken: "The Spanish are too proud to dig into the ground." For the construction of a fortified line around Madrid we assigned a French colonel, a military engineer, who was participating in the war and who worked out a suitable draft. We sent two thousand workers to the area. Caballero ought to have mobilized another twenty thousand construction workers from Madrid, sent excavators, earth-movers, and foremen. In three days we could have dug the main trenches. Largo Caballero promised yet did nothing, and at the moment when work started, he began to dawdle, under the pretext that (he said) there was no money for the earth-movers, there were no transporters for bringing the workers, there was nothing to feed them with, and so on. Greeting the Fifth Regiment and conveying his gratitude for a job well done, he suggested to the command staff that they organize the same kind of military units for all of Spain. With the greatest difficulty we prepared a thousand men in eight days. And Caballero during that time already forgot his request and declared to us that he did not have the money for the upkeep of the new units.

At every step, our party has run into opposition from Caballero. He is completely absorbed in the thought of his political career. It has never occurred to him that if the fascists win, then all his career will turn to dust.

After the defeat at Toledo he changed for the better and began to pay more attention to us.

On the 30th a delegation from the Central Committee, consisting of Díaz, Mije, and both of our ministers, Hernández and Uribe, repeated our proposals to Caballero:

1. The creation of a military committee.

2. An immediate purge of the general staff, which either out of inability or because of the treachery of some elements, was responsible for the lack of success and defeats at the front.

3. The necessity to create an organization that would command operations on the entire central sector. It would be under the chairmanship of Estrada and consist of Asensio, Burillo, Marquesa, Gallo, Lister, García, Mangada, Galán, and many other commanders. This organization ought to answer for military operations on this most important front.

The proposal about the creation of a military committee was rejected by Caballero without any discussion. The second proposal he accepted, agreeing to the introduction of new elements, and even some foreigners, on the general staff.

He also accepted the suggestion about setting up a military operations organization for the central sector but reserved for himself the right to put into it the people that he considered necessary. If only he does not turn the new operations staff into a debate club! That, unfortunately, is the fate of most of our suggestions.

I will conclude: we must carry out as energetically as possible a campaign for realizing the unification of workers and all people.

We must strengthen discipline and bring about unified command—everyone agrees on this.

It is not only Caballero who is dragging out work in the government bureaucracy but also the anarchists throughout the country. This heightens the sense that their party needs to be more responsible and significantly cuts down on the irresponsible criticism from their side.

I am convinced that we can be victorious. It will seem to many that this is contradicted by everything that I have said here. But we must look at this matter dialectically. Caballero turned his back on us fifteen days ago; now he is listening to us more and more. The anarchists threaten us, but they have introduced not a few suggestions acceptable to us.

My proposals:

1. The government and the Communist party must make clear to the people the purpose of the war, as was done in France during the imperialist war. The Republic of the Popular Front of 16 Feb. is not the same as the Republic of 14 April. Caballero said in the parliament that we must give this republic a social content, that we must create a republic of workers, as is written in the constitution. I think that we ought to emphasize more the social character of the Republic. We are not fighting just to destroy fascism, but also for democratic rights and the vital interests of the masses. We must remember what we already have and what we will lose if the fascists come to power. We must decide the question of land. We must strive so that every peasant receives his own plot of land and the right to farm his parcel forever. The anarchists are, with difficulty, coming around to this point. And all the same we must fight for this.

2. Workers' control exists. We did not create this, but since it exists, we need to legalize it, cutting down on its rights and organizing the protection of foreign enterprises, and so on.

3. We must force the government to put into effect measures for social security (protection for old age, for accidents at work, aid for pregnant women, and so on). Measures like this will bring the people closer to the Republic.

Franco has published his program. We must make our program, the program of the Popular Front, known to all the people. We must give freedom to some Moroccans. Until now we have done nothing in that direction. Caballero refused to discuss this question, pleading that he did not want to spoil relations with the French government. All these measures will make our work easier by causing the enemy's strength to disintegrate. The government must come out with a declaration on the Church—freedom of religion for all. Believers ought to know that we will arrest priests not because they serve God but because they serve fascism—that is, they are shooting at the people and spreading fascist propaganda.

We need to carry out radical changes in the work of the state machinery; the government does not control the bureaucracy, which administers irresponsible committees that [supposedly] carry out the functions of the government. We can find a means for strengthening the state machinery that will not affect the democratic form of a constitutional regime. These committees, committees of the Popular Front, ought to help the civilian governors and local government organs.

The anarchists must be drawn into the state machinery, meet more often with us, together work out proposals, and thus strengthen the differences within their ranks. We need to defeat them not with the threat of being shot, as our comrades do, but through the excellence of our work among the masses.

The anarchists have weapons, and we need to take that into consideration. They showed us this in action, arresting not long ago the political commissar of the Fifth Regiment, who was saved from death only by the arrival of our military unit. They arrested one of the commanders of the Fifth Reg., held him for a half hour to show him all of their pistoleros. To fight with them in the face of fascism—this [would be] the end. This means that we should not stop at conceding something to them, and after victory we will get even with them, all the more so since at that point we will have a strong army.

Regardless of the seriousness and difficulty of the military situation, regardless of the possibility of new partial defeats at the front in the near future, I think that, thanks to the steps we are taking, in three weeks the situation will have changed radically.

VLADIMIR GOREV

The military attaché and main GRU agent in Madrid, Vladimir Gorev (code name Sancho), confirmed Marty's opinions about Largo Caballero and gave a professional's view of Spanish military incompetence. In **Document 16,** a report dated 25 September, Gorev commented on the characteristics that least endeared Largo Caballero to the Communists: his attempts to limit Communist influence and his refusal to implement the "proposals" submitted by the party and the Soviet advisers. On the political scene, the GRU agent decried the activities of the anarchists and the "hooligans, criminals, [and] fascists" that had joined up with the CNT after the war began. They used blackmail to force others to follow their policies, and their units fought very badly at the front. Gorev would have liked to take "active measures" against them, a term that could include executions, but the anarchists were simply too strong for that "now." In fact, he noted, the influence of the anarchists in Catalonia was "almost absolute." They could act as they wanted in the province, and it was obvious that the people were also with them. This was an astonishing admission from a senior

Soviet official, because in their public pronouncements and speeches the Comintern and PCE downplayed the role of the anarchists. Gorev's writing, like that of Marty and Ehrenburg, showed that the Soviets were willing to acknowledge privately what everyone else in Spain knew: the Communist party was an insignificant force when compared with the deeply ingrained power and appeal of the anarcho-syndicalists.

The course of the war also provoked nothing but impatient criticism from Gorev. There was no command and control; the staff cadres were pitiful; rations and supplies were not distributed, and there was no sign that the Spaniards were doing anything to improve the situation. Yet Gorev was not completely without hope. He thought that the masses were ready for a broader social revolution and an end to the chaos of multiparty government; the creation, in fact, of a People's Republic. Finally, his constant reiteration of the Republicans' need for military technology (the corresponding Russian word means aircraft, tanks, and heavy artillery) may have helped to convince the Politburo and Stalin to authorize the first shipments of this type of hardware to Spain.

A few weeks later, Gorev analyzed the situation in the Spanish high command and in **Document 17** highlighted the serious problems caused by differing strategic views and personality conflicts. He concluded that the two main actors in the Republican army, General José Asensio (commander of the central front) and Major Manuel Estrada (the chief of staff), who fought with each other continually, were undermining the entire war effort. Gorev's description of Asensio is especially important because this was but the beginning of a full-fledged Communist assault on the general, a firm supporter and protégé of Largo Caballero. By early 1937 Asensio would be the center of a power struggle between the Communists and Largo Caballero, who saw retaining the general as a sign of his continued control over the war. Gorev feared that Asensio could become the next Chiang Kai-shek, but it was his description of the Spaniard's actions as "treason" that would eventually dominate Soviet thinking about Asensio. Meanwhile, Estrada, who would shortly fall under the influence of the Communists, had obviously not done so at this point in the war. Gorev saw him as little better than the other old "leftovers" on the Republican staff. In the coming months, the Soviets would push the Spanish government to carry out a thorough purge of the officer corps both to ensure that no fascists remained and to assert and maintain their own domination of the war. Another way to do this was by controlling the ideology and political makeup of the army. In his report Gorev referred to the attempts to set up military commissars; in **Document 18,** he reported success after "protracted negotiations and constant pressure." The new commissars were told about Soviet experiences and given political instruction; their ranks would soon be dominated by the Communists.

Gorev's next report, **Document 19,** shows just how thoroughly the Soviets had penetrated the new Republican army. Agents of the GRU were everywhere, winning "authority," helping with pencil and paper to decide operations, writing the instructions for the new political commissars, and even giving orders. The "psalm readers" were aviation experts who worked both with Soviet-provided "psalms" (that is, aircraft) and in the Spanish air forces; the "fishermen" were advisers working in the Republican navy, and the "incense burners" were tank experts. These three branches of the Spanish military would be the most heavily penetrated and controlled by the advisers. This was not enough for Gorev, who made two requests that would further increase the power of the Soviets. First, he asked permission to break off official contact with the Red Army, so that he and a few other men could take over running the war more directly. He also wanted dozens more advisers in place to oversee and instruct the Republicans. His analysis for why these measures were necessary shows that once again his attitude toward the Spanish officers was impatient and condescending: they *needed* the Soviets in order to win. Although his first proposal would (apparently) be rejected, after this report the advisers began to take a more hands-on approach to the war. Soon they would regard issuing commands at the front as a normal extension of their duties, while pilots, tankers, and naval officers from the Soviet Union took active roles in engagements throughout the war zone.

# Document 16

[Unnamed source (2)]

25 September 1936
Madrid
N° 6

To the Director[36]

1. In one of your telegrams you pointed out the need to give some perspective on the future situation. For a number of reasons I did not have a sufficient basis for evaluating the political situation. Nevertheless, I can report a few starting points.

The most influential parties that must be reckoned with are the left Socialists (Largo CABALLERO's group); the right Socialists (Indalecio PRIETO's group); the Communists, who are not the "bogeyman" here, but rather the most honest government party; the Republicans—president of the Republic AZAÑA's group—and the anarchists. Up to now I have not understood, and no one can clearly explain to me, why there is no strong peasant party here. It must be kept in mind that the union movement here was strong before the development of the parties, and the unions and their influence on the masses must sometimes be reckoned with more than that of the political parties.

AZAÑA and his group, according to all impressions, do not have great influence on the masses, but they are supported by a fairly wide circle of petty and middle bourgeoisie in the cities and somewhat in the countryside. The significance of this group is that they are supported by a majority of the intelligentsia, that they are more accustomed to government work, and, what is undoubtedly important, that a significant stratum of the officer corps that remained on the side of the government is disposed toward the Republicans.

The right Socialists, headed by PRIETO, control the apparatus of the CC of the Socialist party and several provincial committees. The rights have a majority of the leading positions in the Soc. party. They do not have great influence among the masses, but a majority of the intelligentsia with a Socialist view is on their side. According to a great deal of information, the right Socialists are counting strongly on a majority among the Asturians. PRIETO, himself a northerner, is now occupied more with matters in the north and without him, more than anyone else, almost nothing is done in the north. The leader of the northerners, the Socialist Gonzalez PEÑA, who leads all of the operations there, is apparently PRIETO's man.

The left Socialists headed by Largo CABALLERO hold in their hands the main union organization, the UGT. Through this they consolidated their influence over a rather wide mass of the workers and over a significant mass of the a[gricultural] workers and peasants, who also have a union organization.

In the last government L. CABALLERO took an extreme opposition position, and now he himself is in power and it is much more difficult for him because he has not been able to set right most of those things about which he accused the old government. Caballero has considerable influence in the army, among the militia, but he has almost no supporters among the command staff.

The Communists are carrying out the most consistent policy. Helping the government, both the former and the current one, they are attempting to gain the trust of the masses and to broaden their influence. Earlier the Communist party did not have any especially wide range of masses. Now the influence of the Communist party is growing every day. Work is being carried out among both the workers and the peasants. A significant formation of military units is being carried out. Since the units under the influence of the Communists are better organized and fight somewhat better, a certain number of old officers approve of the Communist party's policy on building forces and are demanding that their sectors be given units under Communist influence, and part of the officer corps has joined the Communist party.

The question about the anarchists is special. Their influence in Catalonia is almost absolute. They do what they want there. It is obvious that right now the masses there are also with them. This influence extends to about Valencia. More to the south and in Madrid their influence is weaker. The union organization CNT is in the hands of the anarchists, and a rather large number of good workers have joined up with it, so they are to be reckoned with. One must keep in mind that after the rebellion everyone who wanted to clothed himself in anarchist colors and a lot of hooligans, criminals, [and] fascists joined up with the anarchists.

The government and policy are now in the hands of the left Socialists, who have the principal portfolios. CABALLERO is playing a complicated and dangerous political game. Before entering the government, he held extremist views, insisted on the seizure of power by the workers, on setting up a dictatorship of the proletariat, and so on. Now he is significantly quieter; however, he continues to play on the contradictions. Through all of his policies it's as if he "sics" the Communists on the anarchists, counting on gaining through this. Despite the fact that the Communists are honestly supporting him, he tries in every possible way to avoid strengthening the influence of the Communists, even if this means pandering to the anarchists. Weapons are given to the Communists with great difficulty, proposals by the Communists do not go through, however necessary they may be, and the mistakes of the Communists are overemphasized. The struggle of CABALLERO'S group with the Communist party for influence over the masses is making itself felt everywhere.

PRIETO and his group are biding their time, obviously reckoning on gaining from the struggle between CABALLERO, the Communists, and the anarchists. The more sober policy of the leaders of the right Socialists is far from the demagoguery of CABALLERO and his group, and they are carrying out a more loyal policy with respect to the Communists, understanding that at the current stage of the revolution the Communists are against all of the extremist tricks of the "leftists."

The Republicans are keeping to the sidelines, obviously wishing to give the "Marxist" parties the opportunity either to cut their own throats or to win the war with great difficulty so that then they can somehow or other seize power.

The anarchists are carrying out an ever more active policy. Not long ago they came out with a proposal to reorganize the government into a defense council based on the unions. Now they have apparently decided to enter the Barcelona government. Their policy is nothing but the usual anarchist demands. To carry out this policy, they are not squeamish about threatening to recall forces from the front. Their units fight very badly, and those sent to the Madrid front simply opened up the front. In view of the fact that they are extraordinarily strong in Catalonia, we cannot talk about taking active measures against them now.

It is extremely difficult to predict where the revolution will go and through what stages it will pass. It is obvious that the development of the Spanish revolution will be significantly different from the development of the revolution in Russia, for there are many elements here which did not exist there. The broad masses are talking ever more about the fact that it will be impossible to linger at the current stage and that the revolution will inevitably develop into a Socialist revolution. Multiparty leadership is not advantageous, and the masses feel this. Ever more frequently one hears that it is very difficult to get anything done because there are many parties in the leadership and there is a constant struggle for influence, and so on. It seems that formulating the question about the unification of the Socialist and the Communist parties will be correct for the future destiny of Spain (such a unification has already taken place in Catalonia). The organization of power in a People's Republic, for instance, is entirely probable.

In any case, a struggle against the anarchists is absolutely inevitable after victory over the Whites. This struggle will be very severe, and there will also be huge disagreements with the CABALLERO group, which in case of victory will make a lot of extremist "ultra-left" demands. It is possible to work with the PRIETO group and with the more leftist faction of the Republicans.

I ask that you consider this entire section to be for information only, because there is a lot that is unclear to me in these questions. I am giving this section just to add something to the information that you have.

2. The correlation of the combatants' military forces is evident from my last reports and from JUAN's report, which is attached. The government group's situation is very difficult, since the lack of military hardware and—this I consider fundamental—the lack of command cadres, places the forces in exceptionally difficult circumstances. The principal result of these preconditions is that the Whites have the initiative on almost all fronts, and the young mili-

tia units give in at the first strong blow. The lack of commanders, especially noncoms, and the complete lack of political work and political workers means that no one is able to stop panics and a disorderly flight begins, often even without pressure from the adversary. The leadership of operations is in the hands of completely incompetent people, who do not have any experience and who come up with uninspired plans, which often do not even take the terrain into consideration. Communications are scandalous; in the center they do not know what is being done on the various sectors of the front. The last operation near Talavera can serve as an example of this. When the Whites began to attack without support and approached the Guadarrama River, they decided to use the NAVARRO and URIBARRI groups (columns) to strike the blow from the south through Malpica, at which everyone affirmed that the bridge on the Malpica was in the hands of NAVARRO. The order was issued, there was a lot of conversation about this by telephone, and the next day they explained that the columns had not carried out the attack. Why? It turned out that every bridge was blown up. When anyone speaks to the Spanish about the need for communications, intelligence, and so on, they assert that everything is fine, whereas in reality it is going badly.

There is all kinds of heroism. Side by side with the shameful flight near Talavera, the defense of Irún and the actions of the forces at Guadarrama and Somosierra can be cited as instances of brilliant self-possession and steadiness. All of this bears out the thesis that the morale of the government units is immeasurably higher than that of the White forces. But a lack of technology and leadership can ruin the best units.

Despite the fact that the Whites' command is unified, despite the fact that the White command has excellent units like the Moroccans and the foreign legion, despite the fact that almost all of the officer corps is on the Whites' side, despite the fact that the Whites are now several times stronger in technology—they have not achieved a decisive victory, and even if they do achieve one, it will be only with great difficulty. It is sometimes simply incomprehensible why the Whites do not do elementary necessary things—why they do not gather their air forces for a decisive blow to one sector, why they don't gather a strong enough fist which would destroy the government's forces in detail. One cannot in any way reckon that slow-witted people are leading the Whites. There are enough intelligent generals and sufficient will for victory there. The thing is, obviously, that the whole business is hanging by a thread, as with the government. From some odd bits of information (intelligence here is conducted disgracefully) it is possible to conclude that only the Moroccan units and the legionnaires fight as they ought to. And even these do not show any special enthusiasm. Besides this, the Whites have quite a lot of trouble in the rear. There is also information about the great uprising in Morocco. The government is rather seriously working on this matter and, though we are consciously taking little interest in this problem, we have information about serious battles there. Disturbances have sporadically sprung up in the Whites' rear—strikes, even uprisings. The activity of the partisans, whom no one from here is leading, also causes some discomfort. The morale of the regular Spanish units is not high. All of this, obviously, ties the hands of the White command and does not allow them to show the necessary activeness.

What are the perspectives? It is, of course, very difficult to answer this question. The main question, on which the outcome of the war will depend, is the correct resolution of the leadership's political problem. As long as the government will not go over to a more planned leadership for operations, does not give up the panicked throwing of disorganized units to reinforce the front, does not formulate the correct question about securing the forces politically, we will progress in fits and starts. The second question is the question about setting up our own cadres. This problem depends completely on the first, for the government is taking an extremely uncertain position on this. For example, until now almost none of the loyal officers have been promoted. Captains and majors are commanding columns consisting of several thousand men. At the same time, the government has not recognized men promoted from the militia, and there are frequent instances when a militia commander with a detachment of a couple of thousand men is subordinated to an officer of the regular army, who either is stupider or has less strength than he does. In this connection the viewpoint dominates that this is not a civil war, in which a new force that has almost nothing in common with the old army is being created for the government's side, but rather that this is the "suppression of an insurrection," in which the army that has stayed with the true government will not, and does not need to, change. For example, there has not even been a decree about the demotion of officers who went over to the side of the Whites.

Training of cadres for the new command staff is held up by the government's narrowly pedantic policies. They do not understand that it is better not to send several hundred men to the front and [instead] to prepare noncoms. Every attempt to set up a school ends unsuccessfully, since everyone immediately leaves for the front.

The problem of equipping the army with technology is a very important problem for predicting the results of the struggle. The war begins to be reminiscent of a war of columns, where aircraft drive away units and the infantry occupies regions almost without resistance. At this point the technological equipping of the government army is so insignificant in comparison with the Whites' army that we expect a catastrophe any day. I have already reported enough to you on this question and will not add anything.

Conclusion—I believe that the government has enough resources to be victorious. The only thing that is needed is more organization and less panic. At all costs, a reserve group of ten thousand soldiers must be set up; even if it is not well equipped with machine guns and artillery, [it must be] trained and go over to a decisive offensive. There are enough aircraft to strike a serious blow at the Whites on the decisive sector. However, it is plain to you that a bourgeois government cannot show such decisiveness in a struggle and that the war will proceed with continual alarms, defeats, abrupt changes in the situation, and so on. A change in the equipping of the army could play a decisive role.

The loss of Toledo and Madrid would be a catastrophe, but it would still not lead to the defeat of the government. The eastern and southeastern part of the country, not counting Catalonia, would remain in the hands of the government, and resistance could be organized and victory achieved on this foundation. If there is a withdrawal, the principal line from which new forces could be deployed would be Cuenca–Alcázar de San Juan–Ciudad Real–Don Benito. The center would probably move either to Albacete or to Valencia or to Alicante. It is probable that Madrid and Toledo will be held and can be supported for long enough so that they will not be definitively surrendered to the Whites. Some measures have been taken for preparing reserves on this line.

There have been absolutely no proposals made even about broken communications with us, for lines of communication will remain open in any withdrawal.

Naturally, it is impossible to predict how the situation on the fronts will shape up, but it would be incorrect to view it as irreparable. It is very difficult, but this is still not the end—even the contrary. Enthusiasm is so great, the masses are so overwhelmingly on the side of the revolution, that to speak of defeat would be a simple unwillingness to understand the situation. I am speaking about this kind of extreme assumptions because there is a tinge of the inevitability of defeat beginning to creep into some people here, and, according to those communications that I have from France, this point of view is rather strong in government circles there.

Sancho

# Document 17

[Unnamed source (3)]

---

16/10/36
Madrid
N° 26

To the Director

A decree will be published today about reorganizing the military command and about setting up the institution of military commissars. There is much that is doubtful in this decree, but personally I do not believe that it brings anything new to the existing situation.

## Document 17 *continued*

The real state of affairs is that this decree should have resolved the situation that has arisen between the general staff, with Major ESTRADA as the head of staff, and the head of the central front, General ASENSIO. Lately, an almost impossible situation has been created between these two people. All the plans and instructions of the gen. staff on the central front have miscarried, and the gen. staff does not help the front enough.

General ASENSIO thoroughly influences War Min. CABALLERO and is striving to carry out a whole series of his own measures. He accuses the gen. staff of hampering his work—that they are interfering in his operations, that they do not give him reserves when he needs them, that they do not care about supplying him with weapons, and so on. In some of these accusations he is correct; taking into account that the front is moving up toward Madrid itself and that no one pays attention to the other fronts, everyone—the gen. staff included—is occupied with the center. There was interference, and unnecessary interference, by the gen. staff into his work.

On the other hand, ESTRADA has accused ASENSIO, saying that all of his operations have, in the final analysis, come to nothing but a waste of reserves, an improper use of the forces, and so on.

In practice, these relations have yielded nothing good. The gen. staff gives a directive, ASENSIO goes to the war min. and tries to get it countermanded. ASENSIO demands reserves, shells, weapons, and ESTRADA does not give them—ASENSIO goes to the war min., raises a scandal, and receives everything that he requests.

From my dispatch you can imagine what ASENSIO is like. The same is true for ESTRADA.

For the last six weeks on the central front there has not been one victory, and up to twenty thousand men have been used up in battle. Part of them was scattered, a part then was regathered and scattered again. These twenty or so thousand were given to the front in batches of a hundred to five hundred men. To every objection that they ought not to do this, there is one and the same answer—Without this the front will not hold out. ASENSIO is a general of the general staff, well enough trained to understand that for inadequately trained reserves this kind of meat-grinder leads only to exhaustion and to loss of morale among the forces. However, all his operations begin with a good order being issued; [but] there is no supervision to make certain that the order is carried out; there are no communications or coordination; the forces go forward, run up against the defense or a counterattack, stop, the Whites call in the air forces, the forces are rolled backward, and ASENSIO reports that the front is wide open and if they don't send him two battalions, he will not be responsible for the consequences.

He is well enough trained, has a c[hief] of s[taff] with an advanced French education, ought to understand that commanders of columns do not have sufficient military training. You remember how orders were written during our civil war. It wasn't orders that were received, but rather instructions, explaining what to do and how to do it. ASENSIO's orders would provoke few objections from a picky professor at the academy, but the force commanders do not know how to carry them out, and the militia are not strong enough to stand up to White aircraft.

All this impels strong doubts about ASENSIO, and moreover some people are frankly talking about his treason. I cannot so categorically assert this, but I do believe that ASENSIO is now more harmful than useful.

The chief of the gen. staff, Major ESTRADA, is a man of limited vision, an instructor of tactics in the military schools. He is comparatively old, a Socialist, a northerner. He is terribly afraid of CABALLERO and is afraid to put forward anything that [Caballero] doesn't want. He understands military questions rather well; he has a clear outlook on the need for trained and equipped reserves. From the viewpoint of military leadership, of course, he cannot be compared to ASENSIO, but with a strong commander, he wouldn't be a bad c[hief] of s[taff].

There are all kinds of old officer leftovers on the gen. staff, and a reorganization of the gen. staff is now taking place. It is not known if ESTRADA himself will remain, but all the department heads are changing, and in three departments (organization, information, and supply) civilians were appointed, and military instructors for them. This reorganization could revitalize the work of the gen. staff and allow it to begin to work on concluding the assembly of a reserve army and on putting together a plan for a general operation.

As I already said above, the decree about unified military command is the method that CABALLERO wishes to employ to lessen the friction between the gen. staff and the central front. Nothing will come of that, since the friction is now focused on the principal question—the use of the reserves—and on that question the situation is the same now as then.

Today the CC of the Communist party [and] the unions (supporters of CABALLERO) ought to have gone to CABALLERO to announce that they do not trust ASENSIO. It is difficult to say how this will turn out, since ASENSIO has CABALLERO hypnotized.

It is difficult to conjecture about how this situation will turn out. In the meantime, I am working primarily with ESTRADA, Juan with ASENSIO. If ASENSIO is able to throw out ESTRADA and take the army into his hands, become chief of the gen. staff, this could turn out very sadly. He is the focus that unites all the hopes of everything old that remains on the side of the Republic, and he could become something like a Spanish Chiang Kai-shek. That is, if he is simply a nonrevolutionary. And if the suspicions are correct that he is working on FRANCO's instructions, then it is clear how all this could turn out.

Sancho

## Document 18

[Unnamed source (4)]

16/10/36
Madrid
N° 29

To the Director

As a result of protracted negotiations and constant pressure, Caballero made the decision to set up the institution of military commissars. In many units there are already "political delegates" pulled together on the spur of the moment.

I enclose with this letter a rather badly done translation of the decree.

ALVAREZ DEL VAYO, the minister of foreign affairs, a left Socialist who is devoted to and trusted by CABALLERO, has been appointed "general military commissar." He has been given four deputies—dep. gen. sec. of the Communist party MIJE, chairman of the syndicalist party PESTAÑA, deputy of the parliament of Republicans BILBAO, and the chairman of the anarchists. In the meantime, it has been proposed that functions will be distributed [thus]—MIJE— Org. Dept., PESTAÑA—Agit.[ation and] Prop.[aganda] Dept., BILBAO— inspector, the anarchist—to coordinate polit. work on the various fronts.

The state of the mil. coms. [military commissars] is taking shape. Tomorrow up to two hundred men will be appointed to political duties, and before they are sent to the units, a meeting will be conducted with them in which they will be told about the experience of our mil. coms., given instructions on how to work, and given political instructions.

If these mil. coms. begin to work as they ought, they will be of great benefit for making the army a cohesive unit.

Sancho

## Document 19

[Unnamed source (5)]

16/10/36
Madrid
N° 30

To the Director

1. The advising work is now in the following state.

I am continuing to work with the chief of the gen. staff, I conduct all talks on the question of defense with the rest of the "leaders," and so on. There is so little time that it has been a while since I have been to the front. Yesterday could serve as an example of a normal day, where I had to talk on various matters without break from 12 until 3:30 A.M. The talks are not general in nature but are already taking place with paper and pencil. The period of winning authority has turned into a period when it is possible to exploit the results.

The situation of ALCALA [Sveshnikov][37] and LEPANTO [Kuznetsov] have improved, by comparison with when I wrote to you last time. They can already give orders not as a result of pressure but as a result of capable work.

JUAN [Ratner] is continuing to work a half-day on General ASENSIO's staff; the remaining time he takes my place to deal with various routine matters. He has worked out a plan for the PUR,[38] instructions for the mil. coms., and so on. He works a lot, and well.

FRIDO [Tsiurupa] is in Archena[39] at the school. He has to be there at least another ten days, because the new people are still not acclimatized.

PEDRO [Liubimtsev] is dealing with all the technical work; I have sometimes been surprised by his endurance and capacity for work in this. In the meanwhile, I cannot report anything but excellent testimonials about his work.

As I reported to you by telegram, our work is greatly hampered by the fact that we cannot do a great many necessary things because of our official position. If it might be possible for us to be volunteers rather than being in the situation we now are, things would be much easier and better.

Now, for example, every trip to the front must include a number of precautions. To go to a unit, to view training, to give instructions on the spot, to help, are not permitted, so as not to break the rules. It's dangerous to be with various military men too often, in case people talk about it too much. You have to use so many dodges to receive a dispatch in a timely fashion from the groups that it gets to be annoying.

Barbara treats our work very patiently, but even she reminds us and checks up, just in case we dirty our laundry.

As soon as the groups at the front are organized, the staff, which is now just an embryo, must be developed into an apparatus that is able to direct operations and administer all the groups. Communications must be organized; they will come with dispatches, reports, and so on. All of this fits in so little with our situation now that undoubtedly we will either have to forgo our "purity" completely or have to leave the institution of which my apparatus is a part.

All these considerations compel me to report to you the following possibility: I, ALCALA, and LEPANTO will be officially recalled. If it is necessary, it is even possible to make a trip to France for a day, but it can be done without this. So that this will proceed cleanly, a new man will be appointed for here without aides—with only a man like PEDRO. He will maintain communications with you and with me. After all the complications have ended, he will conduct official business. In any case, even before this, there were some of my colleagues whom I had not met because I was so busy.[40]

The transition of JUAN and PEDRO to the status of advisers will not cause any special difficulties.

With this kind of situation, I and my people will stand on our own feet, we will be out in the field (in which, in practice, we already are), and the current inconveniences won't constrain us while we are occupied with our job.

It is, of course, possible to set this up differently—to send a group that will take on all of the work and simply to dismiss us. I believe that this will put the new people in the position of having to go through the very same period of winning authority that, to a significant degree, is already behind us.

It seems to me that this operation could pass off without a hitch; in practice, these kinds of things have happened in other countries. Every minute counts now that things are headed toward the preparation of a large operation. We have to go around to the units, teach the forces, prepare the command staff (and now we even have to beware of conducting lessons with the command staff). Now we have to conduct lessons with the commissars there, and right away we are thinking how to do this so that we transfer experience to them and yet don't show ourselves.

When the institution we are part of makes this decision, we will be completely protected from censure and from any dirty work [by the enemy].

I request that this question be decided and that I be informed about your decision as soon as possible.

2. The situation with the forces is such now that things are very difficult without good military leadership. The Spanish are moving toward appointing young commanders, political workers, civilians in the high command posts, but there is nobody to place as military instructors and chiefs of staff. Everyone, from CABALLERO to the commanders of new brigades, is counting on the foreign advisers. It is clear that the arrival of the advisers just before the operations, supposing that they are treated well, will lead to their getting used to [the advisers] during the operations, and they will begin to listen to them as they ought just as the operation is ending. I reported to you about the possibility for allocating the advisers. In practice, the situation has not changed. Now I believe that it is possible and necessary to have advisers: on the general staff—with the ch[ief] of st[aff], with the ch[ief] of the Op.[erations] Dept., with the ch[ief] of the Org. Dept. In the Military Ministry—with the ch[ief] of the engineers, with the ch[ief] of the Quartermaster Service. In military industry—one for supplying shells and another for aerial bombs. With the head of the defense of Madrid—one to three engineers. With the chief of the PUR—one to two. With the brigades of the army reserve—one each, six in all. With the schools—infantry, artillery, communications. Furthermore, at the disposal of the senior adviser—two artillerists and a commu-

nication specialist for training the forces. With the Air Force Ministry—two. With the Naval Ministry—one.

On the central front—with the commander of the central front, with five to six brigades, which will be created from units of the front.

On the southern front—three to four men on the different sectors.

On the northern front—a senior man and three to four assistants for the different sectors, an artillerist, and a communications expert.

On the Catalan front—a senior man and three to four assistants for each sector, an artillerist, a communications expert, an aviator, and a tanker.

This is a lot, but I am reporting about the maximum required and possible for allocation. Anything that can be is better than the situation in which we now are, where we have to let a lot slip from under our influence because the day is simply not long enough.

If the question about me, ALCALA, and LEPANTO is decided, then [there should be] correspondingly three fewer people.

It is very desirable that these people know the language. There are fantastic difficulties with translators. Without Spanish there cannot even be any thought about starting the work.

3. The "psalm readers" are now partially here—five men, extremely mobile. They are included in the work and working with the "psalms" that we have. Right here in the Air Force Ministry, one man is settled in the Operations Department.

The rest are getting ready.

According to a communication from ALCALA, there is dissatisfaction in the group with RINALDO [Bergolts], who has not been able to create any comradely cohesion, holds himself aloof, and so on. There was a case of bad behavior by one "psalm reader," about which both I and RINALDO have already reported. He drinks, is late from leave, takes the liberty of tactless conduct. Now ALCALA has gone there to supervise the receiving and to investigate this entire matter. If everything is confirmed, I will report and with your permission send [him] back.

4. The group of "fishermen" are in a difficult situation. None of them speak Spanish. FRANÇOIS [Annin] is in the north; he has a translator, and [gathering] from dispatches from him, he is working, teaching people; things are happening. Two others are in Cartagena with LEPANTO, but without any Spanish. I will give him a translator from the first [that arrive].

5. The group of "incense burners" are already all at Archena. GRIGORY came to me. His morale is high. The senior man has still not come to me, but it is obvious that the situation that he is in hasn't quite sunk in. Yesterday he called on the telephone and tried to "settle some questions" with JUAN. The guy has still not learned what can be discussed over the telephone and what is not permitted.

GRIGORY told me that they have an order to "coordinate everything with

## Document 19 *continued*

me," and they told him that I would coordinate with them about every question on their work. This does not completely tally with the instructions that I received when I left that this entire matter would be subordinated to me. I understood that just as with RINALDO, they don't quite understand about this question. I endeavored to carefully explain this to them. I do not doubt that there will be no misunderstandings of any kind.

. . .

Sancho

---

### VLADIMIR ANTONOV-OVSEENKO

The memoranda of Vladimir Antonov-Ovseenko provided the Soviet leadership with a somewhat different view of the political situation, while supporting the contention that the Soviets should assume the conduct of the war. A rather tragic figure, Antonov-Ovseenko was a hero of the storming of the tsar's Winter Palace in 1917, an early member of the Bolshevik faction, and conceivably one of the best candidates to be a Soviet representative working among those imbued with a revolutionary fervor in Spain. Publicly, Antonov-Ovseenko loyally followed Soviet policy. During the ouster of the POUM from the Catalan government, he had threatened that if the Spaniards wished to continue receiving Soviet aid, they would have to act as the Soviets demanded.[41] On other matters, he tried to follow a middle course in Spain. In the following three documents, Antonov-Ovseenko's attempts to work out a compromise with the CNT, to find some good in Largo Caballero, and to mediate the differences between Catalonia and Madrid are striking.[42] Yet, as Document 23 shows, he too hated the "bad" anarchists and thought that the Spanish were incapable of large-scale military action on their own. In **Document 20,** a memorandum sent to the head of the Soviet army as well as the Ministry of Foreign Affairs, the Soviet consul described the incompetence of the Spanish government in organizing the defense of their own country. He concluded that it would be impossible for the Spanish to set up large military units without the aid of (Soviet) specialists and instructors. Unlike other observers, however, he did not believe that Largo Caballero deliberately refused to carry out Communist pro-

70

posals. Instead, it was the Spaniard's misguided attempts to follow a "broad democratic" path that prevented him from carrying out Communist measures. Antonov-Ovseenko also thought that relations with the anarcho-syndicalists (the CNT) were improving, and that the CNT was moving away from its radical anarchist (FAI) core.

His next memorandum, **Document 21,** reported the results of a conversation with an unidentified informant—probably a Communist sympathizer within the ranks of the CNT. In direct contrast to the Soviet consul, "Comrade X." thought that relations between the CNT and the Communists had become more, not less, strained. In some cases there had been armed clashes between the two groups. The CNT also had leaders who were provocateurs, was accepting members without checking their backgrounds, and, most suspiciously of all, had not sent all the weapons that they had seized to the fronts. The killing of scabs by the CNT and the summary execution of priests only added to the violent, and troubling, picture that "X." drew of the anarchists. Antonov-Ovseenko made it clear that he was using "X." to ease relations between the Communists and the CNT, disarm the unreliable elements within the union, and end the worst of the anarchists' "willfulness." His next report, **Document 22,** insisted that the "good" anarchists in the CNT were willing to work with the Communists, even after great provocation by undisciplined PSUC leaders. The mention yet again of Communist attempts to seize all the weapons at the rear (and thus to disarm the anarchists) is another link in the chain of events that would lead to the attempted destruction of the POUM and of anarchist independence in 1937.

In the final report, **Document 23,** Antonov-Ovseenko showed a much tougher side. Buenaventura Durruti was one of the most popular of the anarchist commanders and a good friend of the other famous anarchist activist, Francisco Ascaso (whose brother Domingo Ascaso and cousin Joaquín Ascaso would play active roles during the war). Together they had been involved in numerous violent escapades even before the war, all directed at overthrowing the traditional Spanish order. At the outbreak of the uprising, Durruti had been called upon to lead one of the first anarchist units, more than three thousand men, into battle to defend Catalonia from the Nationalists.[43] For the Communists, Durruti, like other well-known anarchist leaders, presented a special problem. At the beginning of the war, it seemed that he did not intend to yield in the slightest to Soviet pressure on either political or military issues, and yet he enjoyed so much support from the people that it was impossible to confront him directly. Later Durruti would become convinced that unified command was a necessary evil, although, as this document shows, he resisted all attempts to undermine his position on the Saragossa front. The Soviet journalist Koltsov would, in fact, report that Durruti had said, "Take the whole of Spain, but don't touch Saragossa: the Saragossa operation is mine."[44] Faced with this sign of renewed anarchist willfulness, Antonov-Ovseenko was forced to "interfere in a firm way."

The other point of interest in this document is, once again, the extent of Soviet advisers' involvement in planning and carrying out operations. It was the adviser who first conceived of removing Durruti's men from the front; the Soviets who interfered when Durruti would not submit; the Soviets who "frustrated" his plans to arm anarchists with better weapons (on the grounds of the anarchists' military and political unreliability); the Soviets who pressured the Catalans into accepting their proposals on economic policy; and finally, the Soviets who proposed an offensive on the Aragon front. To Antonov-Ovseenko's frustration, the plan finally agreed upon by all parties did not suit his conception of what was possible or likely to succeed. He felt forced to go along with the scheme, however, because of the impossibility of working out a plan with the "worthless" Catalan councillor that he was forced to deal with.

# Document 20

RGVA, f. 33987, op. 3, d. 832, ll. 196–200

General Consul of the USSR in Barcelona                                 Copy
                                                                   Top Secret
Vkh. N° 5827
29/10/36                                              11 October 1936 N° 9/ss

To NKID
HEADQUARTERS
Com. Krestinsky

On 8–9 October I was in Madrid (two hours by plane). Spoke with del Vayo, the minister of foreign affairs, Prieto, the minister of the navy and aviation, and with Caballero. I looked over the barracks for the Fifth Regiment and its staff. I conclude from everything that I saw and from conversations:

1. The strategic situation of the Republican forces is not bad. On the Talavera direction, the best of the White units are attacking with up to fifteen thousand men; their communication lines consist of one railroad and one highway. On the Tajo River, behind blown-up bridges, up to three thousand Republican men are holding out on the flank and rear of the enemy. The enemy is not at all using forces from Estremadura. Meanwhile, Deputat Cordón, thanks to good partisan tactics, is holding down a force of three thousand Whites in the Hinojosa del Duque region with a unit of only four hundred men. With just a few weapons and elementary organization they ought easily to be able to create a serious threat in the Whites' rear in Talavera and thus hamper the Whites' offensive on Madrid.[45] Add action to the southeast of Madrid and also with the Asturians on León, and they might create an encirclement of Gen. Franco's forces, which are trying to surround Madrid. It all depends on arms and organization.

2. The Madrid government and general staff have shown a startling incapacity for the elementary organization of defense. So far they have not achieved agreement between the parties. So far they have not created an appropriate relationship for the government and War Ministry to take control. Caballero, having arrived at the need to establish the institution of political commissars, so far has not been able to realize this, because of the extraordinary bureaucratic sluggishness of the syndicalists, whom he greatly criticizes and [yet] without whom he considers it impossible to undertake anything. The general staff is steeped in the traditions of the old army and does not believe in the possibility of building an army without experienced, barracks-trained old cadres. Meanwhile, the capable military leaders who have been fighting at the front for two months in various detachments, and who might have been the basis for the development of significant military units, have

been detailed all over the place. Up to four thousand officers, three-fourths of the current corps, are retained in Madrid and are completely idle. In Madrid up to ten thousand officers are in prison under the supervision of several thousand armed men. In Madrid no serious purge of suspect elements is in evidence. No political work and no preparation of the population for the difficulty of a possible siege or assault is noticeable. There are no fewer than fifty thousand armed men in Madrid, but they are not trained, and there are no measures being taken to disarm unreliable units. There are no staffs for fortified areas. They have put together a good plan for the defense of Madrid, but almost nothing has been done to put this plan into practice. Several days ago they began fortification work around the city. Up to fifteen thousand men are now occupied with that, mostly members of unions. There has been no mobilization of the population for that work. Even the basics are extraordinarily poorly taken care of, so the airport near the city is almost without any protection. Intelligence is completely unorganized. There is no communication with the population behind the enemy's rear lines. Meanwhile, White spies in the city are extraordinarily strong. Not long ago, a small shell factory was blown up by the Whites; an aerodrome with nine planes was destroyed because the aerodrome was lit up the entire night; a train carrying 350 motorcycles was destroyed by enemy bombs.

Caballero attentively listens to our advice, after a while agrees to all our suggestions, but when putting them into action meets an exceptional amount of difficulty. I think that the main difficulty is Caballero's basic demand, now in place, to carry out all measures on a broad democratic basis through syndicalist organizations. Sufficient weapons, in particular machine guns, are now flowing to the city to raise the morale of the populace somewhat. Masses of peasants and workers are thronging to the city—volunteers. They end up for the most part in the Fifth Regiment, where they go through a very short training course, as they receive their weapons only about two days before going to the front.

It is obvious that without very serious support from specialists and instructors they will not succeed in setting up large military units for the various branches under current conditions.

. . .

6. A number of facts, which I communicated by telegram, are evidence for the stabilization of the government and for the serious attempts by Catalonia to regularize the administration [of the country]. At the same time, relations between the anarcho-syndicalists and the FAI, which depend on the lumpen proletariat, are becoming strained. Relations between the anarcho-syndicalists and the Soviet Union are changing in a fundamental way, one sign of which is an article, "Spain and Russia," in the leading organ of the anarcho-syndicalists, set forth for me in a special telegram. Our speech in London had a special significance.

7. Companys acknowledges that relations between Madrid and Catalonia

## Document 20 *continued*

have improved, "but this is a song from necessity." Not long ago, the Whites in Seville ironically praised Caballero, saying that, because of the discord with Barcelona, he had not evacuated the shell factory to there. In Madrid I was told that Barcelona had held up fifty trucks destined for Madrid. Companys informed me, however, that in the last few days they had sent Madrid three hundred trucks. We need to be careful in assigning blame to either side. There is a great deal of well-founded distrust on both sides and direct lies to us. We need to check up carefully [on matters].

All of this convinces me once again [of the need] to send me the necessary workers quickly, and among their number must absolutely be a worker on foreign trade and a specialist on mobilizing industry.

General Consul of the USSR in Barcelona
/Antonov-Ovseenko/

Correct: [illegible]

---

## Document 21

RGVA, f. 33987, op. 3, d. 832, ll. 201–206

General Consul of the USSR in Barcelona          Copy
14 October 1936          Top Secret
N° 10/s

To Headquarters
NKID—Com. Krestinsky

On 12 October Com. X. and I saw each other. He impressed me as a well-informed and precise man.

1. In his words, the relationship between our people [the Communists] and the anarcho-syndicalists is becoming ever more strained. Every day, delegates and individual comrades appear before the CC of the Unified Socialist Party with statements about the excesses of the anarchists. In places it has come to armed clashes. Not long ago in a settlement of Huesca near Barbastro twenty-five members of the UGT were killed by the anarchists in a surprise attack provoked by unknown reasons. In Molins de Rei, workers in a textile factory stopped work, protesting against arbitrary dismissals. Their delegation to Barcelona was driven out of the train, but all the same fifty workers forced their way to Barcelona with complaints for the central government, but now they are afraid to return, anticipating the anarchists' revenge.

In Pueblo Nuevo near Barcelona, the anarchists have placed an armed man at the doors of each of the food stores, and if you do not have a food coupon from the CNT, then you cannot buy anything. The entire population of this small town is highly excited. They are shooting up to fifty people a day in Barcelona. (Miravitlles told me that they were not shooting more than four a day).

Relations with the Union of Transport Workers are strained. At the beginning of 1934 there was a protracted strike by the transport workers. The government and the "Esquerra" smashed the strike. In July of this year, on the pretext of revenge against the scabs, the CNT killed more than eighty men, UGT members, but not one Communist among them. They killed not only actual scabs but also honest revolutionaries. At the head of the union is Comvin, who has been to the USSR, but on his return he came out against us. Both he and, especially, the other leader of the union—Cargo—appear to be provocateurs. The CNT, because of competition with the hugely growing UGT, are recruiting members without any verification. They have taken especially many lumpen from the port area of Barrio Chino.

X. agreed with me that these excesses, coming from below, were meeting ever greater opposition from CNT leaders and that it was completely possible to agree on joint struggle against such occurrences.

2. They have offered our people two posts in the new government—Council of Labor and the Council of Municipal Work—but it is impossible for the Council of Labor to institute control over the factories and mills without clashing sharply with the CNT, and as for municipal services, one must clash with the Union of Transport Workers, which is in the hands of the CNT. Fábregas, the councillor for the economy, is a "highly doubtful sort." Before he joined the Esquerra, he was in the Acción Popular; he left the Esquerra for the CNT and now is playing an obviously provocative role, attempting to "deepen the revolution" by any means. The metallurgical syndicate just began to put forward the slogan "family wages." The first "producer in the family" received 100 percent wages, for example seventy pesetas a week, the second member of the family 50 percent, the third 25 percent, the fourth, and so on, up to 10 percent. Children less than sixteen years old only 10 percent each. This system of wages is even worse than egalitarianism.[46] It kills both production and the family.

X. told about the oddly forceful impression that this scheme is making among the workers. He himself observed at a place where Barcelona workers take walks—la Rambla—how thousands of workers listened to a speech over the loudspeaker by a representative of the syndicate about the introduction of this system.

Three days ago, the government seriously clashed with the anarchists: the CNT seized a priest (from a Marian order). They agreed to release the priest to France, but for a ransom. The priest pointed out another 101 members of his order who had hidden themselves in different places. They agreed to free all

102 men for three hundred thousand francs. All 102 appeared, but when the money had been handed over, the anarchists shot forty of them. Against the protests of the councillor of internal affairs, President Companys delayed shooting the remaining sixty-two. He stated that he would resign if they continued summary shootings. The sixty-two priests have been entrusted to [the care of] a judge.

Arguments in the government about municipal decrees continued for four days. Companys proposed organizing municipal authorities on the model of the central government—that is, on the basis of government by all the parties. Our people sharply objected, since they have undoubted majorities in almost all the cities and large settlements and since Companys's proposal would give the POUM party (Troskyists) representation in the municipalities completely without grounds, but X. recognizes the need to settle problems about the government of the cities, and our people, although they voted against the government's decrees, decided to remain in the government, publishing a special statement.

Com. Calvet—an adviser on agriculture; he is also the secretary of agricultural workers' syndicate—is preparing a decree on forbidding the liquidation of small-peasant property.

4. Our people are also preparing a decree about putting the housing question in order. Houses in Madrid that are without owners are handed over to the ministry of industry and commerce, and in Barcelona this business has not been put in order at all.

Our people are taking every step to ease relations with the syndicalists. The permanent commission, with three members each from the CNT, the FAI, the UGT, and the PSUC, has resumed working on preparing questions for the government and on settling various conflicts.

Approved in principle: a unified UGT-CNT division with fifteen thousand men, in which there ought to be, according to García Oliver, "iron discipline." The question about the command of this division and about the selection of its people has still not been decided.

X. agreed that the people ought to be checked out through the Combined Commission. They should be members of an organization and have guarantees from two members who belonged to the organization before the 17 July.

The CNT also agreed in principle to a proposal by our people about disarming unreliable elements in the rear: a combined commission will be set up that will hold meetings everywhere, explaining the need to hand over weapons for the front. After the meetings—searches. Putting this into effect has been postponed for now.

X. agrees with me that with this campaign it is necessary to stir up a lot of agitation about the danger of the situation at the front, which is emanating from the slogans of the anarcho-syndicalists themselves, most of all from Durruti (however, some partisan pride is shown by X. on this question).

5. X. sharply criticized Caballero's conduct. In Madrid there are up to fifty thousand construction workers. Caballero refused to mobilize all of them for building fortifications around Madrid ("and what will they eat") and gave a total of a thousand men for building the fortifications. In Estremadura our Comrade Deputy Cordón is fighting heroically. He could arm five thousand peasants but he has a detachment of only four thousand men total. Caballero under great pressure agreed to give Cordón two hundred rifles, as well. Meanwhile, from Estremadura, Franco could easily advance into the rear, toward Madrid. Caballero implemented an absolutely absurd compensation for the militia—ten pesetas a day, besides food and housing. Farm laborers in Spain earn a total of two pesetas a day and, feeling very good about the militia salary in the rear, do not want to go to the front. With that, egalitarianism was introduced. Only officer specialists receive a higher salary. A proposal made to Caballero to pay soldiers at the rear five pesetas and only soldiers at the front ten pesetas was turned down. Caballero is now disposed to put into effect the institution of political commissars, but in actual fact it is not being done. In fact, the political commissars introduced into the Fifth Regiment have been turned into commanders, for there are none of the latter. Caballero also supports the departure of the government from Madrid. After the capture of Toledo, this question was almost decided, but the anarchists were categorically against it, and our people proposed that the question be withdrawn as inopportune. Caballero stood up for the removal of the government to Cartagena. They proposed sounding out the possibility of basing the government in Barcelona. Two ministers—Prieto and Jiménez de Asúa—left for talks with the Barcelona government. The Barcelona government agreed to give refuge to the central government. Caballero is sincere but is a prisoner to syndicalist habits and takes the statutes of the trade unions too literally.

The UGT is now the strongest organization in Catalonia: it has no fewer than half the metallurgical workers and almost all the textile workers, municipal workers, service employees, bank employees. There are abundant links to the peasantry. But the CNT has much better cadres and has many weapons, which were seized in the first days (the anarchists sent to the front fewer than 60 percent of the thirty thousand rifles and three hundred machine guns that they seized).

In Sabadell (the largest textile center) the union, which is still autonomous, voted not long ago to join either the CNT or the UGT. Eight hundred men voted for joining the CNT, and eleven thousand voted to join the UGT.

The central organ of the party in Catalonia (*Treball* in Catalan) has a circulation of twenty-seven thousand. *Mundo Obrero*—seventy-five thousand. In Catalonia another four of our daily papers come out with small circulations. A daily paper in Spanish has been gotten under way.

We agreed with X. that:

1. We will jointly strengthen, using all measures, the permanent conciliation commission with the anarcho-syndicalists.

2. We will support the authority of the present government of Companys-Tarradellas, gradually, systematically carrying out a number of measures to liquidate the anarchists' willfulness.[47]

3. Until measures are undertaken to disarm unreliable elements, we will develop a large political campaign on the dangers from Franco threatening the revolution, and so on.

4. To carry out as urgently as possible the organization of a unified division, carefully selecting the command staff for it and getting uniform arms for it. Weapons coming from outside will go to this division first.

5. To insist that the government create in the rear no fewer than two fortified defensive lines.

6. To struggle against the obviously provocative rumors about an impending landing by enemy troops on the Catalan coast.

7. To take every measure in our power to deploy C. Cordón's detachment as quickly as possible.

8. Not to allow the government to abandon Madrid, at the very least half of its members ought to remain in Madrid until the end.

Information from other sources: 1) relations between the UGT and the CNT are getting better, 2) the UGT and CNT Liaison Commission worked badly because of the "intransigence" of Comorera (Gen. Sec., PSUC), recently resumed work (one meeting); a proposal submitted by our people on 10 Oct. about transforming this commission into an "action commission" was received evasively and then was published in the c.[entral] o.[rgan] *Treball.*

General Consul of the USSR in Barcelona
/V. A. Antonov-Ovseenko/
8 copies/mm

# Document 22

RGVA, f. 33987, op. 3, d. 832, ll. 222–224

vkh. N° 5842 from 29/20/36              Copy
General Consulate of the USSR
   in Barcelona                      *Top Secret*
18 October 1936
N° 13/ss

To Headquarters<br>NKID—Com. Krestinsky

1. My conversations with García Oliver and with several other CNT members, and their latest speeches, attest to the fact that the leaders of the CNT have an honest and serious wish to concentrate all forces in a strengthened

united front and on the development of military action against the fascists. I must note that the PSUC is not free from certain instances that hamper the "consolidation of a united front": in particular, although the Liaison Commission has just been set up, the party organ *Treball* suddenly published an invitation to the CNT and the FAI that, since the experience with the Liaison Commission had gone so well, the UGT and the PSUC had suggested that the CNT and the FAI create even more unity in the form of an action commission. This kind of suggestion was taken by leaders of the FAI as simply a tactical maneuver. Com. Valdés and Com. Sesé did not hide from me that the just-mentioned suggestion was meant to "talk to the masses of the CNT over the heads of their leaders." The same sort of note was sounded at the appearance of Com. Comorera at the PSUC and UGT demonstration on 18 October—on the one hand, a call for protecting and developing the united front and, on the other, boasting about the UGT's having a majority among the working class in Catalonia, accusing the CNT and the FAI of carrying out a forced collectivization of the peasants, of hiding weapons, and even of murdering "our comrades."

The PSUC leaders-designate agreed with me that such tactics were completely wrong and expressed their intention to change them. I propose that we get together in the near future with a limited number of representatives of the CNT and the FAI to work out a concrete program for our next action. According to a communication from Comorera, the Liaison Commission has indeed revived with changes in its membership: from the PSUC—Garci Amatei, from the UGT—Sesé and Vidiella, from the FAI—Escorsa, from the CNT—Eroles and Herrera.

2. The Council of the Catalan government works regularly on putting the rear in good order. After a decree on municipalities, a draft decree on collectivization, put together by Fábregas, came before the council. It was returned to the Council on Economy as ordinary material, since the principle of collectivization was too widely extended. The PSUC repeatedly proposed to the government that weapons at the rear be seized and put at the disposal of the government. Not long ago, military councillor Sandino came out with this proposal and was supported by the PSUC, but the CNT induced [them] to postpone the question.

In the near future, the PSUC intends to bring forward the question on reorganizing the management of military industry. At this point the Committee on Military Industry works under the chairmanship of Tarradellas, but the main role in the committee is played by Vallejos (from the FAI). The PSUC proposes to put together leadership from representatives from all of the organizations, to group the factories by specialty, and to place at the head of each group a commissar, who would answer to the government.

3. The evaluation by García Oliver and other CNT members of the Madrid government seems well founded to me. Caballero's attitude toward the question of attracting the CNT into that or any other form of government betrays

his obstinate incomprehension of that question's importance. Without the participation of the CNT, it will not, of course, be possible to create the appropriate enthusiasm and discipline in the people's militia/Republican militia.

The information concerning the intentions of the Madrid government for a timely evacuation from Madrid was confirmed. This widely disseminated information undermines confidence in the central government to an extraordinary degree and paralyzes the defense of Madrid.

4. The arrival of the *Zyrianin* called forth such enthusiasm and such hopes from the Catalans, accompanied by such demonstrations, that it has created a situation of extraordinary responsibility, demanding from us further measures for the support of Catalonia. The development of operations for bartering will be one of these measures; but this is absolutely not enough. Again I will mention to you the necessity to organize all-around assistance to make Catalonia stronger. Catalonia is Spain's healthiest region, with strong industry and undamaged "morale"—from here we can, and must, urgently organize the rescue of Madrid.

General Consul of the USSR in Barcelona V. A. Antonov-Ovseenko

## Document 23

[Unnamed source (8)]

---

Consulate of the USSR in Barcelona                         *Top Secret*
[illegible] November 1936
N° 26

*On Military Questions.*

1. The dispatch of aid to Madrid is proceeding with difficulty. The question about it was put before the military adviser on 5 November. The adviser thought it possible to remove the entire Durruti detachment from the front. This unit, along with the Karl Marx Division, is considered to have the greatest fighting value. To put Durruti out of action, a statement [was issued] by the commander of the Karl Marx Division, inspired by us, about sending this division to Madrid (it was difficult to take the division out of battle, and, besides, the PSUC did not want to remove it from the Catalan front for political reasons). However, Durruti refused point-blank to carry out the order for the entire detachment, or part of it, to set out for Madrid. Immediately, it was agreed with President Companys and the military adviser to secure the dispatch of the mixed Catalan column (from detachments of various parties). A

meeting of the commanders with the detachments on the Aragon front was called for 6 November, with our participation. After a short report about the situation near Madrid, the commander of the K. Marx Division declared that his division was ready to be sent to Madrid. Durruti was up in arms against sending reinforcements to Madrid, sharply attacked the Madrid government, "which was preparing for defeat," called Madrid's situation hopeless, and concluded that Madrid had a purely political significance—and not a strategic one. This kind of attitude on the part of Durruti, who enjoys exceptional influence over all of anarcho-syndicalist Catalonia that is at the front, must be smashed at all costs. It was necessary to interfere in a firm way. And Durruti gave in, declaring that he could give Madrid a thousand select fighters. After a passionate speech by the anarchist Santillán, he agreed to give two thousand and immediately issued an order that his neighbor on the front Ortiz give another two thousand, Ascaso another thousand, and the K. Marx division a thousand. Durruti was silent about the Left Republicans, although the chief of their detachment declared that he could give a battalion. In all, sixty-eight hundred bayonets are shaping up for dispatch no later than 8 November. Durruti then and there put his deputy at the head of the mixed detachment (Durruti agreed to form it as a "Catalan division"). He declared that he would personally be with the detachment until the appointment [of the new head]. But Durruti unexpectedly pulled a stunt, holding up the dispatch. Learning about the "discovery" of a kind of supplementary weapon (Winchester), instead of sending the units from the front on a direct route to Madrid, he sent these units unarmed into Barcelona, leaving their weapons (Mauser system) at their own place [on the front] and instead calling up reserves (without weapons) from Barcelona. His anarch. neighbors did the same thing. Thus Durruti got his own way—the Aragon front was not weakened. About five thousand disarmed frontline soldiers were gathered in Barcelona, and Durruti raised the question about immediately arming them at the expense of the units of the B.[arcelona] gendarmerie and police (Garde d'Assaut [*sic*] where the Socialists predominate and Garde Nationale where the Republicans are in charge). Through this, Durruti would achieve a continual striving by the CNT and the FAI to undermine the armed support of the present government in Barcelona. Since the weapons seized from the Garde d'Assaut and Garde Nationale (about twenty-five hundred rifles) were still not enough, it was proposed to get them from the "rear soldiers," and instead of weapons of a different sort, the Garde d'Assaut and Garde Nationale would also, according to Durruti, receive Winchesters in place of Mausers. Here the government's decree on the handing over of weapons by the soldiers at the rear has already been frustrated.

With a great deal of effort we frustrated this plan, which, in the best case, would impede the dispatch [of the troops] to Madrid for several days (the Winchesters were still en route). Another motive for our repudiation of the former plan was the military unreliability of the anarchists and the political unreliability of the projected staff leadership. We insisted on the dispatch from the front of the Stalin Regiment, the select thousand from Durruti, and from Barcelona the Libertad detachment, which fought well at the approaches to Madrid and was being re-formed. These units came forward between 8 and 9 November. In addition, a thousand fighters were sent to Durruti and a battalion of Left Republicans were dispatched. In sum, about sixty-five hundred bayonets, twenty-five machine guns, fifty light machine guns, twelve pieces of ordnance.

This entire incident proclaimed not only the huge resentments toward Madrid and distrust of our intentions, but also the extreme clumsiness and ossification of the old Spanish military commanders, and also the organizational confusion (all of the parties are in command, bypassing the staffs, with their "own" detachments). One also senses the possibility of treason (by the staff of the Huesca sector commander, Colonel Villalba, if not by Villalba himself).

2. Characteristic difficulties in connection with the use of our specialists dealing with cartridge matters. Industry here is under the leadership of councillor Fábregas, nominated by the anarcho-synd. CNT. The metal industry is under the worker Vallejo (who is under the influence of the FAI). They treat our specialists with suspicion—we have secret schemes, hostile to the CNT-FAI. I have already told how it was necessary to quash these doubts, which even García Oliver has. But even after talks with the latter, sensible proposals by our specialists were curbed.

In the presence of Companys, I agreed with the first councillor, Tarradellas, that he should summon at his own place a special meeting with our specialists and leaders of military industry. Tarradellas put off this meeting in an extreme way, leaving for Paris. It was necessary to hold it without him at Santillán's. The explanations were rather sharply worded, but a large part of the proposals were approved (Santillán was fully canvassed beforehand).

This pressure of ours also served Tarradellas, on his return to France, as grounds for an attack on me personally, as (he said) "giving orders even to individual factories" (Tarradellas later admitted that he was incorrectly informed).

Thanks to our specialists, production of cartridges (mainly out of old empties) has already been raised fivefold, to two hundred thousand. Further increases have been hindered by the poor quality of the tools, because of a lack of tool steel. Soon a lack of various [other] metals will also begin to be experienced (about which I will communicate separately).

3. The weakening of the opposing forces on the Aragon front which was revealed (the recall, in any case, of the Moroccans and several units of the "Spanish falange" and a unit of aircraft) and also the consideration of assistance for Madrid—prompted us to raise the question about an offensive on the Aragon front. This also coincided with the intentions of the staff. At a meeting held on 10 November at the headquarters, a decision was approved

by all of the column chiefs, except for Villalba. The plan for the offensive was accepted for 14 November. I consider this plan to be a bad one.

. . .

But there should be no reconsideration of this plan, nor should it be worked out in agreement with the councillor that you know well (he is utterly worthless and stubborn besides), in order not to ruin even this kind of decision.

Of course, the timing was bad. Because of this, the offensive should be postponed. A second reason for postponing it is the need to amass cartridges, and so on. A third is the organizational friction (mainly from Villalba, whose suspicious manner hampers the regrouping of units).

There are no tanks on this front, and there is not even one modern airplane. Units have sat in damp trenches for more than two months. To stir and captivate them will be possible only through some potent means of inspiration. Best of all would be to support their attack with modern aircraft.

In the present circumstances, success is extremely doubtful.

General Counsel of the SSSR in Barcelona
        (Antonov-Ovseenko)

*6 Copies*
1—Higher headquarters
2—Headquarters
3—The Boss[48]
4—The Director
5—Dep. Director
6—Archive

IOSIF RATNER

Antonov-Ovseenko's views of the anarchists and of Catalonia were given further confirmation by Iosif Ratner, the assistant military attaché. As he noted in the first paragraph of **Document 24,** the opinions he would express were his own and not agreed to by "Sancho" (Gorev). In his reading of events, the anarchist leaders had become much more reasonable and willing to work with the Communists. Only the anarchist "masses" still showed the old desire to shoot anyone who questioned their right to complete freedom from rules and discipline. He also thought that Catalan claims of unfair treatment by Madrid had some basis and believed that the Soviets could find some way to work with Catalonia. Nevertheless, neither of these two men's opinions changed Soviet views of, and policies toward, the anarchists and Catalonia. Both the Catalans and the anarchists were seen as anti-Communist and untrustworthy; little better than the fascists from whom the Soviets had supposedly come to save Spain. This attitude toward the two groups would come together in May 1937, when the Communists decided to rid Catalonia of all the anarchists, "Trotskyists," and "fascists" that stood in their way.

## Document 24

RGVA, f. 33987, op. 3, d. 852, ll. 324–333

NKO SSSR                                   To the People's Commissar of Defense
Worker-Peasant Red Army                        Marshal of the Soviet Union
Department 1                                       *Com. Voroshilov*
12–14 October 1936
N° 10698

I submit a dispatch received by us from Com. Ratner *on the situation in Catalonia.*
The facts brought forth in this dispatch characterize the comparatively great stability of the Catalan army units.
    Enclosure: Dispatch of 9 pages.

Chief of the Intelligence Directorate of the RKKA
Corps Com.[mander] S. Uritsky

                                                                *Top Secret*
Copy N°
                        *On the Situation in Catalonia*
                              *A Dispatch*

I am writing from Barcelona. I am taking advantage of the fact that the mail leaves from here and am writing to you directly. Consider everything that I set forth in this letter my own personal opinion, not agreed to by Sancho. Tomorrow I am leaving for Madrid, and I will report to Sancho everything that I write in this letter.
    I was in Barcelona three days. I met with the war minister Sandino. I had a protracted conversation with Guarner, the chief of the general staff. I had a protracted conversation with Durruti, the people's hero of Catalonia, leader of the anarchists, commander of the nine-thousand-man anarchist column at Saragossa. I visited with Miravitlles, the state commissar of propaganda. I was

at the front near Huesca, where I rode around to all the units stationed there. I was in the only aerodrome in Catalonia, at Sariñana, where all the airplanes are concentrated. I visited barracks situated in Catalonia.

This gave me enough material on which to base the following general conclusions.

Catalonia, and Barcelona in particular, have a more normal and peaceful existence than Madrid. "Anarchist" Barcelona lives the almost normal life of a European capital—a huge contrast with the anarchy that reigns in Madrid. And this was not only in Barcelona, but in all Catalonia. Catalonia gained several victories on the Aragon front immediately after the rebellion began and pushed the enemy back from the borders of Catalonia and continues even now to enjoy partial success. This influences the cheerful, confident, and peaceful mood.

*On the anarchists.* The anarchists came to power, and they hold three ministerial posts, command large army units, and hold a number of prominent government posts. Having become part of the government, the leaders of the anarchists have gradually changed their tactics. The anarchist press, more than anyone else, began to agitate for unified command and for iron discipline. The well-known anarchist Durruti tried for half an hour to convince me that without unified command and without obedience there would be no victory. To the front near Huesca came the beloved idol of the anarchists, Oliver García [*sic*]. He assembled the anarchist column and began to persuade them that they ought to obey orders and be disciplined. That provoked a general indignation. Threats directed at him began to be heard. He hurriedly left there. On that same day the anarchists shot three commanders in their column suspected of sympathizing with Oliver's ideas. The anarchist masses are still as before, but the bosses have already turned toward a more sober and realistic government policy. On social questions there has also been a great change: at the large factories the anarchists themselves are being compelled to reject egalitarianism[49] in wages. The Left Republicans—influential themselves in the government party—are coming out everywhere for organization, discipline, and order and are forcing the anarchists to come to their senses on these questions.

Between Catalonia and Madrid there is a highly charged relationship. Catalans accuse Madrid of not helping them with anything: during the whole war Madrid has given them only 1,200,000 cartridges and no money; they asked for several dozen tons of powder, as they could put together the bullets and cases themselves, and Madrid did not give that, either. They did however give Madrid in these difficult circumstances twelve thousand men and continue even now to send men and even weapons, in which Catalonia is even more lacking than Madrid. Everything that I enumerate here is complaints aimed by Catalan government officials at Madrid. Apparently, some of this is not devoid of substance. Catalans advanced the following proposition: let Madrid give them two million cartridges, and they would take Saragossa and from there strike at Sigüenza—that would be the best aid for Madrid. Madrid will not go for that, demanding that they send reinforcements directly to the Madrid front. Personally, I think that the Catalans are absolutely right on this question. At Saragossa Durruti had thirty cartridges per rifle left. There's about the same kind of picture at Huesca. If they would arm them more, they could take Huesca without difficulty, in one day, because Huesca is completely surrounded and has four and a half thousand Whites, not unwavering troops, against twelve thousand Blues. After the capture of Huesca, they could send ten thousand for an attack on Saragossa from the north. Durruti assures [me] that he would take Saragossa by himself, without the help of other units, if only they gave him cartridges. The capture of Saragossa would have great political, moral, and strategic significance. In addition, the Catalan units sent to the Madrid front are fighting very badly there. They fight much better at home in Catalonia.

As in all Spain, in Catalonia everyone, even the anarchists, has placed hope in us. They are profoundly certain that we will not desert them. This hope gives them confidence and good spirits. I think that, with the Catalan leadership, as with the anarchist leaders, we may come to agreement on many questions. We can influence them strongly. This is possible because the old politicians are in Madrid, while the majority here are young, very candid, ardent, and less experienced in political machinations.

*Situation on the fronts*
. . .

The Catalan military organization is stronger than that of Madrid. The forces are in general more battle-ready. In the Catalan units, discipline will quickly be strengthened. There is already talk of a re-forming of all the party columns and of transformation into a normal military organization. This, of course, they will not achieve quickly, primarily because the anarchists have still not come to that, but order and organization will undoubtedly be strengthened.

In case of an attack on Madrid, Catalonia can undoubtedly play a huge role as a base for offensive action on Madrid from the north. The largest factories and enterprises are in Catalonia, including Hispano-Suiza. There are large cadres of qualified workers, technicians, and engineers with various specializations. With some help from outside, Catalonia can very quickly get the necessary military industry going. In Catalonia the masses as a whole are of a more revolutionary temper and are more intransigent toward fascism than in other regions of Spain (with the exception, perhaps, of the north).

All these circumstances, undoubtedly, dictate the necessity for closer connections with Catalonia.

We absolutely must have a permanent military worker in Barcelona. There is a lot of work here, and there are a lot of opportunities.

CORRECT: Chief of the I Department of the RU RKKA
    Corps Commissar        Shteinbriuk

## ARTUR STASHEVSKY

The final report from the advisers, **Document 25,** shows the stance the Soviets took toward the Spanish economy. Broué and Témime believe that Artur Stashevsky, the author of this report, was nothing more than the economic attaché who arranged arms shipments to Spain.[50] This document suggests that the more sinister reading of Krivitsky—that Stashevsky was sent to manipulate the Spanish economy—may be closer to the truth.[51] Stashevsky was appalled by the "wild, unplanned work" that reigned in Catalonia (the main industrial center in Spain). The Spaniards in his report are incapable of dealing with their own economy or the saboteurs that were attempting to destroy industry at every turn. In addition to arranging the deliveries of weapons from the Soviet Union, then, Stashevsky set about organizing the Spanish economy for war through "skillful maneuvering and persistence." He tried to make sure that Socialists were in charge of the economic bureaucracy and recommended Stalinist-style planning and the centralization of military industry. This latter effort is significant because, according to Stalin's theories, a centrally planned *military* industry was the basis for a socialist economy. If the Soviets were indeed hoping to create a people's democratic republic in Spain, a transformation of the economy in this way was essential.

The other point that is clear from this report is that the Soviets had no intention of *giving* the Spanish anything. Whatever weapons or other supplies they wanted had to be paid for in hard cash. Not long after the war began, the Madrid government sent more than two-thirds of the Spanish gold reserve, much of it in rare coins, to Moscow for safekeeping. As the war progressed, the Spanish would gradually spend the gold, paying the Soviets for the weapons necessary to prosecute the war. Recent scholarship has shown that the Soviets overcharged the Republican government for these arms, inventing prices to coincide with the amount of Spanish gold in their hands.[52] The government in Catalonia, meanwhile, had no hard currency reserves. This explains Stashevsky's attitude when confronted by the English demand that the Soviets act as guarantors for Catalan coal shipments: the mere suggestion that the USSR would give the Catalans coal to fight their war provoked nothing but outrage.

Stashevsky also followed Stalin's views on sabotage and "wrecking." Accusations of sabotage were at the core of the terror sweeping across Stalinist Russia. In 1928, Stalin had begun an ambitious effort to industrialize his backward country in only four years. The result had been, not unnaturally, many setbacks and failures to fulfill plans, along with a few spectacular successes. According to Stalin's paranoid vision of the world, every failure in industry was the result of a deliberate attempt by Trotsky himself to undermine the achievements of the new Soviet Union. The term used to describe this sabotage was "wrecking," and its use in this document, and others, had very specific political connotations, linking the "sabotage" in Spain with the worldwide conspiracy of "Trotskyists" and "fascists" bent on destroying the Soviet Union and any powers allied with it. Stashevsky thus did not believe that just individual fascist sympathizers were at work destroying the Spanish war effort, but rather an entire "fascist organization among the higher command."

It is also significant that, once again, a Soviet adviser singled out General José Asensio as "a highly suspect man." Like other advisers, Stashevsky, too, warned about the anarchists' secret caches of weaponry, while believing that there were opportunities to work with the CNT. The "better part of the anarchists" were beginning to agree ideologically with the Communists, and he praised a talk given by the minister of industry, Juan Peiró (a CNT leader), as "almost the speech of a Communist."

---

## Document 25

RGVA, f. 33987, op. 3, d. 853, ll. 313, 319–323

Copy No. 5                                                                SECRET
NKVT N° 771 31/12/36

To Com. Stalin
Com. Molotov
Com. Kaganovich
Com. Voroshilov
Com. Ordzhonikidze
Com. Andreev

I am sending a copy of two letters from Com. Stashevsky mainly on the question of the situation with military industry in Spain and on the relations among the various parties.

## Document 25 *continued*

These letters were written before the meeting between the ministers Prieto and Negrín and the representatives of the Catalan anarchists, which took place the other day on the initiative of Com. Stashevsky, and at which some understanding on economic questions was reached.

L. Rozengolts

AP/8e
31/12/36

[ll. 319–323]

COPY
Valencia, 14 December 1936

Dear Arkady Pavlovich,

On the question of relations with Catalonia—I am putting everything into this avenue, because in every area—financial, hard currency, either military industry or economic—the problem of relations is becoming very critical and, without the participation of Catalonia, almost impossible.

1. The other day Com. Malkov had a talk with Fábregas, who is not unknown. The latter related the following: in Barcelona there are coal reserves for industry until 1 January. They recently sent a commission to England with the object of obtaining coal from there. The commission returned with nothing and declared that [England] would sell coal to them if there are guarantees from our side that we would pay for the coal. It is unclear to me how it came about that this kind of conversation was carried on. Obviously, the Catalans are trying to speculate on their friendship with the USSR. However that may be, they still have no coal. Fábregas proposed that in exchange for 150,000 tons of coal, which Catalonia could need for the next six months, they would manufacture twenty locomotives and diesel engines, and so on.

I called Com. Malkov's attention to the harm in carrying out this kind of conversations. I believe that the only way out (since the Catalans do not have any hard currency) is for them to apply to the Min.[istry] of Fin.[ance] with the object of obtaining the latter's consent for payment in hard currency. Every import to Catalonia can be carried out only with the authorization of the Min. of Fin., which in the end can pay us hard currency for the delivery.

Do not connect the questions of export and import; take each problem separately. If we find interesting goods for export from Catalonia, calculate in turn for them in hard currency as well. Make an agreement with the Min. of Fin. on the Catalans' affairs, regarding the means for paying for their import orders.

I think that this is the only correct way to strengthen a unified hard currency policy and from the standpoint of normal hard currency relations. I ask for your directives on this question.

## Document 25 *continued*

2. Questions about mil.[itary] ind.[ustry]. Coms. Gaines, Grishin,[53] and I conversed for a long time with the leaders of the anarchists—García Oliver, minister of justice; Vázquez, general secretary of the CNT and minister of health.

Besides various [other] questions, I raised the question of how they pictured the future development of mil. ind. Could the wild, unplanned work in Catalonia continue in the future, haggling for every chassis (by the way, three hundred Ford chassis from Barcelona have still not been handed over), lack of a unified plan for the supply and distribution of food? They declared to us that they were for a unified supply plan, but they insist that a certain percentage of the military material produced ought to remain in Barcelona. I pointed out that perhaps the one unified center for distribution was the War Ministry, which concentrates matériel according to the degree of importance of the fronts, and that they ought to obtain some influence over distribution in the War Ministry. By the way, Largo Caballero for some time asked the anarchists to send people to the staffs, to the War Ministry, but so far the anarchists have not sent any people.

They decided that in a few days Prieto, I, and García Oliver will fly to Barcelona, where we will find out all of the raw material needs, and from that we will try and put together a plan.

The anarchists asked that I come alone, without Prieto; they cannot stand Prieto.

The other day I was with Prieto. He, for his part, cannot talk calmly about the anarchists. But he promised me that he will conduct himself very fairly.

I am not expecting anything much from this meeting, but I hope that we will secure some elementary normal relations between the central government and the Catalans on military industry.

Without this, it is out of the question to think seriously about military industry here, as the entire principal industry is concentrated in Catalonia.

3. General impressions from this conversation—the anarchists are gradually abandoning their positions, they will look for rapprochement through a possible merging of the CNT and the UGT, and they do not want to lose face politically.

Today I was at a meeting organized by the friends of the Soviet Union, in honor of a Spanish delegation that was arriving from the Union. Among others, the minister of industry spoke (an anarchist). He came down rather hard on the control committees in the factories, and demanded discipline, without any reserve. Almost the speech of a Communist. The better part of the anarchists are in the process of this kind of ideological movement toward us. But the process is very painful.

It seems to me that we must help to accelerate this process through *practical* work.

4. Side by side with this are subversive instances of anarchists' hiding weapons. It is known that even in Madrid fairly large quantities of weapons have been secreted away.

The other day, one of the engineers (a Spaniard from Mil. Ind.) reported to me that there are four caches of mortars hidden away in one place here in Valencia. I received a letter from the minister and today a commander of an International Battalion ought to have seized this ordnance with its shells.

Abnormality, disorganization, carelessness, and laxity are everywhere.

I am convinced that provocation is all around and everywhere; that there is a fascist organization among the higher command, which carries out sabotage and, of course, espionage.

Unfortunately, Gen. Asensino [*sic*] is a highly suspect man; a former military attaché for ten to twelve years, now vice-minister for Caballero, enjoying his exceptional trust.

While working on the military industry, I have met with such a large number of seditious instances of subtle wrecking that it is impossible to ascribe this to the casual wrecking of individual people; an organization is at work.

Now the organization of the leadership of military industry is under Prieto, who has had this laid on him. The influence of the most harmful elements has been temporarily checked. On the whole, the bureaucracy is selected by Prieto from among Socialist specialists, engineers, technicians, and there are some results after two weeks of work, or, more truthfully, huge opportunities for production have been brought to light. If there are raw materials and some machine tools, then in a month cartridges, explosives, armored trains, and possibly even tanks should make their appearance. However, Caballero already has said (under the influence of a report by Asensio) that it is absolutely imperative to use generals (the very same ones that I suspect of wrecking) for the leadership of mil. ind.

That is the situation in which the work on military industry is taking place—this is at the moment when the front is groaning because of a lack of cartridges, when a number of reserve brigades that have already formed up are sitting around without rifles.

The situation, as you can see, is not easy. And all the same, I shall not lose hope that through skillful maneuvering and persistence, we shall succeed in introducing planned development into this work, even if elementary in nature.

I shake your hand firmly.

A. Stashevsky

Valencia
14/12/36
    CORRECT: [illegible]
AP/8e
31/12/36

## THE ADVISERS AND THE PURGES

Almost all the principal advisers sent to Spain at the beginning of the war were dead by the time the conflict ended in March 1939. None of them fell in combat, however; they were victims of the political intrigues so characteristic of Stalin's Soviet Union. When the war broke out, the greatest of the political show trials was just beginning. After the marginalization of Bukharin, Stalin was ready to clean out the last institution to remain untouched by his purges—the army. In May 1937 Mikhail Tukhachevsky, along with seven other high-ranking officers, was arrested and summarily executed. That event began a purge in which 90 percent of the Soviet high command and perhaps as much as 70 percent of the officer corps as a whole eventually died.[54] In the midst of this "whirlwind," Gorev, Berzin, Antonov-Ovseenko, and Stashevsky were all recalled to Moscow, imprisoned, and shot. The motivation for their arrests and executions is far from clear, although there has been a great deal of speculation on this point.

Although the new evidence offers no definitive answers, **Document 26** hints at why one of the victims incurred the displeasure of Moscow. In early 1937 Marcel Rosenberg, the Soviet ambassador to Spain, was ordered to return to the Soviet Union, where he disappeared. Many historians have described a public scene outside Largo Caballero's office in which the ambassador was accused by the Spanish leader of trying to impose his will on the Republican government.[55] Since Rosenberg was recalled shortly thereafter, it seemed reasonable to conclude that the dispute precipitated his fall from grace. There were just two problems with this assumption. First, as the documents in this section show, all the Soviet advisers were busily attempting to take over the Spanish war effort, the economy, the PCE, and, eventually, the Spanish government itself. Rosenberg's efforts to do the same could hardly have provoked Stalin to kill him. Second, Rosenberg was already out of favor by December 1936. That month Stalin sent a personal note to Largo Caballero in which, among other things, he asked whether the Republican government was happy with the Soviet ambassador.[56] The following document sheds some light on why Stalin felt impelled to ask this question. Here Gorev hints at a telegram from

Voroshilov on "all kinds of dirty matters" in which Rosenberg was involved. Rosenberg's response was that he would not change but would act as he saw fit. Gorev also comments on the ambassador's "unhealthy [sense of] self-esteem," his interference in everyone's affairs, and his petty surveillance. It was probably allegations of this sort that brought Rosenberg to Stalin's attention and provoked the mention of him in the December letter.

## Document 26

RGVA, f. 33987, op. 3, d. 832, l. 239

Copy

16/10/36

Top Secret

Madrid

To the Director [Voroshilov]:

I showed your telegram about negotiations on all kinds of dirty matters to Rosenberg. The result was about what I expected. He took it as a personal insult limiting his authority and is writing a letter which says that all the same, he is doing that and does not think it necessary or possible to stop. For the present he decided to continue his former policy for leading the negotiations.

You must keep in mind Rosenberg's unhealthy [sense of] self-esteem. He is terribly afraid for his authority; he is afraid lest someone should do something greater than what he does. The result is that he fritters away his energy. He does the same thing with my business and with my opinions and your directives. And as far as the work with Vintser, that's even worse. There he does not allow him to do anything without checking up on him. All his telegrams go through his inspection, and whatever he [Vintser] wants, he [Rosenberg] simply will not allow him to do.

He is incredibly nervous whenever one of us goes into a situation on his own to handle something. There was one incident when Kuznetsov sat with Prieto with Rosenberg's authority, holding preliminary talks about what their conversation would be, and just then, in the very middle of the talks, he could not hold himself back and burst in. Of course, for us that is [not] of no importance and is not good for affairs here. Too much petty surveillance means that he is missing the forest for the trees.

## Document 26 *continued*

It would not be a bad thing if you could write him a letter with some good comradely advice on this problem. But please do it carefully so that he will not know that I had any part in it.

Sancho

## The Soviets Urge the Catalans to Stay the Course

In addition to seeking to control the conduct of the war, the Soviets also had to stiffen the resolve of their Spanish friends for the fight against "fascism." **Document 27**, a letter by Antonov-Ovseenko on the situation in Catalonia, was written when the war seemed hopeless to the Spanish. By early October, Franco's troops had taken several major cities in the south and north of Spain and were beginning to converge on Madrid. It was obvious that the Nationalists were winning because of the aircraft, tanks, and other weapons that they had received from the Germans and Italians, while the Republicans seemed to have no supporters abroad. Faced with this desperate situation, the Catalan government began to lose confidence in its ability to win the war. In this letter Antonov-Ovseenko tried to provide the Catalans with hope; the letter also offers the student of the Civil War a number of surprises. The first revelation is the doubts Jaume Miravitlles (an Esquerra in the Catalan government) and Companys expressed about the nature of the uprising. Some historians have assumed that the Spanish shared the Communist belief that the Civil War was a part of the overall struggle with fascism. Miravitlles and Companys, like many recent scholars, instead saw it as a war against "militarism and clericalism"—that is, the old army and the Church, rather than as a battle against some worldwide fascist conspiracy. The second revelation is that the Catalans seriously considered making a separate peace with the Italians. None of the sources available to us heretofore has hinted that the Catalan leaders thought it might be possible to come to an understanding with the Italians.[57] On both these points, Antonov-Ovseenko used his considerable talents of persuasion, with the weight of the Soviet government behind him, to convince the Catalans that they were wrong. The war was against fascism; the Catalans could not break the united antifascist front; and Miravitlles had misread the intentions of the Italians. After this conversation with the Soviet consul, the Catalans dropped both ideas and became more committed to the struggle with "fascist elements" in Spain.[58]

The other revelation in this document has to do with the nature of the killings that took place behind the front lines in Republican Spain. The controversy over this point is of long standing. On the one side are scholars such as Gabriel Jackson, Paul Preston, and Antony Beevor, who emphasize the disorganized and spontaneous nature of the terror in the Republican zone as compared with the more institutionalized executions carried out by Franco and his men. Jackson also gives a figure of about twenty thousand total killed by the Republicans—approximately six thousand in Madrid and six thousand in Barcelona and Valencia together.[59] On the other side are men like Hugh Thomas and Stanley Payne who blame both sides impartially for the killings. Payne specifically argues that the old distinction between terrors (one spontaneous and popular, the other organized and institutional) is invalid. The "Red Terror" was also carried out by officially sanctioned groups.[60] In his conversation with Antonov-Ovseenko, Miravitlles supports the latter view of the terror. Not only are Jackson's figures far too low—the Catalans had after all killed eight thousand in Barcelona only nine weeks into the war—but the executions were obviously viewed as part of the war effort and supported by the government of Catalonia. Other documents reprinted in this chapter allude to many instances of unplanned and undesirable executions within the Republican zone. As in Nationalist Spain, however, under the Republican government tens of thousands of civilians were killed as part of the official war on fascism.

# Document 27

RGVA, f. 33987, op. 3, d. 832, ll. 53–55

Copy

Top Secret

Letter No 2/s
Vkh. No 5465 from 11/10/36,6 October 1936
Headquarters
NKID—To Com. Krestinsky

At the very same meeting on 4 October,[61] Miravitlles, specifying that he wanted to ask a "very delicate question," relayed the following: personally he had suggested and suggests that "in Catalonia there is no fascism," that "here the war is with Spanish militarists and clericalism" ("it was enough to shoot five hundred, and they had shot eight thousand in Barcelona alone"). Thus, as general secretary of the Committee of Antifascist Militia, the Italian general consul had presented himself to him with a protest at the murder of several Italian nationals. Saying that the murdered Italians were active enemies of the Spanish Republic, M. expressed the opinion cited above, adding that Italian fascism is "characteristic of youth and national consciousness." The Italian consul reproached M. with the fact that he was not expressing a similar notion publicly and suggested that he come with him to the consulate for a more detailed conversation. M. declined, citing his official position and his isolation on that question in the Committee of Antifascist Militia. Yesterday Companys expressed to him the exact same opinion about the lack of fascist elements in the Franco uprising, adding that they might try to agree with Italy on a cessation of assistance for Gen. Franco. M., according to him, answered that this undertaking was extremely crucial and that he would seek advice from me.

I explained to M. that first, his appreciation of Franco's movement was wrong politically, that second, an attempt at such an agreement with Mussolini was patently doomed to fail. Moreover, this attempt, exposing the weakness of the Republican Front in Spain, would only strengthen the activity of Italian fascism, most of all on the Balearic Islands, and, finally, this kind of escapade would destroy the united antifascist front. To counter this, I suggested a plan to M. for a large campaign around that last subject. England and France were vitally interested in not allowing Italy to seize Majorca, and so on, for this would extraordinarily strengthen the Italian position in the Mediterranean, by placing France's communications with Africa under Italian control, and so on. He had to whip up rumors of an agreement between Gen. Franco and Italy on a concession of Majorca to Italy for its support of the fascist rebellion in Spain. He had to raise a similar campaign in the world press, in parliamentary circles of France and Italy, and so on, obtain a landing of French and English journalists on Majorca with intensified observation of them by the French and English navies, and so on. In this way he might, at least, make it difficult for Franco to use the Balearic Islands, with Italian assistance, as a base (for carriers and submarines) against Barcelona. M. seized on my suggestion and promised to send me all the materials the next day.

The evening of 4 October, Companys set forth the same kind of thought to me on the nature of the "general's rebellion" in Spain and on the possibility of pulling Italy away from Germany, but he offered the proviso that he thought it was now impossible, too late. He also talked about his fierce struggle with fascist elements in Spain, and so on. But he did not express any particular enthusiasm about my projected campaign on the Balearic Islands.

. . .

Along with this, M. and C.'s scheme shows the great confusion of the ruling petit-bourgeois Catalan democrats in the face of a situation that is ever more threatening. It may be that here, and without blackmail directed at us, you can quickly and concretely help, or else we will have to come to an agreement with Italy. At the same time, as Ehrenburg commented, dreams [such as] putting themselves under the protectorate of France are prevalent in Barcelona; now, because of Blum's administration, this opinion has disappeared, but are not the pronouncements of M. and C. signs of a rising tide of pro-Italian opinion, in connection with m.b. and with the great activity of Italo-fascists in Barcelona? I have given myself the task of urgently clarifying that question.

Irrespective of the possibility of blackmail, this is another serious motive for beginning all kinds of work in Catalonia.

Antonov-Ovseenko

P.S. I just found out that Companys has seized on my plan and has already taken steps to send French and English journalists (at Catalan expense) to Majorca and also to Lisbon and Gibraltar (I pointed out the need for a campaign of journalists and . . . these people.
    A. Ov.

## The Spanish Civil War and Espionage

In seeking to control the Spanish revolution and to use the Civil War for their own ends, the Soviets brought to bear their greatest resources: diplomatic, military, economic, and, of course, intelligence. The Soviets were not alone in using this last institution—the

Germans, Italians, British, and French also exploited covert assets to obtain information about their opponents' intentions and actions in the war. The Soviets did, however, seem to have better agents, who supplied the most highly classified documents to their Communist controllers. **Document 28** offers one example of the quality of the material to which the Soviets had access. It also presents a small glimpse into the murky world of espionage that underlay so much of the action in the Spanish Civil War. When the Western Department of SIS generated this document, all of the interested parties were trying to prove, while seeking to shield their own violations, that their opponents were breaking the noninterference agreement. The British used information from reports like this to confront the Soviets about violating the treaty, while the fact that the Soviets had a copy of it allowed them to prepare for public accusations at the nonintervention committee in London. The source who supplied this document is unknown but must have been highly placed either in SIS or in Vansittart's office—a reminder that Soviet intelligence had deeply penetrated the British government during the 1930s.

The SIS report is also important for showing us how the Spanish government managed to obtain arms from abroad. Although by mid-October the Republicans were beginning to receive the first military hardware from the Soviets, the channels through which it came were often tortuous. Tanks and used matériel arrived directly from Soviet ports, but there were other, more complicated routes for smaller weaponry and aircraft. One of these involved using some of the gold sent to Moscow to open a bank account at the Chase American bank in Paris. The Soviets then bought weapons, supposedly destined for an unnamed Latin American country, that ended up in Spain. The Spanish were not entirely dependent on the Soviets, however. As the report shows, they had their own buyers, who used the same American bank to purchase war matériel that was then shipped to the Republic. Czechoslovakia was the other important route for weapons destined for the Civil War. It is notable that while the Czechs were willing to permit the shipment of aircraft and other hardware through their country, they drew the line at allowing the Soviets to test-fly the airplanes in Czech air space, a reminder of a similar stance taken by neighboring countries during the Munich crisis. Finally, the attitude of the Spanish leaders when trying to set up these arrangements is telling. Faced with the need to take an action that could lead to international complications, they were all paralyzed by nervousness. Only Buenaventura Durruti, the well-known anarchist commander, was able to act decisively to obtain the weapons that were vital to prosecuting the war.

---

## Document 28

RGVA, f. 33987, op. 3, d. 870, ll. 35–42

---

*Top Secret*

[Marginalia:] To Voroshilov from Yezhov, 2/11/36

INO GUGB NKVD [the Foreign Department of the NKVD] has received from London the following document from the English Secret Intelligence Service, addressed to Vansittart's secretary—Cordón.

*Translated from English.*

*Secret*

Report No. 23 from 19 October 1936
*Western Department*
*Weapons for the Madrid Government*

Below we will relate evidence, received from three completely independent sources, concerning the supplying of the Madrid government with weapons from other countries. Judging from this evidence, we can conclude that agents of the USSR took a very active role both in Paris and in Prague.

a) Moscow credit in Paris
A highly reliable source, closely concerned with the transactions for supplying weapons, reported the following in the course of the first half of October:

1) In the Paris "Chase Bank" credit was opened for Moscow not long ago in the sum of a hundred million gold French francs. On the weapons market buyers appeared who tried to buy large consignments of weapons and ammunition, supposedly destined for a republic in South America. These consignments included a hundred thousand Mauser rifles with a thousand clips for

each, fifty million cartridges, four thousand light 7.92-caliber machine guns, a thousand heavy 7.92-caliber machine guns and twenty million cartridges for these, twenty anti-aircraft guns with thirty-five thousand bullets. These consignments of weapons were to be paid for out of the above-mentioned credit. It is very unlikely that they succeeded in purchasing such a huge consignment of weapons, for it is well known that almost all the spare weapons in Europe are more or less taken up by orders placed not long ago by both of the warring parties in Spain.

2) In confirmation of this intelligence, information was received supporting the circumstance that the steamship *Sishviya,* which sailed from Danzig 3 October, supposedly bound for Vera Cruz, in fact went apparently to Alicante. The weapons carried by the ship were examined beforehand by Col. Levèque who, according to rumors, works for the French government. The cargo was paid for out of the above-mentioned Soviet credit.

b) *Further activity in Paris*

Below, evidence will be given that was received at the beginning of October from a completely independent Parisian source, who maintains close contact with individuals who deal in weapons.

1) A certain Mr. Fournier and his co-worker Mr. Chenette have demonstrated a great deal of energy in locating weapon supplies. The first has plenary powers from the Spanish ambassador in Paris and has a deposit at the Chase Bank (at rue Cambon 41 in Paris) for five million francs (which may be increased to forty million). The question of the deposit was verified by Mr. Geide (4 rue Francoeur, town of Davalier), and it was determined that this report is in fact true. Mr. Geide tried to conclude a bargain with the Spanish government through Mr. Fournier. The latter, apparently, was especially warmly recommended to the Spanish by the French government, and the Spanish government now looks on him as a "trusted person."

2) As a result of the activity of Mr. Fournier, part of the equipment was bought for the Spanish government at the same time as the other orders were receiving a negative answer. [ . . . ]

3) Another agent of the Spanish government is Mr. Druilgue, who is staying at 4 bis rue Gustave Zédé in Paris. This Mr. Druilgue is a personal friend of Señor Largo Caballero. Since correspondence with Madrid was difficult, Mr. Druilgue, who had a Spanish airplane in his possession, flew to Madrid himself, from which he returned only a few days ago. He determined that Sr. Caballero was very agitated and did not have the time (or even the desire) to occupy himself with these questions. At the same time, since Mr. Druilgue insisted that the question of buying the weapons, the payment, and so on, be on solid ground, Sr. Caballero sent for Messrs. Pietro and Condinis; at the same time, these three were so nervous that they did not succeed in achieving any results.

4) After this Druilgue got in touch with a certain "Durruti" from Barcelona,

who, apparently, is a very influential anarchist leader. After the arrival of "Durruti" everything changed completely. When Druilgue set off, together with "Durruti," to see Caballero, they asked them to wait. "Durruti" however declared, "tell Mr. President that I must be received within three minutes, and if not I will raise a scandal such as has never before been seen here." After that he was received immediately, and "Durruti" came down on Caballero, accusing him of not carrying out his duty and of becoming nothing but an unnecessary hindrance. "Durruti" succeeded in firing up the others present, and it was decided to spend another billion francs on buying military matériel.

. . .

V) *Information from Prague*

The following information was received from a very reliable source, completely independent from all others described above (this source maintains close contact with the secretariat of the president of Czechoslovakia).

1) A certain individual, calling himself Mr. Paul, came not long ago to Prague from Madrid. He had a Swiss passport, but he is known to be an agent of the Soviet government. He stayed on Lotsova St. in a room used by the Soviet embassy when they wish to maintain secrecy. He was received by Mr. Krofta, to whom he reported that he had been sent by the Soviet ambassador in Spain to ensure the supply of weapons for the Madrid government. This plan has the approval of the Soviet government, which, according to "Paul," has completely resolved to render assistance to Madrid. He explained to Mr. Krofta that they expected help from Czechoslovakia, and that it would not risk anything, even if it became known, since formally they were selling weapons to Russia.

2) Mr. Krofta answered that the Czech government had in principle nothing against this plan, but that he still had no reply to the further proposal put by Mr. Paul that Soviet pilots, when sending airplanes to Spain, test them out in Czechoslovakia.

3) On 9 October a specialist from Moscow arrived in Prague and, on the following day, after discussion with Paul and a Spanish syndicalist named García, left for Spain.

This García undoubtedly was in Moscow and received complete authority to act as representative for the Spanish government in the matter of buying military matériel. Mr. Paul was to stay in Prague until the reception of further instructions from Moscow. It is possible that they will attempt to send airplanes by air directly to Spain from Czechoslovakia.

CORRECT

Chief INO GUGB NKVD SSSR

COMMISSAR OF STATE SECURITY

2nd RANK                              Slutsky

## The International Brigades

While the Soviets tightened their grip on the conduct of the war, international volunteers were streaming into Spain for the fight against the Nationalists. Many of the volunteers saw the war in Spain as their chance to take on fascism directly—to achieve in Spain what they were unable to do in Germany or Italy. The movement was at first largely a spontaneous response to the war in Spain and the dire straits that the Republic faced. It was, however, soon taken over by Comintern officials, in communication with Moscow, who organized the men into International Brigades, trained them, and would eventually lead the brigades into battle. Document 29 provides a glimpse into the early organization of the brigades and the answers to several historiographical questions about the units. Here we see that the lowest estimates for the numbers of men available for the defense of Madrid were correct. By early November, Franco's troops were so close to the city that the Spanish government decided to move the capital to Valencia. The transfer was opposed by both the Communists and the anarchists, who argued that the city could and should be held.[62] To bolster the defense of Madrid, André Marty, placed in charge of the international volunteers by the Comintern, formed up battalions and immediately sent the men off to battle as the 11th Brigade. Although two thousand soldiers could not make a difference in the actual fighting strength of the defenders, the effect on Spanish morale was immediate and overwhelming. The presence of the Russians, as they were called, stiffened the resolve of the Madrileños and made it possible to hold the capital.

Marty's request for commanders, and the emphasis on the party affiliations of the brigade members, are also significant. From the very beginning, the Comintern and Moscow wanted these units under their control and saw to it that a majority of the troops, if not all of them, were members of the Communist party. The percentage given here by Marty is comparable to numbers cited in later documents in this volume and with the claims of Communists during the war.[63] Control over the command staff was seen as particularly important. Moscow had already sent a few regular Red Army officers to lead the international volunteers and would now send more in answer to Marty's appeal. So that there could be no charges of Soviet *Russian* participation in the actual fighting, these were always men who had been born outside of the current borders of the Soviet Union. Thus Emilio Kléber, the head of the 11th Brigade, was actually Moshe (Manfred) Zalmanovich Stern, a native of Bukovina who had fought for the Reds in the Russian civil war and then become a staff officer in the Soviet army. General Walter, who would eventually lead the 35th Brigade, was Korol Karlovich Sverchevsky, born in Poland, and a participant in the October Revolution and the Russian civil war. He was, moreover, a regular staff officer in the Red Army and a deputy chief of a GRU sector. General Lukács, whose actual name was Mate Zalka, led the 12th Brigade, though his real employment was as an officer in the Soviet army. Finally, the 15th Brigade, which included the American Lincoln Battalion, was commanded by General Gall (Janos Galicz), another regular officer in the Red Army.[64] Through these men, and other "advisers" sent by the Comintern (among them Luigi Longo and Palmiro Togliatti), the International Brigades became, in effect, a Soviet army within Spain.

## Document 29

RGVA, f. 33987, op. 3, d. 832, l. 309

*Top Secret*

To Comrades Stalin
          Molotov
          *Voroshilov*
          Kaganovich

We received a telegram from Com. Marty from Madrid, through Paris, with the following contents:

"Despite the material difficulties, we have three thousand men for an International Brigade at Albacete; of them two thousand men are already formed into four battalions. By nationality they are Italians, Germans, French, Balkan nationals, and Poles; by party, they are 80 percent Communist and Socialist. The morale of the brigades is strong. Lacking are automatic weapons and ar-

## Document 29 *continued*

tillery; one-third have insufficient military training. The command staff is extremely small and insufficiently qualified.

"We request twenty commanders, from battalion to company commanders, including also four for the artillery, all French-speaking."

The further reinforcement of the brigades will proceed to increase, with the calculation of reaching five thousand men by 15 November. I request your directives.

4/11/36

D. Manuilsky

CHAPTER TWO

# 1937

## The Situation in a New Year

BY THE END OF 1936, a false sense of security prevailed,
leading the Republican government to experience something akin
to a state of euphoria. The first Soviet aid had arrived; Loyalist
troops had managed to defeat Franco's attempt to take Madrid,
and the Republican government had consolidated its forces with
the entry into the Popular Front government of both Communists
and anarchists. The Soviets had achieved what at first appeared to
be many triumphs. They had received a great deal of prestige from
the sending of arms to the Republic. This, in turn, increased the
ranks of militants joining the Spanish Communist party. Soviet advisers began to have the run of Spain, and could be seen almost
everywhere. "Intoxicated by their success," E. H. Carr wrote,
"they suffered from an excess of over-confidence."[1] This overconfidence was displayed most strikingly in the attempt of the NKVD
to destroy all left-wing opponents of Stalin in Spain. In August
1936, Stalin had sent Alexander Orlov to the country and had
given him the task of purging the revolutionary Marxist opposition
to the Communists, the POUM. It was Orlov, his biographers
write, who "*was* responsible for engineering and directing a Stal-

inist purge of the POUM, that led to the death of [Andrés] Nin and [some] of Trotsky's supporters and other opponents of the Moscow-backed Republican government."[2]

The problem facing the Soviet Union was that the greatest part of the Spanish working class was either anarchist or syndicalist, and the Spanish Communist party was a minority movement. The Soviet paper *Pravda* had editorialized in December that in Catalonia, the heart of anarchism, "cleaning up of Trotskyist and anarcho-syndicalist elements will be carried out with the same energy as in the USSR." And a few days before, the Comintern had instructed the PCE, "Whatever happens, the final destruction of the Trotskyists must be achieved."[3] The Communists did succeed in having the POUM removed from the Catalan government, but major problems still existed for the Soviet Union. The Spanish Republican premier, Largo Caballero, and the head of the Navy and Air, the moderate Socialist Indalecio Prieto, both objected strenuously to Communist domination of the system of political commissars in the military. At the same time, anarchist officers fought bitterly with their Communist counterparts.

In **Document** 30 GRU chief S. P. Uritsky informed Kliment Voroshilov of the nature of his discussion about Spanish events, held on the last day of 1936, with the left-wing American news correspondent Louis Fischer. The journalist was later to be famous for his disillusionment with Communism, and for his contribution to the anthology by left-wing anti-Communists *The God That Failed*. In that book, Fischer would write that because Spain was "the front line against Fascism," the civil war "postponed my 'Kronstadt.'" Indeed, in his essay, Fischer argued that privately he had come to have great doubts about the Soviet experiment by the time he was covering the events in Spain, for he realized that the "funeral atmosphere [in Moscow] was blacker than ever." The only factor that prevented him from going public was that to do so would have meant losing his contacts with Russians in Spain and hence his ability to work with the Loyalists. As Fischer put it, because the Spanish Communists had gained "great strength in the Republican camp, a critic of Soviet Russia would not have been welcome in it."[4]

The document that follows reveals that Fischer's service was much more direct than his merely writing propaganda for a Western press that sanctioned the Soviet position in Spain. Indeed, the document strongly suggests that Fischer did not as yet have any real doubts, and while in Moscow, he had presented his findings on internal Spanish events directly to the GRU, the military intelligence service of the Soviet military. Fischer, in fact, did all he could to reinforce a highly optimistic view of the Soviet leadership. "'Vivo Russo!' is written on all the streets," Fischer reported, "and portraits of Stalin are everywhere."

Most important, Fischer gave Uritsky negative information about the Spanish general José Asensio, undersecretary of war and commander of the central front in the battle of Madrid. Fischer told Uritsky that he had personally informed Premier Largo Caballero that it could appear that the high number of Republican military defeats was due to the leadership of the people's forces by "a government of traitors." By this time Asensio had become an open opponent of Communist party policy, and hence the Spanish Communists began to demand his removal from all government and military command positions. To impugn his reputation, they claimed that Franco had almost won Madrid because of Asensio's weak leadership.[5] In this context, Fischer's musings about whether the general was a "traitor" amounted to an endorsement of Soviet and PCE maneuvers to destroy him.

## Document 30

RGVA, f. 33987, op. 3, d. 960, ll. 14–29

Top Secret
Copy N° 1

To the People's Commissar of Defense of the USSR
Marshal of the Soviet Union
Com. *Voroshilov*

On 31/12/36 I had a visit with the well-known American correspondent Louis Fischer. Fischer had returned from Spain, where he had taken an active part in the organization of the international units. The logic of the situation and how it was closely tied to the struggle against fascism had gripped him.

I submit to you a stenogram of his talk, especially valuable because Fischer is an American radical with a touch of skepticism, but a rather honest and straightforward person.

Chief of the Intel.[ligence] Direc.[torate] of the RKKA
Corps Commander S. Uritsky

3 January 1937
N° 4ss
2 Copies
MK

*Stenogram*
of a visit by the chief of the Intelligence Directorate of the RKKA
Corps Commander Uritsky, S.P., with Louis Fischer
*31 December 1936*

*Stenogram of a visit with Louis Fischer*

1. *On our people.* I am not exaggerating—just, in my opinion, objectively establishing that we would not be in Spain, that there would not be a Spanish Republic, if the Russians hadn't come. I don't think that this is an exaggeration. They were already at the gates of Madrid by 7 November. I don't think that without airplanes, without cannons, and without tanks, we would have been able to hold Madrid past, let's say, the middle of November. By then, Franco's government would have already gotten into Madrid, and the Italians, by agreement with the legal government of Spain, would have sent a legion. I don't think that the east could have held out without Madrid. That thought, that the fall of Madrid was a death blow, was already around in September. So I don't think that that is an exaggeration. Of course, things would have gone on. Franco would have been a nuisance for many years, but there would have been no Caballero government. Your help saved the situation.

People. I have to tell you that I have always loved the Soviet people, respected their qualities, but it is truly difficult to find the words to describe the people that you have sent there. And everyone assures me, and I believe, that these are not select people, not the best. I'm seeing just ordinary people there. I know one machine gunner, I don't know his name, but I see him almost every day. He doesn't look very smart, but his work is just excellent. I saw how he teaches. I saw how he collects machine guns. Here, he is just an ordinary guy, but over there he is tip-top. I mean, the most valuable, most excellent people. And they have such discipline. A man doesn't push himself forward, is modest—no one knows who he is, except for those who work with him or run into him.

"Vivo Russo!" [*sic*] is written on all the streets, and portraits of Stalin are everywhere. There was one time when the anarchists were acting really brazenly near Madrid. They were guarding the exits from Madrid, and sometimes it was difficult to leave the city. I was staying in Albacete and came to Madrid several times. I had a Russian pass (it was given to me by a Russian comrade). They saw "Comrade Louis Fischer" and didn't look at anything else. Everyone, even the anarchists, loves the Russians. But, I ought to say, during the first period this wasn't true, when you were sending only food over. The Spanish either didn't believe that it was only food or thought badly of it: "What, are they sending us only milk and sugar? That's very good, but we need something else." There was even criticism in the provincial newspapers. They showed a tank. It fires. On the tank was written, "Russian butter." A plane is flying over, dropping bombs. Below is written, "Russian sugar." At that time, when according to my information it was only milk or sugar, they didn't believe, and those who did believe said, "That's rubbish."

That was the situation at the beginning. And both the anarchists and the Trotskyists heated up this mood. Now it's completely disappeared, and now and then the anarchists have a terrific attitude toward you. The Trotskyists have lost the best of their slogans, of their negative argument that Stalin is a nationalist, that he has forgotten the world revolution, that he isn't helping us.

Our internationalists went through Madrid to the front. Do you know how they greeted them? "Viva Russo"—i.e., that Russia is the best. I'm telling you. You can't imagine the prestige of the Russian. I was telling you about the instructor, how everyone was watching him. He takes a shot—watch. Next, in the navy I know a good comrade. Everyone watches how he works [Kuznetsov].

The Old Man[6] you can only love and respect. He's quiet, knows what he's doing. I know that in our column maybe only two, no, maybe only one man knows him, but when they say the name "Old Man," it's like some kind of saint or something. I know how all your people love him, they won't let people near him, so that he won't work too much, so they won't worry him too much. You know, he has an unusual simplicity in understanding the essence of things. They told me, for instance, how, when Kaganovich came to the People's Commissariat for Transportation, he [Gorev] expounded on transportation matters: steamships, goods cars, passenger cars, people. That's the Old Man. He really knows life, knows the simple things, that have simple meanings: weapons for the Spanish, technology, and everything else, and his comparison of all these forms. He talks with me for ten minutes, and I have a complete picture of the military situation in Spain. The anarchists respect him. García Oliver, the head of the anarchists, who just went into the government, prefers to talk to him often, because he's thorough.

Gorev walks around with a pipe, as if nothing bothers him. He always has time. The Spanish love to get all panicked and it [his attitude] works well on them. They need that kind of calm person. Gorev is the favorite around Madrid.

The pilots. I'm not just paying compliments. I always write the truth about the Soviet Union. I'm not sugar-coating things. The pilots are A-1, first class, as we say in America. You know the story about Tarkhov? That is the most invaluable man.

OK, again about the mysteries of the Spanish, about keeping secrets.

I was gone from Madrid for ten days. I come back. That was about 15 Nov. I come to the hotel. Look for Koltsov. Not there. Look for other comrades. Not there. Spaniards in the corridor were asking me, Who is it you need? I say, "I'm looking for the Russian comrades." They show me. They take me into a room—a man's lying there; near him is a Spanish nurse. I ask, "Who's that?" She says, "A Russian pilot." "What's up?" "He has three bullets in his stomach." I ask the Russians. They tell me the whole story that you know, and it's terrible to think that one of ours killed him. On the next day I'm with him. I ask "How do you feel?" "OK. How are things at the front?" Well, he's still a sick man, so I say that it's good, we're holding out, and the enemy is retreating. "Yeah, it's about time," he says. "I got wounded, want to get back soon." I talked with him for a few minutes. The next day I went back. "Well, how do you feel?" "OK." The nurse tells me to say to him that he shouldn't do what he did: he got up at night, only thirty-six hours after the operation. I ask him, "What's the deal?" He answers, "I felt good. You know, if you exercise a little, you heal faster." I look at his chart: 38.3°. I don't think he died because he got up, but very few people could get over that. He even had peritonitis.

2. *On General Asensio. . . .* I got to know him at the end of September in Toledo. Things weren't going well then, and the soldiers were in a rare mood: everyone was asking, "Isn't he a traitor?" I myself often saw him go up to the defensive lines, a brave man, not afraid of gunshots. He invited me to dinner. There were myself, Adiro (a translator), and Asensio. He started right off with the question: Why isn't the Soviet Union helping us? I answered that I know Soviet policies only as an outside observer and in general the only thing that I could say was my own thinking. We talked for a long time about that. He expressed the desire—or better, stated the opinion—that the Spanish Republic could be saved only if a world war developed out of the civil war. By the way, Franco has the same opinion, that his one and only salvation is in an escalation, in the development of this conflict into a world—general European—war. I, of course, explained that this wasn't advantageous for the world or for Spain. I remember the words I used: "You know, the Soviet government won't willingly or lightly make a decision that may involve the deaths of a million or two million people, which may be the result of a world war." I told him, "Stalin will help you if he knows that a world war won't come out of it."

Well, from that conversation I couldn't get an impression whether he was a saboteur or a traitor. I don't know.

Then I spoke with the Old Man. You know his relationship with him. He said that Asensio sends everything to Madrid so that Franco can take it. That was about the middle of November. He shut down the machine-gun school and sent the machine guns to Madrid when they weren't needed there and the school was what was needed, for training new cadres.

Also, during the second half of November, I spoke with Caballero on various topics. He agreed that the International Brigades need weapons, clothing, better equipment. He said that everything that he had, he would give us and promised concretely to give us five thousand rifles with cartridges, two batteries of cannons, three thousand pairs of Soviet boots and four hundred tons of canned goods. All of this ought to be here in a few days on a Dutch steamship.

Then I talked about the general situation, and particularly, that the international column was created for attacks and that there's a feeling among us against sending the 3rd Brigade to Madrid. He said that without his permission, nobody, not one soldier, would go to Madrid.

That same day I told the Old Man about this conversation with Caballero. He said that either today or yesterday they had sent people to Madrid.

Then the Dutch steamship *Rombon* arrived and was unloaded. We received a phone call: Come to the station at Albacete to get your cargo. I went to the station with some people to set a guard, so that we could unload, and we were already getting ready. Suddenly, some Spaniards appeared and said, "This is our cargo." "Excuse me," I said, "they called us. Do you have documents for unloading the cars?" "No. Do you?" "No, but that's our cargo."

Right there were Tsiurupa and a young artilleryman, a good guy. They also had gotten shells there.

"OK, good," I said. "Let's go to the general staff to decide this."

I went to the staff. There was a colonel there, the chief of staff—I don't know his name—something complicated. Anyway, I told him that Caballero had personally promised all this to me. He said, "I'm very sorry, but read this telegram." I read, "The assistant minister of war . . . " No name was there, but it was Asensio, who ordered that the whole load be taken when it arrived and placed in a depot and that it be given to no one.

This was a concrete example of Asensio canceling an order from Caballero. More than that I don't know. On the basis of that, it's difficult, of course, to say that he's a traitor, but it's something that proves that he interferes, that he has his own politics.

Oh, and one more example.

The Spaniards have an internal cabinet, and an internal Council of Ministers. I attended one meeting with Caballero, del Vayo, and Negrín (the minister of finance), and it was very strange that suddenly Asensio showed up. There was a Communist deputy who is in charge of purchases, who was making a proposal that they ought to buy this, that it was possible to buy that, and so on. I should explain that the international column, and the Spanish army in general, suffers from bad kitchens, that it's difficult to fix food in the field, and we got eight field kitchens from the French Communist party. Now, that made us very happy. So when that deputy said that we could buy so many field kitchens, Asensio told Caballero, we don't need them. And nothing more.

So you can interpret that any way you want to.

And that's all that I know. I don't think that I can say that he's a traitor on the basis of that. But there's something there. Oh, and I should add something else. When things were going badly after the fall of Toledo and the Spaniards were running from village to village, I wrote a letter to Caballero in which I stated everything that everyone was thinking, but which no one could tell him about. I, a brash, independent person, thought that I had to tell him that. By the way, I remember exactly the words that I told him: "If I didn't know that at the head of this government stood a loyal revolutionary of proven worth, I would have thought that this was a government of traitors."

URITSKY—You spoke like that to him?

FISCHER—Exactly like that. Those very words. Then I said that history would judge people to be counterrevolutionaries who gave up Madrid without a battle. I told him that he had lost the popularity of the people lately, that people were talking against him and they were saying that Asensio was a traitor.

That was 12 October. My secretary handed him the letter at 1 o'clock in the afternoon, and at 4 o'clock his secretary called me. I personally thought: Well, it's the end, that maybe he would finally give me a dressing-down: What's the deal that Fischer is interfering? In general, I thought that this was the end of my relationship with him. It turned out that at 4 o'clock his secretary called and said that the prime minister wanted to talk to me. And at 7 o'clock I was at his place. The minister of foreign affairs was the translator. We talked over every word of that letter for a long, long time. By the way, I had asked in the letter, "Why don't you build trenches around Madrid?" He answered, "We don't have shovels." That was really funny. That was in October, three months of war. But that's beside the point.

As for Asensio, he answered me: "I don't have proof that he's a traitor. I just know that at the front, when there was a bombing, he stood quietly and wasn't afraid." I told him that that wasn't proof, that a soldier, even if he is a traitor, has his experience, his soldierly sense of honor; he won't run. Caballero says, "I don't have proof." And Caballero doesn't want to give up Asensio.

URITSKY—Why?

FISCHER—Why? Well, as for Caballero, you can't doubt him, because Caballero is such a strong man. He says, "Prove it."

URITSKY—How do the former monarchist officers behave?

FISCHER—There are very few of them. I saw several of them. They don't instill trust. But then there's Torrejón, a captain from the Foreign Legion, who was wounded twenty-four times in Morocco and who was thrown out of the legion, even locked up in jail because he was a radical, and later a Communist—many soldiers said that when everyone else ran away, he was the last one at the bridge; soldiers tried to talk him into going with them, and he wouldn't go, wasn't afraid.

There are some good ones.

3. *About the head of the Republican air force, Cisneros.*

URITSKY—Do you know the head of the air force?

FISCHER—Lt. Col. Cisneros?

URITSKY—Yes, his daughter is with us.

FISCHER—I know him. I think that Cisneros is a devoted man. His wife runs a children's home, a beautiful woman, from an aristocratic family. I got to know her in April. She was my translator. And I also got to know him then. She said that she rarely got to see her husband, because he slept in the aerodrome, because he was afraid every day and night that there would be a revolt by the pilots. So he was on guard, then, and he was on the side of the Republican government.

URITSKY—Is he a skilled, trained pilot?

FISCHER—About that I can't say. He has authority.

URITSKY—Is he a Socialist?

FISCHER—I don't think so. But I don't think that that is important. These are Spaniards—a great people. When I came here, in September, I saw that the Spanish were running. And at the same time, they were writing in the papers about heroism. Something didn't add up. I asked one guy: "Have you seen any heroism?" "No, haven't seen any." "Have you seen any heroism?" I asked another. "No, haven't seen any." I asked Koltsov, Lavrov, "Have you seen any?" "Yes." "Where?" "In the air force." We had a philosophical conversation and came to the conclusion that where one man is the boss, like the pilot, he can perform heroic actions. BUT, one man in a company where everyone is not a hero, but the opposite, they run away, what can one hero do, where is that hero? That means that heroism without organization, without discipline, can't exist . . .

URITSKY—Absolutely right!

FISCHER—And only now is heroism showing up.

4. *The International Brigades.* At the beginning of November, when the enemy was approaching Madrid, suddenly the fighting value and resistance of the Spanish army improved. This happened as a result of three factors:

1) the presence of the air force, 2) the Spanish fight better in the city, having a city behind them, than in a field, 3) the presence of the international columns.

During the course of October, Spanish units retreated toward Madrid. And here was the most frightening occurrence: there was bombing from airplanes. Despite the fact that they saw and that they were convinced that the bombing was not very damaging, sometimes after a bombing they saw that one or two people were killed; yet all the same, the bombing gave them such a feeling of weakness, of defenselessness, that even the best soldiers from the Fifth Regiment began to say: "There, see how enemy planes can act with impunity. We don't have anything." By the way, it turns out that in the middle of October we had three planes; then there was only one, and the French said: "And that last one is a coffin; we know that sometime we're going to come down, but we have to fly." You can't imagine the bad effect on morale caused by a lack of planes. I myself saw how soldiers wept with joy. I'm not a sentimental man and will never write about it, but I saw how the Madrileños wept on the streets of Madrid when they saw their own airplanes. A strange people: they tell them not to stand in the streets when there's an air battle going on: "They'll fall on you." "No," they say, "We need to see." And they shout for joy: "Ours! Ours!" They know ours by their speed. You know, what they're doing in Madrid is horrible, when, let's say, fifteen Junkers fly over and then eighteen soldiers show up. The Italians don't think about seeking battle, and the Germans aren't very eager to go for that either. This has a huge significance both militarily and for morale. They believe that we are not defenseless, that we have something.

The international column.

The Moors are excellent soldiers. There's even a legend about them that they're unbeatable. I spoke with soldiers around Bargas, where our soldiers were. Our offensive was a hundred meters from Bargas. I asked: "Why didn't you take it with the assault?" "Well," answered the soldiers, "There were Moors there who cut off ears and noses." A tanker told me that on the wheels of the tanks that returned from the battlefield were pieces of flesh and dried blood; that means that the Moors didn't retreat even before the tanks. And then, suddenly, before Madrid, the Spaniards saw the Moors' backs. How did that happen? It turns out that the international column stood and fought. So the international column is a school for the Spanish army, and under its influence the Spaniards fight better.

I was on the front the last time on 7 December. Our second brigade was in the second line of trenches, the Spanish were in the first, and I have to say the Spanish fight wonderfully when they feel that they have strong support behind them, which can protect them and reinforce them in case of strong pressure.

There was this kind of incident.

On the opposite side of the river, by University City, stood the 2nd Brigade. They moved to a more westerly position, but in the chaos, which is inevitable on the front in this kind of circumstances, a group of thirty men was left behind, Poles, with two machine guns. I was present when the chief of the staff of the 2nd Brigade spoke with Kléber. Kléber then called up the head of the brigade that was [now] occupying the position by the river and said that the brigade wanted to have its thirty Poles back. Palacios declared, "I don't want to give them back." Kléber: "We will give you the two machine guns." "No, this is about the Poles." "I will give you three machine guns." "Leave us the Poles and we don't need the machine guns."

I was also present when the 1st International Brigade was replaced by a Spanish brigade.

Everyone was persuaded, and it was especially emphasized, that the enemy shouldn't know that the International Brigade had left and that a Spanish brigade had arrived. How to do that so that the enemy wouldn't know? At night, or at any time, when the enemy fires, the Spanish always respond, whereas the International Brigade has good fire discipline and holds its fire, since the enemy isn't attacking. Everything went well—everyone was in a good mood. In the evening of the same day, the commander of the Spanish brigade came calling and reported: "Com. Kléber, everything is agreed. At night I will relieve the 1st International Brigade. We don't want them to go too far away."

They ought to have gone far into the rear, because they hadn't had a bath for fifteen days; they had been in the trenches. It was proposed that they go to the rear. They said, "No, we won't go until you replace us with a brigade that can hold our sector." And they stayed at the front until our staff was certain that the Spanish brigade could hold that position. That means that everything is fine, everything is in order, there's a replacement, but . . . don't let the internationalists get too far away.

You see how they lean on the International Brigade like an older brother, and they need it for support.

The International Brigade has had huge losses. It bore the brunt of Franco's offensive during the first half of November. There were horrible losses from that. So the first brigade came to the front with 1,900 men, and after a month there were only 1,000 left, and I have to say that on average, 20 percent were killed. The 2nd Brigade came to the front on 12 November. It had 1,550 men. By 7 December, when I was with them, there were 800 men left.

There was this kind of incident.

In University City a building had to be taken. They gave the mission to the Hungarians. There were three hundred of them. They had rifles with bayonets. The Moors had machine guns and hand grenades. The Hungarians lost two hundred of their three hundred men. The building was taken. It was horrible. Now we know that that didn't have to be done. But that incident stirred up thousands of Spaniards—they saw what you can do with heroism and conviction. Now we have another situation: sacrifice people to take a hundred meters of a plaza, and after a day you may hand it back.

But at other times, when we had to repulse the enemy, there were huge losses. The question was, do we reinforce them from the base, from the 3rd Brigade, or not? At the front they were demanding reinforcement from the base, but we wanted to set up a 3rd, a 4th Brigade. So we decided to re-form the first two battalions of Spaniards. A war began among the Spanish: every battalion wanted to get into the International Brigade. Finally, they chose two battalions of Asturian coal miners, who had proved themselves to be the best warriors. Now they've gotten so proud that you can't even talk to them. It's interesting to see that.

Every Spanish unit has trucks, and by the way, during the three months I stayed in Spain, I never saw Spanish soldiers marching: they attacked and retreated on trucks. So the Asturians, as soon as they had been placed in the International Brigade, proudly wrote on their trucks: "Internation. Brigade," and all their badges, which showed their Spanish origin, immediately disappeared somewhere; they quickly became internationalists.

Of course, they will fight better being included in the International Brigade. The International Brigade is a school; it's like a reward for good conduct in battle. I have to say that we have great discipline both at the front and in the rear. There was an incident after the alarm of 30 November when the enemy bombed and then lied, reporting that the Italians had made a [parachute] landing. . . . They of course immediately armed us. Undoubtedly, they were using the incident. So all our men began to shout: "Let us unload the trains, let us, we want to!" They unloaded the train. They armed us. And the next day everyone shouted: "What are we doing here? We want to go to the front! We didn't come here for this!"

I was chief of supply and barely convinced a German that he worked for me in the office. "What I do here," he said, "Paper I will write? Really I came for that? I came to fight at the front!" I told him, "If we have bad organization, then it will be bad at the front too." Somehow or other I convinced him. But somehow or other, even now, it's "I want to go to the front!"

The significance of our international columns is huge. The Spanish know that well.

But in recruiting for the columns we made two mistakes. The first: we have about 80 percent Communists. This is too high a proportion. We ought to gamble on recruiting Socialists, simple workers, antifascists, and all who come, of course, people of proven worth. The second mistake: 70 percent of all internationalists are French and Belgians. This means that the committee that takes care of this matter in Paris worked where it was easy to get people. We didn't work in England, or rather not much, approximately two weeks . . .

URITSKY—Are there Englishmen?

FISCHER—Five hundred men came.

URITSKY—Good people?

FISCHER—I didn't see them.

In America, in Scandinavia we didn't work.

On 1 December there were two Turkish officers.

It's just interesting to note.

Every soldier is given a questionnaire: last name, first name, where were you born, how much military experience do you have, and so on.

So one of the Turkish officers writes: I fought from eight to twenty-two years [old].

And we might be able to get people from Turkey.

We have two brigades at the front, which together with the Russians saved Madrid—that's 3,450 men. What a small number of people can change the situation! And what will twenty or thirty thousand Germans under Franco do?

URITSKY—You think that there are thirty thousand?

FISCHER—When I was there, they were saying: "There are five thousand." In the middle of December I had information that there were already ten to twelve thousand Germans in Spain. I believe that now there are more, and I am certain that Hitler will send more, because he's a smart politician. He understands the significance of Spain for him and for the Soviet Union. I am almost certain that there are twenty to thirty thousand men, or that there soon will be.

Also, I don't think that there will be many deserters among the Germans. We've already printed up leaflets, and we will work, we will agitate [among] them. But? Probably they will send trusted people: they know the danger. Then let's take this example: let's suppose that a German wants to desert to us. His family is in Germany. They disappear. He has no homeland. Where will he return to? Further: if he deserts to us, he is not certain that we won't shoot him, because we've shot a lot of prisoners. So he doesn't know what is waiting for him. So to count on breaking these Germans is difficult.

I repeat: if our thirty-five hundred changed the situation, what will thirty thousand Germans do, who have better weapons than our men. So we have to seriously work on recruiting for the international columns. We always have to work on this.

Now I'm going to Spain for just two days, and then I'm going to America and England. Of course I would like to stay in Spain, because it's much more interesting, but they won't leave me there.

But now in the USSR there is another possibility. There are, first, foreign immigrants, who have foreign passports. Next, it's no secret to anyone that they're demoralized and that they don't have very sweet lives. It would be good for both sides if they went to Spain. So this needs to be speeded up.

They've begun working on this, but very slowly. It's a question of time. But if the Germans begin to attack soon, I am not sure that they will not take Madrid. Of course there's the question of barricades—the city is hard to take—but all the same, it will be bad.

Next—the second category of people consists of foreigners—Hungarians, Latvians, Poles, Germans, and others. It is interesting to note: when a Hungarian comes from Paris or from Odessa to Spain, you soon can't tell which one came from Paris. And here there must be hundreds, thousands, of comrades who speak foreign languages.

As for transport:

When I began to talk to the Soviet comrades in the middle of September about the need to send airplanes, that without this nothing would come of it, everyone said: Yes, yes, but this is a long line of communications, that we don't have steamships. But all the same, they give them. On 30 November I talked with the Old Man about the need to send people from the Soviet Union and also with Petrovich, when there was not yet any talk of the Germans.

How do I interpret that?

We can't allow the destruction of the Spanish government. This is too important for the revolution, for international politics, for the Soviet Union. Well, then, if there are twenty to thirty thousand—forty thousand—Germans, they could decide matters. That means that the question of sending people from here comes up. This, of course, still frightens people, but I think that it might become a reality. I'm afraid that they may be late in deciding this question, also, as they were six weeks late with the shipping of airplanes.

I have to note that the scale of the aid grows with time. So if we had had fifty airplanes in August, we might have won. And now, for victory, we might need three hundred or four hundred airplanes. It's the same with the soldiers: if at the end of October we had had, I'm afraid to say exactly, but approximately maybe five to ten thousand, we might have taken the offensive and gone through the country. Now with ten thousand we couldn't do that. Now we need a reserve of twenty thousand. This means that the scale grows. If we could have given one quick blow at the beginning of October, we might have won decisively. Now you won't take it with one quick blow. The scale grows, and when we put it off, we only make things more difficult for ourselves.

In every International Brigade there is a Slavic company, a company that speaks Russian. In these are, approximately, 20 percent White Russians,[7] who hope to get back to Moscow through Madrid. Then there are Bulgarians, Serbs—where the language is Russian. But again there's a question: Well, and if there were a Red Army man from Tambov, wouldn't he also speak Russian? He, of course, will not come as a Red Army man, but will look like a guy who comes from Paris.

## Document 30 *continued*

### 5. *The Soviet transport of weapons to Spain.*

FISCHER—The quantity of weapons and all kinds of matériel delivered to Spain is huge. How this is done is a puzzle. I will say frankly that I haven't figured it out. Some say that your transports came from Vladivostok, others that it's from Murmansk, that you changed the flags on the way, and the contours of the ships. They say that you have used submarines widely to convey cargo to Spain. The rebels have seized eighteen Soviet ships and haven't found one rifle on any of them, and your weapons just keep on coming. How? Everyone, but especially the sailors, thinks about that Soviet secret. And the Italians and Germans keep on trying to help Franco, a whole spy network has been put into action. . . . Your Soviet operation to break through the blockade is heroism in and of itself and requires a separate appraisal. At the same time, this shipment of weapons through the four to five miles of the rebels' cordon and through the Italian and German navies has created a legend around you that you can do anything, that you have some sort of secret base in the Mediterranean, that you have some kind of special naval weapon. One of the English naval officers told me that he often saw how your ships were overloaded with weapons, but he thought it a miracle that they all arrived safely.

But now everyone is bitter about that, and I'm afraid that if you don't set up a submarine base in Spain, if you don't sink the *Canarias* and the *Ispanets,* they might do a lot of damage.

You have saved the revolution in Spain. There won't be any world war if you send soldiers and submarines.

I personally imagine, as do many others, that you are sending transports from the Far East through the Suez Canal, but not through the Bosporus or Gibraltar. That is more dangerous. You have these ways, of course, but how you work that problem, I repeat, is really a secret, incomprehensible.

### Internal Factional Fights

To cement their control over the military, the Communists fought to establish a formal institutional army that they would command. This would be dubbed the Fifth Regiment; more than sixty thousand men were enlisted in it by the end of 1936. There could be no Soviet Spain, the PCE leaders believed, until the war was won, and that meant developing an armed force led by the Communists.[8]

The Soviet view is apparent in a report from General Yan K. Berzin to Marshal Kliment Voroshilov on 12 January 1937, given here as **Document 31.** Berzin made known his disdain for the anarchists, and his insistence that a new regular army be created. Standing in the way of success, Berzin argued, was the position of the prime minister himself, whom he branded an open enemy of the Communists. After this message, it would be but a short time before a formal push was made to remove Largo Caballero from governmental responsibility, and to create a regime more favorable to Moscow's interests. Predicting victory for Soviet policy, Berzin cautioned that the mood in Spain "sometimes gets downright obscene."

Military necessity worked in the Soviets' favor. Though the Republicans had stopped the Nationalist offensive outside Madrid, both the Italians and the Germans stepped up their intervention in Spain during December 1936 and January 1937.[9] These moves threatened to overturn the balance of power in Spain and made the Republican government feel extremely vulnerable. In **Document 32,** War Minister Indalecio Prieto informed the Soviet ambassador how weak his government was, especially by comparison with the might of the rebellious generals and their German and Italian benefactors. To redress the imbalance, Prieto made a formal request for sixty fighter planes, a hundred bombers, and a hundred other fighting craft.

The military situation did not put a halt to the Soviet Union's desire to control the internal political structure of Republican Spain. Indeed, the Republic's dependence on the USSR made that task much easier. Stalin had already sent both GRU and NKVD advisers to Spain, and they quickly set out to master the situation. In **Document 33** the deputy chief of the GRU in Spain, Nikonov, reported on 20 February 1937, on his effort to purge the armed forces of "traitorous elements" who were engaging in counterrevolutionary activity. These, of course, were composed both of those he calls Trotskyists and active members of the POUM. It is significant that Nikonov attributed the fall of the town of Málaga, a defeat suffered because of both bombing and Italian military aggression, to "treason."[10] Moreover, Nikonov turned the GRU's own desire to smash the anarchists into a need to respond to a purported anarchist plot to stage a secret coup against the Popular

Front. Nikonov's report marked one of the first statements from the military intelligence service of the need to oppose the social program advanced by left-wing opponents of the Communists. His description of the revolutionary POUM, whose armed wing George Orwell fought with, as "the rottenest unit of the entire Republican army" indicated the seriousness of Stalin's plans to destroy the opposition. His complaint that the POUM was receiving "supplies, money, and ammunition" from the government provides evidence for the anarchist charge that the Communists and the Soviets wanted only those units which were firmly under the control of the PCE and the Soviet advisers to receive such supplies. Nikonov's report ended with the chilling assessment that the "scum within the Republican camp" had to be "liquidated."

Document 34 is a report of 22 February 1937, issued by the Soviet plenipotentiary in Spain, Marchenko, to Soviet foreign minister Maxim Litvinov. Again, Soviet concern was focused on the internal politics of the various left-wing groups active in Republican Spain. Most striking was his virulent opposition to War Minister Indalecio Prieto, whom he chastised for purportedly arguing that the Soviet Union had its own private agenda for Spain. Among his grievances was that Prieto evidently had described Foreign Minister Alvarez del Vayo as a "mouthpiece for Soviet diplomacy" who was "subservient" to the USSR, a characterization that scholars acknowledge is essentially accurate.[11]

At stake was the decisive attempt to push the government into accepting Communist leadership of the military, and to offset Largo Caballero's attempts to stop the growth of Communist influence. Marchenko's report also offers further corroboration on the importance to Moscow of the fight against the POUM. In a similar fashion, Document 35 reinforces the impression that the Russians had an overriding concern with offsetting the anarchists' popularity. In the report, issued on 7 March 1937 by the Comintern's chief representative in Spain, André Marty, to the secretariat of the Comintern, Marty privately admitted the success of the anarchist social programs, particularly anarcho-syndicalist mechanisms of industrial organization. Reporting on political problems, Marty attempted to delineate which groups in the Republican leadership could be construed as friendly to the Communists. Marty also expressed his concern over the influence and military prowess of the POUM in Catalonia. At times, some of the Soviet advisers thought that events were not moving quickly and forcefully enough in the direction they favored. In **Document 36** a Soviet tank commander in Spain offers his observations, and he comments that because the other left-wing parties were seeking to gain more influence in the Republic, there was but one obvious solution: "The party ought to come to power even by force, if necessary." Voroshilov thought the comment was important enough to forward the report to Stalin and urge that he read it, because "it's worth it."

For a time, the internal political conflicts were concentrated on the attempts made by the Communists to have General José Asensio removed from his command. Two issues came together in this effort—first, the nature of the army: whether it was to be one based on popular militias, or a formal national army led by the Communists; and second, who would control the army, those in the War Ministry who desired a professional army, as in traditional Spain, or those who favored an armed force led by a commissariat of military commissars, as existed in the Soviet army in the USSR. Such a body would then serve as a liaison to both the PCE and the Soviet advisers and would become what E. H. Carr called "the main channel of contact with the government on the army and military policy."[12] **Document 37** contains a letter to the NKVD and Voroshilov from Berzin, writing under the name Donizetti, which reveals the extent to which Moscow was involved in factional fights. Berzin's report indicates how extensive was the Soviet desire to turn the fight against Largo Caballero as well as Asensio, whom Berzin accused of not desiring to appoint "revolutionary," that is, pro-Communist, commanders. Berzin stressed the need to replace the old officer corps with the system of commissars, and he even proposed that if the changes they desired did not occur, the Soviets should "think how to get out of the game."

# Document 31

RGVA, f. 33987, op. 3, d. 960, ll. 180–189

*Top Secret*
Copy N° 2

Dear Director:[13]

The situation here remains tense. After the stubborn battles around Madrid in the middle of December, in which our opponent expended a significant part of his reserves, it seemed to me that, with the quick formation and arming of ten new mixed brigades (16, 17, 18, 19, 20, 21, 22, 23, 24, 25), two new International Brigades (13 and 14), and also a brigade of tanks and an art.[illery] brigade, we would be able to put together a shock group with the help of which we could throw back the enemy from Madrid and then drive him farther. We carried out all of the measures that depended on us for the fastest possible creation of such a group, for putting together the separate brigades, ensuring command and commissars for them, organizing supplies, and so on. The weapons for these brigades, mainly the rifles and part of the artillery, ought to have arrived as orders from three countries placed in November by the government. I have already reported on these orders. The orders, however, were not filled by the projected date (15–20 December), and the weapons did not arrive. The supplier, who was called in Paris, promised to fill the orders by 28–31 December, which again awakened our hopes, and we set about working up a concrete plan of operations. After that, the Andalusian front (Montoro region) was activated at the initiative of the enemy. General Varela was named commander of that front (Franco had pulled him from the Madrid front for his unsuccessful command there); he gathered seven to eight battalions of infantry and six squadrons of cavalry and struck first at Locubin and then at Alcaudete, but, meeting resistance there, transferred the attack to Bujalance. Bujalance was defended by a column of anarchists led by Zimmerman (a German, of unknown political identity, although he is counted an anarchist). This column had given up Toledo to the enemy. This column could not take the attack and quickly began to retreat, giving up one village after another. Militia units on the flanks were rolled up, along with the anarchist column, and sections of the front were opened to the opponent. This forced the high command of the Blues[14] to urgently transfer there two machine-gun companies from Valencia, [and] another company from Cartagena, and when the disintegration of whole sections of the front was apparent, then another machine-gun battalion, the 4th International Brigade, the 3rd Brigade (Galán), then the 16th, and finally the 20th Brigade from Murcia [were sent]. This reinforcement of the Andalusian front was caused by the fact that the 4th Inter.[national Brigade], sent to the Montoro section, could not halt Valera's offensive. The brigade (inexperienced), rushing directly from their cars into battle, suffered deeply, and in particular the machine-gun battalion was

124

caught unaware. The brigade command, which did not send out scouts in a timely fashion and just put its foot into it, was to blame for this. But it is hard to condemn them: in the International Brigades, the command staff is very small, and in the majority of cases soldiers who have any sort of military experience get involved in command duties. The situation got better with the arrival at the front (after a day) of Galán's 3rd Brigade, and after him the 16th Brigade. In the battles of Lopera and Procuno, the enemy suffered large losses and the offensive stalled. The Blue command, which attached an exceptional economic significance to Jaén Province, did not limit themselves to transferring the appointed 3rd Brigade to the Andalusian front but, against our advice, also threw in the 20th Mixed Brigade from Murcia. All the brigades transferred to the Andalusian front received only their weapons (rifles), which arrived from Gdynia to fill a government order for ten thousand [rifles], when leaving for the front. The 16th, 20th, 21st, 22nd, and 3rd (Galán) and 14th International Brigades were armed with these ten thousand and also part of the cavalry brigade; the 13th International received rifles earlier, from [rifles] that came through with a large cargo from the "village."[15] Machine guns for all the brigades, and also for individual machine-gun battalions that were forming, were also issued from the cargo that came through from the "village." The aforementioned seven brigades were viewed by us as the main nucleus for a future shock group, but the enemy upset our calculations (we reckoned badly!). The four brigades enumerated above had to be dispatched to the southern front, and the 13th International and the 22nd Brigade handed over to conduct the operation at Teruel.

The Teruel operation (the necessity for that operation) obviously provoked doubts from you, but this operation was highly necessary. The thing is that the most advantageous ports (in a tactical sense) for an amphibious landing are Sagunto and Castellón (to the north of Valencia) which are eighty-nine to ninety km. from Teruel. This "narrowest" spot on the littoral would allow the enemy to cut Catalonia off from Valencia with a successful counteroperation from sea and land. If the enemy succeeded in this, then Catalonia would very quickly come to separate negotiations (sooner, perhaps, than Basnia [*sic*] with Franco) and would create an extraordinarily difficult internal and foreign political situation. The possibility of separate negotiations in case the enemy causes a breakdown in communications between Catalonia and Valencia exists; this "idea" is running through the minds not only of the Catalan separatists, but also of the "orthodox" anarchists, who to my question, "What will you do if you are cut off?" answered quite unequivocally that they would try to preserve their independence "by the help of anyone at all." The calculation was on the possibility of destroying the enemy's Teruel group, depriving it of offensive capabilities if they did not succeed in taking Teruel.

The course of the Teruel operation is known to you from our reports. They did not succeed in taking Teruel, owing to only one reason: the anarchists who had stood solidly behind the operation in fact did not go into battle. The anarchist columns that were near Teruel for some three months, quietly sitting, had become so demoralized (having gotten used to the peaceful conditions) that their committee and "leader" Benedito were unable to get them to move into battle. Two brigades (the 13th and 22nd) and a tank company turned out to be insufficient to take a city surrounded by strong natural positions. If the anarchists had attacked the very first day, then perhaps the city might have been taken. We encounter the anarchist units' lack of fighting value and their unwillingness to fight on every sector of the front, everywhere that they are. The anarchists are not only on the Aragon front, but also in the south and lately also around Madrid; at the first pressure from the enemy, they give up the front and fall back. This provokes a natural bitterness among the soldiers of the other units, in particular the regular brigades, and a sentiment in favor of disarming the anarchist detachments, and their removal from the front is growing. Measures are being taken against this sentiment, but it is hard to argue with facts. When the anarchists were taken off their sector of the front at Madrid on 9 January machine guns were pointed at them at Casa de Campo, and some of them were disarmed.

I am dwelling on this question because there are still quite a few anarchist soldiers on the front (the Aragon front, around thirty thousand; Teruel, ninety-five hundred); Madrid, three thousand; Grenada sector, twenty-five hundred. All of this "brotherhood," which does not recognize discipline, does not recognize regular organization, does not carry out military orders, and fights only when it feels like it, must be replaced with regular units. Otherwise there will be no stability at the front and at any moment we can expect surprises from this or that sector. The replacement demands new formations, new purchases of weapons. It is completely understood that the replacement of the anarchist detachments, especially on the Aragon front, will not take place in the near future, but we cannot avoid it. The attempt to reorganize the detachments (not only the anarchists) on the front did not yield any results; the names changed, but the organization remained the same.

The enemy's offensive, which began 4/1 on the right flank of the Madrid front (Pozuelo, Villanueva del Pardillo, Humera), forced us to seek urgently for reserves to assist Madrid and in fact ruined the successful advance of the Guadalajara group to Sigüenza, which was beginning. The latter operation was worked up by the front staff to carry out the directive about local operations, and I agreed to that operation, for I believed that, if it was needed, the 12th International could be returned to Madrid in the space of several hours (a distance of ninety kilometers). The enemy's offensive on Madrid at first did not meet any serious resistance from the Blue units (*except for the 11th International Brigade*); the Barceló, the Persa units, the CNT column, which had been for some time in quiet conditions, were rather easily rolled back. It was mainly the tanks (seventeen from the front reserve and sixteen Renault tanks) that impeded a swift advance by the enemy. Bearing in mind the difficulty of the situation, I immediately put before the general staff and Caballero the question of reinforcing Madrid with reserves: the 21st Brigade from Cuenca, the 14th International and the 3rd Galán from the Andalusian front, the 12th International from Guadalajara, the 13th International and the 22nd Brigade from the second echelon, the Pavlov tank group. First and foremost, the 21st Br., 12th Brigade (International), and the Pavlov group ought to have come to Madrid. The general staff and Caballero agreed and handed out the appropriate order, but little was done to put it into effect; the "music" then began. Instead of the designated units' concentrating in Madrid within a day–day and a half, the transfer took more than three days; in particular the 12th Brigade, which was the nearest to Madrid, took three days to transfer. The bureaucracy, from the general staff to the railroads, sabotaged wherever they could. The generals were not behindhand, in particular Gen. Pozas (reckoned a member of the party) held back in every way, dispatching the 12th Brigade to Madrid and placing under arrest brigade commander Lukács who, to carry out the orders of the chief of the general staff, loaded up the brigade for dispatch to Madrid. I don't want to cry about the difficulties here, there are enough of them, but sometimes my hands itch to take some of these bastards out of their offices and stand them up against a wall. Such unpunished, unbridled sabotage of necessary measures, such sloppiness and irresponsibility as reign here in the general staff and in the bureaucracy of the administration at the front, I never could have imagined before. People simply do not carry out the orders of the War Ministry, or they do the opposite and calmly continue to stay where they are. Up to now I do not know of one case of punishment of anyone in the army bureaucracy for failure to carry out an order, for wrecking, for sabotage, and so on. Largo Caballero has not resolved to punish any of the old or new officers for anything. The only thing that the Old Man[16] does not forgive is active work in the party or close connections with the anarchists. He reduced Estrada to nothing because he entered the party; he hounded Casado out of the staff because he got mixed up in the CNT; he's planning on getting rid of Gen. Monje because he "smells" of FAI; Miaja and Pozas (both entered the party) he will not touch, obviously because he considers them not dangerous politically to him (in particular he considers Miaja an "arrant fool"). Among the brigade commanders are many Communists, but the Old Man has not touched them yet, replaces no one, because he needs to consider the opinions of the brigades. Caballero does not like Communists, suspects and fears them. His long-standing struggle with the Communists is telling here; his terrible dissatisfaction that the Communists are attracting to themselves "his" masses from the Soc.[ialist] party and the Soc. youth, dissatisfaction with the fact that the party, weak not long ago, is growing to great strength, which might eclipse him and push him aside. He fears the exceptional influence that the party has in a significant part of the army and strives to limit this influence.

## Document 31 *continued*

[Page missing from document.] giving the orders to the French supplier, [ . . . ] "forgot" to transfer the money to him in a timely fashion, and therefore the orders for rifles, machine guns, cartridges, guns, airplanes that might have been used by the end of December, beginning of January, have not yet been filled. This kind of attitude toward affairs might seem preposterous, but that's the way it is. It is these facts, petty as they are, that unfortunately shape the entire environment in which we are working.

Dejected or not, we will do everything in our power; we believe that we will win out, but the mood here sometimes gets downright obscene.

Heartfelt greetings,

Donizetti

12/1/37

Copy correct: N. Zvonareva

## Document 32

RGVA, f. 33987, op. 3, d. 960, l. 227

Naval and Air Ministry                                      Valencia, 26 January 1937

To S-ñr Ambassador of the USSR in Spain

The quantity of airplanes that the government air force has at its disposal, by comparison with that of the enemy, is very insignificant. Today we have a hundred fighters, twenty single-motor attack aircraft, and seventeen bombers. These last are extraordinarily few in the face of the huge numbers that the rebels have, which gives them the capability for offensive action. Of the bombers that we have, fourteen are fighting today on various fronts. This does not allow us to bomb very worthwhile objectives.

Experience confirms the impossibility of acquiring aircraft from other parts of Europe, and also from the United States, where they have established sanctions prohibiting the export of weapons.

It is obvious to us that only Russia can put us on an equal footing with regard to armaments with the fascists, who last week were lavishly supplied with aircraft by Germany and Italy.

In conjunction with this, in the name of the Spanish government, I appeal to the government of the USSR with a request to send us the matériel enumerated below. I take the liberty of emphasizing the urgency of this order in connection with the stage that our civil war has entered. We need:

—sixty fighters

—one hundred biplane bombers

—one hundred single-motor fighters.

## Document 32 *continued*

All these airplanes ought to be supplied with the appropriate spare parts.
Minister Prieto

## Document 33

RGVA, f. 33987, op. 3, d. 960, ll. 251–277

*Summary of Informational Reports
on the Civil War in Spain*

*Character and significance of the war taking place in Spain.*

In the course of the seven months of civil war in Spain, a fundamental circumstance is clearly taking shape—that [two groups] are appearing in this war. On the one side are the overwhelming majority of the Spanish people, fighting for a democratic republic, national independence, and freedom, and on the other side are German and Italian interventionists and the military-fascist clique of General Franco, which is striving to stifle the working masses of Spain, to set up a fascist regime there, and to turn Spain into a base and appendage of German and Italian imperialism.

The victory of the Popular Front in Spain undoubtedly will better the position of all democratic countries of Europe, stir up the antifascist movement, and strengthen the will of the broader working masses and all of "advanced and progressive humanity" for the struggle against the fascists' war (Stalin).

Conversely, a victory by the fascists in Spain may create the conditions for strengthening the aggressiveness of all fascist states—first and foremost, Hitlerite Germany—[thus] extraordinarily deepening the danger of war in Europe, especially of an attack by Germany on Czechoslovakia and other democratic countries and a counterrevolutionary war against the USSR.

. . .

*The Correlation of Forces.*

. . .

Analyzing the correlation of forces of the sides, it is possible to say that from the standpoint of the correlation of Spain's internal forces, the Popular Front in the end has an indisputable advantage over the fascist rebels.

The Civil War in Spain abounds with numerous examples of heroism displayed by the soldiers and commanders of the Popular Front. The enthusiasm and determination of a great number of Republican units, and also the readiness of the broad masses of the people to continue the struggle against fascism, resist the stubbornness of the rebels waging a life-or-death struggle for the remaining privileges of the exploiting classes. Especially notable is the fighting value of the Republican units that are on the Madrid front.

## Document 33 *continued*

However, the intervention of the fascist governments—Italy, Germany, and Portugal—on behalf of the rebels has, up to now, given them the opportunity not only to prolong the war against the legal government of the Spanish people, but to hold under serious threat the revolutionary center of the country—Madrid.

. . .

*Evaluation of the Situation at the Fronts.*

1. The Republicans are decisively superior to the rebels (with the exception of air forces and tanks) on the northern and Aragon fronts. In the first place great offensive opportunities for the Republicans are opening up. However, only the northern front, or more precisely, its Asturian sector, is prepared to go over to the offensive. The Aragon front, in connection with the internal party struggle within the camp of the Catalan Popular Front, has proved to be stalemated, despite an overwhelming superiority of forces over the rebels.

2. The rebels have a decisive superiority in forces on the southern front, where they also conducted the operation to capture Madrid. However, at present rebel reserves are being drawn away from this front to strengthen the Madrid front.

3. On the central front (Guadalajara and Guadarrama sectors) the two sides are equally balanced.

4. In the Estremadura sector and the R. Tajo sector, the rebels, fearing for their communications, especially in connection with sabotage activities carried out by Republican detachments at the end of 1936, are forced to use significant forces to secure the flanks and rear of their main forces. These units may be used by the rebels partly as a reserve for the main grouping on the Madrid front at the critical moment of the operation on that front.

5. The narrowest in extent, but the most important in significance, is the Madrid front, which is characterized by Republican superiority over the rebels in men and somewhat (but not overwhelmingly) superior rebel technical forces. With this kind of correlation of forces, and also in connection with the fact that the best forces of both sides are gathered here, the Madrid front is notable for a great intensity in battles and operations. Achieving victory on this front demands from the Republicans great persistence and skill in managing troops and maneuvering men and technical means. The achievement of success on this front will dramatically change the entire strategic environment to the advantage of that side which achieves this success. Not to mention the huge moral-political significance of Madrid, the fact that the Madrid front is essentially the center of all other fronts plays an important role; mastery of the Madrid region confers dominion over the entire transportation system of the country (the majority of the rail and automobile roads of Spain radiate out from Madrid). It is natural that the activity of the Republicans in the future, as it has been up to now, ought to have its center of gravity on the Madrid front. But all the other fronts, notably the northern and the Aragon,

ought to render assistance to the Madrid front through energetic action and not give the rebels the opportunity to transfer their forces to Madrid.

. . .

*Next Tasks for Strengthening the Republicans.*

When further strengthening the armed forces of the Republican government and in preparation for the defeat of the fascists, two shortcomings are major obstacles: 1) the higher staffs and the bureaucracy are choked up with unreliable and partially traitorous elements from the generalitat and the officer corps; 2) the demagogic and antigovernment activity of the anarchist leaders, and also the traitorous activity of counterrevolutionary Trotskyist elements, hamper the creation of a strong, united Popular Front army, the introduction of discipline, and the activation of the fronts in cooperation with each other. The hand of Franco objectively plays a role in this.

Up to now, officers and generals who are politically unreliable have had great influence in the bureaucracy of the War Ministry and on the general staff and the staffs at the fronts. They are hindering and sabotaging measures for the organization and a more rational use of the Republicans' armed forces that would meet the demands of the operative situation. Some of these individuals, for example Asst. Minister of War General Asensio and Chief of Staff General Cabrera, despite repeated exposures of their sabotage in the carrying out of useful measures for fortified fronts, up to now enjoy great trust from the premier and war minister, left Socialist Largo Caballero. Some of them have not been exposed but are undoubtedly agents of Franco. During the heaviest battles and in moments of crisis on the Madrid front and in sectors of Málaga there were cases of whole groups of staff officers going over to the enemy. The fall of Málaga in particular was, for the most part, caused by treason. Not a little harm to the strengthening of the Republican army is caused by—along with these concealed fascists—those generals who may, subjectively, be honest, but their actions emanate not from concern for the public interest, but from an egotistical striving for glory and "laurels."

From the army's lower ranks and front commanders, and also from the party's Popular Front, have lately appeared many organized protests against this kind of situation, and demands have been advanced to purge the staffs of all unreliable elements and agents of Franco.

Up to now, the government has met these demands very weakly. However, satisfying them is vital for guaranteeing victory over the fascists. Conversely, a continuation of the policy of concealing the fascist elements that are sown throughout the upper [ranks of the] staff may have catastrophic consequences.

The second serious task on the agenda is to overcome the demoralizing activity carried out by some leaders of the anarcho-syndicalists and counterrevolutionary Trotskyists.

The anarchists have the strongest influence in Catalonia. Here they have a

131

large, organized political and military bureaucracy. The policy of the so-called orthodox among the anarcho-syndicalist leaders is essentially treason. This policy is characterized by interfering in the transition to an offensive on the Aragon front on the pretext of "insufficient ammunition." In fact the "orthodox" are holding this course in order to stash and save up more weapons and to prepare a way for themselves so that they can seize power in Catalonia or for an even viler goal—there is evidence that the "orthodox" think an armed struggle with the Popular Front camp is inevitable and are preparing themselves beforehand for this struggle, since they know the quality of their opponents—in the first instance the Communists, whose growth in influence and authority they deeply envy. It is true that along with these treasonous elements, there are not a few honest revolutionaries among the anarchists, prepared to support demands for discipline and consolidation of the front. The lower masses of the anarchist military units and organizations are basically healthy, but they need to be liberated from the demoralizing influence of "orthodox" demagogy.

In [their] internal policy (mostly in Catalonia) the anarchists have undertaken a series of measures that discredit the Popular Front in the eyes of the broad peasant masses and powerfully alienate the former from supporting the struggle against fascism. The anarchists repeatedly implemented by administrative means so-called free communism, which is a most extreme caricature of the revolutionary movement. In the villages and provincial towns where the anarchists have seized power, they abolished money, carried out a forcible withdrawal from circulation of every single person's cash, set up a coupon system for absolutely all consumer goods, carried out a collectivization of all property, including domestic birds, and so on. Anyone protesting against this was declared to be a fascist and was subjected to oppression and even massacres. Because of this, there were several small uprisings, which were suppressed by the armed forces of the anarchists.

In battle the majority of the anarchist units prove to be insufficiently steadfast, and, thanks to the organizational carelessness of the anarchist leaders, fascist provocateurs turn up, and so on. There were cases of the anarchists' displaying an unnecessary brutality (chopping off the heads of prisoners, and so on), which discredits the Popular Front in the eyes of the broad working masses and of international public opinion.

Even worse scum is the small group of counterrevolutionary Trotskyists, mainly in Catalonia and in part in the Basque country, who are carrying out vile anti-Soviet activity and propaganda against the VKP(b), its leaders, the USSR, and the Red Army. With the connivance of the "orthodox" anarchists, the Trotskyists (POUMists) at the beginning of the war had their own special regiment with two thousand rifles on the Catalan front. This has now increased to thirty-two hundred men and has received weapons for everyone. This regiment is the rottenest unit of the entire Republican army, but it has

## Document 33 *continued*

nonetheless existed up to now and receives supplies, money, and ammunition. It goes without saying that it is impossible to win the war against the rebels if these scum within the Republican camp are not liquidated.

The local nationalism of the Basques and Catalans also deserves special attention because of the influence that it has had on many questions, in the first instance the question of coordinating the fronts; they are showing a provincial separatism that is harmful to the common cause and are sabotaging the decisions of the central government on assistance for the other fronts.

Dep. Chief of the Intel.[ligence] Direc.[torate] of the RKKA
Div.[isional] Com.[mander] Nikonov

20 February 1937
N 5141s

## Document 34

RGVA, f. 33987, op. 3, d. 960, ll. 303–315

Plenipotentiary of the USSR
in Spain
22 February 1937
Valencia
N° 8/s

Incoming of the Sec'ate *T.-S.*
of the Narkom N° 668
2/3/37

To the People's Commissar for Foreign Affairs
Com. Litvinov, M. M.

Dear Maxim Maximovich,
I am sending to you a short summary, "On the Political Situation in Spain."

Enclosure: 4 copies.

Marchenko

*On the Political Situation in Spain*

Two extremely important events lately—the fall of Málaga and the introduction of international control—have speeded up the regrouping of forces within the Spanish Popular Front that was already taking shape earlier. A month ago (as I already wrote) we had a sharp worsening in relations between the Communists and anarchists on the one hand, and between the Communists and Caballero and the UGT on the other, while in Valencia the UGT and the CNT created a bloc directly against the Communists on the question of forming provincial soviets. In the face of this a certain rapprochement took place between the party and Prieto's group, calculating then on the merging of both parties and the isolation of Caballero. In the last month the situation has changed completely.

Lately, a significant *bettering of relations between the CNT and the party* has taken place (I mean, most of all, the national committee of the CNT and anarchist ministers). This found expression, in particular, in the resolution of both the questions connected with the fall of Málaga (the purges of the high command), and the question of control, as the majority of the anarchist ministers supported the Communist ministers. The anarcho-syndicalist press completely cut out polemics against the Communists and took on a decent tone. Meetings between the leaders of the party and the CNT took place. This improved relationship with the anarchists was the result of a further evolution of the anarchist leaders, which began a change in the attitude of the party toward the anarchists, and partly a result of the worsening of relations between the UGT and the CNT.

The anarchist leaders were especially affected by the fall of Málaga, which seriously alarmed them and pushed them closer to the Communists. The improvement in relations between the anarchists and the party proclaimed itself not only in the speeches of the ministers but also in the harmonious announcements in the press on military questions, in the refusal of the anarcho-syndicalists to carry out forced collectivization in the countryside (it is characteristic that now it is not the anarchists but the left Socialists from the UGT, in particular, Pascual Tomás, the actual head of the UGT, that is for collectivization and against the proposal by the Communist minister of agriculture to parcel out confiscated land), in the permission by anarchists for trade with peasant cooperatives that raise oranges, which were organized by the party, and so on.

There were fewer tensions in relations between the party and the UGT, thanks to the fact that the party agreed to include the peasant federation of Valencia, which was under the leadership of Communists, in the UGT. At the same time, events lately, and the extremely strained relations with Caballero on the question of the high command, prevented a rapprochement between the party and the UGT that was being contemplated.

Together with this, a significant coolness began in relations between the party and Prieto. The latter, who saw that his reckoning on uniting with the party against Caballero was not justified, threw off his mask and showed himself to be the reactionary that he always was. Most of all, he does not hide from anyone his lack of faith in victory, and the stamp of this unbelief lies on all his work in the leadership of the navy and military supply. It may be frankly said that Prieto sabotages the building of military industry and the strengthening of the navy. Lately, he is taking an ever more hostile position toward the USSR. At the last [meeting of the] Council of Ministers, while they were considering the question of control, he attacked the Soviet Union, declaring that we were carrying out a duplicitous policy, that first we helped Spain and now we did not want to help, that we were pursuing some sort of goal of our own here and, having apparently suffered a setback, now wanted to leave Spain; he accused del Vayo of being a mouthpiece for Soviet diplomacy and subservient to us. (I ought to note that Prieto supported Juan López, the minister of the CNT, when the other anarchist ministers, García Oliver and Montseny, spoke against him.)

Finally, I should not overlook the proposal made by Prieto to the English in a joking manner (during a visit between him and an English admiral and the chargés d'affaires) on transferring to the English bases in Cartagena and several other ports.

All of this did not lead to a rapprochement between Prieto and Caballero—but to a bloc of them at the two last meetings of the Council of Ministers, against the Communists and anarchists (toward the latter, as you know, Prieto nourishes a pathological hatred).

The relationship between the Communists and the Republicans, with whom they collaborate, in particular among the ranks of the peasant federation, is fine. At the same time, the Republican ministers, on whom the influence of Prieto lies heavily, did not support the Communists in the Council of Ministers when considering the questions of control and reorganization of the army.

*The purge of the high command.*

On 12 February, in their address, the Central Committee of the Spanish party advanced several proposals for improving the leadership of the army and, with particular intensity, insisted on a purge of the high command. The ten demand-slogans that were advanced during the demonstration of 14 Feb. were essentially proposed by the party (a declaration of complete power to the government, the introduction of compulsory military duty, the creation of a genuine unified command, a purge of the ranks of the command staff, and so on), and were preliminarily approved by all the organizations in the Popular Front, including the CNT.

The central question became the question of purging the command staff. The Communist press, at first through hints, and then more clearly, demanded the removal of Asensio, the dept. minister of war, and Cabrera, the chief of the general staff, from military leadership, both of whom the party viewed as the principal culprits in every military failure, as the "organizers of defeat."

The CNT took an analogous position, and in fairly concrete tones criticized the military leadership, demanding the same changes in the command staff. The national committee of the CNT and its Valencia organ, the *Fragua Social* took a position similar to that of the party: a loyal support of the government, a demand for a purge of the high command, the strengthening of discipline in the army, and so on. A somewhat different position was taken by the CNT organ *Solidaridad Obrera* in Barcelona: it brought under fire, along with the Ministry of War and the general staff, the naval ministry and Prieto, as well, and rather harshly criticized the government for the poor leadership of the naval and war ministries. The organ of the Valencia anarchists (the FAI's organ, not the CNT's) *Nosotros,* went even further, demanding in its lead article, "Caballero Is Old," the departure of Caballero from the post of minister of war and threatening, if unsuitable military leaders were not thrown out voluntarily, to remove them by force. The CNT and its leadership—in particular, its secretary, Vázquez—regard the position of this anarchist paper very unfavorably. This reflects the struggle going on within the CNT and the FAI between moderate and extremist elements. This struggle has already gone rather far and can take on very harsh forms. Vázquez said that at the meeting of the FAI, forthcoming in a few days, he will demand that these papers be closed as harmful.

Today (20 Feb.), *Fragua Social* came out with an editorial that directly names Gen. Asensio and, alluding to a series of Madrid papers, including the *Mundo Obrero* (in the *Mundo Obrero* Asensio was not named, but such a precise description was given of him that everyone understood whom they were talking about) demands the resignation of Asensio.

As for the UGT and the Soc. party, they have taken a duplicitous position on the question of a purge in the command staff. On the one hand, public opinion and the masses are pressuring them, and therefore they agreed to the slogan of purging the command staff, and on the other, they are being pressured by the intransigent position of Caballero; therefore they are limited (as is the Council of Ministers) to obscure declarations, avoiding any kind of particulars, about the need for a purge in the command staff. It is characteristic of this position that on the very same day, an editorial in the Soc. party's organ proved the *presence* of united command and compulsory military service (in accordance with a declaration by Caballero, about which see below) and on the second page printed a slogan demanding the *introduction* of universal military service and united command.

The bourgeois press also is behaving very coyly about this question. The only member of the bourgeois parties who gathered the courage to speak out on this question was the chairman of the parliament, Martínez Barrio, who in a decisive way placed under his protection the institution of the commissars in the army, demanded that people who did not want and did not believe in victory be expelled from the army, and criticized the government (in hazy terms) for its indecisive military policies.

*The position of Caballero.*

In answer to the numerous demands that have begun to come out after the fall of Málaga, from the various mass organizations on the introduction of compulsory military service, and on unified command, Caballero issued a declaration on 11 February, composed in a lavish style. This declaration says that the decree from 29 October 1936 already introduced compulsory military service for all citizens from twenty to forty-five years old, and these citizens are obliged to be at the disposal of the Ministry of War, which will reckon whether it is necessary to call them up. As for unified command, the decree of 15 October 1936 declared that the "minister of war takes upon himself the command of all armed forces as their commander in chief and that the commanders of divisions, brigades, regiments, battalions, and so on, will receive direct orders from the minister of war, as the commander in chief of the army. . . . Therefore, unified command of the army exists."

As for the question of a purge of the high command—in particular, the removal of Asensio and Cabrera—Caballero took a sharply intransigent position. When the organ of the party *Frente Rojo* published a notice the evening of 15 February about a certain general, an organizer of defeats, on 16 February at nine in the morning Caballero sent the Central Committee of the party a letter in which he accused the paper of sowing doubts and distrust in the government and further declared, "I consider the behavior of *Frente Rojo,* which calls itself an organ of our fraternal party, for which reason I turn to you—to be completely disloyal and causing discord. You cannot defend the common cause, the government, and unified command, about which many are yelling, and then sabotage it. Did not the *Frente Rojo* set some people on an ambiguous path? I think—until someone proves differently—that this is so. And this is done so soon after the wonderful demonstration in Valencia the day before yesterday and at a time when the high military council is occupied with clearing up who was responsible for the fall of Málaga, according to a report from three members of the government, one of whom is a member of the Communist party.

I call your attention to this case and very seriously propose that you advise the editors of the *Frente Rojo* that they confidentially name names to me. If this is not done, then it will confirm my opinion that the national will, which was clearly conveyed last Sunday, is being maliciously sabotaged. I tell you that I am ready to pursue trouble-makers, whoever they may be, regardless of the consequences."

It is clear to see from this letter that Caballero perceived the Sunday demonstration, a powerful protest by the people against the "organizers of defeat," as a demonstration of full and unconditional trust in him—in Caballero, personally.

When the anarchists and the Communists placed the question of Asensio and Cabrera before the Council of Ministers, Caballero demanded proof, as he had demanded three months ago. He deflects every accusation directed at Asensio and Cabrera on particular questions, declaring that he himself gave the appropriate instructions. And that is true. Asensio has apparently always tried to have the sabotage that he organized blessed by the signature of Caballero.

A situation has been created that must be defused very quickly, since the campaign developed by the press on this question (perhaps even with some excessive zeal) might provoke a well-known negative reaction from the army, undermining army discipline and trust in the command staff. It was obvious to any soldier—yes, and to simple honest Republicans—that with military leadership like that of Asensio and Cabrera, it would be impossible to win, for, even if we suppose that these people are not traitors, this is the kind of leadership that has to have initiative thrust on it almost by force. For instance, now there is a decision on calling up the fifth-years (this decision by the Council of Ministers was wrung out of them almost by force); however, no one worries about organizing the call-up, the necessary bureaucracy does not exist; moreover, the general staff has already secretly given a directive for ending the acceptance of volunteers, so that the next month or two might see a situation where there will be neither conscripts nor volunteers; that is, the reserves so necessary for serious military operations will not exist.

Given these conditions, Caballero's position has complicated the situation immensely, creating an atmosphere of despair among the young soldiers. A whole series of individuals have told us about the highly dangerous terrorist mood among the young officers—in particular among the Republican officer corps—directed against Asensio. García Oliver warned us about the existence of such a dangerous mood among the Communist officers, as well.

All possible pressure on Caballero has been exhausted: the formulation of questions at the Council of Ministers, a campaign in the press, appeals from frontline soldiers and officers (about forty thousand signatures figured in the appeals from the front), and so on. Finally, yesterday's speech by La Pasionaria was apparently the last straw. Asensio tendered his resignation and the Council of Ministers accepted it. Caballero at this declared that he was making the first compromise of his life and was forced to come to the greatest injustice. He lavished praise on Asensio and attacked the Communists, who, he said, were waging a campaign which was essentially directed against him, Caballero, and not against Asensio.

Thus the question of Asensio has been decided. The resignation of Cabrera is expected any hour. Baráibar was appointed to take Asensio's place. This appointment reflects Caballero's steadfast resolution not to allow Communists into the high military command. Already today, one of the prominent Communist military men has been taken from his work at the center and sent off to the front. Baráibar is considered a good organizer and a solid man. Unfavorable about him is the fact that he is too closely connected to Araquistáin who, as you know, does not inspire any special confidence. The party is taking the course of loyal collaboration with Baráibar, despite the fact that he (or better, Caballero) is trying to get revenge for Asensio.

There are talks going on lately about the possibility of a political crisis which will, of course, not be uninteresting for you. Already a week ago, rumors emerged from Prieto's circle about a new cabinet with Prieto at the head of the Ministry of War. There is also an anarchist variation—a young minister of war, in contrast to the old Caballero, namely García Oliver. Finally, in the speech mentioned above, Martínez Barrio also reminded [us] of his right to power.

*Prieto.*

The anarchists continue to advance the idea of reorganizing the Naval and Air Force Ministry, demanding the unification of all armed forces of the country in a united ministry of defense, with transfer of military industry to the authority of the Ministry of Industry. It is possible that in connection with the appointment of Baráibar they will stop insisting on the transfer of the Naval and Air Force Ministry, but they will [continue to] insist that military industry be put to rights.

Neither the War Ministry nor Prieto, who ought to be dealing with this, understand yet that the introduction of control demands the speedy organization of a native Spanish military industry. Therefore, everything that has been done on this problem in a practical way was done thanks to pressure from the sidelines. It would not be an exaggeration to say that the military industry is now neglected. The party is evidently going to enter seriously into the matter of organizing military industry, for this is one of the keys to winning the war (and, incidentally, this is the key to collaboration with the anarchists, who have raised this question for a long time and insistently).

In the face of Prieto's defeatist mood, in the face of actual sabotage by him in the matter of organizing military industry and strengthening the navy, in the face of his impudently slanderous position, taken by him at the last Council of Ministers (where he in essence repeated almost word for word the attacks of the Trotskyist *La Batalla* against the Soviet Union), it is highly probable that the question of his further holding the post of minister will again be raised by the anarchists, and the Communists are likely to support them.

I must note on this point that the appointment of Baráibar, with whom he has an extremely hostile relationship, was a huge blow for Prieto. This shows that Caballero, at least, is not now in a mood to form a bloc with Prieto.

*On the POUM.*

The improvement in relations between the party and the CNT does not at all solve the problem of cooperation between the party and the anarcho-syndicalists. The extremist elements, relatively weak in Valencia, where the CNT's National Committee is located, are much stronger in the anarcho-syndicalist organizations of Catalonia and Madrid, that is, right where POUM is conducting more active subversive work. It is therefore obvious that, depending on the pressure from these extremist elements, there will still be many hesitations and zigzags in the conduct of the CNT and its related organizations.

The POUM is dangerous now because it numbers within its ranks several thousand people, and it is trying, acting through the extreme anarchists, to inveigle within its orbit of provocative activities a significant stratum of the CNT. It is trying to tear apart the planned rapprochement of the party and the leadership of the CNT in every way possible. Agents of the POUM have already set in motion provocative attacks against the anarchist ministers through the anarchist press.

In Barcelona the POUM has succeeded in taking the anarchist young people under its actual influence. The POUM is sabotaging the Unified Socialist Party there, by proposing and obtaining a nonaggression pact, which the CNT, the FAI, the POUM, the Left Republicans, anarchist youth, and other organizations signed, after which it began to yell on the pages of its press and through its anarchist yes-men that the Communists did not want to sign that agreement, that they were continuing attacks against the POUM, which was (they said) a revolutionary organization, and so on. Under the pretext of defense, the POUM is actually carrying out a savage offensive against the party, in deploying, especially lately, the vilest, most slanderous campaign against the USSR.

It must be frankly said that the Communists do not always display the necessary vigilance toward the Trotskyists. Thus, as was already reported to you, during the Moscow trial of the counterrevolutionary parallel center, in the newspaper *Treball*—the organ of the Unified Socialist Party in Barcelona—an article came out in which Trotsky was extolled as the savior of Petrograd. While the Trotskyists are using the smallest occasion to attack the party, the Communist press is not conducting systematic activities to expose the POUMists. Only very lately has it tried to take the course of isolating the CNT and the anarchists from the POUM, contrasting the frontline soldiers with the leadership of the POUM, and so on. Only now have many Communists begun to understand that only the utter political defeat of the POUM (since police measures alone are not enough) will establish the conditions for a protracted collaboration between the party and the CNT, for the POUM is the headquarters of the provocations, and it has its tentacles in every organization and especially in the CNT and the FAI.

Unfortunately, the party has up to now done nothing to use the sharp internal struggle which is now taking place inside the POUM, a struggle between the frontline soldiers and the leadership of the POUM, between the Valencia organization and the Central Committee of the POUM, between the opposition in the CC and the leadership of Nin and Gorkín. The Valencia provincial committee of the party maneuvered awkwardly, so that even though the Trotskyists in Valencia are an insignificant force, the party suffered a failure in its struggle with them, became isolated from the other organizations in the Popular Front, and was forced, in protest, to leave the structure of the provincial council and municipal council.

All of this was, to a significant degree, the result of an underestimation of the Trotskyist danger on the part of certain comrades. Now, as has already

## Document 34 *continued*

been pointed out above, the party is paying much greater attention to this problem.

In the middle of March the POUM is planning to convene a congress. At this congress the internal struggle, which the POUMists are carefully concealing, will probably come to light.

## Document 35

RGVA, f. 33987, op. 3, d. 991, ll. 27–39

*Top Secret*

[illegible]

*The Spanish Question*
(Excerpts from the report by Com. André Marty
at a meeting of the Secretariat of the Comintern 7 March 1937)

I. *General Remarks*

As all the comrades here know, the principal political question is the concentration of all economic, military, social, and hence political, forces in the struggle against fascism.

In that sphere, in the area of uniting forces, I can vouch for the fact that there have been very solid successes. We have taken very appreciable steps forward, but the development of unity is not moving fast enough, and for that reason the enemy is able to register almost continual military successes.

. . .

II. *General Situation*

*The factories—Who is running them?* The unions, each for itself, without plan, as they see fit. Industry is "syndicalized" on the anarchist model. Each enterprise is working not only without plan but also without bookkeeping. This is organized economic anarchy. . . .

Conclusion: The only solution for this situation is an energetic use of government measures, introducing order by decree: the nationalization of enterprises. Nationalization exists on paper, but in practice it has almost not been implemented. Of course this may not touch the enterprises owned by foreigners, it may keep some rights for them, but in general nationalization is the only means for overcoming the existing anarchy. It is even more necessary as the factories in Catalonia have no more raw materials and no deposits in the banks; now they are demanding that the government advance money to them.

*Food supplies.* The situation in general has noticeably improved. There is enough food for all the population of the regions that are in the hands of the

Republicans, including for refugees and the army. . . . Food is being squandered, however, and its transportation is poorly organized. . . .

*In the countryside.* There is no reason to worry about the size of the area sown. On the contrary, sowing was even greater than a year ago. There are no more large landowners in the countryside. Uribe's decree of 7 October has been put into effect very successfully. Not all land was confiscated on the basis of this decree; only the land of landowners who went over to the fascists, and since all of the large landowners went over to the fascist camp, this decree provided the peasants with land democratically. . . .

. . . . Currently the situation is better than in the previous year. The slogan of the party: AGAINST COLLECTIVIZATION EXCEPT FOR WHEN THE WORKERS WANT IT CARRIED OUT ON LARGE ESTATES—enjoys great popularity, and as a result the party has great influence in the villages. But the anarchists (and the Trotskyist groups) continue to demand and organize collectivization.

I must emphasize that the peasant committees, and they alone, are in charge in the countryside.

*Transport.* . . . . This is in complete disarray (this concerns the railroads and particularly road transport, which is even more important in Spain). It is enough to mention two examples: at the end of January, at the moment when we were preparing an offensive at the front, there was not enough coal for the railroads, and after three days there was no more gasoline . . .

*Army* . . . . . On 27 February a decree was issued on the mobilization of the five age groups and on the introduction of compulsory military service. Nevertheless, the general mobilization still produced very little. Old Spanish tradition must be taken into consideration, and consequently some time will go by before mobilization produces full results.

The construction of a people's Republican army is moving very slowly. The Communist party set an example, disbanding the Fifth Regiment of the militia and pouring seventy thousand warriors into the popular army. True, this number was only on paper, for one would need to take into account those killed. In reality, the party contributed thirty thousand warriors with excellent military leadership; the majority of whom were still workers in July. Therefore, one can say that Com. Carlos, a member of the Politburo, is one of the best military leaders and MOREOVER THE ONLY ONE WHO, UP TO THIS POINT, HAS DEFEATED THE ENEMY AND CONTINUES TO MOVE FORWARD (Jaén). . . .

The army is being constructed in an almost modern form. It already has about twenty regular brigades (including five international ones). The 12th Brigade brings together three divisions. But the military preparedness of the army is still very weak, and the methods that it employs are very old, very backward. So it uses the military tactics of 1902, that is, from the period before the Russo-Japanese War. . . .

*Navy.* Confusion, unwillingness to fight. From that—Málaga.

*Air force.* Superb.

## Document 35 *continued*

*The government.* The best means for a forced speeding up of the unification of all these organs is, of course, the GOVERNMENT.

. . . . Caballero gave a speech on 25 February that indirectly but openly attacked the Communist party and those forces which are helping the Communist party carry out all of the slogans about which I have just spoken. On 14 February at the initiative of the party, the Popular Front organized an immense demonstration in Valencia. This was organized to let Caballero and the group around him clearly see that it was time to take energetic measures, and especially to expel the incompetent, the saboteurs, and the traitors from the general staff. The demonstration was exceptionally immense. The next day Caballero pretended that he still did not understand, and, furthermore, on 26 February, he repeated in a communiqué designed for broad dissemination that the goal of the demonstration was to assure the government unconditional support, but he added: "I will not stay in power if my position is not certain. I consider it secure, but if everyone does not share this opinion, then I will not stand in the way." This means that he openly raised the question of his resignation to the entire press. . . .

### Three Groups Within the Government

1. The Caballero group—Galarza (minister of the police, left Socialist), . . . Caballero, and Galarza depend on the following elements: 1) the UGT union cadres, who run not only the unions but also the factories; 2) the general staff [consisting] of young, ambitious, but also suspect generals, like Asensio; 3) through Galarza, he [Caballero] depends on the large number of functionaries whom he has attracted into police work. They know how to lobby well, but they let fascists do whatever they want in the rear. López, the anarchist "theoretician" and of course minister, uses them to advantage. . . .

After Málaga was captured, Prieto once again was reconciled to Caballero. . . .

2. A core standing for unity (this, it is true, does not mean that they present a unified bloc). It consists of: 1) both Communist ministers, anarchist ministers—the minister of health Federica Montseny, . . . García Oliver, the Socialists del Vayo and Negrín, Peiró the syndicalist, a Basque nationalist, and besides these people, who are throughout the ministries, there is Valdés, the secretary of the CNT National Committee. . . . a young Catalan worker, anarchist, who has been won over to many of our slogans.

I believe that Martínez Barrio—of the Council of Ministers, the chairman of the palace of deputies, is a Republican. . . .

3. Finally, there is some vacillation within the Council of Ministers. An especially threatening symptom is the relative silence of Azaña, the president of the Republic. I must say, however, that Caballero has one positive quality: he always, in every way, openly declares that victory is unquestionable. . . .

### The International Situation and Evaluation of It Within Spain

The *front* worries about two problems: 1. Why can't the rear send us what we need? Why, when we have factories like those in Valencia and Barcelona,

143

are there not enough military equipment, shoes, trousers, wine? 2. Why aren't the democratic countries sending us more help (this doesn't mean the USSR). . . .

*Madrid,* of course, takes the same kind of stance toward the international problem, for there is a struggle going on in Madrid. . . . We do not receive from Spain, the rear, or abroad the minimum aid necessary.

In *Valencia* the situation from an international point of view is completely different. . . . The party says: despite control, we can and must be victorious. We have everything necessary for that: military material, food, people, we need only organization. . . . Some of the anarchists say the same, but add: "However, to use all of these resources, we have to complete the revolution quickly."

The *Socialists*—Caballero and Prieto form one bloc, and their ideas can be reduced to the following: they're abandoning us. It is possible that we will all perish (politically), but then we will drag everyone with us, even if it leads to the unleashing of a world war. . . .

The *Republicans*—Martínez Barrio said to me on 21 February, "What will come out of this blockade (for control is really a blockade)?" But he spoke about it, reasoning sensibly . . . , "If you examine the situation calmly, then you have to say that we don't have the necessary economic strength—engineers, cadres—to produce what we need. . . . With this in mind, I want to ask you if you know what is going to happen with the decision by the London committee, if you know whether they'll put it into effect, whether it will be possible to get around it, for we have to get around it, we have to break the blockade; otherwise we won't be able to hold out. . . ."

*The International Brigades*

. . .

*Dimitrov:* How many Social Democrats are there?

—At the beginning there were no more than 1,200 in all, but many Belgians left after the first battles, seeing that the fascists were "shooting with real bullets."

As for the Socialists, there were 200–250 Italians at the beginning. They were the largest group. There were almost as many French, but they are all splendid military cadres, deeply committed to the cause; as for the English, there were 50 at the beginning, and about the same number of Austrians (Schutzbund).

*Dimitrov:* What is Julius Deutsch doing?

—He is working in the Naval Ministry and is in command of coastal defenses. Up to now, since he's been there, the enemy has taken Málaga and bombed Valencia and Barcelona. . . .

In general the cadres in Spain are good. Unfortunately, there is a tremendous obstacle, highly inconvenient from the military point of view: language. . . .

. . .

## Document 35 *continued*

III. *Current State of Forces*

*Anarchists.* A huge change. An entire wing of the anarchist movement, the wing that I just spoke about, with all its nuances, is going along with the party under the same slogans.

The most important element determining the improvement with the anarchists, including the Catalan anarchists, is the effective aid from the USSR, the presence of steamers with food in Barcelona and Valencia. . . .

The situation is good with the syndicalists who have split from the CNT with Pestaña and Peiró . . .

*Socialists.* . . . After the fall of Málaga, Prieto's newspaper, *El Socialista,* refused to discuss the question of responsibility for four days. . . .

*Republicans.* . . . A huge political speech, given by Martínez Barrio in Albacete on 13 February, was superb in every way. A Communist could not find fault with even one word of his speech; it was phrased in an extremely popular form. . . .

*The POUM.* You know, comrades, the position of the Trotskyists and the POUM, so there is no need to go into that. Now they have added to their general position—in the words of an interview, given by Gorkín to a correspondent of the English newspaper *New Leader* on 19 February—they want to organize a World Workers' Congress on 1 May in Barcelona, and after that an International Workers' Congress.

In the opinion of comrades from the party, they represent an insignificant force. . . . In Catalonia they have several military units. . . . I am afraid that this is not completely true, since in Madrid and Valencia they are making themselves felt. . . .

*The Communist party.* In the regions under the control of the Republicans, the party has 230,000 members. As for the territory taken by the enemy, there is no information. Of the party members, 125,000 (more than half the total)— are in the army, and this is not counting the Unified [Socialist] Youth. Huge influence in the countryside and in the army, where, unfortunately, the losses suffered by the party are huge, because the party cadres command units and are commissars. The party has brought forward several wonderful military leaders. . . .

*The Unified Socialist Youth.* 250,000 members. Its newspaper *Aurora* has a circulation of 100,000. It is printed at the front in armored cars. The influence of the party predominates among the ranks of the Unified Socialist Youth.

*The Unified Socialist Party of Catalonia* is also experiencing a complete ascent. At the last conference of this party, three-fourths of the delegates ended their speeches by demanding the creation of a monolithic Bolshevik party. There are some honest elements in the party that are very far from us.

On 6 November, when the enemy stood at the gates of Madrid, only one party mobilized and armed twenty-five thousand workers, to keep the fascists from bursting into Madrid. Just at that moment, the International Brigade

## Document 35 *continued*

arrived. Then it was established that the city had been saved by the joint action of two forces: the Madrid partisans and the 1st International Brigade. Finally the USSR, with all the things that it was doing for Spain, naturally raised the influence of the party. . . .

The party, which began with so few in 1931, the party, which has grown so quickly, is now face to face with a large war. . . . Everywhere, it is experiencing a huge shortage of cadres. . . .

*The war.* Many of our comrades have become military, political commissars. But we need a hundred times more. The Central Committee still does not have a real military organ that possesses the necessary military qualities.

Finally, the government bureaucracy. All the parties can send their own people into it. We can dispatch and are dispatching people to work with the police, but they are overworked there. These are young people twenty to twenty-five years old; they have to deal with old fascist policemen (Italians, Germans, or French); they get flustered and arrest those whom they shouldn't arrest. . . .

IV. *Perspectives*

I must confirm that a great political event is being accomplished in the antifascist struggle: the unification of forces, a rapprochement with the anarchists, an inclination toward the party. Our political unity, our united political front, attracts everything that is honest: forces united in the struggle. . . . But in practice, the lack of coordination (which is present among the ranks), the sabotage, and all kinds of opposition from top to bottom, continually interfere.

I am convinced that we will be victorious. There are many difficulties, but we must keep in mind that we are in Spain, in a country emerging from semi-feudalism, in a country where the energy of the masses and their readiness for sacrifice is immense. That is why, on the basis of the results already reached, I suggest that we continue our business united, continue to hold the front, since first we have to develop our military offensive—and in this we are certain to succeed—I am convinced that we will be victorious.

## Document 36

RGVA, f. 33987, op. 3, d. 1010, ll. 295–300

[Marginalia:]
To Com. Stalin:
I'm sending you a report by Com. Krivoshein, the commander of the tank group in "X";[17] I ask that you read it—it's worth it. Voroshilov 10/3/37

*The Political Situation*

In Spain there is no steadfast government thirsting for victory over the enemy. The Old Man, Largo, a politician who has gone senile, is influenced by representatives of all of the parties in the government. For example:

1. It took a month to dispatch machine guns from the depot to arm the brigades being prepared for the latest counterassault. Largo gave them out himself. That was at the time when every minute was extraordinarily precious for preparing the forces.

2. Putting the production of armored cars right was extremely difficult, when everything was done and the authority of the Ministry of War in Barcelona was needed to prepare/stockpile the oil and fuel—that took nearly a month. That was just for one little piece of paper.

3. The decree forbidding party work in the army. At the same time, the party (the only party protecting the Spanish revolution on all fronts with the blood of its best representatives) is receiving recognition and authority day after day among the broad masses of the population, army, and officer corps.

The poor state of defense work at the factories and industrial works and among the peasants must be attributed to the weakness of the government. The current lack of a decree on general mobilization, despite the fact that the workers and peasants often talk about it—I'll quote a conversation I had with a worker in Murcia: "Com. Colonel, how do you explain the fact that we have here in Murcia and in other cities a large number of young men wandering around aimlessly, often armed, and there aren't any at the front. Why don't they proclaim a general mobilization to destroy the fascists?"

Out of all the parties fighting among themselves, two stand out for their authority: the party and the anarchists. The growth in influence of the party is determined by the enormous work carried out by the Central Committee among the masses. The influence of the party grows day by day among the masses, but its share in the government does not reflect its authority among the masses.

The anarchists are taking in all the déclassé and criminal elements and are recruiting under the slogan: "Everyone who doesn't want to fight, join the CNT and the FAI." And in truth, only the anarchists are running away at the fronts. They began a flight at Málaga that was completely unwarranted. They ran at Madrid. The Durruti column allowed fascists into University City. They refused to attack at Teruel. All the fascists and their sympathizers that remain in Republican territory join the CNT and the FAI. The broader mass of workers and peasants, who feel a deep antifascism, want to fight, but they don't have enough organization and skill. There is not enough political and party work, which might make the antifascist masses fanatically devoted to Republican Spain. And that this can and should be done is a fact. There are whole regions in which all the rich and the priests have been completely

## Document 36 *continued*

butchered. What will happen to these regions when the fascists take them? That is clear to everyone.

If you add to this that every party is striving for more influence in the government and in the leadership of the provinces, then all the difficulties of the situation will be clear.

*Conclusion.* Revolutionary Spain needs a strong government that is able to organize and guarantee the victory of the revolution. The Communist party ought to come to power even by force, if necessary.

. . .

[signed] Colonel Krivoshein
Correct: [illegible]

## Document 37

RGVA, f. 33987, op. 3, d. 991, ll. 64, 70–75

NKO SSSR                                                               *Top Secret*
Intelligence Directorate                                          Copy N° 1
Worker-Peasant Red Army
Department 1
19 March 1937
N° 10208ss

To the People's Commissar of Defense of the USSR
Marshal of the Soviet Union
Com. *Voroshilov*

I am sending you copies of letters from Comrades Shtern and Berzin. Berzin's letter was sent at the first opportunity and apparently was held up during delivery; it is dated 22 February 1937.

Enclosure: Two letters of 11 pages.
Chief of the Intelligence Directorate of the RKKA
Corps Com.[mander] S. Uritsky

[ll. 70–75]

Letter of Comrade Donizetti from 22/2/37

The pressure of local command, and also of the party and the CNT on the government with the demand to relieve Asensio and Cabrera, did not produce the necessary results. After huge fights in the Military Council and the

Council of Ministers, Caballero in the end agreed to remove Subsecretary [*sic*] Asensio from his post but then had to declare that he in no way thought Asensio guilty and that in agreeing to his removal he "for the first time in his life was permitting injustice in the treatment of a person." In the whole campaign against Asensio, Caballero sees the machinations of Communists and anarchists directed, supposedly, against him and suspects that, having brought down Asensio, the Communists will lay hands on him. In any case, the Old Man is desperately shielding the generals and is resisting a purge of the military apparatus any way that he can. By order of the War Ministry, Asensio is left in Valencia at his disposal, and the Old Man obviously wants to make him his main adviser. If this happens, then the same old story will be repeated, but at a worse level, since Asensio has had any formal responsibility taken away from him. The day that Asensio was removed, the chief of the general staff really took fright and even prepared a letter of resignation. He came to Caballero with the letter, as it was told to me, but the latter obviously reassured him, and he was strutting around again the next day.

Therefore, the pressure did not have the expected results. At the same time, the generals, feeling that Caballero will support them in any way possible, will become impudent and play even more dirty tricks than before. From this I conclude that the pressure has to be continued, and I, for my part, will take steps so that the pressure continues. In particular, I will get the front command to apply pressure—commanders of brigades, battalions, and also the political parties—Communist, anarchist, Left Republicans, and the [Unified Socialist] Youth—let them demand explanations from the Military Council and the government for a number of specific facts. Let them demand a concrete plan from the Minister of War and from the general staff for the further defense of the government. The general staff and the Old Man do not have this kind of plan. He formally adopts our proposed plan on organizational and operative measures, but the general staff doesn't trouble itself much about how he actually implements it. On the contrary, every measure is delayed and sabotaged by the general staff. The sabotage is carried out quite subtly, so that one can't catch them at it directly. There are hundreds of examples. To protect themselves against legal investigation, they get the sanction of the minister for every action, and Caballero, who doesn't understand military affairs well, signs everything that Asensio or Cabrera proposes to him. [ . . . ]

The reformist government, whose character is essentially determined by Caballero, is obviously incapable at the present of rousing the masses for the struggle against fascism. It is not able to seize and shape the people's revolutionary energy, their will for victory over fascism. This government (Caballero) is fighting the leftward movement of the masses and in general suffers from "massophobia"; it (or more accurately he—Caballero) does not like the mass leaders that are coming forward; he is afraid of them; he doesn't like, and fears, the revolutionary commanders that are arising. He (Caballero) is looking for a base and support within the old officer corps, behind which, as he himself says, there are no political parties; who will be wholly dependent on him (Caballero) and therefore will be "loyal" to him. On this rotten concept is built his entire system of "using" the old officer corps. In fact the old officer corps in the person of the generalitat [*sic*] is "using" Caballero and, concealing its opinions, is carrying out its counterrevolutionary and traitorous work.

Despite the weakness of the Republican army that is being born, despite the lack of weapons and ammunition, the enemy can be beaten and a decisive victory reached if every measure, every maneuver is not broken off by Ásensio, chief of the general staff Cabrera, and their ilk. Asensio has been formally removed, but actually he still remains behind the scenes. The current task: to succeed in removing both of them and dissolving the counterrevolutionary officer corps. If this is not done in the near future, then the chances of victory will not be great and we need to think how to get out of the game because our presence here will be useless.

## The Internal Conflict Increases

By the end of February, the famous battle of Jarama Valley had taken place, and it gave the Republican troops a new fighting spirit. Although both Loyalists and Nationalists [together] suffered around twenty thousand casualties, and it was certainly not an untrammeled victory for the Republic, its outcome was still perceived as a success. Jarama was one of the first battles that the newly created Republican army engaged in, and the Comintern's International Brigades also participated. As Hugh Thomas writes, the Republic "had for the first time held the Nationalists in open country." Moreover, being in control of both the new army and the Republican government, the Communists had become "almost the real executive power of the State."[18] Not long afterward, the Republican forces would fare even better, in the battle of Guadalajara, in which the most modern Italian troops were halted and all Nationalist advances toward Madrid brought to a halt.

Perhaps out of overconfidence, Soviet officials began to make a series of errors. Some were to pay the highest price for those mistakes. The Soviet consul in Barcelona, Vladimir A. Antonov-Ovseenko, would now be called back to Moscow and executed as a traitor. The problem that the hitherto loyal diplomat faced was that he had once been a follower of Leon Trotsky; now that Trotsky was seen as the major defector from the Revolution and the archenemy of the people, he had to act carefully. During his time in Moscow in the 1920s, moreover, Antonov-Ovseenko had come to know and befriend Andrés Nin, who was at that time a functionary of the Soviet regime. Nin had come to Moscow from Barcelona as a delegate of the CNT to the Comintern, but while living in Moscow as a Soviet functionary, Nin joined the Trotskyist opposition. Returning to Barcelona in 1930, he led the Trotskyist movement in Spain, but later he broke with Trotsky, and in 1935 he merged his group into the POUM. Antonov-Ovseenko's past association with Nin put him in a precarious position. At times he was given the unenviable task of serving as Nin's translator at public functions, during which the diplomat pretended not to know Nin personally.

Nin would use his past association as leverage against the Soviets. He had translated into Spanish and then published a long out-of-print pamphlet written a decade earlier by Antonov-Ovseenko, in which the old Bolshevik could be construed as favoring the position advocated by both the POUM and the anarchists in Spain, rather than that advocated by the Spanish Communists and Moscow. In that pamphlet, Antonov-Ovseenko had argued that popular workers' militias would provide a more effective fighting force than a regular organized army. That argument, of course, dovetailed with the very criticism of Communist military policy in Spain that the leftist opposition was making.[19]

In an attempt to compensate for his earlier heresy, which had been resurrected, Antonov-Ovseenko made public attacks on anarchist policy. These statements reflected badly on his avowed nonpartisan position as a diplomat to another nation. Hence, the left opposition condemned the Soviet Union for seeking to interfere politically in the internal political life of the sovereign Spanish Republic. Yet when the anarchists criticized the Communist attempts to gain hegemony in Spain, Antonov-Ovseenko publicly reprimanded them. He was to find that his efforts to gain sympathy in Moscow had the reverse effect to the one he intended. In **Document 38,** the Soviet ambassador in Spain, Ivan Gaikis, formally instructed him to avoid creating such controversy. Being accused by

Moscow's top diplomat of giving aid and comfort to Stalin's enemies was not the response Antonov-Ovseenko had hoped for, and the accusation may have led to his death.

By the spring of 1937, the internal difficulties had come to the boiling point. Moscow and its allies had decided that the time had come to intensify efforts to force the fall of the Largo Caballero regime. These concerns are addressed in a report sent to Voroshilov by Comintern chief Georgi Dimitrov on 23 March. Written by an anonymous source identified only as a "political informer in Spain," **Document 39,** since it was translated from the French, was most likely penned by André Marty, whose mark it clearly bears. The report reflects the sentiments of Moscow's representatives in Spain at the highest level and reveals a marked increase in the level of the charges made against the Republic by Moscow. For the first time, the Republican leadership, especially Largo Caballero, is accused of treason. Moreover, it is clear from the report that the author was worried that power in the Republic rested not with the government but with the unions, workers' councils, and local party centers. Spain, he seemed to fear, was becoming the kind of society favored by anarcho-syndicalists, rather than that espoused by Marxist-Leninists. As an alternative, the author suggested the creation of traditional institutions that would be controlled by the Spanish Communist party.

Moreover, he credited defeats in battle not to the impossibility of a poorly equipped army's facing professional soldiers supported by Germany and Italy, but to the treason of those Marty described as "traitor-officers." In making these charges, Marty sought to mask the PCE's lack of either popularity or authority among many Spanish Republicans. Instead, he attributed all governmental failures to "experiments in socializing and collectivizing," measures that the anarchists and other radicals favored but that Moscow opposed. As Marty put it, "uncontrolled people" could not be allowed to assume leadership. Indeed, he demanded a widespread purge as the only answer to Spain's problems, and since the premier harbored collaborators and engaged in "anti-Communist fury," he too would have to go.

The document amounts to one of the first clear statements of Moscow's decision to push the ouster of Largo Caballero. As we have seen, at the start of the Popular Front government, the Communists had portrayed Largo Caballero as the anointed leader of the Spanish working class, and had dubbed him the Spanish Lenin. They had sought to win him over as leader of the Socialist party, the single largest party at the front, and urged him to accept their proposal for an amalgamation of the Socialist and Communist parties. But by the time he had created a new government, in early September of 1936, Largo Caballero had become his own man and was clearly not implementing Moscow's policy in Spain. After a little more than half a year, a campaign against him was set in motion. Although Largo Caballero, once in office, had given up his youthful revolutionary enthusiasms and had tried to create a stable regime that would have the support of the middle classes, he stopped short of favoring complete Communist control of the country.[20]

In this document, Marty complained that Largo Caballero even wanted to remove the foreign minister, Julio Alvarez del Vayo, whom he had accused of mouthing the words of the Soviet ambassador. Among other things, del Vayo had appointed only Communists as military commissars, before they went to the War Ministry for approval. Later, Largo Caballero was to write that del Vayo had been most responsible for pro-Communist measures, although he had "professed to be my trustworthy friend. He labeled himself a Socialist, but was unconditionally in the service of the Communist party and abetted all its maneuvers." Largo Caballero wrote that he had reprimanded del Vayo for appointing more than two hundred Communists as commissars without his approval or knowledge, and that the minister "turned pale as he listened to me."[21] Marty concluded with a clear threat: unless the PCE program were adopted, it might become necessary "to force a reorganization of the ministry with another minister of war or to set up a ministry without Caballero."

Marty's demands were reinforced when Foreign Minister Maxim Litvinov received a report from the Soviet ambassador to Spain, Gaikis, in April 1937. In **Document 40** the ambassador offered his own interpretation of events in Spain. Despite the recent successes, Gaikis worried that without a strong centralized armed force, there could be no real military victory. Most significant is

Gaikis's claim that success depended most of all on the Republic's adopting the policy favored by both the PCE and Moscow. Above all, he reiterated that they had to dispel fears that victory would mean the "communization" of Spain. Consequently, they had to support "law and order and lawfulness," which in effect meant strong opposition to the "offensive" waged by the POUM and the Trotskyists. Most striking is the disdain Gaikis had for the actual military victory won by the Republic in the battle of Guadalajara. One might expect satisfaction and pride at the victory, as indeed was the view of journalist Herbert Matthews and writer Ernest Hemingway, who presented such a picture to American readers.[22] Gaikis, however, saw the victory only as an event that stood in the way of Soviet effort to oust Premier Largo Caballero, because the battle had "increased Caballero's confidence in how irreproachable the current military leadership is."

---

## Document 38

RGVA, f. 33987, op. 3, d. 1932, l. 94

---

| Ambassador of the USSR in Spain | Inc. Sec't Narkom | Copy |
|---|---|---|
| | N° 1042 from 27/3/37 | *Secret* |

21 March 1937
N° 16/s
Valencia

To the Deputy Narkom of Foreign Affairs Com. Krestinsky

Dear Nikolai Nikolaevich,

Despite the most authoritative instructions and the instructions of the leadership of the NKID on the line to be taken in Spain that I personally delivered to Com. Antonov-Ovseenko, the General Consul of the USSR in Barcelona again undertook a dispute with the local organ of the anarchists, *Solidaridad Obrera,* about which you probably already know from TASS dispatches. There is no need to prove the political harm that such polemics cause, especially when undertaken in this period of aggravated interparty struggle in Spain, in which the anarchists, and under their protection the local Trotskyists, naturally are increasing their attacks on the Soviet Union. The interference of the consulate just affords support to our enemies.

## Document 38 *continued*

I therefore consider it necessary for you to send direct instructions to Com. Antonov-Ovseenko not to repeat henceforth a mistake of this sort.
With comradely greetings,
Ambassador of the USSR in Spain
Gaikis
Correct:            Secretary of the Narkom Kozlov

Printed in 4 copies.
   ta.

## Document 39

RGVA, f. 33987, op. 3, d. 991, ll. 81–96

*Top Secret*

Dear Comrade Voroshilov,
I am sending you a report from our political informer in Spain, with the hope that this report will be interesting for you even if there are many things in it that are already well known to you.
The report was apparently written in the first few days of March.
With comradely greetings,
G. Dimitrov

23 March 1937

*Top Secret*
*Translated from French*

[Marginalia, partially illegible: "All this is true, and . . . we know it all."]

Dear friends,
I intend to begin a series of informational letters with a general survey of the situation and the problems that we face. This survey may serve as the basis for my information about current questions. At the same time I must give up for the moment on my intention of sending you a detailed survey. The exceptional seriousness of the situation forces me to limit this letter to the most burning questions of the present time. However, I will send to you soon, in a week at the latest, an extensive report prepared by Díaz for the CC, a report that is serious, detailed, and is a solid survey of the situation, which gives an analysis of the course of events, beginning in July 1936—an evaluation of the activities of the party, the relations of the Communist party with other parties and the organization of the Popular Front—and examines and explains the problems that have arisen, analyzes the difficulties of our present time,

gives the immediate perspectives, formulates the immediate tasks of the party.

The most burning question, which occupies everyone here, is the acute and complex government crisis. Its special characteristic consists in the fact that the crisis is apparently almost insoluble, at a time when the situation at the fronts urgently requires a quick resolution of this crisis.

The government crisis already existed in a latent state at the end of January. At the beginning of February it was unexpectedly aggravated. At the beginning of February Caballero already had made an attempt to come to an agreement with the anarchists and break up the Popular Front. He even suggested officially to Azaña a reorganization of the government on the basis of a syndicalist bloc, a union of the UGT and the CNT, excluding the Communists and the Republicans. Azaña energetically rejected this combination, threatening to send in his resignation from the post of president of the Republic, for such a government, in his opinion, would mean a rupture of the Popular Front and the start of a shady venture.

Several days later, the government crisis flared up again, and in the most acute form. This time the fall of Málaga was the grounds for the government crisis. The masses realized, with the catastrophe at Málaga, that things could not go on as they had up to now, that they [the people] needed quickly to carry out an energetic radical change in the government's policy for conducting the war. They felt and were convinced that if the necessary changes were not made, other catastrophes would ensue.

Everyone understood that the catastrophe at Málaga was a matter of treason. And this was actually so. And even worse, the tragedy at Málaga was only a single instance in a system of treachery. The incident at Málaga exposed before the surprised eyes of the people the cynicism and impunity with which treason is at work, a treason that sits and operates at the very heart of the general staff and that has its own people and inspirers on the staffs of almost all the sectors of the front; treason that is favorable to the operations of the enemy; treason that sits on the staffs of the Republican army and draws up plans for operations that are known immediately to the enemy and are even directly suggested by the enemy; treason that organizes the sabotage of the transport of ammunition, machine guns, rifles, people, and reinforcements; that sends ammunition where it is not needed; treason that uses the law to hide that military orders are signed by the minister of war; treason that, in order not to be unmasked, often takes the good advice of loyal, competent soldiers, issues orders written accordingly, but these orders do not reach their destination or arrive with great delays; treason that, organizing incorrect information on the actual situation at the fronts, assures the center that at some strategically important stop there is a reinforcement, when that is not so; treason that gives orders to attack at such and such a place and in such and such a manner, where the enemy literally mows down the Republican soldiers;

and the officers commanding these units organize panic among their militia-men.

All of this was confirmed in the Málaga sector. Similar things were observed before the fall of Málaga and after it fell and on other fronts. All the civilian populace and the soldiers at the fronts, loyal and true Republican officers, competent soldiers, honest and devoted to the cause of the people, were clearly aware of the fact that in the high command military posts were people that constituted an organization of traitor-officers that was systematically carrying out vile and traitorous work. Everyone—with the exception of the minister of war—understood that facts of this kind were very numerous and glaringly obvious. And how could one not be aware of this when almost every day one learns about new cases of treason and sabotage that almost hit one in the face? How can one not think about treason, when one has these kinds of facts, such as:

1. There was a decision to begin a big offensive on the Madrid front at the end of January. The date of the offensive was systematically postponed: to the first days of February, to 6 February, then to 8 February, then to 10 and 11 February. The preparation for the offensive had already begun in December; however, the enemy knew daily about the progress of the preparations for the offensive. He knew the plans. Everyone here, however, spoke very freely about the prepared offensive. A rather large circle knew many details about the plan. After accepting the operational plan for the offensive, the higher officer corps, which had signed on to the plan and had the responsibility for carrying it out, now began a campaign against the plan. But the most characteristic part of the whole thing was that, when the offensive ought to have begun, the railroads were out of commission because of a lack of coal. Everything was foreseen, with the exception of a lack of coal for the railroads!

I am not even mentioning the many other acts of sabotage that were designed to hinder the offensive. The matter ended as had been foreseen by the loyal and understanding soldiers: the enemy concentrated his men and weapons exactly on the point where the Republican attack ought to have begun. Not [content] to wait passively, the enemy seized the initiative for himself and assumed the offensive both at Madrid and on the southern front. The fall of Málaga was a catastrophe prepared by the enemy, which used the services of agents on the Republican army staff, who were trying to stave off a defeat in the face of the proposed offensive on the central front.

2. Incidents in Málaga. You probably know all the details. I only want to remind you of a few moments. Several days before the fall of Málaga, at the end of January, the chief of the Operations Service of the general staff, General Cabrera, answered a senior officer, who was demanding reinforcements and who was suggesting a series of easily implemented measures to assure the defense of the southern front, that "it was useless to do all that, since the fall of Málaga was inevitable and fated to happen." Five days after the fall of Málaga,

157

that same Cabrera, sent to Almería to take measures to halt the enemy offensive, declared there in front of a number of people, among whom was even one of the Communist ministers, that the fall of Málaga, to speak frankly, was from the strategic military point of view even favorable for the Republican army, since, he said, the front was thus shortened and straightened.

Through all of this, however, the minister of war said nothing!

3. It was decreed fifteen days ago, and under pressure from the masses, to make military service obligatory. An order was issued to organize several brigades from the men called up on the basis of obligatory service. But rather than implement this order, they stopped the recruitment of volunteers! And what is more—that is, what was even worse—it has already been fifteen days since obligatory military service was decreed, but a decree on mustering people has still not been issued. When the workers' organizations and parties showed initiative in this area, they told them: don't interfere in government affairs.

4. The workers have prepared armored cars in fairly large quantity. The workers, mostly anarchists, have worked with great enthusiasm. These armored cars, in the opinion of the specialist-technicians, are wonderful. They can and will be able to render great military service, but they do not use them. And this has continued already for more than a month and even more than two months! The workers are indignant.

5. [ . . . ]

The reason for the great tragedy of Málaga does not lie in the great might of the enemy (all attacks by the enemy might have been repulsed), but in the feebleness in resisting treacherous activity that is prepared, led, and carried out by the chiefs of the higher staffs of the Republican army. Warnings and cries of alarm were not lacking. Efforts and measures taken by comrades on their own initiative as soon as they felt, saw, treachery, were also not lacking. Alas! All these efforts, all this initiative, all the devotion and all the self-sacrifice that the comrades displayed, could not stop the damnable treasonous activity. Why? Because the government, or to speak more exactly, the chairman of the council and the minister of war fanatically rejected everything when talk turned toward the general staff and especially toward its heads; because the minister of war rejected every proposal that did not issue from the heads of the general staff; because the minister of war personally signed all the orders with purely military contents, not thinking about how to verify whether the orders were fulfilled, for often the orders that met the interests of the enemy were carried out quickly, and the orders containing measures or indicating effective operations against the enemy were not carried out but rather remained in the archives, or their opposite was carried out; were lost en route; did not reach their destination; or, if they were carried out, then with such delay that their implementation somehow coincidentally met the interests of the enemy.

The people felt a great and urgent need for radical changes in all areas. The masses and the soldiers at the front submitted their demands and proposals under the guise of dozens of slogans, of which the most important: "All power to the government" and "Purge the staffs and army of traitor-officers, incompetent people, or those not dedicated to the cause of the Republic and the people," "Strengthen the army with dedicated and capable officers and promote officers from among the soldiers," "Obligatory military service and mobilization of industry for the war," and so on.

If the masses and soldiers at the front demanded all these measures, then it was because everyone had realized that the government had shown itself weak and almost helpless; that the experiments to syndicalize industry, transport, as well as the experiments in socializing and collectivizing in the country, had brought the economy of the country to a tragic dead end, threatening the fronts and the rear; that the policy of organizing and training the reserves, which is still being carried out, had failed; that supplies of food and weapons, ammunition, and so on, were insufficient and the supplying carried out in a criminal way; that on the general staff and on the staffs of the sectors there were traitor-officers, who are acting in an organized way in the interests of the enemy; and that in the rear there are quite active fascist organizations and groups. The government is however showing itself to be passive, sluggish, and incompetent, helpless to carry out the energetic policy that the circumstances demand. Most of all, the leader of the government, Caballero, opposes the categorical demands of the people and the soldiers; the consequence of this—a government crisis. Caballero's fear of the masses and contempt for them increases the distrust of the soldiers, and soldiers' for Caballero, for the government as it is now organized. A continuation of this situation is a catastrophe for the fronts. This must not be permitted. The party thinks that it ought to do everything not to permit the defeat of the people, do everything to guarantee the victory of the people over fascism, and it continues to remember every day the need to take every measure to guarantee victory. It continues to inform the masses and the soldiers, since by pressure from the same masses, it hopes to compel the government to manage and lead a war in a serious manner.

The ability of the government to govern is very limited. Everyone realizes the unusual weakness of the government. Everyone—the masses—feels the need for a strong government, a government that will truly govern. The masses and all the newspapers daily repeat the common slogan: "All power to the government." Never and nowhere in history can one find a similar strange situation, where the people are united in their demand that the government govern, that it be strong, that all power be in the hands of the government. Nevertheless, the government is very weak, especially as a result of the government's general practical line of policy. A unified government policy line, which they follow, which they attempt to implement, is lacking.

There is no unified government perspective, no unified government will. The government's practical policy is empiricism, but a rather diversified one. But the basic source of the government's weakness is that it is devoid of the means of administration, it lacks a government bureaucracy. What remains of the old bureaucracy was transformed after 18 July 1936 into an active force to struggle against the people, against the Republic. The majority of the functions of the bureaucracy passed into the hands of the unions, the CNT, and the UGT, into the hands of various committees, councils, local party organizations, and sometimes (although this has become less frequent) simply into the hands of bandits and "uncontrolled people." Industry, trade, transport, and housing are still in the hands of the unions. Economic life has been decentralized in the extreme. Control of economic life is not even shared between two union centers but rather between the thousands of unions and federations that belong to the two union centers. Little by little, slowly and only through developments in the battles at the front and as a result of bitter experience and the large number of defeats that the Republican army has experienced, the militia, battalions, and companies organized by various unions are disappearing (although there are still many vestiges). And despite all of these defects, the Republican army today represents the most powerful and most organized sector of the government bureaucracy. But this instrument of the bureaucracy—the army—is busy on the fronts. The government cannot use it to govern the rear.

In the rear there is a permanent official government or, more truthfully, three official governments: Valencia, Catalonia, and the Basque country. Around these three governments are a number of large and small governments, more or less autonomous, that demonstrate their power. All this is caused by the weakness of the government. But all of this might be highly noticeable and comparatively quickly changed if the government could take a united line and have the will to act as it needs to act, especially in the present conditions, when the masses themselves are demanding energetic government action. The time has come, especially since the fall of Málaga, when not only the soldiers at the front, but the masses as well have outgrown the government and the leaders of the unions in their political maturity.

The government consists of eighteen ministers. The Military Council consists of five ministers, but the government does not govern, and the Military Council does not conduct the war, but either does not take the necessary measures for the war or, when it does make a decision, does not control its implementation, does not have the means or the will to compel its implementation. Every minister administers in his area, in the majority of cases, at his own risk, by his own initiative. The government has no proactive policy as a whole. Inquiry into problems, questions about bills in different areas by the Council of Ministers are, for the most part, only a formality. Once the Ministry of Finance tried to submit for consideration various measures and a draft, which had as their goal establishing some order in government finances and restoring the health of the peseta. The chairman of the council sharply interrupted him and said to him: "Your business, as minister of finance, is to pay. When you don't have money, you say so. The rest doesn't concern you." On 13 February Minister Giral, the former chairman of the council, now minister without portfolio, expressing the opinion of the president of the Republic, asked with the greatest courtesy possible that the chairman of the council and minister of war provide him with some information about what was happening at the front. The answer: "What, you can't read the newspapers? Read the newspapers, please, and you will know everything that interests you." Every time that a serious issue is presented for consideration, the chairman of the Council of Ministers resolves it this way: "My opinion is such and such. I hold this opinion, and since I hold it, it's right. And since it's right, you must adopt it." That is the method that is used for all the ministers and ministries, except for the War Ministry. Questions from the domain of the War Ministry, as a rule, are not discussed in the Council of Ministers. If a minister dares to raise a question on that or demands an explanation or makes a suggestion, the chairman reminds him: "Don't meddle in matters that don't concern you." At best, he answers that the question will be discussed at the Military Council. If the minister insists, as did two Communist ministers, as representatives of a party, then the chairman flares up, declaring: "There are no representatives of parties here; you are ministers of such and such a branch, and nothing more. I don't want to know anything about any parties."

The situation is extremely serious. The army must be purged of traitor-officers and incompetent officers and they must be replaced with dedicated, loyal, and capable officers, who do exist. But Caballero does just the reverse. He favors traitors, praises the incompetent, removes the loyal and capable or does not allow them to be used to the maximum extent possible. The party exposed Asensio and Cabrera—and Caballero became infuriated with the party. With ridiculous obstinacy he opposes demands to investigate the responsibility for the catastrophe at Málaga. Obligatory military service, decreed under pressure from the masses, is sabotaged by the same minister of war.

The mobilization of military industry is proceeding very slowly. Instead of listening to the warnings of the Communist party, to the warnings from the front, to the petitions of the officers from the front, to the warnings of the Republicans, to the cries of the steadfast and honest press, he is angry and attacks anyone who dares to criticize, who dares to show initiative.

In response to warnings by the Communists, Caballero uses ministerial crises as blackmail. Whenever the opportunity arises, he provokes the Communist ministers, permitting himself to say intolerable things, hoping that the Communist ministers will lose self-control and resign. He slights the Republican ministers the same way. He treats del Vayo similarly. He thinks that he can use insults and provocations to provoke the ministers to resign, those who dared to voice and defend their opinions. He is carrying out a campaign, through his people, to coerce the press and organizations, and also undoubtedly all parties, to submit to his personal orders. He is demanding oaths of personal loyalty to him. Meanwhile, he and the people closest to him are making efforts to achieve an agreement with the CNT, to conclude a pact between the UGT and the CNT for forming a governmental bloc of the UGT and the CNT, to exclude the Communists and push aside the Republicans. The UGT and the CNT press are waging a systematic campaign on this. But such behavior by Caballero arouses strong dissatisfaction among the military, engenders and cultivates unrest and discontent among the soldiers at the fronts. The best elements, the most honest and most active of the very leadership of the UGT are also beginning to protest. At the same time, not everyone in the UGT is ready to support the petty intriguing maneuvers of Caballero in regard to the CNT. In the CNT there is also a deep current against these shabby intrigues. The Republicans, terrorized by blackmail and the specter of a CNT-UGT bloc, at first hesitated, but now they are declaring that they are at one with the Communist party. Caballero is making desperate efforts to isolate the Communists. What explains this Caballero's anti-Communist fury? There are many reasons: namely, that the influence and authority of the Communist party are increasing; that the front trusts only the Communists; that the Communists in their campaign against officers and traitors, the direct employees of Caballero, have placed Caballero in such a situation that he himself was forced to say, "If I'm not a traitor, then I'm a fool!"; that the young people are working together with the Communists; that the Republicans are expressing a bias for the Communist party; that the course of events is confirming that the Communists are right and that he, Caballero, is wrong.

The acuteness of the crisis is also increasing, owing to the decision about control, and in particular owing to the pressure of one foreign government. Which government is it that is giving help or promised to help Caballero? To what extent does the interference of this foreign government contribute to the governmental crisis, help or inspire Caballero's strange behavior? Without any doubt, Caballero is receiving support or hopes for support from one foreign government. He has doubtless come to an understanding. What sort of understanding is it? At what expense does it come, and what is it against? Several indications point to England as this foreign government. A series of strange coincidences and events would remain unexplained if we did not think about the hand of England. And the series of strange events began exactly (strange coincidence!) with the recent visit of the English naval vessels at the end of January, after the meeting of Caballero and Prieto with the English admiral and with the British chargé d'affaires. There is Prieto's very widely known comment, which he made to the English guests, "If your visit had not been a protocol visit, I might have offered a deal—take Cartagena, take something else, but help us to drive out the fascists, Germans, and Italians."

## Document 39 *continued*

However, from the end of January on (just a coincidence!) there began a carefully thought out, systematic, but hidden campaign against the International Brigades, against the Soviets, against the Communists, against the Communist political commissars at the front. In the first days of February Caballero approached Azaña and proposed throwing out del Vayo and organizing the ministry on a syndicalist base—that is, [he proposed] making the ministry UGT and CNT, without the Communists and without the Republicans. To that proposition Azaña answered that he preferred to retire immediately as president of the Republic rather than accept such a deal.

The proposal to throw del Vayo out acquires special significance if one bears in mind the cynical comment made by Prieto at a recent Council of Ministers after del Vayo had delivered a report on the decision of the Noninterference Committee, namely: "Everything that you say and propose I heard this morning in the very same words from the mouth of the Soviet ambassador. We would like to know your own opinion and your suggestions as minister of Spain." After this Prieto came out with insinuations directed at the USSR with the thought that the USSR had, so to speak, abandoned Spain and was no longer interested, because it could not achieve its objectives. Then (this is also a new coincidence!) during the first days of February a campaign began with great fanfare on the question of aid from Mexico and Mexican solidarity, with this nuance—at first evaluating Soviet and Mexican solidarity [with Spain] as identical, and then attempting to contrast the "impartial" Mexican aid with "biased" aid from the USSR. Then—the invitation for the Republican government to take part in the coronation ceremony of the English king. Then begins a systematic, ever increasing flirtation of the Spanish Socialists and Trotskyists (POUM). One can sense the growth of a dirty campaign by socialists from other countries, along with the Trotskyists and along with the Gestapo against the Comintern, against the USSR, against the Spanish Communist party. Simultaneously—the huge advertisement by the Second International and Amsterdamites in connection with the dispatch of some food aid to Spanish workers. Then—the censors, who crossed out in articles of *Frente Rojo* every attack on the Trotskyists, especially the arguments that show the counterrevolutionary work, the fascist wrecking done by these people in Spain. Then—the proposal by the UGT (whose president is Caballero) to convene that international conference from which the Communists were excluded and which, according to the intentions of the leaders of the UGT, should have some anti-Communist imprint. Then one story more—the real, unbelievable, hellish pretense of direct aid from England for Republican Spain with the agreement of Germany (I am not giving the details [but] leave it to the bearer of this letter to tell you orally).[23]

Taking into account all these coincidences, one comes to the conclusion that England is beginning to play a very active role in the internal politics of Republican Spain. We therefore are beginning to think that the energetic and spreading campaign, which Caballero and his closest friends began against the Communists, is partially inspired and supported by England and probably by Deterding from Royal Dutch.

Does the commerce between Caballero and England spring from Cartagena or from other territorial and economic concessions? And just from that? Do they have this understanding to sacrifice the party? To destroy the party? But destroying the party means destroying the front, since 130 thousand Communists are at the fronts or fulfilling functions directly or immediately connected with the front. The Communists are the backbone, soul, and muscle of the army. To destroy the party, the party in which the peasants have almost a fanatical trust. No, *no pasarán.* The party represents the great political strength of the workers, peasants, and soldiers. It inspires fear and respect, and the party already has sufficient experience and versatility to allow itself not to be provoked, not to isolate itself from the masses. It will be able to expose the anti-Communist campaign, to upset the plans of the enemy. But it is essential that there be no unpleasant surprise from the front. It is essential that there be no more catastrophes like the one at Málaga. That is why, above and beyond all else, the party is devoting its attention to the front, the army, making a heroic effort to ensure and hasten the victory of the Republic over fascism. The front knows the party, its people, its work, its line, its proposals. The front trusts the party, trusts it more than the government itself, and this angers Caballero and the Socialist leaders and some anarchists. This is a fact. This is the result of consistent work by the Popular Front party. And the Republican party, Esquerra Republicana, and the Republican union admit often and publicly that the party is the strongest party, the most loyal and most energetic soldier both at the front and in the rear.

Such is the situation. A difficult situation and critical; the most complicated, most contradictory events are accelerating, changing with the speed of lightning. Here the situation changes three times a day. The one who doesn't change is the union and the social intriguer who is doing and will yet do much harm to the people.

General summary: to win the war, to prevent new defeats at the front, the front demands radical, rapid changes, which means a purge of the staffs, the organization of military industry, securing transport at the front, securing food for the front, securing the organization and training of reserves, securing the implementation of obligatory military service. Our party will do everything possible to implement all of this because it is vitally necessary. It will do everything possible so that it will be implemented by the government with Caballero at the head. But if Caballero and his friends continue to oppose this, new catastrophes may come. And if, in order to avoid these, it becomes necessary to force a reorganization of the ministry with another minister of war or to set up a ministry without Caballero, then that needs to be done. This is a question of a few days, a dozen days. And on this issue the public opinion of

## Document 39 *continued*

the front is being prepared. And on this issue conversations with the Repub- licans, with the anarcho-syndicalists, with the UGT, with the Socialists, with Azaña are being conducted, adhering to and on the basis of a strengthening of the Popular Front. For this a positive program is necessary, a concrete pro- gram of the Popular Front that addresses immediate, burning tasks, which must be resolved immediately. The party is convinced that it will succeed. The party is a great force. It has 250 thousand members in only twenty-two provinces, 135 thousand of which are at the front. With the party are about 250 thousand members of the [Unified Socialist] Youth besides the Unified So- cialist Party of Catalonia, with 45 thousand members, there are the peasants, who have a fanatical confidence in the party. With the help of the Republi- cans. Keeping in mind that a majority of the UGT masses support the position of the Communist party. The situation is exceptionally difficult and complex, but we are certain that the Communist party can overcome all these difficul- ties and that the Popular Front's cause will be victorious, that the cause of the Popular Front will end in victory.

Heartfelt greetings, V.

## Document 40

RGVA, f. 33987, op. 3, d. 1032, ll. 203–211

Secret

Ambassador of the USSR in Spain
[illegible] April 1937
22/s
Valencia

To the People's Commissar of Foreign Affairs of the USSR
Com. M. M. Litvinov

Esteemed Maxim Maximovich,

1. The most recent battles at Jarama, and the recent defeat inflicted on the fresh and well-armed Italian expeditionary corps, announced the undoubted successes reached in organizing the Republican People's Army, in raising its battle readiness, the selection and training of its staunch command staff, and, especially important, these battles declared the growing capabilities of the Republican army not only for defensive, but also for offensive action.

2. At the same time, these battles exposed the presence of serious weak- nesses and shortcomings that predetermine the impossibility of using the successes achieved to inflict decisive blows on the enemy. These blows

would, to a significant extent, predetermine the future outcome of the war. The lack of sufficient and trained reserves, the shortage of ammunition—in the first place artillery shells, the passivity in other important strategic sectors of the front, the lack of true unified military command—these are the principal reasons preventing the proper exploitation of the military success that has been achieved by the Republican army in the battles of Guadalajara.

3. At the same time as the Republican army is growing, the rebels are [also] becoming stronger, primarily as a result of the ever greater active interference of imperialist powers in the internal affairs of Spain, interference that is already taking the form of open armed intervention.

The war is entering a higher stage, and Republican Spain is confronted with new, intensified demands.

Despite the continuing eight-month war, the basic resources of Republican Spain are far from being affected: there is a lack of food, some industrial raw materials, and so on, but these are primarily the result of poor coordination of the proper organs, and sabotage; the relatively powerful industrial base is almost unused; likewise, manpower reserves have not been fully used: the course of the latest mobilization of five age groups shows that the masses want and are ready to fight.

Despite the presence of serious difficulties both internally and externally, every single objective condition is present for the victory of the Republican government. The main thing still lacking is military leadership and the development of military industry.

4. The present military leadership showed its inability to ensure the mobilization of all material and human reserves of Republican Spain and to ensure the necessary organization of the war. This has prolonged the war and sharply lowered the chances of victory.

The successes in creating a regular Republican army and the growth of its fighting efficiency, especially on the central front, were achieved because of the enthusiasm of the masses and also thanks to their political avant-garde. This was done in the face of real opposition from the military leadership and internal and external forces hostile to the victory of Republican Spain.

5. The idea that there must be a radical change in military leadership, that this is the decisive precondition for victory, is acquiring ever more supporters from among the various parties and organizations of the Popular Front. This idea is, in particular, shared by several of the more far-sighted and politically honest members of the current military leadership. The head of the government himself also supports such a change. At the same time, the implementation of this idea is indissolubly linked with the overall political state of Republican Spain and with the role that Caballero, the current head of the military department, plays.

6. Therefore, the overall internal political state of the country and the placement of its principal political forces must be taken into account when

resolving the issue of changing the military leadership. The current situation is characterized both by the ever more widespread idea of the need to change the military leadership (which was outlined above), *and* by a growing struggle against the Communist party, which has recently been clearly revealed.

Despite the lack of a connection, on first glance, between these two phenomena, they are tightly interwoven, and solving the problem of changing the military leadership is inseparable from the further outcome of the struggle with the Communist party.

7. The current head of the military department embodies, and closes, a defined epoch in the development in the Spanish workers' movement. The more radical position of Caballero and his group during the last year, in comparison with the so-called center and right Socialist parties, does not alter the fact that this group represents the reformist current of the Spanish workers' movement, through its left wing. The only revolutionary tendency of the Spanish workers' movement is the Communist party, which has lately developed into one of the principal political forces in the country. The correctness of the general line of the party, the clarity of its slogans, the selflessness of its members, its ideological relationship with the party of the Soviet Union—have caused a growth in sympathy for the Communist party not only among the working class and peasants of Spain, but also among a significant stratum of the petty bourgeoisie of the cities and villages, for whom the party is the guarantee of revolutionary law and order and lawfulness. The slogans of the party on the creation of a disciplined regular army subordinated to a united military leadership have gained sympathy for the party also from among the honest cadres of the officer corps, the more politically conscious members of which have entered our ranks.

8. The growth of the influence of the Communist party is provoking serious anxiety among the Spanish reformists—no matter what their political stripe. This anxiety is dividing international reformism, in the form of the Second and Amsterdam Internationals, and it was very clearly expressed, in particular, at the last conference of these Internationals in London. In Spain there are currently two permanent representatives of these Internationals.

The strengthening in the anti-Communist positions of Spanish reformism is also shown by its attempts to stir into action so-called European democracy, whose relations with Republican Spain are basically favorable. To do this, it is naturally necessary to dispel their suspicions about a "communization" of Spain.

9. The latest military successes have increased hopes for a successful outcome of the war, the attainment of which Spanish reformism imagines will be possible without the Communist party and even in a struggle with it for the decisive position that it has lost. As a result, there is an offensive against the Communist party, not only in the press but also through administrative measures, which have as their goal a weakening of the influence of the party in the

army and unions. In this struggle the reformists are striving to use forces hostile to communism, especially the syndicalists, whose ideological closeness to part of the left wing of the Socialist party is undoubted. The reformists and the anarcho-syndicalists are not the only ones linking up in the struggle with the Communist party; siding with them are also the local Trotskyists (POUM) who have taken refuge with the anarcho-syndicalists, and the dark forces of Spanish reaction, particularly in the form of the generalitat, which sees a serious danger in the growth of the party's influence in the army.

10. The struggle of the reformist higher-ups with the Communist party is lessened by the subjective qualities of the aged and obstinate Caballero, who is able to act as a political dictator by virtue of especially evil circumstances. Caballero views the well-founded criticism of the actions of the military leadership as a struggle directed against him personally, and he is therefore highly susceptible to the systematic, daily, provocative activities of political schemers who are among his closest circle, and of the reactionary generals. Caballero cultivates an admiration for the highest ranks of this latter group, [meanwhile] adroitly using his abnormal suspiciousness to poison any atmosphere of loyal cooperation with the Communist party.

11. Caballero now interprets in a very abnormal way the smallest pressure on the issue of creating and renewing a hardworking military leadership and, as minister of war, has objectively been converted from the symbol of the Popular Front into the largest obstacle in the path of victory over the rebels.

The latest data (my conversations, the result of Pascua's trips and so on) show that Caballero will not support a radical renewal of the high command, especially as this renewal is inevitably connected to a strengthening of the role and influence of those military heads who either side with the Communist party or are under its influence. But without this renewal, it is impossible to change the current way that the war is organized.

The victory at Guadalajara increased Caballero's confidence in how irreproachable the current military leadership is. He does not see the dangerous situation created as a result of the inertia of the military industry and the lack of an efficient general staff. Meanwhile, the imminent establishment of land and sea control, which will doubtless make the appearance of aid from abroad difficult, even more insistently dictates the need to use the country's undoubted great potential and all of its resources that are present.

12. Therefore, in the near future the question may be posed of either keeping the current military leadership, exposing to the most serious risk a victory that is objectively possible, or ensuring the conditions for victory even if at the cost of the serious internal shock that would be provoked by the forced departure of Caballero from the post of minister of war, if in the end the necessary changes are not successfully obtained. Such a dilemma has not escaped the notice of several people close to Caballero (Araquistáin, Baráibar, Aguirre, and others), who are trying to ensure a way out of the approaching

political crisis through secret maneuvers, in which they would keep Caballero in the post of chairman of the Council of Ministers but with the transfer of the leadership of the War Ministry into the hands of one of them.

The trip by Araquistáin to the USSR and the last trip by Baráibar to Paris were connected to the attempt to find this kind of way out of the situation.

13. Naturally, it would be more expedient politically to resolve the situation by setting up a new military leadership (which would include separating the high command from the War Ministry), with the retention of Caballero in the post of head of the government. However, such an outcome can be thought of only if Caballero himself will agree to it. This agreement, it seems to me, might come about either as the result of a realization by Caballero himself that it is impossible to continue in the current situation, or if the willingness of the principal forces of the antifascist bloc not to give in on a renewal of the military leadership, even in the face of a threatened political crisis, is made clear to him.

14. The principal driving forces of the antifascist bloc at the present stage are the Communist and Socialist parties and the UGT union centers—with Socialists as the predominant influence in the leadership—Caballero's supporters and the anarcho-syndicalist CNT. The Republicans are only a potential force, if one takes into consideration that, given the right sort of developments in the Civil War in Spain, they might become the political spokesmen for a significant share of the petty-bourgeois masses. The Communist party has at its disposal undoubted influence among the UGT members and enjoys sympathy within part of the honest proletarian stratum of the CNT. Meanwhile, because of the weakness of its union work, the party has not succeeded in using this influence and sympathy, as a result of which, the reformists, in concert with the anarcho-syndicalists, have the opportunity to speak out against the party in the name of the UGT.

15. The Communist party is the only organization of the Popular Front that is capable of making the question of changing the military leadership a matter of principle. However, a display of the initiative by the party on this question will complicate the peculiarity of a situation in which its allies would be only the Republicans and, possibly, the center Socialist party (Prieto); the party would be opposed by the UGT and the CNT. It is true that the anarcho-syndicalists agree with the need to change the military leadership—however not at the cost of Caballero's departure from the post of head of the government, since they regard him as a guarantee against a possible turn to the right by the revolution.

The party's formulation of agenda questions about a unified workers' party and the creation of a unified union hampers the scope for maneuvering by the reformists and anarcho-syndicalists and strengthens the party's position. The creation of favorable circumstances for resolving the issue of changing the military leadership depends on the activeness of the party, on the extent to which it is able to work among the masses to unite the proletariat and promote the party's positions.

The outlook on this is undoubtedly more favorable now.

16. The assistance of friends is one of the decisive factors determining the possibility for supplying the Republican army with modern technology and the creation of its brilliant air force and armored forces. Without this aid a catastrophic outcome of the war for the Republican government would already be predetermined.

In no way should the role of the friendly advisers and instructors in Spain be underestimated. It is they who have been there from the beginning, who cemented together an amorphous mass—the Republican army that was forming anew—and transformed it into an organized and trained force. The huge contribution of the advisers and instructors in forming the army, training its cadres, their assistance in working out military operations, and, most of all, in leading these operations through demonstration and personal example has received general recognition.

17. The ever greater demands by the Republican army to reinforce it with military hardware (artillery, machine guns, aircraft, tanks, and so on) and with ammunition supplies (shells, cartridges, and so on) cannot yet be satisfied without further help from outside. This is true at least with regard to any matériel whose local production requires a very protracted period of time to organize.

The deprivation of this aid would lead to a sharp lowering of the fighting efficiency of the Republican army in the near future and would partially or even fully paralyze its more effective matériel.

Likewise, a refusal of further aid in the form of advisers and instructors—in combination with a lack of sufficient competent commanders and the absence of a hardworking general staff—would also inflict serious damage.

18. The significance for overall peace of a victory by Republican Spain is indisputable.

The objective preconditions for a victory by the Republican government are present. Likewise, the outlook has improved, and this facilitates the resolution of the task of creating a new military leadership capable of organizing all the forces of the country to ensure victory over fascism.

The assistance of friends continues to be one of the decisive factors for this victory.

With comradely greetings,

Ambassador of the USSR in Spain
/Gaikis/
*6 Copies*
5 Copies—to the addressee
1 Copy—file copy

Barcelona: The Civil War Within the Civil War

For the Spanish Communists and their Moscow patrons, unfolding events made a campaign against the left-wing opposition the single most important issue. At the heart of the debate were the differences in perspective between the Communists, the anarcho-syndicalists, and the revolutionary opposition Marxists organized in the POUM. "For the dissident communist POUM in Barcelona," historian Ronald Fraser has written, "the war and revolution were inseparable. There could be no triumphant revolution unless the war was won; but the war could not be won unless the revolution triumphed." Hence, POUM members opposed the new People's Army of the Republic and argued that "it was wrong to create a regular army, since to do so was to pose the war in the same terms as the enemy." Revolution had to be waged by a popular militia, not by an armed force commanded bureaucratically by Soviet commissars.

Consequently, the situation in Catalonia was of the greatest concern to Moscow. In **Document 41** an agent of the GRU, who reported under the name "Cid," provided a thorough overview of disturbing events in the anarchist-syndicalist stronghold of Spain As "Cid" revealed, the worry was that the left opposition would obtain "total conquest of the government apparatus," an outcome they had to prevent. "Cid" tried to convey the picture of a weakening in support for the anarchists, but, as he had to admit, in Catalonia their support was "still very strong." Indeed, most unsettling were his figures. By his own count, the POUM and the anarchists had twice the number of men under arms in their militias as the Communists did in the official national army. Those two groups also had the allegiance of the working class. Indeed, "Cid" in fact admitted to the "immense historical tradition" (of the anarchists) and to the "exceptionally strong cohesion and discipline of the anarchist cadres." For this reason, he and other Communists feared a coup led by anarchist troops against the regime of the Popular Front.

The result, as George Orwell told the world in his classic account *Homage to Catalonia* and as Ken Loach portrayed cinematically in *Land and Freedom,* was the dramatic revolution within the revolution, the five-day street battle in revolutionary Barcelona. Frustrated at seeing their revolution thwarted by its own contradictions (especially the belief that power lay in the seizure of the means of production alone), by the difficulties of the war, and by the alliance of the PSUC and the petty-bourgeois Esquerra (the Left Republican party in Barcelona), anarcho-syndicalist militants erupted in the streets in response to a Communist-led attempt to take over the CNT-dominated telephone exchange. The intense battle would end after CNT leaders from the Popular Front government convinced the anarcho-syndicalists to accept a ceasefire. The result, however, would be a reorganized central government led by a new premier, Juan Negrín, and without participation by the anarchists in the CNT. Hence, the Spanish Communist party, Fraser concludes, was "even more firmly in control."[24]

Scholars are in agreement that what precipitated the bloody internal fighting was a blatant and provocative Communist assault.[25] The sequence of events could not have been clearer. "At three o'clock in the afternoon of 3 May," historian Antony Beevor writes, "the Communist police chief, Rodríguez Salas, arrived at the telephone building with three truckloads of armed guards. They grabbed the sentries and disarmed them, but as they rushed inside, they were halted by a machine gun which was trained on them from the first floor. Warning shots were fired out of the window. News of the incident spread across the city. In minutes the whole of Barcelona had gone spontaneously onto a war footing."[26]

The attack was part of the Communists' apparent desire to move against their armed left-wing opponents. Historians do, however, dispute whether the crisis took place because of the momentum of the POUM and the anarcho-syndicalists' revolutionary fervor or because of the intransigent conservatism of the Communists. Hugh Thomas, for example, has concluded that despite evidence that CNT workers honestly feared that the government was trying to gain control of the telephone exchange and take it out of the CNT's hands, it was "wrong to assume hastily that this was a step in a carefully worked out policy to provoke the CNT into violent action, carefully plotted by the Russian Consul-General Antonov-Ovseenko and the Hungarian Communist [Erno] Gerö, the chief

Comintern representative in Catalonia." An open clash between the CNT and the Communists in Barcelona, Thomas speculates, "was the one contest which the Communists could not have been sure of winning."[27] Writing more recently, historian Antony Beevor disagrees, and argues that those who believe the attack on the telephone exchange was "a carefully planned provocation to give the Communists the excuse to crush their enemies" adhere to a "reasonable hypothesis."[28]

The most recent thorough discussion of this issue appears in the work of the economic historian Robert J. Alexander. He begins by asking whether the seizure of the telephone exchange "was a deliberate move by the Stalinists and their allies to provoke an uprising by the anarchists, so that they could be crushed once and for all." Quoting the 1936 account by NKVD defector Walter Krivitsky, he notes that according to this leading intelligence agent of Moscow, Stalin could not gain control of the Republic without bringing Catalonia under his rule and ousting the government of Largo Caballero. At the time, an agent of Soviet intelligence infiltrated into anarchist ranks had told Krivitsky that he was instructed to become an agent provocateur and incite the Catalonians to rash acts, to provide an excuse to call in the army, "as if to suppress a revolt behind the front." Krivitsky went on to argue that the secret police instigated the attack, provoking syndicalists, anarchists, and socialists to fight against each other.[29]

At the time, other Communist and PSUC leaders made statements indicating that they had to take Barcelona, and still others wrote years later that the PSUC executive committee had made such a decision several days before the attack on the telephone exchange. Naturally, many anarchist leaders suspected that such a deliberate plot would be hatched as a pretext to crush them. Hence, Diego Abad de Santillán, an anarchist leader, wrote, "We had the impression, hour after hour, that the events had been ably provoked, and that certain sectors were unhappy at our ability to dominate our masses."[30] But was this suspicion accurate? Alexander writes that in conversations with key anarchist leaders who are still alive, he had been told that before the May events, anarchist ministers in the Republican government had been notified of meetings in Paris and Bordeaux between PSUC leaders and Soviet agents, and that they feared a provocation was being planned as a ruse to suppress the POUM and the CNT. Alexander concludes, however, as follows: "It remains unclear whether the Catalan Communists, with or without direction from Soviet officials, either by themselves or in conspiracy with other anti-anarchist elements in Catalonia, planned the seizure of La Telefónica as a deliberate move to provoke an anarchist reaction. All that is clear is that that move did provoke such a reaction."[31]

The recently acquired Soviet documents finally provide an answer to this historical dispute. **Document 42** is the text of a long anonymous report sent on 15 April by Comintern chief Dimitrov to Marshal Voroshilov in Moscow. The importance of the report, written by either André Marty or another Soviet Comintern representative resident in Barcelona, is indicated by its having been passed directly on to Voroshilov, and therefore to the highest authority, Stalin himself. The report began with the observation that the PCE's left-wing opponents were in effect "fascists or semifascists" who hoped for "a victory by the enemy." Certainly, if such were the case, drastic action to eliminate them was called for. The writer noted that the directive or advice of Moscow was "absolutely correct on every question," and declared the eventual "political hegemony of the Communist party in Spain" to be a "natural and indisputable" eventuality.

The writer, however, deduced that sometimes what is historically inevitable nonetheless requires a little human intervention. Specifically, the author of the report noted that the Communists had decided not to wait for a crisis, but to "*hasten it and, if necessary, to provoke it*" (emphasis added). He ended by informing Dimitrov that "the party is waiting for your advice on this question." In these words, which precede the attack on the telephone exchange by a little more than two weeks, we have the proof that the view held by the Communists' opponents was essentially correct. The Spanish Communist party, with the support and knowledge of the Comintern and Moscow, had decided to provoke a clash, in the full understanding that the outcome would give them precisely the opportunity they had long been seeking.

On this score, the Communists had a distinct advantage. Although the POUM had approached the anarchists to suggest that they act together to resist Communist power in Catalonia while they had a chance, the suggestion had been firmly rejected by the anarchist leaders. The anarchists felt obliged to the Republican government, and they reasoned that standing firm behind Largo Caballero and the non-Communist majority of the UGT was the only meaningful brake on the Soviet threat. "But at a time when even those who had been in politics all their lives were being manipulated," Antony Beevor puts it, "their few months' experience of government left them mere children in such matters against the Communists."[32] Once the fighting stopped, the Communists proceeded to engage in a barrage of spurious propaganda. Most outrageous was the charge that the attempt to hold the telephone exchange had been precipitated by Franco agents working with the POUM and the CNT. José Díaz, head of the PCE, proclaimed that the "Trotskyists" of the POUM had inspired the "criminal putsch in Catalonia." And Díaz went on to say that because they were "disguised fascists who talk of revolution in order to spread disorder," they "must be swept away!"[33] The American Communist journalist and artist Robert Minor reported to American readers as well that the May fighting was a "fascist uprising led by [Andrés] Nin and [Julián] Gorkín."[34] The Communist account became widely accepted. It was so influential that decades later, the American ambassador to Spain during the Civil War, Claude Bowers, wrote that "in early May, the Loyalist government moved against [the anarchists] with cold steel. A crisis had been provoked by the anarchists and the POUM, which was composed of Trotsky Communists. It was generally believed that many of these were Franco agents. In factories, they were urging the seizure of private property and strikes to slow down production in the midst of war."[35]

The propaganda approach was first laid out in a document labeled "Top Secret" and was sent to Dimitrov and Manuilsky by a Comintern representative in Spain, possibly Codovilla, who was still running the PCE for the Comintern. Written on 11 May, **Document 43** is the very first report to the Comintern on the May events. According to the Comintern representative, the central government could have put down what he termed the putsch, had not Largo Caballero failed to act for two full days, allowing "the anarchist-Trotskyites" to mobilize and carry out their "fratricidal affair." Although he ascribed the events to the work of the POUM, libertarian-anarchist youth, and the FAI and the CNT, the writer also cited *"very interesting documents proving the connection of the Spanish Trotskyists with Franco."* Positing a conspiracy, the writer claimed that evidence existed linking the POUM with fascist groups in Madrid; he saw the POUM as an "organized detachment of Franco's fifth column."

Indeed, the importance of the document lies in the writer's insistence that the POUM-fascist connection be acknowledged by all elements of the Republic, and the assertion that the people—that is, the PCE leadership—were "demanding energetic and merciless repression," to be instituted by the convening of a *"military tribunal for the Trotskyists!"* (writer's emphasis). In other words, the call was out for the creation in Spain of the equivalent of the Moscow purge trials, which of course were occurring simultaneously in the Soviet motherland. Notable is the disdain with which the writer viewed those in the Republic, including many of its leaders, who were defending the POUM as a legitimate working-class party, and his concern that Largo Caballero himself was not ready to take the active measures required. The writer moreover expressed the impression that many people saw the fighting as a preemptive attempt by the left opposition to counter a future Communist attempt to gain hegemony and institute a Soviet dictatorship. The writer noted that as a result of public PCE protest, the Communists were certain that a ministerial crisis would occur and that a new, less anti-Communist government would be formed.

In fact, the turn of events that the Comintern called for would occur at the cabinet meeting held on 15 May. At the session, one of the Communist ministers in the Republican government demanded the suppression and arrest of POUM leaders. To his credit, Premier Largo Caballero refused to comply. Largo Caballero saw the demand as a threat to working-class unity, and he responded that he would not act against a legitimate working-class political party against which only unproved charges were being made. At that point, two of the Communist ministers stormed out of the meeting, followed by their obedient supporters, the right-wing Socialists Juan Negrín and Indalecio Prieto, as well as by Foreign Minister del Vayo. The dramatic walkout on Largo Caballero was the first in a series of moves to force him out and to create a new government friendlier to Moscow and the PCE.[36]

In this context, a report for the Comintern on the May events, prepared by Goratsy, assumes great importance. **Document 44**, sent to Voroshilov on 19 May, presents the official argument that the "uprising" carried out by "the extremist wing [of the anarchists] in the bloc with the POUM" was prepared in advance over a "long period of time." In this fashion, contemporary history was immediately rewritten. An armed internecine war between the PCE and the POUM, precipitated by the planned takeover of the telephone exchange, is thus transformed in Comintern mythology into an anarchist-POUM coup attempt.

Despite his claim that the Communists had averted an anarchist coup in the offing, the author revealed that Communist forces favored a "final reckoning with the anarchists," for whom he admitted they had "terrible hatred—even greater than toward the fascists." He also assured Moscow that the PCE had plans "for action in the city in case of an uprising," a claim that contradicts their own propaganda that only the POUM, the anarchists and Trotskyists were plotting to implement their own agenda.

The second striking fact about the report on the May events is Goratsy's claim that the POUM and the anarchists were "masters of the situation." Yet in the very same report, Goratsy praised the appointment of General Sebastián Pozas as military commander of the Aragon region, where the CNT and the FAI were the dominant forces. Goratsy wrote that the appointment was an indication of "the loss of influence by the anarchists on military questions." Actually, the appointment of Pozas was far more sinister, for as Bolloten writes, it effectively "nullified the Catalan councils of defense and internal security and, along with them, the cherished autonomy of the region."[37] To call Pozas's command a "positive thing" is, to say the least, a great understatement from the Communist point of view. Finally, Goratsy hoped, the time would be near for "liquidating the POUM divisions." (A detailed listing of forces has been omitted from the section of the document before the "General Conclusions.")

The end result of Soviet efforts was evident by 17 May 1937, two days after the ill-fated cabinet meeting. When Prieto and the

Left Republicans supported Communist overtures to Juan Negrín to assume the job of prime minister, the die was cast. The new cabinet created by Negrín appeared to be truly representative of all political forces; only two minor ministries were formally in the hands of the PCE. The new government, however, in taking a law-and-order stance against the policies favored by the POUM and the anarchists, Beevor explains, left "the NKVD-controlled secret police unhindered in its persecution of persons who opposed the Moscow line and to sacrifice the POUM to Stalin in order to maintain arm supplies."[38]

## Document 41

[Unnamed source (9)]

Dear Director:

I arrived in Catalonia at a moment when the political situation was extremely aggravated, when a crisis that had been brewing for a long time in secret was disclosed with unprecedented force. It is, of course, not just a matter of the usual government crisis, but of deep internal contradictions within the political bloc that was smashed here. In a sense Barcelona is anticipating the political conflicts that will take place (and partly, in an attenuated form, are already taking place) in other parts of Spain.

What is now happening in Catalonia?

The anarchists went over to the offensive against the Popular Front government and primarily against the Unified Socialist Party of Catalonia (a section of the Comintern), which is the principal force of the Popular Front. The anarchists are, as an ultimatum, demanding for themselves these portfolios in the new government: 1) military councillor, 2) councillor of industry and transport, 3) trade and provisions, 4) finance, 5) agriculture; besides that, the posts of 1) general director of all police, 2) commissar of police for the city of Barcelona, 3) a number of posts of chiefs of regional police. Besides that, a demand was put forward that a board be set up and attached to every councillor (minister) with the anarchists to make up half the members on these boards. Thus all the key posts in the government would go to the anarchists. Therefore, this is about the total conquest of the government apparatus, an actual seizure of power. To the masses, the anarchists justify their present actions by the fact that the "revolution is subsiding," that the "government has been seized by reformists and petty-bourgeois elements," and that it is necessary to improve the condition of the masses further through socialization and collectivization. There is furious speculation and demagoguery about inflation (in fact, prices for foodstuffs have risen 60 to 100 percent, there is not enough bread, there is no coal, and so on), the PSUC was portrayed as responsible for the inflation; Comorera, the general secretary, holds the post in the government of councillor for provisions (a very unfortunate maneuver). The actual motive for the present actions by the anarchists is their striving to seize power, while it is not too late, while the strength of the PSUC and revolutionary order have not yet been firmly established. And this strength is growing rather quickly and at the expense of, and to the detriment of, the anarchists. It is an indisputable fact that the anarchists' political influence has decreased over the last few months. The anarchists have alienated the peasant masses through their "collectivization," the Catalan peasantry hate the anarchists, and not too long ago the peasant union ("Union of Rabassaires"), which has around 100,000 people in it, went over completely to the PSUC. The position of the anarchists among the working masses is gradually beginning to weaken, although here it is still very strong. The UGT (which here is completely under the influence of our colleagues, that is the PSUC), has grown from 150,000 to 450,000 members—and the PSUC itself from 8,000 to 50,000, and mainly owing to the workers of Barcelona. The growth in the party's political influence—and not only political influence—is also obvious in the army. In the Durruti Division (anarchists), for example, of 6,500 men around 1,000 are PSUC and UGT members or sympathizers.

The growing authority of the party, which has come out as the embodiment of revolutionary order and discipline and the only force in Catalonia that is striving for a turning point at the front—this is the reason for the present action by the anarchists. These actions are accelerated, it seems to me, by the fact that the new draft (mobilization of 1932–1936) should undoubtedly strengthen the position of the party in the army. A majority of the mobilized (mainly peasants) do not sympathize with the anarchists. Thirty thousand new soldiers, as they are infused into the regular divisions of the People's Army that are forming, this is patently a movement of the real armed forces to the detriment of the anarchists, who now have at their disposal around 65 to 70 percent of the Catalan army. If up to now the correlation of armed forces shaped up this way:

| *The anarchists have* | | *The Popular Front has* | |
|---|---|---|---|
| 1. Durruti Division | 6,500 | 1. Karl Marx Division(PSUC) | about 8,000 |
| 2. Ascaso Division | about 3,000 | 2. The Macià Companys Regiment | about 2,000 |
| 3. Jover Division | about 8,000 | | 10,000 |
| 4. POUM Division | about 4,000 | | |
| | soldiers 26,500 | | |

then the formation of three new divisions will clearly change the picture. And it is not without reason that at several call-up points (for ex. in Barbastro) anarchist agents swooped down and began to "recruit" their own supporters, attempting to remove them immediately for their own divisions.

The anarchists are still very strong in the unions. The railway union, the transport workers' union, [and] the construction workers are in their hands. They control 50 percent of the unions for textile workers, food industry workers, and chemists. In the military industry (that is all heavy metal and chemical industry) they have around half the workers. The strength of the anarchists in the workers' movement lies in their old union cadres, in an immense historical tradition, in the exceptionally strong cohesion and discipline of the anarchist cadres, and in impetuous demagoguery—which will of course, weaken over time (about Barcelona, as I recall, Engels wrote that this was a city, which had known greater barricade battles than anywhere else in Europe—and those battles were led by anarchists). In the FAI's organization there reigns an iron discipline, which other Spanish organizations can only envy. At the front, for example, not one anarchist division commander takes one step, carries out one measure without obtaining permission beforehand from his party center. What this center is, is still not exactly known by us. The "preachers"[39] have told me about a lot of incidents. In the unions, in the factories—among the committee members, in the government apparatus—the very same factional discipline. Lately, some weakening of this discipline has been observed (that is, in connection with the process among the anarchists of internal demarcation), because of which the "preachers" are hoping to secure some sort of local operations at the front.

In the anarchist camp, they say that a struggle is taking place between two tendencies (all of this owing to that weakening of the anarchist position within the masses which I mentioned above, a weakening caused by the failure of their "free communism" peasant policy, by failure at the front—all the best factory workers know that the front is in the hands of the anarchists and that the front is shamefully inactive—by the economic impasse that is approaching in industry "socialized" by the anarchists and not organized according to planned principles, and finally by ideological failure—the participation of the anarchists in the government, contrary to all of their theories, and so on). There are "moderate" anarchists (in the leadership)—a number of people, workers with revolutionary pasts, who understand the difficulties of implementing the anarchist platform at the present time, who understand the need for a real organization of the front, and who are therefore disposed toward collaboration with the PSUC and with other parties of the Popular Front.

Among the lower ranks, as our comrade colleagues say, this kind of disposition is still more widespread. But even the "moderate" leaders have found themselves at a dead end, and they are only now beginning to think through the prospects. Durruti once said in a candid conversation, "If the fascists win, it would be bad for us. If the Republicans (Esquerra) win, then it would also be bad for us. And if Largo and the Communists win, then it would also be bad for us."

Another group of leaders is the "extremists"—consisting in the best case of fanatics with permanently dislocated brains, and mainly of *pistoleros,* people with criminal or semicriminal pasts. *Pérez Comvina* is one of these—the leader of the union of transport workers; *Eroles*—the present chief of police; *Chena*—the ringleader of Hospitalet, the anarchist propaganda organization; *Portela*—the chief of frontier security; and others. Even the acknowledged leaders of the movement such as García Oliver and others are rather afraid of them (according to the admission of several of them).

At the present moment, the anarchist leadership is apparently keeping the extremists in line. It was these people who, enraged not too long ago by a (Catalan) government decree about the creation of a unified corps for internal security and the liquidation of the union and party "security patrols," forced the present crisis and are the authors of all the latest ultimatums. It cannot be ruled out that these elements are trying to organize a putsch. The preparations for an armed action are, in any case, going forward. Lately, weapons have been delivered over the Pyrenees; at several factories that are under the control of the anarchists cartridges are being intensively manufactured; and it is also known that no small number of weapons are being amassed in secret warehouses. On the prospect Passeo de Gracia the other day, across from the Karl Marx House, where our CC colleagues have been put up in two buildings (where the anarchist unions are situated), machine-gun nests were constructed (dugouts with sandbags), which will ensure flanking fire on the building (and the approaches to it) belonging to the friendly organization. And the anarchists have enough will, military knowledge, and weapons for this!

It is extremely difficult to say how the current crisis will end. *Variant N° 1:* The PSUC and Companys (a character who wavers, as befits a petty-bourgeois politician, between warring factions; he sympathizes more with the PSUC than with the anarchists but fears the latter) do not give in, and then the anarchists either leave the government and remain in the opposition or carry out a putsch.

*Variant N° 2:* The PSUC and Companys make a concession—a compromise—and then the old correlation of forces is basically preserved in the new government, with some increase in the strength of the anarchists.

*Variant N° 3:* Companys gives in to the anarchists and makes a concession that is unacceptable to the PSUC, and the latter leaves the government.

*Variant N° 4:* The old correlation of forces is restored.

As you see, none of the four possible outcomes is an improvement in the situation, and the political situation in each one of them becomes more complicated.

This circumstance answers the question that has always worried us: "Why is there no action on the Aragon front?" The anarchists were until now (and still remain) the real main force on this front, and the anarchist center absolutely purposefully did not want to fight—not, as is advanced on the outside, because "we have first to carry out a revolution and then to win the war," but because the anarchist center does not want to mess up its armed forces at the front, which are in the first place intended to seize power and to place constant pressure on the remaining organizations in the Popular Front. There are always enough pretexts and excuses for refusing action on the front: there are not enough forces, not enough weapons, no cartridges, no aircraft and tanks, and so on.

The Left Republicans (Esquerra)—also one of the component forces of the Popular Front—who have their own military unit (the Macià-Companys Regiment, around two thousand men) and who have significant political influence among the officer corps, have their own "reasons" for passivity at the front. A regional, narrowly nationalistic Catalan approach to the questions of the war is characteristic of them [the Catalans]. The most important thing is to defend Catalonia and the army deals with this task (since the adversary is not advancing!). They do not especially want to sacrifice their own units, to use up cartridges for the sake of Valencia—and all the more so as the local nationalist circles feel very resentful toward Valencia, which up to now has officially reduced the national autonomy of Catalonia in questions of shipbuilding, schools, and so on.

The POUMists (Trotskyists), who have their own division (four thousand men) and are developing furious agitation and propaganda activity, are yesmen for the extremist anarchists on all the main questions. They are now promoting the slogan "Worker-Peasant Government" and a number of demagogic demands ("A reduction in the salaries of high-paid white-collar workers," "Against a raise in prices," "For an offensive on the Aragon front," "For real aid to Madrid," and others). In actual fact, of course, these are inveterate enemies of the Soviet Union and the Spanish Popular Front—provocatively ruining all the measures capable of hastening the victory of the Spanish democratic revolution.

There is only one remaining force prepared to activate the front, and that is the PSUC, its K. Marx Division, and its cadres that are scattered throughout other units. But by itself the K. Marx division will not conduct operations on the front, and it ought to be held back because of the situation that has arisen, and not be exposed to a blow by the fascists.

Thus, the situation on the front is such that each unit is avoiding initiative and activity, fearing that setting out [for an operation] will leave it without the support of its neighbor who is from a different party. During the operation (offensive) at Almudévar, for example, the following characteristic episode occurred. Units of the K. Marx Division, anarchists, and POUMists took part. The anarchists agreed with the Marx members that as soon as the latter (who set out first) had occupied some point, a flare signal would be given, after which the anarchists would immediately go over to the offensive. Several hours after the beginning of the operation the flare did appear. The anarchist commander began the offensive. Then a doubt seized him: he checked; it turned out that the point was not taken at all. Then he called a halt to the offensive, which was developing successfully. Were you cheating him? And the operation was ruined. If reserves are urgently required at some point, then without fail one battalion each from the K. Marx, the anarchists, and the POUM must be gathered on an equal footing. Every plan for an operation is scrutinized without fail, with an eye to its advantage for this or that unit. All of this reminds one of the tactics of the old Chinese warlords, who united in a "union" in which each strove to use his neighbor and as far as possible avoided military action himself.

Meanwhile, among the lower ranks, the mass of soldiers and middle commanders, even in the anarchist units, the mood is not bad, is militant. Before my trip to the Aragon front I imagined that the anarchist forces were demoralized by eight months of idleness, undisciplined and incapable of fighting. In Valencia I got an impression of the famous anarchist "Iron Column" ("Columna de Hierro"); (I went to their meeting, where the question of reorganizing the column into a regular brigade was decided, and became convinced that this is a regular gang, half of it consisting of criminals. Time and place do not permit me to give a detailed picture of this mob now—I will tell you about it in person). And then the Catalan anarchist units were completely different from this "column." With all of the weaknesses inherent in them (lack of discipline, weak training and so on), these are, all the same, military units roughly like the Madrid units (taking into account their lack of experience, [certain] elements demoralized by sitting in trenches, and so on). According to testimonials from the "preachers" and my own personal observation (superficial and cursory, of course), the soldiers in the anarchist units are entirely fit for military action. The most important thing is that they have not yet lost their will to carry out an offensive. The soldiers want to fight. On the road I managed to overhear (with the help of the driver) a conversation between soldiers from the Ascaso Division (anarchist): "There was a discussion in our trench yesterday," said one, "and we decided to disperse for home if they hold us at Huesca a long time and if we don't attack. We're tired of this!"

In another unit of the same division at Huesca, the commander of a battalion of foreign anarchists (240 Italians and several dozen Frenchmen), a former Italian officer named Cieri, told us with indignation, "My battalion cannot stand this stagnation any longer. We foreign anarchists came here to fight and not to rot in trenches with a city before us that is almost empty of enemy forces." He showed us the disposition of the enemy, who is fortifying his position with impunity (in several places the enemy trenches are eighty to a hundred meters away) and said that the enemy's strength is almost nonexistent, that a night or an unexpected day attack could still easily dislodge the enemy, but that he [Cieri] cannot do this since there is a strict prohibition from the division staff. "I am a disciplined anarchist and follow orders."

Cierri [*sic*] made a very good impression and is sincerely indignant. "If it continues like this," he growled "we will move off and go to Madrid."

I cite these conversations to illustrate the mood. The "preachers" confirm with one voice that, with some exceptions, the majority of the soldiers and middle officers really want an offensive. How they will behave in battle is another matter, how much steadiness they will show in a fight, but it is important to establish though this fact—the desire to fight in the lower ranks, with a patent unwillingness of the upper ranks to organize seriously and carry out this fight.

The center of the problem of the Catalan front, consequently, is in the political situation. It is possible, through great pressure, to achieve an activation of the front by means of local (and small) operations, even given the current situation. As you know, a little is already being done in this direction. It will probably be possible to achieve something more serious only after reserves are trained (*if* they manage to keep them safe from the anarchists) and with the aid of technical means from Valencia.

Given all these circumstances, what can be done is to teach the troops. The "preachers" are not doing much about this. Why, for example, are the regiments of the K. Marx Division, the [units] most dedicated to the Popular Front, not made models for all of Catalonia? With this monthslong sitting at the front, with this paralyzing calm, it might be possible to manage to do a lot, despite the fact that the division is occupying the front and there aren't many units in reserve. To instruct the junior officers, the sergeant-majors, the sergeants, to teach the middle command to be technically literate, to teach the soldiers to shoot accurately, and so on—all this can be done. This charge ought especially to be laid on the "preachers" (they, by the way, agree with this), and it would be good if you could specially remind them about this task.

Cid

Correct:
2 Copies.

---

## Document 42

RGVA, f. 33987, op. 3, d. 991, ll. 150–188

---

G. M. Dimitrov                                                                15 April 1937

To Comrade *Voroshilov:*

I am sending you a detailed report by our political informer in Spain. Apparently this report also expresses the mood, opinion and circumstances of the CC Politburo itself, since oral information made to us on behalf of the

# Document 42 *continued*

Politburo by a comrade arriving from Valencia coincides with the contents of this report.

With comradely greetings,

G. Dimitrov

N70/10

*Top Secret*

6/MK
Translated from French
N° 4
from 28/3/1937

In this report I shall dwell in detail on the questions concerning *the internal situation of the party, both in connection with the plenum of the CC CPE which just took place, and in connection with the problems of union and political unity of the Spanish proletariat.* To give precise information, however, I must first of all describe the situation both from the military viewpoint and in connection with the development of a hidden government crisis that is now brewing.

*The situation at the fronts.* [ . . . To win the war,] we need the government really to govern the country; to carry out a war policy, we need a government that would bring about a maximum unification of all the people's forces that entered the united Popular Front. We need a real minister of defense, working on the war, securing for the front all that is necessary. The questions of an offensive, securing all conditions that will help end the war quickly and successfully—again arise not only as purely military problems, but also as questions that are basically political. Already there is a Republican army which, despite all its weaknesses and shortcomings, has proven its great endurance and fighting value. Its fighting value is better than the enemy's, despite the fact that the enemy army is better armed technologically. All of the objective conditions are also on hand (people, arms, and the possibility of producing ammunition). The necessary reserves can be prepared in a very short space of time. The difficulties of the present time are explained by the lack of a firm government policy line, the lack of a war ministry that is concerned exclusively with military questions.

2. *The weakness of the government,* the lack of a firm government policy on war issues—at a time when the situation at the fronts demands a quick transition to the offensive—all of this creates the conditions for the imminent *government crisis,* which is manifesting itself in a very acute form. This concealed government crisis and its often acute manifestations have not been a

185

secret either for the population or, even less, for the army in the field. Everywhere a mood of expectation and nervousness is being created. Arguments in newspapers, discussions at meetings and demonstrations, conversations and negotiations, political maneuvers and intrigue—all of this is increasing daily. This creates a very alarming mood among the units at the fronts. Not only are the soldiers at the fronts insistently demanding a resolution of the government crisis to strengthen the fighting efficiency of the Republic's might, but also on several sectors of the front there are repeated instances of collective threats against the government and personally against Caballero. People from the front are formulating direct charges against the minister of war, giving him a negative political evaluation. From all directions they are demanding a quick end to the sabotage, negligence, incapability, and bureaucratic tyranny that reign in the War Ministry. At the same time, among the broader masses a dissatisfaction with the economic and administrative policies of the government is growing—a dissatisfaction that attests to the growing discrediting of the experimental syndicalist policies—policies that the government at times not only supported but also encouraged. I must also add another circumstance that is magnifying this hidden government crisis: it is an increase in the difficulties with supplies. Besides this, the prospect of an ever more real possibility of winning the war is provoking among some elements a growing anxiety about how to divide among themselves the spoils, the glory, the political credit that would come from a victory. There is also intensifying pressure from France and especially from England, which is pushing and demanding "policies that might decide the Spanish problem," as well as pressure and a widening campaign by the Socialist and Amsterdamite Internationals. What kind of new facts evidence the aggravation of the government crisis? First of all, the terrible campaign against the Communist party by Caballero and supported by his friends and by their press. Caballero's daily newspapers *Adelante, La Correspondencia de Valencia* (Valencian organ), *La Claridad* (Madrid organ)—publish articles against the Communist party, against Hernández, against the leaders of the Unified Socialist Youth. At the same time, the minister of war continues a real crusade against the Communists. After he expelled the Communists working on the central general staff, he continued a pogrom against the Communist political commissars. Several of them were demoted, dismissed from holding posts, and replaced by Socialists or anarcho-syndicalists. By decree, at the military school that trains cadres, only people sent by the unions are being taken on as students. Day before yesterday two Communist commissars in the navy and two committees of sailors were arrested, just because there were Communists among their number. Fifteen Socialist political commissars were appointed in the air force despite the fact that there is not one Socialist soldier in the air force—the Communist political commissars are forced to play the role of guards at the aerodromes. They stopped issuing the air force's political-technical organ. They appointed eight inspectors for the army at very high salaries, with the right to invite for themselves five to six assistants each. Of these eight inspectors, six are Socialists and two Trotskyists, expelled several years ago from the Communist party. At the beginning of March a decree was put into effect on the militarization of transport; a transport battalion was organized, at the head of which were placed 111 political commissars—all Socialists. In the transport workers' union, the overwhelming majority of which consists of Communists, the leaders of which are Communists, political commissars were appointed who were all Socialists. At the same time, they are making an unbelievable effort to smash the Catalan UGT (General Workers' Union), as well as the federation of transporters of Catalonia. This operation benefits only the anarcho-syndicalists. The leaders of the UGT (president Caballero) are waging an intensified campaign against the Communists in the unions. Worst of all: Chevenels, Stoltz, and other leaders of the Amsterdamite International and the Second International are traveling around Spain, and, judging by the words of Pretel (one of the secretaries of the UGT, a very frank and honest man connected with the Communist party), they came to offer their services to Caballero and the leadership of the UGT for the fight against the Communist party. Simultaneously, Caballero, his supporters, and the leaders of the UGT are making a huge effort to break up the Unified Socialist Youth and to create a new federation of Socialist young people, organically tied to the UGT and the Socialist party. The bitter struggle is taking place in Madrid for the Madrid municipality. This municipality should have thirty-five councillors; the Caballeristas are demanding twenty posts for the UGT, and the remaining fifteen would be distributed among the Communist party, the Socialist party, the FAI, and the Republican party. They make this demand despite the fact that they know very well that the Communist party of Madrid is politically the strongest party and that if elections were held, then the Communist party could receive 50 percent—more votes than all [the rest]. Simultaneously with the campaign directed against the Communists, the Socialists (supporters of Caballero) are waging a campaign against the Republican party, primarily directed at Azaña. But in this campaign the roles are divided: the anarchists are waging the bitterest and most systematic campaign against the Republican party, mainly through their newspaper *CNT* (daily organ of the anarchists in Madrid). I must say that this newspaper, with a circulation of 100,000–150,000, became the newspaper read chiefly (like all the other newspapers of the CNT and anarchists also) by all the anti-Republican elements, by all the fascists or semifascists who call themselves independent or apolitical, but who are waiting and hoping for a victory by the enemy. I must also speak of the attempts and intrigues carried out by them to create a government of the syndicalist type—UGT and CNT. These attempts, however, proved unsuccessful. Organs of the CNT and the UGT were forced to beat a retreat the last ten days and to take a defensive position on this question.

## Document 42 *continued*

In these circumstances, in full agreement with the advice received from home, to repulse all attempts to isolate the Communist party, the Communist party ought openly to raise the issue of political unification and of unification of the unions, the question of merging the Communist party with the Socialist party in a unified party of the proletariat.

Our comrades talked with Caballero, with Araquistáin, and with del Vayo. Until the last moment, these conversations did not have positive results. Caballero, who declares that he will not oppose a unification of the proletariat, is conducting a shameless policy against the party, against the military competence of the "Russians." But he does not want to hear anything, or to accept proposals and observations that the party considers necessary, the questions neither of reorganization of the general staff apparatus nor of the War Ministry nor of those organizations that directly maintain military action. You advise the party to find a way to convince Caballero about the need for bettering the situation in these organizations, but it would be an illusion to think that Caballero agrees with any of the advice and proposals on these matters given by the Communists. He does not want to accept even the simplest, most inoffensive measures of a practical nature. All of the proposals, all of the advice, in however cautious form they might be expressed (even without any criticism) are taken by Caballero as an attempt to lessen his power and as the most disgusting intrigue. He has said, and declared and emphasized that while he is boss of the government and the War Ministry, he will fully and energetically use his rights to appoint his own employees. He even declared several times that he will use "his right" to choose and personally appoint the ministers that he likes and, as a result of this, he continues to conduct a campaign against Hernández, demanding that we replace him, for he is the only minister who demands explanations about the military situation and makes concrete proposals that would help the army.

Several "left" Socialists from Caballero's faction, like del Vayo, Pretel, old man Carrillo, greet with enthusiasm the idea of unifying the two proletarian parties. The other Socialists, Caballeristas, like Araquistáin (Republican ambassador in Paris) agree with the proposal but declare that "a new united proletariat party ought to join the Second International," despite the fact that the Second International, in the words of Araquistáin, "presents the appearance of a clique led by corrupt people, cheats, and notorious bureaucrat-reformers." At the same time, judging from the information coming from del Vayo, the Caballero faction would accept the proposal to unite the two parties, with the condition that the center and right wings of the Socialist party be excluded—that means with Negrín, Prieto, Lamoneda, and others excluded. This means that the Caballeristas conceive of the unification of the proletariat, or, more correctly, the idea of political unity, as a weapon for factional struggle against the other factions of the Socialist party. In actual fact one gets the following, and one needs to take it into account, that in the course of the last several months there exists a practical, regular cooperation between the Communist party and "centrist" Socialists (Negrín and others) to put into effect the measures useful for the army. This may seem strange, but it is a fact, proven by eight months of joint work in the process of the war, that the former division of the Socialists into "left" and "centrist" has not justified itself. The Socialists belonging to the "centrist" faction have shown themselves significantly better than the "left." They behave better from the standpoint of rendering active aid to the army and incomparably better in their relations with the Communist party, just as in their relations with, and evaluation of, the military competence of the "Russians." The Communist party cannot consider the issue of political unity and discredit this idea by accepting the intrigues suggested by some of the leaders of those who call themselves leftists. The argument that is often used by the leaders of the Communist party in talks with Largo Caballero, that he is regarded as Spain's central figure, that he is the symbol of the Spanish people, that he can play the role of a person under whose banner all the working forces will unite, that the Communist party of Spain and the Communist International are the only forces making his name universal, creating sympathy for him throughout the world—to all of these arguments Caballero makes the following retort: "I know all of that, I know that all of that is true, but I also know that the more that you praise me, the more that you exalt me, the more quickly and easily you will throw me off the pedestal on which you've placed me." It is clear that Caballero will continue his policies in that same spirit. In the best case he will agree to some maneuvers, changes in the makeup of the ministries, but only if these changes do not introduce any improvements but, on the contrary, lead to a worsening. What kind of maneuvers might there be? Caballero leaves the post of minister of war and remains only president of the Council of Ministers, but in the post of minister of war he puts a man like Baráibar or Araquistáin. Friends of Caballero—Araquistáin, Baráibar, Aguirre—agreed that Araquistáin may be the only acceptable candidate for Caballero and for other participants in the Popular Front. As regards this, an article was published in the newspaper *Le Temps,* completely prepared by Araquistáin with correspondents from *Le Temps.* But to grant the post of minister of war to Araquistáin or Baráibar means no improvement at all. And what is more, this will result in new surprises and complications, even more unpleasant and dangerous than the situation in which we are now. I forgot to say that Díaz and Dolores had a personal talk with Azaña. Azaña also thinks that matters cannot continue as they have up to now, and that with the present state of affairs it is impossible to win the war. Azaña thinks that the number of ministers needs to be lessened (eighteen ministers in this small parliament!); that the War Ministry needs to be separated from the presidency of the Council of Ministers; that in the process of the war, in the War Ministry there is enough work with which the minister of war cannot deal if he is occupied with other affairs; that, what is more, it would be necessary for other ministers to be occupied more with military questions. Azaña declared that the Communist party is the most powerful party, the most disciplined, that it sees the situation better than others and that therefore it has the right to more representation in the government than currently, that it ought to have an official opportunity for more practical influence on the government. He also said that the Communist Party of Spain may unite around itself the majority of the Spanish people. But he bows to the fact that, from the point of view of the international situation it is necessary that the main government not be Communist now, despite the fact that he himself is ready to cooperate actively with the Communist party in every condition, taking into account that the Communist party is the central power and guarantees success in the struggle of the Spanish people.

Therefore, all of what has been said above must be taken into account, as with everything that I wrote in the previous letters; the military victories of the past days, which provide a breathing space, must be taken into account, and the fact that this breathing space is being used by Caballero to conduct a pogrom against the Communist party, instead of concentrating all efforts on securing a new offensive; taking into account the proviso that the enemy will not sleep these two-three weeks, and will prepare its forces; taking into account that Caballero, ascribing to himself every military success, attempts to isolate the Communists and create his own military bureaucracy, not in the interests of the war but in the interests of the struggle against the Communist party; taking into account the bad attitude of Caballero toward the proposals of the Communist party on uniting the two proletarian parties; taking into account the basic fact that time is a factor of great importance both in the war and in the political situation and that in two weeks to twenty days, no later, the government crisis must be completely settled and gotten past. All these circumstances place before the party the question, Ought it to remain an observer of the unfolding crisis, not energetically intervening to hasten its resolution? One may put the question, Is the position of the Communist party correct, out of caution, out of disinclination to complicate the unfolding situation, to be content with only some articles in the newspaper, some public appearances and speeches? Is the party right not to answer the continuing crusade against it? Will it be right if the party does not put a stop to the disgraceful campaign conducted against the "Russians"? Will it be right if the party, which patiently, but energetically, demands that the army be purged of the traitors, saboteurs, and incompetents, remains a passive spectator, watching with internal bitterness and anger the demotion of the best officers, the best commanders, the best political commissars, replaced by incompetent people, upstarts, questionable and suspect elements, and even reactionaries and monarchists? If the party took such a position, it would fall into two dangers: on the one hand, it would undermine the conditions for victory; on the other hand, it would compromise itself. If the army took such a position, then

the front and the army would suffer in the first place, the army would find itself in great danger both from within and from without. The party will seem
discredited. Lately, especially after the Málaga catastrophe, which exposed
the weaknesses of the government, the eyes of the soldiers, as well as the eyes
of the greater part of the civilian population, have turned toward the Communist party. They are waiting for the party: what will it say, what will it do? The
party spoke. The party pointed out the path that had to be taken. The party
brought forward the tasks and pointed out the measures that had to be
adopted. Later, on the critical days, when real danger threatened Madrid—
the party again saved the situation. Ought the party to be silent now? Can't the
party, to avoid a ministerial crisis, repulse the crusade directed against it,
against its best officers and political commissars? Can the party be silent
when it sees that all heavy industry, all the factories that might produce the
best shells, are replaced by the production of toys and beds? Can the party be
silent, seeing the hundreds of facts just like these, be silent before acts that
even during peacetime deserve the most severe punishment? Can the party be
idle when officers and soldiers, not Communists, people of very great value,
absolutely dedicated to the people's cause, hold out their hands to it [the
party] and openly declare that the head of the War Ministry is conducting
policies to destroy the army? Can it be silent just to avoid a ministerial crisis?
These are the kind of questions that are before the party. The leadership of the
party fully realizes that a ministerial crisis is not entertainment. The party
knows that to raise the issue of changes in the government, built on the foundation of the Popular Front, is not an easy thing; that here we have a game
with unknowns—this is clear, and it is also clear that there will be a great
struggle, much internal friction, that this will lead to new misunderstandings
and will create some internal danger. The party studied this issue with the
utmost caution. The breathing space must be used to put into effect all of the
measures that will guarantee a successful conclusion to the war and the possibility for a transition to the offensive. In the specific present case, the necessary changes in the War Ministry and in the policies of the government
must be obtained. And this cannot be put into effect without changes in the
makeup of the government. I insist on this matter, and not only in my own
name, but in the name of the entire leadership of the party. The party does not
want to come to such a state of affairs that you would rightfully be able to declare that it did not conduct itself as active Communists ought to conduct
themselves, responsible for their party, but like schoolchildren, regarding directives from the Comintern as the letter of the law, putting them into effect
even when circumstances change. Everyone here agrees that the directives
and advice of the Comintern are absolutely correct on every question; only
one question has already been overtaken by events, this is the question concerning the possibility of finding a common language with Caballero. Here
everyone agreed to recognize that further agreement is impossible, that every

possibility has been exhausted, that the leading position must be seized, to force Caballero to relinquish the post of minister of war and, if it becomes necessary, the post of chairman of the Council of Ministers. This does not in any way mean that the comrades want to refuse to continue personal conversations with him or with his supporters.

How does the party explain the political position of Caballero, his bitter campaign against the Communist party, his obstinate opposition to all measures recommended to him for securing victory? The party says the following. Here it's a matter of the complete political conception of Caballero. One must not explain everything that happens by Caballero's personal characteristics, his weaknesses, his individualism, his personal ambitions. One must not explain this by the individual traits of Caballero's character, since all of the rest of his supporters, with the exception of del Vayo, support and approve of the most unbelievable tricks and policies of Caballero. *Caballero does not want defeat, but he is afraid of victory.*[40] He is afraid of victory, for victory is not possible without the active participation of the Communists. Victory means an even greater strengthening of the position of the Communist party. A final military victory over the enemy means for Caballero and for the whole world the political hegemony of the Communist party in Spain. This is a natural and indisputable thing. This indisputable perspective horrifies Caballero. And just Caballero? No, this perspective inspires fear also in the anarcho-syndicalists. And most of all, the perspective of final military victory over the enemy (a victory that might be gained only thanks to the Communist party; a victory that guarantees a preeminent position for the party) inspires fear also among the reactionary French bourgeoisie and especially in England. England apparently explains the situation to itself thus: it would be a great evil to have in prospect a fascist Spain under the fist of Germany and Italy. This must not be permitted. But a Republican Spain, raised from the ruins of fascism and led by Communists, a free Spain of a new Republican type, organized with the help of competent people, will be a great economic and military power, carrying out a policy of solidarity and close connections with the Soviet Union. This is what England does not like. England is striving to push its policy—that means to maneuver such that the war in Spain ends in compromise, which does not mean the complete military defeat of the fascists. England is prepared to help Caballero's government, especially with promises, but provided that he does everything possible to check the growth of the Communist party, to lessen the role and influence of the Communist party in Spain. A union conference in London took place in this spirit; according to the same plan, a conference of the Second International was held. It is no coincidence that the delegates in London were occupied with studying just one issue: how to explain the growth of the Communist party in Spain and what measures might be taken to stop that growth. It is possible that, thanks to this, the organizers categorically spoke against the participation of representatives of the Communist party and Communist International in this conference. Many new facts confirm the likelihood of this hypothesis. In the Communist Party of Spain, in its leading circles there exists an opinion about a fundamental, intimate connection between Caballero's policy and the policy of the English government and also the policy of the Second International on questions about the conditions for the further course of the war, and the continuation of the struggle against the Communist party. Thus the party is now experiencing a critical period in the development of events in Spain, a time when Caballero's policy has hit a turning point, a turning point in the policy of conducting the war, when all of Caballero's attention is occupied not with the front, not with the army, not with the struggle against the enemy, but rather with the struggle against the Communist party. This issue would not be so terrible if the party had the tiniest grain of confidence that, despite the campaign and pogrom conducted by Caballero against the party, Caballero had firmly decided to prosecute the war to a victorious conclusion. The comrades do not have this confidence. The comrades are beginning to fear that, if everything remains in the present situation, then new surprises and dangers await the party. Every day lost in the matter of securing the necessary preparation of the reserves, in the matter of increasing military production, represents a loss for the Republic and a win for the enemy. What needs to be done?

This is approximately the line that the party has adopted:

1. To continue talks with the leaders of the various Socialist factions, including Caballero and his supporters, with the goal of obtaining agreement on questions of political unity and a merger of the two proletarian parties.

2. To continue publicly, in the press and reports, the campaign for political unity, for the unification of the two parties into a united party, and in the same way to continue the campaign for union unity, for the unification of the two union centers.

3. To continue the campaign to mobilize the masses and their pressure on the government to put into effect the principal measures that will secure military victory: a) a purge of the military apparatus, b) [and] of the general staff, c) the appointment of officers to posts in the high command who come from the people, who have distinguished themselves at the front by their aptitude and dedication, d) the mobilization, organization, intensification of military industry and industry that might become military, e) to secure provisions for the front and the correct distribution of foodstuffs, f) to ensure military training, both quantity- and quality-wise, for the necessary reserves, g) to strengthen and rationalize the construction of fortifications and strategic roads, h) to ensure order in society, i) to create a unified command on all fronts, and j) to ensure for the people of Catalonia and the Basque country the security of their national interests.

4. To continue loyal and fraternal connections with the Republican party.

5. To continue contact with the president of the Republic.

6. To attempt to improve connections with the leaders and active members of the anarchist unions.

7. To continue, maintaining as before the necessary civility, to raise issues, to demand explanations, to introduce concrete proposals in the Council of Ministers and personally to Largo Caballero.

8. At the same time, in accordance with internal party order, to inform all the party activists about the situation that is being created, about Caballero's political line, about the perspectives that flow from this, so that the party activists are ready, if necessary, for possible changes in the makeup of the government.

9. To notify in advance all commissars—Communists and sympathizers, at the fronts about Caballero's policies and measures.

10. To begin a critical campaign openly, cautiously, but confidently, against the poor policies of the little bosses around Caballero. To expose the scandalous facts about the removal of dedicated and capable military workers and their replacement by upstarts, incompetents, and suspect elements. To take under our protection the soldiers and best organizers of the sanitary and quartermaster services who were removed unjustly.

11. To expose the campaign and maneuvers undertaken to split the Unified Socialist Youth.

12. To expose the campaign and maneuvers which attempt to disorganize the unions in Catalonia, some of the federations and the UGT itself.

13. To continue to expose the maneuvers which are leading to a weakening of the Popular Front.

14. To strengthen the work of the unions among the young people. To organize throughout the country, in every city, public gatherings to explain the need for political unity, a unity of unions that will significantly strengthen the Popular Front, that will create a military unity of the Spanish people.

All these campaigns ought to be conducted simultaneously with the formulation of a question in the Council of Ministers and before the head of the government about the need to carry out internal changes in the government.

In a word, to go decisively and consciously to battle against Caballero and all of his circle, consisting of some leaders of the UGT. This means not to wait passively for a "natural" unleashing of the hidden government crisis, but to hasten it and, if necessary, provoke it, in order to obtain a solution for these problems; not to wait for an attack at a critical moment at the front then beat one's breast, tear one's hair out, and reproach oneself that one ought to have foreseen it and known earlier, and to have freed oneself in good time from people who were leading [the country] to defeat. The leadership of the party is more and more coming to the conviction that with Caballero and his circle the Republic will be defeated, despite all the conditions guaranteeing victory. The comrades are more and more coming to the conviction that Caballero and

## Document 42 *continued*

his circle are a government group to which all the elements that are afraid of victory and desire the defeat of the Republican army are attaching themselves, elements that oppose putting into effect all the measures necessary for the successful conduct of war. The party is waiting for your advice on this question. The situation is very complicated, very serious, and your point of view will be exceptionally valuable.

. . .

## Document 43

RGASPI, f. 495, op. 74, d. 204, ll. 128–140

Informational letter of a member of the CC CPI with supplementary information on the political situation in Spain recently

11 May 1937

Top Secret

Dear Friends: Four days ago I sent you a long letter. Today I hasten to take the rare opportunity of being able to communicate to you supplementary information on the recent political situation. As you already know, the Catalan putsch was put down relatively rapidly. I say "relatively," because this putsch could have been taken care of significantly more rapidly if the central government had wanted to do so. The governmental decree putting into effect the urgent measures necessary to put down the putsch was signed by the president of the Republic already on 2 May, but the chairman of the Council of Ministers, Caballero, kept this decree in his pocket for forty-eight hours. And, in the course of those forty-eight hours, the anarchist-Trotskyists carrying out the putsch used the time to mobilize all their armed groups and to concentrate them at the most important strategic points in order to complete their fratricidal affair. Over the course of three days (2, 3, and 4 May), when it was necessary to act with the utmost speed and energy, Caballero showed the utmost passivity and paternal feelings for the anarchist ministers. You have undoubtedly already received detailed information on the putsch directly from our friends in Barcelona, and therefore I will not dwell on a description of it. Everyone knows that the initiators, inciters, organizers, and leaders of the putsch were the Trotskyists (POUMists), the libertarian anarchist youth (many Trotskyists among them), and the extremist faction of the FAI (Iberian Anarchist Federation), with the aid of some groupings and leaders of the CNT. Apart from the pro-fascist actions of the Trotskyists, all their literature, appeals, demonstrations, public declarations, all this, including the putsch in Catalonia, is an illustration of the most destructive missions of the fascists.

## Document 43 *continued*

*There are very interesting documents proving the connection of the Spanish Trotskyists with Franco.* The former chief of public order in Catalonia, Comrade Valdés, with whom I had a long conversation yesterday, asserts that there are documents of a sensational nature proving the connection and activities of the Trotskyists. He promised to send all these documents here to me within two or three days. At the 8 May session of the Council of Ministers, the minister of internal affairs, Galarza, stated that he had proof that the POUMist-Trotskyists maintain regular contact with the fascist espionage-provocateur organizations located in Madrid, working not [*sic*] for Franco. No one has any doubt, either, that the Spanish Trotskyists represent an organized detachment of Franco's fifth column. And the Catalonia putsch demonstrates this once again. The preparations for the putsch began even two months ago. This is also proved. Even if there were not all this evidence, it would be sufficient just to listen to Radio Burgos, Salamanca, and Seville. Every evening after 11 o'clock, this radio station broadcasts propaganda. And almost every evening for these two months now, this radio station does not forget to send several compliments addressed to the Trotskyist POUMists, encouraging them, calling on them to save their forces for the struggle against the "red Bolsheviks of Spain." Very often the fascist radio from Burgos, Seville, and Salamanca repeats the following formula, "Attention, comrade POUMists, the red Bolsheviks have decided to destroy you, and after your destruction, they will begin to destroy the members of the FAI." The masses of the CNT did not take part in the Barcelona putsch. The number of armed participants in the putsch amounted to approximately eight-to-ten thousand persons. The basic armed force of the putschists consisted of controlling patrols of *around two thousand men* who had armored cars. At the time of the battles, eight armored cars were destroyed by bombs. The public forces were surprised by the putsch. They did not even have ammunition. In the words of Valdés, our fraternal unified Socialist party of Catalonia at the outbreak of the putsch had neither the technical material nor the necessary people to respond quickly to the putschists. There were no cases of units being pulled back from the front (with the exception of small groups). I add this in order to correct the information *that I sent on 7 May*. At that time, when I was writing, it was asserted that there were anarchist military units who had left the front and gone over to the side of the putschists. It turns out that this was not true. However, it must be noted that if that was not the case, it did not depend on the anarchists or the Trotskyists. Because, according to the information that we had, even in Madrid itself some elements and anarchist groups were prepared *to leave for Catalonia, but they were not able to do so.* The immediate political consequences of the putsch are very great. Above all, the following one: the Trotskyist-POUMists revealed themselves to the nation as people who belong totally to Franco's fifth column. The people are nourishing unbelievable animosity toward the Trotskyists. The masses are demanding energetic and merciless repression. This is what is demanded by the masses of people of all of Spain, Catalonia, and Barcelona. They demand complete disarmament, arrest of the leaders, *the creation of a special military tribunal for the Trotskyists!* This is what the masses demand. Among the POUMists themselves, sharp disagreements have appeared. One of the members of the POUM leadership, a certain Dr. Tuso, immediately upon the outbreak of the putsch made contact with the Unified Socialist Party of Catalonia, worked under the orders of the Unified Socialist Party of Catalonia, and said that Nin is a provocateur, etc. The POUMist organizations in Sabadell, which had a radio station, broadcast on the radio a manifesto condemning the putsch and the POUM. The POUMists of Tarragona, against the directives of their own central headquarters, let themselves be disarmed without firing a single shot. In this manner, we see the internal splits in the POUM. However, despite the evidence and the obvious facts on the POUM's being an organization of fascists, provocateurs, spies, bandits, and murderers, regardless of the hatred of the POUM by the entire nation, this organization finds defenders. In the first rank of their defenders and accomplices are the fascists. The anarchist press is making unbelievable efforts and occupies itself with conundrums and sophistry, wanting to defend the POUMists. In particular, the newspaper *CNT,* published in Madrid, and the *Castilla Libre,* also a Madrid paper, stand out. It is known that there are several Trotskyists and professional provocateurs among the editors of these two newspapers. But even the central organ of the CNT, *Solidaridad Obrera is taking up the defense of the POUM and its newspaper Batalla.* It must be said that the minister of internal affairs, Galarza, a "left" Socialist from the Caballero faction, who has many times said and publicly repeated that the POUM is an organization of provocateurs connected with the fascists, is becoming a "conspiring" *defender of the POUMists.* But something more must be said: the closest *circles around Caballero and Caballero himself are not preparing to take energetic measures against the POUM.* On this point, it was not very long ago at all that Caballero and his secretary Llopis publicly flirted with one of the POUM leaders, with Gorkín. The Catalan putsch, on the other hand, disclosed and intensified differences of opinion, conflicts, and contradictions with the CNT. At the time of the putsch, at a time when one of the parts of the anarchist extremists in the CNT leadership took a very active part in the putsch, another part of the CNT leadership (such as the secretary of the regional Catalan headquarters of the CNT, Mas; the general secretary of the CNT, Vázquez; and others) made great efforts to prevent the working masses from taking part in the putsch. The anarcho-syndicalist ministers, it is said, worked in this spirit, but with markedly less energy: García Oliver, Federica Montseny, and Peiró. (This is according to information from Comrade Valdés; the information that we have here speaks of the fact that these three ministers played a double role up to and during the time of the putsch). Whatever the case, one thing is clear, that the internal discord and the struggle within the CNT is not much more intense. On this point, one of the reasons that pushed part of the FAI leadership to participate in the preparations for and leading of the putsch was the great losses in CNT members. You know that a great number of the members of the trade unions and union organizations remain in the CNT only thanks to terror on the part of the fascists. Now, after the putsch has been put down, particularly after the disarmament of the FAI (if they succeed in carrying this out), after breaking up the uncontrolled terrorist groups, after crushing the terrorist system of the anarcho-syndicalists, it is possible to expect great loss in the CNT's influence. Hatred of the anarchists and the fascists has become a widespread and enormous factor. The inhabitants of Barcelona and the other cities in Catalonia are warmly greeting with applause the military forces sent by the central government to restore public order. Very often the masses shout to the shock troops, "Show no mercy to those anarchist bandit rogues." In order to counter the threat of losing the influence of the CNT and its members as well, the leadership of the CNT is trying to deceive the people and weaken the hatred of the masses. In the first days of the putsch, having seen that the "business" was lost, the leadership of the CNT made several pacifistic declarations and confessed that the workers had been misled by agents and provocateurs and condemned the group of "*friends of Durruti,*" etc., after they had *begun to maneuver.* They already (in their press) depict the Catalan putsch not as a putsch, but as an "uprising incited by provocateurs and enemy agents," and even as an unfortunate misunderstanding that caused fratricide between two antifascist forces! In their cynicism, they go further and state that guilt for the putsch falls on the harsh policies, which were excessively strict, and the Communists' desire for hegemony. They are developing the "theory" that, disregarding that the actual fighting was started by the armed forces of the POUMists, anarchist young people, and fascists against the government, etc., in actual fact this armed struggle means neither more nor less than a legal effort by the POUMists and anarchists to defend themselves against a future danger, and particularly against the effort by the Communist party to seize the movement and the workers' organizations in their hands; that the Communists want to push aside all other political movements and establish their hegemony and dictatorship.

How did the other parties conduct themselves and how are they now conducting themselves in relation to the putsch; how are they conducting themselves in relation to the POUMists and anarchists? I have already spoken about their positions in relation to the POUMists and Trotskyists. In point of fact, I forgot to mention the fact that the majority of the trade unions and union organizations in the UGT of Valencia at the end of April approved a resolution in which they spoke of not allowing a person simultaneously to be a member of a trade union and a member of the pro-fascist organization called POUM. Let us get back to the anarchists. The Republican party decisively condemns the anarchists. It blames them for the putsch. It condemns them for their behavior at the front (deserters, people causing disorganization, thieves, etc.). They condemn them for organized banditry in the towns and villages. They condemn them for the fact that the anarchists are continually threatening to drive the bourgeois parties out of the Republican government. But the ones that are the most malicious toward the anarchists, against all anarchists, are the Socialists from the former faction that called itself the centrists, from the Prieto faction. Prieto is rabidly *hostile to the anarchists*. It is the same with Negrín. It must be noted here that the incident preceding the start of the putsch was the armed clash between the anarchists and Negrín's border guards in Puigcerdá. This conflict came about because the carabineros, on the decision of the central government, set out to occupy the border posts and customhouses, where until recently the anarchists controlled the smuggling route. The relationship of Caballero and those surrounding him to the putsch and to the anarchists has been, and continues to be, totally different. Two of Caballero's secretaries continue to express practically the same point of view as that of the anarchists. Aguirre and Llopis (two of Caballero's secretaries) have several times said the following, "As a matter of fact, we do not understand why there is so much uproar, why the Catalan incident is considered such a tragedy. The matter is strictly an armed conflict between the anarchists and the Communists. If each of them knocks the other one around, this does not cause any harm but on the contrary can bring good results, as both of the extremist elements are weakened by it." *This shows that there is some kind of contact and mutual agreement between the leaders of the FAI and the CNT and Caballero.* This is another piece of evidence shedding light on the anti-Communist campaign that the anarchists and Caballeristas conducted together, beginning in the second half of March. But there is also other evidence. At the Council of Ministers on 8 May, the following was revealed totally openly: four anarcho-syndicalist ministers (Oliver, Montseny, López, and Peiró) took the same positions as did Caballero and Galarza. They defended the same positions. The following came out against them, and this also means against the position of Caballero (with a definite condemnation of the putsch, the people involved in the putsch, the Trotskyists and the anarchists): del Vayo (a long and very powerful speech), Uribe, Hernández, Giral, Irujo, Negrín. Prieto did not speak out and explained this silence in the subsequent discussions with the following arguments: the criticism and condemnation was directed exclusively against the *Trotskyist-POUMists* at a time when I hold to the point of view that it was necessary to concentrate the attack on the anarchists. Everyone expected that the Council of Ministers would end up in a governmental crisis. All the more so since, on the previous day, 7 May, there were talks between the Socialist party, the Communist party, and the Republicans. In addition, the president of the republic talked with Díaz and Dolores (from the Communist party), Lamoneda, Cordero, and Vidarte (from the ExCom of the Socialist party); with del Vayo, Negrín, Giral, and other political figures. All of these conversations were devoted to questions of the events in Catalonia, military policies, etc. And all of them ended with a unanimous conclusion: we cannot continue with such a policy, it must be changed, and this means that it is necessary to change the makeup of the government, yet remain within the framework of and on the basis of the Popular Front! However, as I have already said above, the Council of Ministers ended without leading to a crisis. After several hours of discussion, during which Largo Caballero did not speak a single word, he declared that everyone was in agreement and formulated a resolution of a compromise nature. The next day, on Sunday, 9 May, in several cities meetings were held, organized by the Communist party. The meeting in Valencia, at which there were speeches by Valdés from the Unified Socialist Party of Catalonia, José Díaz, Uribe, La Pasionaria, Hernández, and Gitton (from the Communist Party of France), can be considered a most important political event that will have enormous consequences. The meeting was beautifully organized. Four theaters were occupied for this purpose. The speeches were made in one theater, and the public in the other theaters heard it on the radio. Actually, the speeches were broadcast throughout the country. We still do not know why or *in what manner it happened that it was not broadcast in Madrid.* Furthermore, the speeches were broadcast through loudspeakers set up at three large squares in the city of Valencia. The theme of the speeches was "the relationship of the party to the war and the revolution." This was an answer to the anarchists' campaign accusing the party of placing in the forefront the mission of "winning the war," which means, as they say, that the party is forgetting about the revolution. But the specific and basic content of the speeches was to give a political *evaluation of the putsch in Barcelona,* an evaluation of the government's policies. The party pointed to the path that must be taken. Valdés, in his speech, described the putsch, underscoring the fact that at a time when there often are not enough rifles, machine guns, and ammunition at the fronts, the enemies of the Republic have seized these weapons and ammunition for a fight against the Republic. He described the nature of the Trotskyist-POUMists. Uribe spoke of the agrarian policies of the party, of the democratic people's substance of the Spanish revolution, criticizing in a very popular form the banditry and plundering of the anarchists in the villages under the guise of collectivization, etc. But the hit of the meeting was the speech by Díaz. First of all, he briefly touched on the policies and activities of the party since October 1934 in order to show the role of the party in the creation of the Popular Front. Then he showed why it was not possible to prevent the uprising of the fascists and the generals. Then he brought in specific facts to explain the nature of the social substance of the Spanish revolution, both in the cities and in the countryside. He analyzed the social composition of the Republican army and the social composition of the enemy army, the command corps and class role of both armies, emphasizing that the Republican army is the living force and the *armed force of the revolution*. When we have won the war, we shall win the revolution. The other main points of Díaz's speech were: the Trotskyists are allies of fascism and instigators of the Catalan putsch and the necessity of disarming those who want to stab the People's Army and revolution in the back. Then Díaz criticized the behavior of the FAI and one faction of the CNT leadership, making a distinction between those who took part in the putsch and those who fought against the putsch. Formulating a demand that the CNT carry out a rapid purging from its ranks of the Trotskyists, provocateurs, fascists, both secret and open, etc. etc. He explained that the party does not oppose the CNT and that, despite differences, the party is always ready to work as closely as possible with the CNT in the struggle against fascism, etc. Then Díaz gave an analysis of and criticized the policies of the government, revealing its passivity in implementing the most necessary matters, the lack of a unified command, not carrying out a purge of the military bureaucracy, not carrying out centralization and intensification of the military industry, and questions about the reserves. He criticized *Adelante,* which is trying to underrate the assistance of the Soviet Union. Those who do this, said Díaz, should go to the front and look at the markings on the butter that the soldiers are eating, in order to convince themselves of the assistance that the USSR is providing. Then he spoke on the necessity of rapidly bringing into existence the unity of the two parties of the working class, on trade union unity, on still greater strengthening of the Popular Front, and on the unity of the peoples of Spain. He ended his speech by revealing the meaning of the policies of that campaign which is being conducted against the Communist party. I will not even give a brief résumé of the report, as I am convinced that you already know it, thanks to the telephone communiqués of the press. The basic points of the critique in his report concerned how the current government is not fulfilling its duties by comparison with the fight that must be carried out against the agents of the enemy and by comparison with the necessity which calls for conducting the war and ensuring victory. *He stated that this government can step down* and that another government of the Popular Front can be found that will be able to fulfill its duties. This meeting made a great impression on the entire country and among all elements of the population. For three days now, everyone has been talking about this meeting. People from various parties concur and speak with a single voice, as if they had agreed upon it, "That is excellent! We have not heard such words for a long time. Now we understand everything! We had often felt that something was wrong, but now everything can be understood! etc. etc." In a word, with this meeting, the party won the sympathy of the majority of the people. And the allies? The allies who only yesterday showed great vacillation and worries, quickly and firmly closed ranks around the party. Of course, with the maneuvers to isolate the Communist party that were carried out by Caballero and his company over the course of two months—this means that there is an end to the prospects for a favorable completion of these maneuvers. The party has again become the center of attraction, the strongest and most powerful force in the Popular Front.

Several results are already visible. The leadership of the Socialist party came to the CC of the Communist party both to congratulate it on the successful completion of the meeting and to propose close cooperation in implementing general measures and that it was time to end, finally, the politics of passivity that had been conducted up to that point. They expect that over the next several days a ministerial crisis will occur as a result of that meeting. They are already putting forward a concrete proposal on the composition of the future government, but without Caballero. The draft for the composition of the new government (like all drafts, it has no decisive meaning): president of the Council of Ministers and minister of finance, Negrín (Socialist); minister of foreign affairs, del Vayo; minister of national defense (including the navy and the air force), Prieto; minister of internal affairs, Hernández (Communist party); minister of agriculture, Uribe (Communist party); minister of industry, trade, and labor, Pascual Tomás (vice-secretary of the UGT); minister of national education, Giral (Republican). In addition, the plan foresees three posts for the CNT (Oliver, Montseny, and Peiró); one more post for the Republicans, and two ministers without portfolio—one for the Basques and the other from Catalonia. According to the draft plan, in the War Ministry there will be several governmental secretaries appointed to manage the basic branches; one spot, at least, is supposed to be given to the chairman of the Communist party. The Republicans, it seems, are in agreement with this plan. As I said already, it is only a draft. Everyone believes that *over the next few days we will have a new government.*

Today Pascual Tomás had a long conversation with Díaz and Checa. The talk was about the meeting on Sunday. Pascual Tomás spoke as an envoy from Caballero. He wanted to know what makes the leadership of the party "tick," what this meeting means, and how to explain the strong words spoken against the government. Díaz did not change anything from his presentation, saying that his speech was not improvised, but, on the contrary, it had been a carefully thought out and weighed report. *Pascual Tomás let it be understood* that this speech meant that the party was recalling its ministers and placing itself in opposition to the government. Díaz said that it was not the case, that the party stands for the Popular Front, and that the party is for active cooperation with the government, but that the government was not governing as it was necessary to govern. The feeling is that Caballero is maneuvering. He is preparing some kind of trick. In general, since Sunday the people around Caballero have been very worried. They are afraid that the Communist party will unify exclusively with the "centrists." They say that *Araquistáin wrote Caballero a letter* in which he advises him to reach an agreement with the

Communists and to carry out a merger of the two parties quickly, as otherwise there is the danger, judging by Araquistáin's opinion, that Prieto will seize the banner of unity and carry out a merger with the Communist party. It is perhaps because of this that the people around Largo Caballero are saying everywhere that unity without Caballero will not truly be unity, a lasting unity; or that unity can be achieved only with Caballero, or there will be none at all! I ask your pardon for telling you all these petty details, but inasmuch as they can describe the attitude of people, I think that it is useful to inform you of them. Without doubt, the party will not be drawn in by these small, limiting political tricks. For the goal of unity, the party will not refuse to reach agreement with Caballero (particularly if he will not be the president of the Council of Ministers), and, even more than this, it will offer him an honorable post in the future unified party. On the other hand, the party is dealing very carefully with the UGT, in order not to incite it against us. There is a great deal of rapprochement and agreement with the ExCom of the Socialist party. Indeed, this matter is proceeding rapidly and successfully. At the present time, there is rapprochement and agreement with the leadership of the UGT. These are the rules for the behavior of the Communist party in specific and practical discussions with both one and the other, as well. I forgot to tell you that the party *is preparing to publish the speech by Díaz at the meeting in three hundred thousand copies (brochures) over the next two days.* It is curious that the ExCom of the Socialist party requested to have fifty thousand copies sent to them, as they want to distribute this brochure among the members of the Socialist party.

So, here, dear friends, is the very latest information. I am passing it on to you as I got it, somewhat disorganized. Everything, however, speaks of improvements or, at the very least, the possibility of improvements. Do not think, however, that we are nourishing ourselves with illusions. No, here matters move and change very rapidly. We are convinced that "the others" are not sitting around with folded hands. If, in the course of the next few days, we see a radical strengthening of the campaign against the party, it will undoubtedly signify the preparation of new forces for the fight against us, as it is not known to what extent Caballero is tied in with the anarcho-syndicalists or what commitments he has given them. It is symptomatic that the anarchist press in Madrid came out today under the headline, "Long Live the Government of the Popular Front Under the Chairmanship of Caballero." Can the Old Man Caballero take himself in hand at the last moment and not become a political hostage of the anarchists? This is a question that it is not possible to answer. A positive indication is that, for the first time in three months, today the *Frente Rojo* was published without any corrections made by the censors. The censors (a direct agency of Caballero) did not cross out a single line. But unexpected things can happen.

The possibility that tomorrow Largo Caballero will make some irresponsible gesture cannot be excluded at all. Before I close, a couple of words about the situation at the fronts. In general, it is good. If the detachments of anarcho-syndicalists would implement the order they received, and if stupid orders were not given by the command of individual sectors, it would be possible to take Toledo today. It is possible that Toledo will be taken in the next several days. We are beginning to feel better in every respect. Some very promising prospects are opening up on the Aragon front, particularly if we succeed in finally liberating Catalonia from the anarchist bandits. Efforts are being made to reorganize Catalonia radically from the military, economic, and political points of view. In this connection, one can recall the old proverb, "Every cloud has a silver lining." If we succeed in this, we can transform the enormous military, economic, and political forces of Catalonia. This will have to realize the colossal possibilities for action and military offensives, since up to the present time Catalonia and the anarchists have given only difficulties, surprises, and wasted expenditure of forces.

P.S. Why don't you write anything? I would be very glad to receive even a few words. If this seems impossible to you, send a few words by telegraph, perhaps. Clearly, my friends and I are very interested in your health. A few words about that, it seems to me, would not be too much to ask. I personally am interested more in your opinions on the information that I have sent. It may be that what I am sending you does not meet with your approval. It may be that you have comments and advice on those questions about which I have been writing. In any case, I would prefer to receive your comments, criticism, reproaches, etc., now, so that I would be able to show you that I can improve if necessary. Are you receiving the newspapers and the publications from here? I have asked several times already if they are sending you the newspapers and our publications. They have answered me in the affirmative, but I still do not know if you are receiving them or not. In the second half of May, the first issue of the theoretical journal of the party will be published. The journal will publish, at the very least, the decisions of the CC and will come out twice a month. In a few days, a satirical magazine will begin publication (in Madrid). In Madrid, the party has become the owner of the newspapers *El Sol* and *La Voz*. The party is publishing the military journal *Tierra, Mar, y Aire* and many other journals. They assure me that all this is being sent to you regularly. I forgot to tell you a very important thing, which is that there was a decision to hold a Special Plenum of the CC on 11 May to study the political situation and the measures taken to oppose the systematic, rabid anti-Communist campaign that has been conducted since the month of April. In connection with the military situation, and also in connection with events in Catalonia, the plenum has been postponed to the second half of May.

A warm fraternal greeting from my friends and me.
Díaz asks you to pardon him for not writing personally.

1. Julio Alvarez del Vayo, commissar of the Republican army, speaking at the opening of a Soldiers' Home.

2. General José Miaja Menant and Francisco Largo Caballero at an aerodrome used by the International Brigades.

3. Dolores Ibárruri, "La Pasionaria," 1936.

4. Pedro Checa and Jesús Hernández Tomás at a plenum of the Central Committee of the Communist Party of Spain in Valencia, 1937.

5. Luigi Longo ("Gallo") and André Marty, 1936.

6. Yan Berzin, Soviet adviser.

7. Vittorio Vidali ("Carlos"), Nino Nanetti, and Soviet correspondent
Mikhail Koltsov talk with Republican soldiers.

8. Hungarian writer Mate Zalka ("General Lukács") with Soviet adviser Pavel Batov.

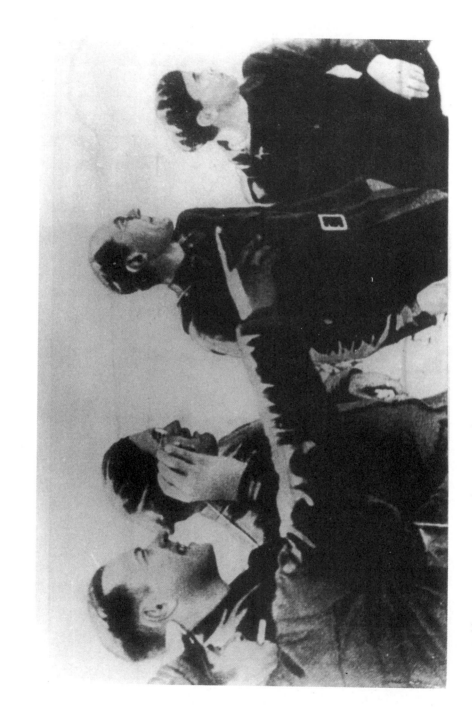

9. Hans Kahle, Ernest Hemingway, Ludwig Renn, and Joris Ivens on the Guadalajara front, May 1937.

10. Anarchist leader Buenaventura Durruti.

11. President of the Republic Manuel Azaña y Díaz.

12. Soviet adviser Vladimir Gorev.

13. Manfred Stern ("General Kléber").

14. Largo Caballero's government.

# Document 44

RGVA, f. 35082, op. 1, d. 132, ll. 500–497

Esteemed Director:
Enclosed I forward a report on the Barcelona events of 3–7 May of this year.

Enclosure: of three pages, N°-09057. Goratsy

*Vkh 2198*
*19/5/37*

## The Barcelona Uprising

### I.

The uprising on the part of anarchists, especially those from the extremist wing in the bloc with the POUM, had been prepared over a long period of time. This is borne out by their repeated speeches in the press, in public demonstrations and on the radio, about the need to suppress counterrevolution and fascism in the rear first, and only then could one raise the question of action at the front. The constant badgering of government forces, the police and national guard, about their (supposed) obstruction and the need to dispatch these forces to the front, bears out the preceding [statement]. Over a long period of time, the antigovernment forces secretly accumulated stocks of weapons, buying them in France and also manufacturing them in military factories in Catalonia. They did not hand over the weapons to the front and did not allow [anyone else] to have any control over them. The secret warehouses of weapons were known to both the generalitat of Internal Security—Ayguadé—and to the PSUC. The "disappearance" of Mosano, the commander of the Durruti Division, and many other workers from the front ten days before the uprising points to the preparation of the uprising even from a military point of view.

In the uprising the anarchists also planned to carry out a final reckoning with the petty bourgeoisie.

I must note, as a positive phenomenon, that the front did not take part in the uprising, with the exception of two to three individual companies from the Ascaso Division and a small machine-gun group from the Durruti Division. The push for individual subunits, groups, and commanders to leave the front and go to Barcelona to take part in the events was quite great, in the units under the influence of the anarchists and also under that of the Esquerra and the PSUC. Whether the current situation would have been preserved if events had not wound down is hard now to determine; but it might have been possible that the Durruti or the Ascaso Division would have found itself, even if not in its entirety, in Barcelona, taking part in the uprising. At the same time, a great desire was evinced in the K. Marx Division to send a couple of battalions in trucks. They were dissuaded from doing so by our comrades.

The opportunity to transfer anarchist units to Barcelona is explained by the fact that the entire railroad transportation system is in the hands of the anarchists.

The influence of the K. Marx Division or Macià Companys on the course of events, being feared, and also the dispatch of armed forces from the central government, communications with the front, [with] Valencia, and also within the city were completely severed, seized under the strict control of persons specially appointed for that, undoubtedly speaking Russian as well.

I personally returned from the front at the height of the events, and must attest to the powerful desire in the K. Marx and Macià Companys Divisions to have a final reckoning with the anarchists, [and to] their terrible hatred for them, even greater than toward the fascists. If there had been a further development of events in Barcelona, it would undoubtedly have been possible to call for the removal of several subunits of these divisions from the front to suppress the uprising.

The anarchists were undoubtedly counting on the workers of the city to participate in the uprising, but here they obviously went wrong. The workers and peasants on the periphery did not follow them, staying in a waiting, or, more accurately, a passive, position, except for some unions, such as the transport union and units of young people who are under the influence of the anarchists. Similar appearances in the villages led to a decisive rebuff of the anarchists by the peasants.

Conclusion—there was no great confidence in the actions of the anarchists, reality confirmed that their calculations about the masses were not vindicated; beside that, the uprising was poorly organized.

II.

[illegible] of May I had a conversation on the question of military work with Com. Pedro, a Comintern representative. The latter announced the city to be in a normal state and, supposedly, scattered incidents happening on the streets had subsided. Reality on the evening of the 3rd and the following days showed absolutely the opposite. Therefore the uprising was undoubtedly completely unexpected by our people. There were no plans to oppose the uprising militarily, although it was not unknown to our comrades that there were preparations for an incident such as the one that occurred. This is indicated by Com. Pedro's appeal to me three weeks ago to consult on a plan for action in the city in case of an uprising.

The leaders of the government units, which had at their disposal some organized forces, did not show the necessary energy in suppressing the uprising, or in seizing the necessary objectives in the city. Government weapons storehouses were plundered; the regional anarchist weapons storehouses were not seized.

The former minister of internal affairs, Ayguadé, undoubtedly with the sanction of and instructions from the president, proposed to begin action to suppress the uprising. They had some forces for this, but because of their confusion and indecisiveness, the government twice failed to implement this course.

The anarchists, especially those on the extreme wing who clearly form a bloc with the POUMists, took advantage of the situation and simultaneously armed and built barricades on the streets, seized a series of objectives, and partially destroyed the national guard.

They seized the radio station, which secured their lines of communication and agitation with the national guard. At first, they noted their neutrality as a positive phenomenon and, afterward, even praised the guard that it had not shown any activity toward those taking part in the uprising. At the same time, they placed all responsibility for the events occurring in the city on the leadership of the PSUC and the minister of internal affairs.

Therefore, dividing the national guard, weakening the government forces, and employing exceptionally provocative methods of struggle, the anarchists with the POUMists were practically masters of the situation in the uprising.

The government, with Companys at the head, meeting almost the entire time, had not decided all the decisive decrees before the arrival of representatives from the center (Valencia), who afterward, together with the president, appealed on the radio to the armed units in the streets with a call to end the struggle and return to their homes. However, this appeal did not take effect, and the extreme wing of the anarchists, along with the POUM, remained extremely hostile up to the last day of the uprising.

III.

The grounds for the beginning of the uprising were a series of individual provocative murders that, with the goal of inciting a struggle, continued throughout the entire course of events. Thus, for example, before the uprising Cortada, the secretary to the executive leader of the UGT, was killed in his car; then Martín, the well-known anarchist, was killed at the French border. To incite the uprising itself, Sesé, the general secretary of the UGT, and a series of other people were killed. In addition to these factors, the occupation of the telegraph-telephone station served as a signal.

All together, these facts served as a call for the anarchists to struggle with "counterrevolutionaries, provocateurs, and reformists." The government forces went into the streets with the mission of protecting revolutionary order. The struggle became more acute with every passing day, gradually enveloping almost the entire city.

It is typical that the entire fascist press spoke of the Barcelona events highly favorably, standing up for all power to go to the FAI and the CNT. Completely secret data, which the PSUC's military section has, confirm the participation of the "fifth column" in the uprising as well as the existence of orders to the latter from Queipo de Llano on the preparation of the necessary supplies of food and weapons and to be prepared for action, mainly as provocateurs.

. . .

## Document 44 *continued*

The ranks of the Guardia are mostly hired guns—as far as morale goes, not sufficiently strong, undoubtedly feeling the demoralizing work of the anarchists within the army. There was no action on the plan that was mentioned above. There was no united leadership to suppress the uprising, and no energy. It will be very interesting to see how the burial of the victims of the struggle will proceed, as it will serve as a striking index of the masses' mood.

The total loses on both sides were about 500 killed and 1,500–2,000 wounded.

*GENERAL CONCLUSIONS*

At the height of the events, a change of government took place under the influence of Valencia. The makeup of forces changed, with the exception of President Companys. From the UGT, Vidiella came in; from the CNT, Mas; from the "rabassaires," Pons; and from the Left Republicans, Feced.

The post of military adviser was given to Gen. Pozas, as representative of the central government, which speaks for the loss of influence by the anarchists on military questions; I must believe that the anarchists will not be reconciled to this appointment and undoubtedly will go through various machinations to compromise Pozas.

For us, the appointment of Pozas is a positive thing, for our influence on military questions will undoubtedly grow through Pozas.

The questions of discipline, organization, activation of the fronts, and study will undoubtedly be decided in a more favorable light, since the former leadership, in the person of Isgleas, clearly sabotaged all these questions, which were repeatedly advanced by us.

The POUM, playing a provocative role in every movement, strongly compromised itself in the eyes of society. Therefore the opportunity has arisen to put before Pozas the question of liquidating the POUM divisions.

Goratsy

3 copies
[illegible], 2-D, 3-G.; lm

## The Negrín Government and the War Against the POUM

The Negrín government moved quickly to satisfy Moscow. In its very first day in office, the order was given to close down the POUM newspaper. When the POUM itself was declared illegal, the Communists took over its Barcelona headquarters and transformed them into a prison for those they called Trotskyists. Leaders of the POUM, including their dynamic chief Andrés Nin, were arrested. Nin himself was killed on the direct orders of Orlov, the

NKVD's man in Spain.[41] The Negrín government proceeded to create what it called Tribunals of Espionage and High Treason, before which dissident figures would be brought. As the Comintern document cited earlier revealed, Stalin had in mind a Spanish version of the Moscow purge trials, most likely to be held in Barcelona.

The Communists' important strength is clearest when one looks at the composition of the security apparatus in the new government. That there were only two Communist ministers in the cabinet drew attention away from the PCE's main achievement—control of the policing functions of the Republic. Not only did the party keep the positions it already held, but also an officer, Lieutenant Colonel Antonio Ortega, became the new director general of security, thereby replacing a supporter of Largo Caballero. Ortega's nominal chief was the minister of the interior, Julián Zugazagoitia—called Zuga for short by all parties. His undersecretary, Juan-Simeón Vidarte, was a supporter of Prieto and friendly to the Communists. In effect, all police positions were completely in the PCE's control. Vidarte later quoted his erstwhile boss Zuga as complaining to him that the Ministry of the Interior and all of security were "nests of spies and confidants of the GPU," Soviet State security.[42]

These events are reflected in **Document 45**, a report written by the same anonymous agent code-named "Cid," who reported to Voroshilov on 22 July. Cid complained of a growing breach between Indalecio Prieto and the Communists, and about Zuga's attempts to sabotage "the liquidation of the POUM." Zugazagoitia had tried to have Ortega, who in effect took orders from the NKVD chief Orlov, removed from his position as director general of security. He also showed concern about Zuga's attempts to end government censorship, which would have interfered with Communist measures to prohibit circulation of newspapers and pamphlets issued by the left-wing opponents of Stalin. Already, Cid wrote, "anti-Soviet and anti-Communist writing" had managed to slip by the censors.

The document is also important for information it sheds on a critical meeting of the Negrín Cabinet that took place after the torture and murder of Nin. At the meeting, Zugazagoitia was quoted as accusing his underling, Ortega, of exceeding his authority when he sanctioned the arrest of POUM members. The Communists, however, had spread false propaganda that fascist conspirators from the POUM had freed Nin from arrest, before he admitted to his Communist interrogators the truth about the conspiracy he had been orchestrating against the Republic. A Communist leader, Jesús Hernández, then retorted that Zuga was not interested in "searching for the criminals who had freed Nin" but preferred to cave in "to the slanderous allusions against the Russian comrades." Hernández then demanded that Negrín "put an end to these dirty intrigues against the Soviet Union." The document thus shows that Hernández, in his own published memoir, lied when he tried to depict himself as an opponent of those who had murdered Nin.[43]

The document also reveals that Negrín tried at the meeting to let the Soviet government off the hook, and preferred to put the blame for repression on the police forces of the Spanish government. This lends credence to the claims of many observers, including Vidarte, that "there probably existed between Negrín and the Communists some kind of tacit understanding, whereby in return for the unconditional political support they had promised him and for the shipment of arms that Spain needed more than ever, Negrín would permit them to carry out *within the law* the liquidation, ordered by Stalin, of a rival party."[44]

Despite this tacit agreement, the report by Cid indicated a growing wariness about the ability of the Negrín government to pursue its assigned tasks, and Hernández was shown complaining to Negrín that affairs were "still unfavorable for the party" and that the fight against Trotskyists was going too slowly. He also found objectionable Prieto's support of a proposed law against proselytizing in the army, a law supported by anarchists and Largo Caballero's former followers. Such a law would, of course, as he put it, "reduce the influence of the party in the army." When they accused Prieto and Negrín of "taking the same path as Caballero," they were in effect threatening the government with precipitating the same kind of crisis that had forced Largo Caballero out of office.

On the last day of July, Dimitrov sent Voroshilov a long report from Valencia. In **Document 46**, the writer reported that despite their success in creating the Negrín government, they still had not attained total control and faced opposition. As the writer put it, "the honeymoon is over." Negrín had become their tool, but he often capitulated to pressure from others and hence did not carry out their policies as promised. In particular, Indalecio Prieto tried to prohibit Communist commissars from being appointed to the army, and was not carrying out the promised purge of "traitor officers" and "suspicious characters"—in other words, left-wing dissidents. Moreover, the navy was in the hands of an officer, Bruno Alonso, who hated the Communists as much as he did the fascists. In essence, their problem was that the administration was trying to denigrate the successes of Communist officers, while promoting incompetent anti-Communists to leadership positions.

Indeed, Dimitrov's source commented that two officers, who were supposed to be turned over to the court and shot, instead became members of the general staff. How, one might wonder, could known fascists be appointed to command of the very army whose main task was to fight Franco's forces? There was only one answer: "Trotskyists," that catchall term used to describe all left-wing opponents of the Communists. In particular, the author of the report cited the case of "the Trotskyist Rovira, commander of the 29th Division."[45] Pozas had him arrested and disbanded the division. Yet Prieto freed Rovira and reappointed him to his command. Had the ploy worked, the author noted, the POUM division would have been back in business, fully armed. Fortunately, he wrote, the PCE's order was implemented and the division was "liquidated." Most striking about the report was that it focused not on the military situation of the Republic, but on the Communists' continuing attempts to gain hegemony.

In arguing that what he feared was Prieto's goal as war minister, Dimitrov's forwarded report again revealed the PCE's actual aim of using an army under its command to create a Spain that the Communists would fully control. Their agenda is clearest from the writer's assertion that Prieto did not like commanders of a "people's army" which would *play a decisive role in determining the economic and social life, the political system of a future Spain"* (emphasis added). The writer stressed that by this point, the Communists were trying to gain support for stepping "beyond the limits of a classical bourgeois-democratic republic." Given that the PCE and Moscow had, however, made it clear that *their* version of a republic did not include revolutionary measures such as those advocated by the POUM and the anarchists, it is evident that they were now trying to advance to the stage of creating what later would be called a people's republic—a government controlled entirely by the Communists, with only one political party.

Moreover, the report's author revealed that with Zugazagoitia still in control of the interior ministry, the PCE had the same problems carrying out purges that Cid had complained about during the Largo Caballero regime. Calling Zuga a "disguised Trotskyist," Dimitrov's source accused the minister of personally sabotaging "pursuit of the POUMists," as well as trying "to turn the Trotskyist spy affair against the party." Thus Zuga had supposedly halted the publication of material exposing the "connection between Nin . . . and Franco's general staff," evidence we now know was fabricated by the NKVD.[46]

The report ended with an evaluation of the different political tendencies in the Republican government. Particularly harsh was the branding of Largo Caballero's followers as "Trotskyist-fascist-anarchists," who wanted "fascism to win, provided that Communism is crushed." Indeed, all political parties except the PCE were described as a group of fifth columnists that favored a separatist regime in Catalonia. Referring to a comment by the head of security that it would be necessary to clean out the anarchist-dominated area in Aragon via a "real planned battle . . . conducted from one village to another," the writer came to the stunning conclusion that the war and revolution "cannot end successfully if the Communist party does not take power into its hands."

The report forwarded by Dimitrov reflected the fact that a strong feeling of disenchantment and disillusionment was setting in. "The spontaneous revolutionary ardour, ill organized and ill coordinated as it was, which animated the Republican armies in the first autumn and winter of the war," E. H. Carr writes, "gave place to a dour defensive struggle to avert disaster, which discouraged any visionary hopes or ambitions for the future."[47] Here, the Communists had a problem. The very revolutionary ardor they sought to capitalize on was in fact the lifeblood of the POUM and the anarchist contingents. Once the Negrín government, responding to PCE pressure, had created a unified professional army, bureaucratization set in and revolutionary sentiment was hard to come by.

Revolutionary-minded troops found it hard to dredge up enthusiasm for the purpose of defending a traditional middle-class republic.

Negrín's government had not yet realized this problem when it launched a new offensive near Brunete. With the participation of the International Brigades and directed by Soviet advisers, the single largest concentration of Republican military strength was brought into play. Despite this, the Nationalists forced the Republican forces to retreat, after brief initial victories. Franco's troops took back Brunete and most of the territory lost by the rebels in the first days of fighting. The Republic's total gain was only twenty square miles, which it achieved at the cost of twenty-five thousand casualties, a loss of 80 percent of its armored force, and one-third of its aircraft. Nationalist casualties were only seventeen thousand men. Although the Communists treated the offensive as a victory and argued that the newly reorganized Negrín army had achieved successes impossible during the Largo Caballero regime, Brunete made it obvious that all was not well with the People's Army.[48]

Two-thirds of Spanish territory was now in Franco's hands. The Republican forces had achieved little or nothing at Brunete, and certainly not the decisive breakthrough that the Soviets had hoped control of the army would bring. Some Spaniards began to talk openly about signing a negotiated peace. By summertime, the dedication of the international Left to Spain had begun to fade. The new tone was most noticeable in the effect it had on the morale of the International Brigades.

## Document 45

RGVA, f. 35082, op. 1, d. 190, ll. 171–181

Secret

Valencia, 22/7/37

Dear Director:

In the last letter I drew your attention to the militaristic tendency arising among the Republican officer corps. Several events that have taken place during the last two weeks not only confirm the presence of these tendencies, but also show this goes much deeper, that this new mood of the officers feeds on and supports a certain political process within the Popular Front.

Isn't it strange that just now, when a large operation is being put together, a breach begins to form between the Communists and Prieto's group? Ten days ago, relations suddenly became so strained that a crisis in the Negrín government was barely avoided.

I will describe these events in detail, so that you acquire a comprehensive understanding of the developing situation. On 14 July there was a meeting of the Council of Ministers, after a long break (a calm began on the central front, and the ministers returned to Valencia). At this meeting Zugazagoitia (a Socialist, protégé of Prieto) systematically sabotaging the liquidation of the POUM and other measures to clean up the rear (which were carried out by Ortega, the head of government security, a Communist) introduced two bills that would reduce the function and rights of Ortega in a vital way. The first law removes from Ortega's authority government security in Catalonia, and directly subordinates him to the Minister; the second deprives Ortega of his fleet of motor vehicles. The Communist ministers spoke out strongly against these bills, declaring that the party can no longer reconcile itself to this policy of sabotaging the struggle against counterrevolutionaries, which the Ministry of Internal Affairs is carrying out; that the proposed bills deprive Ortega of any realistic opportunity to continue the work of cleaning out the rear that had successfully begun; that the Communists consider this step by the minister an attempt to be freed altogether from Ortega, a man who has consistently struggled with counterrevolution. The minister of justice, Irujo, spoke after the Communists (a Basque nationalist, [who] with the fall of Bilbao sent in his resignation in protest and wanted to desert to France). He, supporting Zugazagoitia, spoke out in favor of the need to remove Ortega. After that, Prieto, who did not go into the essence of the bills, spoke, declaring that in this conflict of Zugazagoitia against Ortega, he supported the former, for as a matter of principle he thought it necessary to concede the right for every minister to manage his own subordinates. The minister answers for all of the work, and he has the right to change his own employees. Negrín took a rather indeterminate position, and after all the discussion a majority of the Council of Ministers voted, resolving to remove Ortega from his position, against the Communist vote. After the voting, the Communist ministers declared a protest against this decision. This produced a strong impression, and Zugazagoitia hastened to declare that he was not acting against the party, that he, for instance, agreed to have the Communist Burillo (former chief of Seguridad Catalonia) take the place of Ortega, and so on. Hernández wanted to take him at his word on this and settle the candidacy of Burillo, but Prieto intervened, obviously displeased with Zugazagoitia's indiscrete proposal, and put a stop to the question about Burillo, declaring that "for now there is no need to hurry with the candidacy; we will look into it further," and so on.

At that point in the meeting, Giral (minister of foreign affairs) arrived and reported the sensational fact that the day before a Spanish diplomatic courier's suitcase, which held the ciphers for the Spanish embassies throughout Europe, had been stolen at the Valencia station. The ciphers had been worked out with the help of the Russian advisers (Giral had in mind the "neighbors"),[49] and now, after the loss of the ciphers, "the Russians aren't giving him any rest—they are forcing him to carry out searches in foreign embassies to look for the ciphers" and "in general he was tired of the Russian advisers, who interfere in everything, wanting to know the contents of his diplomatic correspondence," and so on. This completely unexpected declaration by Giral provoked bewilderment and some dismay among all those present. The Communists immediately spoke up, declaring a protest against this statement by Giral, viewing it as an intolerable anti-Soviet attack. At this, the meeting of the Council of Ministers was cut short.

The very same evening, the CC of the party drew up the following tactical line: 1) in view of the acute military situation, not to force a cabinet crisis; 2) however, the Communist ministers, in connection with the Ortega affair, would raise, in all its breadth, the political issue of Zugazagoitia and Irujo's policy, which is ruining the struggle against counterrevolution. In particular, the party would demand the censure and cessation of the permissiveness displayed by the minister of internal affairs with regard to censorship, which has up to now let the anti-Soviet and anti-Communist writing of the press slip by; 3) on the question of Ortega: to agree to his departure, on condition that the government publicly acknowledge his contribution and transfer him to a responsible military position.

Guided by this directive, the Communist ministers appeared the following day at a meeting of the council with the detailed declaration.

They spoke in an unusually harsh and blunt tone. "You know how we work," Hernández declared. "We always put questions before you openly, and if you don't listen to us, we appeal to the masses. Now, we do not want to cause a cabinet crisis, but if the policy of the government does not change, we will find ourselves forced to bring the matter to a crisis, and that we possess enough strength, we have already proven in the replacement of Caballero's cabinet."

Then discussion turned to the question of Ortega. The Communists demanded from Zugazagoitia concrete charges against O., proof of his unfitness and disloyalty. Zugazagoitia dodged a straight answer. Negrín tried to smooth over the situation and declared that the decision about O.'s replacement was not directed against the party, that he suggested in place of O. the candidacy of Burillo. Then Prieto, who was excited, spoke, delivering a speech on the theme of cooperation with the Communists, in which, by the way, he declared, "We will speak openly. It's no use playing. The Communists are capable people. They have a certain way of working. I would not even object if the minister of internal affairs were a Communist. But I would not want to have

Communists as my own subordinates. For the Communist is not a human being—he's a party, he's a line. One cannot say about Ortega that he was good or
bad. It was not he who acted, not he who decided; the committee of his party
decided for him. When a Communist works with you, you don't know with
whom you have to deal: with a person, or with the unseen committee behind
his back. Ortega arrested, Ortega freed—no one ever knows what he did. Who
actually issued those orders? . . . The committee!" . . .

In his speech Prieto answered Hernández rather sharply. Then Zugazagoitia spoke again, charging Ortega with exceeding his authority; for instance, the leaders of the POUM were arrested without enough proof, and so
on. Again Negrín appealed for peace, for an amicable resolution of the conflict. Then the Communists declared that they would not cause a crisis because of Ortega, but they could not allow Ortega to be discredited, and they
demanded an honorable formulation for his departure.

On the question of relations with the Soviet Union and with the Russian
advisers, Hernández made a special declaration, in which, by the way, he
said, "We are tired of the constant anti-Soviet attacks of several organs of the
press; we protest against the Jesuitical relations with the Russian comrades
when something isn't okay—blame is heaped on the Russians, on the people
who came here at your request, who are sacrificing their lives for Spain. For
example, the affair of the liberation of Nin (as you probably know, the arrested
Nin was freed from prison by a group of armed raiders—C.): instead of searching for the criminals who had freed Nin, you caved in to the slanderous allusions against the Russian comrades (a rumor was going around that the Russians, supposedly, abducted Nin—C.). On the matter of the theft of the
ciphers, which took place as a result of the irresponsibility or treachery of
criminal elements—once again insinuations against the Soviet comrades are
being dragged in. The party demands that you put an end to these dirty intrigues against the Soviet Union."

Negrín spoke, excitedly and spiritedly: "While I have been chairman of the
Council of Ministers, I have not allowed the Soviet comrades to be defamed.
In the Nin affair, the Russians are absolutely without guilt, it is our police organs that are at fault. It is the same with the cipher affair, where it was precisely the Russian comrades who rendered great assistance."

Hernández: "But why then did Giral speak that way yesterday?"

Giral fidgeted and said that they had not understood him, that he was fully
aware of the exceptional role of the Soviet Union and of the help rendered by
them to Spain. He was only dissatisfied with one thing—that the Russians intervened in his affairs too tactlessly—but that this could be settled easily and
in a friendly manner.

On this, the meeting ended. After the meeting Negrín in a private conversation with Hernández reproached him for his excessively sharp discussion.
Hernández declared that the main thing was that up to now the government had

not had a clear political program and policy, that almost the same situation was being created as with the Caballero government. Negrín promised (for the nth time!) to raise the question about a government declaration in the near future.

The real result of this conflict, despite the positive results of the political demonstration by the Communist ministers, is still unfavorable for the party. Ortega has to be sacrificed, the post of chief of Seguridad will apparently be taken by a Socialist from Prieto's group, and the struggle with the Trotskyists and other counterrevolutionary forces will go much more slowly and with greater difficulties than up to now.

But the Ortega affair was an important episode, revealing the true attitude of Prieto and his group toward the party.

If in questions of internal politics Prieto wants to push aside the Communists, then this [attitude] was also noticeable in the army.

On 26 June, Prieto published his famous order on forbidding "proselytizing" (I enclose a translation of the text of the order). At that time it seemed to many that this was done by accident, that Rojo or someone else had slipped that law to Prieto and that it was then, as is well known, quickly taken up by the Caballeristas, anarchists, and used against the Communists. But later, during the time of the Madrid operation, it was revealed that Prieto had really actively tried to reduce the influence of the party in the army. This effort took a special form—an overemphasis on the supposed military illiteracy of the Communist commanders, a disparagement of their contribution, and so on. On the third day of the operation, they suddenly appointed the old colonels as "deputies" to Modesto and Lister (Modesto and Lister politely sent them packing). After several days the Madrid newspaper *El Socialista*—Prieto's organ, printed a lead story directed against the Communist commanders. (A translation of the article is enclosed.) The main thesis of the article: those who have military education ought to run the army and command. Characteristic were the following attacks against the party and Communist commanders: "The leaders of the army are forged exclusively through military action, and not by propagandistic speeches; . . . therefore, we repudiate proselytizing in military affairs; . . . those who have no military capabilities are portrayed to us as the military geniuses of the people; . . . the army is not a field for party experiments, but the instrument for victory; . . . party heroes and strategies do not interest us," and so on.

The article (Prieto is considered the author) was of course received approvingly by the Caballeristas. *Adelante* confirmed in an editorial the coincidence of action of the current war minister with the policies of the former war minister (Caballero), which were directed against "proselytizers" (that is Communists).

I think that *Adelante* is not mistaken in this. To the preceding facts, which characterize Prieto's newest position with regard to the party, one might add a large number of other facts from the practice of his work as minister of national defense. Thus, for instance, so far he stubbornly refuses to approve a list of two hundred commissars proposed by the General Commissariat, meanwhile a list of forty commissars proposed by the Republicans was quickly approved. So far, despite repeated representations by the Communists, and also by Sebastian, such traitorous sorts as Mena, the commander of the Estremadura front, Perea, and others have not been removed from their duties. So far, the appointment of old colonels—overtly or covertly fascists—to posts of brigade commander continues. The other day in the 97th Brigade they removed the commander of the brigade, a Communist who had served in battle, and replaced him with an old colonel who wasn't fit for anything. The commanders from the lower classes are stuck at the rank of captain or major, although they are commanding divisions or corps. The other day, by Prieto's order, Rovira, the commander of a POUM division, was freed from arrest. In the navy, the commissar of the navy, the Prietista Bruno Alonso, is conducting a definite policy to expel revolutionary elements—in the first place, the Communists—from the navy and openly protects fascist and semifascist officers. As is well known, Bruno Alonso's policy led three weeks ago to unrest on the torpedo boat *Churruca*. The commissar of the boat, a protégé and favorite of Bruno Alonso, discharged from the boat one of the sailors suspected of theft and arrested him. The entire command came to the defense of the sailor; a violent commotion took place. And the other day [there was] unrest and almost a mutiny on the destroyer *Valdés* (I reported on this by telegraph). So far the head of the naval artillery in Cartagena is able openly to propagandize anti-Soviet vileness such as this among the officers: "The Soviet Union is nothing but a prison," and so on. After the criminal incident with the explosion on the *Jaime I*, despite the demands of the sailors, none of the commanders was made responsible. The morale of the navy and discipline is patently worsening because of Alonso's policy. But Bruno Alonso is not a personal problem. This is a question of Prieto's taking the same path as Caballero.

The Madrid operation accelerated this process. It is possible that after the first days of the operation it became clear to many that the war with Franco was a protracted affair, that huge difficulties still lay ahead to overcome before the final victory, and this prospect provoked new hesitation from the petty-bourgeois participants in the Popular Front, such as the Prieto group. It is possible that another factor was at work here, namely that Prieto, who first came into contact with the army in Madrid, only now was convinced of the huge role the Communists play in the army, the commanders from among their ranks, and so on. Be that as it may, the contours of the approaching new crisis are already taking shape, the new regrouping within the camp of the Popular Front.

The fact that Prieto is now paying our people exceptional attention, at times being very candid with them, readily hearing out military advice and putting it into effect, that it has become in fact much easier to work with him than with Caballero—none of this ought to hide the true situation.

In foreseeing the further hesitations of various participants in the antifascist struggle, the party stood in the right path, gathering the genuine revolutionary forces into a united proletarian party. The matter of uniting the party with the Socialists has lately progressed appreciably. Already, a number of local Socialist organizations, for instance in Jaén, Estremadura, Almería, and elsewhere, have moved in earnest toward merging with the party. Yesterday the plenum of the national committee of the Socialist party, which considered the question of unification, ended. Despite a number of sabotages from the Caballeristas, the national committee made the decision to promote the further rapprochement of both parties. Moreover, it was decided to call to account those local organizations of the Socialist party which refuse without sufficient grounds to take part in local liaison committees. The plenum proposed to the Central Liaison Committee 1) to conduct joint action with the party in the spirit of the military slogans that were formulated in an open letter from the party to the Socialists, and 2) to develop a design for the unification of the two parties. On the question of international policy, the plenum of the CC resolved to maintain close relations with the USSR and to take the course of rapprochement, right up to merging with the Third International.

It became clear from all of the moves of the plenum of the CC of the Socialist party that even in the leadership of the Socialist party there is a healthy nucleus that does not belong either to Caballero's group or to Prieto's group, capable of heading the strong efforts for unity that exist among the Socialist working masses. All of this allows us to view the future of the Popular Front, however the groupings may take shape, entirely optimistically.

Cid

Enclosures:    1. Text of Prieto's order
               2. Translation of article from *El Socialista*

## Document 46

RGVA, f. 33987, op. 3, d. 1015, ll. 92–113

Report from Valencia
G. Dimitrov
30 July 1937

To Voroshilov

### 1. The Government and Its Policies

This is the first question about which I ought to inform you. This assignment has a lot of unknowns. And about the things that are known, one cannot say that they are pleasant or give any hope. The honeymoon is over, and signs of differences in "personalities" are appearing. The government family is far from what might characterize it: friendship, love, and peace. During July, we twice found ourselves on the eve of an explosion, on the eve of a government crisis. Our party had to swallow some bitter pills, come to some compromises to avoid a government crisis. Meetings of the Council of Ministers remind one more of a storm than of an idyll. In the course of July there was not one meeting of the Council of Ministers at which the representatives of our party did not have to wage a real battle. After one of these stormy meetings of the Council of Ministers, Hernández ran up to me and declared: "Write Comrade Dimitrov, write Comrade Manuilsky, let them come here and just look at the beauty of the Popular Front. It's costing us blood and nerves. We have to be on the alert constantly. This is necessary—it is impossible to manage without the Popular Front, but this is a terribly difficult thing: you no sooner succeed in removing one difficulty than twelve new difficulties turn up. If you're not on your guard, then they will fool you twice a day."

It is true that with this government our party has more opportunities for work, for exerting pressure on government policy, than it had with the preceding government. But we are still far from the desirable minimum. And things are becoming strained. After the first month of symbolic gestures and declarations, with the first of July we arrived at a period of "implementation." But an actual united policy does not exist. There are two, three, or even four or more different policies, often diametrically opposed. There is the policy of the Communist party, there is the policy of Prieto and Zugazagoitia, there is the policy of Irujo (Justice), the policy of Ayguadé (Labor) and the policy of the counterbalancing Negrín. Up to the present time it is hard to determine who is boss of the government: Negrín or Prieto. Negrín is full of good intentions, rushes around like the devil, almost always takes the advice of our party, often turns to our comrades for advice, makes promises, takes it upon himself to carry out a number of matters, but does not carry them out, not even 50 percent. Almost never is he not in agreement with our comrades. He always eliminates friction and conflicts. But he does not always succeed in doing this, especially on the fundamental questions, where persistence is needed. He seems an honest person, and honestly, sincerely, and with conviction he is seeking the closest collaboration with our party.

Behind the scenes is that prominent intrigant, Prieto. He has implemented a number of measures directed against the Communist party. So far, more than two hundred Communist political commissars are still not officially approved. But still, despite the official decision of the Military Council, he approved forty Republican political commissars, despite the fact that the contingent of Republican soldiers in the army is minimal. He issued an order against "proselytism" in the army, an order directed against the Communist party, an order giving generals and officers the right to conduct "party propaganda" in the army. By the way, this order has not been put into effect and cannot be put into effect. Prieto himself was forced to recognize that this order was unrealizable, and he is allowing it not to be put into effect. A purge of the military bureaucracy of traitor officers, suspicious characters, and incompetents is not being carried out. We know a large number of cases where officers acting as complete agents of the fascists were not subject to prosecution. There was a case with two officers whom they demoted and promised to turn over to the courts in twenty-four hours and shoot, and now both of these officers are members of the central general staff. The most disgraceful and scandalous fact is the case with the Trotskyist Rovira, commander of the 29th Division. This is a POUMist division and its commander was also one of the leaders of the POUM. He was arrested, and they set about disarming the 29th Division. But by order of Prieto, they freed this Rovira from prison and again appointed him commander of the 29th Division. By order of Prieto, handed down over the head of General Pozas, they returned the weapons to the 29th Division. Fortunately, on the spot they explained this and implemented the order on "reorganization" so that in fact the 29th Division was liquidated. That is at least the latest information that I have received from there.

Another fact—the leadership of the navy from a political standpoint is actually entrusted to the Socialist Bruno Alonso, whose hatred of the Communists is little different from that of the fascists. I will not cite other detailed examples. I must dwell, however, on the new facts characterizing Prieto's conduct during the bitter battles that took place not long ago in the neighborhood of Madrid. Prieto did everything possible to obscure the bravery, abilities, and feats of the Communist commanders: of Lister, Modesto, Campesino, and others. But at the same time, he decided to honor the professional officers, whatever might happen. He issued an order on the promotion of a certain Jurado and showered praise on him just precisely because he showed absolutely no understanding of military matters. This is not a coincidence or a whim of Prieto. He has his own personal view of the army and of command. By the way, he openly acknowledges the presence of such a conception. He does not believe in the military abilities of the commanders who come from among the people. He thinks that the fame that surrounds them is the result of a "certain newspaper's campaign." He does not believe in the professional military, but he tolerates it. He is afraid that the People's Army, headed by commanders who come from among the people, hardened in battle, represents a huge revolutionary force and, as a result of this, will play a decisive role in determining the economic and social life, the political system of a future Spain. For this reason, he would like it if the People's Army were antifascist in an indeterminate way, and far from political activity, especially from Communist activity, and in this the professional military, including Rojo, supports him. He at least wants the command staff not to consist of active revolutionaries.

This policy of Prieto is fundamentally linked to his overall political conception, which does not allow the development of the Spanish revolution to step beyond the limits of a classical bourgeois-democratic republic. Between Prieto and Negrín there are rather sharp disagreements over the military question. This was revealed rather strikingly at the beginning of July, over the order by which the general staff wanted to subordinate the carabineros to itself; Prieto supported the attempt by the general staff. Negrín, backed by the Communists, spoke out energetically against this, declaring that the carabinero corps represented a guarantee in case the professional army forgot that it was at the service of the people. They said a lot of strong and very interesting things to each other, unfortunately awkward to repeat. I must add that Prieto's conception about the army is completely supported by Martínez Barrio and the Republicans.

Things are even worse with the policy conducted by the minister of internal affairs—Zugazagoitia, a follower of Prieto and his friend already from when he worked in the north. This Zugazagoitia, besides the fact that he is a real Jesuit in the way he works, behaves like a real Trotskyist. A number of facts confirm that Zugazagoitia is a disguised Trotskyist. It is still not completely clear to what degree he is acting on his own account and when he is acting at Prieto's behest. Several comrades think that Zuga has his own policy, independent of Prieto, others are convinced that Zuga is an instrument in the hands of Prieto. Zugazagoitia hates the Communists. He organizes one provocation after another against the Communists, and when he is put on the spot, he pretends to be the innocent saint, declaring that he did not know anything and regretting the "misunderstanding" that has occurred. It was he who sabotaged the pursuit of the POUMists. What is more: he himself organized and supported a number of campaigns of a blackmailing nature, provocations whose goal is to turn the Trotskyist spy affair against the party. He forbade and prevented the publication of materials exposing the connection between Nin and the POUMists and Franco's general staff. It was he who removed Ortega, the Communist, from his post as the general director of public security. It was exactly because of this that there was such a strained situation when we were facing a ministerial crisis. The party did not want to bring matters to [the point of] a ministerial crisis, because this happened two days before the beginning of operations on the central front. We sacrificed Ortega. By the way, I must emphasize that Prieto completely supported Zugazagoitia on this question and, what is more, Prieto raised the question as an ultimatum. Zugazagoitia spread slander and lying gossip about Soviet citizens. Our comrades are convinced that the hand of Zugazagoitia was behind the attempt to send back twenty "Mexican" advisers and their staff. It was he who gave the order to search the building of the party Central Committee. They did not succeed in carrying out that search, because we were able to warn the authorities that without the permission of the CC not one person could come into the CC building, and anyone who broke in by force would not come out alive. And that Jesuit Zuga, when they made a scene over this, pretended that he didn't know anything, declaring that this was a misunderstanding, that he never would have dared to have given such an order, and that he had not given such an order.

The deputy secretary of the minister of internal affairs, that is to say, Zugazagoitia's deputy, is none other than Vidarte, a member of the executive committee of the Socialist party. What is Vidarte like? This character trembles with fear every time something serious happens and even when a rumor goes around that something serious is going to happen. His other quality: he is rotten to the core. His office turns into a real bar at night, in which drinking bouts, prostitutes, and wine are a common thing. But this is even more complicated by the fact that Vidarte was abroad for six to seven months, from December of the last year, on a wedding trip. His wife now lives in Paris, takes part in banquets with Cambó, a millionaire, Catalan reactionary, [who] is rendering financial aid to Franco. The father of Vidarte's wife is an intimate friend who has business connections with Cambó. Nice company! A wonderful minister of internal affairs!

And these are the people who have been entrusted with the mission of conducting the struggle against the fifth column, against Trotskyists, against spies and disturbers of public order. To these people have been entrusted the establishment and protection of revolutionary order. I would add and stress that all of this was said and explained to Negrín. It seems that he did not know anything about this. He declared that he would personally see to the matter and take the necessary measures.

The question about Irujo (Basque, minister of justice). Basque nationalist. Catholic. A fine Jesuit, a worthy disciple of Ignatius Loyola. Compromised in the Salamanca-France banking affair. Acts like a real fascist. Especially devotes himself to hunting down and persecuting people from the masses and the antifascists who last year in August, September, October, and November treated imprisoned fascists brutally. He wanted to arrest Carrillo, the general secretary of the Unified Socialist Youth because, at the time when the fascists were nearing Madrid, Carrillo, who was then a governor, gave the order to shoot several arrested officers of the fascists. In the name of the law, this fascist Irujo, minister of justice in the Republican government, is organizing a system of searches of Communists, Socialists, and anarchists, who brutally treated imprisoned fascists. In the name of the law, this minister of justice freed hundreds upon hundreds of arrested fascist agents or disguised fascists. Together with Zugazagoitia, Irujo does everything possible and impossible to save the Trotskyists and to sabotage trials against them. And he will do everything possible to acquit them. This same Irujo was in Catalonia the last few days and with his boss Aguirre, the famous president of the famous Basque republic. They arranged secret meetings with Companys to prepare a separation of Catalonia from Spain. They are intriguing in Catalonia, declaring: the fate of the Basque nation awaits you. The Republican government sacrificed the Basque nation. They will also sacrifice Catalonia.

Two words about the labor minister—Ayguadé. He is Catalan. Negrín himself characterizes him as a bandit. He does everything possible to disorganize work, to create conflicts with the workers. Besides all of this, he is very closely tied to the extremist anarchists. Our party raised the question with Negrín very energetically that things could not go on like this: with such people it was impossible to work. Our party demanded the removal of Irujo, Ayguadé, Zugazagoitia from the government. Our party demands that the government carry out a war policy and general policy consistently and energetically. Our party also is completely dissatisfied with the policy of Giral, the minister of foreign affairs. In the conduct of Giral there are moments that alarm us. Instead of cleaning out the embassies and consulates abroad of traitors, provocateurs, suspicious and demoralized elements, he increased their numbers. To the post of first secretary of the Spanish embassy in Mexico he appointed a Trotskyist. A "nice" maneuver! The demoralization and provocations are continuing in the embassies.

As you can see, things are far from happy. Negrín agrees with our party in principle about the need to reorganize the cabinet and several of the secretariats. He agrees with us also on the question of a need for a flexible, intelligent, and consistent policy in Catalonia (for on this question a great many foolish things have been done here, which might have ruinous consequences if they are not put right). Our party has put the question before Negrín, demanding from him that he force the chairman of the Council of Ministers to recognize his authority, that he have done with indulging those ministers who conduct policies favorable to fascists and destructive to the interests of the workers and the Spanish people. Our party especially insisted on the following three points: to carry out a purge of the military apparatus and to help promote to first place the commanders who come from among the people, and to put a stop to the anti-Communist campaign; to carry out tirelessly a purge of Trotskyist elements at the rear; once and for all to stop indulging the press, groups, and individual people who are carrying out a slanderous campaign against the USSR. If he will not do this, then the party is strong enough, understands well enough the responsibility that it bears, and will find the necessary means and measures to protect the interests of the people.

### 2. The New Political Groupings

Never before have the contradictions, disagreements, and political polemic been so intense as during July. I can say without any exaggeration that a real general crisis is taking place in all the parties and in all of the organizations, except for the Communist party, the Unified Socialist Youth of Spain and the Unified Socialist Party of Catalonia. A very perceptible and rapid transformation is taking place.

## Document 46 *continued*

*We will begin with the Caballerista group.* In the course of two months, this group has come to the point where today it must be considered a triple group: Trotskyists-fascists-anarchists. Caballero, López, Baráibar, Rubiera, Araquistáin, Montier, and a good dozen characters like them, are capable of every crime, of every filth, of every possible escapade, of every treachery, [and] sabotage provided that it defiles the Communists. They have agreed on defeat, they would like fascism to win, provided that Communism is crushed. That old fool Caballero boasted (if I'm not mistaken, this was in March) that he was like Samson, so that if anyone dared to remove him from power, he would destroy the temple and everyone would perish under the ruins. The Caballero clique rushes about the country, organizes demonstrations, meetings, and conferences in the cities and in the countryside; in articles and speeches they are conducting a campaign against the Communist party, spreading slanderous rumors against the USSR, carrying out propaganda together with the anarchists in the countryside, persuading the peasants not to hand over the harvest to the government; they attack the government, are preparing a split in the Socialist party and in the UGT; they blackmail; and so on. This band of intellectuals or pseudo-intellectual, lower-class bureaucrats, lacking any moral or principled foundation, seeing that they are not succeeding in their fight against the Communist party, are spreading rumors everywhere about the fact that José Díaz is not ill at all, but that he was removed from leadership of the party because they discovered that he was a Trotskyist. And that the exact same "fate" awaits Dolores as well. The same kind of fantastic slanderous rumors are being spread concerning other leading party workers and against Communist soldiers.

The Caballeristas are propagandizing now the anarcho-syndicalist conception on the role of unions in the party. Every day, throughout the entire month of July, in Caballero's two newspapers in Valencia (*Adelante* and *Correspondencia Valenciana*) articles have appeared violently attacking the Communists. These articles are reprinted regularly and in full in all the anarchist press, such as *Fragua Social, Nosotros, Solidaridad Obrera, Castilla Libre, CNT,* and vice versa, the most anti-Communist articles from the anarchist newspapers are reprinted in the Caballerista press. At demonstrations organized by the anarchists, either Caballero personally or someone from his band appears. They elicit ovations from the anarcho-syndicalist public. They have already gotten to the point that two Caballerista newspapers, in chorus with the anarcho-syndicalist press, attack the organ of the Socialist party *El Socialista* and the newspaper *Claridad.* More than that, several Caballeristas carry on polemics with other members of the Socialist party through the anarcho-syndicalist press.

If I am not mistaken, in March I wrote to you that Caballero and his clique attracted and organized counterrevolution with a new content. I am recalling this to reemphasize Negrín's words, said by him five days ago concerning Caballero. When we said to Negrín that counterrevolutionary forces were gathering around the name of Caballero, Negrín answered: "Caballero has already become a personality and banner for the counterrevolution, and I will be forced before long to put him in prison, especially as we already have proof that he and Asensio are strongly implicated in the surrender of Málaga." The connections between the Caballeristas and anarcho-syndicalists and the Trotskyists are more obvious every day. More and more they begin to speak with the Trotskyist tongue, with the Trotskyist formulas. Araquistáin and company are preparing to issue a journal, a newspaper, and to write a book. Araquistáin called to Spain the renowned Shapiro, who in 1916–1919 specialized in writing pretentious, slanderous articles in Spain against the Bolsheviks. Later he became an agent and fellow traveler, through literature and journalism, of the [British] Intelligence Service. Several pieces of evidence show that he is connected to the Gestapo. He supports ties with Fenner Brockway. This Shapiro became here the personal secretary and informant of Araquistáin (on international questions). He does everything possible to get at Negrín.

*We will turn now to the Republicans.* The Republicans are beginning more and more to change their relationship with the Communist party. Not long ago, they regarded the Communist party with great respect. In June this began to change. First and foremost, Martínez Barrio and his group. They are drawing ever nearer to the CNT, beginning to get involved with them. There are mutual advances and flirtation. The CNT press "protects" the Republicans from the terrible danger threatening them after the merger of the Communist and Socialist parties. The anarchist press, which has always taken an offensive and slanderous position against Azaña, is beginning to extol him. The Caballeristas are tied to Martínez Barrio. This prominent representative and leader of Freemasonry supports ties with foreign countries, and these ties take him far beyond the bounds of the front. Several Republican newspapers, which never brought themselves to utter a harsh word against the Communist party, are now beginning to bark like little dogs at an elephant, although it is true that [they are] trembling [when they do so]. And their barking now finds an echo in the anarcho-syndicalist press. Another fact is Giral's attitude. He is becoming ever more silent. However, his silence did not hinder him (when one of the office workers "lost" a small suitcase on the street with the government's ciphers, codes, and keys to deciphering instructions) from speaking out against the "Russians," against the "Soviets," in the stupidest way. Another fact: the attitude of the Catalan Left. For a month, with a break of ten days, the Catalan Left has been carrying on a regular campaign against the Unified Socialist Party of Catalonia. Another fact: the speech by Azaña on the anniversary of the war—18 July. Everyone there was very unpleasantly struck by the fact that in the entire speech, not one word was uttered about the USSR. It is impossible to suggest that this was chance, unintentional forgetfulness. If you attentively read through this speech, you will notice that every word in it was well thought-out, considered. In this case to forget to talk about the Soviet Union means to do it in a politically deliberate way.

*On the anarcho-syndicalists.* The internal process of crisis among the anarcho-syndicalists is intensifying. Unfortunately, we are working poorly, we do not know how to work well in order to help the greater part of the working class free itself from the fetters of anarcho-syndicalism. The process of anarcho-syndicalism's crisis has several roots. First of all is the ever greater obviousness of how bankrupt [their] "constructive policy" and "social policy" is, the practice of "socialization" and "collectivization" carried out by the anarcho-syndicalists. Next is the ever clearer revelation that they lack a more or less consistent political line. The working masses, organized in the CNT, feel the need for a clear, consistent revolutionary policy. The anarcho-syndicalist leaders present them with an eclectic, empirical plagiarism, sonorous sentences without any content. The leaders of the anarcho-syndicalists are making an unbelievable effort to transform the FAI and the CNT into political parties. They do not have a program, but instead stunning formulations, which could serve as material for several issues of a humor magazine. They want to declare themselves a political party and at the same time are afraid and ashamed to do that. Their favorite phrase, repeated without end in every article, in every speech, is the phrase "new reorganization" of the FAI and the CNT. This new "reorganization" is viewed by the anarchists as some kind of marvel.

The anarcho-syndicalists wanted and want, whatever may happen, to participate in the government. They have tried to obtain this with all their strength and means. Nothing has come of it. And the workers, members of the CNT, are unhappy that the leaders of the CNT refused in May to participate in the government. To reduce this discontent, the leaders of the anarcho-syndicalists worked up and published a minimum program for the Popular Front government. They invited all of the parties and organizations for discussion of this program. Our party analyzed this program in our press. Our party also took part in the joint meetings called by the Central Committee of the CNT to discuss this program. Later the anarcho-syndicalists and Caballeristas tried to depict these meetings and discussions as action that ought to compel the government to reorganize on the basis of this so-called program discussion. Then our party, the Socialist party and the Left Republican party, except for the Republican Union, refused to participate in the so-called discussion and exposed the antigovernment maneuvers of the anarcho-syndicalists. After this, the anti-Communist campaign by the anarcho-syndicalists began with new ardor. A campaign against the Popular Front also began. Anarcho-syndicalist orators and press put out the slogan "The antifascist front and the Popular Front." The role of the Popular Front was finished after the elections of 16 February 1936, and especially after 18 July 1936. The Popular Front became the political instrument of counterrevolution. It had to be replaced by the antifascist front. And the antifascist front ought to be based on the CNT-UGT. This campaign was fervently supported by the Caballerista press. Moreover, the anarcho-syndicalist press in Madrid proceeded to add to this slogan the slogan "A workers' revolutionary alliance." In the course of several weeks they stupefied the people with this campaign; then, almost unexpectedly, they stopped it. In the course of the whole month of July the CNT, its press, its leaders did not stop carrying out a campaign to protect the Trotskyists. Speeches were delivered; leaflets were issued. In several of these leaflets, the real government is called a counterrevolutionary government. The Trotskyist leaflets were printed on anarcho-syndicalist presses. The illegal workers' office of the Trotskyists was located in no less a place than the office of the regional committee of the CNT in Catalonia. The anarcho-syndicalists want to use and are using the criminal policy of Zugazagoitia to protect the Trotskyist spies and to attack the Communist party. We have at our disposal a number of instructions and circulars and official resolutions of the CNT and FAI leadership, which point out that the main enemy is the Communists and that it is necessary to conduct a systematic campaign against the Communist party. They give practical instructions on how to carry out this campaign, and so on. Throughout the month of July, the sharpest campaign of slander and lies against the USSR has not ceased on the pages of the anarcho-syndicalist press. A rabid campaign of provocations. Everyday, in every newspaper, and—what is most disgusting—the censor allows all of this. And when we energetically protested against this to Negrín, he answered us, "You are right: I am ashamed of these censors, which are packed with either fools or enemies . . . "

In Catalonia, the anarcho-syndicalists, together with the Trotskyists, began a political separatist campaign some time ago, a campaign for the separation of Catalonia from the remaining part of Spain, especially to "be freed from the central Republican government," a government that desires to depict the national interests of Catalonia as imperialistic and threatening. When our comrade Ortega was director of public security and when he succeeded in upsetting the sabotage organization of Zugazagoitia, he did quite good work in disarming the anarchist extremists and Trotskyists. He continued the rather difficult job of establishing order in Aragon and methodically approached the disarmament of the anarcho-syndicalist band in Aragon. But Ortega was removed from his post. On the day of the departure from his post, Ortega, the commissar of public security, declared to us: "To rid Aragon of anarcho-Trotskyist bandit groups, who have arranged large supplies of weapons and ammunition, a real planned battle must be conducted from one village to another. I am afraid that after my removal this work will stop. I am afraid lest ten to fifteen days from now unpleasant events will begin in Aragon." This statement is beginning to be justified. At the moment that I was writing this letter, they informed me that the anarchist units located on the Teruel front have deserted the front, exposing that sector, and that the bandit group of anarcho-POUMists in Aragon has begun military action against Republican power. Simultaneously, they informed me that in several prominent villages of the province of Valencia coups are again in the offing.

History is repeating itself. Every time that the fascist army finds itself in a difficult situation, or every time their army begins an offensive on the Republican position, the anarcho-extremists and Trotskyists come to the aid of the fascist army and organize "uprisings" and coups. Our comrades from the party think that we must once and for all have done with such a state of affairs. At present, our comrade ministers just went to Negrín and Prieto and demanded that they have done with these coups and "uprisings" once and for all. I want to say once again, to repeat and emphasize, that such things will happen and are happening exactly because there is no firm policy, thanks to the indulgence and criminal help that is given by the powers of the provincial authorities (the Ministry of Internal Affairs) and by the military powers to the Trotskyists and "uncontrolled" anarchist extremists. There must be an end to the bureaucratic delays and sabotage that have surfaced over the issues of the need to reorganize the military forces on the Aragon front quickly and [an end] to the indulgence that allows the existence of an independent anarchist and CNT-ist military.

### 3. The Socialist Party

This party is also experiencing a deep crisis. The only salvation for the Socialist party is in unification with the Communist party, in the creation of a united party of the proletariat, and that as quickly as possible. If this unification is delayed, then the Socialist party is truly threatened with disintegration and dispersion into tiny parts. But unfortunately, the leaders of the Socialist party are not hurrying at all with unification. It is true that the last plenum of the national council of the Socialist party adopted a general resolution for unification. But at the end of the gathering of the national council, almost all the orators spoke out in their speeches "for the internal unification of the Socialist party" and directly or indirectly attacked the Communist party. One of the orators, Llanesa—from Asturias, a real Trotskyist, took the liberty of saying even such things as that the Communist party was prostituting itself to increase the number of its members. Another delegate spoke with slanderous statements about the fact that the members of the Communist party who joined the party after 18 July 1936 were elements of the fifth column, who had stolen their way into the Communist party. For three weeks the Caballeristas have been endeavoring to organize a dissenting congress of the Socialist party. Lamoneda, the general secretary of the Socialist party, who up to now has not inspired us with any great confidence in his efficiency on the matter of unity, has now become the most fervent defender of unity. Several days ago, in the name of the executive committee of the Socialist party, he dismissed the provincial committee of the Communist party, which had taken an anti-unity position, and replaced it with another committee that was pro-unity. He also expelled the anti-unity Caballeristas from the editorship of the newspaper *Adelante* and turned *Adelante* into a pro-unity organ of the Socialist party. The internal struggle is becoming more aggravated. A slogan was put out: "First of all, unity within the Socialist party must be achieved." And behind this slogan is concealed the following: "The unity of the Socialist party for struggle with the Communist party." The Caballeristas talk about this openly. They declare their readiness to give up all their disagreements on condition that the unity of the Socialist party be viewed as an instrument in the struggle against the Communist party. However, all of these attempts at a bloc and "unity" with missions like these will lead only to the complete disintegration of the Socialist party. The Socialist pro-unity leaders have displayed neither great activity nor great enthusiasm. They are afraid of unification, afraid that because of unification they will lose the posts that they occupy. In place of energetic, consistent work (propaganda, agitation, organization) on behalf of unification, they prefer to walk a tightrope of intrigue and internal concessions to the various groups and factions within the Socialist party. The main problem is reduced to retention of the posts that they hold in the government apparatus and unions. Instead of reaching an understanding honestly and loyally with the Socialist activists from the "left" wing, who have moved away from Caballero (such as del Vayo, Amaro del Rosal, Pretel, Llanos, and others) and carrying out the active campaign necessary for the political isolation of Caballero and his clique, the leaders of the executive committee of the Socialist party are trying to reach an understanding with the Caballeristas about the Communist party. In this way they will lead the Socialist party to its ruin.

The pro-unity movement of the Socialist workers widens and deepens with every day. In several places (Almería, Jaén, Estremadura, Ciudad Real, Murcia, Albacete, and others) many cases are already counted of local Communist and Socialist organizations that already do not organize separate gatherings but gather together, discuss, work, and together decide political and practical questions of a local nature. The liaison committees in the provinces are automatically turning into committees on merging. The open letter from the Politburo of the CC CPE, sent after the last plenum of the CC to the executive committee of the Socialist party, is everywhere taken as fundamental. Bearing in mind the slowness and modicum of enthusiasm put by the leaders of the Socialist party into the matter of realizing the resolution of the national council of the Socialist party, bearing in mind the opposition shown by them in calling a meeting that would explain the question of unification, our party decided to call meetings of a pro-unity nature ourselves in the majority of the cities of the nation. We must, finally, give the necessary explanations and urge the Socialist and Communist workers on toward unification, to ward off the Caballerista campaign and the campaign by the anarcho-syndicalists. The Unified Socialist Youth also decided to call analogous meetings.

The Caballeristas, who represent a majority in the executive committee of the UGT (and a minority in the National Committee of the UGT) decided to call a congress of the UGT. They thought that at this congress they would succeed in getting a majority and that, consequently, they would succeed in stirring up the UGT against the Socialist and Communist parties. But the non-Caballeristas and Communists make up a majority on the National Committee and the executive committee is appointed by the National Committee. Our party currently is carrying on negotiations with the leadership of the Socialist party to create a bloc in the National Committee in order to expel the Caballeristas from the executive committee of the UGT. At the very same time, our party made the decision to carry out a broad campaign throughout the country on the union question, on all those questions which are on the agenda of the future congress of the UGT, in order to be better prepared than in the past.

### 4. The Communist Party

I am very sorry that in all of my letters I dwell at length on all of the [other] issues and by comparison speak little about the Communist party. However, I would have been able to say and write a good deal, many interesting things both favorable and unfavorable about the Communist party. Unfortunately, even today I will not succeed in answering this question in full, the question of the life and work of the party. I will be able to give you some sporadic data. First of all, some words about the plenum of the Central Committee which just took place (it took place the 18, 19, 20, 21). The principal issue on the agenda was the issue of the political unity of the proletariat. I hope that you are familiar with the text of the speech given by Dolores. Despite the haste in preparing this speech, it was well received, especially well received by the Socialist workers. We were afraid at first that a few parts of this speech were too doctrinal, too historical, and that the Communist and Socialist workers would have difficulty taking it in. But judging by the evidence that we have, the Socialist and Communist workers are discussing and reading it with great interest. They criticize it, wishing to discuss it with Dolores, even the Caballeristas.

Among other questions at the plenum, the question of the role of unions in the organization of industry and the work of the unions, was discussed. This speech at the plenum was listened to with great interest, there was an interesting discussion and all the same, as before the plenum, so after it the issue still remains insufficiently clear. We ourselves have still not investigated it enough. These are very difficult and complicated issues. Chiefly, we do not have enough concrete data. Despite repeated reminders to gather the maximum number of particular facts, the maximum number of particular examples about organization work in business, in industry, about the work of the "managing committee," about the "control committee," about wages, about the role of the unions, and so on, so that it would be possible to do a critical analysis and move to reveal our conception—the issue was discussed more in general outline and remained insufficiently explained. Stubborn sectarianism is constantly substantiated in the work at the factories, in the work of the unions, [and] is indicated by the scant attention that is devoted to the material, practical, everyday life of the workers. At the same time, we have not yet come to a satisfactory agreement on the role of the union in the present exceptional transitional conditions, in the matter of organizing and leading the economy of the country. Personally, I think that outlines and fantastic plans should be avoided and that we must content ourselves with subordinating everything to the central task: winning the war. At the present time the criterion for organizing the economy of the country ought to be how to win the war. The third issue is the cadre policy of the party. This was little discussed, since there was no time. This was already on the fourth day of the plenum. It was impossible to detain the delegates. I was forced to protest, for this meant that the issue was insufficiently clear. To rectify this shortcoming, it was decided that after the plenum all of the regional and district organizations of the party and their cadres would be examined in a systematic way. This decision will really be put into effect. After the plenum the Politburo considered very thoroughly the situation in the Madrid, Murcia, Aragon, Jaén, Valencia, Asturias, Basque, Alicante, Almería, and Albacete committees. Practical measures to overcome the mistakes, to render assistance to the comrades, to reorganize the leadership. But on all these issues a full report must be submitted to you, or you will be incorrectly informed. I want to add only that the issue of the Basque central committee, and so on, was discussed for several days in a row with the participation of Astigarrabía, Larrañaga, Aranaga, Ormazábal. A decision was made to reform the leadership of the party, to remove Astigarrabía from the leadership and secretariat, and a decision was also made to reorganize the leadership in such a way that it would be collective and that it would be led by the entire organization of the Communist party in the north. Furthermore, a decision was made on revising the CC apparatus, the newspaper editorial staffs, the apparatuses of publishers and dissemination of literature, of various commissions. And it was clear, when we got down to work— we were convinced—that everything was far from all right, and that as soon as the verification and investigation are over, a purge and some expulsions must be carried out.

As for the authority and growth of the party's influence—they are unceasing. The influence of the party is growing more and more among the masses, and chiefly among the soldiers; the conviction is growing among them that the war and the popular revolution cannot end successfully if the Communist party does not take power into its hands. Who knows, that idea may indeed be correct. In any case, if our allies continue to drag us backward and continue their petty intrigues, it will be necessary to show courage, good organization, and effectiveness—it is definitely not ruled out that the day will come when the people will begin to demand the transfer of all power to the Communists!

*Some words about the International Brigades.* They are experiencing great difficulties. Many brigades and battalions lost many [men] wounded and killed. In several military units, soldiers and cadres have overstrained themselves. The new contingents are too insignificant to make it possible to carry out serious changes in composition. Relations with the Spanish military powers are not entirely good. Many wounded men and invalids remain without support or the right to it. The commander of the Albacete base was in such a state of depression that we were forced to dismiss him immediately. We set up an almost entirely new council. We worked up service regulations for the international volunteers and took steps so that these regulations were officially recognized by the government. Negrín already officially agreed with them. In these regulations, provisions are made for civilian and material rights, the right to security, to pensions, and so on, for the volunteers, as well as the obligations of the government with regard to them. Without this, the international volunteers were very often treated like recruits for the foreign legion. Political work among the volunteers continues to be very weak. There still remain a large number of wounded or physically sick volunteers who are demanding that they be sent to the USSR. In particular, this can be observed among the Bulgarians and other political emigrants whose families are in the USSR. Cadre work in the brigades, as earlier, is beneath every criticism. Neither in Albacete nor in the CC of the Communist Party of Spain is there any real organ that might devote itself to cadres.

*The health of Pepe Díaz.* Some improvement is noted. But not especially great. He has already added a million and a half red blood corpuscles. He now has three and a half million. Tomorrow he will be subjected to a medical examination to determine whether he may travel to Paris. The comrades from Paris informed me that they have everything necessary to secure the conditions required for the operation. We all feel how the absence of Pepe (Díaz) hinders us in our work. Checa and Hernández, about whom I already wrote you in one of my letters, feel significantly better and are working like Stakhanovites.

## The Decline of the International Brigades

Various historians have documented the growing morale problems after mid-1937 in the International Brigades. The remaining troops, their numbers diminished by battle losses, had been integrated into the ranks of the regular Republican army. One result was the proliferation of mutinies in various brigades, including a near uprising by the Irish and an American mutiny after the devastating Jarama battle of February 1937. In addition, some brigade members left to join liberal and anarchist troops. The volunteers also blanched at being forced into Comintern "re-education" camps, set up by the Soviets and guarded by Spanish PCE members. The troops, although ostensibly all volunteers, found that if they requested to be sent home after their tour of duty, they would instead be sent to the newly created camps. Others were enraged at what they saw as needless slaughter occurring because of the incompetence of their officers. One member of the British battalion, furious at the carelessness of General Gall, stated that he was not "fit to command a troop of Brownies, let alone a People's Army."[50] Harvey Klehr, John Earl Haynes, and Fridrikh Igorevich Firsov have written that "the severe problems with morale and desertion among the American volunteers in the Spanish Civil War and the ideological warfare and personal terror directed at some volunteers by their own comrades need to be honestly examined."[51]

Documents uncovered in the Soviet archives allow us to carry out just such an examination for the first time, not only for the Abraham Lincoln Battalion, but for the European International Brigades as well. Written in Spanish, **Document 47** from Comintern leader Luigi Longo ("Gallo"), a top Italian Communist who was the political commissar for the 12th International Brigade, provides evidence of the heavy sacrifices made by the volunteers. Longo also provides figures that reveal the new integration into the brigades of regular Spanish army troops.

In **Document 48** Grigory Shtern, writing on 23 June, expressed his worry about the state of the brigades, and called for the introduction of a firm leader to get them in shape. The Comintern was regularly receiving reports that could not have been heartening. The writer of **Document 49,** a "Confidential Note on the situation of the International Brigades at the end of July 1937," which was in French, was almost certainly Vital Gayman, a French Communist who went by the name Vidal in Spain. He was replaced as head of the Albacete base at the end of July, supposedly for embezzlement.[52] Gayman confirmed that brigade volunteers were dismayed to find that they were received by most political parties in Spain as "a foreign body, a band of intruders." He makes the striking assertion that arms were given exclusively to Spanish units, and not to the international volunteers, yet they were assigned "the most difficult sector in every battle." The unstated implication was that the brigades were being used as shock troops, for propaganda value, and not as a body seen as a serious fighting force. As Gayman argued, they were "automatically assigned to attack the most heavily fortified centers of resistance." He revealed that the brigade volunteers had been so disillusioned that one captain committed suicide rather than demand the impossible from exhausted troops. That brigade, he wrote, was "not destroyed; it has been murdered." Moreover, Gayman wrote that many of the brigade troops, whose failures were not their fault, were "branded as dangerous, undesirable elements" and denied even one day of rest. Others were "treated as undesirables," handed poor weapons, and sent to the front to be killed. Summing up the situation in the various units of the International Brigades, Gayman painted them as suffering from a serious lack of morale and growing disillusionment with their situation. Some, like the English battalion, had been subject to "collective desertions," which were also affecting officers. The report concluded that without immediate action, the brigades would be unable to perform the actions ordered by their commanders. Hence, the French Communists argued that they should be allowed to work honorably until they could be "removed without endangering Republican Spain."

The Soviets were also aware of the growing problems within the International Brigades. On 21 August 1937, Kirill Meretskov (who would later go on to become a marshal of the Soviet Union) and a Colonel Simonov sent Voroshilov their analysis of the brigades. Voroshilov saw the report, **Document 50**, as so important that he himself sent it on to Stalin, with a note suggesting that Stalin "familiarize" himself with its contents and proceed to give the commander and André Marty instructions on what steps should be taken. In the document, the two division commanders offer Marshal Voroshilov further corroboration of the poor state of the brigades. Reporting on conversations they had held with Comintern representative André Marty, they said that the French leaders complained that the brigades had "stopped being international," that some of their commanders were "in an extremely pessimistic mood," and that the 15th Brigade, in particular, of which the Abraham Lincoln Battalion was a part, had "suffered very heavy losses, which have still not been replaced." Moreover, brigade cadres were subject to "significant fatigue," and Marty confirmed that they were making "mass requests for furloughs." All of this had affected the command staff, and the commissars therefore showed little "confidence in victory." Their report of André Marty's comments, moreover, provides further evidence of how such dissatisfaction among the brigade troops was interpreted by the Comintern's chief in Spain as political deviation. Marty spoke of "increasing activity of provocative, hostile elements," of new "incidents" among the soldiers, and of the need to resolve an untenable situation quickly. The "political-moral state" was unsatisfactory, Marty concluded, and he demanded "that urgent measures be taken."

A report by the Comintern's new main representative, Palmiro Togliatti, which was written on 29 August 1937, confirmed the Soviet officers' opinions. In **Document 51** Togliatti, writing under the name Alfredo, describes the "feeling of fatigue" on the part of the volunteers, when the war had continued longer than they had expected. The initial enthusiasm that had led so many young idealists to volunteer had dissipated. Moreover, since the French government had closed the frontier, it was much harder to bring new recruits into Spain. It was this reality that necessitated putting Spanish soldiers into the brigade units. Togliatti's candid assessment also confirmed that it was the troops from the Western nations, especially France and the United States, that were demanding that they be sent home when their original tour of duty was up. And Togliatti noted that these frequent demands came not only from "bad or demoralized elements" but also from "the broad contingent of volunteers. and in almost every brigade."

Togliatti's view also revealed that the brigades had in effect become "shock troops" whose quality was declining, or even "Spanish brigades with a foreign command staff." Togliatti recommended transforming the brigades into a formal part of the Spanish army, keeping some of the units intact, and uniting the remaining units in a large new corps commanded by a Communist general.

The specific results of the changing composition of the brigades can be seen in **Document 52**, which was written in German. Here the division commander addressed the man in charge of the 11th (Thaelmann) Brigade, a German Communist named Staimer (or Colonel

"Richard") who would later become chief of police in Leipzig. The document shows that by late 1937 units such as the German brigade were in fact composed overwhelmingly of Spanish troops and yet were led by commanders who spoke no Spanish and for whom the troops had little respect. It is also apparent from the report that for those reasons the Spanish troops would not fight but left a small number of Germans to do battle on their own. His solution was to appoint commanders from the ranks of the Spanish troops, which he thought would increase the striking power of the brigades.

## Document 47

RGVA, f. 35082, op. 1, d. 42, ll. 255–249

Commissar of War
Inspector of the International Brigades          Madrid, 19 August 1937
     Madrid
Calle de Velázquez, 63
Telephone 57930 and 57939

Esteemed Comrade,

Attached I send a copy of the proposals for reorganizing the International Brigades and of a plan for a statute which has been sent to the general commissar of war in Valencia and submitted to the organs of government.

Antifascist greetings,

Commissar of War
Inspector of the International Brigades
Luigi Gallo

Commissar of War
Inspector of the International Brigades          Madrid, 19 August 1937
     Madrid
Calle de Velázquez, 63
Telephone 57930 and 57939

*Proposals for the Organization of the International Brigades*

*I. Role of the International Brigades*

The International Brigades played the same role as always in the last offensive: they took part in all of the most important operations and demonstrated

through their successes and their sacrifices that they may be counted among
the best brigades of the People's Army of Spain.

## II. *Troops of the International Forces*

### A. *Troops of the International Brigades(a) [sic]*

| Brigade | Before Offensive | After Offensive | Killed | Wounded | Disappeared |
|---|---|---|---|---|---|
| 11th | 3,555 | 2,390 | 165 | 519 | 200 |
| 12th | 2,134 | 1,658 | 45 | 245 | 87 |
| 13th | 1,957 | 868 | 150 | 480 | 80 |
| 14th | 1,645 | 1,600 | 5 | 30 | 8 |
| 15th | 2,144 | 885 | 293 | 735 | 167 |
| 150th | 1,910 | 1,640 | 121 | 320 | 50 |
| | 13,353 [sic] | 9,041 | 779 | 2,329 | 392 |

### B. *Troops of the other units with international combatants*

| | |
|---|---|
| International Battalion of the 86th Brigade | 1,008 |
| Two Companies of Machine Gunners on the Southern Front | 337 |
| Anti-air Artillery | 1,270 |
| Heavy Artillery, First Group | 264 |
| Heavy Artillery, Second Group | 250 |
| Clero and Peruggini Batteries | 150 |
| Train Regiments | 175 |
| 45th Division [ . . . ] | 1,565 |
| sum and continue | 5,019 |
| previous sum | 5,019 |
| 35th Division | 343 |
| 17th Division | 105 |
| 15th Division | 249 |
| Special Formations | 854 |
| | 6,570 |

### C. *Troops of the organic base* [International Brigade headquarters] *in Albacete*

a) Depot and selection:

| | | | |
|---|---|---|---|
| 1. Comrades preparing to leave for the front on 11 Aug. | 1,238 | | |
| 2. Comrades in treatment (2) | 405 | | |
| 3. Elements for repatriation | 200 | 1,843 | |
| b) Apparatus: | | | |
| 4. Staff, administration, base services | 1,071 | | |
| 5. Military workshops (3) | 435 | 1,506 | 3,349 |

# Document 47 *continued*

D. *Hospitalized Troops*

| | | |
|---|---:|---:|
| In all of Spain | 4,500 | |
| Comrades unfit for any service at the front hospitalized at Albacete | 434 | 4,934 |

Recapitulation of the present forces of the *International Units*

| | |
|---|---:|
| a) Troops of the International Brigades | 9,041 |
| b) Troops of other units with international combatants | 6,570 |
| c) Troops at the organic base in Albacete | 3,349 |
| d) Troops in the hospitals | 4,934 |
| Total | 23,894 |

(1) Neither the sick nor the Spanish battalions, which had been retired from the International Brigades after the offensive, figure in the troops of the International Brigades after the offensive.

(2) In the troops indicated by numbers 2, 4, and 5 figure a high percentage of unfit wounded men from all service at the front.

(3) Can recuperate from the troops of the staff, the administration of the base services, 300 comrades fit for the front, through restrictions in apparatus personnel by the gradual substitution of the fit for the unfit.

. . .

## V. Mixed Battalions

The experience of six months of combat with the international volunteers and with Spanish soldiers in the same brigades has demonstrated that it is necessary as a general policy to organize mixed battalions of internationals and Spanish.

## VI. Immediate Reinforcements

To reorganize and reinforce the International Brigades, it is necessary to provide immediately about 1,500 internationals and 3,000 Spanish, already trained.

These reinforcements ought to be distributed in the following manner to the different brigades:

| | | |
|---|---|---|
| 11th Brigade | 400 internationals | 500 Spanish |
| 12th Brigade | 150 " | 500 " |
| 14th Brigade | 300 " | 500 " |
| 15th Brigade | 400–500 " | 1,000 " |
| 150th Brigade | 200 " | 600–700 " |

. . .

# Document 48

RGVA, f. 33987, op. 3, d. 1056, ll. 27–28

Copy of a letter from Com. Shtern of 23/6/37

Dear Pavel Ivanovich,

I am sending two letters from Negrín and Prieto. These documents are essential, I believe. I informed you about their contents; it is just too bad that there was no decision. It is necessary to insist on a large new consignment of goods for us, for which I beg you—and for the shipment of this consignment immediately—otherwise everything will again be delayed and will produce less effect than it might.

Conditions with us here are more difficult than during any of my time here. The question of officers has presented itself in all its urgency, a segment clearly treacherous, a majority greatly vacillating, in connection with the failures in the north; only a small percentage of the officers are reliable. Every day we talked about this with Negrín and Prieto; our connections with them are very close, we see each other without ceremony three or four times a day. Don't conclude from this that everything is resolved easily, as well, but everyone is succeeding in obtaining a great deal. In an hour I am going to Madrid, and there is therefore no time to write; I will write in detail [in time] for the next post. In general, you work for twenty hours a day minimum, and all the same you don't do all of it. The new people are really weak, especially Lopatin, who is obviously out of place here—he doesn't know how to behave with our people or with the "friends."[53]

Well, all right, we can go into that separately. Just one more thing—I have begun to worry a great deal about the state of the International Brigades. There is a lot going on there: the attitude of Spaniards toward them and of them toward the Spaniards; the questions about morale; the chauvinism of the nationalities (especially the French, Poles, and Italians); the desire for repatriation; the presence of enemies in the ranks of the International Brigades. It is crucial that a big man be dispatched quickly from the big house especially for the purpose of providing some leadership on this matter. I talk about this a lot with our agents,[54] go myself to the brigade, work through our people, but this is too little—we need a strong man on this job. In a few days, at my insistence, the agents are going to lead a meeting of commanders and commissars of the International Brigades.

Your Grigory

Correct:
Colonel Shpilevsky
2 July 1937

# Document 49

RGVA, f. 35082, op. 1, d. 90, ll. 539–533

### Confidential Note on the situation of
### the International Brigades at the end of July 1937

The present note will doubtless appear pessimistic, but it is written by a militant conscious of his responsibilities, who has ceaselessly sounded the alarm, only to go unheard, during the last several months, whenever any threats to the International Brigades have emerged.

I believe that today, at the end of July 1937, I must tell my superiors, those who have military and political responsibility for the International Brigades, what I consider to be the exact truth:

The great majority of officers, noncommissioned officers and volunteers in the International Brigades, are militants or political men who know how to see, judge, and understand. Whether they be Communist or Socialist, Republican or antifascist with no defined political party, today all are consumed by the idea that the International Brigades are considered to be a foreign body, a band of intruders—I will not say by the Spanish people as a whole, but by the vast majority of political leaders, soldiers, civil servants, and political parties in Republican Spain.

Tracing the reasons for this state of mind among Spanish comrades of whatever rank or organization is beyond the purview of this note. What is true is that, at least superficially, numerous facts justify the opinion gradually spreading through the ranks of the internationals. Among these facts, I will cite the following:

• First, it is the prevailing opinion among high officers in the Spanish army, more or less irrespective of political affiliation, that the International Brigades are nothing but a foreign legion, an army of mercenaries fighting for money, who therefore have only one right: the right to obey. Do not say I exaggerate. The fact is known, it is patently clear. It is possible to debate only whether this opinion of the International Brigades is more or less widespread. Certainly the militants in the International Brigades are quite aware of this situation; they cannot help perceiving this treatment as an insult to their antifascist convictions and to the millions of comrades who came with them and have since fallen in defense of Republican Spain.

• The unequal treatment of the Spanish and the International Brigades further justifies the opinion emerging among the international militants, who have been treated like a foreign legion ready to be sacrificed, to which no attention need be paid. This difference in treatment is striking in matters of arms and tactical deployment.

Arms? At the same time that the International Brigades are denied permission to replace out-of-date arms (worn-out machine guns no longer able to function or machine guns destroyed in the course of fighting), they are refused an allotment of mortars and automatic rifles, on the pretext that there are none available. These weapons are provided not only to the new Spanish brigades, but also to the old ones.

Tactical Deployment? When it comes to leave, the International Brigades are treated like no Spanish brigade. There are International Brigades that have remained at the front for 150 consecutive days. For lesser units, seven consecutive months (and they are not going to be relieved any time soon). Even if Spanish units have endured treatment of this kind under extraordinary circumstances, the staff headquarters must realize that it cannot expect an effort of this type, on this terrain, from an International Brigade.

Tactical Deployment? The volunteers in the International Brigades are under the impression that they are systematically entrusted with the most difficult sector in every battle. In the beginning, they ascribed this to the fortunes of war. Today, they no longer accept it when they are told that their situation is a coincidence, and they see instead a concerted effort to annihilate and sacrifice the international contingents.

If the last battles were in fact to be analyzed, the number of losses, or better the percentage of losses, would demonstrate that the International Brigades have always found themselves faced with the centers of enemy resistance. This cannot be ascribed to chance. I am absolutely convinced, as are the volunteers, that the International Brigades are automatically assigned to attack the most heavily fortified centers of resistance. It will be argued this is a mark of trust and honor. The facts I will discuss in a subsequent paragraph, however, demonstrate that far from being appreciated, the heroic sacrifices endured by the International Brigades were held to be the results of their own mistakes, because the internationals did not succeed in removing the fortified targets they were assigned as rapidly as certain Spanish brigades had seized undefended positions.

Tactical Deployment? The international volunteers clearly realize that while Spanish brigades receive enough reinforcements to maintain their battalions at more or less normal strength, the International Brigades receive reinforcements only with the greatest difficulty. Often, on the day before a battle, international units fill out their ranks with an influx of mutinous battalions or untrained recruits. But generally, the International Brigades are never at full strength. They have 40, 50 or 60 percent, maximum, of the strength of a brigade—of the Spanish brigade that relieves them. This does not prevent the International Brigades from being given equivalent missions and a sector of the same size, if not larger; thus every man in the International Brigade will have to do the work of two or three men in a Spanish brigade.

All these facts are known. When the facts I will discuss below intervene, they make the minds of the volunteers propitious terrain for demoralization.

I have just asserted that the fact International Brigades are assigned to attack the most solid points on the enemy line cannot be considered a mark of honor and trust. This is proved by the manner in which certain military leaders of the International Brigades have been treated.

Relieving the commanding officer of the 13th Brigade—after the unit's combat experience at Teruel, on the Málaga front, at Pozoblanco, and after the unit had suffered such frightful losses—is an act that I believe constitutes nothing other than a political and military crime. I do not want to judge the commander of the 13th Brigade. I know his relationship with the mass of men in the brigade was not the closest; though the men had respect and affection for him, he did not develop the popularity that alone distinguishes true leaders. Nevertheless, given the physical and mental condition of this battalion's volunteers after 150 consecutive days at the front, the removal of comrade Gómez on the day before the battle had the following effect: despite their fatigue and exhaustion, the men of the brigade, feeling solidarity with their leader, whom they believed unjustly stricken, desperately fought to the extreme limits of their mental and physical strength. The case of Captain ROEHR is particularly telling. He was a thirty-two-year-old man with a wife and child, who had fought heroically up to that point; he committed suicide in battle because he could no longer accept the responsibility of demanding renewed effort from exhausted men, and at the same time felt he did not have the right to demand rest for his men from his superiors.

I am quite afraid that after the losses suffered in the last battle, and the weakening of morale caused by the removal of Comrade Gómez and subsequent incidents, like the Roehr affair—I am afraid this brigade will be permanently unable to fight.

This brigade is not destroyed, it has been murdered.

Since the battle of Navalcerada and Balsin, the situation of the *14th Brigade,* and of its commanding officer, is not significantly different. Officers and volunteers know that their brigade and their commanding officer are under suspicion. They know they have just been given orders to deliver the guns of their dead and wounded to the army supply depot. These weapons were taken from the battlefield and represent the brigade's only hope of being able to arm its reinforcements, whether they come from Albacete or from other centers of Spanish mobilization.

In the case of the *15th Brigade,* how could the officers ignore the threat made against General Gall after the capture of Villanueva de la Cañada and the crossing of the Guadarrama, a threat made solely because the general did not finally succeed in his attempt to take the two positions of Romanillos and Mosquito—even though the failure of the Spanish brigades marching ahead of him forced him to launch the attack before the established time, and with a reduced troop strength.

These three examples incontestably prove what I have said about the tactical deployment of the International Brigades. They prove further that in matters concerning the International Brigade, it is always their weaknesses and failures, never their successes and sacrifices, that are brought to light. How can men avoid having their morale weakened under these conditions, when in fact the majority of them have nothing to reproach themselves for politically or militarily?

I would like to add the following list of specific facts to those above:

• The treatment of the international elements assigned to the different formations of tanks and armored cars. Only a few dozen of the 200 or 250 men the International Brigades assigned to these formations remain today. The others were killed, [or] disabled by wounds received in combat. Their courage, as far as I know, has never been questioned. The wounded were forced from their units under ignominious conditions, branded as dangerous, undesirable elements who were not even granted a day of rest at the Archena center. Instead, after traveling four hundred kilometers by truck to Archena, they were forced to leave directly for Albacete the evening they arrived. There were officers among them, seriously wounded men, men who will be permanently disabled. Despite all the attention paid to their morale by the military and political militants at the Albacete base, there is no doubt that these forty men are now a factor of demoralization, about which nothing can be done; they were unable to withstand the treatment to which they were subjected.

• It is the same with the artillerymen. The batteries assigned to the International Brigades in November and December of 1936 are now without weapons, which have either been worn out or destroyed by enemy fire. These officers and men have proved both their technical competence and their courage in the course of seven months of war. They were undeniably the best artillerymen in the Spanish People's Army during these last months. Today, they notice that they do not receive new weapons to replace the old. In one case, the commander of an artillery division, a brave and experienced gunner, had only a single gun under his command, which he fired until it gave out—that is, until his worn-out weapon refused to give up its last shell.

Finally, there are the cadres of officers and artillery specialists who have been in Spain, grouped at Almansa, since last February. They were not given guns until July 1937; though they were happy to receive their cannon and leave for the front, the conditions under which the weapons were presented allowed the men to realize they were being given the cannon to be gotten rid of, that they were in fact treated as undesirables.

In addition, for the first time in the history of the International Brigades, the headquarters of the I.B. was not informed when these two heavy artillery groups were armed. The general inspectorate of the Spanish artillery chose the commanding officers of these two artillery groups over the heads of both the commander of the headquarters and the commander of artillery. The inspectorate thus clearly demonstrated its lack of confidence in the leaders of the International Brigades.

• Finally, I will return to the facts already mentioned in the recent memorandum on "several questions that require immediate solution and are of vital importance to the life of the International Brigades."[55]

First, there is the message sent to the commander of the International Brigades' headquarters about the exchange of telegrams between the army chief of staff and the central chief of staff, which took place on 9 July 1937. I do not think a delivery error or a subordinate's mistake caused the documents to be sent to the commander of the I.B. headquarters. I am convinced that this was a characteristic act of provocation, intended to make the men in the International Brigades aware of the administrative staff's opinion of them; not only of the brigades' supposedly "nonregulation" administration, but also of their "inadequate" leadership and their tactical deployment, which logically must be poor as well.

Second, I want to mention the cigarettes sent to the International Brigade volunteers by the Belgian and Dutch SRIs [International Red Help]. The director of the tobacco monopoly used his pen to transform these two million individual cigarettes *into two million packs,* which allowed him to invite all branches of the army—ground, air, and sea—to ask the International Brigades for these foreign cigarettes. Once again, this was an act of provocation, which sent the Spanish comrades the following message: "You do not have foreign cigarettes, English or American, because the internationals have taken them all. Send them your requests."

• I would like to cite one more fact. Last April, via the Madrid artillery depot, General Miaja sent Major Maurice, commander of the artillery groups at the International Brigade base, eight pieces of artillery taken from the Italians at the battle of Guadalajara: two 75-mm. pieces, and six 65-mm., all incomplete.

These pieces were transported to the Spanish Naval Construction Company at Cartagena under the auspices of the I.B. base. At the cost of sometimes laborious transportation, the I.B. base gave this company plans and special steel for the fabrication of breeches. Today, authorization to rebuild these pieces, requested only at the end of July, has been refused. In other words, they prefer to leave eight potentially reparable pieces of artillery unused, rather than see them go to the International Brigades.

Before concluding, I will give my opinion on the morale of each of the International Brigades:

*11th Brigade:* Currently, the international troops of this brigade only account for 10 to 15 percent of its total troop strength. Until now, because of the high political quality of the soldiers, most of whom are German, alarming signs of disintegration and demoralization have not appeared, but it is worth noting that given the composition of this brigade (15 percent international and 85 percent Spanish), the consequences of possible demoralization among the 15 percent international (German) cadres could be more serious here than anywhere else.

*12th Brigade:* The commander of this brigade has recently submitted his resignation. This is a very clear sign that the brigade's morale is suffering. Increasing numbers openly espouse the idea that the four hundred Italian comrades who remain have accomplished their task, and that the time has come to demobilize them, if the officer corps is not to be decimated by Italian emigration.

*13th Brigade:* For reasons I have already discussed above, out of combat at present, and undergoing a very difficult reorganization and reconstitution.

*14th Brigade:* Its commanding officer suspended. Without hope of receiving reinforcements and being returned to normal strength. The brigade's morale is in a worrisome state. In any case, as long as it is not reinforced with troops and arms, it cannot be considered a brigade, because its troop strength is smaller than that of two normal battalions.

*15th Brigade:* Has withstood enormous losses. Four of its battalions have been consolidated two by two, to form only two battalions.

The English battalion has fallen victim to a wave of collective desertions, which has begun to affect the American battalions. The officers are not excluded from this process of demoralization.

*150th Brigade:* Command difficulties. The commanding officer has just been removed. I do not have the details.

*86th Brigade:* Command difficulties, as long as the pseudo-Mexican colonel Gómez's situation is not definitively settled.

*Artillery formations:* Discontent in the batteries supplied with cannon; despite the fact they belong to a brigade (the case of the battery of the 15th Brigade), these batteries are maintained in a sector different from that of their brigade.

Demoralization of artillerymen who follow their brigade when they do not have cannon.

*The International Brigade base.* Demoralization among the unfit or disabled elements who still hope for their cases to be resolved, though this resolution is postponed from week to week.

Demoralization, or at least impatience, among the men in training battalions and their commanding officers (the American training battalion has about five hundred men), who have no idea when they will have to leave, either as part of a new unit or to reinforce old American battalions, because: 1. there are no arms available to equip them either at the I.B. base or in the brigades themselves. (The second American battalion sent to the 15th Brigade on 10 June 1936 [*sic*] was armed with rifles taken from artillerymen, engineers, etc., along with the last reserves from the brigade armory.) 2. because [*sic*] no steps have been taken to add the planned complement of Spanish troops to this battalion, and the chief of staff of the base refuses to create new battalions from 100 percent international troops. Lastly, demoralization of departments like the supply corps, whose members are discouraged by how difficult it has become to obtain authorizations for the purchase of provisions, and for the supply of equipment and clothing required by the brigades or reinforcements assembled at the I.B. base.

The picture of the International Brigades' military and political situation sketched here is not as dark as one might think. Doubtless, these processes of demoralization can be stopped. In some cases, the symptoms indicate potential demoralization, rather than the disease itself. But decisive and rapid action is required.

If these problems are not dealt with efficiently and in a timely fashion, I can say without hesitation that the situation will be the following:

1. Soon, the International Brigades will no longer be capable of performing the military tasks with which they might be entrusted by their commanders. Now, I believe I can affirm that whatever some say their faults may be, the International Brigades still represent a quarter of the Spanish army's shock units. There is not an army in the world that can spare a quarter of its shock units.

2. From a political point of view, a fraying, a disintegration of the units that compose the International Brigades would be an event with international repercussions that need not be elaborated upon here.

At all costs, the International Brigades must be allowed to accomplish their tasks under honorable conditions until such time as they can be removed without endangering Republican Spain; the survivors among the twenty-four thousand volunteers who have come to Spain must not be left with the impression that their sacrifices for the cause were ignored or in vain.

\* \* \* \* \* \* \* \* \* \* \* \* \* \* \* \* \* \* \* \* \* \* \* \* \* \* \* \* \* \*

This is why—though I am convinced that those who will be entrusted with the duties and responsibilities that were mine for ten months know exactly how to meet the demands of the situation and am equally convinced that my departure will not provoke any kind of reaction among the International Brigades tomorrow—I believe it is my duty, at the moment when I must step down from the command of the International Brigade base, to provide a truthful account of the brigades' situation, so that measures might still be taken to avoid regrettable or painful events.

The solution? It cannot be found in partial measures. An overall solution is required that would attack the problem at its root.

## Document 49 *continued*

In other words, the situation of the International Brigades must be treated as a whole, on a political level, as it always should have been.

The volunteers of the International Brigades have certain legitimate interests and rights that must be respected. They can no longer be considered a "foreign legion." Their status must be determined definitively. Their rights must be officially recognized. They must no longer be subjected to the unfavorable treatment they suffer currently, or else the experience of true solidarity in the struggle against fascism, and the heroic conduct of men from all countries of the world, who have possibly saved Republican Spain four times—at Madrid in November and December, at Las Rozas in January, on the Jarama in February, at Guadalajara in March—will leave nothing but a few heroic pages in the history of the revolution, along with the memory of a political failure.

## Document 50

RGVA, f. 33987, op. 3, d. 1033, ll. 95–101

[Marginalia by Voroshilov:]
To Comrade Stalin: I ask that you familiarize yourself [with this] and if possible give the necessary instructions to Coms. Dimitrov and Marty on the necessary steps with regard to the International Brigades needed in "X" (in my opinion, everything is still at an extreme), and on other questions raised here. K. Voroshilov 21/8/37.

*Top Secret*
Copy No. 1

To the People's Commissar of Defense of the Union of SSR
Marshal of the Soviet Union
*Com. Voroshilov, K. E.*

In accordance with your directions, I and Colonel Simonov today had a conversation with Com. André Marty, member of the presidium of the COMINTERN.

Com. Marty reported, through the latest data that he has, on three groups of issues concerning the civil war in Spain.:

1. The state of the International Brigades
2. Questions concerning the naval war and blockade
3. Questions concerning the mobilization of industry

We report a summary of the information and proposals of Com. Marty:

# Document 50 *continued*

I. *The State of the International Brigades*

*11th International Brigade*
German-Austrian. Has three battalions. The fourth is forming. In composition the brigade is only 8–10 percent internationalists (in the entire brigade are around 200 men); remaining composition—Spanish. In actuality, the brigade has stopped being international.

*12th International Brigade*
Italian. Has three battalions. Italians are slightly more than 200 men; remaining composition is also Spanish. Commander of the brigade, an Italian Pacciardi (Socialist) is in an extremely pessimistic mood.

*13th International Brigade*
Mixed composition. Has four battalions, very weak numerically. 1st Battalion (Chapaev) has 90 men, internationalists from the peoples of Central Europe and 300 Spanish recruits. 2nd Battalion—French—has 40 Frenchmen. 3rd and 4th Battalions are Spanish.

*14th International Brigade*
Franco-Spanish. Total number of the brigade is only 1,100 men.

*15th International Brigade*
Mixed composition. Has five battalions. 1st Battalion—English; 2nd Battalion—American; 3rd Battalion—Franco-Belgian; 4th Battalion (Dimitrov)—Slavic; and 5th Battalion—Spanish. In the July battles the brigade suffered very heavy losses, which have still not been replaced.

*16th International Brigade*
Mixed composition. Very weak in numbers and has an insignificant percentage of internationals. Is on the southern front.

*50th International Brigade* (Dombrowski)
Polish. Has four battalions. In the 1st Battalion are only 200 Poles. In the 2nd Franco-Belgian Battalion—100 Frenchmen. In the 3rd Battalion (Rakosi)—100 men of Balkan nationality. In the 4th forming battalion—120 Poles.

*Independent Battalion Dzhurakovich*
Yugoslavian. Has 100 men. Given to the 45th Division.

*Independent American Battalion*
Forming again. Has 325 men. Given to the 15th Division.

*Two Independent Machine-Gun Companies*
French. Weak composition. A long time on the southern front—near Andújar.

*Artillery.*
Besides the earlier formed batteries, six batteries of 155 mm. are forming in Almansa. Of these, three have already been sent to the front.

*Albacete Base.*
*Reinforcement companies*—every five days 120 men are sent to the front from the numbers of returning wounded, sick, and so on.

## Document 50 *continued*

*Reception battalion*—there are about 40 men who are newly arrived in Spain.
*Influx of New Reinforcements.*
Newly arrived in Spain:

| | |
|---|---|
| in April | 200 men |
| in May | 300 men |
| in June | 900 men |
| in July | 700 men |
| (20 days) | |
| TOTAL | 2,100 men (of that number 1,000 Americans) |

For June and half of July on the front 2,400 men were sent in all (both new reinforcements and from the numbers of convalescents).

Next month the dispatch to Spain of about 3,000 men, new reinforcements, is being prepared.

*Political-Moral State.*

Significant fatigue is felt. Mass requests for furloughs to France and to other countries.

Among the units of the command staff and soldiers is a pessimistic mood, and the lack of confidence in victory (the latter has especially strengthened since the operation at Brunete).

Recorded increasing activity of provocative, hostile elements.

The number of incidents of friction and conflicts on an inter-nationality basis have increased.

*Com. Marty's Conclusions.*

On the basis of these facts, and also of all the rest of the information, Com. Marty believes that

1. A systematic process of dispersion of the international cadres is occurring, which essentially threatens the self-destruction of the International Brigades.
2. The leadership of the International Brigades and the international formations has significantly weakened, both in military units and in political ones.
3. Attention and assistance for the International Brigades from our military advisers has weakened.
4. The political-moral state of the International Brigades is unsatisfactory and requires that urgent measures be taken.

*Com. Marty's proposals.*
Com. Marty proposes:

1. To end the dispersion of the cadres.
2. To end the formation of new battalions until the existing ones are reinforced and brought to full strength.
3. To gather the uncoordinated independent battalions and companies and to infuse them to bring the existing units up to full strength.

# Document 50 *continued*

4. To regroup the battalions of the existing brigades so that each brigade has a homogenous national composition.
5. In case of need, from the existing seven brigades to keep only five, but to make these five full-blooded.
6. Not to allow the intermingling of internationalists with Spaniards in battalions and lower. To consider that each International Brigade ought to have no fewer than two to three full-blooded international battalions and no more than one to two Spanish battalions.
7. Using the suspension of control on the Spanish borders in every way possible, to force the influx of volunteers, taking it to a minimum of 3,000 men a month.
8. To ensure for the internationalists, both for individuals and for subunits, a brief rest (furloughs) within Spain.
9. To strengthen the political and military leadership of the International Brigades and the new formations; in particular, to strengthen the assistance from our military advisers to the leadership of the international units and formations.

II. *Questions Concerning the Naval War and Blockade*

Com. Marty believes that the open sea blockade that was begun by the fascists in the last few days and the assaults to sink *all* steamers coming to the shores of Republican Spain are fraught with very serious consequences. In the first place *this threatens to leave Spain without reinforcements of ammunition and weapons for the army, without fuel, and without coal; also it worsens the problem of food.*

Com. Marty believes that not enough measures for the struggle with the blockade have been taken.

From his experience, derived from the World War, he proposes:

1. To revive the operation of the Spanish navy, putting into action all the small and auxiliary ships that, from every kind of often petty damage, remain idle.
2. To organize the escort of mercantile vessels by military ships.
3. To adapt and arm all mercantile vessels (with one to two guns per ship).
4. To take from mercantile vessels untrustworthy individuals and replace them with better [men]; in particular—he is offering Communist sailors in large numbers and of various specializations, ready to voluntarily make for Spain from France.
5. To train the personnel of the merchant marine the elementary tactics of fighting with submarines (Com. Marty argues that with the correct tactics, fighting with submarines can be completely successful).
6. To organize a large-scale network of radio eavesdroppers for the enemy's vessels.

## Document 50 *continued*

7. To employ aircraft for the struggle with submarines (in particular, to use the aircraft carrier that the Republicans have, having repaired it).
8. To undertake attempts to buy small military vessels abroad (in the first place, submarine destroyers).

III. *Questions on the Mobilization of Industry*

Com. Marty believes that, according to the information that he has, the mobilization of industry in Spain is experiencing difficulties. Thus, lately, of the 240 industrial works in Barcelona, only 40 are working on defense, and the remaining 200 are occupied with whatever they like, just not military orders. Com. Marty believes that under conditions of an open naval blockade, this question acquires an especially great significance and proposes to put this matter right decisively.

On the essence of the proposals advanced by Com. Marty we report that all of them, in our opinion, are expedient and pressing. Some of them were formulated by Com. Marty as a result of and in the process of conversations with us.

Moreover, we report that Com. Marty proposes in the near future to head for Spain, not to work permanently, but just by way of getting acquainted with the situation on the spot.

[What was] stated we report for your attention.

Division Commander
Meretskov

Colonel
Simonov

21 August 1937
Moscow

---

## Document 51

RGVA, f. 33987, op. 3, d. 961, ll. 24–33

*Top Secret*
Translated from French

29 August 1937

The situation in the International Brigades as a whole cannot be deemed good. A number of measures must be taken in order to improve their situation.

*One senses fatigue in the brigades.*

The war has dragged on significantly longer than the time that our comrades foresaw. Many volunteers, who came here counting on only a few months, are now worried about their own fate and that of their families and affairs. This concerns most of all the volunteers from legal countries (France, the United States of America, and so on); this kind of talk is being heard: "Should we stay here until, from one offensive to another, we are all killed or badly wounded?" (information presented by Com. Gallo about the 12th Brigade). The question of returning comes up ever more frequently and more insistently. The question is raised not only by some bad or demoralized elements, whom consulates sent home; the question comes up in general and is raised by a broad contingent of the volunteers, and in almost every brigade. The representative of the Communist Party of the United States, for instance, placed before the CC and the secretariat of the Communist Party of Spain a demand that all American volunteers be sent back after a six-month stay in Spain. The arguments that he brought forward were very reasonable (the question concerns comrades who have for the first time left their own country for a long time; several of them received six-month leaves at the companies in which they worked before; and so on. Besides that, almost everywhere we are talking about good party cadres, and, finally, when they enlisted, they were promised, like the English and Italian comrades, that they would be in Spain no more than six months). He added that the American party will continue and increase recruitment to replace those volunteers who are returning to their homeland with fresh people capable in military matters, but who, in turn, ought to be sent home after a six-month stay in Spain. In my opinion, such a suggestion ought to be accepted. The problem takes on an acute quality in the Italian brigade. The brigade commander (Pacciardi—a Republican, a very adroit demagogue, quite close to the soldiers, perhaps even more so than our comrades), at the conclusion of the Brunete operation, openly raised the question about disbanding the Italian brigade. He argued his proposal as follows: "Together with the Garibaldi Brigade, we gained some capital (authority, "glory," and so on); if we remain here longer, we will lose all that, because our losses are more from day to day, because it is difficult to continue recruiting new Italians, because the Spanish recruits that are with us are not fit for anything (in general this guy treats all Spaniards with contempt), and so on, and so on. It would be best of all to send people back home and disband the brigade." After these declarations he left his post and went to Paris, where at a meeting of party representatives, who had created the brigade, he raised the same question as above. At the meeting there were representatives of the Communist party, the Socialists, and the Republicans. They convinced him of the need to return, but it was clear that he would return with the firm intention of actually disbanding the brigade, beginning with sending back the majority of the volunteers; he will not, of course, send the Communists back first. Pacciardi is being supported on this question by Pietro Nenni (openly), and our Italian Communist party already made a lot of concessions at that meeting in Paris. It is true that we must work on the evacuation of the most exhausted Italian comrades, but simultaneously with this we must carry out a new round of recruiting. However, the Socialists (in particular Nenni) and the Republicans openly refuse to carry out a new round). The work on recruiting will have to be carried out exclusively on the strength of our party, with the help of some mass organizations, which exist in exile (unions, committees of the Popular Front, and so on).

The other reason for fatigue, in the opinion of almost all the comrades with whom I spoke, is that the brigades are not always used efficiently. And in actual fact, they view them as shock troops, they send them into all the most important operations, but they do not allow them to rest between two operations, they do not give them the opportunity to re-form thoroughly after especially difficult operations, and so on. This explains the decrease in the fighting value of some brigades and the unpleasant events taking place in some of them (like, for example, the incident during the Brunete operation).

Second remark: *the quantity of volunteers in the brigades is declining every day,* owing to the large losses that they have suffered and the lack of recruiting of new volunteers. The percentage of foreigners in the brigades has fallen to 20 [percent] and what is even more serious, this percentage is lower in the battle units and in the forward positions than on the general staffs, in the rear, and at the bases. If measures are not taken quickly, the brigades will change character and be transformed into Spanish brigades with a foreign command staff. But for a number of reasons, such a transformation is undesirable. Most important, the Spanish government will not agree to it. It is demanding that the percentage of foreigners ought to be 40–50. Second, taking into account the difficulty in bringing foreign cadres closer to Spaniards, these brigades will not be good brigades. Undoubtedly, in such brigades mistrust, discord, and lack of discipline will appear. Thus, from this, it is necessary to dwell on the mission of new wide-scale recruiting; this question is very critical. This means that I completely reject the idea of liquidating the brigades. They have played a paramount role, and it still lies ahead for them to fulfill a great mission, not only as model units, but as an actual real force that is absolutely dedicated to the Popular Front government.

I will now turn to the brigades' organizational problem.

Everyone complains about the fact that the brigades do not have any leadership, and, in actual fact, in this connection the results of a number of mistakes, incorrect orientation in the past, and so on, are felt. This is the result of the interest in the brigades of a number of individuals and authorities whose work was not coordinated by anyone or in any way.

The leaders of the Spanish Communist party recognize that up to now, they knew nothing about the brigades. Up to today, there is still no member of the

CC CPE who would be systematically interested in this problem. Various commanders of the bases have not undertaken the necessary measures to communicate with the leadership of the Spanish party, acting in disregard of or independently from the party.

The base command, for its part, did not have enough authority in the eyes of the brigade command. The latter did not recognize the categorical authority of the base command; at times they even refused to recognize it, sending off defiant letters.

On the one hand, a tendency has long existed and still exists now in the brigades to act independently of the Spanish government, resolving their problems outside it, and this tendency has led to a contemptuous attitude toward all Spaniards in general. On the other hand, you know about the mistrust for the brigades on the part of the government and the Spanish army in the past. This mistrust has not gone away; not long ago at all this came to light even in attitudes toward the brigades by such a person as General Miaja, who used a completely impolite expression about the brigades, the Albacete base, and several brigade commanders, and so on. There were measures taken by him in relation to several elements from the brigades that caused indignation in the brigades (the arrest of Krieger). It seems to me that the comrades commanding the brigades do not always behave in such a way as not to allow friction and incidents. It is necessary to take into account that if several months ago, when the brigades had just gone into action at Madrid, represented a force that was significantly superior to the Spanish units from every point of view, then it is impossible to say that about them today. Today there are already Spanish brigades that are on a level with the International Brigades and, it is possible, even higher than they are. This concerns also the question of discipline: here's an example—I saw how the Lister Brigade threw itself into the Aragon front and I formed a better impression (as to the physical state of the soldiers, their bearing, neatness of uniforms, state of discipline in general) than about the two International Brigades (the 11th and 12th) that I saw marching to that same front. Taking into account the new state of things, it is easy to understand why among the Spanish officers, chiefly, there is a dissatisfied element that grumbles that the International Brigades consider themselves some kind of special force, and of course they use every opportunity to annoy the international volunteers.

The problem of the brigades' internal organization is complicated by the various [sorts of] interferences in its life by fraternal parties. Every party representative is naturally interested in the first place in the cadres of his own party (tries to promote them, protect them). This is right. But taking into account the lack of central leadership, which would coordinate all this work, all of this leads to confusion. Thus, for example, today the brigades are full of officers. In the 11th Brigade there are 250 officers for 2,000 men. The base in Albacete is full of people who have not even once been to the front, and the

Spaniards (the army general staff) are protesting against this situation. Comrade Franz—who is working hard among the cadres of his party—sent the chief of the brigade general staff (Renn) abroad without letting the appropriate heads of the army know. On his own initiative, on the eve of an operation, he pulled the 60 best comrades out of the 12th Brigade and sent them to the party school. This is a wonderful method for preserving the cadres, but for the organizational work within the brigade, it was disorganization. Look at the case with Pacciardi (12th). He went to Paris and there at a meeting of the Italian party decided the question whether he ought to remain commander of the brigade. No one thought about the fact that this question ought to be raised and resolved in Spain, with the agreement of the Spanish party and with the leaders of the Spanish army.

*Political work* within the brigades is inadequate. I have formed the impression that all the comrades who are here to conduct political work have been drawn into military work, at which, by the way, they are not completely competent. Mainly, there is not enough systematic work on bringing the foreign comrades closer to the realities of Spain, so that they can get to know the Spanish problems. They do not read the Spanish press. It is easier to find a brigade of Spaniards who read some Polish or German than the other way around. The cadres of our party that are in the brigades do not understand that in Spain they can learn a great deal. As for the representatives of the fraternal parties, who come here from time to time, it would not be a bad thing to recommend that they also communicate more with the Spanish Communist party, since they also have a lot to learn. This means not to limit themselves to tours of the front, but to begin by asking the Spanish party to explain to them first of all the situation as it is today and on this basis to help draw the foreign volunteers closer to the situation in the country.

How to improve the situation? The central problem that must be resolved is the problem of *leadership.* At one of the meetings, which we called here to study various problems concerning the brigades that we want to place before the government, a proposal was advanced on creating a "Soviet Brigade" with Gallo, a base commandant, and three foreign comrades. I was against that kind of proposal, which can lead only to an intensification of the "separation" of the brigades—this is a tendency to create an army within an army, and so on. The Spanish comrades backed me up, and the proposal was not accepted. The policy that must be conducted consists of continuing to infuse the brigades into the Spanish army as component units of the Spanish army, destroying any form that will lead to separatism, and so on.

The Spanish government has already decided that five brigades ought to continue to exist (11th to 15th) as shock brigades consisting of 40–50 percent foreigners. At the same time they recognize the Albacete base as an organizational and training center for the brigades, and they are permitting [us] to organize special quartermaster and sanitary services to serve the brigades within the framework of the sanitary and quartermaster services of the army. This decision by the government ought to be taken as the basis for resolving all the remaining problems concerning the brigades. As for the question of *leadership,* with the goal of improving the current situation, I advanced the proposal that three brigades be formed into one corps, more precisely in the corps that is under the command of a Communist (Modesto). This kind of solution to the problem will put an end to the existing disorganization. The brigade and division commanders will turn to the corps commander for the resolution of all their problems, and, for their part, the command of lower units will be controlled and supported by the corps command.

The consistent carrying out of this directive requires:

1. That the recruiting of new volunteers be continued and increased, not only to support the percentage established for the composition of the brigades by the government's decree, but also to send the fatigued volunteers for a rest, to give a temporary leave to those who want to fight. I hope in a few days to give you the figures for the number of volunteers who will have to be accepted before the end of the year. Directives do not have to be issued for recruiting specialists; only elements fit for military service are needed. The problem of specialists is rather complicated. For example, as to artillerymen, taking into account that the brigades do not have artillery, artillerymen sent for the brigades are in an uncertain position. If they express a desire to remain in the brigades, then they do not receive weapons. The people that it is unnecessary to send here are the old party cadres who are not able to fight. There are rather a lot of them here, and it is not possible to use all of them.

2. The base leadership ought to be reinforced by one *Spanish* comrade, if possible a member of the party CC, who will work as the chief of the general staff or as political commissar. This decision, already made a long time ago, has not yet been put into effect. We must insist that it be put into effect.

3. One member of the politburo of the CPE ought systematically to devote himself to the problem of the brigades, putting an end once and for all to the situation that only representatives or "political advisers," sent by the executive committee of the Comintern, know and decide questions about the brigades.

4. The Albacete base must be energetically purged. Send to the front all the people who are able to bear arms. Strongly reduce the bureaucracy. Reduce the functions of the base, giving to the government various workshops, and so on and so forth, and reorganize the base chiefly on the basis of five training zones (one for every brigade), retaining only the most necessary services. The current base commander agrees and is already working toward that. I have formed a favorable impression of him.

5. Up to now, the cadre section is mainly performing the work on registration and some work on exposing suspect and enemy elements, and so on. But today it is not able to help the base command staff to resolve all cadre questions. You ought to send a very strong worker to lead this work—this would

## Document 51 *continued*

be a very great help. The cadre section is completely unconnected to the CC of the Spanish party; this shortcoming must be corrected and is connected as well to the cadre section of the CPE.

6. The party representatives ought to direct their work toward preserving very close connections between their own cadres and the cadre department and the base command.

7. The policy on introducing the brigades into the Spanish army ought to be conducted very skillfully, courteously, in order not to provoke friction even over trifles, so that there will be no pretext for any kind of misunderstanding whatsoever, and so on. For example, on the question of ranks, I consider it intolerable that the foreign comrades receive the rank of "general," while at the same time the Spanish comrades do not have a right to a rank higher than (senior) commander. It seems to me that all general ranks have to be abolished in the brigades, and that on these matters we must advise our comrades to be much more modest.

8. As for political work, take concrete measures to strengthen the study of Spanish problems in the brigades, without which our comrades will never be able to maintain good relations with the Spaniards and carry out good, consistent political work among the Spanish recruits, who will be arriving in the brigade.

9. On the basis of the government decision, check up on all the brigade cadres, beginning with a checkup of the brigade, division, and so on, command staffs. Perform this work together with the military advisers who know the capabilities of each one, and under the leadership of the CPE secretariat.

At my request, the base commander wrote a detailed account, which I am sending to you.

*Enclosure*

Composition of the brigades on 9/8/1937:

| | | | |
|---|---|---|---:|
| 1. Arrived | | | 18,216 |
| 2. Losses | | | |
| | A. Killed | 11th Brigade | 624 |
| | | 12th Brigade | 502 |
| | | 13thBrigade | 238 |
| | | 14th Brigade | 240 |
| | | 15th Brigade | 290 |
| | | 20th Bat. 86th Brigade | 36 |
| | | 150th Brigade | 115 |
| | | remaining | <u>613</u> |
| | | TOTAL | 2658 |
| | B. Disappeared | 11th Brigade | 191 |
| | | 12th Brigade | 131 |
| | | 13th Brigade | 170 |

|  |  |  |
|---|---|---:|
| | 14th Brigade | 117 |
| | 15th Brigade | 80 |
| | 20th Bat. 86th Brigade | 5 |
| | remaining | <u>2</u> |
| | TOTAL | 696 |

| | |
|---|---:|
| C. Evacuated | 1,500 |
| D. Wounded | 3,287 |
| General number of lost | 8,141 |

Present on 9 August 1937

|  |  |
|---|---:|
| 11th | 555 |
| 12th | 500 |
| 13th | 300 |
| 14th | 550 |
| 15th | 600 |
| 150th | <u>650</u> |
| | 3,155 |

| | |
|---|---:|
| General staff and divisional services | 260 |
| Cavalry 15th Division | 37 |
| Cavalry 35th Division | 40 |
| Cavalry 45th Division | 150 |
| Artillery 15th Division | 80 |
| Artillery 35th Division | 120 |
| Artillery 45th Division | 215 |
| 1st Group Heavy Artillery | 217 |
| Anti-air artillery | 600 |
| Reserve Bat. 45th Div. | 80 |
| *Albacete base* | 3,657 |
| Commissariat in Madrid | 200 |
| 1st Regiment armored trains | 215 |
| Sanitary units | 639 |
| Unfit for service | <u>150</u> |
| TOTAL PERSONS | 10,015 |

Departed abroad:

|  |  |
|---|---:|
| In April | 1,103 |
| In May | 1,203 |
| In June | 1,341 |
| In July | 895 |
| In August (till the 2nd) | <u>110</u> |
| TOTAL from 14 April to 2 August | 4,652 |

# Document 52

RGVA, f. 35082, op. 1, d. 92, l. 3

To the Comrade Brigade Commander and War Commissar of the 11th Brigade

The order of the day for 10/11/37 for your brigade reads in the paragraph "The reorganization and reinforcement of the battalion staff" that *only* internationals exclusively will be appointed officers for all responsible posts.

It is not conceivable that a brigade that consists of no less than 80 percent Spaniards should be led only by international officers, who as a rule do not command the Spanish language and consequently cannot bring about the proper contact with the soldiers. Imagine yourself in the place of the Spanish soldiers, and you will easily understand that the Spanish soldiers must have the impression that their national pride has been hurt. And perhaps rightly so, for these are the same Spaniards in whose land we are taking part in our struggle. Imagine the future struggle in your own German land, then it will be quite clear to you how an honest German antifascist would feel if he were to fight in a Spanish International Brigade with the same majority of German antifascist soldiers, led exclusively by Spanish officers.

It seems to me, and I am convinced of this, that the way to strengthen the political framework and the military power of our International Brigades is not through national restrictions, but rather in the most resolute collecting and training of the Spanish element for command posts in the International Brigades. To allow them (the Spanish officers) a true, authentic, proper equality in the leadership and not merely the right to die.

As a result of this, the character of the International Brigades will not in the least be lowered, but on the contrary, its striking power will be increased. Also, from the standpoint of the international development of the Spanish soldiers, this kind of measure will truly unite and cement the brigade, and ease the differences in national habits. A broad introduction, a doubling in the number of Spanish officers in the leadership, would satisfy their national demands, so that they would go into battle with you and not leave the German comrades all alone with the enemy, [a situation] about which you yourself have often complained. Because this by no means has anything to do with an "innate" timidity of the Spaniard, as people seek to explain this, who "do not want to" or are not able to understand the immense significance of the national question in the International Brigades. If the Spaniards do not go with us, then it is because above all they feel like strangers around us. The result is that we lose more than is necessary from our not too abundant material of international soldiers.

With this letter I want to help you to regain your practical experience on the national question and to avoid thereby a future repetition, which would absolutely not lead to a strengthening of the brigade.

At my command post, on 12/11/37
General, Division Commander
[illegible]

## The GRU, the Soviet Advisers, and Control of the Republican Army

In the midst of these various machinations, the Soviets continued to use every institution at hand to make certain that they would retain their influence over the new regular Spanish army and thus over the conduct of the war. The principal mechanism for running the war remained the thousands of Red Army "advisers" in Spain, all of whom doubled as GRU agents. They reported back to the "director" (Voroshilov) frequently, detailing their progress on their assigned tasks, the state of the Republican army, and the war effort in general. Voroshilov forwarded the reports on to Stalin, the Politburo, and other top Soviet officials, showing the importance that the leadership attached to their observations and their work. From the dispatches it is clear that the GRU continued to do much more than simply advise the Republicans. Throughout 1937 they endeavored to purge the army of unreliable elements, trained and promoted men that they could trust to positions of command, worked up plans for operations, and used their influence to guide the army (and the war) in the directions that Moscow desired.

The breadth of the tasks that the Kremlin leadership set before the GRU, as shown in **Document 53**, was extraordinary, and it demonstrates just how much the role of the Soviet advisers had evolved over the previous year. By early March, when Semyon Uritsky (the new head of the GRU in Berzin's absence) sent this directive to Berzin and Shtern, the war had taken several ominous turns for the Republicans. Most important, the major city of Málaga, and a large portion of the southern seacoast, had fallen to Italian and Nationalist forces in late February. At about the same time,

Franco's troops managed to force a crossing of the Jarama River near Madrid. For a few tense weeks, it seemed once again as though the capital would fall. As in November 1936, International Brigades helped stiffen the resolve of the Republicans and would achieve even more stunning results at Guadalajara in early March. This letter, while acknowledging the bleak outlook for the Blue army (as the Republicans were known), also emphasized the achievements of, and possibilities for, the GRU. The main point of the letter was that the Republicans could not accomplish anything without the aid of their Soviet advisers. "Preachers" (i.e., agents) of the GRU were training the command staff, purging their ranks of traitors (as ordered by Stalin himself), and preparing reserves. The replacement of Asensio was a direct result of their action and quite an "achievement," as Uritsky acknowledged.

The other major task that the advisers were to carry out was the promotion of trustworthy new commanders to replace the old "lumber." Uritsky asked for a list with short descriptions of young officers on whom the Soviet Union could depend, and **Document 54** was almost certainly the fulfillment of his request. This presentation of the entire Spanish high command is interesting, for several reasons. First, there were relatively few positive characterizations of officers who did not belong to either the Communist or the Socialist party. Conversely, only one Communist (Emilio Bueno) was described in a negative way. It is obvious from the list that only Communists could be depended on to fight well *and* support the policies set by Stalin. Second, although a large number of Communists already held positions of authority in the Republican army (the central front in particular, the most active and important of the fronts, was more than half Communist), the Soviets saw that number as unacceptable. Moscow viewed it as imperative to increase the percentage of Communist (and consequently reliable) commanders throughout the war. This report thus acted as something of a hit list. The Soviet advisers (and behind them the Soviet Union) would at one point or another attack almost all those men of high rank who were portrayed here as anti-Soviet, untrustworthy, or incompetent and would seek to replace them with "reliable" (Communist) officers.

An example of these instructions in action is provided by **Docu-**

ment 55, a telegram sent by Voroshilov to three of the highest-ranking Soviets in Spain: Grigory Shtern ("Sebastian"); Nikolai Kuznetsov ("Lepanto"), the adviser for the Republican navy and later head of the Soviet navy; and Yakov Smushkevich ("André"), who would become head of the main directorate of the Soviet air force. The background for this document is the infamous bombing of the German battleship *Deutschland* in late May 1937. The Germans had stationed ships at Ibiza, one of the Balearic Islands, ostensibly so that they could take part in the control system set up by the Non-Intervention Committee. On 29 May Republican aircraft bombed Ibiza and hit the *Deutschland,* killing thirty-one and wounding seventy-four German sailors.[56] Hitler, infuriated by the assault, ordered the shelling of the Republican port Almería in reprisal. For a few days, Europeans feared that Germany would enter the war against the Republicans openly, or that the Republicans, angered by the shelling, would risk war by retaliating against other German ships. Fortunately, cooler heads prevailed, and the danger that the conflict might widen into a general European war passed.

The telegram Stalin wrote on this occasion grants us several insights into this incident. For instance, it is clear from the document that, as historians have believed, the *Deutschland* was not the target of the air raid. The Republicans were supposed to attack Palma (on Majorca), but two aircraft (Soviet-made, and probably Soviet-piloted, S.B. aircraft) had bombed Ibiza rather than the chosen objective. The most important aspect of the telegram and "inquiry" is, however, the attitude taken by Stalin, Sebastian, and the other advisers toward their Spanish "friends." The Soviets expected the Spanish to follow implicitly Stalin's order, conveyed by Voroshilov, that it was unacceptable to bomb foreign ships. It is also plain from the inquiry that Sebastian had been in charge of the raid that had gone wrong; it was he, after all, who had ordered the bombing of the port at Palma only. It was also Sebastian who would, if so required, "restrain" the Spaniards from bombing Cádiz, even though the order to do so had come from Prieto himself.

A more in-depth look at the Soviet advisers themselves, how they saw the war and their role in it, is provided by the next few documents. The first of these, **Document 56,** is a short report from

Gorev on the work being done by the GRU in Asturias and the Basque country. The tone taken by the Soviet adviser is an important aspect of this letter. As in his reports from 1936, Gorev assumed that an adviser should arrange to be in a position where the Spanish would "carry out his decisions." The example to follow was that of "Lavedan" (the code name for David Kovalev, a Soviet officer), who had won influence and authority among the Spanish and then used the recognition he had gained to resolve even political differences. Meanwhile, officers who did not have the light touch necessary to win over the Spaniards and convince them to do as Moscow wanted, men such as "Frapio," could not be permitted to stay in positions of high responsibility.

Even less desirable was the petty squabbling between the three advisers in Bilbao, which compromised the Soviet officers in the eyes of the Spanish. The intrigues in which these men engaged may seem trivial and even amusing to the outside observer, but they were much more than that in the context of Stalin's Soviet Union. As many works on the purges have shown, accusations and schemes such as these led to the downfall and eventual execution of more important men.[57] This was especially true after the events of May 1937, when Mikhail Tukhachevsky and seven other high-ranking commanders would be accused of treason and summarily executed. Tukhachevsky's fall set off a bloody round of scapegoating that would lead to the virtual destruction of the Soviet officer corps.[58] Thus, the way that Gorev, although hesitating to assign blame for the "ludicrous" way that his men were behaving, singled out "Orsini" (real name, Kirill Yanson) as the villain who had blackened his name with the Spanish would have special significance. It may explain why Yanson, who had already been recalled to Moscow, would shortly be arrested and shot. When Gorev was summoned back to Moscow and executed in January 1938 as an enemy of the people, the rules of the purges meant that men of whom he had spoken favorably would automatically fall under suspicion. The arrest and killing of the "good" officer Kovalev in 1938 thus made a certain twisted sense.

A hint of the coming storm is provided by **Document 57**, a private letter from Uritsky to his predecessor as head of the GRU, Yan Berzin. Here, in what amounted to a "friendly warning," Uritsky attempted to set Berzin straight on a number of accounts. After reminding Berzin of the importance of the task before him, Uritsky noted two salient failings in the intelligence officer's work, either one of which could have been Berzin's undoing. First was that Berzin did not always "appreciate the essence" of the instructions handed down by his superiors, a subtle reference to a failure to follow orders. Always a touchy subject in any military setting, this was clearly grounds for disciplinary measures and, within the excited atmosphere created after May 1937, for summary execution. Second, he charged Berzin with harming the interests of the "firm" (the GRU). This was an even more serious accusation; however, Uritsky softened the blow. The motivation for Uritsky's letter also sheds light on the abnormal atmosphere that prevailed during Stalin's regime. Although he chose to emphasize his close friendship with Berzin and his desire to help his predecessor, the first paragraph of the letter (and the fact that it found its way into the Soviet archives) hint at another explanation: the need to protect himself from charges of being too soft on wrongdoers. Having already provoked suspicion for his treatment of Primakov, Uritsky could hardly afford to risk the same with Berzin. Unfortunately, this letter was too little, too late for the unfortunate head of the GRU. A few months after writing Berzin, he would be arrested and shot, yet another victim of the post-Tukhachevsky purges. Berzin, perhaps because he had been accused by an "enemy of the people," would manage to survive into 1938 before finding himself before the firing squad.

To make certain that the Soviet officers followed the party line precisely, Moscow sent commissars to Spain who reported back on the behavior and political orientation of their men. The following two documents, **Document 58** and **Document 59,** are the extensive reports by two of the political workers. They not only detail numerous breeches of party discipline and "Socialist" morality committed by the Soviets but also show the atmosphere of faultfinding and accusation that prevailed after May. Krotov had little good to say about any of the leading advisers he met: the previous commissar's work was "weak," the behavior of Shtern (Grigorovich) was suspect, Slutsky traveled too much, Grigoriev "completely went to pieces," and so on. Even though he admitted that most of the men were behaving "as befits a Soviet citizen," the numerous mentions of drunkenness, lack of discipline, and illegal use of funds (not to mention embezzlement) show that a large number of the advisers did as they pleased once outside of the reach of Stalinist legality. The other point that is clear from this report is that the advisers saw themselves as purely technical assistants who should not meddle in local politics. Krotov tried to correct this misinterpretation, pointing out that it was wrong for the Soviets to see the "friends" committing political mistakes without doing something to "correct" them. Finally, his decrying of the commanders who took up arms themselves shows that there was a widespread tendency for the advisers, in addition to leading operations, to take an ever more active part in battles.

In Document 59 Kachelin emphasized the delicacy of the position in which the advisers found themselves. The Spanish high command still contained politically unreliable people, and the army (and general populace) had noticed how thoroughly the Soviets had penetrated the Republican military. Thus, although there had been some notable successes (the army was now a more professional force, with tank and reserve cadres trained by the advisers), much work remained to be done. In particular, Kachelin recommended that the Soviet Union send more advisers, pilots and sailors. He also thought that it was necessary to push the advisers to do more than "just" narrow operational work, to take on, in fact, "all of the current army work." Other parts of the report show that the Soviets were already more involved than they admitted in fighting the war for their Spanish "friends" and acknowledges, for instance, that Soviet pilots were indeed flying combat sorties.[59] Finally, while stressing that most of the advisers were doing their work conscientiously and to the utmost of their ability, Kachelin felt compelled to mention some of their failings as well. In addition to noting that some officers "behaved disgustingly," Kachelin's main criticism showed how out of touch he was with the current atmosphere in Moscow. Unlike men who were more in tune with new Stalinist views, he denounced the Soviet propensity to treat the Spanish as if the dictatorship of the proletariat already existed and condemned the overuse of such terms as "wrecker" or "fascist." It is possible that the reason for these assertions can be found in his repeated statement that it was very difficult to discover the correct political orientation (the Moscow party line) in Spain. Later that year Kachelin's failure to keep up with the latest changes in the party line would catch up with him, as Mikhail Koltsov (the Soviet journalist and adviser to Stalin) would denounce him for delivering "demoralizing provocative reports . . . at a meeting about the arrests in the Red Army."[60]

The final report in this section, **Document 60,** sums up the experiences that top advisers had while working in Spain. Written by the man who was known as Emilio Kléber, the report illuminates the battlefield, political, and personal difficulties that the advisers faced throughout the war. "Kléber" (Manfred Stern) came to Spain in the first months of the rebellion and would leave in December 1937. During this period he would command several different international units, be hailed as the savior of Madrid, and be reviled as a dangerous interloper into Spanish internal affairs. Stern came into contact with almost all the other leading Soviet advisers (including Alexander Orlov) and, as a keen observer of human frailty, had much of interest to say about their successes and failures. From the very beginning, he placed emphasis on how much influence the Communists (whether Spanish or Soviet, or from the Comintern) had over military affairs, and how the Republicans tried to combat this influence. He noted that early on in the war the party had "succeeded in having Largo Caballero appoint five comrades from a list made by the party to work in the general staff in order to have their own eyes and ears in the central leadership of the army." This penetration was not enough, however. Soon Stern, first appointed in the Operations Department, would be called on to lead a unit in the new International Brigades. This move forced him to take on a new name and identity, and even to pretend he did not know fellow Soviets like Gorev, in order to hide his true identity as a regular Soviet officer.

Not long afterward Stern found himself caught up in the complex, and devious, world of the Comintern and Soviet advisers. His insights into the personal jealousies, suspicions, and conspiracies that characterized this world are fascinating and add to our understanding both of that community and of the effects that Stalin's paranoid new society had on Soviets stationed abroad. The report also shows just how much latitude Stern had to affect the course of individual battles and the war itself. As a commander in the brigades, Stern (and a few other Soviet officers) had the opportunity to intervene more directly in the war than most advisers. Soon he was planning operations and carrying them out, arguing forcefully for his way (or that of the party) with the Republican high command, and even disobeying orders when he felt that his Spanish superiors were mistaken. Other Soviet advisers, like Comrade "Fritz," the code name for P. I. Batov, were, as Stern wrote, "the secret" commanders of the units to which they were attached. Republican officials, intimidated by the powers they knew were behind men such as Stern and Batov, were unable simply to dismiss them. Thus, though he would be "asked" to leave his first command, Stern was soon back in charge of an international unit and once again doing as he pleased. When Rojo attempted to remove Stern from the 45th Division, Stern was advised to turn to the party for a resolution of the problem, rather than consult the Republican government. In addition to attempting to affect the conduct of the war, Stern also advocated interference in the government to "save" Caballero from Asensio, using the army and "youth" as fronts for the actions of the party.

Equally important for broadening our understanding of the war are Stern's comments on the internationalists and the International Brigades. In his report, international comrades are falsifying reports and feuding with the base command at Albacete, while treating the Spanish soldiers in the brigades as second-class citizens in their own country. As he also shows, the internationalists were not solely to blame for the problems that the units suffered. The Comintern and Soviet agents in charge of the brigades, through their poor use of these forces in battle and their decision to deny almost every request for leave or return home, occasioned a huge drop in overall morale within the brigades. The resulting discouragement and desertions had almost ruined the brigades as a fighting force by the time Stern left the country.

Yet it is interesting to note the freedom with which Stern disagreed with higher party officials, argued with his supposed superiors (both Communist and Republican), and generally had his own way. As other documents in this volume have shown, Moscow was not responsible for all the actions taken by its agents in Spain. Stern's outright disobedience to his party superiors demonstrates that there were even times when actions affecting the war as a whole were not ordered or even desired by the Communists. This document should, therefore, modify somewhat our understanding of how much actual control Moscow had over events in Spain. Away from the "Center," Soviet agents at times did as they wished and justified themselves afterward. When looking at specific examples of Soviet disobedience to the Spanish command, or Communist attempts to take over control, one must therefore keep in mind that this may be the action of one person (or a small group of people) acting beyond the reach even of the long arm of Moscow. Freewheeling "un-Stalinist" behavior like this may also explain why so many men, like Stern himself, were recalled to Moscow for reprimands or worse.

Most of this document is, in fact, evidence adduced by Stern to exonerate him from charges leveled by his "comrades." This was, of course, the wrong tack to take in Stalinist Russia. As J. Arch Getty and Oleg V. Naumov have pointed out, the only correct response to such charges was a ritual apology consisting of self-criticism, admission of complete guilt, and a declaration of repentance.[61] Accused of supporting the anarchists over his Communist brothers, of being a "Napoleon," of disobeying orders, and of indulging in self-aggrandizement, Stern should have admitted his mistakes and pledged to do better. Instead, he defiantly justified his actions. For his failure to bow to the demands of Stalinism, and for his behavior in Spain, Stern would disappear into the maelstrom of the purges in 1938. One point of controversy in particular is worth noting in light of later events. Throughout the report, Stern claimed that he had always supported a "Hispanization" of the war—that is, replacing fallen internationalists with Spanish soldiers, training Spanish officers, and creating a Spanish army to take over fighting the war. Stern's reputation was exactly the opposite. By 1938, as a later document will show, he would be branded an enemy of the people. A deviation named after him (Kléberism) was associated with Soviet officers who, supposedly like Stern, favored the internationalists over the Spanish. Here, however, Stern argued that he had been falsely accused, and he cited several instances where he appointed Spanish officers or attempted to integrate Spanish soldiers into the International Brigades. In Stern's version of events, it was the other "comrades" in Valencia who discriminated against the Spanish and marginalized them in their own war.

## Document 53
RGVA, f. 35082, op. 1, d. 119, ll. 36−34

*Encoded.*
*By mail.*

Dear Donizetti and Sebastian,

1. As a result of the offensive on the Valencia road, which was not unexpected by us, the Whites[62] again won a piece that places them in an advantageous position vis-à-vis the Blues.[63]

If you add to this the fall of Málaga, then the result of the winter, even if not very shining for the Whites, is at the same time highly depressing for the Blues. We clearly perceive that it is only thanks to you and the efforts of all of your "preachers"[64] that things have not turned out even worse.

2. On the current problem: the incapacity of the Blues for offensives. This question is held up by the weakness of the command cadres. Undoubtedly you have worked very hard on training these cadres. Much depends on success in this area.

Do not fail to give detailed, comprehensive data on the work carried out in this direction.

3. The second problem by number and the first in importance is the mission of purging the staffs of saboteurs, agents of Franco. We see from here the prodigious work that you and all our people are doing in carrying out the decrees of the Boss[65] on this question, but the results do not match the effort expended. The majority of the old lumber still occupies its positions and causes harm.

The replacement of Asensio is an achievement, but how does his substitute present himself (write about this).

I would like to emphasize, with all cogency, the necessity for boldly promoting young commanders to the highest command posts.

Incidentally, I ask you to communicate by the next post a list with short descriptions of those young rising commanders on whom we can depend.

4. You must report on what results there were from the fall of Málaga. What practical conclusions can one draw from this.

5. The main mission—preparation of reserves, which you are now working

## Document 53 *continued*

on. The battle readiness of these reserves also depends on receiving military supplies in a timely fashion.

Those three X's[66] which we sent to you, are coming this time with a great deal of effort: the antagonist this time is more rapacious, not to mention the fact that even the elements have turned against us, the X's are coming in through a force-11 storm. For some reason my heart is especially worried about these X's. May they arrive . . .

6. The current uncomforting picture in Catalonia. You should not await salvation from the appointment of Pozas. Perhaps we should have sent several of our strong people there, but, in the first place, several influential Catalan leaders, in a quite undisguised form, grumble about us, and several even permit anti-Soviet attacks; therefore, in the second place, if we send our people, we ought to ask the Catalans and the central government, and if this is possible, then send the appropriate petition with reference to the request by the Catalans and center.

. . .

We sometimes address some small questions on the situation and various details to Zende. This is done in order to not pull you away from your work. I think that you will not object to this.
I embrace you. Strongly shake your hand.
Yours,

D.
3 March 1937

## Document 54

RGVA, f. 33987, op. 3, d. 960, ll. 124–1250b.

*List of the Command Staff of the Spanish Republican Army*

| N° | Post | Surname and rank | Short description |
|----|------|------------------|-------------------|
| 1. | Mil. Min. | Largo Caballero[67] | Leader of the left Soc. 67 years old. Fears influence of the Communists. |
| 2. | His asst. | Baráibar | Socialist; lacks mil. training. |
| 3. | Minister of av. and air forces | Prieto | Leader of the right Soc., good org[anize]r. Long opposed the Popular Front. |
| [. . .][68] | | | |
| 5. | Ch[ief] of Gen. Staff | Gen. Cabrero[69] | Lacks mil. train. Treats our advisers poorly. Sabotages. |
| [. . .] | | | |

| 9. | Ch[ief] 2 Dept. | Lt. Col. Estrada | Good, young, competent commander. Soc. |
|---|---|---|---|
| [. . .] | | | |
| 11. | Ch[ief] 3 | Lt. Col. Casado | Well trained. Politically suspect. |
| [. . .] | | | |
| 19. | Ch[ief] of air force | Lt. Col. Vidango Cisneros[70] | Communist. Good worker. |
| [. . .] | | | |
| 23. | Gen. Commissar | del Vayo | Soc. Activist in the Popular Front. |

*Northern Front.*

| 24. | Com. Front | Llano Encomiendo[71] | General. Weak character. |
|---|---|---|---|
| 25. | Ch[ief] of Staff | Ciutat | Captain. Student of mil. academy. |
| 26. | Com. Bis.[72] Sec. | Arambary | Captain. Adventurer.[73] |
| 27. | Com. Ast.[74] Sec. | Linares | Captain. Good commander. |
| 28. | Com. 1st gr. | Abad | Officer. |
| 29. | C-r 1st gr. [*sic*] | Cisrones | Socialist. |
| 30. | C-r 3rd gr. | Sempura | Lt. Colonel. |
| 31. | C-r 4th gr. | Claudio | Communist. |
| 32. | C-r 1st Brig. | Pirvaro | Socialist. |
| 33. | C-r 2nd Brig. | Caron | Officer. Nonparty. |
| 34. | C-r 3rd Brig. | Victor | Anarchist. |
| 35. | C-r 4th Brig. | Doria | Officer. Nonparty. |
| 36. | C-r 5th Brig. | Viejo | Communist. |
| 37. | C-r 6th Brig. | Garcival[75] | Officer. Soc. |
| 38. | C-r 7th Brig. | Cangas | Officer. |
| 39. | C-r 8th Brig. | Ladreda | Communist. |
| 40. | C-r 9th Brig. | Deago | Socialist. |
| 41. | C-r 10th Brig. | Domian | Communist. |
| 42. | C-r 11th Brig. | Sereso | Officer. Nonparty. |
| 43. | C-r 12th Brig. | Trabanco | Communist. |
| 44. | C-r 13th Brig. | García | Communist. |
| 45. | C-r 14th Brig. | Coleja | Officer. He also commands the 5th Group. |

*Central Front.*

| 46. | Com. Front | Miaja | General. Indecisive in action. |
|---|---|---|---|
| 47. | Ch[ief] of Staff | Col. Rojo | Good military worker. |
| 48. | C-r 3rd Corps | Col. Burillo | Communist. Actively fights with the fascists. |
| 49. | C-r Div. "A" | Col. Walter | Our Communist (Sverchevsky). |
| 50. | C-r Div. "B" | Col. Gall | Our Communist. |

| | | | |
|---|---|---|---|
| 51. | C-r Div. "C" | Lister | Communist. Finished school in Moscow. |
| 52. | Com. Div. | Lt. Col. Juan Arce | Communist. |
| 53. | C-r Div. | Col. Men[a] | Fought well at Madrid. |
| 54. | C-r 4 Div. | Major of the militia Guilloto Modesto | Good commander. |
| 55. | C-r Div. | Juan Modesto[76] | Worker. Com[munist]. Fin.[ished] sch[ool]. in Moscow. |
| 56. | | Carlos | Com[munist]. Go[od] organizer. C-r 5th [illegible] |
| 57. | | Castro | Communist. General. Was ch[ief] of gen.[eral] staff. Go[od] organizer. Commanded 5th I[nfantry] R[egiment]. |
| 58. | | Mangada | Gen. Popular among the militiamen. Behaves well toward the Soviet Union. |
| 59. | C-r 9 Div. | Ruber | (temporarily in command) |
| 60. | C-r 1st Lister Brig. | Glemas | Communist. Fights well. |
| 61. | C-r 2nd Lister Brig. | Pando | Communist. Good c-r. |
| [. . .] | | | |
| 63. | C-r 3rd Brig. | Major Galán | Fought stubbornly at Madrid. |
| [. . .] | | | |
| 65. | C-r 5th Brig. | Major Gaquo | Fought well at Madrid. |
| [. . .] | | | |
| 67. | C-r 11th Brig. | Lt. Col. Hans | Communist |
| 68. | C-r 12th Brig. | Lukács | Communist. Our writer Mate-Zalka |
| 69. | C-r 13th Brig. | Gómez | Communist. |
| 70. | C-r 16th Brig. | Martínez Capri | Worker. Communist. Deputy in the Cortes. |
| 71. | C-r 18th Brig. | Juan Modesto | Worker. Communist. |
| 72. | C-r 19th Brig. | Manuel Márquez | Major. Communist. |
| 73. | C-r 20th Brig. | Mejias López | Captain. Young Communist. |
| 74. | C-r 21st Brig. | Palacio Gómez | Major. Communist. |
| 75. | C-r 22th Brig. | Francisco Achevan | Captain. Communist. |
| 76. | C-r 23rd Brig. | Alberto Calderón | Lt. Col. Left Republican. |
| 77. | C-r 25th Brig. | Major Dus | Fights well. |
| [. . .] | | | |
| 79. | C-r 35th Brig. | Nino Nanetti | Lt Col. |
| [. . .] | | | |
| 84. | C-r 40th Brig. | Antonio Ortega | Lt Col. Communist. Hero of Madrid. |
| 85. | C-r 41st Brig. | Emilio Bueno | Lt Col. Communist. Drinks a lot. |
| [. . .] | | | |
| 88. | C-r 66th Brig. | Parapar | Major. Communist. Energetic, tough c-r. |
| 89. | C-r 68th Brig. | Campesino | |
| 90. | C-r 69th Brig. | Durán | Communist. |
| 91. | C-r 70th Brig. | Ksanch | Anarchist. Fights well in the Jarama group. |

## Document 54 *continued*

| | | |
|---|---|---|
| 92. | C-r brig. s[outhern] fr[ont] | Burguete | Communist. Is waging battle in the encirclement, after the fall of Málaga. |
| [. . .] | | | |
| 94. | C-r Brig. "B" | José Vega | Major. Tough commander. Exp.[elled] from the Com. party. Is striving to join once again. |

*Aragon Front.*

| | | | |
|---|---|---|---|
| 95. | Defense Councillor | Francisco Isgleas | Anarchist. From the miners. Lacks mil.[itary] training. |
| 96. | Adjutant | Jiménez Labrador | Captain. Socialist. Energetic, intelligent officer. |
| 97. | Dep. defense | Molico | Anarchist. Behaves loyally to the USSR. |
| 98. | Ch[ief] of the gen. staff | Vicente Guarner | Colonel. Mason. We[ll] trained. |
| 99. | His dep. | Colonel Matilla | From a revolutionary family. |
| 100. | Ch[ief] of the op.[erations] dept. | Major Guarner Pene | Brother of the ch[ief] of staff. |
| 101. | His asst. | Major Beseda | Nonparty. Good staff officer. |
| 102. | Ch[ief] of the inform.[ational] dept. | Major Martínez Ingliada | Nonparty. |
| 103. | Asst. ch[ief] of org.[anizational] dept. | Captain Guarner | Brother of the ch[ief] of the gen. staff. Deaf. |
| 104. | Representative from Valencia | Col. Beriol | |
| 105. | " " | Inertal | Anarchist. |
| 106. | Com. of the front. | Pozas | General. From the first actively fought against the fascists. |
| 107. | Ch[ief] of staff. | Col. Brincas | |
| 108. | C-r of the Ascaso Div. | Juvert[77] | Anarchist. |
| 109. | His dep. | Vivancos | Lacks mil. training. |
| 110. | C-r of the Durruti Div. | Mensano | Anarchist. 40 years [old]. |
| 111. | C-r of the Karl Marx Div. | del Barrio | Communist. Good organizer. |
| 112. | C-r of the Companys Div. | Col. Peresales[78] | Republican. |
| 113. | C-r of S. | Ebro Ortiz | Anarchist. 33 yrs. [old]. Talentless, coward. |

## Document 54 *continued*

| | | |
|---|---|---|
| 114. C-r of the POUM R[egiment] | Rubida Piket[79] | Trotskyist. |
| [. . .] | | |
| 117. C-r of the Gerona div | Col. Martínez Valesny | Nonparty. Behaves well toward the USSR. |
| [. . .] | | |
| 119. C-r of the Tarragona Div. | Col. Mendran | Nonparty. |
| [. . .] | | |
| 121. Ch[ief] Com. | Col. Jiménez | Nonparty. 58 years [old]. Twice convicted. |
| 122. [illegible] of def. | Oscas[80] | Anarchist. Opponent of reorganization of the army. Good orator. |
| [. . .] | | |
| 124. Ch[ief] of front air force | Reyes | Communist. |
| 125. Mil. adviser | Gleser | Anarchist. |

## Document 55

[Unnamed source (15)]

Copy Valencia—to Sebastian
Cartagena—to Lepanto
Encoded—Murcia—to André

The Boss[81] considers it unacceptable to have planes bomb Italian and German ships, and this must be prohibited.

In the case of operations against ships of the mutineers, it is essential that beforehand careful reconnaissance be carried out, in order not to hit foreign ships.

The Director.[82]

### *Inquiry*

1. On 28 May [19]37 Sebastian reported (No. 1315) that the air force had received orders to bomb Palma. Com. Sebastian ordered that only the port, but not the roadstead, be bombed, which, according to the fliers, was supposedly what took place.

3. [*sic*] Sebastian (tel. no. 1348) reported on 29 May [19]37 that two S.B. aircraft of the Republicans bombed Ibiza and there were hits among the ships, including German ones.

2. On 28 May Sebastian (tel. no. 1327) communicated Prieto's order to bomb Cádiz on 29 May. Sebastian inquired whether the Spaniards should be held back (restrained) from such operations.

The resolution of the people's commissar forbidding bombing operations was received by me on the night of 29–30 May [19]37. I ordered the chief of the Spanish department to send a telegram. Because of a day off, this telegram to Comrade Shpilevsky was sent only on the morning of 31 May.

It must be taken into account in this matter that the bombing of Ibiza in any case could not have been prevented, as it took place on 29 May.

## Document 56

[Unnamed source (16)]

*Top Secret*
Copy No.2

*LETTER FROM BRIGADE COMMANDER COMRADE GOREV*
*ON THE CONDITIONS FOR WORK AT THE NORTHERN FRONT*

My impression is that these days it is extraordinarily difficult to do an evaluation of the people who are working here and of the work that has been done by them.

I consider that, under the conditions we have had here, there has undoubtedly been a lot of work accomplished, and in some sectors it has been exceptional. Particularly distinguished has been the work in Asturias, where Lavedan exercises absolute authority. He knows the situation, they know him at the front, and they turn to him as an impartial person for resolution of even internal political differences. He is tactful in relations with our "friends,"[83] knows how to conduct himself, and knows how to implement what he wants without thrusting this on people. He has very good relations with his group. One feels the great cohesion of the comrades, and Lavedan's skill in working with people. True, the conditions in Asturias are easier than in Biscay, and it is easier for him to carry out his decisions, but it must be said that in Asturias we act solely through influence and authority. I believe that Lavedan can be appointed senior adviser to the northern front; he can handle the work and will make use of the recognition both with our "friends" and with our personnel.

The appointed adviser to the Santander corps, Frapio, is weak as an adviser, somewhat crude, and not always tactful. With constant guidance, he can work as a deputy adviser to a corps or as adviser at headquarters, but he will have to be replaced at the corps. When he was working in Asturias, he demonstrated a decent knowledge of his job, but it is difficult for him to work independently, as he can get rattled and make mistakes. In Santander, his appointment was not greeted with any great enthusiasm.

An especially complex situation has been created in the relationships of our work in Bilbao. Orsini, considering himself to be an adviser to the Basque government, stayed a long time in Bilbao and has just gone to Santander, where the front headquarters is supposed to be. I do not know for what reason, but a very unhealthy atmosphere of unfriendly work has developed in our military group in Bilbao. People have all sorts of attitudes, and there is talk about there being no way out, that everyone here is condemned to perish, etc. This situation in the military group was further aggravated by the squabble that took place between Orsini, Tumanov, and Vintser. Which of them is right and which is wrong I do not want to figure out, and I will not try. They all blame one another for thousands of mortal sins, gather facts, even the smallest ones, about one another, and accuse one another of interference in what is not their affair and of an absence of an attempt at amicable work. I am convinced, however, that all three are guilty and that the basic reason for this squabble is an inability to distribute the work, an inability to overcome difficulties, and a desire to shift bad results over to their neighbor. In this squabble, all three grown people and experienced agents[84] have carried things to a ludicrous point. For example, Tumanov with his staff of three people occupies a huge three-story house, Vintser with one driver lives in another, two-story private residence, and Orsini has a third house. Even if it is, shall we say, useful for Orsini to live separately, it is beyond understanding why Tumanov and Vintser cannot live together. Every kind of trifle and nonsense they elevate to matters of principle and try to present as serious things. All this has a direct negative effect on matters and does nothing but compromise us in the eyes of our "friends." Disregarding this, it must be said that our participation in constructing the Basque army has brought great benefits and our work has had substantial results. How much more we could have done here if there had been harmonious work by all our people.

The question of Orsini's personal affairs, about which I reported to Donizetti, stands apart. With Orsini's departure this problem will take care of itself automatically. It is understood that I could not get involved in delving into this matter, but there is too much talk about it among our people, and the Spaniards to assume that it is really so.

What help does our military group need? Advisers must be assigned to the corps. It is contemplated that five corps will be organized. Advisers are needed for all of them. In Biscay, it is necessary to replace Pavlovich, who is tired and worn out; it is necessary to replace Frapio in Santander; and it is

## Document 56 *continued*

necessary to replace Lavedan, if he will be assigned as adviser to the northern front. In all, we need five advisers who are colonels or even majors with education at an academy. Each corps adviser must be given at least one assistant, whom he could send to the division to carry out an operational mission. In this way, we would need five division advisers who are majors or captains with training at an academy. Machine-gun instructors are needed, perhaps one per corps and two to three at the military schools that already exist.

An artillery instructor is needed for the artillery school. In the group at the front, currently it is essential to have an artillery adviser for the front, one to two military engineers, one captain or major, and one lieutenant, signals adviser.

Having received this number of people, it will be possible to organize the army successfully and to carry out any operational mission. It goes without saying that all the advisers will need translators. It is very urgent to get a specialist in organizing the military industrial effort, as the possibilities in the north in relation to military industries are simply exceptional.

*Printed in 2 copies–*
No. 1—Comrade Voroshilov
No. 2—File copy
[boxed date—23 May 1937]

## Document 57

RGVA, f. 35082, op. 1, d. 167, ll. 204–200

15/4/37
Donizetti
N° 118

Dear Donizetti:

I think it necessary to talk with you[85] frankly about several questions. I will save you from any beating around the bush, confident of my relationship with you. I suppose that you yourself are sufficiently aware of all that, and that our friendship, which began in our work more than fifteen years ago, has never once had a shadow cast over it. It seems to me that it was always based on a mutual and united understanding of our duty toward the work that they entrusted to us. It is enough to mention my attitude toward you after I had been put in your unfortunate place by the will of the firm.[86] In general, it isn't my way, when taking a new position, ever, even in the least way, to denigrate my predecessor. I remember my entire career path. I took over posts from such people as Sheko, Griaznov, Antoniuk, Primakov; and if there is something that someone could charge me with, it was that I (so to speak) overdid the "ethics." You yourself understand that if I had been more vigilant and less "ethical," I ought not for instance, to have smoothed things over after Primakov, but, rather, sharply raised the question of all his work, which had, at the very least, a shady character, which attested, at the very least, to his poor attitude toward affairs. But all of that is, so to speak, behind us, in the past.

Sitting in your place (you know in what conditions), I naturally, like every new man, saw a lot of shortcomings, of course. If someone comes after me, he will probably find not a few of them, and maybe even more. But the question, as I understand it, is not about that, not about shortcomings, but about the great work that was accomplished and which cannot be criticized because of individual shortcomings. You remember that specific moment when we took up with each other in this business; you remember my attitude toward all of your work; you also know how I expressed my attitude everywhere that I was asked about it. Our Boss himself,[87] as I told you somewhat, repeatedly mentioned with satisfaction my more than loyal attitude toward my predecessors.

I won't pat myself on the back; I don't want to multiply the facts that bear out my attitude. I repeat that I don't doubt that you already know this well, and that you can't have any doubts about this, and most likely you don't. I'm writing about this for this reason. You are now carrying out a titanic task. To call all of what you have to go through, the conditions in which you are working, "difficulties" would be but a weak expression of the actual, at times inhuman, difficulties that you have to endure at your post. I understand all that and very often experience those adversities with you. If sometimes because of this you receive demands expressing dissatisfaction on these or other grounds—or just to rectify unavoidable mistakes—understanding well the need to rectify such mistakes decisively, I quickly put myself in your situation and kill myself trying to solve the task presented, trying to see how to rectify the mistakes committed, how to find a way out of the situation. The affair you have control of is already too great—what am I saying?—immense, to carry out without mistakes. This business is not easy for our brother, and every instruction from above is necessary, without which we would not be able to act as higher interests demand.

That's why it seems to me sometimes that you, taking these instructions to heart, that you compare them often to the circumstances in which you must live and work and sometimes do not appreciate the essence of the instructions that come from here; more than that, you sometimes don't take account of where they emanate from (and the majority of the time they emanate from a place where people who are smarter and better than we are understand the tasks). It sometimes seems to me that this has on these grounds created a bad mood in you, even that a sense of grievance has appeared. You, with your characteristic modesty, never write about that, but I feel it and take it very much to heart.

Therefore, I always ask you and now repeat, if you have some kind of bewilderment, lack of clarity, write me, please, and I will put all my effort into helping to resolve the problem. I do that all the time. This is part of our relationship.

Now with regard to work. With all frankness, I will tell you, my dear friend, that sometimes I am grieved because it seems to me that you sometimes harm the interests of our firm, which you represent there. I have in mind the special work[88] by Piru and Johnson and also the special work of Faber. More than any other you know how difficult it is for us with people. I don't need to explain that to you; as if ripping out our hearts, we've torn away the best of our people, we've sent [them] to you to put together a solid intelligence and covert action group, but all of this up to now has not been united, unified enough, does not work to full capacity, does not produce the necessary full value, for the simple reason that there has not been the strong master's hand that is so needed for this. What is more, I understand, my friend, that you often didn't feel like it, but you won't bear me a grudge if I say, From whom can I expect purposeful help in our work if not from you? You know, up to now I thought that you and I were working in the same business, that we belonged to the same firm. For me it doesn't have any significance who is subordinate to whom. I am speaking to you completely honestly, and I'm ready to confirm this where appropriate, that I am ready at any time to be subordinate to you, and I consider you my superior. Therefore, I am very hurt if I see that you don't take a leadership role in our work. I don't want to spend my time nitpicking, but the system of work that has prevailed up to now with respect to the activities of the workers transferred to me is dissipating their activity. The diversion of people for no purpose inevitably reduces the quality of their work, in spite of all the effort expended by us.

Dear friend! I felt it vitally necessary to clarify this problem with you and am counting on the fact that you will not take offense with me for putting the problem so straightforwardly. I ask you, and this is your duty—if not often, since commitments will not allow you, then at least systematically—to help our people, to facilitate their completion of the tasks in front of them, not to let them be distracted from the tasks that have been set before them. Incidentally, I note that you are in fact the most experienced of our people and ought not just to keep an eye on the completion of the tasks set before our people, but to spur them forward, setting new tasks, striving for decisive successes. Naturally, without this help of yours, our work there will not go on. You yourself understand that apart from you, I do not have anyone so experienced in our work there—yes, and do not need one: that would be absurd.

You understand yourself that this has not been very easy for me to write, but you know relationships between people, you know people and ought to agree that it is better to write everything in a straightforward manner, that it is better for me to be troubled than to keep it to myself. It is just this kind of

## Document 57 *continued*

frankness that characterizes a true corporate[89] friendship. I do not doubt that you answer, and will answer, me with complete candor also.

On that I will end, my friend. I wish you success in all your life of many difficulties. You can count on me to carry out as far as possible all of your wishes, to facilitate your work. I end this letter on that. I will return to other questions in a separate letter.

I once asked you whether you had any wishes with respect to Andrei, especially taking into consideration the coming summer period. You didn't answer me on this question. Does this mean that I ought to make a decision based on my own judgment, or do you have definite views?

I embrace you.

Your D.

## Document 58

RGVA, f. 33987, op. 3, d. 961, ll. 207–220

*Copy*

TO THE DIRECTOR

I arrived at the site 6/8/37. Having become acquainted with the situation, I gave a talk at the party meeting about the June plenum of the CC. At that very meeting (12/8/37), Com. Grigorovich presented me as the party organizer, sent to work among our people, except for the tankers and pilots, declaring that my principal work ought not to be in Valencia, but on the periphery. A question was posed about the election of the party organizer, but the meeting legitimately demanded an accounting from the former party organizer Com. Kaminsky, and concerning my candidacy, they were simply in a quandary: how could Krotov, they said, be the party organizer in Valencia and carry out his main work on the periphery, and so on. There were proposals that I be considered an instructor in party political work. Com. Grigorovich and Feder (sent by the CC for work among Communists in the Russian column and formally at the head [of] the party leadership with the military men) could not give the meeting a precise answer about my situation. The issue remained unresolved. The accounting and the re-election were postponed, and everyone was given a telegram concerning me from Com. Grigorovich, the answer to which was received by local workers at an unexpected time. My situation is now defined in this way: I am not elected, but rather appointed as party organizer, heading up the work among all of our Communists, except for the tankers and pilots. Organizationally, the party organization is set up in this way: in Valencia a party group with an elected party organizer at its head; the central front, the Aragon front, Teruel, Cartagena are set up analogously. The

281

southern front and Albacete will be set up in the next few days. Thus we will have seven party groups with elected party organizers, five of them already set up. The account/re-election meeting in Valencia was held 16/8/37. Com. Kaminsky's report was given the evaluation: "Consider his work satisfactory." But in fact his work has been weak, especially lately, as is obvious from the facts stated by the Communists in the discussion:

1. The independent people, who work on the fronts, were not involved. Kaminsky, who has a crucial part of his work in official business, could not do this, and no one was concerned with party-political work any longer. Especially with the Communists who were at the fronts.
2. Until recently, most Communists did not pay membership dues, and they did not even know whom to pay them to.
3. People were not studying, for it was thought that everyone who came was "squeaky clean," thoroughly checked-out, did not require any kind of work on themselves. And this led to a number of unhealthy phenomena among part of the Communists. Although attention was paid to individual anti-party faults of the Communists, the question was resolved in cabinet (secretly); these questions were not submitted at the party meetings; the party organization was not mobilized.

   . . .
6. There has been no self-criticism in the party organization. The Communists talk among themselves, discuss the faults of particular individuals; but at the meetings they just talk in general terms.

The meeting showed that the Communists do not know the principal tasks, on which our party is now working. None of them are oriented on these questions. Moreover, the majority of our comrades do not know the political situation of the country in which they are working. The repeated inquiries of the Communists themselves are evidence of this.

. . .

The conduct of Com. Grigorovich (Shtern) appeared somewhat strange to me at both of the meetings. He uttered not one word, not about my report, not about Com. Kaminsky's report, whereas I had already raised a number of questions concerning the blunting of class vigilance among the Communists who are working in Valencia; I cited particular examples, and also those speaking in the debates at both meetings pointed out a whole series of shortcomings, gave political evaluations of the unhealthy phenomena [manifested] by individual Communists. Com. Shtern kept silent, did not promote the development of self-criticism in the party organization, did not propose political aims for further work, although he was informed in detail by me about the situation of things in the "village"[90] and individual conclusions of mine in the report had been agreed upon beforehand with him.

Com. Nesterenko I got to know only after his speech at the first meeting, five to six days after my arrival. Before that, I was directed by Com. Grigor-ovich to Com. Feder, who knows the working conditions of our comrades very poorly, for she works at the embassy, is not at the fronts, and in general is not with our people anywhere, except Madrid, and is even rarely in Alborai (Valencia). At her suggestion, I took it upon myself to do a report on the plenum, but when I came to agree with her about the main questions [to be discussed], she gave me a directive about the third issue—that is, to say nothing about the internal party situation. I did not agree with that. Despite repeated invitations, she did not come to the second accounting/re-election meeting, and Com. Kaminsky worked under her direct leadership. I believe that this was a diplomatic stunt by her, for my situation had already been defined by telegram, and at the discussions the comrades pointed out the shortcomings of her work as well. Com. Stukov was elected as party organizer in Valencia through secret balloting. The meetings projected a number of particular measures for further work. Now Com. Slutsky [Stukov] often takes off, traveling from Valencia to carry out official errands, which undoubtedly affects the quick elimination of shortcomings in party work and its improvement.

. . .

My first trip was to the south on 20–24 August of this year. In Cartagena, the party organization was set up with a new leadership in May. The bureau was elected through secret balloting, with a three-man composition, and now it has been decided to organize a party group, as well, in the motor-torpedo-boat division, with the introduction of a party organizer as a member of the bureau. The organization has kept to itself; during the entire time, Com. Grigorovich came to them once in May, and then on a specific piece of business. They do not know the situation in the "village" or with the neighboring Communists. Party political work was weak; a number of scandalous outrages occurred in the organization on the part of individual Communists, and there was no response to this at all. Example: the Communist Grigoriev (Anin) completely went to pieces, and Com. Kuznetsov did not give this matter over to an investigation by the party organization but decided the question secretly; did not mobilize the party organization for a struggle against the anti-party faults of individual Communists. With the departure of Kuznetsov, the party organization began to approach a more reasonable response to the anti-party faults of the Communists and, in doing so, dramatically improved the conduct of its members.

> *Examples:* 1. *LARIONOV*—Head of the motor-torpedo-boat division and his chief of staff *NARTSISS* got drunk and late at night took it into their heads to go out to sea to look for the enemy. Com. Ribas disciplined them, and the party organization pronounced a severe reprimand with a caution.
> 2. *GAVRILOV*—a signals engineer who repeatedly caused riots when drunk, also received a severe reprimand with a caution.

This sobered up the other Communists, and, having received their punishment, they are correcting their mistakes through practical work and not doing badly. In particular, Com. Gavrilov's punishment has already been removed. Nartsiss is also improving. Larionov must be worked on more, but even he is already not throwing himself into his earlier escapades.

This party organization exists relatively peacefully—no particular military operations are being conducted there; the entire mass of Communists has the opportunity at any time to gather and decide this or that question. I gave a report to them on the situation in the "village," heard with great interest; there were many questions asked.

. . .

From 26 August to 11 September 1937 I was in the Aragon operation. I worked independently, I did not receive any assignments from anyone at all, and the main thing is that Com. Grigorovich was completely uninterested in my work, although we saw each other daily, as a rule at the end of the day. There were forty men of our people at the operation; with the exception of individual comrades, I was with everyone, got to know [people], told the news, heard them out. All the people behaved well during the operation. Some comrades, who had just arrived from the "village" and went directly to the front, did not know their place. In particular Com. Bondarev, who is an adviser for a brigade commander, deserted him during the battle, left the battalion, was himself firing a machine gun, throwing grenades, and so on. The principal complaint of all the "old men" was that they were isolated, received no current literature and little help from the main advisers. There were individual complaints about a lack of harmonious teamwork. For example: Com. Kharchenko just arrived and was sent as an adviser to Kléber. The latter declared to him that he—that is, Kléber—did not need any advice. After this, Com. Kharchenko went to submit his suggestions to the brigade, but the very existence of this kind of relationship—and, still more, between two Communists—I consider disgraceful. Some comrades turned to us for help with [finding] a car, with [obtaining] translators, and so on. These questions I posed to Com. Grigorovich, although I repeat once again that he himself did not ask me about anything. He settled a few questions favorably [for those who raised them]. For example: I reported to him about the incident between Kharchenko and Kléber, thinking that this kind of relationship between two members of our party was abnormal. Com. Grigorovich declared that Kléber had graduated from our military academy and was not in need of advice (then why were they sent advisers?), and when I recounted the incident—how Kléber, during the offensive in his sector by two anarchist battalions from the 26th Rifle Division, which were very close behind Kléber's division and running away, ordered the machine guns to open fire, and Com. Kharchenko, believing that a misunderstanding might occur among the divisions, advised Kléber not to do this, and the latter agreed—Com. Grigorovich simply interrupted me in the presence of the other comrades, [to say] that I did not know the role of our intermediary, that he was not a commissar, and so on, but only a technical assistant who worked out operational plans and wholly subordinate to the commander for whom he was an adviser. I answered him that the question about commissars was far-fetched and I thought that our adviser, working out this or that operation, could not take into account the political situation, and especially when two of our comrades were working. I am forced to describe all these facts owing to the fact that there was no one to resolve them here. Com. Grigorovich, who left for the "village," did not even consider it necessary to become acquainted with the state of the party organization and what kind of situation our individual (isolated) comrades were in. And he knows their needs and moods very inadequately. I reported the main questions to Com. Perpich, but he is working in isolation, without any contact with Com. Grigorovich. Their relationship is strained, manifestly not normal. For example: leaving for the "village," Com. Grigorovich did not listen to even Com. Perpich about the state of the political work in the Republican army. But it is still early to talk about any sort of personal elements; indeed, that is not what our task is about, but first of all the circumstances oblige [one] to form the objective conclusion that Com. Grigorovich has not valued party-political work to the degree that is necessary here among our people. The impression is created that they view party-political work as merely taking an elementary political education course,[91] and so on. The conditions that I have run into compel a thorough investigation of the work of our comrades in all its facets. Indeed it cannot be otherwise. When you come upon a comrade in the course of a battle or during a lull in the trenches, he recounts in the first place his work, relations with the "friends," brings forward a number of everyday questions, not to mention the fact that he greedily listens to the news about the "village." People know the political situation of the "friends" very inadequately. They turn to you with all these questions, and naturally it is necessary to resolve them to one degree or another. I have a question that is not clear: What is my relationship with Coms. Walter and Kléber—they are members of the VKP(b)—command International Divisions. Com. Grigorovich has recommended them for decoration to our government, but he told me that as far as the party goes, I have no relations with them. But in practice they turn to me with a number of questions. The party organization for the Aragon front was set up by me and Com. Buksin during my stay at the Aragon front. Com. Grigoriev was elected to be the party organizer.

From 14–21/9/37, Com. Buksin and I conducted three party meetings (Valencia, Albacete, Úbeda); at the latter two, party groups and two discussions were set up (Cartagena, Totana) with the principal question: the situation in the "village" in light of the decision by the plenum of the CC VKP(b) and our tasks in local conditions. People were very attentive toward the speech, which many of them were hearing for the first time; many posed questions and discussed questions widely in debates. The principal moments from the debates were the following:

1. The decisions by the CC VKP(b) were approved by all the comrades;
2. They branded the Trotskyist band of Bukharin, Rykov, Tukhachevsky, and others traitorous German-Japanese spies against the motherland;
3. The question of mastering Bolshevism was correctly tied to an increase in class vigilance, to the development of Bolshevik criticism and self-criticism, without respect of persons;
4. All the meetings emphasized the leitmotiv that we were striving to send to Spain nonparty men and people who were concerned only with technology, which led to the fact that we were working without any political orientation, disregarding political factors in the country and the provinces.

*Examples:* 1. *MELNIKOV* (Valencia) says: "Com. Grigorovich in a discussion said to us that we had come here as military specialists and should not carry on any kind of political conversations . . . "
2. *ARKADIEV* (Albacete) "Abramov organized the dispatch of wrecking, they tried to get all party spirit out of us." . . .
3. *NESTEROVICH* (the same) "A large group of us came from the "village" and in Valencia no one would talk with us. Up to now we have not felt any kind of political education.
4. *KOLMAN* (Úbeda—main adviser in the 9th Rifle Division)— "They told us in Moscow to forget about our party spirit."
5. *LIASHCHENKO* (Úbeda) "Com. Grigorovich said to me that we were here as specialists narrowly defined and no politics at all." . . .
6. *VOROPAEV* (the same) "In the artillery group it came to individual comrades hiding their party spirit from one another."

5. There was talk about the disgraceful conduct of individual Communists who were dirty blots among our comrades, who, as a rule, work honestly, conscientiously, and behave as befits a Soviet citizen. Among the most striking examples of breaches in party ethics figured drunkenness, liaisons with women, embezzlement of government funds, pillaging.

*Examples:* 1. *LAMPEL* got drunk, tried to shoot Com. Tsvetkov (artillery group), and then resorted to his fists.
2. The most striking example of a breach of party ethics was the conduct of Rable, who has a wife in the "village." He got married here to the daughter of some kind of Socialist who has a fortune and has lived with her for six months already, considering himself officially married a second time and completely normal. Evidence was not [*sic*] brought forward against him

about desertion from the front, about acting like a grandee. He occupies a separate villa and lives with his "young" wife. He does not want to go out as an adviser to the brigade, considering that this post is not enough for him, and prefers to work as an instructor a little farther from the front. To all these questions which were presented to him by the Communists at the meeting he answered in a petty-bourgeois manner. People were indignant at his conduct; a decision was submitted to investigate the question of Rable at a party meeting. Rable explained his marriage here not in the way a Communist should, but gave a political evaluation for this fact, declaring that, as he said, in the party there are no laws forbidding a member of the party to get divorced and married. And to the question that he is still not divorced from the first wife who is in the "village," he cynically answered that technical conditions would not allow that. Rable also declared that, on the question of his marriage here, he had appealed to Com. Grigorovich and the latter, warning only about vigilance, had answered him that this was a personal matter.

3. A certain Liubimtsev, who was actually a lackey of Gorev in Madrid, expended without any accounting (embezzled) fifty thousand dollars, and this was sanctioned by Gorev and Grishin [Berzin]; now Liubimtsev has left for the "village."

Shekhter (anti-aircraft gunner) got his apartment renovated for him through the "friends"; around eighteen thousand pesetas were spent on one piece of equipment for this.

Citing these facts, the comrades showed that individuals among our great leaders here are living like lords, isolated from the masses, and do not know their everyday conditions of living. Many of these tendencies pointed at Com. Leonidov (the main adviser on the Aragon front).

4. A striking example of pillaging was the conduct of sailor Grigoriev. Analogous examples were cited also with regard to the conduct of Kulik, who several times went hunting and every time brought new guns; before his departure to the "village" he would go to a government institution and "delicately" try to beg for all kinds of knickknacks.

The expenditure of government funds in a number of cases was carried on without control; some individuals manifestly indulged in this to excess, losing their party conscience and forgetting that they were representatives of the homeland of workers of the whole world. The people openly call some individuals *petty tyrants*. Many conversations were held about the work with

287

translators. In addition to the fact that there are not enough translators, there are two policies regarding them:

1. In a number of cases they are severely criticized without reason, especially the internationalists;
2. And in the second case, there is fraternization between some of our advisers and the translators.

But as a rule, those who have translators do not work on educating them, and many complain about the political unreliability of the translators, especially the internationalists. The problem with the translators is still not resolved. The organizational school here has not justified itself. Recruitment was unsuccessful, people were not vetted, the leaders of this school (Olga Nikolaevna and others) were not suited for their appointment. Now the school has been let out and enrollment has started again; a new leadership is being appointed.

Instances of cowardice were noted as exceptions on the part of individuals (Rable, Maximov, captain in the 1st Division, and individual translators).

Comrades of the unit who have been sitting around for eight to nine months and more are homesick. These people, as a rule, are already tired, are in a nervous state and undoubtedly require replacement. The question of wages, which with our people here are highly irregular, is attracting attention. The pilots have high ones, the tankers lower, the general advisers still lower.

> *Example:* The main adviser for the 9th R.D. [Rifle Division], Com. Kolman, who receives wages from the "friends," has a lower salary than the radio operator who is working with him, who receives his wages from Moscow. A radio operator in the navy receives 70 percent less than an operator who works in Valencia, not to mention an operator with the pilots.

The question of wages now requires adjustment, owing to the fact that life has become more expensive by 100–140 percent. I think a subsidy is *essential,* especially for the group of lieutenants who are big men here (advisers for the brigades, and so on), and receive eight hundred pesetas each, owing to which newly arriving comrades cannot properly fit themselves out (a proper suit costs three hundred to four hundred pesetas). Individual comrades are already in debt.

. . .

Everywhere the lack of party-political work, the isolation of our people, in particular the Communists, from party life, was pointed out. People welcome the sending here of party-political workers and the putting right of party-political work. Now Com. Buksin and I are on the whole acquainted with all our comrades. My impression about the basic mass of workers in its overwhelming majority is most gratifying. With the assistance of the party group, and in-

## Document 58 *continued*

dividual party and nonparty Bolsheviks, we have begun decisively to put right the shortcomings here in the work of individual comrades. The majority of our people correctly understand their task, but the situation created earlier by a number of incidents did not allow the opportunity to get correctly oriented, as a result of which mistakes were permitted in local work in the provinces. The principal one of these must be considered the fact that our people, as a rule, observed mistakes on the part of our "friends" but did not help them correct them, considering themselves exclusively narrow specialists. And at the same time, individual comrades buried themselves, took upon themselves the role of commander, losing their place in organizing of victory for the revolutionary army. In a considerable number of incidents, the question of the relationships of our advisers with the "friends" arose, on which an exhaustive answer was given by Com. Buksin.

PARTY ORGANIZER—Krotov
22/9/37

Correct:
Col. Shpilevsky

## Document 59

RGVA, f. 33987, op. 3, d. 1033, ll. 174–183

NKO SSSR                                                                     *Top Secret*
    Intelligence Directorate                                    Copy N° 1
Worker-Peasant Red Army
Department __
22 October 1937
N° 222ss

To the People's Commissar of Defense
Marshal of the Soviet Union
*Com. Voroshilov*

I submit a report by the division commissar Com. Kachelin on political work among our people in "X."
    *Enclosure:* A report by Com. Kachelin of 9 pages.

Dep. Chief of Intelligence Directorate RKKA
Sr. Major of State Security
Gendin

*Report of Com. Kachelin*

By now I have already been to every corner of Republican Spain where our people are spread out. I have talked with the people everywhere and held party gatherings. Many observations have been accumulated, and there is a need to draw a number of conclusions about the work of our people.

It seems to me that the working environment for our people today has changed appreciably. These changes are conditioned by a whole series of circumstances, namely:

Today Republican Spain has its own regular army and, in particular, select cadres on the command staff; moreover, these cadres are present in the technical forces as well. A significant stratum of the higher command staff (which we have to deal with) consists of the higher officer corps—members of the Republican, Socialist, [and] anarchist parties and nonparty men. Part of them are skeptically minded with regard to Republican Spain, and some undoubtedly regard Franco sympathetically. There is indisputably an increased feeling of national consciousness among the command staff. Among the commissars are also many non-Communists. Each party is striving to consolidate its own influence within the army and the command staff is under the constant pressure of its own parties. In these conditions we have to help the "friends" to put together an army for victory on the basis of the slogans and program of the antifascist Popular Front. Great tact is necessary, political perspicacity, [and] sensitivity, so that they cannot accuse us of taking command, of Communist propaganda, and so on. Together with this, skill [and] knowledge are demanded from us to help our "friends" from day to day to cultivate their own cadres, and in the conditions of war, moreover.

The failures on the northern front undoubtedly intensified the hesitations among the petty bourgeoisie; these hesitations find their echo in the army as well. The persecution of Communists by the fascist elements and their accomplices has intensified.

Moreover, it must be noted that, as a rule, the persecution of the Spanish Communists is combined with a demand to "drive out the Russians." These same elements are trying to sow provocative rumors that, as they say, the Russians cannot help [us] now (in connection with the sea blockade) and that, in case of anything, "they will make off and Franco will hang us." There is also talk like this, "that if there were no Russians, then the war would have ended one way or the other long ago." All this fascist agitation undoubtedly also demands a heightened perspicacity from us and tact in our work. The enemy endeavors to use all our slips for their provocative purposes.

By the way, Prieto also is interested in what Com. Grigorovich will come with, that is, whether and to what extent the USSR will supply the Republican army with weapons and ammunition.

Does this mean that the Republican government has radically changed its attitude toward us and that the work of our people here is impossible today? There is no foundation for such a conclusion yet. Our people can and ought to remain here and can work with the greatest benefit. But it is also beyond doubt that the conditions for our people working here have become complicated, and we ought to make greater demands on ourselves. In particular, it is necessary to consider seriously whom we will send and for what purposes.

I personally believe:

1. It is necessary to give up sending tankers (except for advisers); they have their own cadres in sufficient quantities here.

2. The number of pilots must be increased, since the opponent has numerical superiority in the air force.

3. Keep the number of our gunners approximately at a level of thirty to thirty-five men, including the anti-aircraft gunners. There is a need for gunners.

4. [There is] great demand for sapper-engineers. There are not quite enough of them among our people.

5. The sending of lieutenants and first lieutenants *as general arms advisers* should be decisively given up.

It is, of course, necessary to use those who are here; in the future, send lieutenants and first lieutenants in small numbers—in the capacity of rifle/machine-gun instructors; moreover there is no point in attaching them [to units] for the entire time, but it would be better to use them for training rifle/machine-gun instructors from among our "friends." Send qualified comrades to be corps and front advisers. I believe that it is necessary to send comrades from among the best regiment commanders to be corps advisers. In my opinion, we ought not to strive to send advisers for every division. Here, in my opinion, we ought to limit ourselves to sending advisers for those divisions where our "friends" have fewer division commanders prepared; in particular we ought in the first place to provide the Communist division commanders with advisers. Send comrades with a rank no lower than major to be division advisers. As a rule, it is necessary to give up on sending advisers for brigades: this requires a huge number of people. In individual cases it is possible to send one assistant, from among the well-prepared captains, for each corps and division adviser in those divisions and corps which are covering especially important sectors of operation.

6. Two to three comrades should be sent to be advisers for the general staff: one as the main adviser for the chief of the general staff, the other as the adviser for the air force, and a third as an adviser for the intelligence department. Moreover, these comrades ought to sit on the general staff and not only work on narrow operational questions but take in all the current army work. Today our influence is on the whole reduced to working up operations. Dubrovin, as the adviser of the chief of the general staff, sees Rojo from time to time and is absolutely uninterested in the staff's current work in all its amplitude.

One of our majors is always at the staff, but this is an absolutely helpless and useless person. In these conditions we not infrequently have to work blind.

7. As before, the question of the translators is acute. There are not enough of them; part should go home and part of the number of "internationalists" must be expelled as suspect.

8. The replacement of those sailors who have been here already around nine to twelve months should be carried out urgently.

9. It would be good to reduce the number of radio stations in communication with the "village"[92] and likewise reduce the number of our people who have no direct connection with military work. The tankers and aviators themselves can make do without direct and immediate communication with the "village." Let them send detailed written dispatches through their command; in other respects they can send dispatches through us in case of need. I am afraid that at present, given a whole series of radio stations, we ourselves could be violating military secrecy.

10. The matter today stands like this: that commanding the tank forces will be accomplished by our "friends," and this is proper, for our tankers are about eighty men all together and only in the B.T.[93] regiment.

I believe that there is no sense in keeping Com. Korolev as adviser for the commissar of the tank forces. I ask to use him as my assistant. Com. Fotchenko is also in an equivocal situation, since in the B.T. regiment, side by side with Fotchenko, is another commissar from among our "friends"; moreover, the latter has two assistants. I believe that in good time Com. Fotchenko must also become an adviser for the B.T. regiment commissar.

Com. Agaltsev believes that he needs one commissar for each of the Russian squadrons. I do not agree with this, for in each squadron there are only eleven to thirteen men from our people. But it is indisputable that it is very difficult for Com. Agaltsev to work, and I ask you to send him assistance, even if it is only one worker.

11. Once again I ask that you elaborate on the question of dispatching and assigning [rank to] the engineers who are working in the factories.

The sending of internationalist citizens of the USSR should be approached more carefully; to be more precise—not to strive for quantity. If for some reason or other it is impossible to put them at the disposal of Com. Grigorovich, then one thing is absolutely obvious to me: that we ought to be interested in and influence a more expedient utilization of them and ensure a more precise accounting for these comrades for the staff of the International Brigades.

How are our people working and what is the state of their political morale?

Our tankers, and in particular the pilots, are working under a great deal of stress. It is a very common occurrence for each pilot to be compelled to fly four to six sorties a day. Enormous moral and physical endurance are expected from the comrades, but I did not encounter any complaints about fatigue. Our Soviet people are astonishingly excellent. The [regular] gunners,

## Document 59 *continued*

anti-aircraft gunners, engineering-technical staff work tirelessly and courageously. Matters stand somewhat differently with the general arms advisers, who *are working on their own* and have an extraordinarily large amount of work. The majority work well, but they might work to even greater advantage if systematic control were set in motion and it proved to be a great help for them with their work. A number of advisers are wonderful examples in their work, as, for example, Comrades Fedorenko (3rd R.D.), Volikov (34 R.D.), Bondarev, and so on. But due to the fact that the higher advisers have weak control and are not exacting enough, individual advisers loaf around and have even become demoralized. Like, for example, Com. Shvartsman, for whom I am sending a corresponding description together with a dispatch. Some comrades make a perfectly good showing on the battlefield but then behave disgustingly once off it. To this number belong, in particular, Comrades Yarkin and Panov.

Observing the work and behavior of our people, one also clearly detects the shortcomings of our educational work. One thing is indisputable: that our people are very confused about what in fact the capitalist encirclement means and under what circumstances one has to carry out the struggle of the international working class and the fraternal Communist parties. Our people are very confused about how in fact the antifascist Popular Front is being realized. They are accustomed to a situation where the dictatorship of the proletariat exists, a leadership of one Communist party, that there is a leader Com. Stalin, and another order of things they somehow or other cannot even imagine. In one of the squadrons, they suspect that the chief of staff (from among the Spaniards) has fascist sympathies. One of our pilots asked me whether I would let him "crack" this chief of staff on the spot. Another lieutenant saw two translators from among the White emigrants and began to shout that he hanged all White emigrants. Similar things not uncommonly result in our people's not doing well in their appraisal of the people surrounding them, and they really overdo it with tacking on the labels; they say that this one is a "fascist," that that one is a "wrecker," and so on. The harm in these kinds of judgments (although they do not even go beyond the circle of our people) is obvious. There is still a vast amount of political work lying ahead [for us] to do here.

Material from the fascist newspapers, where the testimony of our captured pilots Khoziainov and Kirsanov is cited, was sent to you. Undoubtedly, the authenticity of this kind of testimony must still be carefully verified, but if the nature of these testimonies is confirmed, then this fact also deserves the most serious attention.

The question of strengthening military discipline among our people was presented to me very pointedly. The lack of proper discipline undoubtedly led to the deaths of the pilots Coms. Sileverstov and Gudenko.

. . .

The state of political morale among our people is strong. But I must say that the failures on the northern front have engendered alarm among part of our people about the outcome of the war against the fascist rebels. I believe that in this area it is necessary first of all to strengthen explanatory work, but at the same time I want to draw attention to the fact that our advisers do not always approach operations after careful consideration.

It seems to me that there is a lot of impulsiveness and thoughtlessness in our operational-military work.

Take just the latest two operations, which were proposed but for a number of reasons miscarried. After Belchite, it was decided to conduct the Teruel operation. I should frankly say that the scope proposed for this operation was immense, but its execution was absolutely not ensured; it was clear beforehand that the missions that were set would not be successfully executed. The very same picture was repeated with the second operation, where the seizure of Saragossa was proposed (because of the rain, the operation had to be postponed). Intelligence was set up abominably poorly. We knew little about the opponent. A lot was said about setting up reserves, about training the troops (and these questions are crucial at the present time), but our advisers, in my opinion, did not display sufficient persistence in resolving these questions. Self-criticism is still not highly thought of here; in particular, the senior advisers pay very little heed to the voice of the advisers under [their] command. It is bad that individual advisers issue orders to the advisers under their command, thereby forcing the latter to become commanders. I'm trying to create a situation where all of the orders go through the appropriate chain of command, while it is the business of the advisers to aid in carrying out these orders. It seems to me that it is necessary to control the work of our senior advisers more, even in the "village." With this objective in mind, it is necessary to recall people to the "village" more often, and it is moreover necessary to recall only the main military adviser: his deputy and the front advisers can report on his behalf. In my view, having received clear instructions from the "village," we sometimes do not entirely clearly grasp how these instructions can be practically implemented. Personal contact is best to help resolve these questions.

In conclusion, I request that you enlighten us more often concerning the immediate tasks in the Socialist construction of the USSR and questions on the international situation; otherwise, it is very difficult to work: there is nowhere to receive an orientation here.

As usual, I am awaiting additional newspapers, literature, military books, and magazines.

Com. Zilberg requests that you allot his family a better apartment.

The wife of Com. Kliuss (the Military-Medical Academy) complains that there were very large deductions from her husband's salary and she is forced to sell things; moreover, she is extremely ill and needs treatment at a serious health resort.

I ask you to intervene in this matter.

Correct:
Colonel Shpilevsky
21 October 1936 [*sic*]

## Document 60

RGASPI, f. 495, op. 74, d. 206, ll. 91–146

An account by M. Fred on work in Spain
14 December 1937
Top Secret.

Comrade Manuilsky, talking with me after my return from detached duty, suggested that I write a report characterizing the general military situation in Spain and questions connected with the International Brigades.

He advised that I deal with facts concerning my personal work in a separate report.

I decided, on the basis of the instructions received, to write three separate reports, of which this is the first, inasmuch as the Personnel Department is interested primarily in this question, *an account of my work.*

I set forth below in the greatest detail and in chronological order all the most important facts that I gathered during the year I spent in Spain.

*September–October 1936*

Until I left for my new work, I was posted as the political assistant in the secretariat of Comrade Kuusinen. When he sent me off on my trip, Comrade Manuilsky said some words that I have not forgotten after all this time: You have to report for work in the CC of the Communist Party of Spain and you will do whatever work the comrades entrust you with. But you know, it is not necessary to sit in the office; rather, you can go to the front, and the sooner you earn a position in the army, as a soldier, as a commander, the better. This is what is asked of you in Spain.

After several days, having met beforehand in Paris with Comrade Luis, who was going home with a report, I reported to the CC of the Communist party in Madrid (15 September 1936). Comrade Gerö presented me to the members of the politburo and went with me to the apartment of Comrade Díaz, who is ill and rarely leaves his apartment. Comrade José Díaz described the range of my future work: to assist the CC on military questions and to work in close contact with the leadership of the Fifth Regiment. Comrade Frid (died later in the battle of Madrid) who had arrived a day earlier had already begun work in the Fifth Regiment with the mission of teaching the cadre personnel military matters. In the Fifth Regiment, I found an Italian comrade, *Carlos,*[94] whom I had not known earlier, who told me that he worked in Moscow in the MOPR, and also one Hungarian by the name of De Pablo, who represented the Society of Friends of the Soviet Union in the country. Also working there as a secretary was a Polish Jew, *Juanita, and her husband,* also a Polish Jew.

I quickly fell into the routine of work in the Fifth Regiment, where I was assigned military-operational and organizational work on the headquarters staff. The more active workers in the leadership were the Spanish Communists Lister, Modesto, Castro, García, Ortega, and the Italian comrade Carlos.

Dividing my time between work in the CC, where Comrade Marty, together with the French comrade Vidal (Gayman), was already working on military matters, and work in the Fifth Regiment, almost every day I was called upon to attend the sessions of the politburo and to take part in discussions or make reports on the military situation and on the usual military-organizational questions, sometimes on the instructions of the politburo itself and sometimes on the instructions of the leadership of the Fifth Regiment.

I met with the military attaché, Comrade Gorev (with whom I was acquainted from earlier work abroad on Fourth Directorate[95] matters), in the embassy, because I had been assigned, together with the member of the politburo Mije, for liaison with Gorev and with Gaikis, who was at that time the secretary of the embassy.

The party also had at its disposal separate groups of comrades who had arrived from abroad. Comrade Alfred from the Comintern arrived, and after some time the German comrade whose new cover name was Gómez. Comrade Alfred began to work at the CC on personnel matters.

Comrade Frid, having been unable to work in harmony with the leadership of the Fifth Regiment, was sent to Albacete with the mission of training cadres there. Comrade Gómez took his place. But he could not get along with the leadership either and subsequently, before the critical days for Madrid, received permission to go to Albacete.

The Hungarian comrade De Pablo somehow disappeared from the scene, and by various truths and untruths found himself in Paris. Juanita, because of suspicions of contacts with the Polish embassy, and her husband were dismissed from the Fifth Regiment.

Together with Comrade Alfred and Checa, the member of the politburo, we assigned the new comrades who had arrived from outside to various jobs, some (Comrade Kurt and other Yugoslav and Bulgarian comrades) to Estremadura to establish partisan detachments, others (Comrade Karl and others) to the workshops of the Fifth Regiment to manufacture [supporting] weaponry, hand grenades, mortars; and still others were sent to Albacete to the internationalists, gathered there gradually in the first battalions of the future International Brigade.

During the course of my work, I often went to various sectors of the front—accompanying Modesto, Lister, Carlos, and García, checking up on individuals detached from the Fifth Regiment, and acquainting myself with the situation at the front. Thus, in the course of the first month, I got to know the front commanders: Paco Galán, Burillo, Márquez, Cavada, Moriones, Arregi, Escobar, Mangada, Barceló, Arellano, López Tienda, Heredilla, and many other column leaders, honorable officers who had already been in the Fifth Regiment or had been drawn to it because they had lost faith that the army was being correctly led by the commander in chief of the armies of the center at that time, General Asensio. I had already been able to acquaint myself, personally, on the spot, and from information from the individual commanders, with the situation regarding matters at the central army's front, from Somosierra-Guadarrama to Toledo. And I [had formed] the definite opinion that General Asensio was a dangerous wrecker. This view was confirmed with each passing day, as I studied the operations up to and after Talavera and the facts reported by the commanders of the Fifth Regiment. These facts and the opinion of the leadership of the Fifth Regiment were brought to the attention of the politburo which, in turn, on the basis of its own information, concluded that Gen. Asensio was a dangerous person.

In Madrid itself, the Fifth Regiment encountered instances of wrecking: a workshop for hand grenades blew up, killing the workers and the chief engineer, an American who sympathized with us; commanders of the Fifth Regiment were arrested and their bodyguards disarmed; permission could not be obtained for a workshop to produce mortars; fortification work in the environs of Madrid was forbidden, even though the party and the Fifth Regiment had mobilized thousands of volunteers, men and women, who came to do the work; weapons that were held in the storehouses were acquired for the battalions of the Fifth Regiment only with great difficulty, and only just a few hours before they left for the front; the forces of the Fifth Regiment were used piecemeal at the front to no purpose, by battalions at various points, so that they could not be gathered into a powerful striking force at a given sector of the front, and so forth.

At one of the politburo sessions, it was decided to bring these facts to the attention of Comrade Rosenberg, the political chairman, and get to Caballero with agreed-upon steps concerning Asensio and his other petty accomplices. The Socialists, in their own turn, likewise did not trust Asensio and people such as Pretel, Virgilio Llanos, Almendros (all from Caballero's inner circle) began to look for contacts in the Fifth Regiment, so that joint friendly pressure on Caballero would help him free himself of Asensio. Comrade Mije and the Communist ministers Uribe and Hernández were instructed by the politburo to put pressure on Caballero in this matter. Asensio could not show himself at the front, because the commanders and the soldiers there already hated him.

In connection with the question of Asensio, I was once called to the embassy to see Rosenberg. They told me there that it was necessary for us to go along with Asensio and that it was necessary to do everything possible to support his authority. Rosenberg has already succeeded in discussing this approach with Comrade Mije and, it appears, also with Comrade Marty. I tried to explain to Rosenberg and Gorev why this could not be done and the fact that, with such deep mistrust as the front shows in relation to Asensio, this must not be done. Even if Asensio had been an honest person, it was still better not to appoint him to command an army that has no faith in its commanding officer.

After this meeting with Rosenberg, I stayed for some time in Gorev's office, where he continued to try to convince me of the necessity of "giving in," as if it depended on me that the army's mindset was against Asensio. The secretary of the embassy Gaikis and Comrade Orlov (who works with the neighbors) were present.[96] I explained to Gorev and Gaikis that the matter did not depend on either me or the Fifth Regiment and that even José Díaz had expressed his bewilderment in the case of Rosenberg's intercession, using the following words: "I do not know if he (Rosenberg) feels it is necessary to protect Asensio from the party at the demand of Largo or to protect the party from this traitor."

This was my first falling out with our comrades. It is true that I said at the time that Rosenberg had spoken to me in a way in which a Bolshevik should not speak . . . This phrasing of mine, which Rosenberg found out about, was, of course, excessive. Comrade Orlov, who disapproved of the tone when Rosenberg and Gorev were speaking to me, later reminded me several times that I had let myself be provoked into using harsh words and that this became the reason for the hostility shown me by Rosenberg in our further relations.

At that time, the party had succeeded in having Largo Caballero appoint five comrades, from a list drawn up by the party, to work on the general staff, in order to have their own eyes and ears in the central leadership of the army. I was on that list as General Kléber for work in the operations department of the staff, and Comrade Gayman, as Major Vidal, was to go to the organizational department of the staff; the other three were Spanish comrades. I received an official appointment from the ministry.

It is necessary to explain how I became a "general," for this also caused dissatisfaction and mockery on the part of Rosenberg. It must be said that even I was astonished when José Díaz and Hernández returned from a regular visit to Largo and said that it had been necessary to present us with a definite rank, since otherwise we would be undercut in the ministry. Largo, resisting the proposal by Comrade Díaz, objected that there are not any generals, colonels, and so on, in the party who could occupy such positions. Then Comrade Díaz answered him that the party had such people. So I became a general, in order to impress my co-workers in the staff more. This leap upstairs was excessive, you know. It would have been more fitting to have become a colonel or a major, and I would have been fully satisfied with that. But the step had already been taken, and the appointment took place. There was no way to take it back. Comrade Gómez, it seems, was also on the list as a general, but Largo refused to accept more than five Communists on the general staff, since candidates were approved from the other parties according to a certain ratio.

Before this new assignment of mine, I managed to get to the battles at Toledo, driving there together with Lister, in order to help him (secretly), and Lieutenant Colonel Burillo, again appointed commanding officer of the Toledo group. In Toledo, we—that is, Burillo, Lister, and I—were again convinced of the ridiculously poorly hidden treason on the part of Asensio. Until he got this assignment, Lieutenant Colonel Burillo, an honest man devoted to us, commanded the Guardia de Asalto police forces in Madrid. The party put him up as a candidate if Largo agreed to get rid of Asensio. Asensio, learning of this, decided to "wreck" Burillo, assigning him to the chaos in Toledo three days before the city was taken by the enemy. Asensio had the same views about Lister, who, as commander of the Fifth Regiment, had too much power in Madrid. The removal of Burillo and Lister from Madrid was in itself a sign for the party to be on guard against the plans of Asensio in Madrid itself.

And what about Toledo? Within the city, there was a siege against the cadets in the Alcázar, while the anarchist units and units of the regular army sabotaged each attempt at storming the Alcázar by the people in the Fifth Regiment. Each time the troops storming it were repulsed, being met by mockery from the indifferent anarchists and army soldiers, who were living quite well in Toledo, which was being plundered by them.

From the direction of Talavera, the column of Yagüe, consisting of selected Moroccans and legionnaires, was rapidly approaching. Under the circumstances that were developing, it was necessary to stop the pointless storming of the Alcázar, to limit ourselves to a siege of the cadets, and to throw the maximum forces against the enemy columns that were approaching the city. This is what Burillo and Lister decided to do at my suggestion. However, the Alcázar had to be taken, whatever the cost, or else Burillo and Lister would be put on trial; this is what all the orders said, in writing and by telephone, which were received from Asensio. Entrance into the city was controlled by posts of the POUM gang. The day before the city was lost, this gang, halting our car as we were entering the city, arrested Lister and me. If it had not been for our Mausers and the fact that our comrades' car raced into the city where they informed our people, who rushed to assist us, our stay on this earth might have ended then in Toledo.

We did everything that we could to hold back the enemy from outside and to take the Alcázar by a new assault. It was already too late to do either. We stayed one more day in the city, conducting the battle with Yagüe's column and with the cadets in our rear, who were beginning to make sallies out from the Alcázar. Contact with Madrid was broken off. There, in the report of the general staff, Toledo was already considered taken by the enemy. We continued to hold on for twenty-four hours more. At 3 P.M., Burillo and Lister advised me to leave the city by the only bridge, but it was not known whether or not it had been seized by the enemy. Along with my translator Durán (now with division commander rank and the chief of the Special Section of the Army of the Center), we stepped on the gas and, under machine-gun fire, rushed across the bridge in a southerly direction. We got through. We sped on further, and . . . the car flew off the road embankment at full speed and we flipped over several meters below the embankment into a vineyard. I had only minor injuries. Durán and the driver were unhurt, and even the car was all right. We could continue our escape. Burillo broke through behind us, I don't know how. And Lister stayed on inside the city, in order to break through the encirclement with his detachment under cover of darkness. In street fighting late at night, Lister led the remnants of his detachment out of the city.

In Madrid, Asensio gave the order to arrest Lister and Burillo. They were to be put on trial . . . for surrendering Toledo to the enemy. Asensio most probably did not know about my presence in Toledo.

I returned to Madrid and started working in the operations department of the staff. Sabotage was everywhere. The chief of the main staff, a Socialist and an honest worker named Estrada, was helpless against Asensio and his henchmen. Every proposal by Major Estrada, agreed to by Comrade Gorev and by us, met with resistance on the part of Largo Caballero, who consulted only with Asensio, whose proposals were approved without any [reservations].

Encountering Gorev and the other Soviet comrades in the headquarters, we acted as if we did not know each other. Then later they officially presented me to the Russian comrades. A proposal worked out by the staff and us was made to the military minister on the creation of the first brigades. Largo for a long time did not agree to sign it. At that time, there was another clear case of betrayal by Asensio: the five-thousand-man group [at Mangada], which was commanded by the combat commander Márquez, was almost totally surrounded by the enemy in the hills. The flanking units pulled out. Márquez requested assistance or permission to pull back to the next good position before it was too late. He requested permission from Asensio to withdraw at least his artillery battery, for which there was not even a single shell left (or any hope of receiving any shells). Asensio refused Márquez on all counts, ordering him to stay put until the last possible moment. Márquez in despair showed up at the headquarters of the Fifth Regiment. The matter was clear; retreat was necessary, before it was too late. We set forth the matter to Comrade Díaz and we advised Márquez to pull out of the position that same night. Thus a five-thousand-man group was saved. At dawn the enemy ordered an attack from all sides, but struck only empty space. The detachment of Márquez appeared unexpectedly from the rear and had comparatively great success, forcing the enemy to reduce somewhat his headlong rate of advance on Madrid. The result—Commander Márquez was removed from his duties and placed before a tribunal. Asensio wanted to extract one admission from Márquez: had he received the order for his action from the headquarters of the Fifth Regiment—specifically, from Kléber [?].

All these facts, which were known to the comrades from the CC of the party, caused great indignation. Rosenberg continued in his role as reconciler, considering me responsible for the attitude against Asensio. At that time, Comrade Marty was no longer in Madrid. Remaining there alone, Comrade Gayman-Vidal still insisted on leaving for Paris, which caused indignation in the politburo. Comrade Díaz proposed making the Communist Party of France aware of the matter and demanding the expulsion of Vidal from the party for cowardice. Comrade Marty departed—he was recalled home—but he left Madrid rather with impressions from talks with Rosenberg than with an evaluation of the situation as it was at the time in the politburo.

Delegates from all the fronts came to the CC of the party with information on the situation and with requests for assistance. Comrade Cordón from Estremadura, who was a member of the CC, Comrade Uribe from the Teruel front, Comrade Comorera from Barcelona and the Aragon front, comrades from Málaga, and many other comrades, including commanders with no party affiliation and commissars who were Socialists, came. Working simultaneously on the general staff and in the military department of the CC, I had much fuller information from the fronts through the CC than through the general staff. On the basis of this information and personal questioning of people on the spot, I evaluated our forces and opportunities and the forces and opportunities of the enemy much more precisely than did the general staff, which maintained only poor contact with the fronts. I, like the other Communists sent to work together with me on the staff, considered the continuation of my work on the staff a waste of time. I requested that Comrade Díaz release me from this unpleasant duty, which made me a hostage to the saboteurs on the staff. I requested that I be sent to the front, where people were needed. Comrade Luis, at that time returning to Madrid from his home, found me in this mood. He did not approve my departure from the staff, rebuked me, and said that it was necessary to continue working on the staff, however unpleasant it might be.

I worked up a plan of operations and submitted it to a session of the politburo, at which this plan was approved. It was decided that Mije, Uribe, and Hernández would seek an audience with Largo Caballero. I was supposed to explain the military plan of operations that the party was insisting on carrying out, and I discussed this plan with Comrade Gorev beforehand. Up to that time and for a long time after that, the staff did not have any kind of plan of action at all. It simply recorded events and did even that badly, never knowing exactly what was going on at the front.

According to my plan, in the middle of October 1936 we could and should undertake a very promising offensive on the Teruel sector; another in Estremadura, in the rear of the enemy advancing on Madrid; and a third, coming down from the hills, in the direction of Talavera, thus threatening the open flank of the enemy advancing on Madrid. All questions were closely studied with Comrade Uribe, the military leader at Teruel; with Comrade Cordón, the leader of Estremadura; and with other comrades who came at the summons of the CC—and they returned to their positions in order to prepare for their operations.

Along with Comrade Mije, I was received by Largo Caballero and explained this plan to him. Largo heard out my oral report very unwillingly and offered his conclusion that the plan was unrealistic. That was, at least in his words, Asensio's opinion, to whom he had given a written report for his conclusions.

A week later I had to report another plan to the war minister. This time it was a plan for the possible defense of Madrid. This plan had been coordinated beforehand at the embassy. Rosenberg was very skeptical about the possibilities for the defense of the city.

To reinforce the units of the Fifth Regiment and the detachments of workers mobilized by the party for the defense of Madrid, I requested the addition of two brigades out of the nine brigades that we had succeeded in forming with the military minister.

The directions of the comrades at the embassy were that units of the new brigades could not be thrown into Madrid and that it was necessary to gather a large strike force together, even if it was at a much later time—that is, to strike with a large force after the loss of Madrid, if at that time it had been lost.

I expressed categorical opposition to this line of thinking and said that the basically true principle of striking with maximum force was in this particular case being wrongly applied. Having lost Madrid, we would not get it back even with twenty brigades, and we would simply be conducting a rearguard action, which would very soon reach its end, that is, the full defeat of the Republic.

Comrade Díaz insisted on assigning the new brigades for the defense of Madrid. Along with our minister Uribe, I had to report on the plan for the defense of Madrid to the war minister. Caballero simply waved his hand and called the plan a fiction. At that time, I told my translator, Comrade Durán, to inform the war minister that Madrid would defend itself, but the government, if it did not take every possible action, would lose its authority in the country and in the army.

With that, our audience was ended. The party mobilized feverishly and sent the best comrades to the front, in order to have an effect on the units that were retreating headlong. All the members of the politburo spent those days at the front, returning to the CC in the evenings for meetings and work on mobilizing the masses. New Soviet comrades arrived from home, and they dismissed the policy held earlier at the embassy regarding the utilization of the new brigades.

Comrade Marty returned to Madrid with Gayman-Vidal and the next day left for Albacete in order to begin the formation of the International Brigades.

The first tanks appeared in battle on our side. Showing incredible bravery, they, and only they, delayed the rapid advance of the enemy.

One of the new brigades went into battle, the first brigade of Lister, in whose formation Carlos, Castro, and I actively helped him, while remaining in the leadership of the Fifth Regiment.

Comrade Modesto and Comrade Márquez, with their detachments, conducted a rearguard battle at the approaches to Madrid. The detachments of López Tienda and Escobar retreated from Navalcarnero utterly defeated. With Comrade Durán, my translator, I drove around to all these detachments, giving advice on the course of the operations and laying out lines along which the workers' battalions of Madrid hurriedly dug trenches in the rear.

At night, up to a hundred of the various frontline commanders would gather at the Fifth Regiment to consult with us (Castro, Carlos, and me) on possible actions.

Asensio's headquarters let the direction of operations slip out of their hands and occupied themselves with secretly transferring the weapons that remained in the artillery stores to everyone except the battalions of the Fifth Regiment and the detachments of the Communist party.

At the nighttime gatherings of commanders in the Fifth Regiment, to which the politburo had delegated Comrade Mije as its representative, the outrage against Asensio knew no bounds. Some called for going and arresting Asensio. One must assume that someone among those present at the gatherings was regularly informing Asensio about all this.

In the battle at Seseña, I participated in Burillo's detachment, which was advancing from Aranjuez. The enemy had already reached Getafe.

Lister's brigade and the others thrown at the enemy in direct frontal assaults had no success. Here, by the way, Comrade Frid was killed; he had been called up from Albacete in order to assume the duties of chief of staff in Lister's brigade.

Madrid needed help, and Comrade Díaz got Caballero to approve my assignment to command the international units which had been formed in Albacete under the numerical designation of the 11th Brigade.

In the last days of October, I drove to Albacete with the mandate of the CC and Caballero's signed order in my pocket.

In Albacete, I reported to Comrade Marty. Here I became acquainted with Comrade Nicoletti, the brigade commissar, with Comrade Gallo, and with others. Vidal was carrying out the duties of the chief of staff. Before I arrived, Comrade Marty appointed a Frenchman, who, after Irún, came to Albacete with a group of his people. Comrade Marty, along with other comrades, did not trust this commander much, even though they had assigned him to the post. He was suspected, not without cause, it seems, of being an agent of the French Deuxième Bureau.

The question arose about how to remove this commander and how to help me take up the position without offending the self-esteem of the boys in the French battalion, where the commander of the brigade had his own people.

Comrade Marty proposed calling a gathering of the commanders and commissars of the battalions at which he would present me as the brigade commander appointed by the government. In order to apply greater authority against the friends of the previous commanders, Comrade Marty suggested to me that I provide him with some data from my biography. In giving the information about myself to Comrade Marty, in the presence of Commissar Nicoletti, I warned him that not everything that I was telling him could be repeated at the gathering of the commanders. The commanders had already begun to gather in the next room.

I had a meeting with my rival in private and was convinced that there was no danger from him, for he was ready to turn over the position to me without a fight and wanted to leave for Barcelona and the anarchists there, who had proposed that he form a strong detachment.

Comrade Marty, praising me at the meeting, still stayed within bounds and did not say everything that he knew about me. Then I came before the commanders and corrected Comrade Marty on those points in his speech where he had gone too far in disproportionate praise that I did not deserve. I then proceeded right to the tasks before us and named a time the next day when I would check up on the condition of all the battalions at a tactical exercise in the field.

Over the course of two days, Comrade Marty and I spent time with each battalion and checked them out in a tactical exercise. The first, the German battalion, was commanded by Comrade Hans (Kahle), of whom the commissar had said to me that the German Communist party did not trust him particularly. The battalion did well. The second, the French battalion, was commanded by Dumont, whom I knew from Madrid, where he had not made a good showing (being assigned to the Fifth Regiment as the commander of the machine-gun company in Lister's brigade, at the last moment before a battle he refused to go into battle and, without the knowledge of the Fifth Regiment or Lister, got permission from Comrade Marty to go to Albacete with his people, where they there and then assigned him to command a battalion).

## Document 60 *continued*

The third, the Polish battalion, was commanded by the remarkable soldier Comrade Bolek, and the commissar working there was Comrade Matuszczak, one of the unassuming heroes of the battles to come.

The fourth, the Italian battalion, was commanded by the Italian Galliani, who had come from America, an honest fellow, but an incompetent commander and a romantic windbag.

The brigade still had no weapons. On the fourth day that I was in Albacete, I got some weapons issued—just rifles—for the brigade through the president of the Cortes, del Barrio, who was in charge of weapons.

Russian advisers arrived to inspect the brigades, and they were satisfied with the exercises and night maneuvers that I had conducted.

We secured the necessary railroad trains to move the brigade to Madrid.

I want to report one fact here that in my opinion played some role in the dispute that arose later between the first International Brigade and me on the one hand and the comrades who stayed in Albacete on the other.

When matters had progressed to the point of loading the brigade into the railroad cars, people began to exert an influence on Comrade Marty, telling him that the battalions were still not ready for battle, that it was necessary to train longer, and that it was necessary to wait until the machine guns were received. Once we left, we would supposedly not be given any additional weaponry.

At that time, when people who knew the tragic situation at the front in Madrid were straining to get into the fight there as soon as possible, the chief of staff of my brigade, Vidal, and, together with him, Commissar Nicoletti and Gallo, pulled back, and even Comrade Marty hesitated, in turn. In dealing with these comrades, I was forced to retreat, in the final account, so that the first three battalions were put on the train and the fourth battalion remained in place, with the agreement that it would entrain in two days. The Italian comrades were waiting for the arrival of a new commander from Paris, the Republican Pacciardi, who was supposed to replace the incompetent Galliani. Pacciardi arrived and in my presence conducted exercises with his battalion. Not having succeeded in getting acquainted with his battalion as he should, he declined, if you please, to leave for the front with us. However, Commissar Nicoletti convinced him that it was better to remain two more days.

On 3 November, the three battalions left in the direction of Madrid. The chief of staff of the brigade, Vidal, an incredible coward, concealed the fact by throwing dust in people's eyes. He always knew everything better than everyone else. Thus, he was always finding fault with everything, and he made himself intolerable to Comrade Díaz and the others at the CC. Having left with a great show for Paris with the opinion that everything was already lost, he then returned to Spain with Comrade Marty and with his own wife. He did not want to leave Albacete and his wife. Vidal had great influence over Comrade Marty.

The brigade left for the front without Vidal. To replace him, Comrade Marty recommended to me a retired major from the French services, Vicente, who came to Spain under a contract with the Spanish government. In accordance with this contract, he received the rank of lieutenant colonel in the Spanish army, and they paid him a large salary in hard currency. This old man had no relationship whatsoever with the International Brigades and he landed in Albacete (by mistake!?) because the government, having sent for him from France, had nothing for him to do at that time. Comrade Marty approved his trip from Madrid and brought him to Albacete.

And so I had a chief of staff Vicente, who began to put under his signature the word "colonel."

An excellent fellow, intelligent and devoted to the party, a young party member, Comrade Durán, who served as my translator throughout the time in Madrid and at the fronts, I made my adjutant and, in fact, the chief of staff. Colonel Vicente was simply an unnecessary "decoration" for our brigade and he stayed away from the front. One could not find fault with Vicente's knowledge of military affairs. But he was an alien person to us, with great pretensions, moreover, and quick to take offense, who hated Durán, but restrained himself in his relations with me and outwardly behaved in a disciplined manner.

Vidal remained in place at Albacete with the mission of organizing the expected internationalists and sending them after us, submitting reports to me by courier, and receiving instructions from me.

I went by car to Vicálvaro, near Madrid, sooner than my battalions. Having met with them and deployed them beforehand, I went to Madrid, where, with the help of our comrades from the embassy, I received the long-awaited machine guns. I sent a courier to Albacete with the order to send me the Italian battalion immediately.

In Madrid, there was chaos. The government and the staff had fled without giving anyone the authority for the defense of Madrid. In Chinchona, the anarchists arrested Caballero and Asensio but soon released them.

In the headquarters of the Fifth Regiment and in the provincial committee of the party there was feverish work—direct the construction of barricades, dig trenches, disarm some and arm others, liquidate the known hotbeds for the Fifth column, and so on.

The party members were in good spirits and did not allow themselves to be drawn into the general flood of running away. The party on the spot turned around some individual comrades who had been fainthearted right from the start.

With the help of the party, a "Junta de Defensa" was formed. General Miaja joined it, and his chief of staff was Major Rojo. Otherwise, the buildings of the ministry and the staff were empty. The former life had come to a standstill.

I presented myself to General Miaja and Rojo, and the latter ordered me to move the brigade into the city.

6 November. Madrid is burning after the latest bombing by the enemy air force. The scene at night is terrible. My three battalions entered Madrid in the morning, and after a short speech I sent them in the direction of the University. We know that the enemy is preparing for a triumphal entrance into Madrid. By noon we are already at University City. My headquarters (that is, Durán and I) was set up in the department of philosophy and literature. On my right was the French battalion, in the center the Polish battalion, and on the left the German battalion; we stretched to the Manzanares River and partially into the Eastern Park and the Casa de Campo, on the side of the river where a fierce battle with the Moroccans was breaking out.

The enemy air force flew in and bombed us thoroughly. The enemy artillery took aim at University City. My people stayed calm. The first day went by, and nothing else of note . . . The brigade needs assistance. The combat strength has gradually dropped to 45 percent of the previous numbers. In some companies, there were no more than twenty-five men left. The commander of the Polish battalion had been wounded, and Comrade Petrov (from the Comintern) had replaced him. Many company and platoon commanders could not be accounted for. The exhausted people were falling asleep in the face of the enemy, even in the hottest moments of battle and on the move. They were becoming indifferent to everything. It was not possible to give orders. It was only possible to remind them that they were Communists and to ask them to exert, once again, the last of their strength.

Durruti arrived with some unstable units. Durruti was killed, and things got even worse. Where is our Italian battalion, why doesn't it come? I had already sent three couriers to Albacete, but they did not come back. Comrade Beimler arrived, and I sent him as the fourth courier to Comrade Marty in Albacete.

My commissar Nicoletti and the chief of staff Vicente were sitting out the battle somewhere in Vicálvaro and did not show up at the front. There was champagne in Vicálvaro, and Vicente really liked a tasty meal. In the scraps of reports that reached me, he and Nicoletti kept referring to some matter or other.

The commander of the second battalion, Dumont, disappeared from the front. I thought that he had been killed but, as it turned out later, he was sitting in Vicálvaro. There were no commanders who could take over the second battalion. I took over command of the companies of that battalion directly, until Ludwig Renn arrived on a visit and I transferred command of the French battalion to him.

Hans Beimler returned from Albacete angry and swearing. Comrades Marty and Vidal had met him with rebukes over why he had come and why he was mixing in what was not his business. The Italian battalion was made part of the newly organized 12th [*sic*] International Brigade, and Comrade Lukács was in command of it. Kléber had no right to give orders to the base at Albacete.

They did not want to give Beimler gasoline for the return trip, since he had come to Albacete on his own initiative, without being summoned there.

Several more days passed. We were fighting with the last of our strength. The enemy outflanked us. It was necessary to move the German battalion from the left flank to the right. A Spanish unit was entrusted with the position of the German battalion, and this unit retreated, letting the enemy to slip through into the Eastern Park to seize the French Club and other buildings and drive a wedge right up to the Model Prison. I sent the French battalion from the left to the right (the battalion commander Dumont had returned to the ranks), in order to plug the gaping hole. The enemy drove a wedge into the center at the French Bridge, at the Veterans' Institute, and at the [Palaceta].

I had to move the headquarters back, into the building of the Golf Club. The Fifth Regiment sent its battalions to me. The battalion of Asturians commanded by Heredilla gave us our first support. Heredilla was killed, and the battalion wavered . . . trouble again.

Out of nowhere, a group of Spanish Communists appeared and included themselves in our brigade. On our flanks, we acquired new and more stable forces. Paco Galán appeared on the left, but he was soon wounded. Ortega took his place and firmly consolidated the position. On the right, a new brigade of carabineros and another detachment of anarchists, with the energetic Commissar Mera.

Gradually, our front was brought under control and stabilized. The International Brigade had finally exhausted its strength.

Nicoletti came with a photographer and took pictures of us. He brought the news that the 12th Brigade, after an unsuccessful assault on Angelos Hill (where it did not distinguish itself), should arrive soon to relieve us. Separate groups of soldiers fleeing the Angelos area had already arrived at our positions before his news and had joined in the battle. It does not matter; they fought well.

Comrade Petrov, the commander of the Polish battalion, could hardly stay on his feet. I took him on as my assistant and appointed the Frenchman Rivière in his place. An excellent fellow, a bourgeois, but an honest antifascist. He took the battalion to a dangerous location, in order to take back part of the Palaceta building from the enemy. A battle broke out, the most terrible combat episode during all that time. The Polish battalion clashed with the Moroccans with hand grenades and bayonets. A terrible fight took place on the stairways and floors of the building. Of the sixty men in a Polish company, one platoon of which was Bulgarians and Yugoslavs, only five or six men were left alive. The battalion commander Rivière shot himself, after less than three days in Spain.

November drew to a close. (I am writing this from memory and note that the events of those days appear before me involuntarily in what is not a strict chronological order. It is entirely possible that there are errors in the dates.)

## Document 60 *continued*

The 12th Brigade came under my command. An antitank battery arrived. Another battery was added to the one that was with me. Now there were two, the battery named for Thaelmann and the one named for Liebknecht. We depended entirely on them in close combat, as they served to support the infantry directly, at a time when the Spanish artillery acted only on a centralized basis, not in connection with the infantry.

The soldiers of the 12th Brigade, particularly the German Thaelmann Battalion and the Italian Garibaldi Battalion, were not at all inferior to our soldiers. It was a somewhat worse matter in the Franco-Belgian battalion. By chance we turned up a fascist organization directed from Belgium. Among the Belgians, the commander of the antitank battery had a compromising intercepted letter that was addressed to Dégrelle. And there were actually cases in battle of clear acts of sabotage with the antitank weapons, which were manned predominantly by Belgians. It was a similar situation in the field artillery battery, where there were also Belgians. This battery was always firing short and hitting our people. The battery commander had to be shot and appropriate actions taken.

I began to command an extensive sector in which, besides the two International Brigades, there were also six or seven brigades reorganized by me at the front from the members of former ill-assorted detachments.

Since I had no possibility of directly commanding my own 11th International Brigade, I turned over the command of it to Comrade Hans, the commander of the German battalion named for Edgar André.

The Madrid newspapers were talking about me. If I am not mistaken, the first was the newspaper of the right Socialists, Prieto's organ, *Socialista*. In an editorial speaking of a unified command, the newspaper pointed to Kléber. The ballyhoo was picked up by other newspapers as well. At the start, the Communist newspapers stood aside from this.

I must add to this that by now the first issue of our brigade newspaper, which was [put together] by Comrade Nicoletti, had been published (either in Madrid or in Albacete).

Nicoletti did me a disservice with the picture he painted of me. Not only did he blurt out everything that he had heard in Albacete when I revealed myself to Comrade Marty; he added on to it and embellished the facts, so that a simply scandalous history resulted. The newspapers began to reprint this story.

All kinds of correspondents came to me, but I would not receive them. I simply did not have enough time. In one case, however, I gave in to the requests of my adjutant, Durán, who day after day was visited by a correspondent that he knew from the newspaper *Claridad,* at that time the organ of Largo Caballero.

In order to dispel the harm caused by our Nicoletti, I began to answer questions in such a way as to blur over and deflect interest in my past in the USSR. This is where the interview with General Kléber came from.

## Document 60 *continued*

Some time passed, and the English parliamentary commission arrived in Madrid. Nicoletti, who was always lounging about somewhere, but not at the brigade itself, showed up and said that it would be necessary to receive this commission, which would get information from me. I flatly refused to do so, for the simple reason that I was afraid that my English would hardly stand up before the Englishmen as Canadian, which is what the newspapers took me for. In addition, there was a limited number of generals in Canada, and it would hardly seem possible for any of them to be on the side of the Communists.

Two days passed after I had explained my reasons to Nicoletti. I looked up, and people were pouring into the room and being introduced by my adjutant, one of them a representative of the ministry of foreign affairs and another a representative of the English parliamentary commission. They came into the room where I was sitting down to lunch, simultaneously presenting their calling cards. It was already too late to hide. A group of a dozen men, the delegation, stood in front. I asked them to come in and take a seat at the table. The questions began. I laughed matters off, avoiding a serious conversation. Accompanying the delegation to the door, I was exposed to several photographers, who were rapidly cranking the handles of their cameras. And so I got caught a second time.

When all this came out in the newspapers, but in a garbled fashion, it is understandable that back home they were perplexed and considered me some kind of adventurer.

As far as I know, the comrades right there did not at first assign this any particular significance, rather considering it to be good propaganda for our cause. Only Comrade Gorev chewed me out for all this sensationalism. After that, there was another blunder. This was at the coffin of Hans Beimler. I was standing honor guard with Comrade Gorev, and the photographers had been told that pictures were not allowed. Then I spent about an hour more in the building of the CC. On my way out, they again included me in the honor guard at the coffin. The next day I saw myself in the *Mundo Obrero*. I had not noticed it when the photographer took our picture.

I am going into some detail here about these instances because I know what damage this harmful ballyhoo did to my reputation in the eyes of the comrades. Not wanting to justify myself, I still have to say that nobody could have succeeded in totally avoiding any publicity under the circumstances in which I found myself at that time. Of course, it would have been possible not to give the interview. I did that only because I wanted to dispel the nonsense put out in our brigade newspaper. There was no way to avoid instances of ending up on a photographer's film. I recall a case where one German photographer of the Komsomol press caught me in a general's hat. I ordered the sentry to chase the photographer away. By the way, recently it came out that this photographer was an agent of the Gestapo.

For a long time, the English military attaché in Madrid sought to visit me. He would come to El Pardo, where my headquarters was located. Presenting his calling card, each time he would receive the answer that I was not at home. I posted a special sentry whose duties consisted of warning me if he saw a car with an English flag approaching.

It appeared to me that I had established good relations with the command staff of the 12th International Brigade that was subordinated to me. Comrade Lukács, the brigade commander, Belov, his chief of staff, Fritz, the Russian adviser assigned to him (and in fact the brigade commander) were subordinated to me and my headquarters. They accepted all my actions to increase their combat capabilities after an explanation of this or that measure. For example: there was a cavalry squadron in the 11th Brigade and another in the 12th Brigade. The combat conditions required unification of these forces for joint operations on the flank. We also consolidated our artillery into a single unit and controlled it on a centralized basis in combat, one time serving the 11th and another the 12th Brigade, depending on which of them occupied the crucial sectors.

And still, even though the command staff of the 12th Brigade knew the necessity of such measures, some of them still had a tendency toward a "small owners'" attitude, saying, this is my battery, my squadron, and so forth.

Unfortunately, it so happened that my chief of staff, Colonel Vicente, to whom I had given orders to work out instructions for better work by the rear services, signed the instructions thus: by order of the commander of the International Brigades, General Kléber—chief of staff, Colonel Vicente.

The word "international" (in the plural form) became the subject of the first protest on the part of Comrade Lukács. In vain, I explained that I had not given such orders to my chief of staff and that, in reading the completed instructions, I did not pay any attention to the signature. I ordered the chief of staff to correct the error and thought that the matter would end with that. But no, it was reported to Albacete where, in all probability, they began to record Kléber's sins of commission and omission.

During that time, the 12th Brigade had gradually been reduced in numbers in the battles to the same low level as in the 11th Brigade. Together with Comrades Lukács and Hans (temporarily commanding the 11th Brigade), I, as the commander and chief of the sector, discussed the situation of our brigades, and we asked for replacements from Albacete. Over the course of the entire time, up to January 1937 and after, when I had left Madrid, we had received no replacements from the base. The ranks had wasted away, and the numbers in the battalions had dropped down to two hundred men or even fewer. The rear services of both brigades, however, had not had any significant losses and maintained their numbers, so that the proportion between the combat and service troops became 1 to 1, and even greater in favor of the rear services.

## Document 60 *continued*

In Albacete itself, as was passed on to me, they were carried away with the formation of new brigades, the 13th, the 14th, and so on.

A dangerous situation had arisen, where the first two brigades, for lack of replacements, could disappear from the scene once and for all, which would have been a powerful blow to the prestige of the International Brigades.

After the death of Hans Beimler and considering the situation, I presented my views to the responsible comrades at the embassy:

To that point in time, we had sacrificed in battle the best cadres of the Communist parties, particularly the cadres of the illegal parties, which was a great loss for the revolutionary movement of the affected countries. Our role in Spain was not only to fight but to teach people to fight and to help to build a Spanish people's army. We had to take care of our valuable cadres. This could be accomplished in the following way: accept Spanish replacements into the ranks of the International Brigades; survey our swollen numbers in the rear services with the goal of replacing some of the comrades shot in the battles on the front lines with others; and in particular, protect the cadres of our illegal parties by not sending them into battle as concentrated units and in the role of rank-and-file soldiers.

My experience of joint work with Spanish units had shown me that the fear of losing combat capabilities through a dilution of the ranks of the internationalists with other elements, as they feared in Albacete, was not justified.

I also pointed out that the formation of new brigades in Albacete based on the arrival of people from outside leads to the creation of a Tower of Babel in each of the brigades and battalions, where dozens of different languages are represented. It is almost impossible to command such brigades. One cannot rely on the objectivity of the translators in combat. The headquarters cannot issue orders in several languages. The Spanish language should be the common one for everyone, for a number of reasons, if only because everyone can learn the language easily.

My plan was considered a great heresy by the comrades in Albacete. They brought up petty fears, even of a nationalistic and chauvinistic nature, which even good Communists are sometimes not free of. I tried to get through on a direct line to Comrade Marty and was finally successful. But I was very disillusioned when Comrade Marty on his end of the line said that he did not want to listen. I hung up the telephone.

I do not know why none of the responsible comrades, neither Comrade Marty nor Vidal nor anyone else, ever deigned to come to Madrid to acquaint themselves on the spot with our situation and with our needs and requirements, that is, with the requirements of the first two International Brigades.

They not only did not send replacements to our brigades but at that time even stopped providing us with clothing, footgear, cigarettes, and so forth, taking care instead primarily of supplying the new brigades. Such a relationship to us on the part of Albacete outraged not only me, but also Lukács,

Hans, and in general all the comrades from the 11th and 12th International Brigades.

Our wounded who had ended up in Albacete after getting out of the hospital were forcibly sent to other units, and they more than once took trucks from the battle in order to reach their old brigades.

On many questions, the front did not understand the policies of its base, and the base did not consider the legitimate demands and requirements of the frontline units.

With the full agreement of Comrades Lukács and Hans, the commanders of the two brigades, we proceeded to exchange battalions between the brigades, with the goal of getting rid of the multiplicity of languages in each and the occasional friction between the Germans, the French, and others. In each of these two brigades, there were one German and one French battalion. If the chief of supply in a brigade was a Frenchman or a German, then he would in actuality set up a bureaucracy of representatives of his own nation, which would result in unfavorable criticism in the battalions. To the German soldiers, it seemed, without basis or sometimes with some basis, that the French chief of supply was robbing them of food, clothing, bedding, and so on, and favoring his own Frenchmen, and vice versa. The Poles and others considered themselves treated badly by both sides. There was another, more important, reason for which I ordered the transfer of the German battalion in the 12th Brigade to the 11th Brigade and the French battalion from the 11th to the 12th Brigade, which Albacete perceived as a crime that could not be allowed to go unpunished. This reason was the deep-seated difference in tactics and in the German and French models for military deployment. The action of small units in group tactics of the one and the other has its own peculiarities. To retrain the one in the methods of the other would be harmful to the cause and, more important, too late.

So, with the full agreement of the brigade commanders, I regrouped the Germans with the Germans and the Frenchmen with the Frenchmen. The Polish battalion was transferred to the 12th Brigade because it was made up predominantly of Polish émigrés to France and the Polish tactics were close to those of the French. Furthermore, the Poles understood the Russian language as well, the only language in which Comrade Lukács could explain himself to his people.

I also transferred individual Spanish companies and battalions that were subordinated to me to these International Brigades.

The International Brigades had an enormous attraction for the best part of the Spanish young people. After the death of Hans Beimler, I decided to take advantage of the developing sympathy campaign and proposed (with the approval of the party) the slogan "Ten soldiers from each battalion into the 'Hans Beimler' International Brigade"—that is, the International Brigades would welcome the sending of up to ten volunteers from each battalion from all of Republican Spain, with the goal of forming a brigade named the Hans Beimler.

None of these actions were understood in Albacete. After evaluating the situation on the Madrid front, during the course of December 1936, I considered that it was necessary for us to take advantage of the shock that the enemy forces had suffered during November and to go over to the offensive on the far-right flank, that is, in the region of the Escorial. Making use of the wintertime, when the passes through the Guadarrama mountain chain could be defended with weak forces, we could pull the inactive units down from the mountains to the Escorial in order to strike a powerful blow against the lines of communications in the rear of the enemy besieging Madrid. The military units in Guadarrama-Somosierra, amounting to more than forty thousand men, were at the time the strongest, for they were made up of the original volunteers and had not been subjected to demoralizing desertions, as the other units south of Madrid had been. I wanted at least to replace the units in the mountainous sector of the front gradually with other units that had been demoralized and had suffered great losses. There, on a quiet front, they could sit things out and get themselves sorted out, giving us the possibility of bringing a strong reserve force down out of the mountains. It seemed to me that our splitting hairs and wanting to patch up the front in Madrid itself had led to our forming too great a concentration, unnecessary if we wanted to limit ourselves in Madrid to just defensive actions.

The indecisiveness of the command staff resulted from not believing that we had actually had a great victory over the enemy, a victory—or, more correctly, the first half of a victory, which the second half should follow. It was a matter of the enemy's having been shaken and bled white at Madrid in November. This was the first half of our victory. The second half could be achieved if the enemy was not given time to bring up new forces. And as it turned out, the enemy only in the first half of December began to show new activity on a large scale, that is, only after the famous meeting of Göring and Mussolini, after which fresh forces of the interventionists began to arrive in Spain.

I brought these views of mine on our operations to the attention of the comrades who had influence over the course of the operations.

With what did we actually occupy ourselves on the Madrid front during the course of December and after? We came up out of the trenches (and often also did not come up) right in front of us in order to storm the inaccessible Garabitas Hill or the buildings of Carabanchel, expending great amounts of blood for meters of territory, which, in the final analysis, had no significance whatsoever for the course of the war.

In one such battle, units of my sector were supposed to storm the Garabitas Hill. We had been given about two dozen tanks. The time was set for the assault. The infantry was ready and the tanks did not come and did not come.

Finally, the tanks arrived. The infantry, having moved forward once without tanks and having achieved nothing, did not want to go a second time, even with the tanks. An uncoordinated attack resulted where some went and others did not. This very thing happened with a brigade of anarchists, who were generally difficult to get moving forward. And then the tanks stopped in front of the enemy trenches and did not move forward or backward. *It turned out that the tanks had gone into battle without filling up with fuel.* The enemy antitank guns dealt with the immobile tanks as they liked. After the battle, the person guilty of this criminal negligence, the tank commander, put together a report that the tanks were lost because Kléber had wrongly assigned the missions to the tanks. Later, the actual cause came out, and the guilty party was sent home. This was the origin of my conflicts with individual comrades of the Soviet personnel.

Another instance: the enemy was attacking the Casa Quemada point with a battalion of Moroccans. I requested by telephone that the artillery open fire. I gave all the data about where and how to fire. Everything could be seen from the artillery observation point, clearly spread out before their eyes. A Russian comrade came to the telephone, and I repeated everything to him in Russian. He answered that it was our battalion, not an enemy battalion. I said to open fire immediately, and I would take all the responsibility upon myself; did he think that I did not know if a battalion was mine or the enemy's? But he continued to insist on his view and advised me to send out reconnaissance in order to clarify the situation. Well, how could we not end up swearing at each other in such a case? I cussed him up and down. It was only after an hour that I succeeded in getting the artillery to open fire and then only through bypassing that comrade. And at home that comrade was a corps commander, Comrade Kulik. I did not know that and did not recognize his voice over the telephone. After some time, this comrade appeared at my headquarters in order to acquaint himself with the situation. I gave him all the information. And he, I saw, was searching for something to find fault with. Finally he found it, when I explained how I was carrying out the reorganization of the International Brigades, withdrawn by me into the reserves. (This was the swap of the German and the French battalions between the brigades about which I spoke earlier.) The comrade flew into a fit of rage. With all kinds of words, including "Wrecker! I will arrest you and send you home under guard," he attacked me in the presence of my co-workers at my headquarters. If you know what kind of authority I exercised in the army, it will be understandable what kind of impression that made on those present. Comrade Durán, at that time my adjutant, asked me in English if I would order him to throw that comrade out. I maintained my self-control (which, by the way, I was not always successful in doing) and told the comrade that all these questions had been agreed upon with Comrade Gorev and even with Comrade Grishin, the chief adviser. This statement again threw the comrade into a rage. He shouted, "I am the chief adviser here, not Grishin. Why didn't you tell me about this? I forbid you to transfer the battalions. Who do you think you are? Who appointed you the chief of the sector? I would not even entrust you with a company," and so on, in the same spirit.

By the way, I was right from start to finish, not he: Grishin was the chief adviser; he wasn't. The transfer of the battalions was a measure dictated by all the circumstances. I had received approval to carry out this measure. Everyone was satisfied. Moreover, everything had been done and completed. This comrade, fortunately, did not continue to work for long and was sent home after several incidents, not all with me.

I had no conflicts with the Spanish commanders, that is, with Miaja and with Rojo. On the contrary, Miaja, who at the time did not involve himself in matters, usually greeted me in a friendly manner. Comradely and even friendly relations and mutual respect had been established with the chief of staff, Rojo.

Among the commanders of the Spanish brigades, my subordinates, I exercised unquestioned authority. They liked it that before I gave them written orders, I would call them together and explain my thinking and only then give them the order.

Once, Nicoletti attended one such meeting of commanders and commissars at my headquarters in Aravaca. I don't remember exactly for what reason the anarchist Mera, commissar of the anarchist brigade, spoke out against Nicoletti, who in his own words just said, "We are Communists, we are Communists . . . "

The anarchist Mera was offended by Nicoletti's words and in turn reproached the Communists, with the accusation that they think a lot of themselves, that they think only about their own propaganda, and so on. Both commissars were wrong, but Nicoletti more so. I interrupted their argument and said, "I do not know and do not want to know who here is a Communist and who is an anarchist. We are all soldiers, commanders, and commissars. All antifascists are the same."

Later, Comrade Antón, the front commissar, in reference to that meeting, asked me if it was true that I had taken the anarchists' side against the Communists.

There were other incidents. Here is one of them. The brigade chief of supply, Comrade Duprès, a Frenchman, who was in general not a bad worker and comrade, allowed himself to use a crude and untactful phrase in addressing Rojo, the chief of staff of the army.

The matter was like this. Duprès came to Rojo to get his signature on a requisition for ten thousand rations of butter. Rojo asked him how many men he had. Duprès lied, naming an exaggerated number, and then said, "How can the Spaniards refuse to give the International Brigades butter? When the International Brigades die at the front, nobody asks for numbers, but when it is

## Document 60 *continued*

a matter of butter, they ask for the exact numbers. We came to help you, and you . . . " The unfortunate Duprès showed inappropriate zeal as the chief of supply, in order to get a bit more butter for his units. Rojo called me up about this, and I gave Duprès an official reprimand for lack of discipline and untactful conduct before the chief of staff, Rojo. Duprès then realized his mistake and accepted the punishment. However, Comrade Marty, the one time that he came to Madrid, brought up the incident with Duprès and another incident, "the removal of the battalion commander Dumont from his duties and the assignment of Ludwig Renn, a German, in place of Dumont," as evidence . . . of my dislike of Frenchmen. Comrade Marty said nothing about the fact that Dumont had fled the field of battle and left his unit to the mercy of fate.

Before the arrival of Marty in Madrid in the month of December about which I am speaking here, I had learned that Albacete was distributing various circulars in the 11th and 12th Brigades, addressing them to Lukács, Hans, and my commissar. For Albacete, Kléber had ceased to exist as an addressee. Instead, they began to pick Kléber apart. I was told that at Lukács's headquarters during dinner, one comrade, an adviser on troop reconnaissance matters, made some scornful remarks aimed at me. Some comrades became indignant and asked him why he was doing this behind my back. The rumor was started that I was . . . a Trotskyist.

Once the commissar of the Edgar André Battalion discovered several soldiers of his battalion at the moment when they were getting ready to leave to serve in a neighboring unit of anarchists. When questioned about who had given them permission to leave the unit of their own volition, they stated that General Kléber had given them permission, which was, of course, a lie. During the search of these soldiers, anarchist leaflets in the German language were found on them. So I became an anarchist, as well.

All these incidents, suspicions, and reservations were calculated to discredit me with the party and to destroy the authority that I exercised in my own units.

I did not know that at the time Largo Caballero in Valencia, wanting to make short work of the Junta de Defensa, had demanded, among other things, that Kléber be recalled from Madrid because he was intriguing with the Fifth Regiment against the government. Caballero raised such accusations not only against Kléber. Similar accusations were made against Antón, Carlos, Castro, and others, even against Miaja.

Largo Caballero had just one formal cause for all this, the meetings of the command staff. But it was not a matter, as they thought at the time, of meetings of the command staff at my headquarters, which were of a narrowly organizational, military-tactical, and instructional nature. At these meetings, no one ever said anything against the government or members of the government. Largo Caballero had in mind the meetings at the headquarters of the Fifth Regiment, which were conducted under the chairmanship of Comrade

Mije, a member of the politburo. The higher commanders, predominately Communists, were invited to these meetings, and Comrade Mije, as a member of the Junta de Defensa, provided information about the situation and actions of the junta and the government. At one such meeting, it was made known what strained relations existed between Madrid and Valencia and why this was so. The recurrent demand of Valencia, that is, of the assistant to the war minister, Asensio, was to give up six brigades from the army of the center for the other fronts. At that time, this could not be done. There was information that the enemy was contemplating a strong new offensive on Madrid. To weaken the defense of Madrid by these six entire brigades was rightly de-, scribed to all those present as an act of betrayal. The meeting approved a resolution against this action dictated by Valencia. Carlos and Castro composed the resolution. I came to this session very late. I did not speak at it and did not take part in composing the resolution. I do not know why the CC, considering this resolution to be in error, considered me to be a coauthor of it. As far as I know, there was never a tendency on the part of the leadership of the Fifth Regiment to place themselves in opposition to the Central Committee of the party. The CC attributed this tendency to Comrades Castro and Carlos at the same time and considered me to be in an alliance with them. No one ever accused me directly.

To get back to Comrade Marty's visit to Madrid in December: both International Brigades were held in reserve at El Pardo at that time. I and my headquarters were also there, to whom these brigades were subordinate. Comrade Marty spent the entire day in El Pardo visiting the brigades. He set up a conference of the commanders and commissars, about which I was not informed and which I was not invited to attend. In everyday life, one might not take offense at this, but under military conditions and at the front, I considered that it was an unpardonable emphasis on his relationship to me that would soon reach the units. A commander who has to be removed should be removed, but as long as this is not done, he should be respected as the commander, for tomorrow he will have to lead the units into battle and give orders. What kind of discipline will there be if the commander is deprived of his authority?

Fortunately, my authority was not shaken by this. Commanders and commissars came to me and recalled the matter with a lack of respect for Comrade Marty for his demonstration.

Comrade Lukács, who perhaps had more basis than any of the others for being dissatisfied with me, since I had more than once criticized his actions in battle, told me later that he regretted that he, too, had succumbed to sentiments against me.

The night after the visit by Comrade Marty in El Pardo, a conference was called in Madrid on questions concerning the International Brigades. I was also invited. Comrade Marty spoke critically against the amalgamation of the International Brigades with Spanish units, against unifying the brigades from the standpoint of language, and so forth—that is, against all my work. There were printed handouts worked up by Comrade Marty at hand for those attending. Glancing at them, I was amazed by one phrase which said, "the International Brigades in Republican Spain play the same role as Franco's foreign legion . . . ," an argument for the thesis on why we could not be mixed in with the Spaniards.

I spoke up against such theses and asked Comrade Marty to send a copy of the handouts to Moscow so that they at home would know the essence of our arguments.

The end of December approached. For the entire time, the enemy had had no success in my sector. . . . The quiet Nino Nanetti, at that time the commander of a battalion in one of the Spanish brigades on the right flank of my sector, correctly noted that in the section of his battalion at Villanueva it would be possible to start an offensive on the enemy's flank with success. (This is the same place where in July 1937 we undertook the operation on Brunete.) I consulted with Rojo. He allowed us to commit not more than three battalions and himself allocated three batteries for it. We took the enemy position, occupied Villanueva de [la] Cañada, smashed the enemy battalion, and entered Brunete. The battle developed very successfully, and we had practically no losses. Then suddenly the brigade commander received an order directly from Asensio (over the head of Rojo and avoiding me) . . . that he should retreat and that the three attached batteries should immediately cease fire and vacate their positions. I refused to give permission to carry out this order. Then I received confirmation from Rojo that the batteries were pulling out of their positions because in Valencia they would not give permission for an offensive "a fondo," that is, for a deep offensive. The matter was clear to me. My battalions, having received the order not to continue the offensive and to quit Brunete, demanded the investigation and execution of the guilty party, clearly an agent of the fascists, who had given the order to break off the attack. This agent was the assistant to the war minister. And it was not possible to tell the battalions who it had been.

Comrade Gorev informed me that Comrade Grishin (Berzin), the chief adviser, had arrived and wanted to speak with me. I reported to him. Along with Comrade Grishin in the room were Gorev, Gaikis, and the comrade who some time back had called me a wrecker and promised to ship me home under escort. I thought that the discussion would be about that, in fact, and about the fact that he had said to me at that time that he, and not Grishin, was the chief adviser. I was mistaken. Comrade Grishin began listing my sins: they said that I was making some kind of Napoleon out of myself, intriguing against the government, turning the Fifth Regiment against the CC, not obeying the instructions from Albacete, creating undeserved fame for myself, and that, if Madrid had defended itself, I had had nothing to do with it. And therefore, he ordered that I would leave for Málaga, as that was the decision of the party.

Málaga? Involuntarily, I remember how a few days before I had been listening to Radio Seville and heard the words of General Queipo-de-Llano that . . . "this little General Kléber, who will still not escape the bullets, to be removed from his post and sent to Málaga . . . " I remember something else. In his own time at Toledo, General Asensio submitted the candidacy of Lister for the post of civil governor in Málaga. They also wanted to send Burillo to Málaga.

I asked Comrade Grishin what I would do in Málaga.

"You will be an adviser."

What kind of adviser, to whom? Really, to appoint me an adviser means turning over our cards and showing that I am a Russian. I could not go along with this and reckoned that the comrades had not thought of that. Then Comrade Grishin corrected himself and said that I would be an adviser to the party in Málaga. And here I objected to Grishin, saying that a person who is accused of such sins as directing party members against the CC could not be an adviser. Then one of those present said, "Look, he is afraid to go there, the coward."

"I will go to Málaga," I said, "but only as a common soldier."

"That is a theatrical gesture" said the same voice. I kept silent, since it was hard to prove the opposite.

No one relieved me of my duties. It would have been somewhat unwise at that time for the military minister in Valencia. As if to do me a bad turn, at that time the city council in Valencia had renamed some street or other with the name "Heroic General Kléber." The Popular Front in Castilona sent Kléber a new car as a gift, and Rafael Alberti wrote a poem, "Kléber, the defender of Madrid . . . "

Around the beginning of the new year, divisions began to be formed from the brigades. They formed three divisions from the brigades in my sector. The sector headquarters ceased to exist, and in the new list of division commanders, Kléber did not show up.

I departed for Valencia without the knowledge of my units. In saying goodbye to Rojo, I had the impression that he honestly regretted my leaving the Madrid front.

The archives of documents of the 11th and 12th International Brigades and the first Madrid sector from 7 November until the end of 1936 I turned over to the headquarters of the advisers for shipment to Moscow.

*January–May 1937*

Having arrived in Valencia, I reported to the CC of the party. I did not call on the assistant war minister, Asensio, as etiquette required. It may be that this was a mistake on my part at the time, or more correctly an undiplomatic omission. The chief of the general staff at that time, General Cabrera, told me as regards this incident that Asensio was "offended" by it. I simply could not force myself to shake hands with this enemy of the people.

Being uninvolved and at a certain distance from events, I could quietly evaluate the time spent in the Madrid posting. Even before this, it was clear to me that there was no point in my remaining at my post in Madrid. It could have caused some discomfort for the party.

If one were to speak of my relationship to the government, at that time of Largo Caballero, no one knows better how matters really stood than Comrades José Díaz and Luis. During November and December in Madrid, where Díaz, La Pasionaria, and other members of the politburo often came, I explained my view of the government in approximately these words: the government is a government of the Popular Front. Largo has great influence with the masses. We cannot and should not act against him. The fundamental mission of the government is to win the war. This basic question cannot be resolved, however, as long as the assistant to the war minister, and the only person whom Largo believes, remains General Asensio. Even if there were no fundamental reasons to suspect Asensio of treachery, his promotion from the duties of commanding officer of the army of the center to the duties of assistant war minister, that is, in fact the commander in chief, is a challenge to the entire Popular Front and, above all, the Communist party and the army. The fact that Asensio has remained at his new post demoralizes the army. Largo Caballero, needing Asensio for the struggle against the Communist party, has in fact become a prisoner of Asensio or, more accurately, has become a screen behind which the forces of [Chiangkaishekism] are gathering against the party, against the revolution, and against the people. What do we Communists need to do? To move against Caballero? No. This is not the mission of the party, and, even if it were, the party does not have sufficient strength for it. Largo has maintained significant, although rapidly decreasing, influence with the masses. Largo Caballero's influence with the masses is shrinking specifically because he has become a pawn in Asensio's hands. We need to direct our fire against Asensio in such a way as to separate him from Largo and help the latter free himself from the destructive influence of Asensio on the army, on the war, and on the government. It is not just that the interests of the war and the revolution are dear to the Communist party, but it is also a friend to Largo Caballero, whom it will save from political suicide. Through the Popular Front government, the sole possibility for a government in Spain, the Communist party is joined with Largo Caballero by a "Catholic marriage," that is, one that is difficult to dissolve. It is true that at one time, after the government of Giral, the party rushed to [support] Largo Caballero. The last card had been played, if one can express it that way. The most "leftist" of the possible governments of the Popular Front had been formed, after which, if the government were compromised militarily, there were no other variations for a governmental combination within the framework of the Popular Front. Two possibilities remained: either power would end up in the hands of the anarchists, which they were willing to pursue but which we, the Communists, could not allow; or in the course of events we, against our will and understanding of all the circumstances, would take power, which would contradict the aims of the Seventh Congress of the Comintern. Once we had been bound by the earlier "Catholic marriage" with the "savior," Largo Caballero, we had to support him as long as the left wing of the Socialists, the trade unions, and the youth were behind him. At the same time, the party did not want to sign on to the policy of suicide, which was where Caballero's friendship with Asensio was leading. It was therefore necessary to break up this friendship by any means. And we *had* to succeed at this, for our position in the army was strong and the position of Caballero's government, which found itself now in Valencia (where they received him with an undisguised lack of enthusiasm and even with hostility), was unenviable. Whereas Largo Caballero earlier, as soon as he had [landed the fish], even threatened the Communist party with his retirement, he would not now be fooling around in Valencia and would fear to threaten the party with his usual blackmail. We must be capable of surrounding Largo Caballero with our support (whatever that means), so that people like Asensio do not have access to him. Largo must become a prisoner of those who will save him from Asensio and the counterrevolution. We will be supported in this by the Socialists, the trade unions, and all the youth, who have great influence in Spain and whom Largo does not suspect of hostility toward him. Thus, the active pushing in the desired direction should be done by *the youth and the army,* so that the Communist party does not involve itself prematurely in the action of "sanitizing" the government and the way it conducts itself.

What I said to the comrades from the politburo was not, of course, anything like discovering America. In fact, since October 1936 the party had been going just that route. There was a covert struggle going on in the minister's front lines. Caballero then personally took each such démarche of the party to the Council of Ministers. There he threatened resignation and tried to drive the Communist party into opposition to the government as such. Comrades Uribe and Hernández had difficulties in their roles as ministers. On the one hand, it was necessary to achieve practical resolution of the everyday questions, and on the other hand, a cause for the government's falling from within had to be avoided. Usually Caballero came out of these encounters as the "winner," and then he would scoff at the Communist ministers and allow himself to express his scorn for the Communist party.

The one, in my opinion, who did a bad job of backing up our ministers was the member of the politburo, Comrade Mije. Comrade Mije did not take an official post in the government. This was the advantage of his situation. The Communist party contacts with Largo Caballero and with the prime minister basically went through him. Comrade Mije also represented the party in the trade unions. Facilitated by this influence, he could likewise speak with Caballero as the representative of the trade union exec.[utive] com[mittee]. Comrade Mije, in addition to this, was the main representative of the party on the general staff in a secret position and officially a commissar. Comrade Mije did a poor job of representing and pursuing the interests of the party. He talked a lot but did not follow up his words with deeds. It usually went like this: at the politburo they would assign Mije the task of pushing some assigned question through with Largo. Mije would assure the politburo that he would get it done right away. It was a trifle for him, Mije, since he said that Largo would not refuse him. It was another picture when Mije was with the prime minister. A strange awe would fall over him before his excellency. Mije would hesitate, feeling himself to be a poor relation begging for charity from the all-powerful uncle.

It could be that I am mistaken in my evaluation of this comrade. My evaluation is put together from seeing Mije both at the politburo and at his reception by Caballero or from his work on the general staff. Mije reminded me of Figaro. I think that the politburo, in the final account, understood the true value of this work by Comrade Mije, who at the time the plenum was expanded in the spring of 1937 already was not playing as comprehensive a role as earlier. Together with Alvarez del Vayo, at his post as commissar, Comrade Mije brought the party only disappointments.

My mistakes in Madrid, about which they loved to talk in the plural in Albacete, were not specifically formulated by the politburo into any accusations of me as a party member, as far as I know. In any case, if there was a trial of the Kléber case, it took place without me, and I cannot say exactly of what the CC of the Communist Party of Spain could have accused me.

Therefore, I want to examine myself regarding how the individual members of the CC related to me.

In Comrade José Díaz, I always saw a comrade who valued my work and generally expressed solidarity with my opinions about this or that military matter. On questions concerning the International Brigades, I can definitely state that for the most part he was on my side more than on the side of those who criticized my work. Even after my quarrel with Comrade Marty during his December trip to Madrid (on the questions of the amalgamation of the International Brigades with Spanish contingents; simplifying the language muddle in the brigades; the policy of preserving valuable cadres, primarily of the illegal parties, and so on), Comrade José Díaz, having come to Madrid, listened to the other side, that is, to me, and said that I was entirely correct and that he and the party had full confidence in me. Right from the start, there was also no difference of opinion between him and me on the question of Asensio.

Concerning my evaluation of the military situation and the proposals and plans resulting from it, I can state with pride that Comrade Díaz always listened attentively to me, corrected me where it was necessary, but basically approved my proposals.

In evaluating the role of Largo Caballero, he could sometimes remain silent where I would formulate my definitions too sharply. He, of course, knew better than I how difficult it was to fight with this person.

Comrade Uribe, whom I personally value highly, related to me about the same way as José Díaz.

Comrades Dolores and Hernández, both of an impulsive nature, were even less shy than I was about expressing their feelings when it was a matter of some one of the usual dirty tricks on the part of Asensio and Largo Caballero. They [Dolores and Hernández] always met and greeted me warmly.

I was somewhat unfriendly with Comrade Mije as the facilitator, on the one hand, and from seeing his moments of weakness before the minister and the general, on the other. It was painful for me to watch as Asensio sometimes in the hallways of the ministry condescendingly patted Comrade Mije on the back, expressing in doing so his malice and disrespect, and he, Mije, was grinning with pleasure at the "honor" shown him. I could not refrain from pointing this out to Comrade Mije. Possibly this offended his pride.

Comrade Checa, always a silent one, never refused me in any matter whatsoever, and we established good and comradely relations.

Comrades Antón and Diéguez, leaders of the Madrid organizations, often came into conflict with me both at the CC and in the Fifth Regiment on questions of preparation of the party organization and the workers of Madrid for the difficult days before them and [of enduring] those days. They did everything that they could. It sometimes seemed to me that it would have been possible to do even more.

We could sometimes argue about material matters—say, the assignment of certain specialists is going too slowly, the management of the Saturday volunteer work on digging trenches is weak, and so on. I had no lingering bad feelings from these differences, nor, I think, did they.

I still have to speak of the relations between Comrade Gerö, who later went to Barcelona after the arrival of Comrade Luis, and me. Comrade Gerö, a thoughtful and serious person, worked with his usual calmness even on busiest days, with a very cool head. He valued my work in the military specialty and, together, we more than once had an opportunity to see how damaging to the politburo's work the interventions of Comrades Marty or Rosenberg were. Comrade Marty, suddenly taken with some kind of "genius" idea, would one day make a mountain out of a molehill and the next day the reverse. This jerked the politburo [members] around and made them nervous. We all noted with great relief, as an important event, the telegram recalling him home. In the final account, it was not Comrade Marty about whom the comrades had bad feelings, but his evil genius, Vidal-Gayman, all of whose views Comrade Marty pushed through.

Comrade Luis, after his arrival, brought his own style to the work. The sessions of the politburo became less democratic. And this was a good thing. However, he—again in my personal opinion, which I never told to anyone—shifted the lever to the other extreme. He had been used to working earlier with the comrades from the CC when the party was still young, small in numbers, and leadership was exercised personally and directly. At that time the conditions for the representatives of the Comintern were also different. Now there were totally different conditions. The party had grown and taken upon its shoulders the service of its people at the most complex moment in its history. With the growth of the party and its tasks, the people, the leadership of the party also grew. The earlier methods were no longer suitable. Comrade Luis had personally worked with the comrades from the politburo long ago and his authority was not disputed by them. But if another comrade had worked with the methods of Comrade Luis—doing everything himself and overshadowing the personalities of the comrades in the politburo—he would long since have failed and have brought down difficulties upon himself, even in a case where the leadership was objectively correct.

And so in Valencia, Comrade Luis, alone of all the comrades, in a conversation with me once laid out just what my sins in Madrid were. The basic one, in his words, was not so much my interview as its content. The real state of affairs behind the interview was known to him, and he could not hold me guilty of divulging facts from my life. In relation to the content, he reproached me for "prophesying" a great victory at the beginning of the new year. It is true that Marxists should not engage in prophesies.

He further said that no one disputed the services I had performed, but the party had been forced to take measures because an unhealthy situation had developed in the leadership of the Fifth Regiment in their relation to the party leadership. The leaders in this, so to speak, were Comrades Carlos and Castro, with whom, as was known, I worked in close contact.

The comrades from the Fifth Regiment mentioned above did not, either at that time or now, need me to defend them. Afterward, at the expanded plenum, they honored them as heroes. They gave reports, and Comrade Castro was elected as a candidate member of the CC. I considered it necessary to state, and I repeat it here, that, as far as I knew, there was no such situation in the Fifth Regiment and that neither Carlos nor Castro ever spoke with me about any kind of dispute between them and the CC.

In relation to Largo Caballero, he showed me the article in *Pravda* and said that, even though I had given my characterization of the government in a closely held meeting, he could not agree with my definition of the role of Largo Caballero.

On the questions that arose between Albacete and me, neither he nor the Politburo blamed me, but rather they perhaps agreed with me.

In the entire party leadership, it was not considered necessary to approve any sanctions whatsoever against me, and the politburo, particularly Comrade Díaz, did not agree that I should be sent home. I could remain at the CC in Valencia and work in the military commission. The party considered that the matter of Kléber and its results were part of the general business of the campaign by supporters of Largo Caballero against the people in the Communist party.

## Document 60 *continued*

At the time of this conversation with me, the comrades in the politburo knew that a delegation had arrived in Valencia from Madrid to request that Kléber return to work in Madrid. The situation was that a few days after my departure from Madrid, the enemy began an offensive on my former sector and broke through the front in the region of Las Rozas-Majadahonda-Aravaca. What the enemy had never succeeded in doing up until that time, he succeeded in doing this time. One of the comrades in the CC proposed that I go back to Madrid. The party leadership did not go along with this.

Being in Valencia, I also reported in to Comrade Grishin, who received me rather coldly, because he figured that the suspicions in connection with the Fifth Regiment were not without some basis.

In Valencia, there was a strange relationship with me on the part of the minister of finance at that time, Dr. Negrín. While I was still in Madrid, I once received a letter from him, brought to me by one of the commanders of the brigade of carabineros, Sabio. This Sabio did not inspire a great deal of trust. I reported this incident to Comrade Gorev. I also informed him of the content of all the conversations that I had with this Sabio. Sabio was always exploring for fertile ground and finally informed me that he was personally acquainted with General Mola from previous service in the army and that Mola was a Freemason and that under certain conditions Mola would turn his army against General Franco. Comrade Gorev, consulted with as he should have been, instructed me to take an interest in this story. Then a meeting was set up between Comrade Gorev and Sabio with me present. Here Sabio repeated the story about Mola. He also laid out plans regarding a carabinero corps (border guards) subordinate to the minister of finance, Negrín. This was all while I was still in Madrid.

Having arrived in Valencia, Sabio came to me and invited me to lunch in one of the restaurants on the beach, where Minister of Finance Negrín would be waiting for me. The meeting took place. During lunch, an intimate conversation took place about this and that, and Dr. Negrín, expressing "his pleasure at making my acquaintance," invited me to a dinner being held the next day in my honor at the Ministry of Finance.

I informed Comrades Luis, José Díaz, and Grishin about this. All of them advised me to accept the invitation and to develop this new acquaintance with him. The conversations with Dr. Negrín took place in German and in English. He sometimes showed off his knowledge and his Russian, telling me about his travels in the USSR as a delegate to an international conference of biologists and about the fact that his wife was Russian.

I was a guest at Dr. Negrín's four or five times. He told me about his disappointment with Julius Deutsch, whose services he had used in the matter of organizing the carabineros. He requested me to accept his proposal of becoming the person in charge of organizing the carabinero corps for him and spoke of the possibilities that he had as minister of finance for purchasing weapons in France, independently of the war minister. Knowing that I did not receive a salary from the War Ministry, he proposed to me the use of the services of the Ministry of Finance to whatever extent I considered necessary. I declined this last suggestion. In other respects, I continued to stay in contact with Dr. Negrín with the knowledge and approval of the party and Comrade Grishin. When I implied to him that the meetings with me could become the subject of suspicions on the part of Caballero's people, he assigned one of his sons for contacts with me.

During my stay in Valencia, I was invited to the academic house Casa de Cultura, where a luncheon was given in honor of General Kléber. Academics, writers, and artists—Bergamín, Macho, Prados, and others—praised the "defender of Madrid" to the skies and gave me their works with the appropriate inscriptions of dedication.

I formed a friendship with the poet Rafael Alberti and his wife, María Teresa León. They introduced me to the former director of the Seguridad and prominent member of the Left Republican party Manuel Muñoz, who held the high thirty-third degree in the organization of Freemasonry in Spain. Muñoz expressed in front of Alberti his indignation that in whatever situation the conversation turned to General Kléber, the political representative Rosenberg would say with significance that he did not know "that gentleman." In Muñoz's words, the minister of internal affairs and a henchman of Caballero's, Galarza, took this to mean that in relation to Kléber it was not necessary to be shy about the matter, and he had the insolence to state that this Kléber was an unknown rogue and adventurer and that he, Galarza, would soon put him behind bars. It was also known to Muñoz that Asensio's people were preparing an attempt on Kléber's life.

Once, when I went to the CC, they looked at me with surprise, saying that on that day there had been a rumor going about the city that Kléber had been killed on the street.

The fascist radio did not stop taking an interest in me and thinking up all kinds of cock-and-bull stories.

I [lived] outside of town in the cottage assigned to me by the Valencia municipal authority. I occupied myself with studying the military situation for regular reports to the military commission of the CC, was in charge of short-term courses for military party members, and wrote articles for the [military] journal *Agitprop* of the CC, which were published under the title "Tierra-aero-mar" (Land-air-sea).

Once, a messenger came to me from Dr. Negrín with a request for me to visit him. Negrín presented me to representatives of the Basque government and Asturias who had come down from the north—Aguirre, Peña, and others. They proposed that I fly to the north with them and take up military work there.

In connection with the threatening situation in the Málaga sector, comrades from Málaga had come to the CC and spoken with Comrade José Díaz about

## Document 60 *continued*

his sending me to Málaga. Finally, he got Largo Caballero to name me officially to command a sector of the Málaga front. I was summoned to the chief of staff, General Cabrera. Comrade José Díaz, and also Comrade Grishin, told me beforehand that I should, studying the available information on the particular situation in the south, ask Cabrera to allocate from the party an additional eight thousand rifles and a detachment of armored cars for Málaga. Comrade Grishin, for his part, promised to support this request. I learned from the party members who had come from Málaga that the headquarters of the Málaga front was politically unreliable and that it would be necessary to request the appointment of other co-workers for the headquarters.

General Cabrera, to whom I reported, conducted a discussion not about Málaga, but about the International Brigades, saying, "They say that you have influence in the International Brigades. How do you explain that in such and such a case the 12th Brigade did not carry out orders at Guadalajara or the 13th Brigade in this case at Teruel . . . ," and so on, in the same vein. I answered that I had had no relationship whatsoever with the International Brigades from the time I had left Madrid and that I knew of no case where these brigades had not carried out the orders of the command staff. We switched the subject to Málaga. Cabrera appeared not to have heard anything about my assignment. He suggested to me that I come back during the course of the day. On my second visit, Cabrera confirmed the orders by Caballero. I tried to shift the discussion to the rifles needed and asked him to appoint as my adjutant Durán, my old translator. Cabrera did not want to hear anything about it. He said that I should depart that same night and made the remark to me that the discipline of the Spanish army required fulfillment of orders without any conditions or reservations. In order to get time to warn Comrade Grishin about this new turn of events, I said to Cabrera that, being sent on such important work, I would like beforehand to study the situation according to the materials he had and to receive directions from him. Cabrera broke off our conversation and left the room for a while. A half an hour later (probably spent with Asensio), he returned and gave orders to his adjutant to prepare orders and travel documents for me. Having received the papers in my hands, I read: Mr. Kléber is assigned to the headquarters of the Málaga sector for use in one of the subsectors at your discretion. This meant that I was not going to command the Málaga front as had been the agreement of Comrade Díaz with Caballero. Under these specific conditions, of course, there could be no talk of the release of weapons for Málaga. The former Russian adviser to Cabrera, Ivan, tried to persuade me to accept the assignment. I went to Comrade Díaz to inform him of what had happened and to ask how to proceed. He was outraged by the change and advised me not to go. Comrade Grishin also did not advise going to Málaga. Cabrera was convinced that I, having taken the documents, had left for Málaga.

The next night, tuning my receiver to the Radio Sevilla station, I again had the pleasure of hearing Queipo de Llano, who was being witty about the course of events in Málaga and General Kléber, who had left "to save Málaga . . . " What intelligence!

Málaga was lost several days later. The army headquarters at the time of the battle went over to the enemy. Later, foreign papers wrote about me that I had been taken prisoner in an attempt to flee from Málaga.

After the fall of Málaga, I decided to write a letter to Caballero, explaining to him the reasons I could not agree to accept the appointment offered me by his chief of the general staff. Comrades Díaz and Luis were in agreement with the draft of the letter.

Largo Caballero did not delay in answering my letter or, more correctly, he did not delay putting his own signature under the answer composed in his name by General Asensio. After the jesuitical introduction, "Dear Friend and Comrade," the text of the letter was ignoble, along the lines: There was no misunderstanding in your assignment to Málaga as you have said in your letter. My assistant war minister and chief of the general staff keeps me informed of even the smallest details, and I make the decisions. It is true that I appointed you to high positions in Madrid. It does not follow from that fact, however, that I confirmed you in the rank of general. (Note: I have on hand the first appointment, signed by this same Caballero, where he addresses his excellency Brigade General Don Emilio Kléber). Those assigned to work on the general staff, the letter goes on to say, enjoy the rights and salary of a captain. And I therefore propose that you do not appear in a general's uniform. I hope that in the future you will be well disciplined and that you will give me the opportunity to make use of your valuable services in the glorious army of which I am the head, as its supreme leader, and I also hope that in the future I will not have any cause to doubt the sincerity of your antifascism. Yours in [the cause of] antifascism. Signed: Francisco Largo Caballero.

(Note: As far as the pay is concerned, I never received any, either as a general or as a captain. In general, I did not think about this at the front. When I arrived in Valencia and had to live in a hotel and feed myself, along with my driver and his family, who had been evacuated from Madrid, in the ministry they answered my adjutant by saying that Kléber was not in their personnel records. The ministry asked the base of the International Brigades in Albacete whether the base was paying "the so-called General Kléber." Vidal-Gayman answered the ministry's inquiry by saying that since December 1936 he had no longer been on the personnel roll of the International Brigades.[)]

Caballero and Asensio showed particular attention not just to me, but also to Modesto, Lister, Carlos, and other commanders and Communist commissars. A string of vile attacks took place against the institution of the commissars and personally against Comrades Antón, Carlos, and others. After the important demonstration of the proletariat of Valencia against the loss of Málaga, removal of Asensio from his position was achieved. Caballero put a vile letter into the press in which he apologized to Asensio for being forced to dismiss his personal assistant. After his removal from his position, Asensio remained as the anonymous man behind Largo Caballero, which was even more dangerous. General Cabrera left for the north . . . to help surrender the country of the Basques to the enemy.

Another time when I was with Caballero, the discussion was about my possible assignment to military work. Comrade Grishin asked me whether I was ready to go to the north. I was, of course, ready. Caballero seemed to agree to give his approval. Some days passed waiting for an airplane, on which I was supposed to fly to the north. At that time, the CC proposed that I go up to the Teruel front together with Comrade Castro, so that we could acquaint ourselves with the situation and report to the CC. Arriving at the front, we found a strange situation there. The commander of the 22nd Brigade, Comrade Paco Galán, complained that he had been ordered to pull back at a time when, according to all the information, the enemy in front of his sector was weak and could not be thinking about an offensive. Paco Galán said that recently a partisan group of his brigade had blown up an enemy train and afterward he had received an order from the main staff in Valencia in which Galán was called to task for having carried out an operation without having sought permission from the main staff.

In answer to Comrade Galán (with whom I had become friendly right in the first days at the front at Guadarrama) asking what he should do, I said that if I were in his place, I would advance, together with the comment that there was no reason at all to withdraw. Galán right there gave the order to his troops to advance on the village of Sellades. By the end of the day, he had encircled and taken the village, capturing in it five hundred prisoners of war, four hundred rifles, two dozen machine guns, four field guns, two heavy guns, three antiaircraft cannon, and more than a million rounds of ammunition.

The next day I returned to Valencia. And the following awaited me there: they called from the general staff to ask on what basis Kléber had gone to Teruel? Because Kléber had meddled with matters of command, the minister had refused to give his permission for Kléber's trip to the northern front, that is, again he had spoiled his "friendship with Caballero." This time it was doubly painful for me—once because I could not take part in the defense of Bilbao, for which I had already mentally prepared, having talked things over with Comrade Gorev before his flight there, and again because this time Comrade Grishin was displeased with me, believing the reports that I had meddled in the command at Teruel. Comrade Fritz, the adviser on the Teruel front, was absent from the front on that day, having gone to Valencia with a report. Meeting him, I asked just what was causing the displeasure of the senior comrade Grishin. He answered that he was ready to testify that my advice to Galán was correctly given and that, if he had been in my place, he would have acted just as I had done. The comrade was a corps commander in rank at that time and a respected commander. I was content with his evaluation. However, there was no further talk about going to the north.

Comrade José Díaz tried once more during the Caballero era to get me into work at the front lines. That time the talk was about taking command of the Karl Marx Division at the Aragon front. Comrade Comorera, general secretary of the Unified Socialist Party of Catalonia, several times put this question before the CC in Valencia. There was no hope of a favorable decision as long as Caballero remained as war minister.

The chairman of the Council of Ministers, Caballero, did not want to understand the purport and the demands of the inspiring national demonstration in Valencia, which took place within a framework of loyalty to the Caballero government only thanks to the political strength of the Communist party. Deceiving himself, he construed the meaning of this demonstration as an expression of strength for him personally, for Largo Caballero. After the demonstration, Caballero took the bit between his teeth and dashed off unrestrained on the path toward getting rid of the forces of the Communist party in the army and in the masses. Caballero tried to transform the demands of the masses to purge the army of traitors into the opposite, into a purge of the Communists from the army and its political staff. The Communist party, which in the interests of preserving unity had, over the long months of the war, made concessions on personal questions concerning Communist cadres, could no longer allow Caballero his arbitrary management of questions regarding the army. Whether Largo Caballero wanted it or not, his actions led directly to "an embrace of Vergara," that is, to a reconciliation with General Franco. And even at the subsequent meeting called by the Communist party, the criticism by the Communists did not go so far as to demand the resignation of Largo Caballero. That meeting set as its goal reminding Caballero of the actual significance of the people of Valencia's demonstration. The last "momento!" was when Caballero, having interpreted everything in his own way, seized on the speech by Jesús Hernández, who in the heat of his polemics diverged somewhat from the concept of the speeches of the previous orators. Caballero demanded that the Communist party repudiate its own ardent minister. Caballero did not threaten his own resignation but rather demanded of the Communist party that it pull its two Communist ministers out of the composition of the government. Being used to concessions on the part of the Communist party, he did not this time correctly judge the bounds of the possible and failed in this. The May putsch in Barcelona was, in addition to everything else, a putsch by Largo Caballero against his own government. This putsch was supposed to free Largo Caballero's hands from the confining framework of the alliance with the Communists and, so Caballero thought, allow him to head up a government of the syndicalist type. Where such a putsch would have led him if it had succeeded is a subject for its own article, and Largo did not ask himself that question. The Communist party, having reckoned that it was better to have Caballero in the government than in the opposition to the government, after the May putsch had to say to itself that it could not be any worse. Even though it had built "golden bridges" to keep Caballero in the new government, the new government was formed without him, thanks to the excessive appetite of Caballero himself.

And so the political history of Spain, after a ten-month interlude with Caballero, returned in the makeup of its government to the same situation which had appeared to be a real solution to the crisis in the last days of the government of Giral back in August 1936.

A government of the parties in the Popular Front was finally formed, in which the central pivot was the forces of the right Socialists of Negrín and Prieto.

If I [continue to misuse words], in my further exposition of my account I want to recall the days when, after a resolution of the governmental crisis, the beautiful Dolores, beaming like a child, came into the room of the military commission where I was working and greeted me with the words, "Well, Kléber, now you too will work." Comrades Hernández, Uribe, and others, even Luis, considered it necessary to say to me that I could be happy with the new turn of events. Comrade Stepanov in a conversation with someone else formulated his conclusions about the "Kléber question" thus: In general you were right, but you moved too soon and were too fervent and therefore were incorrect. And so they trumped you.

*June–October 1937*

The party leadership was talking about assigning me to the duty of commander of an excellent division of Communists, the Karl Marx Division, whose previous commander had left to direct the trade unions in Catalonia. I considered this the best solution for my "personal" questions. It was not necessary for me to begin work on the Madrid front again, where General Miaja had already become tired of listening to the fascists' radio constantly warming over the history of Kléber. The fascist propaganda on the radio cleverly played on the nationalistic feelings and on the pride of the Republican officers. For this evil propaganda, Kléber was a windfall. If there had not been any such Kléber, they would have invented him. So they constantly returned to the hackneyed theme that Miaja was not in charge in Madrid, but Kléber was, standing behind his back. This was especially true during those months when I had no relation whatsoever to the affairs of the army, either in Madrid nor in any other location. The Karl Marx Division was a Catalan division on the Aragon front. I could have worked successfully on the Aragon front because the anarchists would not have considered my appointment a challenge to them on the part of the Communists. The fact of the matter is that while I was still in Madrid, I got along with the anarchists better than the other Communists did. Beginning by meeting Durruti, I afterward continued my friendship with Mera and Palacios, whose anarchist brigades gradually became disciplined under my general leadership and began to accept "my" officers assigned to their units. In the difficult days in Madrid, the anarchists at one time were contemplating a coup. The party gave me the mission of getting close to the anarchists and influencing them. An opportunity presented itself at the funeral for Volpiansky, one of those internationalists killed in battle (by the way, a politically questionable type), whom I had assigned as chief of staff in an anarchist brigade. At the funeral for this chief of staff, Mera brought me together with the leadership of the confederation [the CNT] and the FAI. Not wishing to exaggerate my role, I would not, it seems, be mistaken in saying that the leaders of the anarchists were sincerely happy with my comradely conversation with them. The anarchist newspapers referred to me warmly and not once did they make any attacks on me as they did against the other Communist commanders. For the Aragon front at that time, after the events in May, it was very important to have commanders toward whom the anarchists were not hostile. At the time when I was awaiting final formalities in my appointment to the Karl Marx Division in which the party was directly involved, Comrade Grigorovich, who had become the senior adviser after Grishin, summoned me and told me that he was trying to obtain from the ministry my appointment as the commander of one of the brigades. The truth is that I was not very happy about this step by Comrade Grigorovich. Not because we were talking here about a brigade when the party had succeeded in getting me the command of a division, but because in all probability they would assign me to one of the brigades of the Madrid front. And I was trying to avoid that, in order not to give any cause for new sensationalism. I laid out my view of matters to Comrade Grigorovich, who had received me in a comradely way and who said to me at the very first that "at home" the Boss was satisfied with my work and that all these slanders were in the final account nonsense. I said that I was absolutely delighted that they were letting me work at the front at all, and I thanked him for his help in the matter. It was not a matter of ambition, by the way, and that aspect has to be taken into account. The comrades who were commanders of companies and battalions in the group of brigades I had led earlier were now already commanding brigades and divisions. Even my interpreter and adjutant, Durán, was an absolutely worthy commander and commanded a division. It would not be expedient to assign me as the brigade commander in one such division. For the party, Kléber represented, rightly or wrongly, a valuable asset that must be utilized in keeping with the interests of the party. If the comrade advisers had doubts about my command capabilities as the head of large units, it would not be difficult to attach to me a prominent comrade, an adviser whose instructions I would carry out without reservations. If I reminded myself of Negrín, he was going to trust me completely at that time with leading a corps of carabineros, as he earlier proposed to me. I considered that appointing me the comman-

der of the Karl Marx Division was the best way out of the situation for everyone.

The news came that Comrade Lukács, the commander of the 12th International Brigade, had been killed at the front at Huesca. The brigade remained
in the battle without a commander. Learning of this, the party decided to send
me to the 12th Brigade. Thus I again found myself at the head of one of the International Brigades. I wanted this least of all. First of all, because this assignment was received to replace a comrade who had been killed, second, because it was in the 12th Brigade that it was said that the party would remove
me for Trotskyism, and third, I knew what kind of a reputation that brigade
had in the eyes of the Spanish commanders. Colonel Rojo, the new chief of
the general staff, more than once wanted to disband that brigade and remove
Comrade Lukács, whom he hated. And mainly, I knew that the comrades in
Albacete, considering me to be finished and relating to me correspondingly,
would not be pleased that the party had again sent me to the international
units.

I have to include all these details because it will be easier then later to understand the matters of the last phase of my work in Spain.

At the party CC, they made me aware of the fact that Colonel Rojo wanted to
see me at 9 P.M. At the general staff, I saw Rojo for the first time since we had
parted in Madrid as good friends. At the time in Madrid, he had said how it
had been a pleasure for him to work with me and that they were replacing me
with old fools who understood little about military affairs. Now Rojo met me
in a dry and official manner and without any extra words presented me with
a proposal in the name of Minister Prieto that I would be appointed to command the 12th International Brigade, which would become the basis for the
formation of a new division.

One must know that Rojo, during Lukács's life, had done everything he
could to prevent the 12th Brigade from being expanded into a division. In response to Rojo's question whether I was happy about my appointment, I answered that I could not be particularly happy about taking the place of a fallen
comrade. When would I leave for the front? he asked. I answered, This very
day.

I went to the CC to say good-bye to the comrades. Comrade Luis offered me
some parting advice: Don't try too hard to get out in front (in saying this, he
had in mind the death of Lukács). As far as the comrades in the brigade and in
Albacete are concerned, they will be given instructions that undermining the
authority of Kléber will not be allowed. The party has complete trust in you.
You, of course, know yourself that it is not necessary to give any interviews.
The brigade newspaper itself should take care of the popularity of its own
new commander.

The following night I arrived at the headquarters of General Pozas, the commanding officer of the eastern front. I knew General Pozas from my time in

Madrid, when, before the arrival of Miaja, he was the commanding officer of the armies of the center. He joined the Communist party somewhat earlier than Miaja. He bore a great grudge against General Miaja, for he reckoned that he had been removed from the command of the armies of the center only with the help of Miaja. While I was still in Madrid, Pozas twice congratulated General Kléber in his orders for the success of the latter's units; he did this to spite General Miaja. He considered Kléber, like himself, to be the innocent victim of intrigues by the national hero Miaja. This is why Pozas was particularly well disposed toward me.

Pozas straightaway appointed me to command a group of five brigades attacking Huesca from the north. I asked him to forgive me for turning it down, but it was now midnight and the attack was to start at 6 A.M. I did not know the situation, nor did I know what units I had, who the commanders were, where they were; I had not yet seen the terrain, I had not yet been in my own brigade, which did not have a commander, etc.

Pozas did not like the objections.

I went to Comrade Leonidov, the senior adviser to Pozas. He briefed me on the situation. I learned from him that tomorrow at dawn our offensive would in essence be an exact repetition of the unsuccessful attack on the enemy fortifications at Chemillas and Alerre that had taken place a few days before. All the orders had already been issued, and the units were already preparing. I objected. I asked whether it was not possible to put it off for twenty-four hours, so that I could familiarize myself with the terrain during the daylight. After all, we could not repeat the unsuccessful attack with the same units and at the same place. If we did not take the enemy positions earlier, then we would not take them now either, after suffering up to 30 percent losses. It was necessary to rework the plan and to select another place for the attack. This required a delay in the beginning of the attack of a minimum of twenty-four hours.

Comrade Leonidov agreed with my reasons, but he could not help me.

I went to the commissar, Virgilio Llanos, whom I knew from Madrid.[97] He also agreed with me, but . . .

This "but" was Bilbao, which had to be helped by drawing enemy forces away from them toward us. Bilbao was living through the last critical days before its fall. All my objections had to be withdrawn because of this consideration.

The battle developed unsuccessfully for us. On the right flank, we had some success with the 98th Brigade, which took a plateau dominating the enemy position. In the other sectors, the attack had no success. The 12th International Brigade (which, after the death of Lukács, was commanded by two Bulgarian comrades, Petrov and Belov), having lost around seven hundred soldiers and many of the senior and mid-rank command staff, was again repulsed from the concrete fortifications of the enemy at Chemillas and Alerre.

The southern group did not help us at all. Basically, all the fighting was done just by the northern group under my command. In this battle at Huesca, there were also many other [preexisting] circumstances that led to our lack of success. There were POUMist units alongside us and in our rear who were infuriated by the events in Barcelona in May. They incited their commanders to fire on the rear of the International Brigades, which they did. When our units, having failed in their mission and lost many troops, withdrew to their former positions, they were met with a hostile coldness and gloating over their misfortune from the POUMists sitting things out in their trenches.

Another reason for our lack of success was the wrecking done by the chief of staff of the Eastern Army, Lieutenant Colonel Guarner. He and his brother, Captain Guarner, had worked out the first plan for the operation. They then insisted on repeating the operation without any changes in the plan whatsoever. They targeted the International Brigade especially for a frontal attack on the concrete fortifications and barbed-wire obstacles. After completion of the operation, they heaped all the blame on the unhappy International Brigade, in which there was only about 50 percent of the personnel left.

The Guarner brothers were later removed from their posts at the request of Commissar Llanos. They now are imperturbably working in Valencia on the general staff. The older of them is the chief of the operations section, that is, one of the closest assistants to Rojo. On the Aragon front, it was not a secret to any of the comrades that the brothers Guarner were fascists or, in the best case, rascals in alliance with those who provoked the events of May in Barcelona.

I got acquainted with my own brigade in this battle under the tragic conditions of depression at the loss of the commander, Lukács, the commissar Gustav Regler (seriously wounded), the brigade commander Niburg (an excellent old Hungarian Communist killed at Chemillas), the battalion commander Batistelli (an Italian Republican who died later in the hospital), and many other comrades.

With the remnants of the brigade, I withdrew from the battle at Huesca and loaded the units onto a train. At the town of Tortosa, I was supposed to receive new replacements from the ranks of the new recruits, train and arm them, and convert the brigade into a division. I had been given only a few days for all this work.

While awaiting the replacements, I took on first of all a reorganization of the headquarters as left behind by the late Lukács.

One should not say anything bad about deceased comrades. Comrade Lukács was an excellent person who took good care of his people, and they loved him for that. But Comrade Lukács was a weak commander, who more than once had to be censured, for the most part justifiably, by the higher authorities. Under the command of Lukács, the brigade had learned to "collect things." They drove the best vehicles, which they had acquired by hook or by crook. They had large stores of clothing and food for which they had not accounted to anyone. In matters of money, there was no accounting and, as a consequence, a lot of abuse. All of this gave Lukács's brigade a bad reputation among the other units. He got away with a lot because they had a good combat record, especially after Guadalajara.

As long as Comrade Fritz was the adviser, and in fact the secret commander, of the brigade, everything went well. After Comrade Fritz left and while Lukács was alive, all the combat work landed on the shoulders of Comrade Belov, the chief of staff. By the time that I arrived, Comrade Belov was totally exhausted. He began to have nervous attacks during battle. It was necessary to give him some basic recuperation. After being wounded, Comrade Petrov, another Bulgarian comrade and a good combat commander, arrived back from the hospital. Comrade Petrov, however, had one important defect, as he could express himself with the brigade personnel only in the Russian language. There were a lot of other people at the headquarters, but few workers among them.

Having begun the reorganization of the headquarters, I ran into an understandable guardedness on the part of Comrades Petrov and Belov, who still did not know about the party's opinion in regard to the previously "used-up" Kléber. Having gone to Valencia, Comrade Belov, after meeting with Comrade Stepanov, returned with a total eagerness to help me in the work. The same with Comrade Petrov; however, Belov had to be given leave, and Petrov had already been assigned to other work while he was in Valencia. I remained alone. The other workers in the headquarters unwillingly submitted to the order that I imposed, feeling that I was trying to do away with the traditions of the late Lukács. In the end, the headquarters began to function, but the young and inexperienced chief of staff, temporarily replacing Belov, was not up to the task.

In forming the new 150th Brigade, we ran into sabotage by one of the battalion commanders, the Spaniard Pardo, who turned out to be connected with the Trotskyists. The late Lukács had left this Pardo at the rear with the assignment of receiving and training the expected new recruits. Pardo secretly carried out a vile campaign against the International Brigades, turning the new Spanish recruits against the other battalion commander, the good Bulgarian comrade and combat commander Khristov (Malinov). At the time of my return from Huesca, the worthless Pardo had already succeeded in convincing them in Valencia to appoint him commander of the 15th Brigade and to transfer to him all the new recruits and all the weapons allocated for the division. Playing on the nationalistic feelings of the officers who were Rojo's closest assistants, Pardo succeeded in suspending the order for the formation of a division based on the 12th Brigade. We had to arrest Pardo, take the new recruits and the weapons, and protest to Rojo about his co-workers who had helped Pardo in the matter of breaking up the brigade. Rojo was a nationalist and not a friend of the International Brigades (especially Lukács's brigade). He disavowed his co-workers and Pardo. Thanks to this trouble with the 15th Brigade, we lost several valuable days of those few that were intended for the formation of the division and for training the new recruits.

When the order was received to load the division onto trains and move to Madrid to join Miaja's forces, the new division set off on the trip with untrained new recruits and with poor cohesion.

An inquiry into the question of commissars came to me from the leadership of the International Brigades' base at Albacete. After the commissar Gustav Regler was wounded, the commissar of the Italian battalion, Barontini, became commissar of the 12th Brigade. When the brigades (12th and 15th Brigades) were converted into a division, Barontini hoped to become the commissar of the division. Comrade Gallo, the inspector general of the International Brigades, encouraged Barontini's hopes in this matter.

Considering that 70 percent of the division personnel were Spaniards, I requested that the CC of the Communist party assist in having a Spanish comrade who also knew foreign languages appointed. A good commissar was appointed, a Spaniard, Comrade Vidal (not to be confused with the Frenchman Vidal-Gayman in Albacete). Comrades Gallo and Barontini were dissatisfied with my action. The political bureaucracy in Albacete and the commissar of the 12th Brigade, Barontini, began to sabotage the new division commissar. When my new 45th Division arrived at the Madrid front, the operation at Brunete had already begun. The division was placed in the reserve forces operating at Brunete.

Reporting to the commanding officer of the armies, General Miaja, I encountered there the ministers who had come to the front, Negrín, Prieto, and Hernández. Dr. Negrín, whom I had not seen since the new government was formed, greeted me like an old acquaintance and introduced me to Prieto.

The division went into battle. One battalion, helping other units to surround and take Villanueva del Pardillo, distinguished itself in the battle and was mentioned in the orders of the day for the army. The remaining units of the 45th Division did not have any particular success in the course of the battles. The lack of training of the new recruits and the disruptive work by the Trotskyist Pardo, about which I spoke earlier, had their adverse effect on everything. There were cases of individual new recruits going over to the enemy side, leaving behind them stereotypical notes in which they explained the motives for their conduct, "We do not want to serve or to fight because we are commanded by foreigners." It was necessary to take stern measures, and the leaders who were discovered were executed. The incredibly high number of self-inflicted gunshot wounds also speaks to the weakness of the units and the political situation. An incident took place where a group of deserting new recruits took a Polish comrade with them by force in order to turn him over to the fascists as a Russian. In a word, the Trotskyists and fascists did better work on our new recruits than we and our political bureaucracy did. The internationalists, fearing betrayal or simply the weakness of the new recruits in battle, did not act as decisively as before. And at Brunete an even more difficult battle developed! The division, entering the battle, immediately ran into an unexpected situation when one battalion of a flanking unit fled before the enemy. Before we could carry out our own mission, we had to restore the situation on the flanking sector of the 11th Brigade. We had to attack the famous Mocha Hill, strongly fortified by the enemy. In front of the hill and the barbed-wire obstacles of the enemy was a deep ravine with steep banks. Our tanks got to the ravine and could not go any further. At that point, the enemy antitank cannon were firing well-aimed shots. My infantry got into the barbed wire of the enemy and could not move any farther forward. In order not just to sit in the ravine under enemy fire, the battalions during the night returned to the original jumping-off positions.

I reported to the command staff on the situation and proposed that the following day we carry out an attack, not directly on Mocha Hill, but to the left of it on the village of Manilla, and I pointed out that the approaches to it were much more advantageous and that, by taking Manilla, we would achieve a winning position in relationship to that damned Mocha Hill as well.

The command staff did not agree and ordered a repeat of the attack on Mocha, in which all commanders were ordered to go in front of their battalions and lead the people in a bayonet attack. The time was set for 11 A.M., at which time they promised there would be support from our artillery and air force. The battalions went forward simultaneously, with their commanders in front, and there was no support at all—neither the air force nor the artillery. With new sacrifices, particularly among the ranks of the commanders, the battalions again pulled back from the barbed-wire obstacles of the enemy. Returning from the field of battle to my command post at 1300 hours, I found out that an order had just been received from the command staff that the attack arranged for 11 o'clock was being postponed because of the flight time of the air force and that it would be repeated at 1900 hours, at a time when the participation of the air force could be ensured. The notification of the delay in the morning attack had been received too late. It had already taken place. The vagueness of the orders and the losses suffered made all the combat personnel of the division extremely irritated and rendered problematic the chances for success in repeating the attack designated to take place at 1900 hours. By telephone, I communicated how things stood and the greater possibilities of an attack on Manilla than of a new attempt to attack Mocha to the corps adviser, Comrade Ivon, who until that time had been an adviser at the general staff in Valencia. Comrade Ivon, with a sergeant major's approach to all questions, perceived in my report an attempt to avoid any new attack at all. He conducted the conversation over the telephone with me accordingly. Giving me a totally inappropriate lecture, he asked me to stay on the telephone because the corps commander Casado would also speak with me.[98] The telephone receiver was not hung up, so I could hear what Comrade Ivon was saying to the corps commander Casado through the interpreter, that he should not allow such willful disobedience by Kléber, that he should point out to Kléber the laws in wartime that those disobeying orders can be brought before a field court, and so on, in that vein. Corps Commander Casado then, picking up the telephone handset, conscientiously expounded on everything that Ivon had prompted him to say, and in addition he also complained about Kléber to General Miaja.

Miaja summoned me the following day for me to explain things. At that time, at 1900 hours, my units again stormed the ill-fated Mocha Hill, and the assault ended with the same results that the previous two attacks had.

On the following day, obviously basing his actions on the report by Corps Commander Casado, Miaja again demanded a repeat of the assault on Mocha. I reported to General Miaja why there would be no results from repeating the attack. Miaja insisted on it, saying that it was necessary to attack *at whatever cost.* (The previous attacks had already cost my division seven hundred men killed and wounded. The command staff had 50 percent losses. There were only eighteen hundred men left in the division.) In order to forestall the final destruction of the division, I expressed myself to General Miaja in the following words: "I understand that there are cases when it is necessary to sacrifice entire divisions in order to break through the front in a designated sector, through which fresh reserves can then pass in order to develop a strike in depth. However, in this case I know that there are no reserves available for this purpose. Even if my division takes the hill—which given its present condition is even less probable than at the start—there is no one behind it who could exploit the success. The slightest counterattack by the enemy will force my weakened units back, and the enemy will exploit this in order to carry out a strike in depth on our rear. If the general orders that we repeat the attack, then I, knowing the morale and physical conditions in my own units, must warn him that I cannot encourage his hopes of our successfully carrying out the orders received." General Miaja said in response to this, with annoyance, "What, are you resigning? I will not accept any resignation; I know myself when to remove a commander from his position." With this, our conversation, unpleasant as it was for both of us, terminated. No order for a new assault on the hill was received. General Miaja, however, in reporting this to the comrades in the Communist party leadership, pointed out the unacceptability of Kléber's not carrying out orders and resigning . . .

Comrade Ivon, who had caused me all this trouble, had another incident that very same day with one of the Finnish comrades, the adviser in a division on my flank. This comrade, a very brave and resolute commander of the Red Army, pointed out to Ivon the impossibility of carrying out the absurd orders of Corps Commander Casado. Comrade (?) Ivon, in answer to him called the headquarters guard, ordered them to disarm the Red Army commander and then began to beat him unmercifully in the presence of the guard. They removed Ivon and sent him home for this. Relations between General Miaja and me became strained. And the main thing was that the comrades in the CC actually believed that I did not want to obey the orders of General Miaja. Still remaining with my division in our positions, I undertook an attack on an enemy fort located between Majadahonda and Manilla, that is, in the direction I had been pointing out from the start as the axis promising better results than an attack directed at Mocha Hill. With part of my weakened forces, the fort was taken at dawn. Not having received the necessary support, we could not secure this success we had achieved.

In the following days, Corps Commander Casado, contrary to the instructions of the higher command and of our advisers, thought up a complicated and unnecessary exchange of some units with other units along the entire front of our corps. This action, which was not justified by anything, cost all the units of the corps their combat readiness for a period of five days, until this entire procedure of replacement was completed. At a meeting of the division commanders called for this matter, I pointed out to the corps commander the danger in case of a counterattack by the enemy on Brunete. The corps commander stuck to his plan. On the third day, the enemy carried out its counterattack at the dividing line between Casado's corps and Modesto's corps. Lister's division wavered. The withdrawal of Lister mushroomed into a general flight of several divisions. Hurriedly gathering three battalions and my squadrons of cavalry, I occupied a line and began to halt those fleeing from the front. How difficult it was to fight against the mass panic can be seen just from the fact that my cavalry squadrons occupied with restoring order had three men killed and fourteen men wounded in the "battle" with the panicked floods of armed people fleeing to the rear.

Seeing such unprecedented panic among the units, the command staff decided to begin fortifications on the rear boundary line. This would have resulted in giving up to the enemy almost all the territory in the region of Brunete that we had recently won in battle, including the towns of Villanueva de [la] Cañada and Quijorna. It seemed there was no other way out of the situation at hand.

I sent one battalion into Villanueva de [la] Cañada and dug in on the forward line with another battalion positioned somewhat behind it and, with the remaining forces gathered into a strike force, awaited the enemy. With the actions of my division and Walter's division in the region of Quijorna, the general panic was localized and the forward line was preserved behind us. I can state that we were able to achieve this accomplishment thanks to the fact that I did not carry out the orders of my corps commander. Corps Commander Casado, during the days of the panic, lost any kind of control over his units. He "took sick" and left for Valencia.

My units remained in these positions without relief for thirty-nine days.

## Document 60 *continued*

The divisions of Lister, Walter, Campesino, and others were pulled back one after the other in reserve and for rest. My division remained in position. The burden of battles, difficulties with food and water, constant bombardment by the enemy air force and artillery, unbelievable heat—all these, taken together, exhausted my units to the last of their strength. There were days when individual soldiers literally went mad. Suddenly they would leap out of the positions and run about in insane terror in no particular direction. The doctors diagnosed it as obvious madness caused by the terrors that they had lived through, along with deprivations and physical exhaustion.

It was in this condition that we got a new order, according to which my division was supposed to be loaded onto trucks and transported to the Aragon front for participation in an operation at Saragossa. Before I get into the events on the Aragon front, I want to continue with some incidents connected with the period when the division was at Brunete.

The commander of one of my brigades, the 15th, had to be replaced during battle. This comrade, whose last name was Gerassi, an artist by profession, had been appointed to the position of brigade commander by the late Lukács, even though he had no experience whatsoever in military affairs or in commanding a unit. Earlier, in the battle at Huesca, I had already seen that Gerassi, despite all his other, good qualities, could not be allowed to remain at the head of a brigade. In the Brunete battle, his unsuitability was again confirmed. General Miaja requested that he be removed from the brigade. The whole brigade was satisfied, knowing that the Polish comrade Janek, commander of the Dombrowski Battalion, would be appointed in place of Gerassi. The removal of Gerassi displeased several Russian comrades, advisers, who had become friends with him and his wife, who worked as a translator in the advisers' organization. Comrades Gorsky and Loti (advisers for transport and intelligence) took Gerassi's side and held me responsible for his removal from command of the brigade. The matter was soon settled when other, higher-up comrades agreed with my conclusions in the matter of Gerassi.

It was a more difficult matter with the commander of the 18th Brigade, Pacciardi. Pacciardi, an Italian Republican, was not a bad commander and had earned himself a prominent reputation as the head of the 12th Garibaldi Brigade. In Lukács's division, brigade commander Pacciardi, an extremely proud and capricious fellow, did just as he pleased and did not take into account Lukács's opinion. Pacciardi totally stopped considering the Italian Communists in the 18th Brigade. Even though the Communists were an overwhelming majority in the brigade, Pacciardi put together his headquarters only from Republicans, anarchists, and Socialists and conducted policies against the Communists. The conduct of Pacciardi and [his] setting of some against the others threatened a rupture in the unified front among the representatives of the various parties of the Italian émigrés fighting under the banner of the Garibaldi Brigade. The Italian Communists were right to be on their

342

guard in their relationships with Pacciardi. They made their mistake when they began to fight against Pacciardi's influence along sectarian lines, and clumsily, losing their comradely contacts with the Socialists and anarchists and alienating them. A strange situation developed in the 18th Brigade: on the one hand, the Communists (and not all of them, for part of them fell under Pacciardi's influence) and on the other hand, Pacciardi with all the Republicans, Socialists, anarchists, and nonaffiliated in a single front against the Communists. In order to fight against Pacciardi's dominance, Comrade Gallo, the inspector general for the International Brigades, appointed the Communist Platone as chief of staff of the brigade. Brigade Commander Pacciardi became even angrier at the Communists, at Commissar Barontini, and at Inspector Gallo for having appointed his chief of staff without having asked for his opinion. If the new chief of staff, Platone, had been well placed as a chief of staff, then it could be that everything would have come off without a scandal. Unfortunately, Platone, a good comrade, proved totally unsuitable as a chief of staff. Pacciardi completely stopped having anything to do with Platone. This was an old story and lay in the past when, after the death of Lukács, I took over the division.

At the time of the Brunete battles, the "Pacciardi affair" again became a current one. This time Pacciardi became the mouthpiece for the feelings about demobilization among the Italians in his brigade. After the events of May in Barcelona, the attitude among the Italian anarchists became openly hostile in their relationship to the Communists. The Chief of the operations section of the staff of the 18th Brigade, an anarchist named Braccelare,[99] became the person most trusted by Brigade Commander Pacciardi, and both of them expounded the following theory to the Italians in their brigade: "We Italians created the Garibaldi Brigade. Now we have a total of only 300 to 350 men remaining. The Spanish replacements, the new recruits, are only spoiling the good name and the tradition of the Garibaldi Brigade. Instead of waiting until the former glory of the Garibaldi Brigade is dragged down, we Italians should draw our own conclusions, which are that we will all pull out of the brigade and take along from it the name Garibaldi. We will go for leave in France. You are all very tired, and we need a long rest. In France, in Marseilles, in Nice, and in Paris, the Italian émigrés will honor us as heroes and Garibaldists and there we can carry out a new recruiting campaign. Then we will return here with new, fresh forces, and the Garibaldi Brigade will again become a powerful combat unit in the fight with the fascists. If the Communists, bound by their own party discipline, do not agree with such a plan, then we, the anarchists, the Socialists, the Republicans, the Catholics, and those without party affiliation will nonetheless go to France in order to carry out our plans without the Communists."

This concept of Pacciardi and Braccelare also reflected the attempt to get away from the battles (which is what attracted many of the Communists, tired of battles) and clever propaganda against the Communists and fascist agitation (conscious and unconscious) and the personal ambition of Pacciardi, and much else.

Inasmuch as the Italian personnel overall represented the cadre of the brigade, the commanders, commissars, political officers, and logistical officers, this plan of Pacciardi's would lead to the destruction of the 18th Brigade as a combat unit.

In combat, Pacciardi made every attempt to protect his cadres, by which he drew suspicion upon himself on the part of the Spanish comrades (rank-and-file soldiers, Spaniards from the machine-gun company of the 18th Brigade, came to me and asked that I remove the Italian company commander and Italian platoon commanders because in combat they hid and stifled the combat spirit of the Spanish comrades). If one of the Italians was wounded or killed in battle, that fact was used as evidence of the necessity of leaving soon for France, as Pacciardi proposed.

I summoned Pacciardi and pointed out to him the unacceptable nature of such agitation in the face of the enemy. In front of me, Pacciardi, referring to the objective conditions of general fatigue, tried to prove that the Communists were guilty because of their sectarian policies, which had alienated all the honest antifascists from them, and [because they] wanted to run the 12th Brigade themselves.

Pacciardi, seeing that he could not behave with me as he had with the late Comrade Lukács, gave notice of his resignation, and hoped, in doing so, that after him all the commanders he had persuaded would follow his example and give notice of their resignation also. The matter threatened to become a political demonstration against the Communists and against the united front with the Communists.

I did not accept Pacciardi's resignation and suggested that he ask for leave owing to illness, which he did. Thus, the political matter was transformed into a personal matter of an ailing Pacciardi. Pacciardi went on leave, and the other commanders remained at their posts, waiting for the return of Pacciardi from leave.

The story of Pacciardi called for serious analysis. It was necessary to find a new way to increase the combat capabilities of the International Brigades. It was a matter not only of the Italian brigade but also of others, particularly the 14th Brigade, made up of Frenchmen, and the 11th Brigade, made up of Germans, which were experiencing their own crises at that time to a greater or lesser degree. With a background of general fatigue and great losses in the ranks of the internationalist soldiers, they began to ask themselves questions: How long will we continue to suffer and bear our losses? We have been fighting for a year, and that is enough. Let some others come and take our places.

Letters from wives in France in which erotica played a large role (you know, if you don't come back soon, I won't be able to stand it any longer and will give myself to another . . . ) contributed a great deal to the low spirits. Since the international cadres occupied all the command positions in the brigades, and the rank-and-file combat personnel were exclusively Spaniards, this crisis among the cadres became a general crisis for all the International Brigades. The difficulty in communications between the internationalist commanders or commissars and political officers who were also internationalists and the rank-and-file Spanish army members because of language gave rise to many other undesirable and even dangerous phenomena, particularly nationalist antagonism. The fascist propaganda and Trotskyist demagogy seized upon these tendencies and fanned their flames even more.

Under these conditions, I decided to act more boldly than previously in promoting new commanders from among the Spanish ranks. Good soldiers, people devoted to the party and to the cause of antifascism, I began to promote to command positions as the commanders of squads, platoons, and companies. I requested that the Unified Socialist Party of Catalonia send me trusted Spanish comrades from among those completing the officers' courses in Barcelona. Comrade Comorera, the general secretary of that party, sent me thirty men personally selected by him. I began to assign these comrades to the companies and battalions and in the headquarters of the brigades and the division. In addition to this, I created a division cadre school where, in the rear area right behind the front lines, hundreds of new Spanish cadres were trained under my observation and leadership. All command and political positions in the division and the brigades were doubled up, that is, there was a Spanish deputy assigned alongside the internationalist. I gave the internationalist personnel a directive that our mission in Spain was not only to take part in the fighting directly, but also to help the Spanish people create their own combat cadre. Since our International Brigades were made up of 80 percent Spanish personnel, we did not have the right to occupy all the responsible command positions. Some internationalist commanders looked down on their Spanish soldiers and related to them on the average as the officers of the imperialist armies related to the soldiers in the colonial armies. For similar behavior, I removed an internationalist commander and replaced him with his Spanish deputy.

All these measures very rapidly brought the desired results, as the combat capabilities of the International Brigades were increased. Low spirits became less and less common. The Spanish personnel had received a new stimulus and began to fight no worse than the internationalists in battle. We began to smooth over nationalistic differences. The new Spanish cadres grew before our very eyes and felt themselves responsible for the combat capabilities of the brigades. The language of command became Spanish. Fascist and Trotskyist propaganda about the demoralization of the International Brigades lost its fertile ground and was soon revealed for what it really was. It became much easier to fight against.

All these measures undertaken by me in the two International Brigades of my division apparently were not understood by the comrades from Albacete. Passing through Valencia, I was at the CC of the party and gave an account there of the essence of the difficulties with the International Brigades, reporting what measures should be taken to fight this dangerous situation. The comrades from the CC were fully in agreement with me. They began, in accordance with my requests and to the extent of their power and capabilities, to send to my division Spanish political workers and comrades who could become commanders, if some work was done with them.

In Albacete, some comrades considered that the actions taken by me would lead to the "destruction of the International Brigades as such." As it turned out later, these comrades complained about me to the CC. I will tell about this later.

At the time of the Brunete battles, there was a scandalous incident with the 13th International Brigade, which had arrived from the southern front under the command of Comrade Gómez (a German comrade who had worked in the Comintern and the MLSh). This brigade, which had always been isolated from all the other International Brigades, arrived at the Madrid front in a deplorable condition of physical exhaustion and fatigue from the previous battles in the southern zone. Comrade Gómez, arriving at the front at Brunete, reported on this, in the process perhaps describing the condition of his units in excessively dark tones. They removed him from command of the brigade. Another commander led the brigade into battle. In the course of the operations, they then appointed Comrade Krieger (an Italian comrade, now in Moscow) to command this brigade. The 13th Brigade was given one of the most difficult sectors, at Romanillos, and, despite its fatigue, it generally fought no worse than the other units. Even so, a misfortune befell it; one battalion of this brigade, not standing up to the enemy's pressure and being pounded by the enemy air force and artillery, fled from the front. With regard to this, the battalion in question was not the only one in this operation to do so. It also happened with other brigades, which enjoyed a good reputation for combat.

Colonel Rojo decided to disband the 13th International Brigade as punishment.

When I learned of this, even though I had no direct relationship with the 13th Brigade, I asked for a meeting with the inspector general of the International Brigades, Comrade Gallo, and requested that he take all steps to rescind this shameful punishment. I gave the following reasons to Comrade Gallo, who seemed agreeable to sanctioning the proposed action by Colonel Rojo in relation to the 13th Brigade: Gallo knew as well as I did how Rojo behaved toward the International Brigades overall. Rojo and the entire War Ministry in general considered that the International Brigades were one of the stronger supports of the Communist party in the army. They were not against weakening the strength of the party in the army in general. We could not create a precedent. We had to maintain the existence of the 13th International Brigade. It would be a huge political mistake to agree to disband one of the International Brigade units. The enemy would exploit that fact as a great victory. It would be possible to preserve the existence of the brigade if he would join with Comrade Antón and with the advisers and request of General Miaja that this severe action not be taken. We had to achieve permission to withdraw the brigade to the rear and have it undergo a reorganization there. Comrade Gallo heard me out, but from his words in response I got the impression that in his heart he agreed with Rojo and that his intercession could not be relied upon. He began to lay out for me his "plan" for disbanding the 13th Brigade. He said that the Germans would be sent to the 11th Brigade, the Poles to the 160th Brigade, the Frenchmen to the 14th Brigade, and the Spaniards would be given to Lister and Campesino. And everything would then be in order.

I objected again and asked Comrade Gallo to take into consideration that a combat unit is an organism with a combat tradition (the 13th Brigade had a good tradition), an organism with its weapons, logistics, and so on. Handing out such punishment to one brigade as an "example" would reflect badly on the other brigades. This brigade did not deserve such a reprisal against it. I requested that he give me the unit (since the table of organization called for me to have three brigades), and I would guarantee that the 13th would not fight any worse than the others. General experience had shown that at the given point in the war, independently operating International Brigades were used as a stop-gap that any commander of a Spanish division in which such a brigade found itself temporarily and by chance would try to exploit in every way, send it into the most difficult situations, and, in addition, try to profit at its expense by taking [away its] weapons, transport, medical supplies, and so on. Operating within an organized division (such as my division, the 45th, Walter's 35th Division), the individual International Brigades could bear adversities more easily, they often relieved each other, and they could get better rest and better provisions. They could be taken more firmly in hand through political indoctrination.

To this proposal to include the 13th Brigade in one of the existing international divisions, Comrade Gallo objected that he was in principle against international divisions, even though some already existed. I tried in every way to show Comrade Gallo that he was overlooking many things if he was in principle against organized [international] divisions. Just take the question of the artillery. The International Brigades existing within the framework of a division had support from the division artillery and other combat equipment of the division. Brigades operating independently could not always count on their own artillery. When all was said and done, it was not a matter of the title. Look, it would be better to rename the existing divisions brigades, for in actuality, according the number of soldiers in them, including the Spanish contingent, they did not exceed the numbers for a fully manned brigade. It would be better to have less talk and more action. Instead of the six weak International Brigades, which in many ways deceived the eye and created internal political complications, it would be better to have *two* international divisions of three brigades each and to rename these divisions *brigades.* What was now called a brigade could be named a battalion. This would be unpretentious and a matter of more action and less talk.

With what I have written above, I have tried to give an account of one of the root organizational questions about which the comrades from Albacete, in particular Comrade Gallo, were not in agreement with me. Hundreds of times I had thought these questions over and checked out my view, taking into account the situation and my combat experience. And each time I was more and more convinced that the comrades from Albacete were not right about this matter.

What happened with the 13th Brigade? Colonel Rojo ordered that at the disbanding of the brigade it be cordoned off by carabineros and that it be disarmed. Comrades Franz Dahlem and Gallo arrived and they began to implement the order on disbanding the brigade. Anyone who felt like it began to pilfer the weapons taken from the 13th Brigade—machine guns, antitank cannon, vehicles, medical supplies, and so forth. The carving up of the living corpse took on a disgraceful character. Like vultures, both designated and uninvited "heirs" pounced on the belongings of the unhappy International Brigade from all directions. The heirs began to accuse each other of swindles. In a word, it developed into a repulsive sight for everyone within several kilometers of the forward line of the front.

Comrade Krieger, the commander of the disbanded brigade, was first arrested, then released. The Slavs of the International Brigade became a laughingstock for those who had borne a grudge against the internationalists. It was no secret to anyone that certain, even influential, circles in the ministry did not refrain from expressing their political views, in the sense that they said the Italian and German intervention had been caused by . . . the existence of the International Brigades. In other words, if there had been no International Brigades, there would also not have been any Italian and German forces on the side of Franco. There were quite a few such "friends" among us in Spain.

Individual groups of soldiers from the 13th Brigade came to me and, weeping, said: for ten months the fascists at the front were not able to break up our brigade, and now we have been destroyed by our "friends." Some of them had hidden their weapons, in order not to surrender them to the inspectors.

I consider that *the disbanding of the 13th International Brigade and the method by which this action was taken was one of the greatest mistakes committed by the responsible comrades from Albacete.*

If in Madrid at the time Comrade Dolores or someone else from the CC of the Communist party had stood up for this brigade with General Miaja, it would not have suffered such a fate. Really, the brigade did not deserve it. In comparison with the others, it had the same high percentage of losses in the Brunete battle.

Comrades Franz Dahlem and Gallo reiterated one thing: the Germans had to be sent to the 11th Brigade, the French to the 14th Brigade, and so on. In the final analysis, it turned out that they were all scattered in different directions. My 45th Division received eighty-one disarmed Poles and Czechs from the former Mickiewicz Company. And by order, the number 13 was transferred to the 150th Brigade of my division, which was not very happy about this gift. The comrades considered that the 160th [*sic*] Brigade had its own combat tradition, and with the number 13 it was inheriting all the "glory" of the brigade that had been recently disbanded.

Some time passed, and Comrades Franz Dahlem and Gallo came to my headquarters in Torrelodones. Before they explained the purpose of their visit in words, I could already guess from their faces that it was something bad. They required me to explain the matter of my "cadre policy," which, in their words, was leading to the elimination of the International Brigades. For this, they said, I would soon be called to task before the party. But this was not my only sin. In other matters, such as, for example, the mail, they considered that I was deliberately hampering the work of the base in Albacete.

What had happened with the mail?

It turned out that the division commissar and I had committed a new sin. The matter was as follows. All the mail of the International Brigades, incoming and outgoing, was collected in Albacete for inspection by the censor. On the basis of an agreement with the main censor, the base of the International Brigades had its own organization for censorship and mail. More than a hundred persons worked in this bureaucracy under the leadership of one colonel, two lieutenant colonels, and other high officials of the Albacete post office.[100] In spite of this, the post office functioned wretchedly, and in the brigades at the front there were always justifiable complaints about the workings of the post office. Letters for "unknown" addressees piled up in pigeonholes in Albacete. People said that once Comrade Marty took an interest in this matter and went to the post office to check on its work. In the pigeonhole, under the letter *M,* he found a pile of letters and newspapers addressed to him, Marty. They were lying there waiting for the unknown addressee to turn up.

The division commissar and I, getting constant complaints from the soldiers about how the postal service was working, decided to suggest some kind of improvements to the Albacete post office. The proposals consisted of assigning a field section of the Albacete censor's office to Madrid (all the International Brigades were on the Madrid front). This separate censor's office should collect all the letters and classify them along these lines: addressed abroad—send to Albacete for censoring; addressed within the country, check on the spot and stamp "inspected by the censor," then pass to the post office to send to the addressee. Before this, all letters from the front addressed to the city of Madrid were first transported to Albacete, and from there they returned (if they returned at all) to Madrid after a fourteen- to eighty-day delay. When it was taken into account that the majority of the personnel in the International Brigades were Spaniards and that, among them, the majority were residents of Madrid and its environs, it was understandable to what degree the proposals by my commissar and me would eliminate one of the reasons for dissatisfaction of the soldiers and their families.

Strangely enough, the censor's office in Albacete agreed with this suggestion. A field section was assigned, and it began to operate in Madrid. It seemed that everyone could be satisfied with this solution.

But it did not turn out that way. Being "thrown out of work," the postal workers in Albacete protested and complained to the authorities, asking on what basis Kléber was meddling in our Albacete affairs.

And so a new sin had been committed by Kléber, for which Comrades Dahlem and Gallo felt he should answer to the party. In the words of Dahlem and Gallo, this restructuring of the work of the censor's office and the post office hid dangers within it and indicated that the division was trying to avoid the censor's office in Albacete.

Another action that elicited suspicion on the part of Comrades Dahlem and Gallo was my ordering the centralized dispatch and receipt of mail for the entire division. In actual fact, before this order each brigade was sending a vehicle to Albacete daily with the mail. And so I decided to save gasoline and not to have vehicles unnecessarily running back and forth, and I ordered that the mail for all units of the division would be collected at the headquarters, from where one vehicle would regularly take it to Albacete.

Such centralization contradicted "in principle" the situation envisioned by Comrades Gallo and Dahlem, in which each brigade, and not the division, was supposed to be the unit with which Albacete wanted to do business. In the words of Dahlem and Gallo, I wanted to promote the division as a unit by whatever means possible.

It was with such accusations that Comrades Dahlem and Gallo came to me and demanded the involvement of the party.

Comrade Stepanov came to me at the front to investigate what was going on. Checking out the facts on the spot, Comrade Stepanov got a real laugh out of it and did not spare his remarks about those complaining. His words at the end were, "Well, what idiots!" Stepanov asked me whether it was true that in recent days I had been at my headquarters in Torrelodones and not at the forward command post. I confirmed that I had, in fact, for the most part been in Torrelodones, three kilometers behind the front, for things were quiet at the front and I was busy training cadres in the division school. I was connected with the command post by telephone. There were headquarters personnel at the command post day and night. In ten or fifteen minutes I could be at the front and command my units. Comrade Stepanov again laughed and said, "And in Valencia they had complained to us that Kléber is sitting in the rear and does not go up to the front."

Comrade Walter, who had learned of the new "war" between Albacete and me, looked in on me at the headquarters. "What can I do," I asked him, "when they come here and search for something to find fault with and then go and complain to the CC—as if the party and all of us did not have more important things to do!" Comrade Walter answered, "And then you should do as I do. I simply throw all such visitors out by the seat of their pants." No, I was not prepared to imitate Walter's actions in this matter.

Well, those thirty-nine days when my division was at the Madrid front were filled with such additional squabbles and annoyances.

An order was received from Colonel Rojo to send all three batteries (Thaelmann, Liebknecht, and Gramsci) to the ordnance depot, where they would have their equipment replaced. We lost those three wonderful batteries, the pride of our division, forever. Having taken the batteries away, Rojo then ordered them never to return to the division.

Thus, without artillery, with seriously weakened brigades (losses of up to a thousand men), and with physically exhausted people, I pulled out of the positions at Brunete and loaded up my units for transportation to the Aragon front. We were facing participation in the operations at Saragossa.

After sending my units off to their new assigned location, I remained at the division cadre school. After completing the course of instruction, these new cadres were supposed to receive and train two thousand new recruits, whose arrival I expected from one day to the next.

Traveling to the front, I stopped in at Albacete to make arrangements with Comrade Belov (who had replaced Gayman-Vidal) about some things. The base for the International Brigades at that time had worked out a new agreement with the War Ministry on the status and operating procedures for the International Brigades. It had been decided to maintain five International Brigades, in which the base had committed itself to bringing the number of internationalists up to 40 percent of the overall personnel.

In connection with the new agreement, there were all kinds of organizational changes in the composition of the International Brigades in the works; in particular, the André Marty Battalion was supposed to be transferred from the 13th Brigade (the former 150th Brigade) to the 14th Brigade, and the Dimitrov Battalion, made up of Balkan Slavs, was supposed to be transferred to my division from the 15th Brigade.

In Albacete, I met with Comrade Ercoli, with whom I had a brief conversation about our matters. Since I had to rush off, we agreed that I would write him a letter. Unfortunately, subsequent events did not allow me to keep that promise. I felt very bad about this, because it seems to me that if Comrade Ercoli had been better informed about the nature of my previous arguments with Albacete, he would not have allowed things to develop as they did later.

Continuing my journey, I was able to satisfy myself that in the CC of the Communist party the comrades did not share the opinion of Comrades Dahlem and Gallo with regard to the complaints that they had lodged against me.

Brigade commander Pacciardi, returning from his leave in France, arrived in Valencia at the same time that we did. I had earlier arranged with the brigade commissar Barontini that, in case Pacciardi did return from leave, I would not allow him to take command of the Italian brigade but would bring him into my headquarters, in order not to give him an opportunity to continue his business of breaking up the brigade. Comrade Gallo considered that I should appoint Commissar Barontini as brigade commander in place of Pacciardi. I did not agree with Gallo for the following reasons: first, Barontini did not have the knowledge and habits of a commander and would not be up to the new task. Second, everyone knew that Comrade Barontini was frightened in battle and behaved like a coward. At Guadalajara, Barontini, crying and trembling with fear, cut a very sorry figure and became the butt of sneers and bad jokes from his own soldiers. Third, the Communist Barontini, with such poor qualities as a commander in battle, would compromise the Communist party at a time when the entire clique around Pacciardi was trying to show that the Communists were striving to seize the entire leadership of the brigade in their hands and to remove all the other antifascists from their posts. Assigning the Communist Barontini to replace Pacciardi would only reinforce the existing tendency and could lead to a demonstrative break in the united front with the Communists. Acting from these motives, I appointed the non-party-affiliated commander Penchienati, the most senior among the battalion commanders, to perform temporarily the duties of commander of the 18th Brigade. And to Comrade Barontini I gave the task of increasing his work as commissar, in order to get rid of the attitude that had remained in the brigade after Pacciardi.

So over the course of a month Battalion Commander Penchienati had been leading the brigade. Now Pacciardi had again appeared on the scene after his leave. What should I do with him? Simply to throw him out of the division was not something that I formally had a right to do. It was also necessary to keep in mind that Pacciardi was the secretary of the Italian Republican party and that he had returned from Paris together with Pietro Nenni, a member of the exec. com. of the Second International who had already succeeded in getting to War Minister Prieto, together with Pacciardi (Prieto was a personal friend of Pacciardi's from when they were both in Paris as émigrés). If I ran Pacciardi out of the division, I could be cooking up a fine kettle of fish, not just for myself but also for the Communist party. You had to know how Prieto would make use of the slightest false step on the part of the Communist party in order to fight against the influence of the Communist party in the army. In relation to this, Prieto was that much smarter and therefore that much more dangerous for the Communist party than Largo Caballero had been in his time.

Comrade Barontini, having met first with the returning Pacciardi, told him everything that he knew right then and there. He told him that he, Pacciardi, could not be permitted to command the brigade and that Kléber had in mind using him for work in the division headquarters. Pacciardi, together with Pietro Nenni, came to me to demand an explanation. I calmed them both down and told them that it was an unfortunate misunderstanding. I said that I did not have it in mind to deprive Pacciardi of his command, but that I had simply taken into consideration that Penchienati had done a good job with the duties entrusted to him during Pacciardi's absence; I had in mind asking the ministry to confirm Penchienati in the position and to promote Pacciardi in rank and keeping him with me as assistant to the division commander until such time as the minister appointed him to the position of commander of his own separate [division].

It is most probable that on that same day Pietro Nenni reported all this to Minister Prieto and Colonel Rojo.

When I went to the CC, I found that Comrades Barontini, Roasio, and other Communists had already come there to ask Comrade Luis how to proceed with Pacciardi. It was quite a delicate matter. I explained the essence of my conversation with Pacciardi and with Pietro Nenni to the comrades. Comrade Luis approved my approach. This was the best way for us to avoid a conflict with Prieto on the matter of Pacciardi and, especially, we would not give him any opportunity to continue his work of breaking up the 18th Brigade.

In the War Ministry, I was received by Colonel Rojo, who, considering the condition of my division, said that the division would be temporarily in the reserve of the front command and that it would be given an opportunity for replenishment with new personnel. In any case, before going into battle, the division would be given a fresh brigade and it would have artillery and tanks attached.

Arriving at the front at Saragossa, the division came under the command of Corps Commander Modesto. It turned out, however, that one of the divisions on which the command had been counting to arrive at the same time had been delayed en route somewhere, and it could not take part in the operation as the plan had called for. To replace it, my division was being included in the first echelon of the attacking forces. Three groups were supposed to advance on Saragossa simultaneously. The right hand group was the Karl Marx Division, comprising a powerful force of sixteen thousand men with attached tanks and artillery; the left group was the divisions of Lister, Walter, Gallo, and others, with an overall total of more than eighty-five thousand men, which had been given the maximum technical forces of tanks, aircraft, and artillery. The third group in the center consisted of my 45th Division, totalling not more than eighty-four hundred men and arriving here from the positions at Brunete deprived of its own artillery. To replace this artillery, I was given nine cannon from a local anarchist division. It had been promised that there would be 160 trucks to move my division from the sector of Modesto's corps to its new sector. In fact, there was a total of only 40 trucks, and they came eighty-four hours late, so that the assembly of the division at the new sector was continuing at the time that its forward units were already supposed to be going into battle.

In a meeting [I had] with Comrade Walter, he did not at all agree with detaching the Dimitrov Battalion from the 16th Brigade subordinated to him, even though the decision of the party and the International Brigade base had been that it was to be transferred into my 45th Division. He argued that the detaching of that battalion would disrupt the calculations and the plan of action that had already been drawn up. He promised to reassign that battalion to my command after the battle had ended.

With great difficulties, owing to the lack of transport, the division was concentrated in the area of its jumping-off position. The area was unusually deserted, and there was not a drop of drinkable water. Potable water had to be brought over a hundred kilometers by cistern trucks.

I had a meeting with Comrade Leonidov, the adviser to General Pozas, in the town of Lérida. At the time, General Pozas already had a different chief of staff, Lieutenant Colonel Gordon, a member of the Communist party. Comrade Gordon was, of all the professional officers, perhaps the most valuable man for the Communist party. He knew his business, had authority in the army, and was a sincere Communist, putting the party above all else.

Comrade Gordon explained the mission of the upcoming action, and I left for the front. In carrying out a reconnaissance of the ground together with my commanders, I became convinced that the lay of the land definitely required one basic adjustment to the preliminary plan of attack as developed, which was that the offensive should be carried out by our left flank, in place of the earlier designated direction on the right flank. All the ground on the right flank was a flat plain, which could be observed and fired on for entire kilometers, over which loomed isolated hills and mounds occupied by the enemy and fortified with concrete positions and protective forts. On the left flank of the ground, it was hilly and partially covered by blackthorn overgrowth, which would permit us to hide from aircraft better and to move to the objectives of the attack unnoticed. I decided to regroup all my forces on the left flank and to cover the right flank with just one battalion. I informed the high command of this decision.

In addition, when I saw the terrain, I began to doubt that it would be possible to make use of a motorized detachment as had been foreseen in the general plan. According to the plan, it was intended that each of the three advancing groups would keep part of its forces on trucks, which, after the breakthrough of the enemy front, would suddenly rush directly at Saragossa from three directions.

In my section, the only road, and a narrow one at that, that led to Saragossa was under oblique fire from heavy enemy batteries, which brought accurate fire down on even individual vehicles appearing on the road. Considering that the drivers of the trucks were civilian drivers from the local anarchist organization, I had strong doubts whether they would drive the trucks under artillery fire. Hearing the artillery hit even one vehicle, the entire column would come to a standstill on the road, from which it would not be able to move either to the right or to the left. A hit to the head of the column would hold up the entire column; a hit to the tail of the column would block any chance for the rest of the column to turn back, and a hit in the middle would cut the column in half. In addition, there was a great risk in keeping a column of two battalions on truck on the single road open to the view of enemy aircraft.

On the strength of these considerations, I requested that Comrade Leonidov, who had come to my sector, agree to some deviations from the original plan. These deviations would not, in the final analysis, have any adverse effect on the course of the offensive of the other attacking groups, but would on the contrary assist in the fulfillment of the overall mission even more.

Comrade Leonidov agreed entirely with the approval of my decision and I began to issue orders and directives for the upcoming offensive.

Several hours later, I went to the headquarters of my brigades to check up on how things were going in preparing for the offensive. To my complete astonishment, I found Comrade Leonidov in the headquarters of the 12th Brigade, where he was showing Brigade Commander Penchienati on the map the advantages of advancing by the right flank, that is, the exact reverse of the decision that had already been made.

I pointed out to Comrade Leonidov the unacceptability of such interference. It would be better to have just one decision, even if it seemed a bad one, than two contradictory decisions. In addition, Comrade Leonidov should have known that he was supposed to discuss such matters with me and not with the commanders subordinate to me. Comrade Leonidov stopped short and said that he did not, if you please, have any objections to my decision.

The division offensive began during the night. I passed one battalion after another through my position, standing at the ten-kilometer point on the road where they were supposed to turn *to the left* off the road and assault the enemy forts. To my complete astonishment, I found out that some time before, the 12th Brigade, turning off half a kilometer from me, had turned not to the left, but to the right off the road—that is, it went just the way Comrade Leonidov had advised brigade commander Penchienati to go.

Comrade Janek, the commander of the 13th Brigade, following my orders exactly, broke through the enemy fortifications, and at night, using only bayonets, pushed deep into the enemy deployment areas. By morning, it became clear that a yawning gap had been created between the 12th and the 13th Brigades as they had followed divergent directions. I was able to hold back one battalion of the 12th Brigade and send it in the right direction. The other two battalions found themselves in the morning to be in a hollow, cut off from all directions. The enemy opened heavy fire on them from the hills, and by the following night both battalions, remaining on the low ground, in a situation where they could neither push forward nor retreat, had sustained losses.

At my question about who had given him the right not to carry out my orders, Brigade Commander Penchienati answered that both battalions . . . had made a wrong turn in the night and that it was an unfortunate accident and not a deliberate act of not carrying out orders.

At that time, the 13th Brigade, having pushed two battalions into the rear area of the enemy, proved too weak to break through the enemy forts on the next ridge of the heights with what forces it had remaining. No assistance was forthcoming on the part of the 12th Brigade, because it could not help. For an entire day, we had to direct the fire of our artillery at enemy targets that were preventing the two battalions of the 12th Brigade from pulling back from the difficult position in which they had landed in the accursed low ground. While we were doing this, six of the nine cannon broke down.[101] There were no means by which we could give artillery assistance to the 13th Brigade.

Two battalions of the 13th Brigade, namely the Dombrowski and Palafox[102] Battalions, devised a night raid and seized the town of Villamayor de Galero and came within three kilometers of Saragossa. In Villamayor they captured an enemy headquarters with 150 prisoners of war, mainly officers. Among them were also four Germans with three interpreters. A panic started in Saragossa. The fascists sounded the alarm, and all night long the church bells were ringing. Strong detachments of troops appeared on trucks from Saragossa. The Polish battalions met them in a friendly manner, with machine-gun fire. The battle in Villamayor de Galero continued until 1700 hours, when the enemy, advancing with tanks, forced the Poles from the town. They were already running out of ammunition. At dawn the next day, the Polish battalions, reduced to 60 percent, began to arrive at our deployment area in groups, carrying with them their wounded and four dozen prisoners. The other captured officers had been shot by them when the prisoners refused to go with them and tried to escape under the cover of night. Separated groups of soldiers made it back through the enemy lines for four or five days more. From Saragossa, the enemy threw three camps of Moroccans at my division, then three battalions of infantry, then five. Rapid-fire batteries and dozens of tanks. Since my groups had gotten closer to Saragossa than the other groups, the enemy considered that the greatest danger to them threatened from that direction, and therefore he threw his reserves specifically at my group. Fierce battles broke out before the individual forts, and the entire weight of the battles was borne on the shoulders of the 13th Brigade and my reserve battalion, the Dzhuro Dzhakovich Battalion, made up of Bulgarian and Yugoslav comrades. Over the course of the next few days, only fifty men were left out of that battalion, and there were already more than eight hundred corpses of Moroccans in front of the fort, which had been taken and held by that battalion, despite all the counterattacks.

I threw in the last of my reserves, a squadron of dismounted cavalry made up mainly of Russians (former White Guards). A night assault by these cavalrymen succeeded in pushing the enemy out of the most important fort on Petruso Hill.

At night we began to improve the fortifications at the fort for ourselves. In order to have some reserves free for further action, I pulled the cavalrymen back at night and sent a battalion of anarchists attached to my group into the fort.

At dawn the enemy carried out a counteroffensive on the fort with ten tanks. It did not take fifteen minutes before the battalion of anarchists fled from the fort in panic, leaving it to the enemy practically without a fight.

Besides the heroes of the Dzhuro Dzhakovich Battalion, in which all the officers and political workers were either killed or wounded, the André Marty Battalion also fought extremely well, not giving up to the enemy the fort it had captured, despite heavy losses.

In response to my requests, the higher command promised reserves and tanks. They began to arrive in a scattered fashion, averaging one battalion per day. But these were anarchist battalions and battalions of new recruits. One commander of a tank battalion, having arrived at the front line, immediately took his group of people over to the enemy side.

In the final analysis, we gave back to the enemy (besides Villamayor de Galero) three of the five forts we had captured. And the situation stabilized at that point.

The right-hand group, the Karl Marx Division, moved forward to the Zuera point and could not go any farther.

In the left-hand group, Lister's division got stuck before Fuentes de Ebro, leaving behind it Belchite and Quinto. Walter's division surrounded these points of resistance and took them after a five-day battle.

Not one of the three groups of motorized detachments justified itself, precisely owing to the fact that the drivers of the vehicles were civilian drivers.

Evaluating the results of the entire battle at Saragossa, I have to say that the 45th Division under my command did everything that it could have done under those conditions. It drew down upon itself the greatest possible number of the enemy, thus making it easier for the other groups to achieve success. Not wanting to belittle the accomplishments of the division that Comrade Walter commanded, I must say that in taking Quinto and Belchite, about fifty guns and an entire group of tanks participated, under cover of our entire air force. If my group had had even one-third of those forces, we would have held on to the forts that we had captured and Villamayor de Galero. By the way, we must offer thanks for the taking of Quinto and Belchite primarily to the Dimitrov Battalion, that very battalion which in fact had belonged to my division.

After the fourteen days of battle at Saragossa, all the attacking groups went over to the defense. The remnants of my division, in all not much more than a thousand soldiers, were relieved and withdrawn to the rear for rest and reorganization.

I should go further into some aspects of the battle for Saragossa.

It is no secret to people who know the real state of affairs at Saragossa that the chief of the general staff, Rojo, did not, to put it mildly, contribute to the development of the successes that were achieved at the start. He was affected by his "jealousy" in relation to the chief of staff of the eastern front, and actually its commanding officer, Comrade Gordon. The entire operation, conceived for purposes of drawing the enemy forces away from Santander, was considered at the general staff in Valencia to be an operation that was directed by and carried out by the forces of the Communists (Gordon, Modesto, Walter, Lister, Gallo, the Karl Marx Division, Kléber). The Communist party exerted all its mobile forces to the utmost here. It threw in all the best political workers, organizers, and agitators. The Saragossa operation had great internal political significance for the Communist party, because it presented the opportunity to put an end to the anarcho-Trotskyist-FAI dominance in Aragon. It is no wonder that the party demanded the utmost exertion of effort from all its members. It is also understandable that the party could not be satisfied with the results achieved. Outwardly, it might seem that Kléber's division, along with others, had not lived up to the hopes that had been placed on it. But everyone knew why the two battalions of the 12th Brigade had "made a wrong turn," why Villamayor de Galero and two forts taken at the start were given back to the enemy, why the artillery broke down, why the enemy so easily took back the Petruso fort, and so on.

The day after the capture and loss of Villamayor de Galero, Colonel Rojo came to my command post. After my report on the course of the operation, he said, very meaningfully, "There is still the question of whether your units were actually at Villamayor." I did not want to answer this question at all. I asked him where the brigade that he had promised me in Valencia was and where the three batteries that had been taken away from me were.

To this, Rojo replied, "If you take Villamayor, you will get it all." I rephrased his words, saying, "If everything had been given me on time, you would be having this conversation with me today in Villamayor de Galero, not here."

There are some other incidents that took place during the operations at Saragossa which I should also include here.

Being at the command post of my own 13th Brigade, from where I directed the battle the entire time, I could observe the entire battlefield. I noticed in several cases how the commander of the 12th Brigade, Penchienati, carried out my instructions. He would report to me that one of his battalions had launched an attack. At the same time, I could see with my own eyes that the battalion had not moved from the spot. I swore at Brigade Commander Penchienati over the telephone for giving me false information and threatened him with unpleasant consequences. At the time, Comrade Gallo, the inspector general for the International Brigades who had come to the front, was with Penchienati.[103]

Later I found out (it was reported to me by the chief of staff of the brigade, a French Socialist named Bernard) that Penchienati, instead of carrying out the orders he received from me, began to criticize my actions in front of everyone, including Comrade Gallo. Penchienati even found time to write out a complaint against me, which he gave to Gallo. Gallo assured Penchienati that I would soon be removed from the division. Gallo, as well as Penchienati, expressed his doubts about whether the Polish battalions had really been at Villamayor de Galero. Comrades Gallo and Barontini began to question the soldiers about Villamayor de Galero, in an obvious attempt to prove that the Poles had not reached it. Having found out about this, the Polish battalions were highly incensed at the conduct of these Italian comrades. They, in turn, when they captured a prisoner or got hold of a deserter, questioned him about Villamayor and thus collected evidence from twenty various prisoners who confirmed that they had captured that town.

I don't know why Comrade Gallo found it necessary to cause friction between the two brigades. I can only suppose that he needed material to use against Kléber.

I found out about this when the division was already outside the battle and resting at the little town of Samper de Calanda. The division commissar got interested in this, having learned all the details from the political officers of the companies and battalions. At a conference of the senior command staff to analyze the operations at Saragossa, I asked Penchienati and Barontini to express their opinions. They could not find anything to say against my leadership in the operation or against the actions of the 13th Brigade. I pointed out the sacrifices of one brigade and then those of the other, analyzing the operation day by day. In the 13th Brigade, around 800 men were killed and wounded and in the 12th Brigade about 250 men, mainly on the day that the "lost" battalions found themselves on low ground with no way out. Penchienati, seeing that in the face of these facts he could not defend the accusations raised by him in his complaint, stated that his nerves had suffered in the battle and that he was requesting leave in Valencia for several days. It appeared that he wanted to take back his complaint, which he had given to Comrade Gallo.

A few words should be said about Pacciardi who, at the time of the battles, was hanging around my headquarters. Pacciardi told the commissar and me that he did not have any work assigned and did not consider that there was any purpose in his remaining at the division. Having consulted with me, the division commissar asked the army commissar, Virgilio Llanos, to recall Pacciardi for work at the army headquarters. When he was already at army headquarters, Pacciardi met with Prieto and Rojo, who asked him not to do anything. Rojo was indignant that Pacciardi had been removed from the division and ordered him to return, saying in doing so, "There is still the question of who must be removed from the division, Pacciardi or Kléber." Pacciardi returned to the division and told me about his conversation with Rojo and Prieto. In doing this, Pacciardi told me that, knowing Rojo's relationship with me, he did not want to remain any longer for two reasons, those being out of respect for me and also because in the case where I was removed and he was appointed in my place, he would not have the support of the Communists. After the battles were over, Pacciardi went to France, resentful toward the Italian Communists, particularly Gallo and Barontini. As for Penchienati and his conduct in battle, Pacciardi said that Penchienati had confessed to him that he regretted having fallen under Barontini's influence and having let himself be used in intrigues against Kléber.

I am ashamed to be writing about all this here. I was ashamed to be talking about this subject with Pacciardi at the time. Subsequent events, however, confirmed the words of Pacciardi himself, who in parting with me "in a comradely manner," considered it necessary to warn me that they were preparing to remove me from command of the division and that he was not prepared to take part in this game.

Despite the losses suffered, the morale and political condition of the division improved with each day of rest, the first received after many months of hard battles.

I ordered the division cadre school to report to me from Madrid. More than a thousand almost trained new recruits arrived with the school. Comrade Gordon also sent around two thousand new recruits to the division. From Albacete, Comrade Belov sent several hundred internationalists. For the first time, the division had brought together around six thousand men. The work of organization and training was in full swing. Good work was done with the local population, frightened by the previous anarcho-Trotskyist dominance. General Pozas and Colonel Gordon came to inspect the division and were satisfied with it.

At this time, I began to receive strange telegrams from Valencia, along the lines of: "The commander of the 45th Division is to turn over all the automatic weapons he has received, specifically, thirty-two heavy and seventy-two light machine guns," or "Report what you have done with the antitank battery which you illegally took from the disbanded 13th Brigade." (I had never taken an antitank battery, legally or illegally, from anyone.) One fine day, they sent me a detail of four hundred additional new recruits from Valencia. My officers detailed to receive them returned with the new recruits and reported with horror that these were not new recruits, but *the cadres of the Trotskyist organizations* just released from prison, where they had been imprisoned for their participation in the May putsch and brought together from all over. A nice gift for the international division! I sent these new recruits back to where they had been taken from.

A strong party organization began to work in the division. Earlier the Communists had not been organized into cells, and now each company already had its own cell. Elections of the party committees had been carried out in the battalions and in the brigades. A division party conference was held. Massive contacts with the populace were carried out. The division newspaper the *International Bayonets* was recognized as the best of the existing army newspapers. In a word, we had reason to be pleased with our successes, achieved during the time of the two-, almost three-, week rest period, the first that had come the way of our division.

I was able to achieve the return to the division of the three internationalist batteries taken from us. The two squadrons of cavalry were being brought up to full strength. Finally, I brought into existence the old dream of our internationalists, particularly the Yugoslav and Bulgarian comrades, by working to create a third brigade in our division, which was to bear the name of Comrade Dimitrov. The basis of this brigade was to be the Dzhuro Dzhakovich Battalion that was in the division and the Dimitrov Battalion, which I was supposed to receive from the 15th Brigade. I had not encountered any objections to creating this brigade, either from Comrade Belov, responsible for the base in Albacete, or from Comrade Gordon, the chief of staff of the front, or from other comrades of the CC of the party or from the bureaucracy of the advisers. Of the three brigades of the 45th Division, the Garibaldi, the Dombrowski, and the Dimitrov, the latter was supposed to become the strongest and most capable of combat. I had already collected sufficient weapons for this brigade, making use of secret connections with the anarchists' depots, where we received rifles and machine guns in return for gifts of cigarettes.

In connection with the matter of the transfer of the Dimitrov Battalion, I went to the 15th Brigade to see Comrade Walter. I did not find him at the headquarters. Then I looked for Comrade Čopič, the commander of the 15th Brigade. Čopič, did everything possible to avoid meeting with me and did it in a rude manner. Finally, I was able to catch Čopič, who had been avoiding a meeting. It turned out that, contrary to all the decisions, he was not about to give up the Dimitrov Battalion to the 45th Division.

At the headquarters of the 15th Brigade, they were generally surprised at my arriving there and being involved in the business of the 45th Division, since they had information that Kléber had been removed from the command of that division.

It turned out that Franz Dahlem, upon arriving from Albacete, had told the comrades in the 15th Brigade that they had removed me from command of the division. The rumor about Kléber's being removed had gone around all the internationalist units and they had begun to talk about it even in my division. Officially, no one had informed me that they were removing me. Comrade Dubrovin, the deputy to Comrade Grigorovich, came to my division. I asked him if he knew anything about their removing me from the division. He shrugged his shoulders.

But rumors are persistent things.

Comrades Belov and Gallo came to hold a conference with the commanders of the International Brigades. They invited the division commissar and me to this conference. After the business part of the conference, I asked Comrades Belov and Gallo what was going on and whether it was true, as the persistent rumors had it, that I was being removed from command and that Comrade Hans would be appointed to replace me. Both these comrades, who should have known the actual situation, assured me that the rumors were groundless.

On the way back, the division commander said with indignation that the "innocent face" of Comrade Gallo was a lie and that the rumors were being spread specifically by Comrades Gallo and Franz Dahlem. The division commissar revealed to me that he, when he heard the rumors, had tried to get in to see someone from the CC of the party in order to draw their attention to the rumors, which were dangerous for the morale and political condition of the unit. He was made aware of some kind of leaflet written in Italian that was being passed around among the political elements of the 12th Brigade. In this leaflet, it was said that Kléber had been removed from command. My adjutant, sent by me on division business to the general staff in Valencia, returned and reported to the commissar that the assistant to Lieutenant [sic] Colonel Rojo had asked him if he were leaving the division together with me.

A week went by like this. Everyone was whispering, and no one had officially informed me of anything. I imagined what consequences such rumors could have if the division had to go into battle and hear the orders of a commander, when everyone knew that not he, but someone else, had the right to give orders.

I met Comrade Franz Dahlem and called on him to speak openly. With unpleasant malice, Franz went through the entire list of my sins; here he brought up the old story about the "cadre policy" and my accepting Spaniards into the courses. Then he added in some new sins for my attempts at creating the Dimitrov Brigade, with which he fundamentally did not agree. In the opinion of Comrade Franz, there should be five separate brigades, which would be the German, the Anglo-American, the Italian, the French, and the Slavs. Instead of this mixing together of all the Slav contingents in one brigade, I was for assigning the Balkan Slavs, the Greeks, and the Romanians to a separate unit. This was my mistake. In general, my division was undergoing an internal crisis for which he held me responsible (for example, the case of Pacciardi). I was supposed to answer for all these matters soon before the central committee in Valencia and the Comintern at home. The matter had already been settled at Albacete and among the general staff.

Comrade Walter and Comrade Richard, commander of the 11th Brigade, were present during this conversation.

I pointed out the following to Comrade Franz:

I considered, as did many comrades in the CC, that as far as my cadre policies and relying on Spanish cadres were concerned, all the actions I had taken were correct. The unhealthy incidents that had taken place in the International Brigades, particularly in the 11th Brigade, in relation to the Spanish contingents, which made up from 70 to 85 percent of the total combat personnel of the International Brigades, simply could not be permitted.

Concerning the "Slavic" brigade, it could be stated that it would have been a great political mistake to lump them all in together. It was necessary to take into account what significance, for example, a Polish-Ukrainian-Belorussian brigade named for Dombrowski would have on the development of an antifascist unified front in Poland. Letters, newspapers, and information about the "Dombrowskis" would get through to Poland and elicit an enormous positive response there. To deprive this brigade of its clearly expressed image and make it into just a Slavic brigade would mean to make a turn into the wrong course. The combat alliance between the Poles and the Spaniards was based on a healthy political formula: We are helping you beat the fascists in Spain. When we finish with them here, the Dombrowskis-Spaniards will come with us to help us beat the fascists in Poland.

This was how all the International Brigade units should be set up, starting with the companies and battalions.

The flow of new internationalist soldiers would be best ensured through just this course. The Poles would go into their own brigade, the others likewise. I, for example, considered it an erroneous principle that was applied in the 11th, the so-called German brigade. A generally valid principle, the language, could not be carried to absurdity. In the 11th Brigade, they were all mixed into the same pot—Germans, Austrians, Swiss, Alsatians, Flemish, Norwegians, Swedes, and so forth.

In my opinion, we should have separated the Sudeten Germans from the 11th Brigades and made up a battalion of them, together with the Czechs and Slovaks, named for Masaryk. There would have been greater political sense in this than in moving ahead of the racists Hitler and Henlein and in Spain joining the Sudeten Germans with Germany and carrying out the annexation of Austria by Anschluß earlier than it actually happened.

As far as the Dimitrov Brigade was concerned, it had to be taken into account that the Dzhuro Dzhakovich Battalion that I had created was carrying out a decision made even before I took command of the division. The Dzhakovich Battalion was the newest in the division, but proved to be one of the best in battle. It existed [as a kind of] reserve battalion under my direct control. As division commander, I had the right to create a reserve unit.

The Dimitrov Battalion transferred from the 15th Brigade (Anglo-American) also already existed. This battalion was perhaps the very best of all the battalions of the International Brigades. I had thirty-two Maxim machine guns in reserve, and I wanted to create a reserve machine-gun battalion on the basis of the present Dimitrov Battalion. I had already detailed the best Spanish recruits, who were getting intensified training, for this purpose.

With such a machine-gun battalion in reserve, I could always occupy a large sector of the front with them, and the remaining brigade personnel would be given a chance to rest up and to be concentrated into a strike force for a powerful blow. The military advantages were apparent, to say nothing of the political importance of the Dimitrov Brigade, in which would be concentrated all the Bulgarians, Yugoslavs, and so on, scattered all across Spain. In this brigade, there would be a Bulgarian-Spanish battalion, a Yugoslav-Spanish battalion, and a Hungarian-Spanish battalion (the latter also existed within the 13th Brigade, called the Rakosi Battalion). In the battalions listed here, there could also be a company of Romanians and a company of Greeks.

The influx of new soldiers would be assured and not worse, but probably better, than to the German or Italian brigades. Balkan emigrants were arriving from the French emigration and particularly from the Americas, both North and South, and would be more willing to fight in the Dimitrov Brigade, where their cultural life would take place in their own language, than in the Anglo-American or French brigades.

Regarding the statement by Franz Dahlem to the effect that the 45th Division under my command was undergoing an internal crisis, I asked him to go around to the battalions and the companies and to get to know the soldiers and the commanders. There was no crisis, particularly because I was carrying out that personnel policy which Comrade Dahlem considered a mistake. The rest they had received, the intensified political work, and the exercises, all this had greatly improved the spirits of all the personnel, including even the Italian soldiers whom Pacciardi's work and his fight against the Communists had agitated. The "Pacciardi affair," as everyone knew, had existed even before I came to the division. We came out of it without any scandal, and the 12th Brigade had been brought up to the level of the other units. If a crisis had recently existed in the 12th Brigade, it was only in the minds of some of the comrades at the top, but not in the lower levels of the brigade. With the departure of Pacciardi and the dismissal of Penchienati, this "crisis" also disappeared.

I did not convince Comrade Franz Dahlem with these arguments.

In conclusion, I also reminded him that he should have known what kind of struggle with the war ministry the party had to deal with in the matter of the Communist cadres. After the battles at Saragossa, they took his former divisions away from him and transferred them, including my division, to a new corps commander, the notorious Casado (former commander of the 21st Corps in the Brunete operation). They wanted to remove Comrade Lister from his division, and the party kept him there only with difficulty. They permitted themselves a vile attack against Walter, stating in official communiqués that his units "were engaged in plundering" in Belchite. It was clearly a lie fabricated by the Trotskyists in their attempts to discredit Walter and his units. A campaign was waged against Comrade Gordon. They even wanted to remove the commissar to the Socialists, Llanos, from his post. Were the people that Rojo wanted to put in their places going to be better than these comrades?

If Comrades Dahlem, Gallo, and the others considered it necessary to remove Kléber from the division for whatever sins, they should not have done it right at the time when those most interested in doing so were the enemies of the party. If I were in Comrade Dahlem's place, I would not want to play into the hands of a certain clique in the ministry and the general staff, and I would choose for myself a more suitable time to remove Kléber from the division. "You are seeing ghosts!" said Dahlem. "And do you think that you are seeing the present situation correctly?" I asked him.

The division commissar, Comrade Vidal, returned from Lérida and passed on to me that Comrade Gordon wanted to see me. In Lérida, Comrade Gordon told me that the rumors were being confirmed. Colonel Rojo had proposed to General Pozas that he remove me from the 45th Division. Pozas, in the words of Comrade Gordon, did not agree with this. Comrades Gordon and Llanos advised me to go to Valencia and to clear up this matter with the party.

I left for Valencia.

In the division at that time, after the return of the commissar from Lérida, the party organization met to discuss the situation that had developed. The party organization unanimously (with two abstentions from voting—the commissar of the 12th Brigade, Barontini, and one other comrade) approved a resolution to send a delegation immediately to Valencia, to the CC of the party, to clear up the entire matter and to request that Kléber be kept in the division.

The delegation, made up of three internationalist and Spanish party members, arrived in Valencia almost simultaneously with me. I found out from them about the resolution approved at the party meeting.

In the CC, Comrades Dolores, Ercoli, and Stepanov received me. Before hearing me out to the end, Dolores asked whether it was true that I had set the Poles against the Italians. Instead of answering the question put to me, I requested that they ask the comrades who had come here in the name of the division party organization. I left the room and the three comrades who had come from the division went into the room. Their conversation with Comrade Dolores lasted about an hour. When they came out, I again went into the room to find out the decision of the CC. Comrade Ercoli took me aside and said to me, "In general, there is nothing to be held against you. But it is simply that a telegram has been received from back home that you are being recalled for other work. It could be China . . . " Comrade Ercoli's words did not sound too convincing.

Cutting into our conversation, Comrade Stepanov advised me to go to the headquarters of Comrade Grigorovich, where they could tell me more. I went there as Comrade Stepanov had suggested.

Comrade Grigorovich was not at the headquarters (he had departed for Moscow). His deputy, Comrade Maximov, was not there either. They expected him back any minute. Comrade Dubrovin received me. He did not know anything about a telegram from back home. "You know," Comrade Dubrovin said, "here Rojo, Prieto . . . the comrades from Albacete . . . unsuccessful operation . . . You need a rest . . . and we decided . . . " "What did you decide?" I asked Comrade Dubrovin. "How we get out of this situation? The anarchist newspapers will have a field day with this. We have to be careful . . . " "What has to be done?!" "We still have to speak with Rojo. We want him to give the appropriate orders in which Kléber is thanked for his work . . . You know what, it is better for you to go to Rojo . . . " "What am I supposed to say to him?" I asked again.

Another comrade, whose name I did not know, joined into our conversation, "Kléber, report yourself as ill."

I thought about it and said, "I cannot report myself as ill at this time. After all the buzz everywhere that I was already removed from my position, it would be inappropriate, even for the customs of Chinese ceremony, to report myself as ill. If Comrade Dubrovin had suggested that to me two weeks ago when he was at my division, I could perhaps have done that."

"So, this means that you refuse. Hey, old man, don't joke around with this!" burst out of my partner in this conversation.

"Understand, comrade, that nobody needs to have me present myself like the widow of a noncommissioned officer."

Comrade Dubrovin ended this unpleasant conversation with, "OK, I will call Rojo, and he will tell you to report to him."

A day or two went by on waiting for the summons from Rojo.

At that time, several commanders from my division came to me at my apartment. It turns out that there was another delegation. The Spanish commanders, led by Captain del Río, had come to protest against pulling Kléber out of the division. As they explained to me, they had already succeeded in getting to the CC of the party. As party members, they requested that they be told what this was all about. In the military commission of the CC, they answered that there was nothing known there about Kléber's being removed. Kléber was the commander of the 45th Division.

And so, after the explanation they received in the CC, they had come to me to request that I return to my place in the division. If it was necessary, they were ready to go to Prieto to protest . . .

What was I supposed to do?

I told them, "No protests are necessary. You should go back to the division. I have to take care of a few things here. When I am finished, I will return to the division."

These comrades gave me about a dozen letters brought by them from the division in which the command personnel expressed individually and collectively their great respect and their regrets at the "unworthy intrigues." There was a dangerous note in these letters, in which they stated that they would leave the division if I did not remain as its commander. These letters had to be answered and the comrades told not to do anything stupid and to remain at their posts, carrying out the orders of the command staff. I requested that they show the new commander, if one were to be appointed, the same confidence that they had had in me.

Rojo summoned me to him. He met me with exaggerated courtesy, "Mi general. Should I announce your arrival to the minister?" "Why bother the minister," I said.

"Yes, his excellency has decided to appoint you to the position with residence in Barcelona."

"I regret that I will not be able to accept this appointment, since I have come to request permission to leave the country."

"Too bad, too bad. I will immediately inform the minister of this."

The advisers' office took care of providing travel documents and money for the trip. I came to say good-bye to the comrades in the CC. To my question about what I should say if they ask me at home why I had come back, Comrade Stepanov answered me, "You can say that the CC of the Communist Party of Spain has nothing against Kléber."

Comrade Maximov, having replaced Grigorovich, also received me prior to my departure. In his words, "Kléber did not work badly, if anyone analyzes whether Kléber or the comrades from Albacete were right. He worked for more than a year, longer than all the rest, and it was time to go home. They need people with our experience at home."

Comrade Dubrovin (who had just returned from the 45th Division, where he had gone together with Comrades Gallo and Ercoli to present it with its new commander, Comrade Hans) said, "It is an excellent division. Good people. I saw the letter that you wrote to brigade commander Janek. You don't say anything; it is the kind of letter that a Bolshevik should write."

On the day of my departure, I saw Comrade Ercoli again. He now had a direct idea of what the division was like, since he had visited it. It seemed to me that this gave him the opportunity to see the entire "history of Kléber" in a somewhat different light. He told me that Barontini had been removed from his position as brigade commissar.

"You are also to blame for some things," he said in parting; "basically it is a fact that the people in your division became attached to you personally."

This may be; however, this was not something that I did deliberately or in a calculated way.

Captain del Río came to say good-bye to me and to ask me to give his greetings to his son, who was studying in Moscow at a school for Spanish children. He passed on the details of how the meeting of the command personnel had gone, at which Comrade Gallo had spoken. Comrade Gallo had outlined the history of the International Brigades, paid tribute to the late Comrade Lukács, and praised the future commander of the division, Comrade Hans. Since Comrade Gallo did not say a word about Kléber, one of the commanders stepped up to correct Comrade Gallo. The entire hall shouted demonstratively, "Long live Kléber!"

Recalling these details here, I do not want to show off at all. I want to say by this only that, despite all the unpleasantness, I remain deeply satisfied with the work that was done. I am also satisfied that the comrades who fought together with me at the front really respected and loved me.

## The Year Draws to a Close

By September, the government of the Spanish Republic had moved from Valencia to Barcelona. This action strengthened the hand of the central government over the anarcho-syndicalists of Catalonia and came at the expense of the Catalan governmental authority, the generalitat. As Palmiro Togliatti wrote in a report to Moscow, the masses were longing for peace, and this sentiment created pressure for a negotiated settlement with Franco. In Barcelona especially, he reported, people were advocating defection. Moreover, the Argentinean Comintern adviser Vittorio Codovilla and Comintern leader André Marty were both having a negative effect on the Spaniards.[104] Codovilla, a.k.a. Luis, left Spain in the summer of 1937. After that, the most important Comintern leader on the scene was Togliatti, later the head of the Italian Communist party, who in the meantime was the virtual chief of the PCE while in Spain; he wrote the speeches both of PCE chairman José Díaz and of the famous Dolores Ibárruri, who was popularly called La Pasionaria. In his testimony to the U.S. Senate Subcommittee on Internal Security in 1957, Alexander Orlov, the NKVD chief in Spain from September 1936 until his defection in July 1938, emphasized

Togliatti's importance. Togliatti, he told the Senate, "directed the Spanish Communist Party and the Spanish Communist military forces on behalf of Moscow."[105]

Seeking advice, Spanish Communists submitted questions to Georgi Dimitrov for him to pass on to Moscow. **Document 61,** which Dimitrov forwarded to Marshal Voroshilov on 8 September 1937, asked a number of questions for which the Spanish Communists desired answers. Most interesting was their candid admission that although they were doing what they could to defend the Popular Front, they considered the current government a "republic of a new type," a "people's democracy." They acknowledged, however, that in this regime a "democratic life of the masses" did not exist. The central concern of the PCE was how to gain full control over the Spanish government without openly appearing to disrupt the would-be unity of the Popular Front coalition. Moreover, party leaders feared that military losses would cause the government to lose "its authority among the masses" and result in further challenges from their left-wing opponents.

This document is particularly instructive in its characterization of what challenges the PCE thought it faced from those on the Left. Even though the party's leaders branded their opponents "premature revolutionaries" for calling for revolution before the PCE declared it was time, they bemoaned the reality that the war had taken on "a deeply class character," making the population vulnerable to calls for socialization and collectivization. What made the program of the Left so popular, according to the writers of the document, was that landowners and factory owners stood on Franco's side, and union and worker committees ran most factories. Drawing an analogy to the French Revolution, the Spanish Communists revealed that they were being hurt among the populace by charges from the Left that the government and the revolution had entered a period of Thermidorean reaction, exemplified by efforts to destroy the POUM and other left-wing groups.

Despite their complaints, the Spanish Communists had in fact achieved a major victory for Moscow—control over the armed forces. By September 1937, the People's Army had a combined force of 575,000 men, who were divided into 152 different brigade units. Integrated into this force were the once autonomous International Brigades. Moreover, the army was now effectively under PCE control. Sixty percent of its personnel were members of the PCE, as were five of the eleven corps commanders and fifty-six of the seventy-two brigade commanders. The commissars, who were in charge of ideological and political control, came from the PCE or from among pro-Moscow Socialists. By summertime, the PCE had representatives in every military unit, thus ensuring that officers were loyal to the program of the Popular Front regime.

The response to this control created new problems, which prompted Dimitrov to forward four different reports to Voroshilov from the leading Comintern and PCE leaders working in Spain. Two were from Togliatti—one on 29 August and the other on 11 September; one was from PCE Politburo leader Pedro Checa and the Comintern representative Codovilla; and another was from the Hungarian Communist who later briefly became head of the postwar Hungarian Communist regime, Erno Gerö, known in Spain as Comrade Pedro. **Document 62** reproduces Dimitrov's cover letter along with one of these reports, the 30 August dispatch from Togliatti.

Togliatti's reports are of special importance. It is clear that, unlike other apparatchiks, Togliatti was extremely candid and forthright in his observations. Indeed, much of what he reported highlights the weakness of the PCE's propaganda. Togliatti revealed that even when the PCE-dominated army had won a battle, such as the one at Brunete, there was no "decisive victory" of the type that would give the people confidence that it could win the fight. Even the creation of a unified regular army was not satisfactory. No matter how hard the party had tried to eliminate them, "traitors, suspect people," and factions were in the ranks, including "agents of the enemy." Togliatti's language also revealed him to be a loyal follower of Stalin, anxious that more be done to purge the ranks of enemies.

Moreover, Togliatti was worried that even in Catalonia the bad situation was "just as acute" as it had been during the Largo Caballero years, and in fact was "more dangerous than earlier." Togliatti feared a new opposition bloc of POUM members and anarchists, who had great influence in the unions that ran "almost all the economy"; under their leadership, he thought, a new left-wing movement could lead "dissatisfied groups of the population." Indeed, Togliatti revealed that negative characterizations of social life were well grounded. Noting the existence of food lines and an increase in the cost of living, he confessed that the population was not happy. To deal with these problems, Togliatti demanded once again that General Asensio be arrested and that tougher measures be taken by the government against those he branded "enemies of the Popular Front."

It is clear that the Comintern, despite its success in forcing Largo Caballero's replacement by Juan Negrín, was not satisfied with the results. Togliatti's fear that some in the government secretly sympathized with the attacks of the POUM led him to advise a strategic slowdown. Demands that were too firm might work only to split a tenuous alliance, and his major concern was to keep the PCE in control of the government apparatus. The party, he informed Moscow, could not afford to lose "even one of the positions won by us." Thus Togliatti cautioned against the party's raising "the question of its *hegemony*" just then and instead preferred that the issue be put off until a more favorable time. A shrewd tactician, Togliatti realized that calling for total power would only force those in the center "to take up a position against us." At the same time, in Catalonia, Togliatti called for a policy of reinforcing the moderation of the Popular Front, rather than demagogic appeals to a revolution-minded populace. If the anarchists tried to move toward open revolt and stage a coup, he advised one solution only: "We will finally do away with them." While publicly advocating attempts at cooperation with opposition anarchists, Togliatti noted that their leaders were "scum, closely tied to Caballero," and had to be fought via "large-scale action from below."

In **Document 63** PCE leader Pedro Checa presented a political analysis of the war's meaning. In it he made the claim that two Western powers, Britain and France, sought a compromise with Hitler and Mussolini that would result in a republic or a monarchy, and eventually in military dictatorship, rather than in a popular (that is, Soviet-style) people's government. He claimed that all the interested European nations hoped to carve up a helpless Spain, a claim that has no support outside Checa's statement. All those who did not see the Soviet Union as Spain's "only reliable friend" were thus written off as servants of Western imperialism. Therefore,

Checa claimed, because the Socialist International treated Negrín as an instrument of the PCE and the Soviet Union, it too was to be considered part of the imperialist camp.

Clearly, Checa was motivated by fears that the Western-oriented Socialists were trying to force a break with the PCE and, as he put it, to gain "liberation from the influence of the Soviet Union." Their anti-Soviet policies, Checa argued, were based on the claim that the Spanish Communist party "wants to seize all power for itself in order to set up a dictatorship and that the Soviet government intends to make Spain an appendage of the USSR." Checa's use of language is striking. The documentary evidence, as we have shown, suggests strongly that such indeed was the goal of both the PCE and Moscow. Perhaps what worried the erstwhile Spanish Communist leader was the uncanny accuracy of the Socialists' analysis.

The remainder of his report provides further evidence for this view. He went on to indicate the PCE's dissatisfaction with the Negrín government's inability to implement measures favored by Moscow, including the removal of "suspect elements from the army" and the total liquidation of "the remains of the May putsch"—that is, a complete purge of the POUM. Checa argued that the Negrín government was putting the PCE program into effect "very slowly or not at all." Because of this, the failure of the Republic to win its battles against Franco could be blamed on Negrín's indecisiveness—not on Moscow or the PCE—as typified by the government's continuing desire to create a professional "apolitical" army, rather than the "People's Army" led by Communist commissars that Moscow wanted.

By June, the government had begun to officially act against the POUM. It had announced the creation of a special tribunal for espionage, intended to be used against the remaining POUM leadership. Andrés Nin had already been tortured and murdered, and other key leaders of the organization, including Julián Gorkín and General José Rovira, had been arrested. A month later, more than a thousand militants had been arrested, yet the organization continued to exist. As historians of the POUM have explained, its strong local base allowed its members to gain protection from other worker militants. Some CNT members gave union membership cards to POUM cadres so that they could work, and CNT militia brigades let them into their units to protect them and keep them out of Communist brigades.[106] Yet by autumn, as a leading historian of the war, Antony Beevor, has written, the Republic "witnessed the continued decline of anarchist power, the isolation of the Catalan nationalists, discord in Socialist ranks, and the development of the secret police. Negrín's government presided over these developments, and as a result of Communist power the repression of dissenters was far greater than it had been" during the dictatorship in the 1920s.[107] It was during this period that the security services consolidated into the Servicio de Investigación Militar (SIM), which was run by the Communists and became the mechanism of control by the GRU and NKVD units operating in the Republic. According to Beevor, its methods were particularly brutal: The SIM "evolved beyond beatings with rubber piping, hot and cold water treatment, splinters inserted under nails, and mock executions. The Soviet advisers made the procedures more scientific. Cell floors were specially constructed with the sharp corners of bricks pointing upward so that the naked prisoners were in constant pain."[108]

The SIM sought to be as effective as possible. During the Negrín years, tribunals tried opponents of the Communist line as fifth columnists. Historians have argued that the PCE was successful in exercising great control over the Negrín government, even though the party held only two minor ministries in the premier's cabinet. Yet the more the PCE exercised control through terror, the greater the opposition its tactics produced. Soldiers became furious when they found that non-Communist wounded were often refused medical aid; officers learned that if they did not follow PCE policy, they would not get the weapons they needed. Indalecio Prieto claimed that Socialists fighting in PCE units were even shot for cowardice or desertion when their only "crime" was having refused to join the PCE.

Part of the weariness of the Comintern representatives stemmed from their inability to attain their foremost goal—the complete destruction of the left-wing opposition. In **Document 64**, Erno Gerö, writing on 16 August 1937, presented a comprehensive report on the military and political situation in both Catalonia and Aragon, areas of anarchist and POUM predominance. Gerö's frustration is apparent in his call for a harsh policy that would purge army units of anarchists. He went so far as to claim that despite all that had been done to it, "the official POUM was not disbanded," was publishing illegally, and still had representatives in the Catalan *municipalitat*. Moreover, he provided evidence that the population was not cooperating with the Communists and was acting to protect POUM members who had been arrested. And as a result of successful Communist maneuvers to control the trade union federation, former POUM members were trying to resurrect the predecessor organization of the POUM, the "worker-peasant bloc."

In his final dispatch for 1937, dated 15 September and given here as **Document 65**, Togliatti once again acknowledged the growing despair felt by members of the Spanish working class. Their wages were falling and, as good trade unionists, workers sought redress through union militancy. Here Togliatti pointed to the sectarianism of the Spanish Communists and their inability to gain ground among the workers. He complained that the Communists ignored the working masses and instead sought influence through "gaining posts in the leadership," while "ties with the working masses in the factories are weak." Indeed, Togliatti argued, despite all that the party had done, the followers of Largo Caballero still dominated the trade unions and were continuing their war against the PCE. The party responded by trying to take over the labor press and the union leadership, an attempt that he predicted would only backfire and create even more resentment against the Communists. Togliatti stressed that the Spanish Communists alienated all sides through their intransigence. As an example, he cited the PCE's continuing false charge that Largo Caballero's followers were simply counterrevolutionaries. Since Togliatti knew that this charge and the anti–Largo Caballero campaign originated with Moscow, he was clearly sending a message to the Comintern and Stalin that perhaps they should consider advancing a different line. Finally, Togliatti blasted Codovilla's leadership in previous years, conveniently putting the blame on him for the PCE's many problems. Codovilla became an easy scapegoat for Moscow, and he was soon replaced by Togliatti.

# Document 61

RGVA, f. 33987, op. 3, d. 1033, ll. 123–133

Dear Comrade Stalin!

The Spanish comrades have formulated by letter questions, which they are placing before us for discussion and on which they are asking appropriate advice and instructions.

I am sending to you their memorandum in connection with a forthcoming conversation.

With comradely greetings

G. Dimitrov

8 September 1937

*Translated from French*

*Questions for resolution.*

Taking into account the reflections presented in our report on the current situation in Spain with regard to both national and international relations, we convey the following questions for discussion by the Comintern, so that the Comintern might give us its advice and assistance in resolving them:

1. *On international relations.* How to achieve a rupture of the bloc that currently exists against Republican Spain, and how to achieve a change in the policies of democratic countries?

We believe that, first, it is necessary to strengthen the international campaign for aid, not only for material aid, but also using mass action so that the democratic governments force the fascist governments to stop their policy of armed intervention in Spain.

Taking into account the hostile attitude of England and France in regard to the Spanish Republic, what sort of concessions might be made with respect to them—concessions combined with the existence of the democratic republic—to change their attitude?

We do not have any clear thought concerning this.

2. Taking into account that the most reactionary elements of the Second International are collaborating with the imperialist policy of the governments of their countries, what sort of proposal may be made to the Second International with the goals of exposing their reactionary leaders and winning over the masses, who sympathize with the cause of the Spanish people, for joint revolutionary action?

The Communist Party of Spain, together with the Socialist party and the UGT (General Workers' Union), signed an appeal, the result of which was the Annemass Conference. Lately it [the party] made a new appeal in the same spirit. What more might it [the party] do in this direction? What can the fraternal Communist parties do in this regard?

3. The fascist governments of Germany and Italy are conducting open war in Spain, using forces of their nationalities and colonies; in these conditions, we believe that the International Brigades have a huge role—not only for their political significance, but also for their use from a military point of view. We believe that it is necessary to reinforce the five International Brigades that currently exist in Spain with new foreign comrades and at the same time to increase the recruitment of foreign volunteers, to create new brigades.

The system of mixed brigades, Spanish and foreign, has produced very good results in the conflict, and through this system, little by little, we have succeeded in attaining the introduction of the International Brigades into the Spanish army. (Currently, it may be said that in fact the International Brigades make up part of the Spanish army.)

With the goal of raising the fighting efficiency of the International Brigades, it is necessary to give them military leaders who are more capable than the majority of those who currently command them. Can the Comintern help us to obtain such officers?

4. At present the tactics of the enemies of the Popular Front, leading to the creation of an opposition bloc, are directed toward the goal of sabotaging the actions of the current government and provoking a crisis to remove the party from the government and isolate it from the masses. The Communist party is straining every nerve to maintain the Popular Front and is doing everything to enlarge its base. But up to now it has not reached this goal.

What tactics does the Comintern advise to reach completely this goal?

5. Despite the fact that there exists in Spain a democratic and parliamentary republic of a new type (a people's democracy), the democratic life of the masses as a whole almost does not exist (with the exception of the political activity of our party, meetings, press, and so on, there are no other opportunities for the masses to express their willingness through democratic forms).

The parliament does not function, but even if it functioned, the deputies who presently exist mostly do not represent the will of the people of Spain. In Russia at the time of the revolution the masses expressed their democratic will through the soviets, in other democratic countries through elections (municipal, cantonal, general, and so on). In the present conditions in Spain they do not believe that they can allow elections, since the most active part of the population is at the front. After the elections of 16 February 1936 throughout the whole country committees of the Popular Front were set up, which devoted themselves to counteracting the reactionary municipalitats and which little by little concentrated in their hands the entire political and administrative life of a given locality. After July all of the reactionary municipalitats were abolished; new municipal councils were created from above by order of the Ministry of Internal Affairs. These municipal councils took into their hands the functions of committees of the Popular Front—with the exception of a few—and in practice abolished the work of these committees.

Is it possible to set up this form of organ at the present time, so that the masses might express their democratic will? We have still not found a solution for this problem. We are asking advice from the Comintern concerning this.

6. Taking into account that it is necessary to strengthen the authority of the government of the Popular Front and to increase the membership of the government so that it may obtain a great deal of help from the entire working population; and also taking into account that, to conduct a policy that is capable of winning the war it is necessary that the decisive posts in the government be in the hands of the party of the proletariat, our party proposes to create the conditions to strengthen the present government. (Of course without causing a crisis.) We believe that, having once created a united party of the proletariat, it will be necessary to secure a majority for it in the government of the Popular Front, drawing into the government representatives from the UGT and the CNT (the National Labor Confederation), especially the CNT (taking into account that the UGT is represented in the government by the Socialists and Communists). We also believe that the present minister of justice (Irujo)—who by his reactionary policy is alienating the masses and discrediting the government—ought to be dismissed as soon as possible from the government. The Basque nationalists ought to be represented in the government by individuals connected to the people's wing of Basque nationalism (from among "Acción Nacionalista Vasca" or "Basque Solidarity").

Does the Comintern consider such a position of the party correct? In any case we ask advice from the Comintern: Which tactic should we follow in order to raise the authority of the existing government and to enlarge its base? On the other hand, if the proletarian situation worsens, as a result of military defeats, and the government loses its authority among the masses, the opposition against the government will strengthen, what way out can there be in such a situation?

7. Up to now we have not met any difficulties—on the principal questions, programs, questions of structure, and so on—over the formation of a unified party. The Socialists in general accept our proposals. Up to now we have not come to a discussion of how the unified party ought to be named and to which International it ought to belong. The CC of our party is of the opinion that the unified party—before the congress—ought to be called the Unified Socialist and Communist Party. Why? Because this name gives satisfaction to the Socialists of the old tradition, since the party retains the name Socialist party, only adding the name Communist. On the other hand, the name Communist satisfies the vast masses of heroic soldiers who are in our party and who are deeply attached to it and to the Comintern.

As for the problem of joining the Second International, our CC considers it permissible for the unified party to support simultaneously relations with the Third and Second Internationals, fighting to unify these two organizations. (By the way, in the action program of the two parties, which is already accepted, the necessity of struggling for the unification of the two Internationals is prescribed.)

Does the Comintern consider our opinion correct? What is its opinion on these questions?

8. Our party correctly fought against various endeavors of premature revolutionaries in the cities and villages (against socialization, forced collectivization, against egalitarian[109] communism). But it must be taken into account that the majority of these incidents occurred because the civil war in Spain has taken a deeply class character and the masses, in general, wanted to produce and lead production on their own. One must bear in mind that the vast majority of landowners—large and medium, large employers, representatives of financial capital, and so on, took active part in the struggle on the side of fascism, part ran away, abandoning [their] land and factories, the other part was virtually liquidated by the masses. At present the overwhelming majority of industry is managed by the unions, by factory committees, in several places by elections, in others created by order of the unions—or finally by workers together with former owners.

Production is not coordinated, not led on the basis of a national or regional plan, nor of a plan for branches of production. Each factory or group of factories produces as it wishes and for an unknown market (goods are produced that are not needed, and they do not make goods that are very much needed). But in any event the factories are working and, in general, the workers in some form or other of leadership are running the factories, and several among them rather well.

In such a situation, the party sets the goal of nationalizing the large industries, carrying through on the principle of planning, setting up coordinating committees for production, and, where the factories are working normally, recognizing the existing system of leadership set up by the workers.

We ask the advice of the Comintern concerning this issue.

9. There exist at present in the countryside various systems for cultivating the land: collectives of agricultural workers and small peasants, who together exploit the land of plantations that earlier belonged to large-scale landowners; collective peasants, who cultivate the land jointly with common agricultural implements; agricultural cooperatives—it is true, very little developed, with the exception of Catalonia—which comprise production, purchasing, selling, credit for their members; the cultivation of land with joint participation in the profits (municipal land, land of Republican owners, and so on)— those who cultivate this land get paid by the day, and at the end of the agricultural year they take part in the profits, in very diverse proportions; farmers

of Republican properties, who work with their families—in accordance with a decree issued lately by the minister of agriculture, these farmers will not pay taxes this year, in the expectation that the government will give a definitive structure to land ownership; and finally, individual peasant farmers who received free land, which belonged to the former landowners, the churches, and so on, and who work on their own, sometimes with the help of several day laborers.

There are still no exact statistics on the various forms of land tenure. The system changes according to the district (in Catalonia, Valencia, Murcia, Alicante, and Castile a large part of the land belongs to individual peasants; on the contrary, in the provinces of Jaén, Ciudad-Real, Albacete, Estremadura, Toledo, and Madrid agricultural ownership, for the most part, is collectivized).

The policy of our party and our minister of agriculture at present is the following: assistance for the existing collectivization, set up voluntarily by the agricultural workers and peasants; the reorganization of collectives that were set up by forcible methods, granting peasants and workers the freedom to participate or not participate in them; the democratization of the collectives (elections of councils, accounts, and so on); the establishment of prices for the chief agricultural and industrial products and control over carrying out these decisions by the government organs.

10. We still do not know exactly the present military situation in the north after the transfer of part of the enemy forces, which ought to have been sent to the Aragon front. We believe that if the quantity of enemy forces drawn off to the Asturian front is significant, then now, when winter begins in Asturias and the enemy air force and army will not be able to be used on a large scale, Asturias may be defended for the course of many months by forces from other fronts, allowing us to deny them assistance from [other] Republican units. For this it is necessary to secure arms for the soldiers and supplies for them and for the civilian population of Asturias. The arms may be sent to Asturias through various ways: by sea, by air, from the Valencia government, and also from our international buying commission. As for sending food to Asturias, we believe that the International Committee of Aid to Spain may be used here to send food from European countries and America. In case of an attack by the fascist navy, this will provoke strong indignation from the masses of these countries and still more solidarity.

The other urgent problem in the north is the evacuation of the population fleeing to Asturias. If this evacuation is not carried out immediately, the possibility of defending Asturias is terribly weakened. (The steamers chartered by the Committee of International Solidarity may be used for this.)

The approximate number for evacuation from Asturias is at least two hundred thousand people. Fifty thousand are already in France. The government of that country lately resolved to repatriate them to Spain through Catalonia.

The return of these refugees, terrorized and demoralized by defeat, to the rear of Catalonia and the Levant, represents a very serious problem not only from the point of view of lodging and food, but also because they may become a demoralizing element in our rear. Therefore we think that the Communist Party of France, depending on the strength of the Popular Front, ought to conduct a campaign for the right to asylum for the refugees and, simultaneously, to organize aid for them. Furthermore, the sending of refugees to various democratic countries must be organized.

We also ask—if it is possible—that the Soviet government permit the entry of part of the refugees on its territory.

11. The food reserves, which are presently on Republican territory for supplying the army and the civilian population, are sufficient only until the middle of this winter. According to an approximate calculation, for feeding the army and the population it is necessary that Republican Spain import 3 million quintals of bread, 1.5 million quintals of grain (peas, lentils, and so on), 1,100,000 quintals of sugar, 7 million quintals of potatoes. Moreover, it must be borne in mind that in the Republican zone, with the exception of livestock that give wool (already rather scarce), there is very little livestock left. Meat is needed, especially for the half-million in the army, and milk, butter, and so on, for the civilian population (12 million people). Above and beyond the purchases that the government makes officially for the army and the active part of the population, it must be kept in mind that women and children are not receiving enough nourishment. International aid, which—with the exception of the USSR—up to the present has not been much, has almost stopped, from the lack of activity on the part of our party, and also from a criminal campaign conducted by the Trotskyists and reactionary elements of the Second International against aid.

We believe that it is necessary to strengthen the activity of the international committee for sending food for the women and children of Spain.

12. Taking into account that international Trotskyist spies, together with all counterrevolutionary elements that are still tied to the international workers' moment, Brockway, Maxton, Pivert, and so on, are developing a disgusting campaign against the government of the Popular Front, accusing it of conducting a counterrevolutionary policy under pressure from the CP of Spain and the Soviet Union; taking into account that these elements are trying to fool that part of the masses which are under their influence, saying that Spain is smashing "revolutionary" organizations (the POUM; organizations of Trotskyist spies; uncontrolled groups, connected with the anarchists, and so on); taking into account that they are demanding that the masses refuse to help and defend the democratic policy of the Spanish Republic, that according to them the Republic is in a Thermidor period; we consider an international campaign necessary for fighting with the political positions of all these elements connected with Trotskyism (toward these goals, our party is publish-

ing in a few days a book with materials showing the counterrevolutionary and espionage activity carried out by Trotskyists in Spain).

13. Taking into account the continuing growth of our party and the need to raise its ideological standards, our CC asks the Comintern to send us some professors capable of working in party schools and also to help create cadres of Spanish instructors.

Checa
Luis

8/9/37
Zlsas

---

## Document 62

RGVA, f. 33987, op. 3, d. 961, ll. 5–23

---

Dear Comrade Voroshilov!

I am sending to you the following materials on Spain:

1. A report by Com. Ercoli (Alfredo) [Togliatti] from 30/8/37 on the situation in Spain and the problems of the Communist Party of Spain.
2. A report by Com. Ercoli from 29/8/37 on the International Brigades.
3. A report by the Spanish delegation (Coms. Checa and Luis).
4. A report by Com. Pedro, political adviser in Catalonia, from 15/8/37.

With comradely greetings,

G. Dimitrov

11 September 1937
N° 107/ld

*Top Secret*
*Translated from French*

The proposal made by me on sending you one of the representatives of the P.B. and one of the "political advisers," who were sent here by the secretariat, brought forth the evaluation that I present the situation in the country, which demands very deep study. As for the particular information, comrades will carry to you the largest quantity of material possible. I will dwell on my personal evaluation, chiefly concerning the policies and work of the party.

It is beyond doubt that the fall of the Largo Caballero government and the creation of the Negrín government set up a more favorable environment for solving the tasks before the entire Spanish people on how to win the war, and also for the work of the party. In several sectors, thanks to the new environment and the policies of the new government, there have already been successes. The party succeeded in strengthening its authority among the people and in the eyes of the other parties, especially after it defeated the offensive by Caballero and his group. A positive side in the current environment is also the fact that a number of measures against the POUM were successfully adopted. This makes strengthening the rear easier. The disbanding of the Council of Aragon also was a blow against "irresponsible" and "responsible" elements of anarchism and produced the same positive results. What is more, the fact that the anarchist organization was not able to oppose these measures of the government, which were directed precisely against them, helped to lessen their authority and sowed dissension among their ranks. As for the army, almost everyone here was of one opinion; everyone agreed that the change in chief of the general staff created a more favorable environment. Despite all of this, it would be incorrect to think that with the arrival in power of the new government, and with the coming of a new policy, we have succeeded in solving the serious problems of organization of the army, of military industries and industries of the rear, problems whose resolution depends on victory. On the contrary, large parts of all these problems are still not resolved.

As for the army, you have more information than I do. I will make only a few remarks. The new government has led several operations. The most important of these was the operation at Brunete, which, by the way, is one of those that up till now has given the best results, compelling the enemy to reform and shift its forces and giving us the opportunity to occupy better positions and so on. But not one of these operations has ended in a decisive way, neither in the sense of a final decisive victory, nor in the sense of gaining such a victory that might influence the mood of the population, convincing it that the People's Army is able to smash the enemy and drive it from Spanish land. This is a result of the fact that not one of the missions set before these operations was accomplished. Why did this happen? The competent people will give you a detailed technical explanation. But the basis of the matter was the fact that the transformation of the party militia into a real regular, organized army, capable of fighting against a modern army, has still not taken place, and if it has occurred, then it has done so only partially and formally. A lack of coordinated action by the separate units and separate commands, a huge difference in fighting efficiency of the individual units, in discipline (and indeed the general staff was forced to recognize that only the "Communist" units and

International Brigades were capable of offensives), the acute problem of re-serves (every commander of fronts, armies, divisions, wants to have *his own* reserves), incidents of treason, refusals to go to battle, and so on—all of these facts prove one basic thing: the success attained in creating a united People's Army, with a united command, with strong discipline and a great will for of-fensives, is still not enough. The army is riven by an endless number of inter-nal conflicts: between the old and new officer corps, between the anarchists and Communists, between the nationalists (Basques and Catalans) and other parties, and so on. In the army are still a lot of elements not dedicated to the cause of the people and the Republic: traitors, suspect people, agents of the enemy, and so on and so on. However, the work in purging the army and in unification is often a *political* action that is decided in the rear, through strug-gles of parties, groups, committees, and individual people that are character-istic of the rear. The future of the war and the army depends on politics. This of course in no way means that I dismiss completely the need for material aid, now more than ever (arms, instructors, perhaps even soldiers, and so on). But even with the greatest amount of aid we will not succeed in defeating the en-emy if we do not develop a politically consistent work to create unity in the rear and in the whole country.

The second remark on the army: the existence of military literature, sol-diers' newspapers, and so on. An open, consistent effort to bring the army nearer to the people, and the people to the army, almost does not exist (com-pletely does not exist if one speaks of government measures); the problems of the army are not raised before the entire people. The whole population is not mobilized for solving those tasks, which would raise the enthusiasm of the people and thus transform the war into a general people's war against the ag-gressor. The lack of such activity explains many shortcomings in the army, the lack of an offensive mood, and so on. The military communiqués, even when they speak of victory, are written in a coldly bureaucratic style. The commentary in the government newspapers always bears a defeatist charac-ter toward these military communiqués. The government itself never ad-dresses the people with appeals, speeches, declarations, and so on, about the war. The impression created is that the government either does not exist or, if it exists, then it consists of bureaucrats and people who do not believe in the possibility of victory, people living from day to day and just waiting on events.

The same picture goes for military industry. Some successes, not especially large, but there is no consistent and serious effort from the government in this direction. It hesitates, makes decisions but doesn't put them into effect, and acts from day to day.

The difficulties in this area stem largely from the fact that the government is running against the opposition of the unions, and also because poor rela-tions have arisen with the government of Catalonia, where a large part of in-dustry resides. I will return again to these two questions. It must be empha-

Document 62 *continued*

sized that where the unions are in the hands of the Communists and where there is no opposition, the government has not made up its mind to take measures for nationalization or militarization or, even less, simply for centralization and control, which might ensure the military industry production.

Let us return to the main question, to the question of the rear, or to be more exact, to the question of the general political situation in the country.

The overthrow of the Caballero government without a doubt brought us out of a dead end, but presently, in the new environment, the difficulties against which the party fought under the Caballero government have acquired a new form, although they remain just as acute. From several points of view, the situation today is still more dangerous than earlier.

It is dangerous that in the current situation there exists a tendency, ever more obvious, to create an opposition bloc against the present government, which at the very same time is a bloc of the most vicious enemies of the Communist party. This bloc has an illegal wing, consisting of Trotskyists and anarchists. The latter also acts illegally, illegally publishes newspapers, which are sold as organs of the Iberian Anarchist Federation (FAI). In the illegal press of the Trotskyists and anarchists, the Negrín government is called "the government of counterrevolution," it is said that this government must be overthrown, and there are published appeals for an uprising. Legally in the bloc are the Caballeristas and anarchists, acting in close association. They have connections with the Republicans (unionists) and with the Catalan nationalists (Esquerra or the Catalan left). Through Pestaña and his syndicalist party, the bloc apparently has some sort of connection with the government. Neither the anarchists nor the Caballeristas talk openly about the need for overthrowing the Negrín government, but, concentrating all of their offensive against the Communist party, they declare the need to include in the composition of the Republican government representatives of all mass organizations of the country, complaining about the fact that the unions have found themselves outside the government and so on. The anarchist newspapers openly raised the question about the need for even anarchist participation in the government. However, on the eve of the Aragon operation, the anarchists sent to all of the parties and to the government a memorandum in which they subjected the activity of the Negrín government to violent criticism, especially on the military question, with the goal of proving that the lack of success is explained only as a result of mistakes made, and chiefly due to the influence of the Communists on the government on the military question.

The danger of the actions of the opposition bloc comes from the following:

1. The bloc depends on the two union centers that essentially run, if not all, then almost all the economy of the country.

2. The anarchists and Caballeristas may at the right moment prepare and head up a movement of separate, dissatisfied groups of the population. It

must not be forgotten that the war has dragged on for over a year and that part of the population is already beginning to feel fatigued. Lines (for bread, milk, tobacco, and so on), a rise in the cost of living, lack of small change, and so on, are not making the population happy. The defeat in the north also will have serious consequences on the mood of the masses, especially if one takes into account the fact that the government is not doing anything to explain to the masses the reasons for the defeat, so that the appropriate lesson might be learned from this and morale raised.

3. The Caballerista slogan that, due to the influence of the Communists on the government, the democratic countries no longer have any sympathy for the Spanish Republic and this isolates Spain, may bring the vacillating stratum of the petty bourgeoisie, the rest of the bourgeoisie nearer to them. This slogan now unites all of the dissatisfied and the reactionary scum.

What are the plans of the opposition bloc? There is talk of a "putsch" and it is indisputable that several groups controlled by them are conspiring and preparing armed action or individual acts of terrorism. But the leaders of the bloc must understand that if they resort to arms, then undoubtedly they will be smashed. Apparently, and this seems more like reality, their plan consists of using some failures by the Negrín government to begin a campaign and demand the resignation of the government. With this goal Caballero went to Martínez Barrio, demanding a convening of the Cortes, since he wanted to appeal to the Spanish people through the tribunal of the Cortes. It is clear that the campaign will be accompanied by acts of violence. In the last few days, after the offensive began on the Aragon front, the Caballerista and anarchist press changed their tone somewhat, announcing the need for harmony, condemning polemics, and so on. But this cannot be trusted. Apparently the intent behind this new maneuver was to win to their side the part of the masses that was tired of the constant polemics of the parties and then more confidently to begin to act against their opponents.

The danger of the intrigue campaign of the Caballerista-anarchist opposition bloc would be significantly less if the government for its part carried out a more consistent Popular Front policy. It might be possible to hinder, or in any case make more difficult, a union between the Caballeristas and the anarchists, proposing, for example, that the latter participate in the government. Several weeks after the crisis some of the anarchist leaders were ready to accept an offer to enter the government, and participation in the government, today, is their highest wish and principal demand. As for the Caballeristas, it would be enough to begin a serious investigation into the reasons for the fall of Málaga (to arrest General Asensio, who is the inspiration of all antigovernment conspiracies), to present them with great difficulties and even perhaps to paralyze their activity. The government has done neither one nor the other. As for the unions, to take a number of measures with the goal of attracting the unions toward collaboration with the government, organizing order in the area of leadership and control over the economic life of the country (for example, the creation of a higher council, local economic councils, and so on), would produce differentiation within the unions and improve the position of the government. But this they do not do. The same remarks might be made in every area of the government's work. But what is even worse is that the government does not carry out an uninterrupted, consistent policy on mobilizing all of the masses for resolving the economic and political problems that stand before the country in the rear, in order to smash and expose the open enemy, in order to isolate and paralyze the activity of the open enemy of the Republic. There is no Popular Front press led or inspired by the government. There was introduced a proposal to create such a press, but despite the fact that it was accepted by Negrín, it was not put into effect. If the Communist press is excluded, then all of the rest of the newspapers are either newspapers of the opposition (anarchists and the majority—Caballerista) or newspapers that take a rather cool position on the matter of defending the government and do not struggle with the enemy. The government press also vacillates, listlessly, spinelessly. The government very rarely undertakes open action against the enemies of the Popular Front, and at times these positions are rather ambiguous. For example, the declaration by the government against the anti-Soviet campaign was greeted as if it were an act of victory, but it was so composed that it suggested the idea that the government did this only because it was giving in to some kind of pressure!

What are the reasons for such an attitude by the government?

It is not enough to say that Negrín has a weak character. The reasons are political. They consist not only of the fact that the composition of the government is very diverse, but also that several elements of this government sympathize with the campaign against the Communists being carried out by the opposition bloc. To this it is necessary to add a number of secondary reasons (sabotage from the government bureaucracy, subversive work by enemy agents, and so on and so forth), but without a doubt I place the political reason higher. This means that at the appropriate moment, under the influence of events (military failure or other) or under the influence of some foreign powers, or even only under the pressure from the opposition bloc, some of those who are currently our allies and collaborators in the government may turn against us. This possibility must be taken into account when determining the tactics of our party. This means that the possibility must be considered that too energetic pressure from our party, in order to obtain changes in the attitude of the government, demanding that it take measures that are provoked by necessity, may cause not only a split in the composition of the current government, but also a split in the Popular Front in general, which will create a number of complications and increase difficulties.

Before turning to the character of the party's policy, I want to make one additional remark on the issue of the organization of Spain's political life in general at the present time. The thing that is more striking than anything else is the lack of democratic forms that would permit the broad masses to participate in the life of the country, in policy. The parliament already represents almost no one in present-day Spain; on the other hand, it would be foolish to think now, in the current situation, about re-elections. The municipal councils (*ayuntamientos*) and the provincial councils are created from above, by the governors, who distribute the posts among the various parties, with the agreement of the local leading organs of these parties. The committees of the Popular Front at a certain moment were set up everywhere, but they took on a governmental function, and subsequently these were forced to hand over this function to the municipal councils. From that time on, the committees of the Popular Front in fact ceased to exist, with the exception of several places where they continue to exist, not being, on the other hand, elected by the masses. Factory committees exist, but it is very difficult to determine if they are elected or appointed from above by the leadership of the unions: it seems to me that in the majority of the cases they are appointed from above. In these unions, which have become huge economic organizations, there is also very little democracy. The political parties, with the exception of ours, conduct very weak political activity among their members. The political life of the country develops outside of mass control. The political questions are decided at meetings, discussions, systems, in struggle between the different "committees," parties, unions, and so on. The press reflects this situation: it is full of polemics that do not always interest the masses and that sometimes are accessible only to a single person. The only organization that has a democratic character is, essentially, the Communist party, whose internal life is very intensive (its members discuss, work collectively, and so on), and the army, in which the Popular Front and every political trend is propagandized. If these trends are still not merged, then in any case they have converged. This peculiarity of political life in Spain at the present time makes especially difficult the strengthening of the Popular Front and complicates the solution of all the political problems. A deep rearrangement of forces in favor of the Communist party and for the victory of the policy recognized by the Communists is taking place among the masses, but the bureaucracy of the old parties is opposing with all its strength this regrouping of forces, fearing that it will infringe on its position in the representative organs, in the leadership of the union bureaucracy, in the government bureaucracy, in the army command, and so on.

Despite all the difficulties, it is absolutely imperative to conduct Popular Front policy in a very broad and intelligent way. The circumstances demand this. The example of Bilbao and Santander showed that where the Popular Front policy was not carried out it was impossible to hold out against the offensive of the enemy. Apart from the offensive of the enemy, legitimate Spain in the coming months will experience very serious economic difficulties. A hard winter lies ahead. The difficulties with supplies are beginning to make themselves felt. The peasants are reluctantly giving their food to the government. On this question, very serious work must be carried out in the country, and high prices must be paid, which will increase the cost of living for the workers. They are demanding an increase in their wages, wanting the unions to protect their interests (the unions are not occupying themselves with this now, because they are busy managing production), and so on and so forth. The rise in the cost of living deeply injures the middle stratum and the petty [bourgeoisie] of the cities, the craftsmen. If the government and the parties within it do not carry out a consistent Popular Front policy, a policy of unity of all Republican forces, a policy that will not give breathing space to the enemies of the Republic, to the people who are sowing discontent, and so on, a policy that on the contrary raises the masses, mobilizes them to endure every difficulty, prepares them for the necessary sacrifices—if such a policy is not carried out, then the prospects will be very difficult. We must at all costs put into effect such a policy. Does our party understand this and is it doing everything possible to achieve this goal?

The party has radically changed. It has become a large party and undoubtedly contains the best part of the people. It is full of military spirit, enthusiasm, and initiative. Its authority has grown extraordinarily. Its leaders expound in a very popular form everything that the people know, want, and feel. For this reason, it is popular and beloved by the people. Our party is at present the only organization with a mass character in Spain that has a revolutionary program for victory in the war, and strives to put this program into effect. At the decisive moment (Madrid in November) and on the decisive problems (peasant question, the army), our party proposed to conduct a definite political line and action, which saved the situation. But despite these positive aspects of the party and the recognition of the historic role of our party in the war and revolution, we must not close our eyes to the shortcomings still existing in the party's work, so that they may be eliminated in time. These shortcomings are connected to the difficulties of the situation, to the rapid development of the party, and to the weakness of its cadres, the majority of which are still very young and inexperienced.

The party understood one thing very well: that it ought to conduct a consistent struggle to broaden and strengthen its position in the army, in the police, in the government apparatus, and so on. The strengthening of the party's position within the army (chiefly) and in the government bureaucracy is one of the principal guarantees of victory. In my opinion, this struggle must continue. It is quite impossible to lose even one of the positions won by us, and everywhere we must win new positions. If one may reprove the party, it is for its inability to use the fall of the Largo Caballero government to win important new positions.

The party has not yet mastered how to carry out political maneuvers to disrupt the enemy's forces by implementing a consistent Popular Front policy. In this area, it seems to me, some improvements in the party's policy must be made.

The success in overthrowing the Largo Caballero government has undoubtedly turned the heads of some comrades. They decided that the success belongs exclusively to the party, forgetting that the centrists (Prieto) played a very large role both in the preparation and in the resolution of the crisis. This mistaken evaluation resulted in the appearance of an opinion that the party could already raise the question of its *hegemony,* openly struggling for hegemony in the government and in the nation as a whole. When the difficulties with the new government arose, these comrades thought the only way to overcome these difficulties was to create a government with a predominance of Communists. The anti-Communist bloc, which began to form based on the correct observation that the struggle against the Communist party was a result of its growth, later slipped into the "theory" that it was inevitable and fated that all of the non-Communist parties ought, one after the other, to take up a position against us. It is enough to speak with our comrades and attend their discussions to be convinced that even today they have not achieved sufficient clarity on this question. One of the tasks laid upon us is to explain this to them and to help them clearly understand this. In Catalonia this confusion has led to the comrades placing as the central task that of "struggling for the destruction of all capitalist elements" and "preventing the strengthening and revival of capitalist elements," arriving, of course, at the conception that such a task can be accomplished only by a purely proletarian and Communist government. I will send you one of the copies of the pamphlet (an open letter to the UGT) in which this theory is propounded. It is clear that with such a confused understanding, the comrades could not see that after the fall of Caballero their tasks were, on the one hand, to exert pressure on the government to obtain from it an implementation of Popular Front policy, and on the other hand to prepare for a widening of the government's base by stimulating through the appropriate political work a differentiation in the ranks of the anarchists and Caballeristas. Now, and throughout the course of the entire forthcoming period, this is the only line that can lead us to victory. The party has undoubtedly hesitated lately in implementing this line.

On the question of merging with the Socialist party, we have now succeeded in making up somewhat for lost time. The preparatory work for merging is already quite significant. But opposition from the Socialist leadership (I am speaking of the centrists, Caballeristas, who, as you know, are desperately opposing this) is still very strong. Surprises are possible. We must continue the work of convincing the centrist leaders with simultaneous pressure from below, protecting the party with all of [our] strength from a split [caused] by actions that are too sudden. As for the Caballerista group, it is clear that they will not come into a unified party: we must maneuver to isolate them.

As for the anarchists, on this question, in my opinion, we have not merely hesitated, but made absolutely real mistakes in our tactics. The party as a whole does not have a correct orientation on this question. On the road from Barcelona to Valencia, I posed the question to the comrades accompanying me. Their opinion was very simple: the anarchists have lost all influence, in Barcelona (!) there is not even one anarchist worker, we are waiting until they organize a second putsch, and we will finally do away with them. This opinion is very widespread in the party, in particular, unfortunately, in Catalonia, and when we stick to such an idea, it is impossible to carry out a policy of rapprochement with the anarchist masses and differentiation of their leaders. The party as a whole, at best, does not know which problems the party is raising on this matter of organizing the anarchist masses. They do not know either the CNT, or their leaders, or their internal questions, or the tendencies, or the crises, and so on. I have not yet been able to find even one comrade who could tell me the names of the members of the leading committee of the CNT. Moreover, not long ago, when three members of the secretariat of the CNT came to the party secretariat, where they talked with three members of the secretariat of our party, it turned out that one of these three was completely unknown to our comrades. Even today they still do not know the names of the people that they were speaking with! Thus the problem of anarchism remains completely sidelined in the agitation and propaganda of the party. Anarchism, for its part, is carrying out very intensive propaganda. In practice there is very little collaboration with anarchists. In Madrid nothing has been done to the People's House, which is in our hands, and so on.

After the overthrow of Caballero, the party did not understand the need to move the anarchists nearer to us, to prevent their rapprochement with the Caballeristas. We hesitated. At the beginning of July we started negotiations, then suddenly, for no apparent reason, the Communists withdrew. A letter that explained the reasons for ending the negotiations and the departure of the Communists disappeared from the party's archives, whereas the anarchists are continually citing passages from this letter to prove that we, the Communists, did not want to work with them. But even more serious mistakes, in my opinion, were made in connection with concluding the UGT-CNT pact. The fact is that the party was against this pact, thus making Caballero the champion of trade union unity in the present circumstances; the anarchist press is printing whole pages of resolutions on unity while we are regarded as the opponents of unity. The party did not understand that the pact forged against us might have been used against those that created it, if the party had taken up a position as the head of the movement standing for the rapprochement of the two union centers.

Now the comrades understand the need for rapprochement with the anarchists, confirming that they will put it into effect. But to do this will not be easy, both because party forces will have to implement a real change of direction and because some of the anarchist leaders are real scum, closely tied to Caballero, and are the most vicious enemies of the party and the Popular Front. Only large-scale action from below will make it possible to isolate and paralyze any attempts at violent action against the government.

Closely tied to the question of the anarchists is the problem of trade union work. I will write about this after a more thorough study of the problem. What is already clear is that this is the weakest part of the party's work. At the very same time this is one of the questions around which all our difficulties are accumulating. The trade unions have attained great economic power and this must be taken into consideration. The difficulties we have met when conducting the campaign about nationalization lie chiefly in the unions. I ask you to work on this problem precisely in this connection. Is it possible to find a slogan that is an intermediate organizational form that would not remove immediately the trade unions from running industry, but that would allow the government's organs entry into this leadership, which might prepare for nationalization? I am posing this question because implementing the nationalization slogan means, in fact, the expropriation from the unions of wealth that was given to them by the revolution, that they consider their own. In some cases the workers agree and it will be possible to carry out nationalization with the workers' support, and with the aid of the government. In other cases it will be impossible to carry out this task and therefore we have to agree temporarily to a compromise. The unions in Spain have their own traditions, their own history, and this must be taken into consideration.

The Popular Front. Only through the work of the party will it be possible to attain an improvement in this area. This means: the work of the Popular Front committees that already exist must be revived, new committees must be created, and so on. But this will not lead to a decisive improvement. I would like it if on this question you examined with the comrades the possibility of assuming responsibility for a democratic initiative, through which it might be possible to involve the broadest masses in this work, to mobilize them organizationally to support the government, for putting into effect military policy and so on. I am not thinking about the possibility of elections (of the Cortes or the municipal councils), since this is impossible because of the military situation, and elections would end with weapon fire. But it might be possible to find some form of connection with the Popular Front committees that would rouse the masses. One might advise the president of the Republic, and other party figures, to appeal for the creation of a mass patriotic organization that would put up resistance to the enemy, provide aid and propaganda, and that would take on the task in the rear of raising the morale of the masses, enlarging the support base for the government, promising the latter the backing of all decent Spaniards.

The government. The difficulties of collaborating with the government are surmountable if the party gets down to work, mainly among the anarchists, [if it] gets to work on rapprochement with them, if it succeeds in smashing the opposition anti-Communist bloc through mass action by the Popular Front. On the other hand, merging with the Socialists without a doubt poses the question of reorganizing the government and, it seems to me, we ought to use this situation to (1) introduce representatives of the CNT into the government (in this connection you see from the pamphlet of the UGT in Catalonia that there is already a tendency to create a theory about the impossibility of trade unions participating in the government), (2) obtain several new posts for the party so that the party might more directly influence the government's policy thanks to its situation. To expand the government's base and expand the position of the Communists within it. You examine with the comrades the possibility of putting this into effect.

Finally, some words about the work of the party's central committee. There is much confusion and improvisation. The leading comrades spend entire days in conversations among themselves and with various people, workers in the ministries, the army, and so on. It's a permanent meeting, which goes on without any plans, in which a number of decisions are reached, but after which no one devotes themselves to checking to see if the decisions reached are carried out. All of the leading comrades are tired, overworked, sick. This is also a result of their way of working. The bureaucracy, which ought to help them, is weak and inadequate. Plenary sessions of the politburo with prior preparation are rare. The result of such a situation is felt in the party's policy. It acts from day to day, without all the political actions of the party being based on and issuing from a firm, established political plan; at times questions are decided without preliminary calculation, whatever may be the consequences. As a result it turns out that, despite the fact that the party's line is correct, the actions to put this line into effect are inconsistent. From this come the various mistakes and hesitations, about which I have already told you. One must not close one's eyes to these shortcomings. In the current situation in Spain, the little mistake or the decision that is made and not put into effect can have serious consequences. I implore you to study thoughtfully the events in the north, how the fall of Bilbao and Santander occurred. The Popular Front broke up; at the same time as the opponent began a general attack, a fight of everyone against everyone began, which paralyzed any resistance and opened the way for the enemy. Our party in the north did not play the role that it ought to have played. If it had played that role (a role like the one during the offensive against Madrid), then the north would have resisted significantly longer. But responsibility does not only fall on the northern comrades. Responsibility falls on the entire party, which did not see all the problems in time, which did not make the necessary decisions, and when it did make them, then they were not put into effect.

We must demand from the comrades a radical improvement in the work of the center and help them with this. The help that you might render consists of sending several comrades (instructors) to expand the party's central school and strengthen the training of new cadres.

I do not want to conceal from you my own impression that the responsibility for the poor work of the center partially lies with our "advisers." In particular, we must convince L.[110] about the need to radically change his method of work. The Spanish comrades have grown: this must be understood and they should let them walk on their own, limiting themselves really to the role of just "advisers." Concretely demand from L. that he stop being the workhorse for the entire CC, that he hand over operational work to the Spanish comrades, that he stop being the kind of person without whom no one can do anything or knows what to do. This would give the Spanish comrades a feeling of greater responsibility and would greatly help them to work better. Second: the role L. is playing here now keeps him from taking a critical approach to things, and this is the principal role of an "adviser" of the Comintern. It is thus inevitable that criticism will be directed against him. Third: demand from L. that, as a rule, all meetings with members of the Spanish government, ministers, leaders of parties, and so on, be carried out by Spanish comrades. It is intolerable that Caballero found out about the *party's* decision on raising the question about merging with the Socialists through Comrade U., and then through L. and only after a month through Pepe Díaz! As for Moreno, I have nothing to say except that he ought to influence L so that he'll be convinced of the need to change his method of working. With the perspective merging with the Socialists in mind, the question about the need to change L.'s way of working ought to be resolved as swiftly as possible.

With heartfelt greetings,
Alfredo
30/8/1937

# Document 63

RGVA, f. 33987, op. 3, d. 961, ll. 34−56

Secret.

*Some facts about the situation in Spain.*

The current situation in Spain has led to significant changes both in international and national relations that demand a deep analysis to determine the party line that is appropriate for this new situation.

1. The war in Spain, which began as an uprising of the most reactionary military cliques, who rose up in union with the large landowners and the large-scale industrial and financial bourgeoisie, with the support at first of the German fascist government, developed into an open war of the fascist governments of Germany and Italy, who were striving, on one hand, to place the Spanish people under a national fascist dictatorship, and on the other to use for themselves Spanish sources of raw materials. Spain's strategic position is very advantageous for them in connection with preparing for a world war. The French government and English imperialism in particular, which at first supported a policy more or less truly of noninterference, are currently not resisting the invasion policy of fascist imperialism, and are even protecting it with the goal of dismembering Spain to gain within it zones of influence. Thanks to this imperialist aspiration, France and England are not responding to the policy of sea blockade of the Spanish Republic that is being carried out by the fascist powers, despite the fact that this blockade is harmful for them. The goal of this policy is to compel the Spanish Republic to capitulate, so that then they will intervene as mediators to suppress the people's revolution and receive their share during the division among the four imperialist powers of zones of influence and sources of raw materials.

2. France is carrying out a special separatist policy in relation to Catalonia with the goal of separating this region from the rest of Spain and subsequently setting up its own protectorate over Catalonia.

The majority of the Catalan representatives of financial and industrial capital are concentrated in France (with Cambó at their head). They are connected to the most reactionary circles of the French bourgeoisie, who are collaborating with them on this objective. In France are also several leaders of the Estat Català party,[111] which supports ties between France and Catalonia and receives help from France to carry out separatist propaganda in Catalonia. In France is also Casanovas,[112] who with his group is also tied to the French government and is working on this same objective.

On the other hand, the French government is practicing an intensive economic policy of import and export in Catalonia, much more active than normally, which it is not doing with the Valencia government. It has facilitated a whole series of trade transactions with Catalonia in order to increase its popularity among the population of this region.

England, which is directly tied to a large part of the Basque nationalists, representatives of financial and industrial capital, during the course of the entire period of the war has given all of its means to the Basque government, which hindered an activation of the northern front. When the offensive began in the north, England pushed the Basque government to capitulate, offering to act as mediators with Franco. As a result of English influence, the nationalists with all their strength impeded the destruction of large-scale industry, mines, and factories situated in the Bilbao zone, which subsequently passed into

Franco's hands. Part of the nationalists capitulated in the face of the fascist forces.

As compensation for this, England made a compromise—it would pull strings for the interests of the large financiers, ship owners, and large industrialists (the evacuation of Basque capital to English banks; the recognition of English affiliates for several Basque banks; the right for the former owners, who had taken English citizenship, to continue to exploit several Basque factories). England took under its flag the merchant marine of the north, in particular the Sota and Aziar fleet, thus keeping it safe for the large Basque capitalists. All this [was done] to preserve traditional English interests in the Basque lands and with the desire to reach a compromise with the fascist government of Germany for joint exploitation of the wealth in this region (iron pits, forests, the production of canned goods, and so on). At the same time, England, wanting to eliminate German fascism from this zone, promises the Germans its support for their introduction [instead] into Morocco, the Canary Islands, and the Galician coast.

Compromises with Italy also come into this general plan for the partition of Spain: the recognition for it of rights to the Balearic Islands and the southern coast of the Mediterranean Sea (Málaga, Almería, and so on).

Portugal will be permitted to change the borders in its favor, annexing some Spanish territory from Estremadura and Miño (Galicia).

4. This change in English and French policy in relation to Spain was expressed in the démarche issued by them under the Negrín government, which would grant to them rights of mediation to end the civil war in Spain. The goal of this interference was to secure compromises with the fascist powers and also with England and France and to set up a regime in Spain that was capable of smothering the people's revolution (England proposed to set up a "democratic" constitutional monarchy, as a form that would unify all the peoples of Spain. To "pacify the country," France proposed setting up a "democratic" republic that would precede a military dictatorship.)

With this policy England and France made several allies in the Popular Front who did not particularly believe in the victory of the Republic, conscious of the frightening difficulty and length of the war, and revealed the social character of the people's revolution.

5. On the other hand, since the current government has not achieved any significant military successes in the latest operations in the center of the country and in the east (Aragon), since it was unable to render the necessary help to the north and thus impede the seizure of Bilbao and Santander, as well as the encirclement of Asturias, the opposition groups (Caballeristas, anarchists, Trotskyists, and other concealed enemies) were able to begin a covert campaign against the government of the Popular Front and against the Communist party, which is the most visible political force in the country, in order to sow defeatism and to shake some of our allies (the Republicans).

They are united by fear in the face of the influence and organization of the Communist party, which continues to increase in the army, the air force, the navy, among the carabineros, the assault detachments, police, government apparatus, in the villages, industry, unions, and so on; in the face of the strengthening and development of the revolutionary achievements of the proletariat and popular masses, despite the disorganization of the country's life, provoked by the poor policies of the Caballero government; in the face of the growth in sympathy and devotion of the Spanish masses for the Soviet government, which is viewed as their only reliable friend. This is why the bourgeois elements—the old and new bourgeoisie, the Caballeristas and the professional bureaucrats who go with them as well as a large part of the CNT leadership, which continues to lose its influence among the masses—are striving to form an opposition bloc, in which apparently part of the old cadres of the centrist Socialist party will take part as well. The objective of the bloc—bitter struggle against the party and the Popular Front government, the removal of the Communists from the government, the weakening of the USSR's influence in Spain, that will facilitate the mission of English and French imperialism, which is striving for the capitulation of the Republican regime.

The opportunities for this opposition were increased when the leaders of the UGT and CNT unions left the Negrín government.

6. In all these processes of regrouping of national and international forces, the Second International plays a very active role.

It is well known that the Second International views the Negrín government and Negrín himself in particular as an instrument of the Communist party and the Soviets (despite the fact that the policy of the Negrín government is actually more moderate and constructive than the policy of the Caballero government). The Second International, through a number of "friendly" intrigues, is pushing the Negrín government toward a rupture with the party and toward liberation from the influence of the Soviet Union. It must be pointed out on this issue that the Second International, which earlier acted distrustful of Caballero, now bitterly defends and supports direct, straightforward relations with him and his group. The anti-Soviet and anti-Communist policy of the Second International may be summarized in the following way: down with Communists in the government, down with Soviet influence in Spain. The Second International and the democratic countries of Europe have pledged aid to Republican Spain[113] only on the condition that there be no Communists in the government.

7. Those in opposition to the party, the Popular Front government, and the people's revolutionary forces are striving to form a group on the pretext that the party wants to seize all power for itself in order to set up a dictatorship and that the Soviet government intends to make Spain an appendage of the USSR. In the opposition bloc have come the Caballeristas, part of the anar-

chist leaders, the nouveau riche, bourgeoisie and reactionary elements that are on Republican territory, Trotskyist spies, and so on.

8. The Negrín government, despite the fact that there are representatives of the UGT and the CNT within it, has arisen as a real Popular Front government, since it depended on the masses and in particular on the army, which was indignant at the policies of the Caballero government. This government, despite making serious steps forward in organizing the economic life of the country, the organization of the army, the restoration of public order, and so on, did not prove to be a strong government capable of carrying out a consistent policy in every area and, consequently, to arouse in the masses confidence in a victorious conclusion to the war.

The Negrín government carried out a more active policy in organizing a regular army and activating the separate fronts (Teruel, Aragon); they created a united general staff, which is carrying out planned military operations (Brunete, Aragon); they used the military cadres better and removed some suspect elements from the army; they followed a more consistent policy with the reserves; they took serious steps in relation to military industry.

To establish public order, they organized and used assault forces and police, restored public order in Catalonia and Aragon, liquidated the remains of the May putsch in Catalonia, did not allow the putsch that was preparing in August to break out, took under their control the borders and ports, outlawed the Trotskyists and their activities.

In the countryside they facilitated the carrying out of the party's policy on guaranteeing the safety of peasant property.

In the economic sphere they succeeded in establishing order in a large part of foreign trade and centralizing into their hands the hard currency received from export, which had earlier remained in the hands of the unions and committees.

The Negrín government, as a result of having fewer members in the cabinet, functions better than the Caballero government. It considers and accepts a large part of the proposals made by our party on resolving the problems that the country is facing.

But despite this, it must be said that this improvement is not a result of the government's consistent policy, which might have helped to raise its authority, but is a result of the consistent policy and activeness of our party, which is a strike force for accomplishing the tasks that even the government itself faces. The negative side of this government is that, although it accepts almost all of our party's proposals, it puts them into effect very slowly or not at all. This slowness or incapacity of the government to implement the necessary measures to gain victory and to strengthen the revolutionary achievements complicates the situation, taking into account that the speed of implementation of these measures does not correspond to the seriousness of the situation.

9. In general it may be said that the army, with the exception of its northern units, is not an organization that is uniform. Side by side with the regular

units are still military formations that more resemble a militia than the units of a regular army.

In the north, the breathing space created by the operations at Brunete was not used to reorganize the military forces and transform them into a regular army. This was one of the reasons that the military operations in this region did not produce the proper results.

A firm and consistent purge of the command staff has not been carried out. And still today in the high command there are suspect people (the central general staff: Guarner, Garrico, and so on); suspect and even traitorous elements exist also in the army staffs (the latest operations on the Aragon front showed this).

There has been no policy carried out to unite the professional command cadres with the command that has been promoted from the people; on the contrary, the policy being carried out has led to an increase in the friction between the new and the old command (the commanders promoted from the militia are not able to have ranks higher than major; military units led by professional commanders are separated from those led by commanders who come from the militia).

A policy of mass preparation of military cadres—especially of middle cadres—proportional to the development of the People's Army has not been carried out.

There is a misunderstanding about the character of the People's Army; there is a tendency to turn the People's Army into an "apolitical" army of a professional sort. A struggle is going on against the institute of political commissars, which are the spirit of the army and the guarantee of its development and organization; they are trying to turn this institution into a bureaucratic organ to take away its revolutionary character and to discredit it in the eyes of the masses of soldiers. They speak out against the commanders that have come from among the people, against their promotion and the political education of the army, against the work and creation of the organization of the party in the army, despite the fact that they recognize that the party is the best guarantee to preserve the popular and revolutionary character of the army (Prieto reflects this policy in the government). They are not carrying out a quick and consistent formation of reserves; this ruins military operations and spoils plans (as the operations at Brunete and Aragon showed).

A rational employment and distribution of armed forces on the various fronts has not been set up. There are fronts from which masses of soldiers could be transferred without weakening, in which case there would always be well-trained forces in reserve for use on other sectors.

A policy for transferring units from the front for rest and after rest back to the front does not exist (there are units that have been in the trenches for eight to ten months without a break).

## Document 63 *continued*

There is still no *general* military plan based on study of the situation at all the fronts. Military policy is conducted from day to day.

The *navy* has not been used and improved. There is no school for preparing cadres for the navy. Systematic obstacles to the work of the party in exposing incompetent commanders and sabotage have led to the gradual liquidation of the navy's fighting efficiency.

Despite the removal of the major obstacles that were hindering the creation of a strong military industry, despite the fact that the workers themselves have offered their strength to the government for organizing this industry, from lack of a plan by the government, from sabotage and bureaucratism, military industry is not working at full capacity.

The bureaucratic apparatus of the government has not undergone a thorough purge, and its lack of flexibility delays quick implementation of government decisions. During a war that demands large-scale financial expenditures, the expense of the bureaucratic apparatus is heavily burdening the country.

A coordinated economic council exists only on paper and does not manage the economy of the country.

A consistent and energetic struggle against the internal enemy—fascists, Trotskyist spies, saboteurs, and so on, who act almost freely throughout all Republican territory—is not being conducted.

Only under pressure from the party did the government take a number of measures against the Trotskyist spies, and the government does not regard them as a force of espionage and counterrevolution.

The government has not taken energetic measures against speculation, carried out in the majority of cases by bureaucrats in the unions, resulting in discontent among the population and creating the grounds for provocations.

Despite the fact that the government as a whole declares its disagreement with the policy of Irujo, who is using the Ministry of Justice to restore the old, reactionary justice, and using it against the revolutionary workers and antifascists, at the same time as he is freeing fascists from prison, the government does not take any measures to hinder this policy.

The government has proved incapable of carrying out a consistent national policy and therefore could not prevent the reactionary forces of the Basque nationalists from disorganizing the military forces, stirring up the Basque nationalists against the central government. It could not establish political and economic ties with Catalonia, strongly binding the fate of Catalonia to the rest of Spain, in order to thus cut short any separatist policy.

The government did not apply any effort to attract the union organizations, in particular the CNT, to participate in the economic organs of the government; in fact it did the opposite, resisting their participation.

Because it advocates the use of administrative and police measures rather than political and economic ones, the government attempts to resolve complicated problems through administrative means rather than through the support of the masses. This is shown by the government's attempt to declare martial law in Catalonia, and its latest proposal to transfer the residence of the central government to Barcelona to take in its hands the direction of this province, which would have led to conflict with the generalitat of Catalonia.

10. The government is not carrying out a consistent Popular Front policy and is not displaying readiness to reconstruct the municipalitats, which were formed by the Caballero government from sectarian and antipopular elements. The majority of the municipalitats are in the hands of the UGT and the CNT with very limited participation of the rest of the popular forces.

11. The foreign policy of the government as a whole is pro-Soviet. However, there are various methods for carrying out this policy. *Negrín* has come out for this policy openly and unreservedly. *Prieto* agrees with it, lauds it publicly, but in personal conversations has some reservations. *Giral* (Azaña) accepts it honestly as the only correct policy. *Giner de los Ríos* (Martínez Barrio) accepts it, publicly praises it, but internally prefers aid from democratic France (Franco-Masonry [*sic*]) in order to avoid "Soviet influence" on Spain. *Ayguadé* adheres to the very same policy as Giner de los Ríos. *Irujo* clandestinely fights against the Soviet policy, does not do this openly for fear of the masses, but does not miss an opportunity to overemphasize English policy, and lately also that of the French—"its good intentions in relation to Spain"—and from time to time comes out with proposals on opening negotiations with these powers. *Zugazagoitia,* despite the fact that he denies this, is a Trotskyesque and anti-Soviet element and does everything possible to influence Prieto as regards this.

The government as a whole has searched and is searching for the support of the French and English governments, proposing to them economic and also territorial concessions, compatible with the existence of a democratic republic. Negotiations between Negrín and Delbos and emissaries of the English government took place in Paris with this objective; talks between Azcárate and Eden, Ossorio y Gallardo and Delbos, and so on.

As yet, however, the government of Spain has not received any favorable answer that would mean any kind of aid for the Republic. It has received only vague promises to intervene later to prevent a final victory by Franco (declaration of Eden and Delbos to Negrín, Alvarez del Vayo, and Ossorio y Gallardo).

12. The present military situation may be characterized in the following way: the armed masses are organized in regular units but are not formed into a united army, do not have the same military preparation, do not have a real command staff. Our army has been formed in the process of defensive tactics. Because of a lack of the necessary mechanized arms and of a policy of

fortification work, over the course of a long period of time tens of thousands of people were irrationally concentrated on one front. At the same time as fronts exist that are manned by a very small quantity of soldiers, on the others there are 50 percent more than are needed. These people are not doing anything, and it would be possible to transfer them to the reserves, to train and organize them (Madrid front). The culprits in this tactic are Rojo and Miaja, who are interested in concentrating the maximum number of forces on the Madrid front.

Taking into account that the enemy is currently regrouping his shock units, in particular transferring the foreign units from the north to other sectors, it is necessary to quickly verify the situation on the various fronts, to strengthen our positions, to allocate the mechanized arm more rationally, to group the units that ought to occupy defensive positions and to recall from the various fronts the maximum forces to reorganize and reinforce their military training and especially to prepare them for offensive tactics, to check up on and add to their arms, and to prepare from among them maneuver and strike forces.

It is necessary to prepare in the course of [the next] several weeks reserves of 150,000 men to assume the offensive and to inflict a decisive blow that would affect the enemy's rear, which is not that strong. This mobilization of recruits is possible in view of the fact that it is possible to mobilize another 650,000 men from twenty-seven to thirty-five years of age in the Republican zone.

13. The main reasons for defeat must be sought in the lack of a plan to organize operations, which in the majority of cases are just provoked by enemy attacks or the desire to divert his forces from one front to another; in the unequal fighting efficiency of the various forces; in the lack of reserves and in the lack of a decisive and reliable command; in the lack of fighting efficiency of several military units as a result of the recruits' insufficient military training; in the lack of uniformity in the arms of individual units; in the lack of discipline and desire to fight among the anarchist units; in the lack of coordination between the various types of weapons and between various commands; in the exhaustion of units as a result of the lack of rest, and also as a result of poor organization of supplies; in the lack of versatility and good organization when transferring units from one front to another; and finally in the treachery on the part of several commanders and staffs.

In the north we suffered defeats because, on one hand, a regular army was not successfully created, and on the other because our party and other antifascist organizations were not able to break the mood created among the nationalist soldiers [that is, national formations, of Basques, Catalans, and so on] by traitorous commanders, which said that they ought to occupy Vizcaya with defensive positions pending the resolution of the war on other fronts, and that everything must be done so that it was possible to have few human and material sacrifices in this province. The defeat also resulted because there were not enough reliable and proven political commissars there (among these the majority consisted of Catholic priests), and because of the lack of energetic struggle for a purge of the command staff, a lack of a united command leading all the military operations in the north, and, finally, the insufficient quantity of aircraft.

On the other hand, a firm class policy prevalent in the government of the Basque bourgeoisie, which did not give anything to the masses, in particular the proletariat, led to the fact that the broad masses did not fight with enthusiasm for the independence of the country (at the same time, the industry in the hands of the large-scale industrialists produced large deals, using the war, for exports abroad, to England and France, and large-scale profits; the workers worked more than earlier for less pay, and the peasants continued, as before, to pay leases for land and there was no distribution of land among peasants in the north).

On the pretext of avoiding political discussions and the need to concentrate all efforts on victory, all democratic freedom was abolished (public meetings, gatherings, freedom of the press, and so on). Consequently the masses could not actively participate in the resolution of the problem of the war and revolution.

Largo Caballero's policy—"noninterference in the affairs of the north"—resulted in the north not being rendered any serious help, [and in] a policy that favored the reactionary strata of the large-scale Basque bourgeoisie, turning this province into a sort of crown estate, independent from the other parts of Spain.

Despite the fact that the CC of our party signaled the incorrectness of the line carried out by the leadership of the Basque party, [and] many times discussed together with the Basque comrades the situation being created and attempted to correct these mistakes, this led nowhere. Despite the fact that the CC sent several political and military workers to the north to help the party resolve military and political problems, the CC of the party bears part of the responsibility for the situation created in the north, since it did not put this problem with the necessary force before the mass membership of the Basque party, and did not manage to compel the leadership, under pressure from these masses, to change its policy (later we discovered that this harmful policy was carried out by Astigarrabía, the general secretary of the Basque party, who revealed himself as a Trotskyist, deliberately fighting against the policy of the CC CPE).

14. The International Brigades played a very important role in the defense of Madrid and in other military operations; at the beginning of the war they served as an example for the creation of a people's army and for raising morale among the soldiers and population of Madrid. On the other hand, the fact that foreign fascist forces were met in battle by volunteer units from their

own countries to a great extent helped to demoralize the fascist units and to partially defeat them (Jarama, Guadalajara).

But it must be said that the leadership of the International Brigades did not understand in good time the need to introduce these brigades into the regular army, did not place them in the same conditions of existence with the Spanish units of the Republican army that crystallized at that time. Some leaders of the brigades were not able to create the necessary conditions for establishing fraternal relations between the Spanish units and the volunteers and for avoiding the friction with the units and commanders of the Spanish army, to whom it seemed that the commanders of the brigades looked down on them (the incident with Kléber, Dumont, Gómez, Gallo, Vidal).

Reinforcing the International Brigades with Spanish recruits led in general to good results, although there were incidents when, due to the inclusion in the brigades of recruits that were insufficiently trained militarily, the fighting efficiency of the brigades decreased (the blame for this falls not on the leadership of the brigade base but on Largo Caballero, who reinforced the units only at the last moment before they left for the front).

Experience showed that the mixed brigades (national and foreign) ought to be organized on the basis of nationality or language to avoid misunderstandings when giving orders and especially so that units might trust the commanders of their nationality or those who speak their language, taking into account also the presence of the different military tactics of the various countries.

It is necessary to attribute the lack of permanent, methodical political work in the brigades to shortcomings in their functioning. Although in Spain there are many permanent representatives of the various parties, sent for political work in the brigades, and every party from time to time sends delegations to Spain—all these do not communicate enough with the leadership of the CPE, are insufficiently informed about the political and military situation in the country, which hampers the conduct of the necessary political work in the brigades, which is based on pressing problems.

15. The activity of our party from the beginning of the war is well known in general. When the mutiny broke out, the party had only just succeeded in getting out of the underground work—it numbered only around twenty thousand members. At the beginning of the mutiny, thanks to its consistent Popular Front policy, the party began to enjoy some political influence (in July the party already had 118,763 members). Advancing the slogan "Win the war, and this means the revolution too," the party concentrated all its activity on the work at the fronts, sending there its best people. The party created the Fifth Regiment, from which subsequently grew the Spanish People's Army. Along with this, the party set about forming the institution of political commissar, sending to the front hundreds of the best organizers, who have subsequently played a decisive role in organizing the army. The party therefore now has hegemony in the army, and this hegemony is developing and

becoming firmly established more and more each day both in the front and rear units.

During the first four months after the beginning of the mutiny, our party was the only one working at the front. At that time the left Socialists, anarchists, POUMists, and others were occupied with carrying out the so-called revolutionary experiments (socialization, collectivization, control, and so on). Thus a sort of division of labor was established: while the Communists fought at the fronts, the rest "made revolution in the rear."

The criminal policy of "revolutionary experiments" sowed disquiet in the villages: there were incidents in which not only individual peasants but entire villages went over to the enemy, just to save themselves from this disastrous policy (Toledo, Aragon, Guadalajara, Cuenca). At that very same time, the party began the slogan "with face toward the villages," mobilizing all its strength in the rear to put it into effect. At the front the Communists, establishing a linkage [smychka] with the peasants, also helped to put this policy into effect. The results of this policy are well known. After 4–5 months of intensive work in the countryside, the party acquired decisive influence there. It succeeded in attracting the peasantry to the Popular Front policy and did not allow outbreaks of uprisings in the villages (this was helped by decrees on land, on agricultural credit and the creation of peasant unions, on agricultural cooperatives, and so on).

The noticeable evolution of Caballero and the anarchists toward the use of the unions for an adventuristic policy (the intention to create a government of a trade union type, the attempt at a putsch, and so on) put the party on its guard and compelled it to make a quick turn in that direction. The results are on hand: 55 percent of the members of the party came to us from the UGT, which is under the leadership and influence of the party.

Despite the fact that the party during the year of war has concentrated its strength in working in these three basic directions, it did not cease its activity on other sectors as well, thanks to which it has been transformed into a mass national party, but in its program, and in its policy, into a party that the huge majority of the working masses supports.

The current situation of the party is the following: 328,978 members, of which 167,000 are at the front. Social composition: industrial workers, 116,372; agricultural workers, 91,210; peasants, 91,463; intellectuals and professionals, 8,580; urban petty proprietors, 21,215 (from the general number of members of the party, women, 30,000). To this number must be added another 64,000 members of the Unified Socialist Party of Catalonia.

The CC of the party consists of forty-five members and twenty candidates, the P.B. of seven members and four candidates, and the secretariat of three members.

The CC is organized into the following commissions: Organizational, Personnel, Agitprop, Military-Political Commission, Union, Commission of Rear Forces, and Women's Commission.

At the head of each of these commissions is a member of the P.B. or CC. Each of these commissions has its own apparatus. The largest is the Agitprop Commission.

The party has a central party school, eight provincial schools and four regional, twenty-seven newspapers of which ten are daily, one more daily paper especially for soldiers, and sixteen weekly. The party publishes a theoretical journal, a military magazine, a magazine for the air force, a police magazine, and several professional weeklies for specialists. The party has four publishing houses: [one each] for the Popular Front, the party, young people, and international literature. The party has two telegraph agencies and several radio transmitters, and so on.

16. The Unified Socialist Youth at present numbers 350,000 members. It publishes two illustrated daily newspapers and several weeklies.

17. MOPR numbers at present 517,000 members, enjoys huge influence and popularity among the population.

The UGT—2 million, of them 758,000 agricultural workers (480,000 in Catalonia).

The CNT—has around 900,000 members, of these 120,000 in Catalonia.

There is an autonomous peasant organization: the peasant federation in Valencia, 75,000 members, in Alicante, 32,000, and the union of rabassaires in Catalonia, 80,000.

The executive committees of the UGT and the CNT signed a nonaggression pact not long ago [but] in fact this pact is an attack on the Communist party. This pact does not contain one constructive point on the questions of conducting the war, production, improving the living conditions of the workers, and so on. This pact only establishes good relations between two union organizations, which ought to be subordinated to all the decisions promulgated by the two leading centers.

The party openly criticized this pact, which was very badly received by the masses of the UGT and the CNT, who refused to set up liaison committees in the lower organizations. The CC of our party explained to the Communists the need to participate in the organization of these liaison committees. But our party, partly subject to these moods, committed the mistake of not carrying out a campaign on setting up these committees, which might have been used for developing the unity of action of the two union centers.

The correlation of forces within the UGT is the following: 20 percent Prietista, 25 percent Caballerista, and 55 percent Communist. The influence of the party within the UGT is growing every day. As a result of every meeting, every congress, the Communists gain new posts.

Caballero's supporters, elected to leading posts already in 1932, are carrying out an internal union dictatorial policy, they infringe upon union democracy, refuse to convene union meetings and congresses or dissolve them when they see that the Communists have the majority (the case with the congress of agricultural workers of Madrid, with the union of workers of hotels and restaurants).

On the other hand, despite the fact that the centrist Socialists are our allies, they are refusing to convene union meetings, fearing the election of Communists (the incident with the congress of the metalworkers union, the leadership of which has a huge majority of Communists).

Lately, thanks to unified action with the centrist Socialists, Caballero's supporters have found themselves thrown out of the leadership of several unions, and also of the leadership of the daily newspapers *Adelante, Claridad;* now it is possible [that they have been thrown] out of the leadership of the UGT in Valencia and the newspaper *Correspondencia* as well. In agreement with the centrist Socialists, a demand was advanced to convene quickly the national committee of the UGT to call Caballero to account for his anti-unity and anti–Popular Front policy and for the exclusion of him and his group from the leadership of the UGT.

19. As for the CNT, despite the fact that this organization still enjoys great influence, it is possible to ascertain an ever greater reduction in this influence. The influence of the CNT organization grew significantly during the first months after the mutiny. The CNT seized a great number of the factories and their raw materials, as well as the financial means of their former owners. Since the CNT was not concerned about increasing military production, it was able to better in many places the living and working conditions of the workers—forty-four-hour work week, daily payment of wages even if the working week was not completed. Thus the CNT put pressure on workers to join the CNT so that they might obtain work.

But now, when the situation has become ever more normal, the workers are deserting the CNT and going over to the UGT.

Despite the fact that our party has turned the corner in union work, that it has gained a serious position within the UGT, it has not succeeded in dealing with the difficulties and putting right work within the CNT. There is still not a large number of unions led by Communists; within the organization of the CNT are still very few [Communist] union factions.

The relationship of the party and the CNT has lately been very strained, which happened because the Communists were forced to intervene in and settle the conflicts provoked by the disorganization introduced by the CNT in economic, political, and military arenas, since the Popular Front government was incapable of establishing order (the liquidation of the Catalan putsch; the restoration of order in Aragon; the disarming of the Trotskyists and irresponsible bands; the reorganization of the Teruel front; the normalization of some social services, which were disorganized by the CNT; the struggle with fascist and Trotskyist espionage flourishing within the CNT organization; the organization of the police together with "control patrols," and so on).

Despite this, the party also sought contact with the leadership of the CNT, trying to differentiate the honest leaders from the bandit adventurers, but did not obtain significant results in this regard. At present there are favorable conditions for establishing contact between the party and the healthy part of the CNT. Today in the CNT it is possible to point to two loose affiliations. One seeks rapprochement with Caballero (this grouping is connected also with the Trotskyists—Mariano Vázquez, García Oliver, Juan López, and so on), struggles against the CP, against the Soviet Union, and against the Popular Front, and carries out putsch tactics. The second grouping does not want a putsch, because it does not want to lose the war, and on the other hand, it feels the strength of our party (Antona, Peiró, Mas, and so on) and is striving for unity, although it is not finding the courage to declare this publicly.

As a result of the constant hesitations in the CNT leadership, the contact that is being established between us has repeatedly fallen through. It is possible that this contact will now be restored, taking into account the agreement by the libertarian youth to participate in the national youth alliance.

20. During the first months of the war, the Socialist party not only did not develop, but it lost the greater part of its members, who moved to our party. The war compelled the Socialist party to the height of factional struggle, and when it was forced to temporarily suspend this struggle to avoid friction the leadership of the Socialist party paralyzed all the party's political work.

This situation of political passivity of the Socialist party continued until the beginning of 1937.

In the course of several months, the Soc.[ialist] party acquired several thousand new members, but in the present period it is dragging out a miserable existence because of the tense struggle between factions, provoked by supporters of Caballero.

There are no precise figures for the number of members of the Socialist party. Because the Socialist party was always a party composed of cadres, it had the opportunity to lead a union movement (the UGT) and to have in its hands a large part of the government apparatus.

Before the mutiny three tendencies held sway in the Socialist party: the center, and right and left wings. At present, there are the following tendencies: the center, left wing, and Caballeristas. The center consists of the current leaders of the Socialist party (Prieto, Negrín, Peña, Lamoneda, Bugeda, Cordero, Vidarte, and so on), who, although they do not enjoy the trust of a huge majority of the party's members, still lean on their support, thanks to which they are carrying out a policy of united action with the party. The left tendency is represented by Alvarez del Vayo, Del Rosal, and others. This tendency are [*sic*] consistent supporters of unity. Caballero still has some influence on part of the old cadres of the Socialist party, but he is losing influence more and more on the masses, and his group is turning into a sect. He bitterly struggles against unity. When unity has been accomplished, one can say with confidence that Caballero and his group will not enter into a united party, and will seek an opportunity to keep back part of the Socialists together with the Trotskyist elements, uncontrolled anarchists, into their own party.

Within the executive committee of the Soc.[ialist] party there is no one openly speaking out against unity. How is the situation actually with each of them? Negrín, Bugeda, and Peña honestly stand for the unification of the two parties and are struggling for the realization of this unification in the new future. Lamoneda and Vidarte, who are declaring their political solidarity with the Communist party, despite this, are carrying out a number of maneuvers to put off this unification. Cordero and Anastasio de Garcio, old Socialists, accept unity as an inevitable sacrifice. Prieto declares everywhere that he will not stand in the way of unity, but taking into account his individualistic petty-bourgeois character, his ties with the liberal circles and petty-bourgeois stratum, it cannot be ruled out that at the decisive moment of unification he will begin to construct obstacles or to move away from a united party.

Despite all of these variations on the unity questions, it is possible to establish that as a whole, the present leadership of the Soc. party is moving toward unity under pressure from local [members], who want to bring about unity as quickly as possible and who in several cases (Jaén, Albacete, and Almería provinces) have brought it about in practice.

The liaison committees for unification of the Communist party and the Soc. party are functioning almost throughout the Republic, and in many places both parties organize joint meetings and discuss problems of the war, production, union questions, and so on.

The national committee of liaison already regularly functions as a coordinating organ for the political activity of both parties. This committee has already approved the program of united action, which will serve as the basis for the united party, and is already discussing the principal questions and statutes for a unified party.

In general, the Socialists accept all of our proposals with some changes; we have met only some opposition on the national question and the question of the need to attract the anarchists toward united action.

All the conditions for quick creation of a united party are on hand, but its creation is being postponed because the large part of the leading cadres of the Soc. party fears being swallowed up by the unified party, and they want to receive every kind of guarantee of their positions and future utilization. In any case we believe that unity will be realized very quickly, because if unification is not realized there is the danger of disorganization of the Soc. party, the entry of a great number of the Soc. party's lower organizations into the Commu-

## Document 63 *continued*

nist party, and also the danger that Caballero will attempt to draw into his group part of the Soc. party.

---

## Document 64

RGVA, f. 33987, op. 3, d. 961, ll. 57–64

*Emo bens*         -

*Top Secret*
*Translated from French*

Dear friends, I wanted to write you immediately after the Third Conference of the Unified Socialist Party of Catalonia to inform you about the political line of the party, about the military situation, to determine what kind of technical and political opportunities are opening before us. The situation in the country (in Catalonia and Aragon) has significantly changed on all fronts.

1. *Changes in the military situation.* At present the Eastern Army is occupying the line of the front of sector. . . . . . . . [*sic*] from the French border to Teruel; besides that it is attending to three Catalan sections and the decisive parts of the three Aragon provinces, which are located under Republic dominion. This army consists of several divisions, which are trying to hold in check the enemy's attempts at advancing and in sum numbers up to 132,000 soldiers; to them must be added another 40,000 men of the unified army, consisting of units that are occupied with working on fortifications, transport, artillery, aircraft, quartermaster services, units that are awaiting transfer, and so on. You know that up to the May putsch, the anarchists had their units on almost the entire front of Aragon. But this situation changed later. Influence in the ten divisions is allocated in approximately the following way:

There are now three divisions (88, 80, and 90) under the control of the CNT. Under the absolute influence of the Unified Socialist Party of Catalonia with the PCE are two divisions (27 and 11). The Unified Socialist Party of Catalonia has decisive influence in four divisions (30, 31, 43, and 44). The CNT has relative influence in one division where this influence is divided among them, the FAI, and the POUM (32).

The Esquerra (Left Republicans) have influence in several units, but nowhere completely. To make it easier to present what ideological influence in the army means, I will give you an approximate picture in numbers of the composition of these army units.

3 army corps: one under the influence of the CNT, one—Esquerra, one—PSUC.
10 divisions     CNT—4, PSUC—4, total—8; Socialist Party of the Republican Union—1, PCE—1.

29 brigades     CNT—11; Esquerra—2; PSUC—11, PCE—3, total—14; Socialist
Party of the Republican Union—2.

116 battalions     CNT—49; Esquerra—7; PSUC—42, UGT—14, total—56; Socialist
Party of the Republican Union—2; Catalan government party
(Estat Català)—1; Syndicalist party—1.

The majority of the representatives from the companies are members of the
PSUC or the CP of Spain. We also have a majority in the quartermaster units,
with fortifications, and we are beginning to gain a majority in the artillery.

As for the air force, the situation there is not completely clear, because although we have a majority there, this majority is not impressive. Among them
there are many questionable elements, although also members of the PSUC
and the CP of Spain.

The situation in the area of purely military cadres is not too good, since we
have very few new technical cadres, even fewer than the anarchists. The
party is putting forth a great deal of effort to form cadres, and the party envis-
ages the transfer of a number of commissars who have displayed military ability and bravery in battle to command posts.

As the correlation of forces on the front changes within the Eastern Army,
the army itself has improved and its fighting efficiency has increased. This is
why we see the new phenomenon on the Aragon front. It has already been
two months that the Aragon army has not remained stationary, as it was earlier, but it is launching [operations] almost everywhere, a little at a time—local operations, small sorties, which demand matériel that we still do not have
at our disposal. The arms of the 10th Division are still very much inadequate:
they have about sixty thousand rifles.

In any case, the presence of three divisions that are completely under the
influence of the anarchists represents a huge danger from the military point of
view, as experience has shown that all the anarchist divisions fight very
badly, very often will not go over to the offensive, and when the enemy attacks are among the first to desert their positions, as happened not long ago on
the Teruel front. On the other hand, the divisions that are not under anarchist
control are still backward from a technical point of view and, despite the fact
that unified command is more in force every day, very often, because of a lack
of appropriate conditions or due to bad organization, they do not carry out the
command's orders. *The Eastern Army is still not a real army that might take
upon itself the execution of large-scale operations,* but it can execute serious
missions on the scale of one sector or two. This could be done significantly
faster if there were no systematic sabotage from the War Ministry, which despite the changes taking place continues to resist a rapid reorganization of the
Eastern Army.

After Valencia's large hesitations (Prieto), they finally decided to disband
the armed forces under the control of the POUM (59th Division with two
brigades). But as a result of these hesitations, the POUMists were able to

conceal part of their weapons; on the other hand, disguised members of the POUM stole their way into anarchist units, in which they continue their provocative work. I think in general that even from a military point of view it is necessary to set about purging the anarchist military units (this must be done to others as well, but the anarchist divisions more than the others are littered with all kinds of provocateurs). But this is impossible to accomplish if purely anarchist units remain in existence in the future. The only way to put this into effect is to include anarchist brigades in divisions that will have two non-anarchist brigades for every anarchist brigade, and at the same time to carry out a number of changes in the composition of the command staff.

Experience has shown the great value from a military standpoint of brigades that are organized with a majority of recruits who were drafted into compulsory military service; in the makeup of these units, usually as the nucleus of the battalion, are the so-called veterans, which means people who have gone through several months of service at the front. We must note, however, that there has been a significant growth in desertion (from both sides), this is especially seen among the new elements, who entered the army not long ago through conscription.

To sum up, we can say that in the area of military organization, we have significant improvements in the Catalan and Aragon armies in comparison with the former situation. But the improvement is going *very slowly,* taking into account the opportunity that is present and the need not to give the enemy the opportunity to fortify and extend his positions, and he is not losing any time. The recent dissolution of the "Aragon soviet," which was under the absolute leadership of the most sectarian-minded anarchists (with forced collectivization, with attempts to carry out "libertarian communism," with massive murders of antifascists, peasants, with a real regime of terror and robbery of the peasantry), significantly increases the opportunities to move forward more quickly. But I must say that *until very recently, the Republican government, and even our comrades from the CC CP of Spain, extraordinarily underestimated the Catalan-Aragon problem, did not render the necessary assistance, and even now are not doing everything that is required to change the situation quickly. I am repeating all this mainly because I foresee very serious military difficulties.*

2. The second question about which I wanted to inform you briefly *is the question about production and in particular the question of military industry.* Immediately after the May putsch, a significant improvement in production was noted, particularly in military industry, [but] up till now a radical change in this area has not been successfully attained, despite the fact that a huge majority of the metalworkers (sixty-three thousand in round figures) and almost half of the workers in the chemical industry are members of the UGT—that is, they are under the influence of our party. This is explained, apart from the

weakness of party and union work, mainly by the fact that the government of the Republic is taking a position that cannot be explained by anything, a position held by Prieto and Negrín, who display indecisiveness all the time, thanks also to the system (allowed originally) that is implemented on this important question. Therefore, up to today, despite the repeated and persistent demands from the PSUC and the UGT, a united leadership for military industry in Catalonia has not been set up (despite the fact that everyone agrees [with this], even the generalitat government and the CNT). Thus several managing centers exist that have not stopped the internal arguments, often compete with one another, and still more frequently sabotage one another's work. Besides this, there is a large dispersion of businesses as a result of "syndicalization"; a significant reduction of individual productivity, as a result of the introduction of a system of egalitarianism [uravnilovki] in the question of wages; a lack of competent technical leadership (businesses in the majority of cases are led by "Business Councils" or "Control Committees," which in practice are almost equivalent). Our party—the PSUC—demanded that the central government militarize all the military factories and at least nationalize those that employed more than fifty workers. Two to three months went by without this elementary measure, and a number of other additional measures that we proposed to the government and publicly defended, being carried out. It seems that now at last the government has decided to publish a decree on the introduction of the united management of military industry in Catalonia (which is decisive for the country) and on the nationalization, not of all military industry, but only of some businesses that they consider the most important. The national party conference advanced a number of proposals on increasing productivity (published in a speech by Comorera that came out in a brochure). That is why I do not want to go into detail on this question in this letter.

3. *The question about the POUM and the struggle against the Trotskyists.* We are moving forward very strongly on this question, but there are still many difficulties that must be overcome. The official POUM was not disbanded, and moreover it still has its own representatives in the municipalitats and in some other official organizations. Despite the fact that the POUM does not have any legal press in Catalonia, it issues a whole series of illegal publications, which are ever more openly fascist. In publishing it receives assistance from the anarchists and mainly from the libertarian young people. The government is not arresting people who distribute the POUM's and the FAI's illegal literature, and moreover, they set them free when our comrades turn them over to the police. Several members of the government openly play into the hands of the Trotskyists, as are Caballero and company, and the majority of the leadership of the CNT and the FAI. However, it is possible to confirm that the POUM lost its influence in the unions, mainly where we seized the majority of its positions, and among the POUM's ranks a very

strong disorganization is noticed. In some places POUM members are asking that they be accepted into the ranks of the PSUC (the party is very careful on this question), and in some places they talk about the need to restore the old worker-peasant bloc ( . . . ), as a reaction against the Trotskyists who, in the words of this group, destroyed the worker-peasant bloc. The Catalan government is now discussing a draft for a new municipal decree, which will give them the capability to expel POUM representatives from the Catalan munic-ipalitats.

4. *There are great difficulties beginning again with the peasantry.* This time they were provoked by the question of prices. The Catalan government with the agreement of the Valencia government set the prices for wheat at the rate of seventy pesetas for one hundred kilos, obliging the producers to sell their grain to the government at this price without fail. But the peasants, who re-ceive twice this price for the very same grain on the black market, are refusing to sell wheat at the price set by the government. The fascists, Trotskyists, and in general all the counterrevolutionary elements are developing strong agita-tion around this question, inciting the peasants to declare a strike on selling. To correct this situation we suggest the introduction of a system of "maxi-mum" prices, strong measures against speculation and breaking the law, and along with this to carry out a series of measures to encourage and develop co-operation.

5. *One of the problems demanding a quick resolution is the problem of a wage plan and the workers' standard of living in general.* The workers are liv-ing with difficulty, because prices have risen greatly and wages remain the same. This is creating great difficulties and facilitates the work of agent provocateurs. It is clear that with the introduction of a system of piecework payment, and with the introduction of differentiated wages, it may be possi-ble simultaneously and significantly to increase the productivity and to im-prove the state of the workers.

6. *Relations with the CNT* are still far from wonderful. The reasons are var-ied. On one hand there are still strong tendencies in the party against merging with the CNT, and these tendencies have their representatives in the most re-sponsible circles of the party. On the other hand, the Caballero-CNT-FAI bloc openly defends the Trotskyists, the POUM, and this makes merging with the anarchists terribly difficult. And finally, a new danger of a putsch has ap-peared in the past few weeks, which is being prepared by the leadership of or-gans of the CNT-FAI-libertarian young people, and a series of attempts, pre-pared by the leading elements of the FAI against [the lives of] our comrades—these are not elements that are conducive to the realization of the work on merging. It seems to me that the danger of a putsch is not unpreventable now and we ought to do everything possible to isolate the provocative elements and to merge with the more honest elements.

In the party (PSUC) there was a moment of very tense relations with Esquerra (the Catalan left), but the situation was successfully settled. This is important also because Esquerra together with our [people] make up a majority in the Catalan government.

7. *The party* continues to develop as does the *UGT*. Of course this growth is not as great as in the first few months, especially as touching the UGT. The UGT can increase its ranks now only at the expense of the CNT, since, as you already know, everyone is organized already in one of the two centers. Despite this, the UGT continues to grow. Thus, for example, the UGT union of metalworkers in Barcelona now has approximately fifty-five thousand members (I say approximately because it is very difficult to have even approximate statistics). On the situation at the *front:* There have been significant changes here and of the most varied sort.

The party conference in general was good and showed that we have a large party in Catalonia. It is natural that, from an ideological and organizational point of view, many demands may still be put on the party. I regret very much that you did not send your greetings to the conference. The Valencia "friends," for their part, also did not put forth the effort to send an appropriate delegation to the conference.

To end this letter, and such a long one, allow me to pose a personal question and, at the same time, not a personal one. With some breaks, I have been here already more than a year. It seems to me that it would not be bad to change places with comrades working in the country. Thus, for example, I might go to Valencia, Madrid, or to the north (where the situation is very serious and moreover all this time completely abandoned by the party). It is clear, of course, that this is only a suggestion, which you may accept or not accept, but in any case, it seems to me that someone absolutely ought to stay here, since the party is still very young and militarily a very difficult spell lies ahead for us to go through.

The most heartfelt greetings to all the comrades, I remain always at your service,

Pedro

Barcelona, 16 August 1937

# Document 65

RGVA, f. 33987, op. 3, d. 961, ll. 104–110

Letter from Com. Ercoli from Valencia

*Secret*
*Translated from French*

15 September 1937

Dear Comrades:
Several words about what has been done lately to put into effect your advice and directives.

The declaration of the P.B., in which the politburo intends to make the first steps to correct the tactical line of the party on a whole number of questions, will appear today in the party press.

The document was prepared after the departure of Luis. Later I will explain to you why it was impossible to do this earlier. The first critical remarks were *openly* made by your friend Alfredo at a meeting of the politburo on the eve of the departure of Ch. and L. [Checa and Luis], but unfortunately no practical actions followed. I want to add that I was very dissatisfied with the speech and position of L. at this meeting. Whereas Checa's information and the speeches by Hernández and especially by Uribe directed the discussion on the correct path of self-criticism and an investigation of the way to improve the tactics and work of the party, Luis's speech, in which he raised a number of practical problems, so to speak, on the question of the government's activity in various areas, utterly confused the comrades and concealed the principal problems on the need for the party to conduct a consistent Popular Front policy. After the departure of Luis, we continued the conversations and discussions in the secretariat and politburo, and I was left very satisfied with [their] method of considering these questions. In the process of these discussions and conversations, I myself became convinced that it was necessary to radically change the method of work of your "advisers" who are here. Besides Díaz, who is not here, as you know, and Checa, there are a group of comrades here (Uribe, Dolores, Hernández, Giorla) who are able to lead the party themselves, and lead it well. But for this it is necessary:

1. That your "advisers" not confuse the comrades, pushing them down the wrong path by improvising incorrect theories or bringing in unnecessary irritations into a policy that comes to an end due to the irritation and to the Spanish comrades' gradual impairing of the party's tactics.

2. That your "advisers" stop considering themselves the *"masters"* of the party, that they actually stop viewing the Spanish comrades as people not capable of anything, and on the pretext of doing things better and faster not to

take their places, and so on. This criticism mainly concerns L. If the latter cannot change his methods of working, it would be better if he did not return. With every day I am more and more convinced of the correctness of this.

The document published today is actually a result of the collective work of the entire politburo. The members of the politburo, facing the need for a critical approach to the party's activity, showed their maturity and ability and even took upon themselves the initiative to make the appropriate conclusions from the critical remarks made collectively. An article by Dolores (written by her at her own initiative, without any help or corrections on our part) preceded the politburo's document. This article made a real stir and turned out very well. Two articles by Giorla evoked a great deal of surprise thanks to the changing tone, and this very morning two anarchist newspapers answered them in a very heartfelt note. But I personally consider this, and the document itself, just the preparation necessary to clear the air of the accumulated electricity from the bitter polemics of the past few months. The actual political work will start with the beginning of negotiations with the anarchists from the CNT, which will take place, I believe, in several days. The difficulties will be great, since it will be necessary to bring about a merging with the CNT, not breaking off or hampering relations with the Socialists and other parties of the Popular Front. With some flexibility it is possible to reach the desired results.

But again on the question of anarchists. The situation had become difficult because of the rumors spreading those days about a putsch being prepared by the anarchists. It was necessary to work so that the comrades did not lose their composure. This is what happened (I will dwell on the details because the facts are very significant). Several days ago, we received secret information that the anarchists together with elements from the fifth column were preparing an uprising for 14–15 September. At the same time, our comrades in Barcelona received the very same information. The source: the French police in Perpignan, who intercepted telegrams and letters. The plan for the uprising: the anarchist group would enter Spain across the French border simultaneously with an uprising in the city organized by CNT forces. It is clear that the party took all the necessary precautionary measures, but I advised my comrades, as opposed to what was done in other such cases, not to raise the alarm and not to say anything about this in the press. In giving this advice I was guided by the thought that such an alarm must not interfere with the campaign on merging with the anarchists that was beginning. In reality, a very strange thing happened. It turned out that simultaneously with the warning for us on the inevitability of an anarchist uprising, there were warnings to the anarchists about the Communists preparing an uprising also on the fourteenth or fifteenth of this month. They also took their precautionary measures, and on the night from the fourteenth to the fifteenth, at the same time that all the Communists gathered in the party building waiting for events to unfold, the anarchists also gathered in their organization's building. Fortunately, everything was limited to one sleepless night. But the slightest trifle might have provoked a bloody clash. From this comes the conclusion that there are people who, knowing the mood on both sides, have learned very well how to use it, while the party is not always on guard against these kinds of provocations.

To explain the nature of the corrections to the various points of the document, long, concrete commentaries would be necessary, but I do not have the time now, and moreover I think that a discussion with Checa and L. will clarify all these questions: I would like only to emphasize that, for my part, there ought to be introduced corrections from *two points of view* into the activity of the party: on the one hand, in the direction of conducting a consistent Popular Front policy (the politburo document is the first step in *this* direction), on the other hand, in the direction of devoting a significantly larger place in all its activity to the defense of the pressing demands and aspirations of the working class, the agricultural workers, and the poorest peasants. All of this, of course, within the framework of a Popular Front policy. Here stands the question of working in the unions, on which we have fallen behind very greatly and where matters are going rather poorly. It has already been a month since I came here and during this time the union question has not once been discussed in the secretariat. There is no doubt about the fact that there are a number of burning questions about the unions, as for example: workers' wages and so on—questions the party cannot not be interested in. There is no union rubric in the party press, there is no correspondence from the factories, which emphasizes that union work still takes a back seat and ties with the working masses in the factories are weak. The comrades are mainly interested in the political struggle with the various tendencies within the unions (gaining posts in the leadership and so on), but in this struggle also they still are oriented more toward maneuvering the higher-ups and not mobilizing the masses organized into the unions, on the basis of protecting their interests. This is one of the reasons why Caballero has till now retained significant positions in the unions, and his cadres within the unions remain almost untouched. Let us take, for example, Valencia. The Caballeristas have in their hands the leadership of the regional committee of the city's unions. Therefore they have the opportunity to publish the daily organ *Correspondencia de Valencia*—the organ of Valencia's unions. This newspaper is now Caballero's organ, leading the dirtiest campaign against the Communist party. This question was before the secretariat up to the time that I came here; the comrades are convincing me every day that they are driving the Caballeristas out of the leadership of the union regional committee and from the editorial staff of the newspaper. The comrades want to enter into an agreement with the Socialists (centrists) who are in the leadership of the regional committee, which will give them the majority, and then to make a sort of semi-legal revolution, driving out the Caballerista editors and putting in their place a new editorial staff. They assure [me] that this is possible, that it is possible to accomplish it with the help of the authorities and they promise every day that everything will be done in twenty-four hours. Luis inspires them and energetically pushes down this path. Seeing that the matter was not moving, I finally appealed to the comrades with a request to work on this question once again seriously, exposing their discussion to a meeting of the secretariat. As a result of this discussion it turned out that the authorities never promised to render them assistance in the matter of seizing the journal, that this kind of interference was intolerable to them both from the standpoint of the law and the standpoint of the traditions of the workers' movement; that the only possible interference (after a decision by the judges!) was interference by the minister of labor, who is an enemy of the party and does not agree with this; that the centrist Socialists will not want to enter such a revolution; and that if we insist on this then only one thing remains to be done—to lead an attack against the newspaper with people and means from the party, risking through this the arming against us of the forces of society and that this action will lead to the rallying of a number of Caballero's factions, making more difficult the isolation of Caballero and worsening our relationship with the anarchists, the government, and with part of the working masses. A whole month was thus lost in negotiations with the leaders of the Socialists, with the authorities, and so on, and during this month they completely forgot to carry out the most elementary work among the masses, mobilizing the workers at the factories through union meetings against the newspaper and against the editorial staff, sending protests, delegations, resolutions of the meetings, and so on and so forth. In my opinion this means that they forgot the most fundamental thing, and this gave Caballero the opportunity to organize his offensive against us, eliminating various local organizations and convening a general conference of unions at which we risk finding ourselves in the minority if we do not accomplish a great work from below. And this work from below has not been done.

These shortcomings have revealed themselves in the party's national activity, which was directed at offering resistance to the splitting activity of Caballero. All the work is carried out from above and [the following] remain almost completely forgotten: (a) union work in the grass-roots organizations, (b) they are not making the necessary effort to rouse the cadres of Caballero, even if it is only a part, against his policy (cadres of the former "left wing" of the Socialists). But a new chapter is beginning here. An analysis of the situation in various places compels me to come to the conclusion that in many cases the party is making a mistake in uniting into one bloc all the cadres of the former "leftists," giving them an identical evaluation and struggling against them, not differentiating. They say: the Caballeristas are counterrevolutionaries—enemies of the party and so on, which in many cases does not correspond to the facts. It is beyond doubt that a more flexible tactic might lead to a deep split, even in those groups that stand closer to Caballero. A speech by Caballero (the old man) in many respects, for example, differs from other speeches.

At the last meeting of the UGT ExCom, Galarza proposed that the UGT insist on inviting the Communist International to a meeting in Paris. This proposal provoked strong anger from Caballero. An incorrect tactic with respect to Caballero's cadre may lead to very serious consequences among the youth, since many leaders of local youth organizations still remain tied to Caballero and, of course, will never move away from him if we consider them enemies. The central youth committee has seen this danger now and is beginning to carry out work consisting of: (a) correcting mistakes (some of them very serious: in Murcia, for example, the youth organization is standing on the threshold of a split, it has two leaderships: one—Caballerista in the "Youth Club," and the other—Communist, working in the party building), and (b) systematically winning to our side the old "Caballerista" cadres, drawing closer to them because of specific work with the youth. But the party itself ought to change deeply its relationship on this plane with the Caballeristas.

One of the questions we are working on these days is the question of discipline of the (unfortunately, best) Communist cadres in the army. And here the situation is *very dangerous*. Let us leave details to the side. The principal thing is that the Communist cadres in the army do not feel the authority of the Central Committee. From this—an intolerable struggle among them, which undermines discipline, self-advertisement, and so on. The party, in the name of the Central Committee, decided to appeal to the Communist cadres in the army with an open letter. Simultaneously, the CC is undertaking a number of other appropriate measures.

All the remarks made by me reflect also the opinion of Moreno, whom, I repeat, I do not accuse of anything except for the fact that he has done nothing lately to orient the comrades toward correct self-criticism, to not allow rather serious mistakes by this, and so on. In agreement with Moreno, I raised the question about Luis not coming back. I did not want to judge his work hastily, but now I can say with conviction that *his presence hurts the party*. Reasons: (a) without doubt he is the main culprit for why the party has not carried out a consistent Popular Front policy, ties with the anarchists, and the isolation of Caballero in the past few months. [His] method of formulating the principal questions can only confuse the party. (b) I consider him to be the main culprit for the inconsistency with which party policy was covered in the press (also partially in demonstrations), inflicting a blow now to the left, now to the right, without any kind of plan, which led to the absolute impossibility of consistent political activity to isolate [our] open enemies and to strengthen the Popular Front. (c) As his presence hinders the work of the Central Committee, depriving the comrades of a feeling of responsibility and criticism and so on.

## Document 65 *continued*

I know that when you receive this letter, the question will already be resolved by you, but I wanted you to know my opinion also, taking into account the seriousness of the problem. I think that we have made a serious mistake leaving the Spanish Communist party in the present situation under the guardianship of L.

The most heartfelt greetings.

# CHAPTER THREE

# 1938–1939

## Arms for Spain

WHEN 1938 BEGAN, there were few signs that the war would end soon. Although the Republic had lost a great deal of territory during 1937, most significantly the Basque provinces, Catalonia and central Spain were still under government control. The Republican industrial base was largely intact, the Spanish People's Army had been transformed from a ragtag collection of militiamen into a decent fighting force, and morale was generally high. The leaders of Spain hoped to be able to muddle through somehow, holding out until their conflict was subsumed under the inevitable general European war that everyone felt was imminent. The Soviets too could feel fairly optimistic about the course of the Civil War. With a minimal investment of men and money, they had held off the Nationalists and their foreign allies for more than a year while consolidating Communist control over the war effort. Politically, the "radical" anarchists and "Trotskyists" had been repressed, and the ascension to the post of prime minister of Negrín, a man more amenable to Soviet "suggestions" than either Largo Caballero or Prieto, was yet another favorable sign.

Although they thought the war was going well for the Republicans, Soviet officials believed that the Spanish still required aid if they were to survive. Some scholars have described a steep decline in Stalin's assistance to the Spanish government after the summer of 1937. Given what we now know about Soviet involvement, Stanley Payne's explanation for this drop-off seems to ring true. According to Payne, the Soviet government, having achieved political and military hegemony in the Republic and prompted by broader strategic calculations—the outbreak of war in the Far East, the lack of results in the struggle to build a stronger relationship with the West, the expense of the war, and the risk of direct conflict with Germany—chose to deny victory to the Nationalists rather than to help the Republic win. The Soviets therefore drastically cut the amount of matériel sent to Spain.[1] However tempting this explanation might be, it was not, in fact, true. Although they reduced somewhat the level of aid shipped to Spain, the Soviets continued to send tanks, aircraft, artillery, and tons of supplies for the war effort until the very last months of the conflict. One example of the Soviet response to appeals for aid during 1938 is shown in **Document 66**. The Spanish "command" (that is, army) requested help in acquiring American aircraft, and the Soviets agreed to buy the planes and ship them to Spain. The delivery of the DC-3s and motors would take seven months. That the time delay was not seen as a problem demonstrates Soviet confidence both in the outcome of the war and in their Spanish allies. Voroshilov made it clear to Stalin that he would request financing from the Spanish beforehand, so that the Soviets would not need to pay for the aircraft themselves. Once again, the Soviets made certain that they would not be forced to pay for the Spanish war.

In a memorandum to Voroshilov, **Document 67**, the ambassador of the Soviet Union in London, Ivan Maisky, urged the Soviet army and government to respond positively to the Spanish pleas for aid. In doing so, he clarified some of the reasons for the Soviets' decision to continue providing weapons to the Republicans. First, he thought that if the Republicans were able to inflict a defeat on Franco, Chamberlain and the British would be forced to reconsider their decision not to intervene. Second, "the entire European situation" depended on a successful resolution of the Spanish war. It would be a defeat for reactionary forces everywhere and would "change the whole atmosphere" in England and France. His reference to the "pact of four" (an alliance by France, Britain, Germany, and Italy directed against the Soviet Union) shows how far from reality his understanding of Western political and diplomatic processes was. In the very worst case, Maisky believed that Soviet aircraft and artillery in Spain would at least postpone the inevitable general European war by a few years. Just as important, all this could be achieved by giving the Spanish what amounted to the cost of supporting the Red Army for only a day or two in a large war. His hostility toward both Chamberlain and the French is also illuminating. At the very same time Stalin publicly proclaimed that he wanted a collective security alliance with the British and French against Italy and Germany, Maisky described the British leader as "an extreme reactionary," "the malevolent enemy" of Socialism who wanted Franco to win in Spain. The French, meanwhile, changed policies every few days and were extraordinarily corrupt. These are hardly descriptions of trustworthy allies and friends.

The Soviets had similar attitudes toward Roosevelt, another possible ally against fascism and source of aid for the Spanish government. In early 1937 the U.S. Congress had adopted almost unanimously an addition to the neutrality laws that specifically forbade Americans to supply arms to either side in the Spanish conflict. Enforcement of the new law was difficult, however, because, as Document 66 shows, all the foreign parties involved in the war simply had material shipped to their own nations and then forwarded it to Spain. As a result, American weapons and other military matériel ended up on both sides of the front lines. Yet there was a feeling in the Soviet Union and among leftist circles in the United States that the law was inherently unfair because it treated a legitimate government and rebellious army officers as equals. Nowhere is this feeling better illustrated than in **Document 68,** in which the Soviet ambassador is "nauseated" by Roosevelt's "hypocrisy" toward the war against fascism. On the other hand, he welcomed a proposed change in American policy. The decision expressed here, to allow American goods to flow unhindered through

French ports to any destination, may come as a surprise to historians. Until now it has been believed that Roosevelt tried to loosen the embargo on Spain only once, in early 1938. When his attempt ran into unexpectedly intense resistance from Congress, he backed down and supported the ban on weapons shipments until the end of the war. This memorandum shows that Roosevelt tried to find a way to get around the letter of the law by allowing the "unimpeded export of arms to France 'to any company without verification.'"

This backdoor strategy would allow the Soviets to make good on their decision to supply the Spanish with American aircraft. **Document 69**, the follow-up to the Spanish request for aid, makes it clear that Stalin supported the decision to buy the Douglas airplanes. The other significant fact in Gendin's report is the deception the Soviets planned to use on their Spanish "friends."[2] In his book *Arms for Spain,* Gerald Howson showed that the duplicity of the Soviets with Spanish money was pervasive and continual throughout the war. The Soviets forced the Spanish to pay for every aspect of their involvement, including the cost of transporting, feeding, and maintaining the Soviet advisers in Spain. Meanwhile, they played with exchange rates and the cost of the weapons to ensure that they spent every bit of the Republican gold—and more.[3] As this report shows, they also used Spanish gold to achieve other foreign policy and military goals. For at the same time that the Soviets were involved in the Spanish Civil War, they were supporting the Communists in China. The covert operation to supply Mao, known as Z or *Zet,* was at least as important to Stalin as Soviet aid to the Republicans, and at times, as this document demonstrates, the two were actually linked. The Soviets hoped to buy three DC-3s with Spanish money and then, before delivering them to Spain, use them to evacuate men from China. Their friends would be none the wiser about the reasons for the delay in shipment. The comment about the deicer is revealing in that it suggests yet another motivation for buying American aircraft: acquisition of Western technology with Spanish funding. A deicer was hardly necessary for flights within Spain but would be a nice addition to aircraft flown farther north.

# Document 66

RGVA, f. 33987, op. 3, d. 1142, l. 16

*Top Secret*
Copy N° 2

To the Politburo CC VKP(b)
*Comrade Stalin*

4 February 1938
N° 104ss

The Spanish command is asking us to help acquire several two-motor airplanes and one hundred aircraft motors for Spain, since firms are refusing to sell these goods to Spanish representatives.

Our people in the USA have told us about an opportunity to buy seven DC-3 airplanes from the Douglas firm and one hundred motors from the Wright firm, which could be delivered to the Union and after that sent to Spain.

The timing and conditions for delivery of the aircraft are the following:

1. DC-3 airplanes: price 122,981 Am. dollars each, delivery in three months;

2. Motors: price 7,819 Am. dollars each, delivery in seven months, beginning in April this year.

The cost of the entire order, including transportation of the equipment to the Union—1,725,000 Am. dollars, which we will request from the Spaniards beforehand. Thus financing of the order on our part is not required.

I enclose a draft directive.

[signed] K. Voroshilov
printed in two copies
vp.4/2/38

Correct: [illegible]

# Document 67

RGVA, f. 33987, op. 3, d. 1148, ll. 53–57

Plenipotentiary of the USSR                                25 February 1938
In Great Britain                                           N° 39/ss

To the People's Commissar of Defense—Com. K. E. Voroshilov

Dear Klimenty Efremovich,

The ministerial crisis now breaking out in England will undoubtedly be reflected in Spanish affairs. It is necessary to consider that the policy of the British government henceforth will take a turn that is still more unfavorable to the Republicans than it has been until now. Chamberlain is an extreme reactionary and the most malevolent enemy of everything that even remotely smacks of "Socialism." Moreover, he has linked the fate of his cabinet to the outcome of the Anglo-Italian negotiations. Therefore, his policy will now be—to come to an understanding with Mussolini concerning Spain and to assist Franco's victory in Spain as much as possible. Of course Chamberlain will have to reckon with serious opposition within the country and perhaps with some pressure from France, but for all that, Eden's resignation has in general changed the correlation of forces in the international arena in ways not beneficial to the Republicans.

Given these conditions, Republican successes at the front are extremely important. There is nothing more persuasive than victory. The English are great opportunists and, if the Republicans defeat Franco, then even Chamberlain will be forced to take reality into consideration. From this viewpoint, this coming spring and summer may have a decisive significance for the outcome of the entire Spanish war. Therefore, it is imperative to create as quickly as possible the most favorable conditions for the greatest possible victory by the Republicans. The most important of these conditions is a sufficient quantity of airplanes and artillery. Meanwhile, things are far from well with regard to this matter. The casualties at Teruel, judging from the data that we have here, were caused by Franco's exceptionally enormous advantage in aircraft and artillery. The rebel airplanes flew with impunity over Barcelona, Valencia, Alicante and so on, which is also explained by the fact that Franco has a great advantage in the air, and that the Republicans moreover suffer from an extreme lack of anti-air artillery. [ . . . ] The Republicans have the undoubted advantage in infantry, not only numerically, but also in quality. If the Republicans had an equal chance with the rebels in terms of technology, the Republicans would undoubtedly be victorious, even if the number of Italian-German interventionists remained at their present dimensions.

What needs to be done about this?

## Document 67 *continued*

On the basis of data that I have from Soviet, Spanish, and English (International Brigade) sources, the most acute needs of the Republicans in weaponry are portrayed in the following way:

1) *Airplanes.* [ . . . ]
2) *Artillery.* [ . . . ]
3) *Other types of weapons.* [ . . . ]

Of course, the problem of transport is exceptionally important. It seems to me that the main transit path ought to go through France. The French-Spanish border, generally speaking, is passable given a certain amount of caution and a certain amount of "grease." The difficulty lies in the fact that the French often change their minds and what you can do today turns out to be impossible tomorrow, and day after tomorrow is again permitted and so on. I think that it might be possible to come to an agreement with the French authorities in a nonofficial way—even if on the basis of a certain amount of compensation—about a more extensive admission of military materials through France than is taking place now. Or rather, this is more obvious to our representatives in Paris. I have also gained the impression that lately we have been using the maritime route too little. There is, of course, a risk and a danger connected with this, but it is by no means impossible. Be that as it may, I consider it necessary to draw your attention to the following: if any action is to be taken in this matter, then it must be done quickly, in the course of the next two-three months. On the one hand, that period is dictated by purely strategic considerations. On the other hand, in the course of the stated period, there will be all sorts of dawdling in the Committee on Non-Interference and consequently the Spanish border will not be controlled. One can think further that in the process of negotiations with England, Mussolini will be somewhat more restrained both in his piracy at sea and in various other areas.

I ask you earnestly to forgive me for this interference in a sphere that lies somewhat outside my area of competence. It is possible and even probable that you have much more detailed and better-founded information from other sources on the question that I have touched on. Nevertheless, for the past twenty months I have become so closely tied to Spanish affairs and so closely taken them to heart, that I thought it possible to appeal to you through this letter. The following consideration also pushed me to do this. From here, from London, perhaps, it is more obvious than from any other point, how colossally significant it will be for the entire European situation to have one or the other resolution of the Spanish conflict. I have absolutely no doubt that a victory by the Spanish Republic would completely change the whole atmosphere in England and France and would make various reactionary maneuvers, like the pact of four, impossible. It is well worth it to pay a couple hundred airplanes and batteries to achieve this. You know, in the end, this is no more than a two-three days' cost for the Red Army in case of a large war.

## Document 67 *continued*

And the result would be, in the very worst case, a postponement of that kind of large war for a number of years. It seems to me that the game undoubtedly is worth playing.

With comradely greetings,

The Plenipotentiary of the USSR
in Great Britain

I. Maisky

3 Copies
1 - To Com. *Voroshilov*
2 - To Com. Litvinov
3 - file

## Document 68

RGVA, f. 33987, op. 3, d. 1149, ll. 125–126

Embassy of the USSR in the USA                                   Copy
Washington, 13/4/38                                              Secret.
                                                                 N° 97s

To the People's Commissar of Foreign Affairs
Com. M. M. Litvinov.

Dear Maxim Maximovich,

The Spanish ambassador informed me, highly confidentially, about the substance of his protracted conversation with Roosevelt in early March. In response to de los Ríos's complaint respecting the legalistic reply by the State Department to [his] question about the compatibility of the embargo with Spanish-American agreements and even with the sense of the Neutrality Act itself, Roosevelt replied to the ambassador that one could not count on a lifting of the embargo, but that he promised to give directives not to hinder the export of any weapons to France and not to inquire about the further destination of the cargo. (This has a practical significance because the American authorities, in particular the State Department's Committee on the Export of Arms, which is controlled by the most reactionary bureaucrats, has more than once blocked such exportation of weapons by refusing to issue licenses as soon as there were any doubts about the final destination of the cargo.) I would not have bothered to inform you about this conversation now if not for the fact that, according to the same de los Ríos, Roosevelt had not held a con-

## Document 68 *continued*

versation on this topic with the Mexican ambassador. Despite the fact that the conflict between the USA and Mexico over oil is now at its height, [President Lázaro] Cárdenas [of Mexico] instructed his ambassador to approach Roosevelt and appeal to him in the name of the president to lift the embargo on the export of arms to Spain. Roosevelt announced to the Mexican that he had taken steps to bring about the unimpeded export of arms to France "to any company, without verification" and that he would take steps toward the same unimpeded export via Mexico (against which the same sort of obstacles were created). I do not know what the practical effect of these statements [will be]. De los Ríos trusts them. I will refrain from passing on to you all of Roosevelt's antifascist pronouncements from the same conversation with the Spaniard since, as you have correctly stated in your letter to Com. Troianovsky, these pronouncements are in such striking contrast to [his] actions that it has become nauseating. I will only mention that, sharply criticizing Chamberlain, Roosevelt said that he did not trust the English, not only with regard to Europe, but also with regard to the Far East, and gave me to understand that he was worried that the Englishman might cut a deal with the Japanese.

Signed: With comradely greetings, (K. Umansky)

Correct: [illegible]
two copies tv.

## Document 69

RGVA, f. 33987, op. 3, d. 1104, ll. 76–77

*Top Secret*
Copy N° 1

To the People's Commissar of Defense of the USSR
Marshal of the Soviet Union
*Com. Voroshilov*

I am reporting information regarding the purchase of "Douglas" aircraft in the USA and France:

1. *In the USA.* At this time, as per the decision by headquarters, an order to deliver nine "Douglas" aircraft (DC-3s) to us has been placed through the Department of Foreign Acquisitions (DFA) of Vneshtorg, with the following conditions (order N° 80080 from 31/3/1938):

a) half of the aircraft will be ready for formal acceptance at the factory in June-July, half in August of this year. The acceptance will be carried out by our engineers who are now in the USA (Comrades Borisenko and Kozlov);

b) the firm will use its own means to deliver the aircraft to Leningrad;

c) the total cost of the nine DC-3 aircraft, according to the DFA, is exactly 1,140,547 Am. dollars, which includes the cost of transporting the aircraft from California to New York, their packaging and so on. The price of one airplane is exactly 120,800 Am. dollars;

d) the first of the airplanes that arrive here will be equipped with a radio and deicer, which cost 6,549 Am. dollars above the total amount;

e) in addition, the cost of spare parts ([made] according to precise specifications) is 167,000 Am. dollars. Therefore the total cost of nine DC-3s with spare parts, radio, and deicer (the last two for one airplane as a sample) is 1,314,096 Am. dollars.

2. *In France.* Simultaneously with this, at the request of the "friends," we have inquired through our people in France about the possibility of purchasing in the USA another ten "Douglas" aircraft for later transfer to "X."

By 4 April of this year "Thomson" in Paris finished negotiations regarding the purchase of these ten aircraft under the following conditions:

a) three machines will be ready for formal acceptance at the factory in 14 days, seven machines in 150 days (that is, three airplanes in April and seven in September);

b) to transport the aircraft to the USSR our steamship must be chartered;

c) the cost of one airplane is exactly 120,000 Am. dollars.

3. Without deciding beforehand the question of purchasing all ten aircraft, I gave Thomson a directive to conclude a deal to acquire three DC-3s (ready for formal acceptance in April of this year) in order to use them in the "Zet" operation [in China], where there is now a severe lack of transport aircraft given the increased transportation of people from the Union to "Zet" and the evacuation from there also of a significant number of our people.

With the purchase of three DC-3s for the "Zet" operation we will be able to present a demand to the "friends" about the immediate repayment of the cost of these aircraft to us.

Regarding the remaining seven aircraft, which might be acquired by Thomson, I ask your directive.

Dep. Chief of Intelligence Directorate of the RKKA
Senior Major of State Security
    Gendin

10 April 1938
*Printed in 2 copies*
    ar

## The International Brigades Disintegrate

Despite their firm commitment to supplying their Spanish allies with arms, the Soviets believed that more and better weapons would solve only one of the difficulties that the Republicans faced. Before the war could be won, a whole series of problems—the sad state of the International Brigades, espionage within the ranks of the People's Army, and the failings of the Soviet advisers themselves—had to be settled. Areas of concern almost since the beginning of the war, these issues would now dominate discussions about how to secure victory. One reason such matters took center stage is that, by 1938, the other problems with the war effort that the Soviets identified—poor leadership of the army, bad strategic planning, interference from "treasonous" politicians, and the poisonous influence of the "Trotskyists"—had all been dealt with. Generals like Asensio had been thrown out of the army, the Soviet advisers now did most of the war planning themselves, leaders like Largo Caballero and Prieto who had interfered with Soviet plans had been forced out of power, and the POUM and the anarchists were, for the most part, under control.

The poor condition of the international troops was one of the most troubling issues the Soviets faced. Throughout 1937 the actual numbers of foreigners in the brigades and their significance as a fighting force had declined precipitously. By early 1938, the international units were important to the Soviets and the Comintern only as a means of scoring points in the propaganda war and as bargaining chips in negotiations with the other great powers. Nowhere is this more clearly shown than in the series of documents that follow. In **Document 70**, General Walter (the Soviet officer Korol Sverchevsky) reported on the state of the brigades, describing both their glorious past and their dubious future. There are four crucial points in his report. The first concerns the attitude that the international soldiers had toward the Spanish. In Sverchevsky's words, they believed they had come to Spain to save it from the fascists. This viewpoint had led directly to their superior attitude toward the Spanish, whom they treated like second-class citizens in their own country. As we have already seen, the high command had earlier complained about Emilio Kléber (Moshe Zalmanovich

Stern), the man whom Sverchevsky blamed for creating an atmosphere hostile to the Spanish.[4] By early 1938, Sverchevsky could write pejoratively about "Kléberism," a sure sign that Stern had fallen out of favor and that the party line had turned decisively against the International Brigadists' disdainful treatment of the Spanish.

The poor training and ineffectiveness of the internationalists are also important, not only because they show how little the volunteers were contributing to the war at this point, but also because they highlight the volunteers' tendency to tie their deficiencies to the presence of so many Spaniards within their ranks. In the second half of 1937 and early 1938, the International Brigades, as usual, participated in all of the major engagements, but with a difference. Sverchevsky thought that in earlier battles the foreigners had distinguished themselves for their bravery, but he now wrote of one brigade "fle[eing] with enviable speed" during combat near Madrid, while another was "nothing like what it had been." The 12th Brigade was even disbanded by the Spanish because of its poor fighting abilities. The internationalists tried to blame the decline in their military effectiveness on the Spanish, who "don't want to fight," but Sverchevsky pointed out that there were sufficient problems with the volunteers themselves. For one thing, their units had too many officers (some kept around so that the brigades could claim extra pay from the base at Albacete), and they did not seem to care at all about training, discipline, or even cleanliness. In addition, the 11th Brigade was a "half-demoralized rabble," the Poles had an "intolerable familiarity and uncomradely attitude toward the Spanish soldiers," and the Americans and English were unbelievably dirty and had filthy weapons. The contrast with the Spanish units could not be greater, for while the internationalists were arguing about "saving Spain," the Spaniards were improving themselves as soldiers.

These two points pale beside what Sverchevsky thought was the largest problem with the brigades: the "nationality question." Historians have noted the role that dissent and desertion played in the brigades, but there have been few hints until now of the great friction that existed between the various ethnic groups that made up the international units.[5] Sverchevsky's report gives a glimpse of what he called "this petty, disgusting, foul squabble about the superiority of one nationality over another." The area in which the problem was most apparent was in the negative attitude of the soldiers toward their French, Jewish and, of course, Spanish "comrades." He accused the Germans in particular of endorsing an "openly racist nationality policy," but many of the ethnic groups seem to have expressed national prejudice against certain of their fellow internationalists.

To demonstrate the bias against the Spanish, Sverchevsky noted that the brigadists were just as likely to desert as the supposedly cowardly Spaniards and yet were rarely punished. The data he offered for the 11th Brigade represent the first official numbers on desertions available to Western scholars. Although highly fragmentary, they suggest that as the war began to go badly for the Republicans, the internationalists voted with their feet. The problem had become so bad by December 1937 that commanders in the 11th Brigade began covering up the desertions, refusing to report them. The experience of this unit was not unusual. About 120 men of the 15th Brigade, which included the Abraham Lincoln Battalion, deserted during a movement of the unit from Madrid to Aragon. As we shall see in Document 71, the experiences of these two units were typical of other International Brigades as well.

The next two reports, **Document 71** and **Document 72**, written in French, show the results of the widespread demoralization of the internationalists in one particular brigade, the 14th. Sverchevsky had been the original commander of this unit, but authority had been given over to Jules Dumont, a longtime Communist, in the spring of 1937. Just a few months later, the reinforcements for the brigade were of the lowest sort: drunkards, malcontents, and even one "pederast." Their attitude toward André Marty is especially illuminating. Once viewed as the savior of Madrid for his ability to quickly bring the International Brigades together, Marty's reputation declined rapidly thereafter. His brutal suppression of all dissent, insistence on iron discipline, and belief in using terror to achieve these ends had earned him the name "butcher of Albacete."[6] Now the new recruits quickly learned to mock Marty, sarcastically referred to his creation of punishment camps, and even made death threats. The next report shows that following a drunken binge the unit even terrorized Spanish villages. The comment that one cause of the disturbance was lack of a police escort is also instructive, making it seem completely normal that the assistance of local police was required to keep military troops under control.

The Soviets did not give up on every "malcontent" as a lost cause. In **Document 73** Comrade Gómez reported, among other things, that they generally tried to rehabilitate internationalist offenders. Gómez's real name was Wilhelm Zeisser. Zeisser was a German Communist who had become a Soviet citizen and GRU operative and, during the Spanish war, the head of the Albacete base of the International Brigades. In this report, Zeisser described the work done at the base and gave figures for the total number of internationals in the brigades. One of the tasks assigned to the base was the re-education of unreliable soldiers. Zeisser thought it commendable that through intensive political and military work the base had managed to re-educate up to 80 percent of the men sent to a concentration camp created for that purpose. That 20 percent of the soldiers were not rehabilitated is astonishing, and their fate was probably the same as that of other untrustworthy elements. The number of soldiers who passed through the camp is also staggering—four thousand in just three months—and testifies to the widespread demoralization of the International Brigades after the disastrous battles of the summer of 1937. The final figures that Zeisser presented for the internationalists lay to rest several controversies about the brigades: the total number of foreigners who fought in the units, their nationality, and an approximate number of deserters throughout the war.[7] This last number, given in the second "Information" as the final difference, is extremely large. It implies that one-sixth of the volunteers were unaccounted for by normal means by May 1938—they were either deserters or perhaps "unreliables" who had been executed.

By mid-1938 it was apparent that the International Brigades had outlived their usefulness as military units and, as **Document 74** shows, were increasingly viewed as having little value other than as bargaining chips in international negotiations. In the first paragraph Dimitrov and Manuilsky noted that only five thousand internationalists were still fighting in Spain and that they were so exhausted they no longer had much fighting value. To announce a withdrawal of the troops would be a propaganda coup for the Republican government, however, and might force the "fascists" to do the same. The memorandum confirms that the initiative for disbanding the brigades came from Negrín, but it also reinforces the widespread impression that Negrín no longer had control over the international units. Instead, he had to seek permission from the PCE and the Comintern in order to break up a military force that was supposedly fighting under his direction and for the freedom of his own country. Even then the Comintern could not make a decision on its own to agree or disagree with Negrín's proposal; it had to apply directly to Stalin for permission.

The dissolution of the International Brigades did not mean that the Communists simply forgot about the volunteers who had sacrificed so much to save Spain from "fascism." In **Document 75** Sverchevsky urged Voroshilov to remember these men, not because they deserved special recognition for their service, but because they were ripe for recruitment by foreign intelligence agencies and "Trotskyists." The tortuous reasoning behind this conclusion begins with the Communist belief that, as Sverchevsky wrote, "in a class society there is no political vacuum." If this were true, then it would be foolish to leave the thousands of former soldiers without political support and education in a foreign country, since they "may become the booty of our enemies, class or otherwise." Any relaxation in political vigilance "inevitably strengthens the enemy" and might lead to the internationalists' involvement in "dirty and base espionage-sabotage work against the USSR." The answer was to make sure that the men were involved in the Communist struggle, where they could be watched and ultimately used for more positive purposes.

Notes on the Situation in the International Units in Spain
Report by Colonel Com. Sverchevsky (Walter)
[14 January 1938]

I have worked for a year in the international units, first as commander of the 14th Brigade and from the end of February 1937 as commander of a division through which almost every International Brigade passed, except for the 12th (I worked closely with it for a short time near Las Rozas and at Jarama), and that still contains the 11th and the 15th, that is, the "oldest" and the "youngest" brigades. This year of work allowed me to observe and study these units closely and to come to some conclusions that I would like to share with you.

The military merits and role of the international units in this war are so indisputable and so well known that to prove so would be like trying to knock down an open door. It is enough to remember that it was none other than the appearance at Madrid of the first two International Brigades in those critical days in November that determined a successful defense of that city. In February at Jarama, they, the International Brigades, took upon themselves the brunt of the repeated attacks by the fanatical "Moros" and "Tercios," that is, Franco's most elite forces, at the beginning of the operation. During that slushy and anxious March at Guadalajara, the same Madrid brigades, the 11th and the 12th, were among the most reliable and stable units flung against the victorious, or so it seemed, march of the Italians. This was the first, and still the only but we will hope not the last, loud slap in Mussolini's (and in all of Fascism's) face—a second "Caporetto" that was, to a significant extent, achieved at the hands of the internationalists.

Guadalajara, in my opinion, concludes the most brilliant, most dazzling pages of the International Brigades' combat history. After that there was a decline in their relative importance, a decline that coincided with the arrival into our units of Spanish members, whom many of the international patriots sometimes try to blame for their own weaknesses.

Already during the events at Segovia (end of May, beginning of June), the 14th French Brigade was displaying some symptoms of a weakening of its combat qualities—it is true that this was mainly the fault of its commander—and was inferior to the 69th Spanish Durán Brigade, whose action, despite some weaknesses and failings, was nevertheless characterized by more dynamism than that of the 14th, which heroically, but passively, allowed itself to be slaughtered over the course of five days near Balsain.

Then there was Huesca, where the Lukács Brigade was nothing like what it had been during earlier battles.

All of the International Brigades, except for the 14th, took part in the immense Brunete operation (July), but their presence was not distinguished by anything special compared to the other Spanish brigades, among which were many young units experiencing battle for the first time. Thus, for example, the 11th had a very sluggish start at Brunete, but then after two days, on 8 July, they showed an exceptional brilliance, rushing to the attack on the "Cementerio" in Quijorna and, with the seizure of this cemetery on the morning of 9 July, deciding the fate of the village that the Campesino division had been unsuccessfully attacking for three days. But then again, after a few days, this same brigade, showing a rare lack of talent attributable to its commanders, attempted unsuccessfully to seize Hill 610, which was not very well fortified. In that same operation the number of International Brigades was reduced by one, the 12th (this number was later appropriated by the Polish Dombrowski Brigade), which was disbanded by the Spanish command for its poor fighting ability and for its refusal to carry out a military order.

On the disturbing day of 26 July, when there was a general panic and flight, the International Brigades, except for the 11th and units of the 15th, which held their positions, were not much slower [than other units] in their inexplicable but hasty movement backward.

During the last operation on the Aragon front, the so-called Saragossa operation, in which four of the five International Brigades took part, two extremes in their performance were observable. On the one hand, the 45th Division sat around marking time with the half-demoralized and unbattleworthy 12th Garibaldi Brigade and with the 13th Polish Brigade, which was senselessly, futilely but profusely bleeding; and on the other hand there was the quite good action of the 11th and 15th Brigades, which seized fortified Quinto and decided the fate of the solidly fortified Belchite—the two main keys to Saragossa.

And after a short time in the other sector, the Madrid one, the 14th Brigade could not hold out against weak but unexpected pressure from the enemy and fled with enviable speed, even leaving some of its soldiers at some nameless creek (I don't know the details. I'm passing on this episode in the words of Com. Valsky, the former adviser in the 3rd Corps).

The unquestionable decrease in the military significance of the international units cannot be explained by some relative decline in their numbers in the army, which now has more than two hundred brigades (some of them, by the way, are more orderly, organized, and disciplined than we are). We must also even more categorically reject any attempt to attribute our weaknesses to the Spanish, who now make up a majority in the international units, saying that they "don't want to fight," as some internationalist leaders have tried to assert. In no way is the "saturation" of our units with Spanish members the cause of our troubles. It is impossible to overlook the fact that except for the five International Brigades, there are actually no fewer than two hundred Spanish [brigades] fighting and showing, by the way, their maturity in the operation now going forward at Teruel. It is not, therefore, the "perfidy" of the Spanish that keeps us from enhancing and improving our military performance.

It is completely natural that our role today cannot be as noticeable as it was in the first few months of the war, when we indeed could serve as an example to the small, hastily thrown together Spanish brigades. We must admit now that we are no longer in charge (if it was ever possible to talk about that) and that it is the Spanish performers who are now playing first fiddle.

It seems to me that the fundamental reason for, and primary source of, our troubles lies, first and foremost, in a deeply rooted conviction which stubbornly refuses to die that we, the internationalists, are only "helping," that we "saved" and "are saving" Spain, which, they say, without us would not have escaped the fate of Abyssinia. This harmful theory prevents the German and Italian comrades from seeing the silhouettes of "Junkers" and "Fiats" in the fascist air force; they forget that here, on Spanish soil, they are fighting with arms in hand, that is, in the most effective and revolutionary way, first and foremost against their own enemy, which has already oppressed their own countries and peoples for many years. French "volunteers" do not always notice the direct connection between Franco, De la Roque, and Doriot; they forget that their country is already surrounded by black and brown shirts and that their vital interests lie in preventing a fascist sentinel from looming on the last border, the Pyrenees. The Poles do not completely comprehend that every one of their victories here is a direct blow against the Pilsudski gang, which has turned their country into a prison for the people; they do not understand that the liquidation of Franco is the most practical way to reach a true liberation of their country.

"Kléberism," though formally denounced, in fact continues to exist—in different forms and to different degrees—in every international unit, without exception. The figure of Kléber, the "savior" of Madrid and Spain, despite his physical absence, continues to control the psyches and actions of many, even of prominent internationalists.

From this theory of "salvation" and "aid," which is harmful, anti-internationalist (not to mention anti-party), and insulting to the Spanish, a claim that we are "superior" to the Spanish has arisen, that the Spanish people are obligated to feel some sort of boundless gratitude toward us, that they should allow us freedom of action, even if it goes against their interests. Here, in this theory, lies the foundation of our nationality policy in the international units, a policy that very often feeds our overt and covert enemies with material [to use] against us and fertilizes the soil for their fascist work. Because of this, political work in the International Brigades often does not proceed, as it should, from Spanish circumstances and the interests of the Spanish majority, but rather is based, as a rule, on the principle of satisfying first and foremost the needs and demands of the internationalist minority.

## Document 70 *continued*

The internationalists stubbornly refuse to recognize the fact—a not completely comforting one, but nonetheless real—that they are surrounded by 70 to 80 percent Spanish (only the 15th Brigade is half Anglo-American), and that this fact in and of itself, whether they like it or not, demands a decisive rejection of the forms and methods of work and command [left over] from that time when the International Brigades consisted solely of non-Spanish, with a core of ardent revolutionary fighters, many of whom gave their lives for the best ideals and aspirations of their own peoples and for all of mankind.

We are stubbornly clinging to the old ways of working, which were perhaps not all that bad earlier, but which do not meet the demands of today's tasks, when the situation has radically changed. We are continuing to see the international units as we would like them to be and not as they in actual fact are.

Below I want to present a number of illustrations which prove, in my opinion, that there is at best a misunderstanding of the real processes going on around us and which are preventing us from enhancing the role and significance of the International Brigades to a higher level than they currently occupy. I am convinced that our honest, open, and courageous recognition of the mistakes that we have committed and are committing and their resolute eradication and a sincere alteration in our behavior can increase our fighting quality to an enormous degree and immeasurably raise the prestige of the International Brigades in the eyes of the entire antifascist world.

In the following concrete particulars I will primarily refer to the 11th Brigade, with which I worked longer than any of the others and where our weaknesses and blunders are most clearly reflected. In different forms they are present in every one of the International Brigades, without exception.

1. *Organizational structure.* The Spanish People's Army does not yet have a firm material basis. Every two or three months we receive entirely new tables of organization that, as a rule, are far not only from the actual situation in the units, but also from any prospect of being realized in the near future. The Spanish command has been especially generous with automatic weapons, promising, on paper of course, to bring, for example, the number of light machine guns up to ninety-six weapons per brigade. In the organizational tables they are counting on highly qualified officers, although in practice many of the quite good chiefs and officers are very hesitant to put their signature on documents (aided by the abundant flourishes in Spanish signatures, which sometimes makes it difficult to read the names of even literate people), and several of them, even in this day and age, are somewhat mistrustful of attempts to convince them that a map is the exact representation of a locality.

No matter how unrealistic the Spanish command's draft tables may be today, one cannot deny their tenacity in setting right the structural form of their armed forces. It is a good thing that all of those "columns," ."..." [*sic*], "centuries," and other haphazard[8] forms of military groups and units, which were inevitable during the initial period when the army was spontaneously coming together, have faded into history and that today the People's Army consists of unified types of military units and formations that are even identified as brigades and divisions.

The international units are among the most unruly of the units, and I know a number of the Spanish units as well, especially when it comes to the organization of their staffs and promoting officers. Brigade staffs are so excessively overstaffed that they can easily complicate the already difficult task of managing battalions in combat. It is enough to say that there were up to forty officers on the staff of the 11th during the Brunete battles, which apparently explains why its commanders were so touchingly ill-informed about the disposition of their own battalions and units. There are now "only" sixteen officers in that brigade's staff, a good half of whom could easily be sent off to the front lines. The 15th does things in an even bigger way, outdoing its older sister: it has three majors and twenty-three captains and lieutenants on its staff. Undoubtedly, one of the most important concerns of the command must be finding useful work for this platoon of officers.

That same 11th, not resting on its laurels, introduced, apparently as a scientific experiment, additional staffs at the battalion level with corresponding chiefs and chiefs of operational units (!), or so the brigade order from 11 October 1937 reads. Despite my tenacity, I remain ignorant to this day as to what the roles and functions of these operations captain-lieutenants might be and deeply convinced that these functions are only vaguely understood by these [officers] themselves. In any case the presence of battalion staffs has not sped up one bit the receipt of even the battalion combat lists, for the simple reason that these lists are still a long way from being introduced everywhere.

The overstaffing of the headquarters with officers is in no way evidence that there are an abundance of them in service, and it is far from rare [to find] sergeants continuing to command platoons, since there are not enough lieutenants in the companies.

The total number of officers in the brigade does not formally exceed the prescribed norm (130–40), and the 15th is even experiencing shortages, but first, the officers are not completely correctly distributed within the unit, and second, each of the brigades has a sizable reserve of officers available at Albacete, which the service lists sent to the division headquarters completely fail to mention. The commissar of the 11th recently declared that his brigade has ninety officers at the base.

The procedure for promotion to officer and their advancement in rank does not always take into account the regulations prescribed for this and is, to a certain extent, a secret of the brigade command. This problem was settled for the 15th the moment it joined the division, but I myself cannot clearly conceive of how these promotions are being carried out in the 11th. At Brunete the brigade complained about the heavy losses in the command staff; it lost many cadres at Saragossa as well, but as far as I recall, I sanctioned a very insignificant number of new officers and promoted [few] existing ones, and nevertheless I did not hear any complaints about a lack of officers.

Com. Gómez, the head of the Albacete base, carried out an interesting experiment. An order was issued that all of the officers there, before receiving a salary, first had to report to the base headquarters for a discussion. The results were immediate. The first days that the order was in effect, more than seventy officers reported. They had been sitting around the base without any defined duties, and the majority of them could not give an intelligible explanation for why, by whom, when, and for what reason they had been awarded an officer's rank.

This happened a month ago. It is possible that today there are more of them.

In general, in the cities and villages of Spain, in different delegations, bases, houses, legal and illegal schools, it is possible to assemble an impressive number of officers and other "representatives." A dramatic reduction of their [ranks] would scarcely pose a serious threat to a successful conclusion of the war.

The problem of the overproduction of officers has become especially acute now with the signing of an agreement with the government several months ago, according to which the base and International Brigades are to be wholly controlled by the Spanish command. There are already some Spanish officers at Albacete, and we must expect legitimate pressure from them; in particular a question may arise about verifying the officer corps and about the unconditional subordination of the International Brigades, in every sense, to the laws and decrees that are obligatory for the entire Spanish army.

As soon as possible, we should meet them halfway.

The international units are keeping two books. One is for Albacete and the other is for the division, and the difference between the two is sometimes striking, as can be seen from the following table, in which the data for Albacete are given as of 1 December and the personnel lists for the division are for 26 December 1937.

A small difference in the numbers could be explained by the normal movement of personnel and insufficient precision in their inventory taking, but this huge disparity of 772 men for the 11th and 923 for the 15th was intentional, and this was advantageous to both sides because the brigades receive extra funds (Albacete pays out the money according to these lists); and Albacete also profits from this by withholding 3 percent for each man. The most important thing, however, is that the Spanish command uses these lists to determine Albacete's relative importance; the higher the numbers for the international units, the greater its importance.

By the way, the lists presented to the division do not indicate the contin-

| Units* | Lt. Cols. and higher | Majors | Capts. | Lts. | total officers | Medics | Commissars | Sergeants | Corps. | total noncoms | Privates | total |
|---|---|---|---|---|---|---|---|---|---|---|---|---|
| 35th for Albacete | 2 | 5 | 12 | 37 | 56 | — | 9 | 109 | 135 | 244 | 1,031 | 1,340 |
| 35th in reality | 2 | 4 | 11 | 40 | 57 | 24 | 14 | 106 | 101 | 207 | 1,132 | 1,433 |
| 11th for Albacete | 2 | 5 | 24 | 119 | 150 | — | 31 | 297 | 255 | 544 | 2,882 | 3,626 |
| 11th for the division | — | 4 | 28 | 107 | 139 | — | 38 | 229 | 188 | 417 | 2,256 | 2,854 |
| 15th for Albacete | 1 | 4 | 16 | 66 | 86 | 28 | 28 | 286 | 232 | 518 | 2,755 | 3,386 |
| 15th for the division | 1 | 6 | 115 | | 122 | | | 198 | ? | ? | 2,143 | 2,463 |

*The division headquarters with their services for artillery squadrons, machine-gun and rifle companies, communication companies, and engineering and sanitary units.

gents from the brigades' recruiting centers, which are maintained on Albacete's account.

Everything that has been said about the 11th and 15th Brigades can be extended to the rest of the international units, but I would not blame them exclusively. For this is all a result of Albacete's general system of policy and work, every aspect of which needs to be improved.

I do not want to dwell on many other particulars. I just wanted to present a general picture of the "autonomy" of our units, which do not want to be confined to the limits that are mandatory for the Spanish army.

It seems to me that the international units need to work out an organization that is unified, solid, and standardized, somewhat different from the generally accepted [kind], as it takes into account its specific character. Once this has been worked out, however, it should become absolute law. Albacete could work on this, using, of course, the experience of the units as a basis. By the way, we should expand the officer and commissar corps, taking into account the need to duplicate some functions, which will be discussed below.

Once this kind of solid plan existed, it would be easier for the division to exercise control and further subordinate the brigades to itself. This is difficult to achieve because the latter have their own independent life, dealing directly with Albacete on every question and bypassing the division headquarters. The problem of centralizing every question between Albacete and the divisions is being resolved very slowly, and under these conditions it is really difficult for the divisions to thoroughly investigate and introduce the desired adjustments to the brigades.

If the organizational problems of the International Brigades are not put in order, if they are not completely subordinated to the divisions, it will be difficult to achieve the necessary improvements in all areas of their training and military performance.

They accuse us of being arbitrary, of not wishing to observe and submit to Spanish rules and regulations, and unfortunately there is, not infrequently, a significant amount of truth in this and the reproof is deserved. All of this could easily be avoided by putting our own house in order and honestly subordinating ourselves to the Spanish Republican Army.

2. *The military training* of the International Brigades, despite [making] appreciable progress, especially after the Segovia operation, continues to be unable to keep up with today's demands.

Drill is harder on the international units than it is on the Spanish, who generally conform more easily to military discipline. Earlier, when the brigades were fully international, introducing the daily routine and organizing the most elementary drill quite often required a great deal of energy and frequently succeeded only after the suppression of opposition not only from the soldiers, but also from a significant portion of the officer corps. In January 1937, after Las Rozas, when the daily routine and work were being introduced, there were attempts at open opposition in the 14th Brigade, and a rumor was set about that the brigade commander (me) was a supporter of Franco and wanted (as they said) "to introduce the fascist way of doing things here." They, the volunteer antifascists and not infrequently the Communists, understood the revolutionary army to be an organization built on free principles, without order, without military discipline. We had to give a number of talks to convince [them], using the example of the Red Army, to mobilize all of the brigade's healthy elements and even to take a number of extreme measures against the most zealous "revolutionaries," and only then was it possible to turn the tide.

When I first visited the units of the 11th Brigade in April, they were some sort of half-demoralized rabble (especially the French Paris Commune Battalion). The state of their weapons literally made me shudder. In this huge church, dirty as a cesspool, some sort of ragged, gloomy creatures were lolling about. They did not even want to move a leg when their commander walked past. The German battalion was better, but even they were far from what they should have been. The command staff passively contemplated this scene and thought it completely normal, or, perhaps better, they did not notice or see the depth of the disintegration. Only after a very intense conversation with the officer and the commissar staff, after a special talk with the brigade commander, Com. Hans, after mobilizing the entire brigade for a struggle with their own lack of discipline, did we succeed in giving it another appearance. By the way, at that time they were still discussing the commanders' orders at general assemblies, since the latter found this to be an indication of "democracy" (!).

I first visited the Polish battalion, then still known as the Dombrowski, in May, and my first meeting with compatriots took the form of an intense, one-sided talking to about dirty rifles, about bayonets that were used as tent-pins, about [their] intolerable familiarity and uncomradely attitude toward the Spanish soldiers of the battalion, and so on and so forth. This was the Polish battalion that won the fame it so richly deserved for its heroism at Casa de Campo and Ciudad Universitaria.

Finally, a month ago I was with the English and Canadian battalions of the 15th Brigade. It is difficult to convey in words the state of [their] weapons and how dirty [they were], especially the rifles. The bores of their barrels were not much different from a seventeenth-century musket barrel found at Belchite. No fewer than 95 percent of the rifles had no bayonet or cleaning rod, all lost since time immemorial. There was only a handful of cleaning rags in the brigade.

Until a short time ago I myself was inclined to deny the usefulness of the bayonet, given the local conditions. It seemed to me that it got in the way when troops were being transported by motor (buses), that it hampered the soldiers in the trenches (which are, as a rule, very narrow), in dugouts, and so on. I argued with the brigades, but at the bottom of my heart were various justifications for this kind of "bayonetophobia," especially as I did not meet a unit that would keep them, although one must admit that one sees them more often and in greater numbers in the Spanish brigades than in ours (to the credit of the advisers).

But here, in the Teruel sector, I stopped off at the headquarters of the 96th Spanish Brigade. The brigade commander, a former "toreador," had never before served in the army. For the first time during my work in Spain I saw a guard forming up at the sight of an approaching car with a commander's flag. The guard had rifles with fixed bayonets, and I was literally rooted to the ground at seeing all of those rifles—about 1,350—that still retained their very own bayonets, and that they even had cleaning rags, an object of special concern for the noncommissioned officers and most of all for the soldiers themselves, to whom the significance of these "trivial" objects has been explained. In addition, the condition of the rifles and the machine guns could be reckoned among the best that I have seen in Spain.

I, a Soviet commander, was embarrassed in the face of this half-literate brigade commander: for myself, that I was unable to achieve this in [my] division; for the internationalists; for our criminally loutish attitude toward [our] equipment, toward the weapons which were brought here with such difficulty; and for the rifles, the shortage of which can be felt at every turn (the 15th has 1,200 in all).

To my question about who had fostered in him such a respect for arms, he gave the names of our advisers who had earlier worked in the brigade (Coms. Alexander [Pomoshnikov] and Valsky), declaring that they had driven him crazy with their demands to maintain and respect arms.

After that, the brigade commander pulled out a small notebook in which, like any thoughtful manager, he kept the entire brigade; people, weapons, ammunition, matériel, in a word, everything necessary to know in order to manage it well.

A characteristic trifle: I and my adjutant were with the brigade commander for more than half an hour, and the entire time Karnach stood below on the staircase, fearing to miss the moment of our departure and to be late forming an honor guard to see us off.

And another touching detail: the first thing that struck one upon entering the headquarters was the little statuette of Com. Stalin (the brigade commander and more than 80 percent of the officers and commissars are Communists).

I heard quite a bit about the other, 22nd Galanovsky Brigade, which is even better organized and more disciplined, from our comrades.

It is true that in both cases there are commanders at the head of the brigades who are concerned only with the matters entrusted to them, and not with the key problems of immediately reconstructing the world and saving Spain, about which our internationalists love to argue all the time. There are people who are modestly and honestly devoting their knowledge, energy, and talents to the units entrusted to them, caring for [their] soldiers and weapons, finding the ways and means to better provide for their subordinates and without any quarrels and discussions carrying out the instructions of their superiors. Until very recently we had the nice habit of taking an order received from above as a signal for some inventiveness to somehow or other avoid or delay carrying it out (Lukács at Majadahonda and at Casa de Campo; Kléber in the Saragossa operation; numerous incidents in the 11th Brigade, and so on).

Unfortunately, the examples of the 22nd and 96th Brigades can in no way be taken as typical of the entire Spanish Republican Army. In the majority of the Spanish brigades and units the command is exceptionally formal and callous. Despite the fact that the majority of the line officer corps comes from the militia, their relationship with the soldiers is characterized, in the majority of cases, by lack of even a minimal concern for the fighters. At Brunete and in the Saragossa operation, entire brigades, despite the monstrous heat, were left without water and were fed with canned food, and this was one of the reasons for their lack of steadfastness. Here at Teruel, our division is perhaps the sole exception, its brigades receiving regular hot meals and heated wine. It is difficult to demand more from the soldiers than they can give when, for example, the same 68th Division (and this is not the only one) gives its troops only warm coffee—and this is in winter, in the mountains, with the temperature down to $-18°$ [Centigrade] and with an acute shortage of winter clothing and shoes.

The discipline in the international units was, and in fact still is, somewhat formal in nature. In the 11th it is first of all "party comrades," and until recently the nice, cozy atmosphere of a Quaker society still prevailed in the 15th. In both cases, if nationality or party "contradictions" are not present, relations between commanders and subordinates are angelically peaceful. Being an "antifascist revolutionary" allows you to argue and debate with the commander, as a rule, using the familiar "tú" with your hands in your pockets and a cigarette in your mouth. It was easier to find and recognize "Richard" in the 11th than the commander of the brigade. Beginning with Brunete, a lot of effort has been expended to prove that it is exactly a revolutionary understanding of discipline that obliges one, first and foremost, to [maintain] the strictest military relations and does not give one the right to doubt the effectiveness of orders handed down from above, and that, even if it might be possible to retain democracy at the general assemblies, then it is only in two instances: first, in order to debate how best to carry out the orders received; second, to expose any weak areas that had been allowed when carrying out the order in order to avoid repeating them.

It is true that much has changed for the better in the brigades of our division over the past few months, after the Saragossa operation. The 11th has become much more exacting, and the 15th sometimes seems completely different from what it was just a short time ago. Both brigades have seriously pulled themselves together and do not intend to rest on their laurels.

A relatively short time ago, the International Brigades began more or less regular studies. This change occurred in our division after the Saragossa operation. We began with putting our weapons in order, with discipline, shooting practice, and studying of tactics. The 11th Brigade has made a (relatively) good showing and is undoubtedly the best prepared of all the International Brigades. From the start of October up to the moment the division was transferred to Teruel, it [the division] worked like clockwork, every day, systematically, tenaciously, and, most important, according to plan. The 15th, because of a number of unfavorable circumstances, began studies a good deal later, but even it has achieved highly appreciable successes, first and foremost in an understanding [of the need for] regular drill every day and for elimination of laxity in discipline. Much still needs to be done to raise the quality of work and study, but today it is already possible to confirm that the tide has turned and that attending classes is no longer an act of heroism or regarded as doing a favor, as it was earlier, but rather fulfilling an obligation. The brigades are now convinced that study and classes, besides increasing their battle readiness, are conducive to maintaining order and tighten up discipline, clear out the atmosphere, and raise the troops' morale.

The results can already be seen. The behavior of the 11th Brigade, which has been on the line at Teruel for seven days, and the 15th, which has a battalion and a half in the trenches in the Seladas sector, despite the intense cold, repeated attacks by the enemy, heavy fire from his artillery, and frequent air attacks, the behavior of these brigades deserves the highest praise. The mood of the fighters and even of the wounded is very calm, martial, and, in the opinion of the Spanish command, higher and better than that of any Spanish unit.

Of course, it is too early to say that we are fully prepared. The battle at Teruel saw the onset of a new stage in the war, with massive artillery fire from the enemy and massive and frequent air raids, for which we are insufficiently prepared. Up to now we have oversaturated our front line (and that usually the only one) with soldiers; we use up our modest reserves inexcusably quickly; we dig in slowly and not deeply enough, reckoning that trenches are for the engineering company to deal with; our wonderful 45mm antitank guns have still not become the threat to the enemy's tankettes and machine guns that they should be, nor as the enemy's scarce cannon are to our worthy T-26 and BTs; in a word, we are still very far from the level of preparedness that modern battle demands.

Nevertheless, these facts do not diminish our undoubted progress. If I emphasize our weaknesses so sharply and harshly I do so only because we should and can work much better with our international cadres, with less waste of our valuable, worthy, heroic, but not all too many internationalists, who are needed not only here, but also for future work in their own countries.

Even harsher discipline, systematic work on ourselves and with subordinates, the raising of our military essentials (there can never be too much of that), weapons always ready and clean, better tactical preparation than up to now, daily close concern for the soldiers, their needs and demands, candor in our work, in our relations with subordinates—these are the situation's urgent demands, and we cannot avoid facing them.

3. *The nationality question* is the weakest spot in the international units and is the main hindrance impeding the growth of our potential.

Very little is said about relations between the nationalities within the international units, or, more truthfully, it is completely hushed up, but it is just this [problem] that gives rise to almost all our weaknesses.

Earlier, when the label "international" exactly matched the national composition of the units, the nationality question had not acquired the acuteness that it has now, as the internationalists are becoming lost in the surrounding Spanish masses. It is true that even then there were more than enough petty squabbling and strong antagonisms in the international units. The francophobia was most transparently obvious, for instance (although it is difficult to see why, when in all the brigades it was precisely the French who filled in all of the most unpleasant "holes" during battle), anti-Semitism flourished (and indeed it still has not been completely extinguished), but in general this was, if one can talk like this, a family quarrel, very diligently hidden from strangers', that is, Spanish, eyes. However, the conditions of that period allowed neither the time nor the opportunity to investigate thoroughly this veiled issue.

The International Brigades and units were created literally within the course of one or two days from those volunteers who were on hand at the time (the 9th Battalion of the 14th Brigade was gathered, staffed, and armed in one day; the brigade itself was created by an order dated 23 December 1936, and on that same day, at 1600 hours, the first echelon took to the southern front; there were subunits that contained dozens of nationalities (one of the companies of the 9th Battalion of the 14th Brigade had fourteen); furthermore, all of these were people who were absolutely unacquainted, not accustomed to one another, and right off found themselves in a battle. If you add to this the extremely acute shortage of political workers, the lack of qualified military cadres, and a whole number of other needs, then the weaknesses and the solution to this problem (adequate at that time) are not surprising.

The great, very exalted, and revolutionary objective, armed struggle with fascism, united everyone, and for its sake Germans, Italians, Poles, Jews, and representatives of the world's numerous nationalities, including blacks, Japanese, and Chinese, had to agree among themselves, found a common language, suffered the same adversities, sacrificed their lives, died heroes, and were filled with the very same hatred for the common enemy.

But at the very same time as the volunteers were unifying, this petty, disgusting, foul squabble about the superiority of one nationality over another was going on. Everyone was superior to the French, but even they were superior to the Spanish, who were receiving our aid and allowing us to fight against our own national and class enemies on their soil. The 12th Brigade, during Jarama, was deeply indignant at the "impertinence" of the Spanish command, which dared to hint very cautiously about the desirability of sharing their wealth with their poor Spanish relatives. The command of this brigade was offended by this "criminal attempt" by the Spanish on the "holy property of the internationalists." At that time they had 150 trucks, 66 light automobiles, and 48 motorcycles at their disposal; while not far from Pingarrón the three-brigade 11th (Lister) Division had only a handful of trucks and ambulances at its disposal and could neither remove its wounded nor supply its troops.

I personally saw at Castillo de Alcodea near Madrid the mountains of ammunition (seventeen trucks) thrown out by that same brigade as unwanted, although that same matériel would have met the needs of Spanish brigades.

Alcalá de Henares, a peaceful town about thirty km. from the capital, suffered several uneasy nights when groups of Anglo-Americans and after that the French, withdrawn from the front for rest, regularly roamed about its streets.

When in April, after several days of squabbling, the 12th Brigade finally relieved Durán's 69th Brigade at Casa de Campo, some soldiers from the Garibaldi Battalion required the help of the soldiers they were replacing in order to get down into the trenches and take the place of their Spanish precursors. (Durán, who was at that time subordinate to the division, reported this to me personally.)

No longer ago than yesterday, 13 January 1938, was I able for the first time to receive exact information about the transportation [resources] of the 11th Brigade, still concealed like no other military secret (the frontline register showed twenty, and, after some pressure, thirty-eight, vehicles). It turned out that the brigade had ninety-four vehicles (light automobiles, trucks, and special ambulances, and so on), that is, almost as many as a normal two-division corps would have. By the way, the 216th Brigade of the 67th Division, which is now working with me, has one light automobile, one truck, and nothing else. There is not even one ambulance. And that's for 2,760 men.

Out of the 11th Brigade's transportation wealth, a good half went out of commission, but it was a pity to give up even the dead machines, a shame to give them to the Spanish, who might have been able to repair some of them, and who knows, perhaps the soldiers of that 216th Brigade might have been able to get a hot meal more often than one or two times a week, with the temperatures now reaching a freezing 17° [Centigrade] below zero.

This excessive transportation wealth is the sole reason for the premature decay of the machines because to keep 100 machines in good running order one must have a tolerable mechanic's shop, which the brigade, of course, does not have. But the command of the International Brigade does not want to recognize this fact.

Particulars of this sort could be liberally cited from every area of life, study, and behavior of the International Brigades, and in all of them would be reflected a stubborn refusal to face the fact that we are on Spanish soil, we are subordinate to the Spanish army, that the only boss is the Spanish people and, as we shall see further on, for us Communists, the Spanish Communist party.

With the arrival of Spanish reinforcements in the International Brigades, our own, national squabbles calmed down somewhat, and immediately our attitude toward them, the Spanish, took on the tone of a dissatisfied boss. All of our difficulties, weaknesses, and failures were excused by the fact that there were Spanish present in our brigades. "The Spanish are cowards," "they always flee," "they never want to fight," and so on and so forth, became the internationalists' favorite and most frequent leitmotiv. So much so that if they, the Spanish, all disappeared one fine day, we would be in a really difficult position, what with having to search all over again for other sources of our misfortunes.

The internationalists had and have complete, absolute power, even though in the majority of the brigades and units the percentage of Spanish has reached the impressive number of 60–80 percent. All of the key command and political positions are firmly occupied and held onto by the internationalist minority, and entrance to the command Olympus is attended by such difficulties for the Spanish that only a few of them have been favored with the right and the honor to lead their own compatriots.

This is supported by the figures for the 35th Division cited below, and I will make so bold as to suggest that our situation is undoubtedly better than that in the other international units.

The division headquarters with all of its services and subunits (artillery battalion, rifle and machine-gun companies, engineering and communication companies, cavalry squadron, sanitary unit, quartermaster service, transport, and so on) numbered 1,472 men at the [beginning of the] new year, of whom 338, or 29.6 percent, were internationalists.

| By position: | officers 90 | of whom internationalists | | 53, | or | 60.0% |
|---|---|---|---|---|---|---|
| | commissars 11 | " | " | 3 | " | 27.3% |
| | sergeants 100 | " | " | 47 | " | 47.0% |
| | corporals 127 | " | " | 16 | " | 12.3% |
| | privates 1,038 | " | " | 214 | " | 29.2% |

11th Brigade (figures for 30 November 1937)—2,899 men, of whom 648 or 22.4% internationalists.

## Document 70 *continued*

| By position: | officers 145 | of whom internationalists | 90, | or | 62.0% |
|---|---|---|---|---|---|
| | commissars 40 | " | " | 20 | " 50.0% |
| | sergeants 232 | " | " | 96 | " 42.0% |
| | corporals 221 | " | " | 26 | " 11.8% |
| | privates 2,263 | " | " | 416 | " 18.4% |

15th Brigade (figures for 25 December 1937)—2,463, of whom 1,258 or about 52% internationalists.

| By position: | officers 122 | of whom internationalists | 65, | or | 54.2% |
|---|---|---|---|---|---|
| | commissars 40 | " | " | 23 | " 57.5% |
| | sergeants 198 | " | " | 143 | " 71.5% |
| | corporals and | | | | |
| | privates 2,148 | " | " | 1,081 | " 50.2% |

The data cited clearly reflect the general tendency of our nationality policy, for it should, of course, be emphasized that the higher the position, the lower the percentage of Spanish and vice versa.

If one takes, for example, only the staffs in the narrow sense of this word, then the percentage of internationalists sharply rises in comparison to the general number of officers.

Staff of the 35th Division: has 11 officers, of whom 6 are internationalists, or 5.0%
" " 11th Brigade " 26 " " 20 " " 77.0%
" " 15th " " 19 " " 14 " " 75.0%
data for 7 November 1937

The percentage of internationalists is no less sharply increased in the non-line services and the subunits of the brigades. The picture is the following in the quartermaster service, weapons shop, transportation and sanitary services:

| *35th Div. Staff:* | officers 47 | of whom internationalists | 23, or 46.0%, |
|---|---|---|---|
| | noncoms, soldiers 330 | " " | 104 or 31.6% |
| | data for 7 December 1937 | | |

| *11th Brigade:* | officers 19 | of whom internationalists | 7 or 90.0% |
|---|---|---|---|
| | noncoms, soldiers 273 | " " | 132 or 48.5% |
| | data for 31 November 1937 | | |

| *15th Brigade:* | officers 18 | of whom internationalists | 12 or 66.6% |
|---|---|---|---|
| | noncoms, soldiers 183 | " " | 157 or 87.0% |
| | data for 20 December 1937 | | |

On the line and in the battalions our influence remains intact, but it is much less than in the staffs and in nonline subunits, and what is more we hold complete sway over the command of the battalions (except for the 59th Battalion of the 15th Brigade, where the battalion commander and officers are Spanish), less in the companies and are much weaker at the noncom and private level. This is most clearly expressed in the 11th Brigade.

The proportional relationships in the brigade battalions are the following:

| | | | |
|---|---|---|---|
| *11th Brigade:* | officers 85 | of whom internationalists | 48, or 56.1% |
| | noncoms, soldiers 2,374 | " " | 297 or 12.0% |
| | data for 30 November 1937 | | |
| *15th Brigade:* | officers 63 | of whom internationalists | 37 or 60.0% |
| | noncoms, soldiers 1,625 | " " | 850 or 56.3% |
| | data for 20 December 1937 | | |

The figures cited above speak convincingly of our stubborn domination, of our clinging to positions, a good portion of which ought to be handed over to the Spanish if we want to strengthen the International Brigades.

Beginning when I worked in the 14th Brigade, I tried to convince and I am convincing the command of the brigade itself that the only policy that is correct from every point of view, the most international policy, will and ought to admit and attract Spanish officers into participation in leadership, that it is inconceivable and impossible to retain [our] current positions while we are drowning in a mass of Spanish, that at the very least we ought to boldly duplicate command and political positions, beginning with the company commanders and higher.

I brought this up repeatedly with Com. Fritz [*sic*] Dahlem,[9] the representative of the CPG [Communist party of Germany], and with Com. Gallo, the commissar of the International Brigades (by the way, the divisions and brigades know him only by hearsay), and tried to demonstrate this in Albacete as well.

Everyone agreed, no one denied the seriousness of this problem, but everything stayed the same, and in the 11th Brigade itself, as well as at Albacete, they have become convinced that I am just playing into the hands of the enemies of the International Brigades among the Spanish command. The very same suspicion about me, although it is true that it was more veiled, also prevails among the commissariat of the International Brigades.

We have succeeded in achieving some results, although it is true that these are still inadequate. Almost half of the officers (45 percent) are now Spanish, and in the near future this percentage will grow to not less than 60–75 percent. Unfortunately, matters are not moving quickly enough because I cannot afford to weaken the brigades by transferring good Spanish officers to the division staffs, while Albacete (without my consent) is sending over only internationalists.

The 15th Brigade is meeting us halfway [on this], and for three months has had a deputy brigade commander who is Spanish (Major Crespo). The choice turned out to be an uncommonly poor one, but this does not at all prove that the policy is wrong, and, especially after the experiences at Brunete, Saragossa, and the operation now taking place at Teruel, I continue to be a supporter [of the idea] that attracting the Spanish to command in the international units will strengthen the latter and facilitate the work of the internationalist leadership.

At Brunete, Quinto, and Mediana, the 11th Brigade complained time and again about a number of instances when the Spanish fighters would not attack behind the internationalists or retreated at the slightest suggestion of pressure from the enemy. The 15th complained about the same thing. The only epithets the command of the 11th could come up with for the Spanish were "cowards" and "poor soldiers."

This is just slander. The Spanish soldier over the course of almost a year and a half has bravely fought an unequal battle and knows how to die heroically and quietly. Show him the least bit of warm, comradely feeling, surround him with the necessary care and attention, persuade him by example that you will stand with him in the heat of battle, treat him with humanity, and he will be a faithful, devoted, courageous, and brave fighter, exceptionally obedient and disciplined.

He did not see this from us and today still sees too little of it. But the brigades of our division have lately managed to turn the tide in our relations with the Spanish, eliminating the sharpest edges of antagonism, making them feel like equals, working with them seriously, giving them the opportunity to see us a little bit closer up, sizing them up a little better. The command of that same 11th Brigade confirms that in the operation now taking place at Teruel, when the 11th was on the line from the fourth through the thirteenth of this month, repeatedly attacked by and attacking the enemy, and was under very strong pressure from [the enemy's] artillery and air forces, companies of Spanish recruits—from Catalonia and Madrid—proved to be the best.

We internationalists live our own isolated life. Except for infrequent official visits, we rarely allow the Spanish into our midst. The English and American soldiers not long ago were smoking "Lucky Strikes," not paying attention to the Spanish fighters standing next to them, who had spent days looking for a few shreds of tobacco. The internationalists receive frequent packages from home but are very rarely willing to share them with their Spanish comrades. We have done a good job of providing national foods in the brigades but only recently have acknowledged the right of the Spanish majority to their own [kinds of] food. The sanitary unit at Albacete until recently attended very well to only the internationalist wounded, and as for the Spanish, cynically suggested that we ourselves—the divisions—should care for them. Having wonderful hospitals at their disposal in Albacete, Murcia, Alicante, Benicássim, [facilities] equipped with splendid, first-class personnel and matériel, Major Telge and Captain Franek, the chief and deputy chief of the sanitary service at the International Brigade base, stubbornly and for a long time resisted attending to Spanish fighters who had fought side by side with the international soldiers in the very same International Brigades. I consider it a great achievement that our division was the first to succeed in getting the Spanish wounded of our units treated on an equal footing with the internationalists.

Richard, the commander of the 11th Brigade, reporting on the casualties suffered by the brigade at Brunete and Saragossa, always gave the exact number of dead and wounded and frequently even the names of the internationalists. But he never knew the casualties of the Spanish personnel.

For the first time in the history of the 11th Brigade, Spanish officers have now been appointed deputy battalion commanders; we requested from Albacete a Spanish captain, the former commander of the 4th Battalion, wounded at Brunete, whom we intend to use as second commander of the brigade; for the first time Spanish companies—Catalan and Spanish—were thanked for their conduct in the latest battles; for the first time the new brigade command treated Scandinavians as equals. (There are forty or fifty of them there and, in the opinion of the former brigade commander, they were "riffraff," "drunks," and so on and were rated no higher than the Spanish.)

The *punitive* policy of the international units, and not the disciplinary/educational policy, has its point aimed first and foremost, if not exclusively, at the Spanish. I learned that of twenty-seven internationalists (among whom were several officers) who were given leave by the 11th Brigade command at the beginning of August from Collado Villalba, none of them has yet returned to his unit. Nothing has been done to undertake a search for them, although if one had had the slightest desire to do so, it would have been easy to find their residence (Albacete).

The data, for example, on desertion in the 11th Brigade for October present the following incomplete picture:

| Month | October | | | November | | | December | | | Total | | |
|---|---|---|---|---|---|---|---|---|---|---|---|---|
| | Sp. | Inter. | total | Sp. | Inter. | total | Sp. | Inter. | total | Sp. | Inter. | total |
| Privates | 12 | 1 | 13 | 21 | 11 | 32 | 2 | 1 | 3 | 35 | 13 | 48 |
| Corporals | 1 | — | 1 | 6 | — | 6 | — | — | — | 7 | — | 7 |
| Sergeants | — | — | — | 5 | 2 | 7 | — | — | — | 5 | 2 | 7 |
| Lts. | 3 | 2 | 5 | 3 | 1 | 4 | 1 | — | 1 | 7 | 2 | 9 |
| Captains | — | — | — | — | — | — | — | — | — | 1 | — | 1 |
| | 14 | 3 | 19 | 35 | 14 | 49 | 3 | 1 | 4 | 52 | 18 | 72 |

The November maximum to a certain extent reflected a protest against the harsh pressure for learning and discipline and against the difficult material situation of the brigade at that time. The December figures, on the other hand, reflect not only an indisputable reduction in desertion, but also the poor arrangement for keeping track of it and also partially the brigade command's unwillingness to bring the truth to the attention of the division after serious words had been had with the brigade commanders about this.

During the latest movement of the 15th Brigade from Madrid to Aragon, about 120 men deserted, among whom were internationalists. Whether they returned or not, whether anything was done to return them, and, most important, whether anything was done through political work to prevent absences without leave and desertion, no one knows.

In my memory there has not been one case of a public investigation and punishment for desertion by an internationalist, but if a Spanish [soldier] is absent without leave or is late returning from leave (which does not often happen, as leave is rarely granted), the inexorable sword of justice immediately falls upon the head of the criminal, and not uncommonly he is brought up on charges that the accused did not think were criminal (for example marriage!). In the period November–December 1937 alone, the military court of the 11th Brigade met four times. Three of the cases deserve to be gone into in some detail:

a) Sergeant José Siles González, thirty-eight years old, member of the CP of Spain since 1933. Volunteer since 31 August 1936. In the 11th Brigade since 10 April 1937. Was a company commissar. Injured at Brunete. On 17 October 1937 left the brigade without leave, went home, married, and after fifteen days returned.

On 5 December 1937 the court met (chaired by Major Gustav Schinde, the "cadres' commissar" of the brigade staff).

The accused defended himself by saying that he had been at the front the entire time since August 1936 and had not seen his family since then; he had requested leave three times following standard procedure but had never received an answer; at home he married, for which he had received official permission from the brigade.

The wise judges answered (this is how it was entered in the verdict) that (a) antifascists ought not to desert their units without permission (true!); (b) especially as this was unworthy of a Communist (an official institution, such as a military tribunal, had no right in this case to bring up the party affiliation of the accused; especially as the tribunal might be composed of anarchists); (c) many other comrades had been just as long at the front and nevertheless had patiently waited their turn; you could just as well wait. (This is not true, at least concerning the internationalists, the majority of whom had been on leave; many repeatedly). As for his marriage, the following was noted, verbatim: "Marriage during war is a grave mistake, and the soldier who decides to take this step should not forget the responsibility that he must bear if his wife and child are orphaned."[10]

One can imagine the horror of the accused when they authoritatively and officially explained the depth of his utterly evil deed and his deep gratitude toward the good judges, who had shown such touching concern for the fate of his young bride and future child.

The sentence:

1) Demotion to private,

2) one month of service without pay, and

3) after that another fifteen days in a penal platoon on half pay.

This document has it all: an exceptional callousness, coldness, and heartlessness; the refined, sadistic-pharisaical virtue of impotent men who recommend celibacy to achieve victory over fascism; sectarianism and narrowmindedness over parties. As a whole, this is valuable material for fascist work not only within the brigade, but also far beyond it.

Wouldn't Franco be happy to lay his hands on this kind of document and drop it from his aircraft by the thousands over his and our positions, and wouldn't he be able to add his own suggestive commentary [to it]?

Where were the brigade commander, the brigade commissar, and the commissar of the International Brigades? Where were the brigade's immense political apparatus and its powerful party organization, to permit this kind of real counterrevolutionary insult to a seasoned fighter and honest antifascist?

b) Sergeant Etienne Rovira Leroux, eighteen years old. Volunteer in the brigade since 24 October 1936. Promoted to sergeant on 1 May 1937 for distinguished military service.

On 26 November 1937 he got drunk and refused to serve, declaring (not for the first time) that he couldn't take it any longer and didn't want to stay in the brigade and that he was going to Albacete to request a transfer to another International Brigade. Arrested on the spot by the captain of the company, he took off on the way to the detention cell and walked all the way to Sariñena (about fifty km), where he was detained the following day and returned to his unit. On 17 December 1937 the brigade military tribunal met (with a lieutenant as prosecutor).

In his speech for the prosecution, the prosecutor himself was forced to ask for leniency in view of his [the sergeant's] irreproachable fourteen months' service.

The sentence: (a) demotion to private, (b) fifteen days in the penal platoon at half pay.

No one in the brigade command who ought to look over the sentences deigned to display any interest in finding out why one of their oldest soldiers, of whom there remain dozens, could not go on and so insistently strove to leave the brigade in which he had served more than a year. No one showed the least concern for the soldier, a living repository of the military history of the 11th Brigade. I am convinced that a friendly half-hour conversation with the "criminal" would have helped to clear up a great many things about which neither the brigade commander nor the brigade commissar may know. Perhaps it is necessary to admit that they know all too well the sickness in the unit entrusted to them, but both of them prefer not to take any medicine.

I reversed both sentences while Richard was still around, but my order was carried out only some days after he had left the brigade.

c) Rafael Lores Cucales. In the brigade as a volunteer since 19 November 1936. Received a ten-day leave and overstayed it by twelve days because of his wife's sickness. The tribunal refused to thoroughly investigate the "personal" motive for his overstay and simply demoted him to private, sending him for correction to a penal platoon for two weeks (the matter came before the division staff on 22 December 1937).

The great fighting efficiency of the penal platoon is unsurprising given that it is staffed with "criminals" like these.

There was, it is true, one example of an investigation of an internationalist's case, Lieutenant Elias Ervin Carp (medic), who was accused of instigating a private [to act] against a commander, of failure to carry out the command's orders, and of political unreliability. I have still not managed to obtain the sentence (the tribunal met at the beginning of November 1937), but a complaint reached me from this medic and officer, who was demoted to private and, what is more, was sent to that same celebrated penal platoon. In his complaint he cites two facts about his "crime" that were not denied either by the brigade command or by the tribunal itself. The first of these facts very clearly reflects the intellectual mediocrity of the commissar of the 2nd Battalion (and unfortunately, he is not alone).

In October, when the weather is at its coldest and rainiest, in view of the sickness of the soldiers because of the weather and because of a lack of uniforms in the quartermaster service, he appealed to the commissar of the 2nd Battalion, where he worked as a doctor, to allow him to go to Barbastro to procure warm things for the soldiers, which he wanted to buy with money gathered from the soldiers themselves.

The battalion commissar categorically refused, giving as a reason that if this were done, there might "spring up" among the soldiers "doubts about the work of the brigade quartermaster service" (amazing logic: let the soldiers freeze and fall ill, provided that they remember lovingly their brigade quartermaster). Instead, the battalion officers suggested that he buy things for them. Carp refused and . . . there's your crime.

In the second instance, he proposed changing people's straw after the battalion and rooms had been disinfected and obtained the consent of the battalion commander and company commander to do so. However, on that same day, an order for the battalion saw to it that it would be done the other way around. The doctor legitimately protested this order, and he was charged with insubordination.

The doctor was tried [and convicted], and of course demoted and sent as a private to the penal platoon. However, the real reason for this "trial" was not these "crimes," but rather that (a) he had been a prisoner in a concentration camp and therefore was probably an agent of the Gestapo, (b) as a doctor he might have automatically become an officer, but he wanted to serve as a simple soldier, which meant that he was probably an enemy, and (c) he cared about the soldiers too much and was always with and among them; hence he probably set them against the good commanders. Besides, he was a Jew.

After being demoted, the medic came to Director Arco, the head of brigade sanitation, with a complaint about the poor state of his health. The [director] certified him as sick and inquired of the brigade command what should be done with him. They answered that he, the medic, was probably faking it. They ordered that he be considered healthy and put henceforward in the penal platoon.

I found out about this incident only at the end of December (the brigade did not consider it necessary to bring it to the attention of the division). Demotion requires a review by the divisional court, but in the meantime the [military] operation interfered with that and besides, neither Richard, the brigade commander, nor the head of brigade sanitation knows Carp's exact location.

If only the two facts cited in that suffering man's complaint are proven, then his sentence should be overturned, especially as even from a formal point of view the legal proceedings in and of themselves are utterly illegal because a sentence can be put into effect only after it has been confirmed by the division commander.

Leave in the army always attracts a great deal of interest, and the problem flares up with a special keenness during a war. One would think that the command of the units would be anxious to solve this question correctly, to have a definite policy, granting short-term leaves in strict order to, in the first place, the oldest and most deserving cadres, awarding them as a prize to the best, the most distinguished fighters. This would bind them still more closely to the brigade, stimulate the performance of others, strengthen the most active [soldiers], without whom it would be difficult to command at all. A leave policy of this sort would positively guarantee success in [our] struggle with desertion and reduce absence without leave to a minimum.

There is nothing like that. In practice, besides the extreme limits on leaves by order of the war ministry, according to which no more than 2 percent of a unit can be released, and now even this is forbidden, leaves go to those who are most persistent, often those close [to the commander], and usually to internationalists. They have still not even considered it necessary to answer a request by the Spanish in the 11th Brigade, as is obvious if only from the first tribunal case quoted below. The following facts from the past few days show what that leads to:

At the end of December I received two letters from Private Manuel Rijo Pérez, a signaler in the 2nd Battalion, volunteer since August 1936, who had repeatedly applied to the command for leave but had not been favored even once with an answer. I ordered the commander of the 11th Brigade, Richard, to investigate this matter thoroughly and personally, look into it, and punish [the guilty] and to grant the soldier the leave he requested. I obliged Richard to report to me officially about the execution [of this order].

It goes without saying that the commander of the 11th Brigade did not deign to carry out my order. After Richard left on the tenth of this month, January, I ordered the new brigade commander and commissar to take care of this matter, but it was too late. The soldier had deserted, and, through its own fault, the brigade was deprived of one of its few seasoned fighters.

Beginning in July, the division was in three serious operations: Brunete, Saragossa, and now Teruel. In the intervals between battles, the division found itself in a difficult situation, both in terms of atmosphere and matériel, with epidemics, cold, a reduction in food, a lack of clothing, and so on. People were really tired, they needed to be granted at least a little compensation in the form of short leaves, and it was possible to do this. But thanks to our heartlessness, callousness, and lack of understanding of our own role, nothing was done.

Last month both brigades were on the front lines. The 11th fought at Teruel from the fourth to the thirteenth and from the seventeenth to the twenty-second endured the most stubborn and powerful battle it had ever had to fight. The brigade behaved heroically, enduring eleven attacks by the enemy over the course of three days at a certain El Muletón. The brigade lost about 1,000 men dead and wounded at the battle of Teruel (450 wounded, 150 killed, 300 sick). The battle of Teruel undoubtedly constitutes the most brilliant page in the military performance of the brigade, and the companies of Spanish recruits (Catalan and Madrid) for the first time, showing their very best side, spoke well for themselves, as the brigade command itself attested.

But this brigade came from the front, went into the reserve, and from the very first days desertion began. One private from the 3rd Company, 1st Battalion; three privates and two corporals from the 1st [Company], 2nd [Battalion]; two drivers deserted from the 3rd Battalion; the 3rd [Company], 4th Battalion was deprived of one private and one lieutenant.

The old, dangerous kind of talk has crept back in among the Spanish, who only yesterday were heroically fighting side by side with the internationalists. The soldiers complain about the lack of attention paid to them by the internationalists; the officers complain about the lack of a future in the work and advancement in the service; all of them are demanding leave ever more loudly; and many of them are declaring that they won't return to the brigade from their leave. And in the meantime no steps are being taken to relieve this tension. It is true that it will not be easy to relieve it. For more than a year a German chauvinism has been persistently implanted and cultivated, and all of this time an openly racist nationality policy has been carried out. During all of these months any attempt at Spanish growth has been stifled, and of course the Spanish do not believe that we are seriously going to work on improving relations, that we have so . . . [*sic*] [altered?] our political policy, that it will result in appreciable changes in only one or two months, with the last month spent in battle.

And in fact the new policy is being carried out by the new brigade command very unboldly and timidly, as if for fear of deserving reproof for it.

Thus, for example, a report from the 11th Brigade submitting [names] for awards for the last battle (the lists were presented 29 January 1938).

Twenty-four men were submitted for promotion, of them ten internationalists and fourteen Spanish, so they kept to the proportions fairly well, but unfortunately the internationalists were proportionately given far greater advancement to the higher ranks.

Five lt.    were presented for promotion to captain, of them four intern. and one Sp.
ten serg.  "                    "            "        lieut.   "        two   "      " eight "
nine corp. "                    "            "        serg.    "        four  "      " five  "

To express gratitude, a list of thirty-nine men was displayed by order of the division: nineteen were internationalists and twenty Spanish, but the latter figured almost solely among the noncoms and privates.

| Rank | of whom internationalists | Spanish |
|---|---|---|
| Captains 7 | 7 | — |
| Lieutenants 4    " | 3    " | 1 |
| Sergeants 7    " | 1    " | 6 |
| Corporals 5    " | —    " | 5 |
| Privates 13    " | 6    " | 7 |
| Political workers 3    " | 2    " | 1 |

Six men were recommended for decorations, of whom only two were Spanish. One major and two captains were internationalists; two lieutenants (one of them Spanish) and one Spanish commissar.

I did not accept these lists and suggested to the brigade commander that noncoms and privates be added to it (the recommendation for decorations) and that the percentage of Spanish among the higher ranks (captains) be increased.

The examples cited above on nationality policy in the International Brigades (and I am certain that there are similar instances in all of the international units, without exception) are but a meager percentage of the indicators of our illness. In these, in all of our policies in every area of our work, lies the reason for the low morale of the Spanish in the international units, why they consider themselves offended, why our enemies, almost with impunity, are active among them.

# Document 71

RGVA, f. 35082, op. 1, d. 95, l. 14

ex.—2/14/38 [*sic*]
A.A.

14th Mixed Brigade                                          11 February 1938
"La Marseillaise"

13th Battalion
  Henri Barbusse                        *SPECIAL REPORT*
Commissariat of War

*SUMMARY:*                  Information regarding 14th Brigade reinforcements
            Many drunkards
            Many malcontents
            Many tramps. A few decent sorts lost among the rest, who
must be removed from these surroundings immediately.

The agitators are of two kinds.
Overt agitators. Confessed agitators.

*Ringleaders.*—Silent ringleaders. We mention DONCE Henri in particular; at
the frontier, he asked certain volunteers how and where they would pass.
Two of his friends, whose names I do not know, denounced him at Perpignan.
When searched, his suitcase was filled with anarchist propaganda (pamphlets).

  JAVENEL Marcel supports the ideas of the agents of disorganization and
  drinks a great deal.
  KREITCHNER Joseph, previously in our Brigade Supply Corps. Informer for
  the swindler VOSCO.
  TESSERRE. Inveterate pederast. Previously in the 13th Battalion. Caught red-
  handed at Torres de l'Almeda.

Next are MADANI BEN RANDAN, GUERBOUCH Barconni, SAOULI BEN
CASSEN, MAHOMET BEN AMAR, AMIDOU BEN HOUSSI.

Toffalo, arrested in Villanueva (was perhaps compromised for trafficking in
arms). Two of these individuals claimed to have escaped from Franco. One
appears to have been a sergeant in the fascist army.
One whose name I do not know, wearing a blanket and a sheepskin, face deco-
rated with long paws, engaged in a systematic program of provocation during
MARTY's speech.

## Document 71 *continued*

EXAMPLE: MARTY is fat, he eats chicken while we eat rice.

Another, with a swollen face, has already caused a scandal at TREMBLEQUE. The group of five Portuguese, one of whom claims to have come directly from Portugal; such a claim is not within the capacities of everyone in the group.

*GENERAL IMPRESSIONS.*—A. MARTY's speech was undermined by small groups who questioned the passage about work camps. Marty is wrong to speak of the camps, since he created them himself.

The death threats were not even disguised.

Concerning the Villanueva affair, among the new arrivals there are twelve guys who have escaped from the camp and who have lived by marauding. They were released from prison to be sent to us.

The Villanueva barracks is being tormented by certain individuals who ask if it might not be possible to have an armed revolt there.

My personal impression is that we have a delicate situation to address. It would be good to introduce some trustworthy friends among the new arrivals and have them take down the names of those who seem dubious.

THE COMMISSAR OF WAR.

## Document 72

RGVA, f. 35082, op. 1, d. 95, l. 10

3.ex. - 14/2/38
A.A.

*14th Mixed Brigade*

Lieutenant Colonel DUMONT
to
The commanding officer of the International Brigade Base
*ALBACETE*

REPORT on the REINFORCEMENTS received at the Albacete Base on February eleventh and twelfth, nineteen thirty-eight.

Some infinitely regrettable and exceptionally serious incidents took place while the detachment was in transit (at TREMBLEQUE and MADRID, in particular). At the base's request, an officer and a political commissioner were sent to TREMBLEQUE, but they arrived after the said incidents had occurred and registered complaints from both the fortress commander and the Popular Front Committee: a large number of men got drunk the night before, causing an unprecedented scandal in the city; an assault guard was brutally disarmed and threatened by these drunk men; buildings were damaged, and the entire population was literally terrorized. Finally, while the detachment was marching, sixty men escaped. In MADRID, the events were less serious because of the good arrangements made by the commander of the Pilar de Saragossa quarter.

In our opinion, these events were caused by the following:

1. The convoy was commanded by a Polish captain who had no control over his troops.

2. Radically insufficient supervision—the *nominal* group leaders did not have lists of their groups and did not know the men.

3. TEN political instructors from the base school would have been required; there was not a single one.

4. An even more serious fact: no police convoy was planned.

Moreover, it is important to emphasize the reprehensible dereliction of those who assembled this group of reinforcements.

New arrivals from France and sick, inept inmates released from work camps were placed side by side with soldiers on leave and wounded men returning to the brigade, though the most basic prudence demanded a strict separation by group.

No paperwork was sent to us, even concerning the most dangerous elements, which made it nearly impossible for us to isolate and neutralize the agitators (about ten of whom, having made serious threats against our best comrades, could have been arrested with the help of our intelligence service).

Another sign of serious negligence: many are too old: forty, forty-five, and even forty-eight. One man has proved he has five children. The rule of assignment by nationality has not been respected either: in a preliminary inspection, we discovered two Bulgarians, two Russians, two Czechoslovaks, one Greek, etc. . . . These men, who have barely arrived, ask to be sent to the Balkan Brigade.

Finally, a certain number of them had no blankets; others had no shoes, and all were without plates and silverware.

We notify the base commander of these facts and draw his attention to their extreme gravity, as well as to the negative effects they will doubtless have on the Spanish authorities and the population as a whole, to the detriment of all the International Brigades.

> P. de M. 13 February 1938
> Lieutenant Colonel, Commanding Officer of the
> 14th Brigade.

# Document 73

RGVA, f. 33987, op. 3, d. 1149, ll. 260–265, 268–269

NKO SSSR                                             *Top Secret*
Intelligence Directorate                             Copy N° 1
Worker-Peasant Red Army
Department—
26 July 1938
N° 535307

To the People's Commissar of Defense of the USSR
Marshal of the Soviet Union
*Com. VOROSHILOV*

I am submitting information from Com. Gómez, the head of the organizational base of the international units, about the base's work and the numerical composition of the internationalists who are in Republican Spain.

*Enclosure:* Information on ten pages.

Dep. Chief of the Intelligence Directorate of the RKKA
Sr. Major of State Security                           Gendin

*Information*
About the work of the organizational base of the International Brigades in Spain
(Information from the head of the base, Com. Gómez)

The work being carried out at the organizational base of the International Brigades can be divided into four stages:

First—includes the period from the middle of October 1936 to 1 April 1937. During this time, five International Brigades and other international units were put together, various services organized (sanitary, transportation, quartermaster, paymaster), and the general staff of the base was put together. The people who made up these organizations were, in the first place, internationalist comrades. In February 1937, contingents of Spanish comrades, who were important to the international units, came to the base for the first time. The 15th International Brigade left Albacete in February 1937 as the first with Spanish battalions. Up to and including March 1937, 18,714 internationalist comrades passed through the organizational base for the International Brigades.

In April 1937 a second stage in the organizational base's work began. Organizing complete new brigades became secondary. The basic task was to ensure the dispatch of reinforcements to existing units to replace casualties.

## Document 73 *continued*

The requisite number of people was derived from the contingents of internationalist comrades who continuously arrived from abroad and also from those who were discharged from the hospitals and made up the reserve. For the period from April to July 1937, reinforcements numbering 6,017 men were sent to the front by the base, that is, on average 1,504 men a month. A second, no less important task consisted of supplying the various units that were on the front with necessary matériel. This matériel partially came in from abroad as gifts to the internationalist comrades. All of the internationalists of the various units from the beginning of the foundation of the International Brigades deducted every day a certain amount, which subsequently was fixed at exactly three pesetas. The amounts gathered in this way were used to improve supplies, to buy the matériel mentioned above, and to set up hospital centers, for example, Murcia, Dénia, Benisa, and Benicássim.

In general, the organizational base met the requirements of this work. Of course, over time organizational inadequacies caused by the hasty improvisation of the base began to be felt. It is true that this kind of improvisation was necessary at the beginning, but subsequently this was not eliminated with enough energy. This weakness manifested itself in an extreme bureaucratism. On 31 July 1937, of the free people at the base, 37 percent were employees of the general staff and various services, 23.6 percent guards and transportation, and only 39.4 percent were in various camps for training. Training during this period was relatively weakly developed. There were only two training companies at Madrigueras and Tarazona de la Mancha and a school for officers at Poco Rubio at which short-term courses were given that absolutely did not meet the requirements appropriate for such a school.

The fierce July battles at Brunete, in which almost all the international units participated, somewhat weakened the morale of the forces. This, in connection with the systematic work of the fifth column, resulted in the fact that—at the end of July, beginning of August—Albacete found itself flooded with a large number of more or less demoralized elements who had abandoned their units. The danger threatened [was] that the international units would disintegrate somewhat if we did not manage to hold this in check for the time being.

Lt. Colonel Belov was appointed commander of the base on 1 August. This started the third period. As an urgent measure, a concentration camp for the elements indicated in the preceding paragraph (camp Lukask [*sic*]) was organized. Four thousand men passed through this camp from 1 August to October. With the help of intensive political and military work we managed after two or three months to return up to 80 percent to their units at the front as good antifascist soldiers.

Training at the base was completely reorganized. A training battalion was organized for each brigade as well as a training group for the artillery, which were allocated in the following way:

## Document 73 *continued*

| | | | | |
|---|---|---|---|---|
| Training battalion of the 11th Brigade | | | | Madrigueras |
| " | " | 12th | " | Quintanar de la República |
| " | " | 13th | " | Casas Ibáñez |
| " | " | 14th | " | Villanueva de la Jara |
| " | " | 15th | " | Tarazona |
| Artillery training group | | | | Almansa |

The school for officers at Poco Rubio was reorganized along new lines. Only comrades who had already been present at the front in the rank of officer were permitted to be students. Each course lasted two and a half months. A program based on the one at the military school in Valencia was established.

In every training battalion special schools for sergeants and corporals were organized, and furthermore, special short-term courses for the best marksmen, sighters, and also for work with heavy and light machine guns. For all of these cadres and for the general training of the recruits, a precise, uniform program was established.

At the end of November 1937, six training battalions were organized at Fuente Albilla as the basis for the 129th Brigade, which was being formed that same month.

The success of this reorganization manifested itself in the fact that the number of comrades sent to the front each month increased significantly.

During this third stage, that is, from 1 August to 15 November 1937, the average number of comrades sent to the front rose to 2,223. There is no doubt that the training these comrades received was better and more thorough in comparison to the preceding periods.

Even so, during the third stage a slow reorganization of the general staff and individual services of the organizational base was begun. The result was that after 15 November 1937, only 21 percent worked in the general staff and its services, 14.5 percent guards and [transportation], and 64.5 percent were in training. The organization of the general staff, including the various central services, was during this stage still the weakest point of the general organization of the base. However, even then it was impossible to talk about a genuine general staff organization or to say that its work was normal. On 15 November 1937 Lt. Colonel Com. Belov ceased being the head of the base, and it came under my authority from that date.

Thus began the fourth and last stage of the organizational base's work. After several days the War Ministry detailed several professional Spanish officers to be at the disposal of the base for work in the general staff. In the first place, thanks to the wonderful work of Colonel Verdu-Verdu, the chief of the general staff, the reorganization was finished in February 1938—a quartermaster service was organized that completely met the standards of the people's forces and that satisfied everything that might be required of it. The percentage of those working in the general staff and its services fell to 18.2 percent and as guards and in [transportation] to 11.2 percent at the same time as the percentage of soldiers passing through training rose to 70.6 percent. We also managed to reduce the number of officers and soldiers in the general staff.

The proof of the quality [of these changes] was the fact that during the difficult months of February, March, and April 1938, we managed to transfer in the shortest time [possible] brigades that had suffered significant casualties and that urgently required reinforcements. During the period from 15 November 1937 to 1 May 1938, the base sent 19,472 comrades to the front, that is, a large number during these five and one-half months of the first stage of setting up the International Brigades.

The evacuation of the organizational base to Catalonia by an order of April 1938 was carried out in accordance with the order in a four-day period without any special incident, and more than 8,000 men were transferred to Catalonia, among them almost 3,500 wounded and sick, and a large amount of matériel. This is evidence that with the foundation of the organizational base, an organization that could meet the most difficult requirements was created

Correct: Colonel Grechnev

*Information*

About the comrades who were sent to the front and who passed through the organizational base at Albacete.

| Information by month | No. of volunteers | Average per month | Total |
|---|---|---|---|
| A. | | | |
| Up to & inc. 37 March | 18,714 | 3,415 | 18,714 |
| April | 701 | | |
| May | 1,339 | | |
| June | 2,066 | | |
| July | 1,911 | | |
| | 6,017 | 1,504 | 6,017 |
| B. | | | |
| August | 1,328 | | |
| September | 2,638 | | |
| October | 2,432 | | |
| 1–15 November | 1,383 | | |
| | 7,781 | 2,223 | 7,781 |
| C. | | | |
| 16–30 November | 2,444 | | |
| December | 882 | | |
| January 1938 | 1,339 | | |
| February | 3,514 | | |
| March | 7,033 | | |
| April | 4,310 | | |
| | 19,472 | 3,540 | 19,472 |

Total number of comrades sent to the front who went through the organizational base of the International Brigades                    *52,049*

*Note:* In the total sum of 52,049 are included the wounded who repeatedly passed through the organizational base.

## Document 73 *continued*

*Information*

About the numerical composition of the internationalists.

| By nationality | | Up to 30 April 1938 | | Available personnel on 31/3/38 | |
|---|---|---|---|---|---|
| | | *Sent home* | *Dead and missing* | *Internationalists in various units* | |
| Germans | 2,180 | 189 | 308 | Base | 1,259 |
| Americans | 2,274 | 337 | 276 | Train. battn. | 1,467 |
| Austrians | 846 | 79 | 138 | Almansa and others | 1,104 |
| Balkans | 2,056 | 54 | 96 | Representatives | 145 |
| Baltic states | 862 | 17 | 179 | 15th Division | 17 |
| Belgians | 1,701 | 330 | 185 | 35th Division | 215 |
| Canadians | 510 | 51 | 71 | 45th Division | 388 |
| Czechs | 1,046 | 142 | 133 | DESA | 727 |
| Scandinavians | 662 | 92 | 91 | Artillery | 873 |
| French | 8,778 | 2,301 | 942 | Battn. air defense | 82 |
| Dutch | 586 | 82 | 42 | 11th Brigade | 1,134 |
| Hungarians | 510 | 40 | 56 | 12th Brigade | 826 |
| English | 1,806 | 460 | 124 | 13th Brigade | 1,293 |
| Italians | 2,908 | 335 | 526 | 14th Brigade | 1,568 |
| Poles | 3,034 | 240 | 466 | 15th Brigade | 982 |
| Portuguese | 132 | —— | —— | 129th Brigade | 992 |
| Swiss | 406 | 46 | 78 | Hospital staff | 559 |
| Others | 1,072 | 267 | 864 | Hospitalized | 2,361 |
| Total: | 31,369 | 5,062 | 4,575 | Total: | 15,992 |

[all totals circled by Voroshilov]

*Conclusion:*

| | |
|---|---|
| Total arrivals | 31,969 [*sic*] |
| Present on 31.III.38 | 15,992 |
| Difference | 15,377 |
| Of them badly wounded | 5,062 |
| Dead | 4,575 |
| Difference | 5,740 |

# Document 74

RGVA, f. 33987, op. 3, d. 1149, ll. 284–285

To Comrade Voroshilov

The Politburo of the Spanish Communist party together with Com. Marty put before the Comintern the question of evacuating the volunteers from Spain, who form part of the International Brigades. The grounds on which the CC of the Spanish Communist party bases its proposal are the following:

Negrín insists on bringing out the volunteers who are still in the ranks. During two years of war the volunteers of the International Brigades suffered great casualties. Of the overall number of international volunteers in Spain, 31,000 men, only 10,000 remain, and there are no more than 5,000 soldiers in the ranks. The soldiers of the International Brigades are extremely exhausted by the continuous battles, their military efficiency has fallen off, and the Spanish divisions have significantly outstripped them in fighting value and discipline. The influx of new volunteers is negligible, and the International Brigades have actually ceased to exist as special units. The evacuation of the foreign volunteers will not affect the condition of the Spanish People's Army. Lately Germany and Italy have intensified their efforts to spread their spies under the guise of volunteers. Because of this, Negrín proposes that it is possible to let the volunteers go without damaging the defense of the Spanish Republic. This measure, in Negrín's opinion, will demonstrate the growing strength of the Republican Army and the confidence of the Republican government in victory. Along with this, it will create a situation that is advantageous to the Republican government, by putting pressure on the English and French governments over the question of cleansing Spain of the fascist interventionists, and will ruin Franco's argument that the government of the Spanish Republic also has resorted to the aid of foreign volunteers.

For all these reasons, the Politburo of the Spanish Communist party tables a resolution about the possibility of evacuating the volunteers at the right moment, when both the military and international environments will be favorable. After discussion of this question, we are inclined to accept the proposal of the Politburo of the Spanish Communist party.

We ask your advice and instructions.

G. Dimitrov
D. Manuilsky

29/8/38.
P.S. We have already sent this letter to Com. Stalin.

[Marginalia by Voroshilov:] Inquire of our comrades in Spain. KV. 7/9/38

# Document 75

RGVA, f. 33987, op. 3, d. 1149, ll. 308–314

NKO SSSR                                                    *Top Secret*
Intelligence Directorate                                    Copy N° 2
Worker-Peasant Red Army
Department—
N° 535789
18 November 1938

To the People's Commissar of Defense of the USSR
Marshal of the Soviet Union
*Com. Voroshilov*

I submit a memorandum by Colonel Com. Sverchevsky (Walter) concerning the international soldiers in connection with disbanding the international units in Spain

Dep. Chief of the Intelligence Directorate of the RKKA
Div.[ision] Com.[mander]
Orlov

REMARKS CONCERNING THE FORMER INTERNATIONAL SOLDIERS IN CONNECTION
WITH DISBANDING THE INTERNATIONAL UNITS IN SPAIN.

Among the total number of questions put on the agenda in connection with disbanding the international units and the departure of the volunteer internationalists from Spain, I would like to stimulate interest among the appropriate institutions in one factor which, given certain circumstances [and] if not enough importance is attached to it, may become the source of additional difficulties for some fraternal Communist parties and may to a certain extent perhaps affect the interests of our country.

I have in mind that now one apparently ought to expect a sharp intensification of the enemy's intrigues in the French international milieu.

a) Even while the internationalists were in the ranks of the Republican People's Army, secret police agents of almost all nations, and to no less an extent the Trotskyists as well (or rather these were one and the same), were trying to carry out and did carry out demoralizing work in the international units. In a memorandum submitted about three months ago, I cited concrete particulars about the sabotage activities of the fascist elements in the army, taken from the experience of [my] struggle in just one division, the 35th. There is no need to repeat that here, but one may categorically affirm that every single one of the other international units to a greater or lesser extent was the objective of the "concern" of various secret police establishments and counterrevolutionary organizations and groups. Both the organizational base at Albacete itself and any of the International Brigades and units might be cited as no less analogous examples of the enemy's attempts to discredit and weaken the strength of the international movement in Spain. To reckon that the disbanding of the international units will also automatically end the enemy's work among the internationalists would mean, at the very least, a patent underestimation of the adversary. On the contrary. It seems to me that it is exactly now that one ought to expect pressure from them, since the situation in which many groups of internationalists found themselves or may find themselves in France creates highly favorable conditions for the work of class enemies.

b) The recall of the volunteer internationalists from Spain pointedly sets before them the problem of their future. Except for the French, Scandinavians, and Anglo-Americans, who have a real possibility of legally returning to their countries, the situation of the other nationalities, especially the Austro-Germans, Balkans, Poles, Czechs, and some of the Italians, cannot fail to provoke in them a feeling of alarm about their future. None of them will probably escape from Paris, and staying in France without the right to residence and work—for the French government will hardly be inclined to grant them either the first or the second—is fraught with the completely realistic danger that dissatisfaction, depression, and a loss of prospects will arise among some part of the internationalists in these groups. The enemy could easily profit by this and attract to his side the least steady elements among the former international soldiers. It would be naive to suppose that in and of itself the heroic not-so-distant past and the glorious struggle in Spain will provide enough immunity to unconditionally guarantee the internationalist mass against the penetration of the disease-carrying bacillus into its organism. The international movement can and must be regarded as the highest manifestation of progressive humanity's international solidarity with the heroic peoples of Spain. One can confirm that the expensive cost of six thousand dead and the blood of twenty thousand wounded and crippled internationalists in this just antifascist war tied the tight and lasting knot of a fraternal union of workers on the Spanish front lines; one can and must confirm that with the exception of a small group of rogues, adventurers, and scoundrels, a hugely overwhelming majority of the internationalists in Spain were fulfilling their duty as revolutionaries and were conscious of the need for an armed defense of freedom and of their national and class interests. At the same time, however, one should also not forget that the internationalists were a mixed bag, both socially and politically; that there was vacillation all around them; nor the fact that the Spanish Republic appeared to many international soldiers to be their future homeland, with which they associated their personal interests and future. Hence, because they have not had enough political clarification about this (and, unfortunately, political work in the international units was in no way among the [army's] most progressive sectors), the necessity even if only of a temporary withdrawal outside the borders of Spain may be interpreted by a fairly significant portion of the former soldiers with feelings of chagrin as an undeserved insult, of alarm about an unknown tomorrow, and of fear when faced with a return to the wandering of their previous emigrant life with all of its difficulties and privations.

c) The enemy is already trying to exploit these moods. For example: one of our comrades who returned from Spain related that among the internationalists gathered for departure in the Barcelona region persistent rumors circulated that after the obligatory quarantine in France, they will (supposedly) send them not to where they lived before they came to Spain, but to their place of birth. It is not hard to guess what sort of impression these patently provocative rumors might evoke among the internationalists if they are not immediately countered by an extensive clarification on the part of the authoritative institutions and individuals. In Paris, as the former commander of 13th Brigade writes from there, these characters have gone to work attempting to portray the disbanding of the International Brigades as punishment for the "criminal activity" of the internationalist leaders. In both cases, the completely obvious enemy objective is to cause nervousness among the internationalists, to demoralize them, and to weaken their resistance. By the way, both of these examples are also evidence of the fact that, apparently, the former soldiers have not been furnished with an adequate political understanding of the steps and measures of the Spanish Republican government.

There is no doubt that the struggle for the internationalists is only beginning and that it will spread wider and deeper after the departure from Spain of all of the former participants in the battles of the Republican People's Army.

d) It seems to me that out of the entire group of internationalists, conditions are shaping up most unfavorably for the Poles. Although the problem of organizing and caring for the former soldiers of the international units stands acutely before everyone alike who has been deprived of the legal opportunity to return to his own country, the position of the Polish group is also complicated by the fact that in contrast to the rest they are completely, or almost completely, without a political institution or center that might lavish its guardianship upon them, preserve and educate them, and protect them from dispersing and disintegration. When the Polish Communist party was disbanded—as the Poles in Spain told me—those organizations that earlier had carried out work among the Polish émigrés in France were partially abolished and partially reduced their activity. Under such conditions there is a real threat that the thousands of former frontline soldiers returning from Spain will find themselves left to their own devices. And because in a class society there is no political vacuum, then some part of them may become the booty of our enemies, class or otherwise, or go to reinforce the Poles of the foreign legion. This danger is not ruled out in relation to other internationalist groups as well, but there is no doubt that for the Poles it poses the greatest threat because this nationality right now lacks its own organized political center.

It seems to me that the creation of a special apparatus working within and under the most direct guidance and control of the CPF is the most important task and a condition for preventing a loss of part of the international cadres. It will not be difficult to find people for this. Among the ranks of the International Brigades—including the Polish ones—not a few workers have arisen who by blood have proven their commitment to the revolution and the antifascist struggle. Naturally, such an apparatus ought to attract the intent attention of the Comintern and our special institutions [organs].[11]

I am not in the know on the measures taken to organize and arrange the international soldiers. Undoubtedly everything possible is being done to preserve the valuable cadres who have merited, through their two years of military work, the deep gratitude of the Spanish and their own peoples. Nonetheless, it seemed to me not out of place and necessary to report here my views of the situation as I understand it. I am also obliged to do this by my almost year-and-a-half stay in the international units of the Republican Army, where I saw hundreds and thousands of examples of selfless commitment, courage, and heroism displayed by the soldiers of the International Brigades in numerous battles. Fundamentally, the majority of the former internationalist soldiers are very valuable to the revolution. But the history of class struggle, the examples of the past (the Red frontline soldiers of Germany and the Schutzbund of Austria), and especially the experience of our own day teach that the slightest relaxation of political vigilance, in any sector of the work, inevitably strengthens the enemy. This truth is undoubtedly correct. If the former internationalist volunteers are left without the necessary political care and material support, many soldiers who fought for the revolution yesterday may in the coming class battles be found on the other side of the barricades or be recruited for dirty and base espionage-sabotage work against the USSR. This cannot be permitted.

Colonel K. Sverchevsky

20 November 1938

## The People's Army and the Soviet Advisers

Sverchevsky's reservations about the reliability of the internationalists were part of larger Soviet fears of fascist penetration into the Spanish army. These fears were detailed by Sverchevsky in **Document 76**, a listing of thirty instances of "sabotage," "terrorism," "wrecking," and "treachery" by fascist agents and their Spanish or internationalist accomplices. The difference between earlier descriptions of these sorts of problems in the Spanish army and Sverchevsky's report is enormous and has far-reaching implications. During the first year of the war, Soviet advisers blamed Spanish military difficulties on lack of experience and technology, poor planning, the treachery of a few unreliable regular officers, and the work of "Trotskyists" or radical anarchists. Sverchevsky saw the problem as much more insidious. In his opinion, the entire army was riddled with agents who, supported by Germany, Italy, and the fifth column, freely worked to undermine Republican operations. In his report there are no coincidences: an officer who ordered a unit to the front without a machine-gun belt was not simply incompetent—he was part of a vast conspiracy; the rivalry of Lister and Modesto, admittedly of long standing and caused by envy, was somehow part of this conspiracy; incorrect telegrams sent to Sverchevsky were not the result of miscommunication, but the enemy's attempt to distract him; internationalists' demands to return home, Spanish resentment of the foreigners, distrust of the Soviet advisers, and mass desertion were blamed on fascist agitation; the enemy even poisoned chocolate to disable Republican pilots. Of special interest to Americans is the news here that even Robert Merriman, first commander of the Lincoln Battalion and then chief of staff of the 15th Brigade, fell under suspicion for his contact with the American military attaché.

There are probably two reasons for the transformation of Soviet explanations of military incompetence. During 1937 all of the problems that had plagued the new Spanish army had supposedly been dealt with. The People's Army was well trained, had good commanders (selected by the Soviets themselves), and was armed with Soviet technology. The Soviets had crushed the power of the "Trotskyists" and anarchists and were now in control of the war

effort. Yet the Republicans continued to lose. The only rational explanation for committed Stalinists was that the army lacked the
requisite ideological purity to win the war. They truly believed that
the tide would turn only after they had purged the enemy within.
The other reason for the transformation was the increasingly paranoid world that Stalin had created. Historians who have studied
the Soviet Union of the thirties have shown how Stalin's belief that
there were no coincidences, that all adversities were intentional
and somehow linked, led to the construction of elaborate theories
about vast conspiracies, all of which led back to the ultimate
source of all evil: Trotsky.[12] In Sverchevsky's report both these explanations come together in his argument that the army had to be
cleansed of the hundreds of fascist sympathizers and Trotskyists
who had somehow wormed their way into the military.

It was not just the Spanish and the internationalists who had
problems, however. Sverchevsky, as usual, was not backward in
admitting that the Soviets had committed serious errors themselves. In **Document 77,** he not only detailed the many mistakes the
advisers had made but also showed just how much in control the
Soviets were by late 1937. Now problems with the planning and
execution of operations could not be blamed on the Spanish but
were instead the fault of the military advisers from the Soviet
Union. It was they who were in command of the attacks at Brunete,
Teruel, and elsewhere and who had, therefore, to take responsibility when these operations failed. Their greatest error was to become hypnotized by their last victory, Guadalajara, and refuse to
believe that attacks could come from any other sector. Yet there is
an element of self-deception in Sverchevsky's evaluation, for he
then proceeded to list as one of the main errors of the Soviets this
very habit of claiming that they were commanding units, that they
had ordered "their" forces to attack or defend a position. What
was the truth here? In his discussion of this "error," Sverchevsky
noted that the largest problems with this sort of "lavish fantasy"
were (first) that the Spanish took exception to it and (second) that
the advisers, while taking credit for successes, declined to take responsibility for failures. In fact, in another section he deplored
those advisers who *refused* to "actively interfere in situations,
changing them in a direction that we desire." The most important

lesson that the Soviets had to learn was not to lord it over their supposed comrades, an error into which many of the advisers had fallen. Instead, they had to be more "cultured" (that is, civilized), less rude and obtrusive, and willing to try to guide their charges more patiently and covertly.

The obtrusive interference of the advisers was especially apparent in the security services. Scholars of the Civil War have already detailed how the Soviets came to dominate the secret police and intelligence institutions, particularly the Servicio de Investigación Militar (SIM).[13] As outlined earlier, the SIM had been set up by Indalecio Prieto in the summer of 1937 as an independent intelligence service that would be loyal to the government alone, rather than to the Soviets. Within a few weeks the Communists had infiltrated and taken over the SIM. By late 1938, the situation had become so intolerable to many Spanish policy makers that even Negrín felt compelled to ask the Soviets to be more discreet. **Document 78** is a report by Marchenko, the Soviet chargé d'affaires, to Maxim Litvinov on a conversation he had had with Negrín in which the Spanish leader expressed his concerns about the situation in the intelligence services. Negrín's solution—to have the new head of the NKVD in Spain work through him rather than try to maintain direct contacts with the SIM—shows that Negrín disapproved not of Soviet control of these services but of the clumsy, obvious way in which the advisers went about exercising it. Like Sverchevsky, the chargé d'affaires had to admit that there was some justification for Negrín's complaints, and he wrote that men who had been in charge of intelligence work had not understood how necessary it was to change their "methods of work" before the Spanish demanded it.

# Document 76

RGVA, f. 33987, op. 3, d. 1149, ll. 211–226

NKO SSSR                                                          *Top Secret*
Intelligence Directorate                                         Copy N° 3
Worker-Peasant Red Army
Department—
2 August 1938
N° 535343

To the People's Commissar of Defense of the USSR
Marshal of the Soviet Union
*Com. Voroshilov*

I am submitting a report by Colonel Sverchevsky (Div.[ision] Com.[mander] Walter), who is returning from a special mission, on the work of our people in "X" and on espionage work by fascist agents in Republican Spain.

We will put into effect a number of Com. Sverchevsky's proposals, set forth in the first section, when sending our people to "X."

*Enclosure:* Two reports consisting of twenty-eight pages.

Dep. Chief of the Intelligence Director of the RKKA
Senior Major of State Security
Gendin

*ESPIONAGE WORK BY FASCIST AGENTS IN THE REPUBLICAN ARMY*
(Report by Com. Colonel Sverchevsky)

By means of this note I would like to draw your attention to what is, in my opinion, an under-utilization of the events in Spain by our intelligence and counterintelligence institutions [organs]. Meanwhile, these events are presenting us with such rich material on the character, form, and methods of the enemy's work within the People's Army (and no less in the rear) that direct participation of our colleagues in the struggle against fascist agents and a study of the facts, it seems to me, might to a large degree allow us to improve the organization of our intelligence and special institutions [organs].

The active participation of Germany and Italy in the Spanish war, with their rich experience and means of intelligence; the presence in the Republican rear of a powerful, organized "fifth column"; the complexity of the political situation of the people's antifascist front; the weakness, inexperience, and poverty of the protective institutions [organs] of the Republican government and military command; all of this taken together creates exceptionally favorable conditions for fascist agents, spies, provocateurs, saboteurs, and wreckers to work almost with impunity.

477

## Document 76 *continued*

The enemy is seeking to penetrate everywhere and in any way possible. They are trying to use every loophole, to penetrate every fissure, to use every difficulty to weaken, through their demoralizing activity, the military efficiency of the units, to reduce the fighters' confidence in their command, to convince our forces of the numerical and technical superiority of the enemy, to prove that the tactical situation and outcome of the war are hopeless, and so on and so forth. In addition, the enemy profited by the frictions between nationalities within the international units, aggravating national antagonisms, striving to keep and deepen the abyss between the international units and the Spanish, interfering with study, stirring up the command, agitating for the return home of the internationalists, planting secret agents and provocateurs among the internationalists.

The forms and methods of this activity were very diverse, from spreading rumors, stirring up dissatisfaction, slander, and counterrevolutionary agitation to public speeches, wrecking, and the organization of terrorist acts.

Below I shall venture to mention a number of simple, unsystematic particulars from those retained in my memory that may give some idea of the range of this enemy activity.

1. The 10th machine-gun battalion of the 14th International Brigade was sent to the front in December 1936 with its thirty-six heavy Colt machine guns [but] without a single machine-gun belt. It was established that the belts were issued by the International Brigade depot, but some senior officer had ordered them to be left at the Albacete station, explaining to the battalion command, which had little experience, that they would receive a complete set of Colt belts at the front. With a great deal of difficulty they succeeded in bringing them from Albacete only on the eve of the brigade's first battle.

2. In the 14th Brigade, on the night between the first and second days of the battle of Lopera, up to five hundred soldiers and some of the officers were taken from the line, and, in an organized way, all of them went to the rear, to Andújar. They were brought back to the front only with great difficulty. An investigation showed that this was the work of Andujaran anarchists and agents of the fifth column who had penetrated the brigade the first day it was in the city. With promises of money, women, wine, with agreements and threats and by gambling on the inevitable difficulties of that moment, they succeeded in getting that good battalion to abandon its positions.

3. On 1 January 1937, by sentence of the brigade tribunal, De LaSalle, the commander of the 10th Battalion 14th Brigade was shot for demoralizing the battalion, organizing panic and desertion (by the way, in 1919 he worked in Varna against the USSR, holding at that time the post of resident of the French general staff's Deuxième Bureau). Among the soldiers on that same day this sentence was commented upon as an execution [carried out] because De LaSalle (supposedly) "had forced a soldier to attack," which legitimized the

positions of those elements who had carried out agitation against the offensive from the first days of the brigade's founding.

4. At the very beginning of January last year, I received two telegrams from Paris addressed to me. The first of these announced that my two children had fallen ill, and the following day the same kind of telegram from the same source informed me about the death of my daughter. The objective was clear—to distract my attention away from the brigade.

5. On the eve of the start of the Las Rozas operation, the German company of the 10th machine-gun battalion of the 14th Brigade mutinied. The mutiny was the result of agitation by hostile elements who used the difficulties of transferring a brigade from the Andalusian front at Madrid. We succeeded in persuading the company [to continue]: the agitators hid themselves.

6. When the brigade was granted a three-week respite after Las Rozas and I ordered the brigade to get down to studying, rumors immediately began to spread that I supported Franco, and as proof instances of my (supposed) telephone conversations with fascists were cited. When the political department carried out a struggle against these opinions, the commissar of the brigade (Com. André Esler, now a member of the CC CPF and chairman of the Committee for Aid to Spain) was proclaimed to be my accomplice. The studying, thanks to the appropriate agitation, was interpreted as an attempt at "army democratism" and as Walter's desire to introduce fascism. For an entire day and a half the majority of the brigade sabotaged the order; subunits did not begin studies, an epidemic of card playing broke out among the soldiers (which we had not observed earlier), and drunkenness. It took a good deal of effort and drastic measures to secure obedience. The temporary commander of battalion 13, Captain Cavian, was one of the agents who was later exposed.

7. During the urgent transfer of the brigade from Torrelodones to Jarama in the middle of February last year, the Madrid anarchists got the lead 12th Battalion, where the commander of the battalion was the anarchist De Mujen, drunk, and it was not a military unit that arrived at Araganda but rather a drunken mob, which attempted to organize a massacre of the inhabitants and was absolutely incapable that day of any sort of action. The battalion had to be driven out of the city with pistols, and the following day it was with difficulty forced to go to the front line.

8. The first month and a half, the 14th Brigade was armed with obsolete rifles of various types, and its machine-gun equipment consisted of museum-piece Colts, Shoshes, and Lewises. This circumstance provided the basis for agitation against the Spanish, who had supplied the internationalists with these old things on purpose, they said, so that they could be wiped out by the fascists more easily. At the same time as this first "argument" [appeared] among the soldiers, a theory was spread around about the futility of cleaning and caring for these weapons and also that tactical study was unnecessary, for, they said, it makes no difference how much you study or clean these

weapons—no one was going to win with them and even fighting [with them] is useless.

9. On 6 February 1937, the day the brigade celebrated receiving banners from Jaén worker and antifascist organizations, a Spanish officer from the "De la PUA" Battalion, which was at that time part of the 14th Brigade, was killed by a shot out of the blue. And after a few hours, as if in response, a French sergeant was seriously wounded in the stomach. Beyond any doubt, both of these terrorist acts were aimed at provoking an armed conflict between the Spanish and the internationalists.

10. After Jarama, the fascists skillfully used the fact that many recruiting bureaus in France were giving guarantees to those signing up that they were going to Spain for three months only, after which they were to be replaced by new [men] (moreover at many bureaus volunteers were promised as a form of bonus the right to travel to the USSR after their return from Spain). Under the influence of fascist agitation among the internationalists, for the most part French, there began a mass demand for discharge from the army and leave to go home. Moreover, aircraft began to scatter leaflets addressed to the French, in which Com. Marty was declared to be a traitor and enemy of the people, and everyone wishing to go home was called upon to apply to the French consulate to receive a foreign passport and money. As a result, we had a great deal of desertion; a significant number of French from the 13th Brigade, which was then not far from Valencia, made off toward home on a French steamship; the French consul in Valencia began to openly visit the brigade, and a brothel in Madrid that was supplying all those who wished to leave Spain with French passports was exposed. Before we intervened, this "institution" alone had issued more than 250 passports.

11. After I was appointed division commander (at Jarama), agitation began among the officers under me in the 5th and 17th Spanish Brigades in favor of insubordination against the "foreigners." This intensified after I arrested the commander of the 17th Brigade (the brigade at that time was called "De la PUA"), the impostor Lt. Colonel Carrasco. Things got especially tense when I announced in a divisional order a reprimand against Lieutenant Soto, a Spanish artillery officer, for cowardice. The head of artillery in my division fell ill to protest this, the commander of a battery as well, and the head of the corps artillery resigned. At that same time, fascist newspapers appeared in our trenches with a call to the Spanish to drive out of their midst the "Marxist foreigners, agents of Moscow." Only the personal and energetic intervention of Corps Commander Burillo, who was completely on my side, and the aid of the corps' political institutions helped to relieve the tension and expose some of the organizers of this fascist campaign.

12. During the Segovia operation (end of May, beginning of July last year), the 21st Brigade was attached to me to reinforce the division. I subordinated one of the battalions of this brigade, I believe the 3rd, to Durán, the comman-

der of the 69th Brigade. He sent [his brigade], with the battalion, into an attack on Hill "Cabla Grande." The fascist cell in the 21st Brigade battalion killed its battalion commander, and about twenty men went over to the enemy with weapons in hand. The brigade command knew about the existence of this fascist group but did not take any measures to liquidate it.

13. In May last year a mass poisoning of soldiers in the 69th Spanish Brigade took place. Earlier, the same thing happened in the 12th International Brigade, where poison was discovered in the chocolate sent to the fighters. This was confirmed by a laboratory chemical analysis.

14. Before Brunete I received new personnel for brigades, including the 108th, which had been formed two months before. The following particulars speak clearly about the degree and dimensions of its demoralization as a result of fascist work:

a) On the eve of the operation, the entire first (not the second) battalion of this brigade had to be handed over to the 11th Brigade, supposedly to reinforce the latter but really from fear that at the first clash it would surrender. By my command the battalion was divided up by platoon among the companies of the 11th Brigade.

b) Because of this very same apprehension, I removed an additional six heavy and twelve light machine guns from the brigade, under the pretext of needing to create a machine-gun company within the division.

c) On the first night of the operation, it was necessary to disarm and arrest the entire company of one of the brigade's battalions, and eighteen men from it, led by a lieutenant and three noncoms, were shot by sentence of an army tribunal for organizing the company's going over to the enemy.

d) The division commissar and brigade commander (anarchists) were shot by Lister on the second night of the operation for refusal to obey a military order and for persuading their command staff to surrender.

e) Moreover, over the course of twenty-two days, during which the brigade was on the front line, up to twenty enemy agents were exposed and removed from the division. A good half of these were officers.

15. The surrender of Brunete and the flight of many brigades were, to a significant extent, the result of a panic sown by the "fifth column" that the fascists had gotten around our forces. This was repeated to a much greater extent during Saragossa in the 24th Division and during the March battles of this year.

16. The 35th Division's sanitary unit registered several instances of wounded internationalists who were in Spanish hospitals for medical treatment dying because of maliciously negligent or completely unnecessary surgical operations and diagnoses and methods of treating the sick that were patently the work of wreckers.

17. During the siege of Belchite, the fascistlike command of the 12th Corps deluged the eastern front with lying and slanderous telegrams about the rob-

bery and shootings that, supposedly, the 15th International Brigade was engaged in, and about the impossibility of "bringing it up to the front line." At the same time, they provoked clashes between the anarchist elements and the internationalists and advised the commander of the 153rd Spanish Brigade to sabotage my orders. This lie was so insolent and obvious that it even drove the command of the 5th Corps, which is not usually prone to put itself out for us, crazy, and Modesto then started a real row with Gen. Pozas, the front commander, over this and sent a very sharply worded telegram to Gen. Rojo demanding that the culprits be called to account.

By the way, our leading comrades, to whom I turned for assistance to help me end this dirty and undoubtedly fascist campaign against the internationalists, expressed a startling indifference to my request, and Leonidov (Yushkevich) even announced to me that he "would not permit any division commander to get excited and speak in a heightened tone with him, a front adviser" (verbatim).

18. The day that the staff of the 35th Division arrived in Granen, 29 September 1937 (I was at that time appointed corps commander by de Vedao), the password "The scoundrels have arrived" was established by Sánchez Plaza, the head of that city's garrison and the anarchist mayor. The following day it was "Death to foreigners." On the second day of our stay in Granen, they freely let an officer and two privates through to the enemy side. So then on the morning of the third day the fascist air force welcomed us with a bombing. The hostile attitude of the anarchists toward us was expressed in the scattering of POUM literature and newspapers among our units. This called upon our soldiers to go over to work for them, where the pay was higher and the service easier.

19. During the typhoid epidemic in October 1937, which carried off up to a thousand soldiers in just two brigades, when we began to disinfect the water with special chemical tablets, rumors began to spread among the soldiers of the 32nd Spanish Brigade and partly also in the 11th International Brigade that the "internationalist command" was poisoning the water, which led to a number of instances of refusal to use it for food and drink. Only after the brigade command staff, beginning with the brigade commander, publicly and demonstratively, in the soldiers' view, first drank several times from the water that we had purified, and the brigade political section organized and gave a special talk about the harm [caused by] unpurified well water, only then did we succeed in overcoming the enemy's agitation.

20. In the autumn of last year in Barcelona, a Trotskyist-fascist conspiracy was uncovered. Its goal, along with other missions, was to kick Prieto, Modesto, and me out. Two curious features characteristic of the weakness of the Republicans' security institutions can be detected in this incident.

a) The day the conspiracy was published, but before the newspapers had received [the news], an adviser of the 3rd Jarama Corps, Com. Valsky, told me that approximately ten to fifteen days before this, in Jarama, a soldier had tried to go over to the enemy at night, but he got lost in the darkness and came back to our positions, taking them for the fascist ones. He explained to our captain who he was, explained to whom he was going, told about the organization that had sent him to the enemy, gave the secret signal, and, by the way, told also about the fact that all of this was prepared to get rid of Modesto, who was in Madrid, and Walter, whose arrival was expected any day. This latter indicates that there was a member of this organization close to me, in the division staff, for I really did intend to leave for Madrid. And thus despite the fact that the interrogation of the arrested Joaquín Roca, who first testified about the conspiracy, took place on 22 September, despite the incident cited by Valsky that took place about 10 October, neither Modesto nor I was warned by anyone, if only so that some kind of measures could have been taken.

b) More than that, the evening of the same day, when the conspiracy was published in the newspapers, someone shot at me in the courtyard of the home at which I was staying during my visit to Madrid. The shot came from the neighboring cottage, where three characters without definite occupation were living. It was well known that they sympathized with the fascists and that the brother of one of them was shot by the Republicans on the first day of the uprising for taking part on the side of the rebels with weapon in hand. When the police were informed about the attempt on me, they confined themselves to checking their documents, found everything in order, and left them alone.

21. Several days before my departure from the division, I was told by Com. Gallo, the commissar of the International Brigades, and then in more detail by Com. Hans, commander of the 45th Division, about a large-scale Trotskyist spy and terrorist organization that had been exposed in the 14th Brigade. This had branches in all of the rest of the international units and was connected with some kind of center in Barcelona. By the way, one of its main tasks was to arrange the murder of Sanje Hans, the commander of the 14th Brigade, me, and a number of other workers. I immediately called comrades in the NKVD in Barcelona about this (about which, by the way, Com. Marty was subsequently very displeased), but they turned the matter over to one of the internationalists—Stefanovich—whom even the command of the 14th Brigade would not allow to get close to them, and Brigade Commander Sanje took it upon himself to do the investigation. He went to work so ardently and clumsily that the arrested man, a French lieutenant, quickly died during interrogation, taking with him the secret of the organization.

22. The veiled hostility between Lister and Modesto is widely known in the People's Army. Petty, personal factors—envy and rank—are at the bottom of this. Modesto resents the fact that Lister and not he became commander of the Fifth Regiment, so resoundingly known in its time, and that Lister became a commander earlier than he did. Lister in his turn took offense at the fact that

Modesto quickly rose above the level of division and had already received a corps by the end of March of this year. Both of them have provided themselves with special people to shadow and collect compromising material on one another. Modesto has used most colorful language about Lister, and the latter has answered Modesto's criticism as a commander with a stubborn unwillingness to carry out the orders of his corps commander, as happened at Brunete and especially in the Saragossa operation. The abyss between Modesto and Lister, it has turned out, was deepened by the interference of fascist elements who roused mutual hostility between the two and thus weakened the strength of the 5th Corps. At the end of February, [people] demanded that a special meeting be set up with the representatives of the Politburo (Lister, Modesto, Campesino, Delage, me, and, from the CC, Antón and Mije) to reconcile the two. Formally they are now friends, but knowing both, it is impossible to doubt that this friendship is but a temporary truce to [allow them to] accumulate strength for the next opening of military action between them, especially if the enemy worms his way into this incident again.

23. The French military attaché in Spain proposed to Putsou, my former second in command, that he work for the Deuxième Bureau. He asked him, to start with, about providing him with models and blueprints for Republican automatic weapons. Merriman, the chief of staff of the 15th Brigade (who was captured at Batea), was openly friendly with the American military attaché, and the latter from time to time gave Merriman "small presents," such as his leather sleeveless jacket, which supposedly he had worn during the world war. In the very same 15th Brigade a certain Captain Watkins, an English career officer, had worked for a long time. There was almost no doubt that he had connections with the "Intelligence Service," but when I wanted to approach him stealthily in April of this year, Watkins took refuge in the protection of the secretary of the English CP, Pollitt, who then took him away to Barcelona, where he was immediately transferred to an English destroyer.

By the way, this same Watkins managed to so win over the soldiers in the English battalion that they organized among themselves a collection of pesetas to buy him hard currency. The brigade command found out about this only after he had left the unit.

24. And during last year's Saragossa operation and at Teruel our lines were showered from the air with fascist leaflets which appealed, for the most part, to the young Spanish units with the suggestion that they surrender because "your lack of training"—the leaflets said—"and lack of preparation for modern warfare condemn you to be cannon fodder." At the same time increased agitation against the command began among the soldiers. The command was deliberately, they said, "throwing untrained soldiers into the slaughter."

25. 31 December 1937, a difficult, panic-stricken day when the Republican forces fled from the front and almost cleaned out Teruel itself, was to a significant degree the result of a panic organized by fascist agents among our units.

An order from Gen. Rojo openly spoke of this. In it were the facts about the panic and the shooting of seven sergeants who had confessed that they were agents of the fifth column (unfortunately, the Spanish high command, as usual, did not dare to deal with the more serious and dangerous agents in their midst).

26. Our defeats in the March battles, which resulted in an outlet to the sea for the rebels and interventionists, in addition to all of the other general military-political reasons, is explained by the immense and intensive activity and work of the defeatist elements and agents of the fifth column within the Republican units. The most unbelievable and disturbing rumors about our supposed hopeless situation and the treachery of the commanders got out of hand among the soldiers and command staff; they carried out almost open agitation for surrendering and going over to the enemy and forcibly taking their officers and commissars with them; the soldiers were persuaded to throw away their weapons because, they said, every armed [man] caught by the fascists would definitely be shot. The Spanish soldiers in our international units were called upon to break away from the internationalists and not to stay with them because, if they were captured [with them], death threatened them as it did all internationalists; quite often during the battle, at the first shots, hysterical shouts about us being surrounded by the enemy would ring out. Those were the days when the most stinking, fetid, treacherous activity by all the bastards of all shades and colors flourished the most, and it was exactly this that was the reason the forces were so depressed and why their morale fell, so that it was enough sometimes for one lying shout about the approach of the enemy, especially his cavalry or tanks, for the units to flee in panic.

After Caspe, I organized a purge in my division and drove out the hostile and defeatist elements, beginning with the division staff, in which Major Cheverdat was shot for repeated organization of rabbitlike panics. I also cleaned out the brigades, most of all the 13th, but in place of those removed we received new reinforcements from Albacete, among whom were many adventuristic, hostile [men] and some who were simply criminals, the result of which was that in the second stage of the battle of Gandesa our ranks were no less infested than earlier. After the withdrawal to the left side of the Ebro, it was necessary to set up special brigade and division tribunals for another purge of the units.

27. During those same March battles, as earlier at Brunete (18th Corps), Saragossa (24th Division), and Teruel (20th and 22nd Corps), fascist agent-provocateurs widely employed the following modus operandi, which was highly dangerous for us: using the unclear tactical situation, the extreme fatigue and nervousness of the troops, the way that they were scattered around, and most of all the lack of secure communications among the subunits and between the subunits and their commanders, at the tensest and most anxious moment of the battle, unknown officers appeared and, supposedly in the

name of the command, issued orders known to be provocative to retreat and regroup and so on. It is enough to point out that, as a result of the provocations, during the night of 14–15 March the 38th and 139th Brigades scattered from Caspe and sixteen tanks from Lt. Colonel Ressa's group left, opening a path for the enemy to Gandesa. It was only the fortuitous presence there of our division, which had just gotten out of the encirclement, that allowed that city to be held until the approach of units from the 45th Division. Thanks to these same provocative orders, the 31st of the /3rd and the 1st and 100th of the Lister Brigade were withdrawn and left the front at Calaceite, the 12th Garibaldi Brigade deserted its positions at Maella, subunits 11, 14, 15 of the International Brigades fell back and partially scattered on the eve of the surrender of Gandesa, 1 April 1938. At the most acute and crucial moment, part of Modesto's corps artillery was removed from its positions and taken to the rear, supposedly by his order, and that evening at Gandesa, supposedly following my order relayed to the tankers by some captain, six of our T-26 tanks were abandoned by the crews and burned.

During those days the element of provocation represented a significantly greater danger for us, the command, than the living forces and superiority of the enemy.

In a few cases we succeeded in catching the provocateurs red-handed, and they suffered the requisite punishment right then, but the overwhelming majority of the agents, because of the general weakness of the command and the political apparatus and the lack of special institutions [organs], remained undetected and did their base and vile business almost with impunity.

The tricks of the provocateurs were observed on a much greater scale in [illegible].

28. Each of the international units can cite many examples of obvious spies, provocateurs, and terrorists exposed among them. They were deliberately sent to the International Brigades by the espionage and intelligence institutions [organs] of those states whose nationality is represented in the makeup of that unit. Perhaps more than all the rest, the 11th and 13th Brigades were flooded with agents of the Gestapo and Polish Defensiv, although there are quite a few among the French, Anglo-Americans, and Italians.

29. In December last year, when the division was transferred to the Alcaníz region and was waiting to be brought to Teruel, we decided to organize a censor for civilian mail, and to start with, we looked through a couple hundred letters. The results were stunning. Many letters contained, in a completely open way, information about the approach of the military units, artillery, special forces, tanks, and so on through Alcaníz, pointing out in detail the brigade designations, numbers of troops, and quantity of hardware. We arrested nineteen men for this business and handed them over to the Spanish authorities with the documents.

30. In April fascist knowledge about all of our measures was so well orga-

nized that, for example, the most important orders from Barcelona would be repeated by fascist radio stations on the following day. It is curious that when an order was expected on the reorganization of the command in the Ebro sector, and I inquired of our comrades by telephone when that order would reach us, I was informed that I would receive it the next day, but then they warned me the contents of the order and the exact disposition of all our units were already known to the fascists.

I repeat that the citation of these thirty simple and unsystematic particulars from the experience of just one division reflects the great many sides, the versatility and vitality, of the enemy's work in the ranks of the People's Army. They also attest, first and foremost, to the exceptional mediocrity, weakness, and lack of experience of the protective institutions of the Republicans. This is a result, first and foremost, of an acute lack of workers who have even the slightest experience, who know the methods and tricks of counterintelligence work in military units.

Beginning in January this year, I asked our NKVD men many times to give my division, even if only temporarily, an experienced instructor who could organize the special apparatus and get its work going. But because of the acute shortage of people, even among our comrades, I was unable to obtain any practical help. My attempt at improvisation produced some results, but they were very far from what might have been achieved if, instead of a crude, primitive special department, we had had at our disposal an apparatus headed and directed by experienced specialists. We would have been able not only to appreciably weaken the enemy's influence, but also to gain experience as well. This experience, or so it seems to me, might have also been successfully used in practical work in the Soviet Union.

Furthermore, I would like to draw your attention to another circumstance. Our comrades have repeatedly approached me with a request to grant them reliable people of proven worth for special work. It is very difficult and risky to recommend people only by their outward appearance. Let us say that I had in the division my own, experienced apparatus, a sort of special department—among the international cadres it would be possible to find hundreds of first-rate, committed workers who now and afterward might render us service in their own countries.

That is why it seems to me that the Spanish struggle is not causing us to pay enough attention to special policies. In my view it would be expedient to increase and intensify them in the events on the Iberian peninsula.

Correct: Colonel Grechnev

# Document 77

RGVA, f. 33987, op. 3, d. 1149, ll. 227–239

*Memorandum*
### About the work of our people in Spain
### (Colonel Sverchevsky)

My official position as a line commander of a People's Army division allows me to observe the work of our advisers from the, as it were, "consumer's" point of view. Besides this, as a division commander, I, more often and more closely than any other, have run into a very diverse circle of people within the Spanish command. This circumstance, plus a knowledge of the language, has made it possible for me also to be in on the Spanish evaluation of our people's work, evaluations that do not always come to the notice of Soviet comrades.

The sum total of the advisers' work is admitted by almost all the Spanish, without exception, to be very significant and positive. Most of all, the role of our comrades has shown itself in an acceleration in the general construction and organization of the Republican armed forces. This fact, that the People's Army in the course of two years has successfully put up resistance to an adversary who enjoys technological superiority in most modern means of battle, in aircraft, artillery, and tanks, is to a significant degree the result of the work of our comrades, who have expended much energy, effort, and labor to achieve units of one type, their weaponry, the selection and strengthening of the command, the preparation of the officer and noncom cadres, and tactical training for the subunits. To our advisers must be ascribed the considerable contribution of significant progress in the sphere of cooperation among the different arms. And although it is still unsatisfactory today, at the same time it is impossible not to see how far the army has come from that time when every commander acted on the basis, first and foremost, of the interests of his own arm and his own unit, caring either little or not at all about the interests of the battle as a whole.

But all this is history. Despite the large number of serious flaws, shortcomings, and weaknesses in the People's Army, the rebels and interventionists have encountered in it a strength upon which all of their attempts to decisively turn the tide in their favor have, so far, unsuccessfully broken. Moreover, one can confidently talk today about the ever-diminishing results of the fascist gang's onslaught and the growing power and strength of the Republican resistance. The advisers have contributed considerably to this by not losing their heads on the bad days and managing to speed up a turning of the tide in the forces after the difficult failures in March and April.

Then, besides the large-scale *material* assistance provided by the Soviet Union to the Spanish people in their heroic struggle against the fascist aggressors, which is widely known, one should not underestimate the immense significance of the *moral support* to the Spanish command and army that our comrades have rendered. The fact that our people are there in and of itself is living proof to the Spanish that they are not alone in the struggle and that they can lean on the assistance and aid of 170 million Soviet people, and of the largest, most advanced, most powerful, and strongest country in the world. Unfortunately, we underestimate the significance of the moral factor and yet its role in Spanish life is very great. One can cite a considerable number of instances in which the presence of our comrades raised the morale of the Spanish command, increased their energy and decisiveness, reinforced their good spirits and confidence in their strength. This was very apparent, for example, during the black days at Teruel and especially during the tense situation in March and April.

1. However, this general background of our people's work, which is undoubtedly positive, by no means ought to cover up the many disappointing operational blunders committed by the advisers.

I believe that no small portion of the blame for that fool's errand in the park at Casa de Campo in April of last year falls on us. All we achieved were heavy and, most important, senseless casualties and a weakening of the ranks of the Madrid Brigade, a blunder that the Spanish have still not forgotten as an example of how not to organize an operation.

In the Brunete operation we did not show enough tenacity in using the very favorable conditions of the first few days, but then had more than was necessary later on when we were too late. We stubbornly tried to compensate for being caught yawning with local and futile attacks at Villafranca and Mosquite by 18th Corps units that had little fighting value.

At Saragossa we calmly watched the open sabotage of Lister, who did not want to be subordinate to Modesto, and we did not render the necessary assistance to stir up the units of the 45th Division. After a month we agreed to a second operation at Saragossa, one of the most criminal escapades ever. Long before it began there could be no doubt about its sad outcome.

In exactly the same way we ought to share responsibility with the Spanish command for Teruel. The modest tactical successes and the extremely doubtful operative results [achieved there] can in no way justify our heavy casualties and the great weakening and disorganization of almost all the divisions in the maneuvering army and the units in the Levant, which was a significant cause of our later failures.

The adviser's apparatus also proved to be insufficiently prepared for the latest attacks by the rebels and interventionists. Since the fall of last year we have been hypnotized by Guadalajara and therefore obviously underestimated what it meant when the adversary began the March offensive on the eastern front toward the south of the Ebro. We thought it was only a feint and stubbornly continued to expect a general battle at Guadalajara (for that was how we evaluated the situation in the main military council on the evening of

13 March, that is, just before the fall of Alcaníz). Only the Guadalajara bias, in my opinion, can explain the fact that, despite the presence of precise data that we had well in advance about the impending offensive, insufficient reserves were concentrated where the blow occurred. For example, only the weak 15th International Brigade was in the Belchite region, and the 13th was brought to Híjar from Estremadura. We were appreciably late with the transfer of the Madrid division to the eastern front. If we had done that several days earlier, it might have been possible if not to completely avoid [giving] the fascists an outlet to the coast, then at the very least to slow down and delay that and to inflict significantly greater casualties on the adversary than he suffered. For instance, we definitely lost Lérida because we were late with the transfers of the Campesino and Del Barrio Divisions to that sector. They arrived there only after the adversary had seized Fraga.

Finally, the last unsuccessful attempt in May at an offensive operation on the Catalan front (Balaguer-Tremp) also reflects our weakness. No one believed that it could succeed, and yet, nevertheless, instead of our straining every effort to preclude it, it was hastily prepared for and carried out.

2. It seems to me that a significant portion of our operational blunders can be explained by the fact that there is not always a sober and serious evaluation of the actual Spanish realities. If one excludes the (unfortunately) small group of comrades who have a sufficiently clear conception of the army, who know its condition, means, and needs fairly well, a large percentage of the advisers *patently overestimate how knowledgeable they are,* mistakenly supposing that a superficial visit to the units and a conversation with the Spanish officers—and that through an interpreter—is enough to categorically state their opinions about the corps, divisions, and brigades of the People's Army.

A portion of our comrades, and not a small one, who have been in Spain for a good long time and then left have taken with them an impoverished vocabulary and a no less meager conception of the country, the situation, and the army. Yushkevich can serve as an example. He sat for many months on the eastern front like a feudal lord and studied to perfection the quality of the vintages but knew about the disposition of the units at the front mostly by map and about their condition by hearsay.

There are even worse examples. The aviator Lopatin, who was on tour in Spain, began his activities by wasting many hours finding a melodious aristocratic name for himself—Montenegro—and a coat of arms but did not show himself very well in the profession for which he was sent here. He categorically refused, for example, to bomb the cemetery at Quinto, which was occupied by the fascists, on the pretext that "aircraft cannot distinguish between such small targets from the air" (?).

Grachev, the tanker, is a worthy partner for the aviator. He came here in the firm conviction—which he however did not conceal when he was drunk—that "Spain is of interest to us only as a training ground and nothing more."

Moreover this anti-Stalinist interpretation of the role and participation of the Soviet Union in the Spanish antifascist war came, unfortunately, to the attention of the Spanish, and you can imagine what sort of impression such a declaration by such a "representative" of our country might produce on them.

By the way, the Spanish command keep up with everything that happens with us in this country rather attentively and no less intently observe the conduct of our people. A striking example of this is the conversations of the anarchist Perea, the former commander of 4th Corps and now commander of the East, with his friends, in which he advised [them] to behave in a more guarded and reserved manner with the advisers. He gave as the reason for this the lack of guarantees that the advisers' community was completely free of any ill will toward Spain.

I do not in any way want to connect Grachev's statement with the "advice" of Perea, but the example of the latter ought to serve as a constant reminder to us to keep a firm watch on ourselves and to avoid everything that might strengthen the position of our enemies in Spain.

3. Of course, these unfavorable examples, more of which could be cited, cannot in the slightest measure detract from the generally favorable evaluation of the work of our comrades, especially as there were and are a large number of very valuable workers who have merited the deep respect of the Spanish command.

Even now, the names of Coms. Pavlov and Smushkevich—now heroes of the Soviet Union—are remembered with great gratitude. Comrades Shtern, Ratner, Shevchenko (who died), artillerist Klich, engineer Dunavsky, signaler Likhter, Doctor Klus, and others. Malinovsky proved to be a serious, authoritative, tactful, and tenacious adviser and tankers Arkin and Kondratiev worked honestly and quite well.

Of those who are there now, the Spanish regard Com. Maximov well enough and speak quite well of Kachalov's work; Arzhanukhin, the adviser-aviator, enjoys a solid authority, tanker Sedlesky is outstanding, there is good opinion about the work of Trotsenko and Kurbatov, tanker Fotchenko, Colonel Vechnyi, and, finally, there are not a few excellent, invaluable Soviet cadres among our young men of all specialties who honestly represent the Soviet Union in Spain.

Of course, one cannot assert for sure that the Soviet column is free of people who discredit our prestige in the eyes of the Spanish through their work there. Even today one can find a considerable number of examples in which our comrades do not comprehend the environment and situation and, most important, the abruptly shifting conditions, which require them to change their way of working so that they use more tact and more cultured methods and are more serious about their responsibilities.

4. If one is speaking about personal shortcomings in our work, then one must point out, first and foremost, the desirability of quickly eliminating the

condescension and the patronizing tone that a number of comrades have in their attitude toward the Spanish command as a result of a primitive understanding of the People's Army. They hold the deeply mistaken opinion that the army is still in its infancy and incapable of developing without the guardianship of the advisers in the most petty of matters. This is a profound and dangerous delusion. The People's Army threw off its diapers a year and a half ago. Even its enemies have been forced to acknowledge its maturity and growth. Today and even yesterday this was not an infant that needed constant assistance to keep it steady as it took its first timid steps, but rather a young organism of grown-up and strong men. If the Spanish Republican officer asked us many months ago to demonstrate to him the elementary foundations of military affairs, and the advisers frequently had to act as instructors, then today our condescending attitude, as if he were a dilettante with little understanding, grates on him. Our petty, pedantic concern does not satisfy him, and he is legitimately demanding that the quality of our work be *improved and that it be cultured.* He really *only* needs an adviser today, but an adviser who possesses tact, who does not thrust his decisions on him by force, but rather one who helps him most quickly understand the situation, most correctly discover and make a concrete decision, opportunely directs his thought in the necessary direction, inconspicuously introduces a correction when it is needed. And the adviser never, under any conditions, ought to attempt to take the place of the commander whom he has been appointed to help.

Unfortunately, the art of the cultured adviser is a complex art, and mastery of it is not granted to those many comrades who are not able to discover the correct way to carry out their work. Quite often rudeness, obtrusiveness, a lack of respect for the Spanish officer, and so on develop, which leads to a reduction in our authority and a limitation of our influence. What frequently gets in the way is the conceit that one observes among us, the result of our comrades' oblivion to the simple tenet that besides the task of *helping the People's Army,* we have the no less important duty *to learn ourselves.*

Where exactly do our shortcomings show up?

a) I happened to witness scenes like these: our young worker is giving long and tedious, hackneyed lectures and exhortations, talking as if to a pupil. But in fact they are frequently [lecturing] seasoned officers who are honored in this country and well known in the army, like General Sarabia, for example. [Our worker] does not understand when he's doing this the awkwardness of his own situation and the delicate position of the Spanish chief, who is forced, sometimes in the presence of his subordinates, to listen to a translation that is not always competent and to advice that is not always necessary or valuable.

b) In other cases the adviser understands his task as a duty to constantly follow on the heels of the Spanish officer to whom he has been assigned, lavishing on him the most petty guardianship. The officer naturally does not always like this, and he is sometimes not fastidious about using every kind of trick to free himself, if only temporarily, from the wearying presence of the adviser in order to have some privacy or to talk freely with his colleagues.

c) There are also cases in which the adviser has, from the first, adopted an unnecessary imperious tone. It was this, it seems, that Frolov (the replacement with Modesto for the dead Shevchenko) had no luck with. Frolov had to leave then and there, and however much he tried in another place, it was difficult for him to make amends for that original sin. He seems to me, personally, to be a quiet, thoughtful worker.

d) One can often meet hardworking time-study specialists who think that the function of an adviser is to conscientiously record events and not actively interfere in situations, changing them in a direction that we desire. One is most likely to meet this type of adviser on quiet sectors of the front, though now and then they also get into mobile units. Chaikin, for instance, quietly lived for several months in Lister's division.

e) The advisers' community also has distinctive sorts of Oblomovs, who contemplate with apathy and unconcern what is happening around them. They live by the principle, "Don't get on the bosses' nerves and don't tire yourself out." Frequently this sort of person, in the idle intervals between two assaults, conscientiously does research into the richness of the country's wine, and when things heat up exhibits a reduction in personal courage.

f) Finally, one meets workers who reflect not one but a whole number of our shortcomings. One example is Gornov, who began working here in the X[illegible] Corps with Otero, an old professional lieutenant colonel. With enviable swiftness he managed to completely spoil relations between the command and the staff workers so that he had to change his specialty and move to transportation, where he continues to display his former shortcomings, with dubious benefit to the work.

I am convinced that a significant portion of these negative factors in our work might easily be eliminated through better selection and allocation of people and through a serious preliminary briefing of the comrades when they join the work. The new advisers absolutely must become familiar with the personal descriptions of the command and the military unit to which he is sent and also absolutely with the lessons of his predecessor's work. The overwhelming majority of the comrades honestly and sincerely want to be of the greatest possible benefit to the common cause, but often they know neither the methods of work nor the policies, and therefore they commit mistakes that cause vital harm and reduce the effectiveness of our influence and authority.

5. Of the purely personal elements that do not do us honor, I want to point out three shortcomings:

a) The first has to do with the excessive abuse by our advisers of the personal pronoun "I." "I attacked," "I defended," "I ordered my units to attack," "I carried out the operation," and so on and so forth. Besides the clear incongruity of these kinds of statements with the truth, this kind of lavish fantasy reinforces the arrogance of our people and reduces the value of our comrades in the eyes of the Spanish, from whom our bragging is not concealed. Incidentally, I ought to mention an even more dangerous element: our people very eagerly assume responsibility for the successful actions of the units in which they work and shift all the blame for failures, as a rule, onto the lonely shoulders of the Spanish commanders. I am not against a legitimate division of merit, but it seems to me that it is more important to honestly apportion responsibility for blunders and failures. Otherwise our work smacks of a one-sided bias, and it also allows the loss of a feeling of responsibility for the business entrusted [to us].

b) We are not always truthful enough in illuminating the situation in our work. From what I have seen and experienced in Spain and from materials that I have looked through here, it is patently obvious how strongly the difficulties and, in no less a measure, the modest achievements are exaggerated. We frequently exaggerate the difficulties to make our own inadequate activeness not seem so bad. From this come inflated and unverified testimonies about the enormous superiority of the adversary (Brunete, Saragossa, in part at Teruel), and our successes swell to no less a degree (Teruel). For example, the testimony about the fascists' overall casualties for the entire war, which I looked through here, testify to, first and foremost, the very rich and inexpert fantasy of the authors. Meanwhile, the role of the advisers consists exactly of, first and foremost, not only the most veracious approach to the facts and events, but also in teaching this quality to the command staff of the Spanish People's Army. Nothing can exact vengeance so brutally in a war as an erroneous evaluation of the situation.

c) It may be petty, but the vital factor hampering our rapprochement with the Spanish commanders is the slovenly appearance of the advisers. In our country we long ago made ever-increasing demands for a civilized appearance, and it is, therefore, very embarrassing and unpleasant to see in the background of the Spanish staff, close by the Spanish officers who are generally following behind him, the slovenly, unshaven figure of our comrade in a shabby suit, often civilian, that is wrinkled in the extreme. It is clear that this is also not in keeping with an increase in the Spanish officers' confidence in their adviser, and yet without this all of the effort of the latter may be reduced to nothing.

It is true that during the past few months one notices more neatness in personal care than earlier; however, this should not prevent the comrades from keeping in mind very strongly that we represent our homeland here and that the Spanish form opinions about the Soviet Union and the Red Army not only through our work, but also through our appearance.

6. I will now briefly touch on a question that, it seems to me, no one has yet raised, but that in my view deserves thought. I have in mind the policy of recalling comrades from Spain.

The Spanish command reacts sensitively to changes in the advisers' apparatus. They greet the departure of advisers of little value with gladness and relief and part with comrades who have proven themselves to be necessary and useful workers with regret. These factors ought to be taken into consideration in the future, keeping those men who have deserved esteem for their work in Spain as long as possible and recalling them here only to grant them a small respite and rest. *It is necessary to take into consideration especially seriously the situation at the moment of recall.* The departure of Com. Shtern, for example, which coincided with a crisis on the front, was taken by the Spanish command as a slackening of our country's attention on them, and there were even direct statements about his flight. The recall of a significant group of advisers from the fronts in the southern part of Spain not long before the rebels and interventionists got their outlet to the sea engendered suspicion among the Spanish that they [the advisers] had left them to the mercy of fate. The quick departure of Colonel Malinovsky was also regarded by the command of the mobile army as a manifestation of our fear of the future. When I was departing from Spain, after the transfer of the division, the Spanish interpreted my recall as a result of a policy to reduce the international units, which was caused (they said) by a lack of confidence in Republican Spain's prospects and a desire to save ourselves from a sinking ship. This especially provoked suspicion among them as during the very last fascist offensive the question was raised (and they knew about it) about granting me only a furlough and not having me leave completely. The Spanish command, in particular Rojo, repeatedly and transparently hinted that they had no objection to seeing several advisers around them again and it seems to me that *it would indeed be useful to have some sort of stable leading cadre in Spain.* It is rare when one does not experience a shortage of valuable workers. Moreover one ought to bear in mind that the adviser apparatus was, over the past few months, badly weakened by the departure of a number of comrades, such as Shtern, Kalinovsky, Trotsenko, Goffe, and a number of others, and the new ones require a significant amount of time while they are getting up to speed on matters. Therefore the return of comrades who have shown themselves well, even if just a few, seems expedient to me since their experience, knowledge of the situation and people undoubtedly would be, to a great extent, conducive to the strengthening of the adviser apparatus. On the other hand, no less important, the fact that returns were occurring would produce a very beneficial impression on the Spanish, emphasizing by this that the readiness of the Soviet Union to assist and aid the Spanish people and army to the utmost in their selfless, heroic struggle has not weakened, *especially during the crisis* stage the war is now in.

8. The last observation has to do with language. It seems to me that we ought to increase pressure for our comrades to study the Spanish language. It is indeed awkward when some workers stay there up to a year and more and still cannot take a single step without a translator. Meanwhile, if they had had the desire [to learn the language], they could, and should, have been able to converse with the Spanish without outside help. Study of the language ought

## Document 77 *continued*

to be obligatory and taken into account in their résumés when the value of comrades and their attitude toward the job are being determined. This is a question also of the Soviet commanders' political face.

Colonel Grechnev

## Document 78

RGVA, f. 33987, op. 3, d. 1081, l. 16

Incoming to the S[ecretariat] Narkom                         Copy.
N° 31/os                                               Top Secret
17/11/38                                               N° 91/ss

TO THE PEOPLE'S COMMISSAR OF FOREIGN AFFAIRS, COM. LITVINOV M. M.

In my first conversation with him after my return, Negrín incidentally touched on the question of the work of our neighboring workers in Spain. He expressed a desire that the new leader of this work, Com. Kotov, not advertise himself and not acquire a wide circle of official acquaintances (by this he was emphatically alluding to the indiscreet conduct of Com. Kotov's predecessors). He declared bluntly that he thought a connection between Com. Kotov and his workers and the Ministry of Internal Affairs and SIM (the Army's Special Department) was inexpedient. He proposed that Com. Kotov maintain an indirect connection with him, Negrín, because he is creating a special secret apparatus attached to him.

The fact that Negrín, who is always extremely delicate with regard to our people, considered it necessary to make such a remark undoubtedly indicates the great pressure on him from the Socialist party, the anarchists, and especially the agents of the Second International concerning the "interference" of our people in police and counterintelligence work. Unfortunately, as I once reported, a number of workers who have now been recalled did not understand that it was necessary to change their methods of work in a timely fashion and not to wait for the Spanish themselves to demand it.

I informed Com. Kotov about this conversation with Negrín, and he will come to the appropriate conclusions from this [exchange].

Chargé d'affaires of the USSR in Spain
Marchenko
Barcelona, 10 November 1938
Correct:
Secretary [illegible]

## Document 78 *continued*

## The Question of Negrín

Negrín's attitude as described in Document 78 may surprise some students of the Civil War because it suggests that he enjoyed a degree of autonomy from Communist control. There have basically been two opinions of the last leader of the Spanish Republic: on the one hand are those who argue that, although Negrín never officially joined the PCE, he supported Communist policies so intently that he might as well have been a member. On the other hand are those who have seen him as a more independent figure trying to find a way to prosecute the war while keeping his only foreign supporters happy.[14] In this report he opposed the Soviets, but Marchenko took care to note that Negrín was "always extremely delicate with regard to our people." **Document 79,** another report on a meeting with Negrín, makes it clear that the Spaniard's views of politics closely coincided with the Soviets', while the similarities between his vision for postwar Spain and that of the Soviet Union are striking. Negrín thought that because it had been impossible to unite the Socialist and Communist parties during the war, "the very most that might be expected is that the Socialist party will be absorbed by the Communist party at the end of the war." Because this might cause difficulties, he suggested another political solution for postwar Spain: a one-party dictatorship, with his "national front" as that party. Of course, the Communists would be given leadership of important sectors of the party. Meanwhile, all the principal branches of Spain's economy would be nationalized, and the "bourgeoisie" of Catalonia, who desired more autonomy from Spain, would be brought back into line. This document suggests that if the Republicans had won the Civil War, Spain would have been very different from the nation that existed before 18 July 1936 and very close to the post–World War II "people's democracies" of Europe.

# Document 79

RGVA, f. 33987, op. 3, d. 1081, ll. 79–80

To Com. Voroshilov

*Top Secret*

### Conversation with Negrín on 10 December 1938

Negrín asked me to convey a number of his wishes in connection with the communication that he received from Cisneros (I already transmitted the contents of that part of the conversation), after which he had a lengthy discussion with me on a number of other topics.

*The situation in France.* Negrín believes that the French Communists and Socialists committed a mistake in going into battle on the unfavorable grounds of Renault's decree. They shouldn't have committed to the general strike, for it was doomed to fail from the start. One should not push Daladier to the right. One should have maneuvered, attempting to isolate Bonnet, who is more dangerous and harmful than Daladier. It is still possible to tear the latter away from the Right with the correct tactics; one should not forget that he is a weak-willed man. The Pivertists and Trotskyists instigated the strained relations with the government. One should not stand in the way of a direct struggle against the government given the current situation—one must drive a wedge between Daladier and the rightists. He, Negrín, gave the Spanish press instructions not to come out against the French government—Spain cannot take any other position, especially as the Daladier government has treated Republican Spain no worse, up to this point, and perhaps even somewhat better, than the Blum government.

*Pedrozo.* Negrín is very dissatisfied with Pedrozo, declaring that he has very unfavorable information about Pedrozo, and he asked [me] to ask if we do not have the facts about his conduct in Moscow. Negrín is looking for someone to send to Moscow but cannot find anyone. I recommended to him that he look among the representatives of the nonparty intelligentsia. This idea pleased him.

*About the creation of an all-Spain national front.* Negrín told me that he conversed with Díaz and Uribe on the question of creating a united national front, which seemed to him to be a sort of distinctive new party. This idea came to him after he lost faith in the possibility of uniting the Socialist and Communist parties. The unification was unrealizable because of the opposition of the leaders of the Socialist party. The most that might be expected is that the Socialist party will be absorbed by the Communist party at the end of the war, but in this case the higher-ups in the Socialist party—Prieto, Caballero, Besteiro, Lamoneda, Peña, and others—will not acknowledge the unification, and the bourgeoisie will utilize it under the name of the Socialist party.

But what kind of party is the government depending on? To depend on the Communist party is unfavorable from the international standpoint. The existing Republican parties have no future. The Popular Front does not have a common discipline and is torn by interparty struggle. What is needed, therefore, is an organization that would unify all that is best in all of the parties and organizations and would represent a fundamental support of the government. It might be called the national front or the Spanish front or union. Negrín has not pictured concretely how this organization ought to be constructed. It seems to him that it ought to be based on individual membership, and he conceives of the membership in a threefold way: simple members, active members, and leading cadres, who ought to bear the title of full members. He permits a double membership, that is, members of the National Front may remain in existing parties, the activity of which will not be limited.

The Communist party ought to give this new organization workers, but not, at first, from among its leaders—better to use little-known people. The leadership of the new party's organizational and propaganda work must be handed over to the Communists.

He believes that nonparty military men like Rojo, Matallana, Menéndez, Casado, and others must be included in the new party and also prominent representatives of the intelligentsia who are currently outside of the party and hence outside of the Popular Front. In this regard, he said, the Popular Front will be expanded.

Negrín emphasized that he was not insisting on this idea if someone will indicate another way out of the situation. One must think about both the present and future, when the unity of Spain will be restored and the masses now in fascist territory who have been exposed to ideological brainwashing for two years are brought into the political life [of the country]. There is no returning to the old parliamentarism; it will be impossible to allow the "free play" of parties as it existed earlier, for in this case the Right might once again force its way into power. This means that either a unified political organization or a military dictatorship is necessary. He does not see any other way.

He does not propose setting up the new organization immediately, but he thinks that the idea must be disseminated among the masses. "This must be done very skillfully and carefully, and many months will pass before the ground for setting up a National Front will be properly prepared."

I reacted in a very reserved way to Negrín's idea and drew his attention to the difficulties and complications that the organization of a new party would cause.

General impression: the form is unclear to Negrín, but he has essentially thought through the question sufficiently. If there are military successes, he can begin the formation of "his" united-Spanish political party, with the participation of the Communists if they will allow it, and without the Communists (and that means against them) if they refuse.

## Document 79 *continued*

One must take into account, however, that for now all of this is not very pressing, and some time will pass before the question becomes acute.

*Relations with the Catalan government.* Negrín reported that relations with the Catalan government have been temporarily settled, for the Spanish government decided to support [it] financially. He again spoke about the fact that many Soviet workers during the first period had not understood the Catalan problem. The Esquerra is using the national factor to restore the position of the Catalan capitalists. Now it is striving to get the central government to return to the bourgeoisie their homes and some of their seized enterprises, after which it will stir up the anarchists and workers' organizations against the central government. Companys, who portrays himself as a martyr, is a second Miaja, a multiple Asensio, an arch-intriguer. In the countryside the Esquerra depends on rightists and fascists; a number of *alcaldes* [mayors] from the ranks of the Esquerra have remained in power in areas captured by the fascists. The Esquerra has prohibited the Spanish language in Catalan schools. The Catalan government does not concern itself with the children of refugees because they are Spanish. In the countryside hatred against the Spanish has been stirred up. "I am for helping the Catalan government, but I do not want the money that we are giving them to go for the anti-Spanish propaganda of the Catalan bourgeoisie."

It is strange, says Negrín, that a deft politician like Comorera is so reverential toward Companys, as is Moix, the minister of labor, who is an honest and straightforward man. Companys himself speaks of them with the greatest contempt. Comorera does not understand that the Esquerra is striving to return to the situation that existed before 18 July. Such a return will not happen. The bourgeoisie will not recover their positions. All of the principal branches of Spain's economy will be nationalized. And Spain will be disposed least of all to restoring the privileges of the Catalan bourgeoisie.

6 copies printed.
5—to Com. Litvinov; 1—file copy.

## A Final Summing Up and a Footnote

At the end of 1938 Erno Gerö, still working within the PCE, wrote a précis of the current situation in Spain and the prospects for future activity by the Communists. Forwarded to Stalin and other members of the Soviet Politburo, **Document 80** constituted, in many respects, a summary of what the Communists felt they had accomplished in Spain. In each of the areas discussed, Gerö had both good and bad things to say about the results achieved; what is significant is the extent of Soviet and Communist intervention in Spanish affairs and Soviet intentions for the future of Spain.

Because at this point in the war the army faced the most pressing difficulties, Gerö began with an overview of the military situation. By late 1938 the Nationalists had cut off Catalonia from Madrid and central Spain, critically wounding the Republic. Just a few weeks after this report was written, the final assault on Catalonia began, culminating in late January 1939 in the unexpectedly swift collapse of Barcelona. Although the rest of the province held out a few months longer, that event signaled the end of Catalonia and of the Spanish Republic as a whole. Gerö sensed the coming crisis and sought to assure his readers that the Communists had done everything possible to avert a disaster. Most important, they had worked to transfer power over the military into the hands of the only man who could be trusted to run the war the way that the Communists wanted—Negrín. It was also vital that most of the major command posts and a large number of the commissar positions were now held by trusted comrades. The other measures pushed by the Communists—centralization of command, the creation of a disciplined regular army, and extensive purges—had also been carried out and had produced the result Moscow wanted: a large force of trained soldiers who would crush the fascists and then establish a postwar regime modeled after the Soviet example. As in the earlier reports by Sverchevsky, the problems faced by the People's Army were not in these crucial areas. Gerö stressed instead, as the major cause for concern, the interventionists and their increased supplies of technology and men.

Next in importance was the development of military industry, long a focus of Soviet efforts in the Spanish Republic. The Communists had, of course, favored the new law centralizing industry in government hands and were certain that the problems still experienced in the factories were the result of a failure to carry out this measure properly as well as of the interference of bureaucrats (an area of concern in the Soviet Union also) and poor supplies. The government, in contrast, posed fewer challenges, given that the most vital issue—leadership of the country by a man amenable to Communist "suggestions"—had been solved to Moscow's satisfaction.

The situation with the political parties was more problematic.

As we have seen, the Soviets had worked almost from the beginning of the war to unify the Socialists and Communists in one party that they could then control. For many reasons, including the opposition of men like Largo Caballero, this had never happened. In summing up, Gerö again attacked the "Caballeristas" as antigovernment and defeatist and as seeking, like the "Trotskyists," to destroy the Popular Front and the Communist party. The other enemies of victory were the remnants of the POUM. It may seem surprising, given the complete marginalization of the POUM, that Gerö still saw the marginalized party as a serious problem, even more dangerous than the much more influential Caballeristas. As in Sverchevsky's reports, this simply reflected Stalin's belief that Trotsky was at the root of every evil. Only through the utter destruction of every trace of his influence could true control and real Communism be achieved.

Gerö's report was not all negative. He noted that the UGT was more than ever under Communist control and that the "bad" anarchists had suffered a significant defeat at a recent plenum. Although there were reasons for concern, then, he was cautiously optimistic about the future of the Popular Front and the opportunities for the PCE to unify first with the PSUC and then, when conditions permitted, with the Socialists. Given the events that would transpire just three months after Gerö submitted this report, the Comintern agent was, in fact, far more optimistic than he should have been.

In this, their hour of extreme need, the Spanish turned once again to their only consistent supporters. Sometime in late 1938 the Spanish sought more arms from the Soviet Union in order to continue the battle with the Nationalists. Although a few historians have thought that the appeal for weapons went unanswered, **Document 81** shows that in fact the Soviets sold an enormous amount of material to the Republic.[15] The problem was that the French refused to honor the Republican request to ship the arms across the borders. Voroshilov's memorandum to Stalin also shows that by early 1939 the Soviets had given up on the Republic and would no longer intervene on its behalf. The Soviet military leader could now only "deplore" troubles with the French and worry about the weapons falling into the hands of "fascists."

# Document 80

RGVA, f. 33987, op. 3, d. 1081, ll. 30−44

To Comrade Stalin I. V.
  Com. Molotov V. M.
  Com. Kaganovich L. M.
  Com. Voroshilov K. E.
  Com. Yezhov N. I.
  Com. Mikoian A. I.
  Com. Andreev A. A.

We are sending you a report by an ECCI worker who has worked for more than a year in the CC CP of Spain, on "The Current Situation and Tasks in Spain."

The conclusions made in the report on the whole coincide with the viewpoint of the Politburo of the CC CP of Spain itself.

G. Dimitrov

4/12/38
N° 301

7 Copies                                                                      *Top Secret*
25/11/38

*On the Current Situation and Tasks in Spain*

I. *General evaluation of the situation. Immediate prospects*

One must expect that the Spanish Republic in the very near future will be put to the most serious test, by all signs the most serious test that has taken place since the beginning of the war for independence. After the adversary had liquidated the "pocket" on the Ebro, large human and material resources were freed up. During the course of the past month the adversary had already systematically groped for various sectors of front, in particular Madrid and the Levant.

According to intelligence from trustworthy sources, Italy is dispatching a new expeditionary corps to Spain. At the beginning of November, 12,000 fully equipped men were already set for dispatch at the port of Spezia.

It is obvious that a military offensive, which must be expected in the very near future, will be combined with an international diplomatic offensive (the recognition of belligerent rights for Franco; Chamberlain and Halifax's trip to Paris, set for 23 November, has the objective of preparing a pact to smother the Spanish Republic) and with an offensive in internal politics (an increase in the activity of the capitulators and enemies of unity, enemies of the Popular Front governments, Communist parties—that is, Trotskyists, Caballeristas, adventurers from the Iberian Anarchist Federation (FAI), and so on).

To correctly evaluate the Spanish Republic's chances of enduring the three-fold offensive which, by all indications, it faces in the near future, the situation in the country must be analyzed in its most important areas of activity, even if briefly, and the proper conclusions drawn from this analysis.

II. *The Military Situation*

1. The situation on the fronts during the past five or six months has become more stable. This was achieved as a result of the reorganization of the government in April of this year with the transfer of the leadership of the War Ministry into the hands of Negrín. As a result, a more consistent and stable policy was carried out to strengthen the army; to create reserves; to create fortifications in a more intensified way; to train, retrain, and promote the command cadres; to introduce measures for rewarding the best soldiers and commanders; to improve discipline and unity in the army; to introduce the concept of unified command; to partially purge the army; to improve the work of the staffs and to make the military commissariat more active.

The army currently has reached roughly 1,200,000 men, that is, the Republican Army now significantly outnumbers the fascist army. Currently the Republican Army consists of six front armies. Of these, four are in the non-Catalan zone (Army of the Levant, Central Army, Army of Estremadura, the Southern Army) and the unified army group under the command of General Miaja. There are two armies in Catalonia (the Army of the Ebro and the Eastern Army), also unified in the army group of the Catalan zone under the command of General Sarabia. There is a general staff of all ground forces, headed by General Rojo.

There are twenty- [illegible] army corps in the entire land army, of them [illegible]-teen in the non-Catalan zone and [six?] in Catalonia. Of the corps commanders, fifteen are members of the CP of Spain or of the Unified Socialist Party of Catalonia, one of the army commanders is a member of the Communist party and the other is a sympathizer. In the lower command posts, the positions held by the party are approximately the same as the proportion held at the corps level. After the Communists, the command posts belong, first and foremost, to the anarchists, while the Socialists have an extremely insignificant number of command posts, even the Republicans have more. The positions of the Communist party are less strong in the staffs than among the unit commanders. In the military commissariat, at the very bottom the majority of the commissars belong to the Communist party; among the commissars of the large units (corps and armies) the Communist party's positions are weaker.

In general, the army's mood and the morale of the soldiers and commanders are satisfactory, although lately an increase in desertion to the adversary has also been noticed, especially in some armies. The army's good morale in general does not, however, rule out the existence of rather strong symptoms and signs of war fatigue in the army and among the population, and the presence of vacillating and defeatist tendencies in a few sections of the army's command cadres and among the leaders of the parties and organizations of the Popular Front, tendencies that strengthened after the Munich pact.

The improvement in the army has been far from even everywhere. One can regard the Army of Ebro as being on the very highest level, then the Levant, then the Central Army, and finally the remaining weaker armies.

Despite the army's improved situation, one must consider the military situation to be very serious because (a) the adversary has a significant advantage in military matériel, especially in aircraft (the proportion is one to five) and also in artillery (the Republican artillery is not only numerically weaker, but also more worn-out than the adversary's artillery). (b) The expected reinforcement of the intervention will increase this advantage still more. (c) There are still weak sections in the Republic's fronts that can serve as places for the adversary to penetrate. (d) The food supplies of the army and population have deteriorated lately, and there are difficulties with the winter uniforms for the army.

2. The navy has not experienced the same kind of improvement as has been ascertained in the army. Although the Republican Navy roughly equals the fascist navy in matériel (the fascists have more cruisers, more submarines in good repair, but then the Republic has a much larger number of destroyers), the Republican Navy is inactive. On the whole this is explained by: (a) the lack of unified command in the navy itself (the command is split between the navy command and the navy base command) and the lack of a unified general staff, which would unite the staffs of the land, air, and naval armies. (b) The social composition of the naval commanders, who are largely right wing and aristocratic. While the majority of the commanders in the army are new and were promoted from among the people during the struggle, the old naval command staff remains almost untouched. (c) The unsatisfactory work of the commissariat (the naval commissar, Bruno Alonso, is Prieto's right hand; all the commissars are Prietista Socialists or Caballeristas, often with Trotskyist tendencies, who are working, in the majority of cases, not to increase the navy's fighting efficiency, but against the Communists, that is, in essence they are causing the navy to disintegrate). (d) Given these conditions, the work of the enemy, spies, sabotage, and wrecking in the navy are undoubtedly much stronger than in the army. (e) The Communist party did not pay enough attention to the navy; in the navy the influence of the anarchists is stronger than the influence of the Communist party.

3. Some success has been achieved in military industry during the past few months, although the decree about centralizing all military industry in the

hands of the Republican government has still been put into effect only to an insignificant degree. The development of military industry, however, was too slow and was delayed mainly for the following reasons: (a) the bureaucratization of the military industry leadership and commissariat. (b) The still existing syndicalization of many enterprises. (c) The unsatisfactory supply of factories with raw materials and insufficient use of the internal resources of the country and factories themselves. (d) Poor food supplies for the workers. (e) The lack of a unified system of progressive piecework payments and a significant lack of coordination in wage rates. (f) The weakness of the work of the unions and the Communist party in the enterprises.

*Some conclusions:* To improve the fighting efficiency of the army, a unified general staff must be set up for all the armed forces of the Republic with the staffs of the land and air armies and also the staff of the navy, subordinate to it.

It would be expedient to appoint a commander in chief for all ground forces with the objective of [attaining] a more consistent implementation of the unified command principle.

It would be highly desirable to help the Republican Army with aircraft and artillery in view of the significant advantage of the adversary in this area.

A serious purge of the navy must be carried out; as well as a policy for creating and promoting new cadres; and the work of the commissariat must be put in good order by subordinating the naval commissariat to the commissariat of all the armed forces of the Republic.

[It is imperative] to undertake these necessary measures so that the decree on centralizing all military industry in the hands of the government can be put into effect more quickly.

[It is necessary] for the Communist party to undertake a concrete review of the situation in the entire army and on all fronts to expose weak spots and to improve the army's condition from every point of view.

III. *The Government*

The government headed by Negrín was, to a significant degree, consolidated after the partial reorganization of 16 August of this year. The authority of the government increased. One can now consider the situation from this point of view to be relatively stable, although some factors still hinder the normal work of the government. The most essential of these factors are the following: (a) The friction between the Republican and Catalan autonomous governments has not ceased; on the contrary, after some improvement it again intensified in the beginning of November. (b) The Republican government is working intermittently (the government has not had a meeting in five months; the ministers complain that they cannot meet with Negrín and cannot resolve questions about their departments with him). (c) As a result of this situation, many important questions are put off for weeks and sometimes for

## Document 80 *continued*

months without resolution (for example, Negrín agreed to create a high coun-cil for the national economy, yet the decree was not issued; Negrín agreed to instill order in the navy, but the question about the navy has dragged on for months; Negrín agreed to issue a decree that would guarantee foreign credit for the purchase of foodstuffs, but the decree has not been issued, and so on). (d) Despite the increased authority of the government, attacks on it from defeatist elements have not ceased.

*Some conclusions.*

The government headed by Negrín is relatively stable. The government and in particular the head of the government will endure the onslaught of the impending international offensive, although the stability of the govern-ment depends on many other circumstances, such as the situation at the fronts, food supplies, and so on. It is necessary to make every effort to pre-serve and in the future to consolidate the Negrín government, which is one of the decisive factors to gain success in the war for independence. It would be expedient, however, given the proper situation, to raise the question of including representatives of the left Catalan Republican Party and of the Party of Basque Nationalists in the government with the objective of achiev-ing a more complete national unity; achieving a definitive elimination of the friction between the central and Catalan autonomous governments; guaran-teeing the normal activity of the Republican government so that the impor-tant questions of the war will be decided without delay; strengthening the struggle against capitalist elements, isolating them from those who are wa-vering, and taking concrete organizational measures against them.

*IV. The parties and organizations of the Popular Front. Questions of unity.*

There have been no essential changes in the past two or three months in the area of the unity of the antifascist forces of Republican Spain. It is true that during this time a strong offensive has been launched by the Caballeristas, Trotskyists, and Trotskyesque elements of the Iberian Anarchist Federation (FAI) against the Communist party, the unity of the Communist party with the Socialist party, the internal unity of the Unified Socialist Youth, the leader-ship of the Socialist party itself, the Popular Front, the government, the Uni-fied Socialist Party of Catalonia. One can say that although this offensive has impeded and is still impeding the development of a movement for the unity of the working class and all antifascist forces and has created the danger of a split in the Unified Socialist Youth, for now it has still not achieved its main objective. It has not managed to isolate the Communist party or to ruin the unity of the Socialists and Communists or of the Popular Front.

The Popular Front is not active enough. The enemies' attempts on the Pop-ular Front have consisted of, on the one hand, the use of the Popular Front against the government under the pretense that the Popular Front ought to be the institution controlling the activity of the government; on the other hand, the isolation of the Communists in the Popular Front to make the Popular Front a weapon in the struggle against the Communists and against the unification of the Socialist Party of Catalonia. To achieve this goal, the enemies of the Popular Front are trying to use the fear of Communists that exists in the various parties and institutions of the Popular Front owing to the growth of the Communist party's influence among the masses and especially in the army.

What fundamental processes are occurring in the most important organizations of the Popular Front?

During the past five or six months, one can ascertain some consolidation in the Socialist party (the organization of meetings, plenum, and demonstrations; the creation of a number of new local organizations, where the Soc. party earlier did not have organizations). After the plenum of the Soc. party's national committee in August this year, the Caballeroist elements became noticeably more active, strengthening their struggle, together with some of the Prietistas, against the Communist party, against the leadership of the Soc. party and against the unity of the Socialists and Communists. At the very same time, at the midlevel sector (that is, at the regional level) the relationship between the Socialists and Communists somewhat worsened as a result of this anti-unity activity, while at the lowest and national levels there was some improvement. Caballero's group, which has in its hands a number of regional Soc. party committees, turned more and more into a Trotskyist, anti-Communist, anti-Soviet, defeatist, antigovernment, Rasulnich group. Moreover, this is a double-dealing group, as it conceals its true objectives even from its own supporters (for example, it publishes provocative Trotskyist leaflets without signature). Negrín's influence is becoming stronger within the cadres of the Socialist party. At the same time, a rapprochement is taking place between the Caballeristas and the Prietistas.

There is significant disorder within the anarchist movement. There are two tendencies. The adventuristic tendency, represented mainly by the leadership of the Iberian Anarchist Federation (FAI), the regional Catalan committee of the National Labor Confederation (CNT), and also by part of the leadership of the anarchist youth, has close ties with the Caballero group and with the Trotskyist POUM. This tendency suffered a defeat at the plenum of the entire anarchist movement, which took place at the end of October. The other, healthier tendency is represented by the leadership of the National Labor Confederation (CNT) and the majority of its organization. It is standing up for supporting the government, for the Popular Front, for the struggle for the country's independence.

Despite this disorder the CNT is growing, although to a negligible extent, in a few regions of the non-Catalan zone. This is explained by the energetic activity of the lower cadres of the CNT and by the lack of internal democracy in the General Workers' Union (UGT), with its passivity, the bureaucratization

## Document 80 *continued*

of its work, and the weakness of the work of the Communist party in the UGT and at the enterprises.

The Communist party has significant influence on the central leadership of the UGT, and on the whole [they] carry out our line. The Caballeristas, however, lead a number of the largest federations, although they are actually a minority in most of them.

The question about the creation of a unified union center, as a topical question of the war itself, is still not a question for the broader masses. The party has done little up to now to provoke a wide discussion of this question among the masses, the unions, in the enterprises, in the press, and to overcome the opposition of the leaders of the CNT and also the UGT.

More than ever a weariness with the war is felt in the ranks of the Republican parties. There is much wavering in these parties, and defeatist elements are very active in them. At the same time a boundary is being drawn in these parties between the supporters of the struggle for independence and the unsteady, defeatist elements. The main demand of the Republicans is to put into effect the thirteen points of the Negrín government. Many Republican figures are raising the question about the fact that since this is a struggle for a democratic republic, then the bosses in the country ought to be Republicans. (The government, army, economic command posts).

At the beginning of November, a pact containing a number of government measures was concluded between the Left Republican party of Catalonia and the Unified Socialist Party of Catalonia.

*Some conclusions.*

To further strengthen unity, it is necessary to intensify the struggle against the enemies of unity—the POUM, the Caballeristas, adventurers from the Iberian Anarchist Federation (FAI), defeatists—coordinating this struggle with the struggle for a closer unity between the Communist party and the Soc. party, for a union of the youth, for an activation of the Popular Front, and, most of all, for the creation of a unified union center as the vitally important question of the war itself. To achieve this last objective, it would be necessary to concretely raise and resolve the question not only about the further improvement of the party's work in the General Workers' Union (UGT) and in the enterprises, but also about the work in the National Labor Confederation (CNT). This would be done to get some prominent leaders of the CNT, from the most honest elements, to enter the Communist party and the Unified Socialist Party of Catalonia. [We could then] use cases like these to develop a large-scale political campaign.

V. *Some problems of the CP of Spain and the Unified Socialist Party of Catalonia.*

The new tactical orientation developed during August-September (the policy of unifying all Spanish for the struggle against the interventionists, along with raising the policy of resistance to a higher level) met with a very favorable response in the party, among the masses, in the army, and even among the leaders of a significant portion of the other parties and organizations of the Popular Front. In the meantime, however, the policy has barely penetrated the masses in Franco's zone.

The work of the CP of Spain has improved lately, especially in the army and to a lesser extent in the enterprises and the UGT. After a protracted stagnation, there are the first signs of a new inflow of the masses into the party. The party currently numbers about 830,000 members (without the Unified Socialist Party of Catalonia); of these, half are in the army.

The improvement in party work, however, lags behind what the situation demands, and it is impossible to overlook the gravity of this. To improve the party's work and to resolve the question about leadership, the CP of Spain is preparing a national conference for January 1939. Currently the CC CP of Spain does not sufficiently reflect the party's true situation. A significant number of CC members are not equal to the tasks that the party and country are facing at the same time as new, valuable leading cadres of proven worth have been promoted but are not in the CC. A huge majority of regional committee secretaries are not members of the CC.

It is also necessary to reorganize the Politburo. The Politburo now consists of seven members (Díaz, Dolores, Checa, Mije, Uribe, Hernández, Cordón) and four candidates (Antón, Uribe, Carrillo, Delicado). Com. Díaz, however, due to constant illness, cannot participate actively enough in the leadership; Cordón has been a commander in the army from the very beginning of the war; Hernández is a commissar in an army group in the non-Catalan zone; Uribe is a minister, which takes up a large part of his time. Therefore, of the seven members of the P.B., only three can carry on the leadership work full time. I must add to this that the situation demands that the members of the leadership be distributed between the Catalan and non-Catalan zones in order to have the general leadership in Barcelona (the Politburo) and in the non-Catalan zone, in Madrid to have a strong and authoritative enough delegation of the CC, since the party is in fact located there and also more than two-thirds of the population and three-fourths of the army are there. This requires a strengthening of the Politburo. The Spanish comrades (Com. Díaz) foresee the co-optation into the Politburo of the following comrades: Giorla (CC member), Manco (CC member), Diéguez (secretary of the Madrid regional committee, CC member), Palau (secretary of the Valencia regional committee, not a CC member), and Comorera (member of the CC general secretariat, Unified Socialist Party of Catalonia). They also foresee the return of Com. Cordón from the army to work in the P.B.

The Unified Socialist Party of Catalonia foresees a convocation of a congress during the last half of January. Here the question about the leadership is even more acute than in the CP of Spain, since the current leadership cannot completely guarantee the situation. Besides this there exists a danger of factional struggle with the cliques that were created as a result of the recent struggles over the relationship between the Republican and Catalan autonomous governments. The party currently numbers more than seventy-five thousand members (of whom about thirty-five thousand are in the army). The party is especially growing in Barcelona (every month there are eight hundred to a thousand new members in Barcelona, of whom 70 percent workers, 30 percent women; of whom 15 percent from the CNT) and in the army. The party base is healthy and the majority want to have amicable collaboration with the Communist party and consider themselves Communists. However, there are some hostile Caballerista and also nationalist elements.

To achieve a united leadership for the CP of Spain and the Unified Socialist Party of Catalonia, a united secretariat was set up, which is still working intermittently, yet all the same has improved over the past few weeks.

Before the conference of the CP of Spain and before the congress of the Unified Socialist Party of Catalonia, it would be expedient—if the situation in the country permits—to send for Com. Comorera together with a member of the Politburo of the CP of Spain to discuss all of the questions and to definitively settle the relationship between the two parties.

It will also be necessary to send Com. Gallo or Mikhal to Spain to study, together with the Politburo and the leadership of the Unified Socialist Youth, the state of the youth movement and to take appropriate measures that will guarantee the unity of the Unified Socialist Youth and the activation of the Antifascist Youth Alliance.

VI. *The international campaign and activity to aid the Spanish Republic.*

The opinion that the international proletariat are not actually helping the Spanish people, and that one ought not to expect effective help from them, is rather widespread in Republican Spain. On the other hand, one needs to acknowledge that the aid rendered up to now has been insufficient.

In the face of the approaching danger, it will be necessary to undertake every measure to strengthen international aid not only in the form of sending food (which is very significant because there are already rather strong signs of hunger in the country), but mainly through mass action, with the goal of preventing a new strengthening of the intervention, the granting of belligerent rights to Franco, and the implementation of plans by Hitler-Mussolini-Chamberlain-Daladier to smother the Spanish Republic.

E. Gerö

19/11/38

# Document 81

RGVA, f. 33987, op. 3, d. 1266, l. 6

*Top Secret*
copy N° 2

16 February 1939
N. 3084 ss

To the Politburo of the CC VKP (b)
Comrade Stalin

Comrades Surits and Marchenko and military adviser Kolchanov report that NEGRÍN through Pascua is trying to get an answer to his additional request for the delivery of arms for the Republican army. I would suppose that it is necessary to give directives to our people that in case Pascua or other people turn to them about aid with weapons it is necessary to answer, for example, the following:

1. The USSR has always treated the needs of the Spanish government with benevolence and met, as far as possible, their requests for aid with weapons and other fighting resources in a timely fashion.

2. The latest request of the Span.[ish] gov.[ernment] for the sale of arms, which was announced through Cisneros, was, to a significant degree, met by us and if the Span.[ish] gov.[ernment] could not agree with the French government about the timely transfer of these arms to Spain than we can only deplore that.

3. To demand new deliveries of arms for Spain at the present time, when the weapons already supplied by us in enormous quantities are in the territory of France and risk falling into the hands of the French fascists as trophies, is, at the very least, inopportune.

I request directives.

K. Voroshilov
Correct: [illegible]

printed in 2 copies
lz.16/2/39

# Notes

INTRODUCTION

1. Paul Johnson, *Modern Times: The World from the Twenties to the Eighties* (New York: Harper and Row, 1981), 321–340.

2. Alfred Kazin, "The Wound That Will Not Heal," *New Republic* (25 August 1986), 39–41.

3. Murray Kempton, *Part of Our Time* (New York: Dell, 1955), 317.

4. Gerald Howson, *Arms for Spain: The Untold Story of the Spanish Civil War* (London: John Albemarle, 1998), 146–152, 251; cf. Neal Ascherson, "How Moscow Robbed Spain of Its Gold in the Civil War," *Observer* (London) 27 September 1998.

5. Walter G. Krivitsky, *In Stalin's Secret Service* (New York: Harper, 1939), 102–107, 291.

6. See, for example, Burnett Bolloten, *The Spanish Revolution: The Left and the Struggle for Power During the Civil War* (Chapel Hill: University of North Carolina Press, 1979), 110; Howson, *Arms for Spain*, 208–217; Hugh Thomas, *The Spanish Civil War* (London: Eyer and Spottiswood, 1961), 263; cf. Thomas, *The Spanish Civil War*, rev. ed. (London: Penguin, 1965), 337, in which he writes that "Krivitsky's evidence can generally be accepted."

7. E. H. Carr, *The Comintern and the Spanish Civil War* (New York: Pantheon, 1984), 31, 44.

8. The MASK documents were the top secret coded messages deciphered by the British secret service during the war years—the British equivalent of the American decoded Venona documents. The MASK documents appear here exactly as

they were received and released by British intelligence and as they were made available in this country by the National Security Agency.

9. Tim Rees, "The Highpoint of Comintern Influence: The Communist Party and the Civil War in Spain," in Tim Rees and Andrew-Thorpe, eds., *International Communism and the Communist International: 1919–43;* (Manchester, England: Manchester University Press, 1998), 144–165.

10. Paul Preston, *The Spanish Civil War: 1936–39* (London: Weidenfeld and Nicolson, 1986).

11. Burnett Bolloten, *The Spanish Civil War: Revolution and Counterrevolution* (Chapel Hill: University of North Carolina Press, 1991).

12. Paul Preston, *A Concise History of the Spanish Civil War* (London: Fontana, 1996), 108.

13. Ibid., 4. Preston comes down firmly on the Communist side of the argument. He writes (173): "Against all of this stands the indisputable perception of the Communists, the bourgeois Republicans and the moderate Socialists that once the uprising had developed into a civil war, then the first priority had to be to win that war."

14. Stanley G. Payne, "Foreword" in Bolloten, *The Spanish Civil War,* xi–xiv.

15. Preston, *A Concise History of the Spanish Civil War,* 171–172.

16. Ibid., 173.

17. Robert Alexander, *The Anarchists in the Spanish Civil War* (London: Janus, 1999), 1028–1029.

18. François Furet, *The Passing of an Illusion: The Idea of Communism in the Twentieth Century* (Chicago: University of Chicago Press, 1999), 245–265.

19. Stéphane Courtois and Jean-Louis Panne, "The Shadow of the NKVD in Spain," in Stéphane Courtois et al., *The Black Book of Communism: Crimes, Terror, Repression* (Cambridge: Harvard University Press, 1999), 333–352.

20. Furet, *The Passing of an Illusion,* 261.

CHAPTER 1: 1936

1. Carr mentions this as a possible reason for the delay in Stalin's response to the war, as well—Raymond Carr, *The Civil War in Spain, 1936–39* (London: Weidenfeld and Nicolson, 1977), 107.

2. For a good (and short) discussion of Spanish anarchism, see Pierre Broué and Emile Témime, *The Revolution and the Civil War in Spain* (Cambridge: MIT Press, 1970), 54–57.

3. Stanley Payne, *The Spanish Revolution* (New York: Norton, 1970), 232; E. H. Carr, *The Comintern and the Spanish Civil War* (New York: Pantheon Books, 1984), 15; Denis Smyth, "'We Are With You': Solidarity and Self-Interest in Soviet Policy Towards Republican Spain, 1936–1939," in Paul Preston and Ann L. MacKenzie, eds., *The Republic Besieged: Civil War in Spain, 1936–1939* (Edinburgh: Edinburgh University Press, 1996), 95–99; Carr, *The Civil War in Spain,* 107.

4. Hugh Thomas, *The Spanish Civil War* (New York: Touchstone Books, 1986), 338.

5. Carr, *The Comintern and the Spanish Civil War,* 20.

6. The best-known proponent of this view is, of course, Burnett Bolloten. See

Burnett Bolloten, *The Grand Camouflage: The Spanish Civil War and Revolution, 1936–39* (New York: Praeger, 1968), and *The Spanish Civil War: Revolution and Counterrevolution* (Chapel Hill: University of North Carolina Press, 1991), especially 110–113. See also, however, Preston, *The Spanish Civil War, 1936–1939* (London: Weidenfeld and Nicolson, 1986), 130.

7. Broué and Témime, *The Revolution and the Civil War in Spain,* 194.

8. Víctor Alba, *The Communist Party in Spain* (New Brunswick, N.J.: Transaction Books, 1983), 204–207.

9. The major disagreement among these historians is their understanding of whether the Communists were "counterrevolutionary" or whether, as Bolloten has argued, the revolution continued at a slower pace and more hidden from view. Most scholars agree that the Soviets restrained social revolution in Spain, although they give very different reasons (in addition to winning bourgeois support) for the restraint. See Preston, *The Spanish Civil War, 1936–1939,* 130; Smyth, "'We Are With You,'" 100–101; Carr, *The Civil War in Spain,* 107; Payne, *The Spanish Revolution,* 232.

10. All parentheses in MASK documents were placed by the British cryptanalysts who deciphered the telegrams. The indication "([number] group[s])" meant that one or more groups of ciphers either could not be deciphered or were garbled in transmission.

11. Literally, "under the banner."

12. The text of this MASK document was supplemented (in brackets) with material from the original Russian document in RGASPI and reprinted in Chubarian, ed., "Komintern i grazhdanskaia voina v Ispanii, 1936–1939," [unpublished manuscript]. Oddly enough, this was one of the few documents in this collection that did not have an archival citation.

13. See, e.g., Alba, *The Communist Party in Spain,* 205–206.

14. Ibid., 200.

15. There have been three major explanations for this abrupt volte-face. Most scholars have accepted Hernández's explanation that the party consulted with Moscow, received instructions to join Caballero, and then did so—Alba, *The Communist Party in Spain,* 208; Antony Beevor, *The Spanish Civil War* (London: Orbis Publishing, 1982), 119; Thomas, *The Spanish Civil War,* 406. Carr disagrees, pointing out that the ECCI secretariat had left open the question of participating in the Popular Front as long ago as 22 May. He thought that the PCE was simply availing itself of this choice (*The Comintern and the Spanish Civil War,* 7, 19). The new evidence suggests that Broué and Témime were much closer to the truth when they wrote that the Communists "gave in" to an insistent Caballero (*The Revolution and the Civil War in Spain,* 210).

16. The documents for this conclusion are provided in Chapter 3.

17. For a complete discussion of the factors involved in the French change of heart, see Jill Edwards, *The British Government and the Spanish Civil War, 1936–1939* (London: Macmillan, 1979), 25–30; Beevor, *The Spanish Civil War,* 109–110; John E. Dreifort, *Yvon Delbos at the Quai D'Orsay: French Foreign Policy During the Popular Front, 1936–1938* (Lawrence: University Press of Kansas, 1973), 35, 38, 50–54; Robert H. Whealey, *Hitler and Spain: The Nazi Role in the Spanish Civil War, 1936–1939* (Lexington: University Press of Kentucky, 1989), 15; William E. Watters, *An International Affair: Non-Intervention in the Spanish*

*Civil War, 1936–1939* (New York: Exposition, 1971), 38; Broué and Témime, *The Revolution and the Civil War in Spain,* 328–329; Pierre Cot, *Triumph of Treason* (Chicago: Ziff-Davis, 1944), 94, 338, 344–346; Michael Alpert, *A New International History of the Spanish Civil War* (London: Macmillan, 1994), 14, 21–22; Anthony Adamthwaite, *France and the Coming of the Second World War, 1936–1939* (London: Frank Cass, 1977), 42; Dante A. Puzzo, *Spain and the Great Powers, 1936–1941* (Freeport: Books for Libraries Press, 1972), 82–88.

18. We will have to wait for the opening of the Presidential Archive in Russia before we can have definitive answers to many of our questions about Soviet policy decision-making. This archive, which contains all the materials sent to Stalin, is open only to Russian researchers, and very few of its contents have been made public.

19. See Smyth, "'We Are With You,'" 95–99; Carr, *The Comintern and the Spanish Civil War,* 15; Gabriel Jackson, *The Spanish Republic and the Civil War, 1931–1939* (Princeton, N.J.: Princeton University Press, 1965), 258.

20. See, e.g., Paul Preston, "The Creation of the Popular Front in Spain," in Helen Graham and Paul Preston, eds., *The Popular Front in Europe* (London: Macmillan, 1987), 84; Puzzo, *Spain and the Great Powers,* 83.

21. One of these is Burnett Bolloten. See his *The Spanish Civil War: Revolution and Counterrevolution,* 100–101, 104–105.

22. Some will allow that the Soviets may have shipped a few small arms in September as well. Puzzo, *Spain and the Great Powers,* 135–136; Broué and Témime, *The Revolution and the Civil War in Spain,* 367; Alpert, *A New International History of the Spanish Civil War,* 51–52; Carr, *The Comintern and the Spanish Civil War,* 24–25; Payne, *The Spanish Revolution,* 270; Jackson, *The Spanish Republic and the Civil War,* 316; Smyth, "'We Are With You,'" 92–93.

23. Payne, *The Spanish Revolution,* 267; Carr, *The Comintern and the Spanish Civil War,* 15; Thomas, *The Spanish Civil War,* 339.

24. See, e.g., "Information About the Military Situation in Spain, for 8 September 1936," RGVA, f. 33987, op. 3, d. 845, ll. 20–23; Information About the Military Situation in Spain, for 19 September 1936, RGVA, f. 33987, op. 3, d. 845, ll. 46–48.

25. See, e.g., Documents 13 and 16.

26. Hugh Thomas, relying on Spanish evidence, believes that Stepanov established a virtual tyranny over the Central Committee of the party. Thomas, *The Spanish Civil War,* 341. Documents cited in Chapter 3 show that Codovilla acted in much the same way.

27. A common abbreviation for the Soviet Union.

28. The anarchist flag.

29. He probably means Juan José Tarradellas, an Esquerra politician.

30. See, e.g., R. Dan Richardson, *Comintern Army. The International Brigades and the Spanish Civil War* (Lexington: University Press of Kentucky, 1982), 51–52.

31. Alba, *The Communist Party in Spain,* 91–102, 125–139, 195–287.

32. Bolloten, *The Spanish Civil War,* 400.

33. Not the least of which was the antagonism between Largo Caballero and the anarchists and the fact that Largo Caballero had every expectation that he would be able to take power legally.

34. *Politotdely.*

35. The word used here, *vreditelia,* was fraught with political overtones in Stalin's Russia.

36. The title "director" always referred to Voroshilov.

37. The real names (in brackets) associated with these code names were added in the text by Voroshilov himself.

38. The PUR, or Political Directorate of the Red Army, was the parent institution for the Soviet military commissars.

39. The Soviet armored school and tank training grounds were at Archena.

40. I.e., so that they would not know he was a Soviet officer if they met him later commanding in the field.

41. See Bolloten, *The Spanish Civil War,* 411; and Carr, *The Comintern and the Spanish Civil War,* 363.

42. Miravitlles suggested that it was this tendency to support Catalonia, shown clearly in these memoranda, that would eventually lead to the Soviet consul's death (Thomas, *The Spanish Civil War,* 703, n. 1).

43. For more on Durruti's background, see Thomas, *The Spanish Civil War,* 68, 316–318; and Broué and Témime, *The Revolution and the Civil War in Spain,* 58–59.

44. Quoted in Broué and Témime, *The Revolution and the Civil War in Spain,* 185, n. 5.

45. Franco's forces were always referred to as the Whites, and Republican forces as the Blues (not the Reds), by Soviet advisers.

46. *Uravnilovka.*

47. *Svoevolie.*

48. Stalin is always called the Boss in dispatches and reports.

49. *Uravnilovka.*

50. See Broué and Témime, *The Revolution and the Civil War in Spain,* 372–373.

51. Walter Krivitsky, *In Stalin's Secret Service* (New York: Harper, 1939), 96–97.

52. Gerald Howson, *Arms for Spain: The Untold Story of the Spanish Civil War* (London: Albemarle, 1998).

53. Another code name for Berzin.

54. For the complete story of the military purges, see John Erickson, *The Soviet High Command: A Military Political History, 1918–1941* (London: St. Martin's, 1962), 449–473.

55. See, e.g., Thomas, *The Spanish Civil War,* 533–534.

56. Thomas, *The Spanish Civil War,* 533.

57. Although there had been one attempt by a certain Andrés Revertes to come to an agreement with the Italians, this attempt was completely disavowed by the Catalan government—Payne, *The Spanish Revolution,* 286.

58. At the same time, the Soviet official's suggestions about Majorca were apparently ignored by the Catalans, who had more important issues to deal with.

59. Preston, *The Spanish Civil War, 1936–1939,* 103–138; Beevor, *The Spanish Civil War,* 69–78; Jackson, *The Spanish Republic and the Civil War, 1931–1939,* 276–309, 531–533.

60. Payne, *The Spanish Revolution,* 225–226; Thomas, *The Spanish Civil War,*

258–281. Broué and Témime also believe that the terror in the Republican zone was a complex phenomenon: although without question a spontaneous movement initially, it then became a means of prevention and a spur to revolutionary action—parties and unions organized *paseos*. Broué and Témime, *The Revolution and the Civil War in Spain*, 124–125.

61. A meeting with Antonov-Ovseenko, Ehrenburg, and Miravitlles.

62. See Document 21.

63. See Michael Jackson, *Fallen Sparrows: The International Brigades in the Spanish Civil War* (Philadelphia: American Philosophical Society, 1994), 88.

64. These short descriptions are based on biographies provided by the archivists at RGVA, Nonna Tarkhova and Vera Mikhailëva. See also Richardson, *Comintern Army*, 57–59, 67, 72.

CHAPTER 2: 1937

1. E. H. Carr, *The Comintern and the Spanish Civil War* (New York: Pantheon Books, 1984), 34.

2. John Costello and Oleg Tsarev, *Deadly Illusions* (New York: Crown Books, 1993), 349.

3. Quoted in Michael Albert, *A New International History of the Spanish Civil War* (New York: St. Martin's, 1994), 146.

4. Louis Fischer, in Arthur Koestler and others, *The God That Failed* (New York: Harper and Row, 1950), 197–199.

5. Burnett Bolloten has pointed out that the consensus among historians is that Asensio "possessed very great military capabilities and exceptional mental gifts." See Burnett Bolloten, *The Spanish Civil War: Revolution and Counterrevolution* (Chapel Hill: University of North Carolina Press, 1991) 280–281.

6. A common name for Berzin.

7. Not Byelorussians, but rather "White" as in counterrevolutionary. The term connects the Nationalists with the Whites who fought the Reds (i.e., Communists) during the Russian civil war.

8. The first commander of the new regiment, Enrique Castro, told his troops that "only by winning the war shall we achieve the revolution . . . and become another Soviet republic in an area of great importance for Communism in the world . . . that army will be our army, but we alone know this. For everyone else that army will be an army of the Popular Front. We shall direct it, but above all, we must appear to others as combatants of the Popular Front." Quoted in Bolloten, *The Spanish Civil War*.

9. See Hugh Thomas, *The Spanish Civil War* (New York: Harper and Row, 1961), 573, 577–578.

10. Hugh Thomas points out that the 13th Division of the International Brigades could have been sent from Murcia to aid the threatened town, "had not the Communists feared that the Anarchists would take the opportunity of rising in Valencia." And Franz Borkenau, although personally opposed to the anarchists, wrote at the time that Málaga could have been saved, if the people had engaged in a "fight of despair" of the kind that the anarchists "might have led." The problem, Borkenau argued, was that the officer in charge of the army in Málaga viewed his task as purely a military one, "hated the spirit of the militia," and could not com-

prehend the "political factor." Borkenau concluded that the "Spanish Republic paid with the fall of Málaga for the decision of the Right wing to make an end of social revolution and of its Left wing not to allow that." Cf. Thomas, *The Spanish Civil War,* 364; Franz Borkenau, *The Spanish Cockpit* (Ann Arbor: University of Michigan Press, 1963), 228. Noam Chomsky notes that "Borkenau's detailed explanation [for the fall of Málaga] tends to bear out the anarchist 'explanation,' at least in part" ("Objectivity and Liberal Scholarship," in *American Power and the New Mandarins* [New York: Pantheon, 1967], 98–99.

11. See, for example, Gabriel Jackson, *The Spanish Republic and the Civil War, 1936–1939* (Princeton, N.J.: Princeton University Press, 1965), 362–363. Referring to del Vayo's positions in the Caballero administration in 1937, he writes that del Vayo consulted the Soviet ambassador "and the Russian military advisors as though they were unconditional allies who could not possibly have motives and interests different from those of the Spanish Republic." As minister of war, moreover, del Vayo "appointed mostly Communists" to the key post of war commissar, who were supposed to check on the loyalty and political consciousness of officers.

12. Carr, *The Comintern and the Spanish Civil War,* 39.

13. The first copy was sent to Comrade Stalin with a note by the People's Commissar: "Com. Stalin. For your information. K. Voroshilov, 16/2/37."

14. The Republican army. Soviets refused to call the Republican army Reds, because they were not yet completely Communist, nor were they fully under the control of the Communist party.

15. The Soviet advisers often called Moscow the village. We have added quotation marks to distinguish this particular use from its more literal sense throughout the book.

16. Largo Caballero, too, was usually called the Old Man by the Soviets.

17. The term "X" had two meanings. Here it is used to indicate "Spain," but in other contexts it meant the physical shipment of weaponry to Spain.

18. Thomas, *The Spanish Civil War,* 381.

19. See Víctor Alba and Stephen Schwartz, *Spanish Marxism Versus Soviet Communism* (New Brunswick, N. J.: Transaction Books, 1988), 133. They write that "*Editorial Marxista* published it just when the Communists were defending the need to transform the militias into a regular army."

20. On Largo Caballero, see Jackson, *The Spanish Republic and the Civil War,* 311, 371–374; Bolloten, *The Spanish Civil War,* 114–123, 346.

21. Bolloten, *The Spanish Civil War,* quotes Caballero's memoirs, *Mis recuerdos: Cartas a un Amigo* (Mexico City: Alianza, 1954), 212.

22. See Jackson, *The Spanish Republic and the Civil War,* 350–351.

23. Marginalia by Voroshilov: "This comrade has not yet arrived in Moscow."

24. Ronald Fraser, "The Popular Experience of War and Revolution: 1936–1939," in Paul Preston, ed., *Revolution and War in Spain: 1936–1939* (London, Methuen, 1984), 237–239.

25. See, for example, Bolloten, *The Spanish Civil War,* 403–404; 429–461; David T. Cattell, *Communism and the Spanish Civil War* (Berkeley: University of California Press, 1955), 142; Thomas, *The Spanish Civil War,* 424–436; Alba and Schwartz, *Spanish Marxism Versus Soviet Communism,* 188–189; Jackson, *The Spanish Republic and the Civil War,* 369–370.

26. Beevor, *The Spanish Civil War* (New York: Peter Bedrick Books, 1983), 188.

27. Thomas, *The Spanish Civil War*, 425–426. Thomas does concur that once the fighting started, the "Communists would be expected to reap the fullest advantage from what was happening—to take the opportunity, for example, to discredit and destroy finally their old enemies in the POUM." Cf. Alba and Schwartz, *Spanish Marxism Versus Soviet Communism*, 190. Alba and Schwartz suggest that the reason CNT leaders eventually supported a ceasefire is that "they knew they were faced with a provocation and that if the general situation had been favorable to the workers, no such provocation would have taken place."

28. Beevor, *The Spanish Civil War*, 190.

29. Walter Krivitsky, *In Stalin's Secret Service* (New York: Harper and Brothers, 1939), 108.

30. Diego Abad de Santillán, *Porque Perdimos la Guerra* (Madrid: Imán, 1975), 166.

31. Robert Alexander, *The Anarchists in the Spanish Civil War*, (London: Janus, 1999), 938–942.

32. Beevor, *The Spanish Civil War*, 189.

33. Speech of 9 May 1937, cited in José Díaz, *Tres años de lucha* (Paris: Globe, 1969), 432.

34. *Daily Worker*, May 9, 1937.

35. Claude Bowers, *My Mission in Spain* (New York: Simon and Schuster, 1954), 356.

36. See Beevor, *The Spanish Civil War*, 191.

37. Bolloten, *The Spanish Civil War*, 450.

38. Beevor, *The Spanish Civil War*, 193.

39. GRU agents in the field. Quotation marks have been added to show special use of this word, here and throughout the book.

40. This phrase was underlined by Voroshilov as well.

41. "Operation Nikolai," broadcast on Spanish television in November 1992.

42. Juan-Simeón Vidarte, *Todos fuimos culpables* (Mexico City: Fondo de Cultura Económica, 1973), 751, cited in Bolloten, *The Spanish Civil War*, 487.

43. Jesús Hernández, *Yo fui un ministro de Stalin* (Mexico City: Editorial America, 1953), 112–113, cited in Bolloten, *The Spanish Civil War*, 509–510. Hernández claimed that he was actually upset about Nin's disappearance, and that he had opposed the NKVD's secret operation against the POUM leader. Moreover, he wrote that he "detested Orlov and his gang of police," but fearing a storm "descending on our party" (the PCE), he defended the official Communist line even though he knew that it meant he was "implicitly defending a possible crime."

44. Vidarte, *Todos fuimos culpables*, 731, cited in Bolloten, *The Spanish Civil War*, 509.

45. The report refers to José Rovira Canales, commander of the 29th POUM Division, and a member of the POUM leadership. Rovira was soon to be called to Barcelona by General Pozas, who, acting on the order of the Communist leadership, had him arrested. According to the Labour M.P. Fenner Brockway, War Minister Prieto sent a telegram to Pozas protesting that the arrest had taken place without Prieto's knowledge or authority. Prieto ordered his release, but Rovira was rearrested in October 1938. He eventually managed to escape from prison with other POUM leaders before Barcelona was captured on 26 January 1939. See Burnett Bolloten, *The Spanish Civil War*, 500, and note, p. 887.

46. One such document was said to be a memo by General W. von Faupel, the German ambassador to Nationalist Spain, written to Hitler on 11 May 1937. Franco told von Faupel, according to the memo, that a Nazi secret agent had started the street shooting in Barcelona. Robert Conquest has called this charge an "old [Stalinist] canard of inspiration, a charge believed even at the time only by those who also believed that Trotsky was a German agent; indeed the slander on the POUM was part and parcel of the anti-Trotskyist falsification" ([London] *Times Literary Supplement*, letter to the editor, 17 Nov. 1978).

47. Carr, *The Comintern and the Spanish Civil War*, 45.

48. Beevor, *The Spanish Civil War*, 200; cf., Hugh Thomas, *The Spanish Civil War*, 461–466.

49. The KGB was always called the neighbors by the GRU.

50. Quoted in Beevor, *The Spanish Civil War*, 213; cf. Harvey Klehr, John Earl Haynes, and Fridrikh Igorevich Firsov, *The Secret World of American Communism* (New Haven: Yale University Press, 1995), 151–187. Klehr, Haynes and Firsov detail how the Comintern fought dissenters in the brigades. Included is their account of the killing of an American volunteer, Albert Wallach, who had left his own troops to work for a unit aligned with anarcho-syndicalists. They also print a Comintern document called "List of Suspicious Individuals and Deserters from the 15th Brigade," indicating that ideological deviation was considered a crime when discovered among the volunteers.

51. Klehr, Haynes, and Firsov, *The Secret World of American Communism*, 187.

52. Hugh Thomas, *The Spanish Civil War*, 458, 780; R. Dan Richardson, *Comintern Army: The International Brigades and the Spanish Civil War* (Lexington: University Press of Kentucky, 1982), 52–53.

53. The Soviets often spoke of the Spanish as the "friends," in order to avoid naming them directly. Quotation marks added to show special use of this word here and throughout the book.

54. The Russian word used for GRU agents in this document, *korporanty*, can be taken as almost the exact equivalent of the CIA's "company man." It was used exclusively by GRU agents to refer to other GRU agents.

55. This memorandum was not found.

56. For two discussions of the incident, see Pierre Broué and Emile Témime, *The Revolution and the Civil War in Spain* (Cambridge: MIT Press, 1970), 484–486; and Beevor, *The Spanish Civil War*, 202.

57. See especially Robert Conquest, *The Great Terror: A Reassessment* (New York: Oxford University Press, 1990); J. Arch Getty and Oleg. V. Naumov, *The Road to Terror: Stalin and the Self-Destruction of the Bolsheviks, 1932–1939* (New Haven, Conn.: Yale University Press, 1999).

58. The best discussion of this bloody affair remains John Erickson, *The Soviet High Command: A Military-Political History, 1918–1941* (London: St. Martin's Press, 1962), 449–473.

59. This confirms the suspicions of many students of the war. See, e.g., Payne, *The Spanish Revolution*, 325–326.

60. Report by Koltsov to Stalin and Voroshilov, dated 4 December 1937, RGVA, f. 33987, op. 3, d. 961, ll. 224 and 224ob

61. Getty and Naumov, *The Road to Terror*, 79.

62. The Nationalists.

63. The Republicans.

64. GRU agents in the field.

65. Stalin was always called the Boss, just as Voroshilov was the "director," and Moscow (the Center) was the "village."

66. The actual shipments of weaponry to Spain.

67. The Russian spelling has generally been left as it was in the original. Corrections have been made in the notes where needed and when the commanders are known.

68. Only those commanders with no short description have been left out.

69. General Toribio Martínez Cabrera.

70. Hidalgo y Cisneros.

71. Llano de la Encomienda.

72. Biscay.

73. A pejorative term.

74. Asturias.

75. Perhaps Col. García Valiño.

76. The same as above. Modesto's full name was Juan Modesto Guilloto.

77. Possibly Gregorio Jover.

78. Jesús Pérez Salas.

79. May mean José Rovira Canals.

80. Joaquín Ascaso.

81. Stalin.

82. Voroshilov.

83. I.e., the Spanish.

84. *Korporanty:* GRU agents in the field.

85. The form of "you" used throughout this letter is the familiar *ty*.

86. The GRU.

87. Stalin.

88. A term used for spying.

89. GRU.

90. Moscow.

91. *Politgramota.*

92. Moscow.

93. A sort of tank.

94. Vittorio Vidali, who was known as Carlos Contreras in Spain.

95. The GRU.

96. The infamous (or famous) Alexander Orlov. "The neighbors" is the term both the GRU and the NKVD used to refer to each other.

97. Note at bottom of page: "Virgilio Llanos was a Socialist from Caballero's group. After the events in Asturias in 1934, he lived in the USSR. At the beginning of the war, he was sent to Barcelona. From there, he came to the Madrid front as the commissar of a column of López Tienda. Together with López Tienda, who was killed at the front, he soon joined in with the Fifth Regiment. Using his personal friendship with Caballero, Virgilio Llanos urged him without success to part company with Asensio. Later Caballero appointed Llanos commissar of units where it was necessary to fight against the influence of the Communists. Llanos did not fulfill these hopes. While remaining a Socialist, he began to work in close contact with the Communist party."

98. Note at bottom of page: "Casado Segismundo—a regular officer working on the general staff, attached to General Asensio. At the beginning of the war, the Republican agencies had suspicions that Casado was connected with the enemy. Casado's brother was arrested as an active fascist. Casado himself avoided arrest by joining the anarchist organization FAI. Thanks to his connections, he continued to work on the general staff and surrounded himself with suspect types, such as anarchists. At the time of the Brunete operation, he commanded the 21st Corps. At the time of the enemy counteroffensive at Brunete, he sabotaged operations and gave no aid to Modesto's corps. Now he commands the 18th Corps at the Aragon front. Some comrades consider that Casado could be drawn closer to the Communist party. I consider counting on Casado a dangerous mistake on the part of our comrades."

99. Note at bottom of page: "Braccelare [*sic*]—the son of a well-known editor of fascist newspapers in Italy."

100. Note at bottom of page: "A great crowd of antifascists settled in Albacete and thereby steered clear of the front and all its dangers. It was said that when Gayman-Vidal was in charge of the base in Albacete, there were about eighteen hundred men in the internal security, made up of internationalists. The Medical Directorate bureaucracy consisted of eight hundred persons, etc. At the front, there were only some three hundred to four hundred internationalists among the combat personnel in some brigades."

101. Note at bottom of page: "I had received the artillery from an anarchist division that remained at its position. I started an investigation of the causes for the damage to the cannon, for there were strong suspicions of deliberate sabotage. When I was already back in Moscow, I read in *Pravda* of 24 October that a POUMist organization had been uncovered that, among other things, had damaged the cannon attached to my division at Saragossa."

102. Note at bottom of page: "We called one of the battalions made up of Poles and Spaniards by the name of Palafox. Palafox was a people's general who defended Saragossa from the invasion by Napoleon's army. In his detachment at that time, Poles also fought alongside Spaniards."

103. Note at bottom of page: "Any time that Gallo appeared at my division, he would visit only the 12th Brigade (the Italians). This greatly offended the other internationalists (Poles, Frenchmen, Bulgarians, Yugoslavs). They nicknamed Gallo the defender of the Italians."

104. Cited in Carr, *The Comintern and the Spanish Civil War*, 63. Carr prints letters written by Togliatti to Moscow as an appendix, pp. 89–101.

105. U.S. Congress, Senate, Committee on the Judiciary, *Scope of Soviet Activity in the United States* (1957), 3446.

106. Alba and Schwartz, *Spanish Marxism Versus Soviet Communism*, 225–231.

107. Beevor, *The Spanish Civil War*, 209.

108. Ibid., 211–212.

109. The Russian term used here, *uravnitel'nyi,* is a pejorative reserved for undesirable forms of socialism and anarchism.

110. Luis, the pseudonym for Vittorio Codovilla.

111. Note at bottom of page: "Estat Català is a small party with a large tradition in the political life of Catalonia. Despite the fact that its leaders come from the petty bourgeoisie, they represent the interests of a large part of Catalan financial

capital and large industrial works, which are based on the investments of Jesuit capital. It is a pro-fascist party."

112. Note at bottom of page: "Casanovas is the former chairman of the Catalan Palace of Deputies, an adventurer, who already once, when there was a very acute situation at the front, together with Dencás tried to stir up a separatist movement in Catalonia."

113. Note at bottom of page: "The international Trotskyist and Trotskyesque delegation: Maxton, Brockway, Marceau Pivert, Kuriel, and others used the open support of Caballero and the anarchist leaders to protect Trotskyist spies. The Maxton delegation declared to the UGT that it also enjoyed support from the Second International."

CHAPTER 3: 1938–1939

1. Stanley Payne, *The Spanish Revolution* (New York: W. W. Norton, 1970), 273–274.

2. Throughout the war the Soviets referred to the Spanish as friends in order to avoid naming who they were directly.

3. Gerald Howson, *Arms for Spain: The Untold Story of the Spanish Civil War* (London: John Murray, 1998). For further confirmation of Howson's work, see Report to Voroshilov on costs of operation "X," dated 21 February 1938. RGVA, f. 33987, op. 3, d. 1149, ll. 60–63.

4. See, e.g., Verle B. Johnston, *Legions of Babel: The International Brigades in the Spanish Civil War* (University Park: Pennsylvania University Press, 1967), 57.

5. Vincent Brome, *The International Brigades: Spain 1936–1939* (London: William Heinemann, 1965), 184–194, 226–235; Robert A. Rosenstone, *Crusade of the Left: The Lincoln Battalion in the Spanish Civil War* (New York: Pegasus, 1969), 297–312; R. Dan Richardson, *Comintern Army: The International Brigades and the Spanish Civil War* (Lexington: University Press of Kentucky, 1982), 159–176.

6. See, e.g., Burnett Bolloten, *The Spanish Civil War: Revolution and Counterrevolution* (Chapel Hill: University of North Carolina Press, 1991), 571; Hugh Thomas, *The Spanish Civil War* (New York: Touchstone, 1986), 457–458, 881.

7. For a good overview of the numbers offered by several sources, see Michael Jackson, *Fallen Sparrows: The International Brigades in the Spanish Civil War* (Philadelphia: American Philosophical Society, 1994), 60–95. The final number that Jackson arrives at, thirty-two thousand, is remarkably close to the figure cited here.

8. Literally "guerrilla."

9. Should be Franz Dahlem.

10. This quotation was corrected in the margin. The correction is the one given here.

11. The term "organ" and particularly "special organ" as used here means "intelligence, security, or secret police institution." So throughout the chapter.

12. See, e.g., Sheila Fitzpatrick, *Everyday Stalinism: Ordinary Life in Extraordinary Times: Soviet Russia in the 1930s* (New York: Oxford University Press, 1999), 21–22.

13. Gabriel Jackson, *The Spanish Republic and the Civil War, 1931–1939*

(Princeton: Princeton University Press, 1965), 406–407, 453; Pierre Broué and Emile Témime, *The Revolution and the Civil War in Spain* (Cambridge: MIT Press, 1970), 312–313; Bolloten, *The Spanish Civil War,* 546–549, 600–606; Payne, *The Spanish Revolution,* 346.

14. Among the scholars who do not see Negrín as a puppet of Moscow are Antony Beevor and Helen Graham. See Antony Beevor, *The Spanish Civil War* (London: Orbis Publishing, 1982), 193; Helen Graham, *Socialism and War: The Spanish Socialist Party in Power and Crisis, 1936–1939* (Cambridge: Cambridge University Press, 1991), 94. Bolloten sees him as a crypto-Communist. Bolloten, *The Spanish Civil War,* 138–144, 587. A more moderate position is taken by George Esenwein and Adrian Shubert, who argue that Negrín supported the Communists because (1) he thought their strategy (of winning by not losing) was best; (2) he was dependent on Soviet material support; (3) they were too deeply embedded in the military and political fabric of the Republican zone; (4) and in any case, he was not particularly hostile to them or their methods. George Esenwein and Adrian Shubert, *Spain at War: The Spanish Civil War in Context, 1931–1939* (London: Longman, 1995), 253–254.

15. Esenwein and Shubert, *Spain at War,* 256.

# Index